To a very
special friend
who is always there!
God Bless You,
Luv Michael

STORIES
of the
GREAT
OPERAS

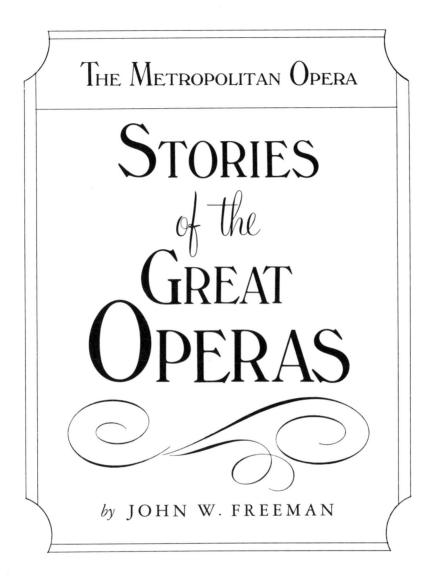

THE METROPOLITAN OPERA

STORIES
of the
GREAT
OPERAS

by JOHN W. FREEMAN

THE METROPOLITAN OPERA GUILD

W·W·NORTON & COMPANY·NEW YORK·LONDON

All photographs courtesy of the Metropolitan Opera Guild except for the following:
Joplin—The Bettman Archive
Hindemith—BMI Archive
Blitzstein, Korngold, Thomson—Culver Pictures
Bartók—G.D. Hackett

The text of this book is composed in Garamond, with display type set in Windsor. Composition and Manufacturing by The Maple-Vail Book Manufacturing Group. Book design by Antonina Krass.

Library of Congress Cataloging in Publication Data
Main entry under title:
The Metropolitan Opera stories of the great operas.
I. Operas—Stories, plots, etc.   I. Freeman, John W.
II. Metropolitan Opera (New York, N.Y.)   III. Title:
Stories of the great operas.
MT95.M49   1984   782.1'3   84–8030

ISBN 0-393-01888-1

W. W. Norton & Company, Inc., 500 Fifth Avenue, New York, N.Y. 10110
W. W. Norton & Company Ltd., 37 Great Russell Street, London WC1B 3NU
3 4 5 6 7 8 9 0

This book is dedicated to
the memory of Dario Soria

Contents

Contents

CONTENTS

CONTENTS

Contents by Opera Titles

FOREWORD

BY JAMES LEVINE

In the world of opera, repertory is a magic word. It refers not only to a system of displaying masterworks one by one in alternation with other masterworks—the so-called "repertory system"—but also to the enormous body of works from which we can choose. This so-called operatic repertory includes not only the standard repertory—*Carmen, Aida, La Bohème, Faust, Don Giovanni, Tristan und Isolde,* and what have you—but a much greater body of works—heard occasionally—which greatly enhance the main diet of the most familiar operas. Beyond these, there lies an even greater body of works that might be called dormant or less active. Of course, not all of these are masterpieces; only a few qualify for that distinction. But a great many are fascinating, stimulating, perhaps ripe for revival and reconsideration.

Yes, the literature of opera is richer than many opera-lovers realize. And the repertory—that magic word—is like a huge storehouse of treasures, only the smallest bit of which an opera house can expose to view at one time. To browse among the scores of operas, imagining how great voices would sound in this scene, how a great designer could make the stage look for that one—is one of the most intoxicating experiences I know.

The artistic director of an opera company, like the chief librarian of a great library, has the privilege, responsibility and pleasure of reviewing this store of treasures constantly. When I became the Metropolitan Opera's Music Director in 1976, I had no trouble coming up with ideas—only trouble deciding which ones should come first. Opera seasons have to be planned well ahead, and there is no point in hoping to do a work—even so familiar a one as *Aida*—unless you can be sure of having the artists you need, and having them for a series of performances, not just a few so-called "festival" appearances. The ideal is great to contemplate, but the practical reality is more challenging—and by far the more rewarding in the long run, because it gives audiences a continuity of great experiences, not just a once-in-a-lifetime occasion. We need to find the repertory our people can do best, as well as find the people who can best do the repertory we want. From this approach—from two directions simultane-

xxi

ously—it is possible to make a balanced repertory, the familiar spiced with the novel.

When I started at the Met as Music Director, I had several broad ideas, such as doing new productions of the operas of Mozart, introducing masterpieces of the twentieth century, refurbishing the standard repertory—making sure the war horses could do their paces in style—and exploring works that may have been out of our repertory for a long time or may *never* have been in it. That's a large order, but we have a large company with a glorious history and resources to match. To live up to our own ideals and those of the public, we have to think clearly and deeply and move ahead. Nothing stays the same—everything keeps developing and changing, and if you rest on your laurels, pretty soon they get dusty and tarnished.

Fortunately, the literature of opera is so vast that it will always invite and sustain an extraordinary range of ideas—broadening the repertory, improving a company's sense of style in any given period, extending forward or backward the periods from which we can select works to present. For instance, until the Centennial season 1983–84, the Met had never staged a Handel opera. The Canadian Government made us a gift of their Ottawa production of *Rinaldo,* and Met subscribers discovered an opera composer whose output is so generous that it would reward any amount, any degree, of exploration—provided, of course, that the works receive superior performances. We have expanded our range of capabilities to encompass this style. It is not unreasonable to imagine that some of Handel's operas will join the standard repertory in our lifetime. Several of them are practically there, or are standing in the wings as members of the occasional repertory.

Older music—that is, from before Mozart's time—has been neglected by today's opera companies until relatively recently, but we have just as much enthusiasm for our contemporary masters, and, yes, even for works from the well-trodden paths of romanticism that have been overlooked. I have found it incredibly exciting, for example, to restore Mozart's *Die Entführung aus dem Serail* (four performances in 1946 had been its entire Met exposure), and to introduce his *Idomeneo* and *La Clemenza di Tito* to the Met stage. Mozart, you might think, is a "sure thing," but our regular audience knew these works only from phonograph records or rare performances by other companies. Verdi too is considered a staple, but when we take a fresh look at *Luisa Miller, I Vespri Siciliani, Ernani,* or *Simon Boccanegra* we are seeing his less familiar side, recognizing the full scope of his genius. From more recent times, the verismo composers of the turn of the century (Mascagni, Leoncavallo, Puccini) have given us repertory stalwarts, but they have also written interesting operas that are less often performed. The Met has restored Puccini's *Il Trittico,* for instance—a masterpiece that had its world premiere with our company in 1918. There are also works by less well-known composers of the same period that repay a fresh look: consider Zandonai's *Francesca da Rimini,* based on D'Annunzio's retelling of a classic Italian story that goes all the way back to Dante's reference to a real-life incident, which we revived in the 1983–84 Centennial season.

As the twentieth century progresses through its last quarter, our perspective lengthens, and we can see what our times have produced. The bulk of the standard repertory is said to be nineteenth-century, but Strauss and Puccini, Debussy and Ravel, Berg and Schoenberg, Poulenc and Britten wrote all or most of their operas in the twentieth. (Verdi, after all, died in 1901.) Under the Gatti-Casazza administration, the Met paid a surprising amount of attention to contemporary works, including many American ones. It need not discourage us that most of these have been forgotten: the mortality rate among operas has been high during all periods, especially throughout the alleged heyday of mid- and late-nineteenth century. The important thing is that the works were written and produced, and that many have survived.

Since the Great Depression and World War II, which made opera much more costly to produce and disastrously affected the continuity of artistic development from one generation to the next, we have been obliged to proceed more cautiously with contemporary repertory, but the enthusiasm remains. We have produced three major works of Benjamin Britten, brought the American classic *Porgy and Bess* to our stage for the first time, introduced Kurt Weill's *Mahagonny*, revived Alban Berg's *Wozzeck* and added his *Lulu*, offered the Met premieres of Stravinsky's *The Rake's Progress* and *Oedipus Rex* and a revival of *Le Rossignol*, as well as two Poulenc operas and Ravel's *L'Enfant et les Sortilèges*. Of course, there is some resistance whenever a new work appears, but for me the overwhelmingly exciting thing is to see this gradually melt away as audiences come to share our enthusiasm. These twentieth-century works are enjoying an unparalleled success and finding an ever larger following. It is often said that opera audiences are conservative, that they like what they know. Perhaps—but they are getting to know more and more of the boundless riches of the repertory.

I have been speaking mainly of the Metropolitan, which is closest to my heart and mind, but I am convinced that the trend toward a broader standard repertory, plus greater curiosity toward the nonstandard, is worldwide. Today's classic was yesterday's novelty, and many of today's novelties will be tomorrow's classics. Opera is a mainstream art, and the stream keeps moving. It is illuminating to remember, for example, how long it took for *Così Fan Tutte*—totally accepted today—to be "rediscovered" in the twentieth century after years of relative obscurity. When I was growing up, the Verdi standard repertory meant *Rigoletto, Il Trovatore, La Traviata,* and *Aida,* but now we see and hear *Otello, Falstaff,* and *Don Carlo* (all masterpieces) just as frequently.

The person who loves opera usually cannot get enough of it. Here is a book with the stories of 150 operas: to read any of them fills me with excitement and rekindles my imagination, for each is not only a musical experience but a dramatic, poetic, historical, psychological, and in every way a passionate one as well. Some of these operas are thrice familiar, some are encountered only occasionally, but all are richly stimulating. I commend them to you and hope you will have a chance to hear and see them all, plus perhaps many more, because there is no such thing as too much of anything so varied and rewarding as opera.

INTRODUCTION

BY PETER ALLEN

"I would have you serve the poet better than the composer."

*Giuseppe Verdi to Felice
Varesi, his first Macbeth*

In a good many years behind the microphone, including ten with the Texaco–Metropolitan Opera radio and television broadcasts, I've made a fair number of introductions, but this one gives me particular pleasure, partly because I have long admired John Freeman's writings on opera, and partly because I'm so keenly in sympathy with the purpose of this book. That purpose is, simply, to help people—not just aficionados, but even those who may be a bit skeptical about opera—to enjoy what I and many, many others feel is one of the great experiences of our civilization.

I can speak with authority about "those who may be a bit skeptical," because I was once one of their number. As a youngster I was lucky enough to be able to play in string quartets, quintets, the school orchestra (even the marching band!—cymbals and bass drum). I took pleasure in making and listening to all kinds of music. That is, *instrumental* music. Opera was a different story. In fact—and I blush a bit to say it—when it came to opera, I was indifferent or even somewhat scornful. The little I knew of it was that the plots were often ridiculous. I was also a young actor and drama student, and so, ironically, my prejudice was strengthened by my love of both music and drama.

Music and drama. Had I known then that Richard Wagner rejected the very word "opera" and called his works "music dramas"—had I known that he contended vigorously that music was only the means to serve the higher purpose of drama, and then went on to give us gigantic works in which the reverse is arguably the case—I might have been moved to look more deeply into this paradox. It is more likely, however, that I'd have shrugged off the whole question with my prejudice even more deeply rooted, in agreement with the venerable Dr. Johnson, who some two centuries ago labeled opera "irrational."

xxv

Well, the plots that are the subject of this book have not changed since I was a youngster; why is my reaction so different today? It would beg the question to say that since those days I've heard some operas. What is it about the operas themselves? It is simply that the miracle of music can transform a seemingly unworthy story into a profoundly satisfying emotional experience. And even successful stories and plays have been given deeper and more lasting success by transformation into operas—*La Bohème, Carmen, La Traviata, Tosca, Madama Butterfly, Rigoletto,* are but a few examples.

Nonetheless, despite the powerful role of the music, even the least impressive of stories is vitally important in an opera, not only for the audience but also for the composer. One of the Titans of music, Beethoven, wrote only one opera—a masterpiece, but only one. In the more than twenty years left him after the first performance of his *Fidelio,* he sought in vain for a story that could serve him for a second opera. The tale of a devoted wife's heroic love stimulated this wifeless man in a way he could find in no other story. Yet to us today, the heroine's last-minute rescue of the unjustly imprisoned hero (to mention only one of *Fidelio*'s dramaturgical shortcomings) seems decidedly melodramatic and naïve. True, last-minute rescues and unjust imprisonments did not seem unbelievable in those turbulent days during and shortly after the French Revolution (and perhaps they don't seem strange today, either), and true, the story attracted three other composers before Beethoven, but that kind of apology hardly makes it more palatable to the modern theatergoer. Nevertheless, in the opera house, the last-minute rescue, even as our twentieth-century credulity may be strained a bit, stirs within us an intense, noble exhilaration.

Curiously, Beethoven "summarized" his opera in the overtures John Freeman refers to, and which are by themselves favorites in the concert hall. But satisfying as these orchestral works are, they can never displace the experience in the opera house. And not simply because they are much shorter than the opera: even brilliant concert readings of an entire opera are, finally, lacking in the dramatic impact of a staged performance.

But surely, some readers may be saying, all of that can be taken for granted. After all, was not opera invented, in Florence just before 1600, by men trying to restore what they thought were the methods of the Greek dramatists—that is, the use of music to reinforce speech? Yes, but Wagner's argument for the supremacy of drama over music in the opera house was prompted by operatic practices he felt disregarded that goal and sacrificed dramatic values, not only to the music but even to mere vocal display. As an extreme example, a singer sometimes, quite regardless of the plot, would insert a favorite old number in a brand-new opera, merely as a showpiece for the performer. (They were called "suitcase" arias, because they traveled with the singer from opera house to opera house.) Or consider Verdi, who boycotted the Teatro alla Scala for many years because its management reversed the sequence of two acts in one of his operas.

Perhaps singers no longer dictate as freely as they used to, but cries of anguish on that score (no pun intended) have come from the ranks of composers even now, while this book was being written. And stage directors still sometimes wield capricious authority. I have seen a production—not at the Met—in which the famous, beautiful, golden, long hair of Mélisande was short! When her frustrated husband seized her by the hair to shake her from side to side, as the score calls on him to do, his hands held nothing. In the same production, the delicate music Debussy wrote for scene changes, to be played by the orchestra with the curtain down, was played with the curtain up, as women in black changed the sets. This may have shown a knowledge of Oriental stagecraft, but it defeated the music.

I was lucky enough, however, to see Debussy get revenge, at least at one performance. When the women of simulated invisibility were wheeling away the injured, bedridden husband, the wheels of the bed became tangled in the carpeting. Poor Golaud, feeling the frantic tugging going on about him, lifted his head, raised his eyebrows to the audience, shrugged his shoulders, and got out of bed just in time to lift it clear of the obstruction, as Pelléas walked onstage, staring in disbelief, to sing the next scene.

It would be unfair to end this without taking note of a point of view contrary to that of Wagner. It comes from no less a composer of opera than Mozart. He wrote, in a letter to his father, that in an opera the words must be "the obedient daughter of the music." Well, a century and a half after Mozart, a worshipful admirer of his, Richard Strauss, said musically in *Capriccio* what is probably the last—if still indecisive—word on the subject, as John Freeman points out near the end of his preface. At any rate, even Mozart, like all composers of opera, always began with the story. It's the right place for us to begin, too.

PREFACE

As an adolescent, when I first fell under the spell of opera (having liked instrumental music since childhood), I was given a pocket-size book, no larger than the palm of your hand, called *The Story of a Hundred Operas.* Many of the operas it contained were not in repertory then, and there was no way to hear them on records. The book was like a set of picture postcards from some distant, exotic corner of the world, and it sparked a lifelong desire to travel and explore among its treasures.

Mindful of what that little book meant to me, I have written a bigger one, sharing the opera stories at greater length. The purpose of this book is to make available the stories of a large number of operas, both the standard ones and those likely to be met occasionally. The task sounds simple, but as one moves away from familiar territory, there is many a judgment of Solomon to be made. Fortunately, I had plenty of help.

Sparked by the excitement of the centennial season of the Metropolitan Opera, my employer of nearly a quarter-century, the Metropolitan Opera Guild, reactivated the long-nourished idea of such a book. Its prime movers were Geoff Peterson, the Guild's director; merchandising chief Paul Gruber; and a free-lance book producer, Leslie Carola. Mrs. Carola set the project in motion by soliciting a basic list from the editorial staff of *Opera News.* The resulting list consisted of every remotely interesting opera anyone could think of, and the next step was to pare it down. There would be room in the book for 140 operas, so people were asked to vote again, singling out the titles most likely to be encountered. Not all the operas, of course, have been presented by the Met, but that was no obstacle. It seems appropriate for a major world opera company to offer such a list of stories to opera-lovers at large.

Discussion followed, anticipating the inevitable "But what about . . ." and "How dare they omit (or include) . . ." type of reaction. Meanwhile, the list was reviewed with W. W. Norton's music editor, Claire Brook; with last-minute deletions and additions swelling the total to 150, it was as final as we could make it. If compromises were inevitable, we were able to feel they had been fairly weighed. If some of the marginal operas may still be questioned, the core of the current world repertory is here.

On to the next step: how best to tell the stories? In most opera synopses, the aim is quick information or memory refreshment—no room for details. To restore details at every hand, however, would cause the main plot line to disappear. Keeping the serious listener's needs in mind (those quick digests in the theater program are still of vital help as the house lights are going down), stories were evaluated as they went along, clarity coming first, but with reasonable completeness a close second. If a key prop or bit of stage business is integral to the plot, it should not be taken for granted. If an aria or ensemble goes on for several minutes while action is suspended, the listener needs a clue as to what the characters are expressing.

It should be emphasized that our stories reflect the composers' and librettists' intentions, not necessarily current stage practice. There is no accounting for what a stage director and / or designer may do. Wagner wanted his Valkyries riding and his Rhinemaidens swimming, but such effects are seldom attempted literally. The *Ernani* text asks the hero to leap down from a parapet, but few tenors would attempt so reckless a feat. A production of *Les Troyens* in which the Royal Hunt and Storm is staged the way Berlioz wrote it, as a ballet pantomime, would be hard to find. The reader should be prepared for such deviations and, especially in foreign productions, for finding the *Ring* set in a factory or *La Forza del Destino* in a hospital ward. A recent *Faust* in its native city used sets and costumes that would have been just right for *Louise.*

Though the score and libretto had to be our last court of appeal, it was a surprise to find how cavalier composers and authors could be. By no means are the time and place of action always specified, and lapses of time between scenes are often left to be inferred. Occasionally we found ourselves with no alternative but to fall back on the time-honored catch-all of "legendary antiquity."

Two favorite marathon-argument subjects in opera are translation (the opera-in-English controversy) and the literary merit of librettos. For this book it was decided to adhere to the language of the original insofar as practical (we stopped short of Cyrillic typography), both for the titles and for the characters' names. There are a few exceptions. No English-speaking person refers to *Prodaná Nevěsta* as anything but *The Bartered Bride.* Several originally French operas *(La Favorite, Les Vêpres Siciliennes, Don Carlos)* are almost invariably produced in Italian editions authorized by their composers; for the sake of intelligibility, these are given in the form most often encountered.

Slips of the composer's, copyist's or compositor's hand also had to be accounted for. Donizetti could not cope with the name Ashton, writing it as "Asthon" in *Lucia di Lammermoor.* Within the score of *Les Contes d'Hoffmann* as originally published, it is possible to find "Dappertutto" spelled with either one "p" or two. Not all mistakes start at the source: many develop later, such as the popular pastime of adding a definite article before *Tosca, Götterdämmerung, Pagliacci* and *Dialogues des Carmélites.* The case of Ponchielli's *(La) Gioconda* is still arguable, since one authority (Loewenberg's *Annals of Opera*) gives the title without the article, but annals of La Scala from the era of the premiere give it with.

Mythology and history, those two mainstays of the librettist's art, pose the knottiest problems. Students of literature know Dido, Aegisthus, Jokanaan and Philip II, but Berlioz, Strauss and Verdi (and their onstage characters) deal with Didon, Aegisth, Jochanaan and Filippo. Since this is a book about operas, not about Vergil, Sophocles, Wilde or Spanish history, and since operas are usually performed in their mother tongue, the published versions have been kept. To do otherwise would open the door to calling Lucia "Lucy" or transliterating Madama Butterfly's name as "Cho-Cho-San." Designations other than proper names, however—kings, counts, messengers, flowermaidens—have been translated.

Dramatic plausibility is the area in which librettos are most often held up to ridicule, but even a casual sympathy with opera should make clear that the aims of this art form don't include literal accuracy. If one stops to think about an opera plot, as distinct from experiencing it as a series of emotional climates, one will soon be in trouble, perhaps even in stitches. If Manrico in *Il Trovatore* has been captured while trying to rescue his mother from the stake, why is she in prison and not among the cinders? If Silva in *Ernani* has already faced the king as his ward's would-be abductor, why does he seem so surprised when Ernani later tells him the king is their rival? In *Les Huguenots,* Nevers, placed under house arrest for refusing to join in the St. Bartholomew's Day massacre, nevertheless manages to get killed in the fighting. In *Wozzeck,* we cannot help wondering who is Marie's baby-sitter; classical operas such as *Medea,* with their parade of confidantes and ladies-in-waiting, obviate such a problem, though they pose others. There are countless non sequiturs, and every opera-lover has his favorites, but they never seem to interfere with the expressive effect of an intelligently staged, well sung performance.

Problems of time sequence are also legion. Scarpia's minions could not possibly get to Mario's villa and back in the few minutes allotted them in Act II of *Tosca,* and so forth. The most intriguing question of time is perhaps that posed by Elina Makropoulos in Janáček's opera that bears her name. Toward the end she gives her birth date as 1575 but then changes it to 1585, ten years later. Is she just being a prima donna about her age?

Since ours is not a book about librettos per se, any more than it is a book about the music, there is no need to evaluate literary quality—a pursuit open to anyone who reads librettos. The most highly estimated examples of the genre—those by Da Ponte, Boito, and Hofmannsthal, for instance—are good reading, and so are many of the more workaday examples, such as *Andrea Chénier.* Interestingly enough, however, the best reading is the libretto that can stand by itself, and which therefore is perhaps by definition not the best libretto, in the sense of inviting a partnership with the music. Two of this class, Boito's *Mefistofele* and Hindemith's *Mathis der Maler,* are by the very composers who wrote the music. One, Clemens Krauss' witty *Capriccio,* is by a musician and man of the theater. Two others, *The Rake's Progress* and *Francesca da Rimini,* are by ranking poets (Auden, D'Annunzio) who loved music so much that they longed to collaborate with composers.

The point argued in *Capriccio* is that the question of which takes primacy—the words or the music—cannot and should not ever be settled. Many opera-lovers are primarily voice fanciers, and some admit they would rather not be concerned with understanding the words. Composers, on the other hand, usually insist on translation when their operas are performed abroad. Today we can follow a recorded or broadcast opera with printed text or synopsis and have the best of both possible worlds. But the real moment of truth comes in the theater. By trying to clarify what happens there, we hope to have eased the way for many operagoers past, present, and future.

JOHN W. FREEMAN

ACKNOWLEDGMENTS: The author wishes to thank Claire Brook and Otto Sontag for their diligent, discerning help in editing. For help in finding, checking and clarifying rare source materials, he is indebted to Erika Davidson, Yveta Synek Graff and Mrs. Jan Peerce.

STORIES
of the
GREAT
OPERAS

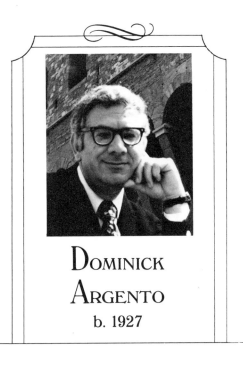

DOMINICK ARGENTO
b. 1927

*A*n American composer with eight performed operas to his credit is something of a curiosity, but the description fits Dominick Argento. Born in York, Pennsylvania, of Italian immigrant parents, Argento from the first revealed an affinity for vocal music. In 1975 he won a Pulitzer Prize for one of his song cycles, *From the Diary of Virginia Woolf.* His most ambitious stage work to date is the imaginative opera *The Voyage of Edgar Allan Poe* (1976), introduced by the Minnesota Opera, of which he was cofounder when it started as the Center Opera Company. Minneapolis has been his base of operations since 1958, when he was appointed to the faculty of the University of Minnesota, where he teaches composition and the history of opera. In addition, he spends part of each year in Florence, his "adopted spiritual home."

The Minnesota Opera also served as midwife for his one-act *Postcard from Morocco* (1971), the best-known of Argento's operas. Considered a major breakthrough in his work, this "symbolic fantasy" laid the groundwork for *The Voyage of Edgar Allan Poe* by establishing a kind of evocative whimsy in place of the neo-verismo that has informed so many American operas. "I've never been intrigued with musical problems and solutions per se," the composer has observed. "The interest is in people. Words are people." Though he studied in Italy with Luigi Dallapiccola on a Fulbright scholarship, Argento has chosen to write in what Nicolas Slonimsky describes as a "constructively eclectic" style, "ranging from expansive Italianate cantabile to tense and acerb

1

polyphony." Another writer, Peter Altman, says Argento "is conservative and literary and believes unapologetically that music should be 'expressive.' "

In his foreword to John Donahue's text for *Postcard from Morocco*, Argento compares the work to Wagner's *Der Fliegende Holländer*, since both are concerned with wandering voyages by persons who are, each in his own way, condemned. "The scene is like a memory (1914)," Donahue specifies in his own foreword to the text—"like an old postcard from a foreign land showing the railway station of Morocco or some place, hot and strange, like the interior of a glass-covered pavilion or spa. . . . Around this waiting room are scattered the people. Some are real, and some are not. . . . We see each one trying hard to protect whatever small part of himself he has in his suitcase, the symbol of his secret or lack of secret, his dream or lack of dream. . . ."

POSTCARD FROM MOROCCO

ONE ACT
MUSIC: Dominick Argento
TEXT (English): John Donahue
WORLD PREMIERE: Minneapolis, Center Opera, October 14, 1971

CHARACTERS

The Mirror Lady Operetta Singer	Coloratura Soprano
The Cake Lady	Soprano
The Hat Lady Foreign Singer	Mezzo-Soprano
Mr. Owen, painter	Tenor
Old-Luggage Man First Puppet Operetta Singer	Lyric tenor
The Shoe Man Second Puppet	Baritone
The Cornet Man Puppet Maker	Bass

Entertainers, puppets, dancers, passengers

A group of characters is discovered at the curtain's rise, each identified with some pet possession or eccentricity, chattering among themselves without communicating. All seem to be en route to various destinations and jealously guard their luggage. The Mirror Lady explains she always carries a mirror: it helps her to see things in unlikely places. To entertain those waiting, a continuous floor show takes place, starting with puppets who discuss building a ship; at first they have fun talking about the various kinds of storybook boats they could make, but then they begin fighting about it. The people watching take a cautious interest, intrigued by the idea of sailing away. Abruptly the time changes, and instead of the puppets there is a Foreign Singer, offering a song in some incomprehensible language, followed by a "fascination" dance. When the Cornet Man comments on the Old-Luggage Man's suitcase, the latter explains that old luggage is less likely to be stolen. The Hat Lady, thinking they all look like birds on a fence, makes bird noises, while the Cornet Man mentions (but refuses to show) the instrument he carries in his case. The Hat Lady parries questions about her hatbox, saying she makes special hats to order. As the band strikes up a Wagner medley to accompany magic tricks by the entertainers, the Shoe Man remarks that he is not carrying his own clothes: he is a salesman, with samples of every kind of shoe, which he refuses to show except by appointment (*You'd think a person could travel lighter than this*). As two operetta singers offer a duet (*Bubi, Bubi, Mädi, Mädi*), some of the group inquire about the Cake Lady's cake box, which she mysteriously says contains her lover. Mr. Owen, a shy painter, hesitantly ventures that he once saw her with her lover and sketched them (*And I traced that smile*), but she denies it, though he describes the scene in detail. Then he addresses one of the inanimate figures seated in the room, telling of a magical sailing vessel he imagined as a youth, before mundane concerns deprived him of his fantasy. The Puppet Maker appears behind the puppet stage, saying he designs his creations by observing people in real life. Sensing that Mr. Owen is the most vulnerable member of the group, the others badger him to paint their picture and press their inquiries about what he carries in his box. The Old-Luggage Man announces that Mr. Owen will paint a group portrait, for which the Cornet Man requests a Moroccan setting. Mr. Owen protests (*Oh, no, no . . . I'm afraid I don't*), but they jostle him until he drops his box, which flies open and is seen to be empty. Mr. Owen lets out a cry of anguish, like a train whistle, but the others unconcernedly resume their meaningless small talk, then leave him alone on the small stage with one puppet who has just knocked out another in their ongoing argument. Mr. Owen assumes the role of captain of an imaginary ship (*All hands! Move quickly*). He steers it toward parts unknown.

SAMUEL BARBER
1910–80

*S*amuel Barber, a nephew of the Metropolitan Opera contralto Louise Homer and himself a professionally trained baritone, was the most prominent American songwriter and conservative symphonist of his generation. Though content to write in traditional forms, to which he contributed music of patrician lyric eloquence, he was slow to undertake an opera. In 1954 he finally joined forces with his lifelong friend Gian Carlo Menotti, who agreed to write a libretto for another composer (all his others he set to music himself). The resulting work, *Vanessa,* won the Pulitzer Prize for composition in 1958 and had its world premiere at the Met, with Dimitri Mitropoulos conducting, Eleanor Steber in the title role, and Nicolai Gedda as Anatol. It was recorded by this cast, but Barber later revised and slightly cut the score, reducing it from four acts to three, and in this version it was performed at Spoleto U.S.A. shortly before the composer's death.

VANESSA

THREE ACTS
MUSIC: Samuel Barber
TEXT (English): Gian Carlo Menotti
WORLD PREMIERE: New York, Metropolitan Opera,
    January 15, 1958

CHARACTERS

Vanessa, *beautiful baroness, about forty* . . . . Soprano
Erika, *her niece, about twenty* . . . . Mezzo-Soprano
The Old Baroness, *Vanessa's mother and Erika's grandmother* . . . .
. . . . Mezzo-Soprano
Anatol, *man in his early twenties* . . . . Tenor
The Old Doctor . . . . Bass
Nicholas, *the majordomo* . . . . Baritone
A Footman . . . . Tenor
The Young Pastor . . . . Mime
Servants, guests, peasants

ACT I A luxurious drawing room in a "Northern country" suggestive of
Russia or Scandinavia, around 1905. Erika dictates a dinner menu in French
to her aunt Vanessa's majordomo. Evidently an important guest is expected;
Vanessa worries that he may lose his way in the snowstorm that is raging. The
Baroness, Vanessa's mother, who has not spoken to her daughter in years,
silently goes to bed as Erika walks to the window and looks out (*Must the
winter come so soon?*). Almost immediately thereafter the guest arrives; as he
stands silhouetted in the doorway, Vanessa addresses him as her lover of twenty
years ago (*Do not utter a word, Anatol*). But to her shocked amazement, she
discovers he is not Anatol—Anatol has died, and in his stead his son has come,
curious to meet her (*All through my youth I heard that name, Vanessa*). Angrily
refusing to see this "imposter," Vanessa goes upstairs, leaving the young Anatol with Erika, who reluctantly agrees to have supper with him.

§ On a Sunday morning a month later, Erika confesses to the Baroness that
on the night of Anatol's arrival she let him seduce her. He has offered marriage, but she feels him incapable of love—and besides, Vanessa now seems
infatuated with him. As if to confirm this, Vanessa and Anatol enter happily

from skating. A family friend, the Old Doctor, who has come to join them for chapel, recalls the gaiety of the house in olden times and tries out a dance step with Vanessa (*Under the willow tree*). Vanessa confides to Erika that Anatol has come close to proposing; then she joins the Pastor, who has just arrived, for coffee. The Baroness warns Erika that Anatol will "choose what is easier," so the girl confronts him when he comes back from the adjoining room, asking whether it is true that he proposed to Vanessa. He replies that his offer to marry Erika is still good, laughing at her old-fashioned sentimentality (*Outside this house the world has changed*). Disillusioned by his shallowness, she does not reply, and when the others return en route to chapel, she stays behind, uncovering the mirrors and a portrait of Vanessa, all of which have been hidden for years. As a hymn drifts in from the chapel, Erika declares to herself that she will not marry Anatol: Vanessa, who waited so long for so little, is welcome to him.

ACT II On New Years' Eve, in the entrance hall, guests arrive for a festive evening. Slightly inebriated, the Doctor confides to the majordomo, Nicholas, that he missed his calling: there is not much poetry in medicine, but he has a poet's soul. Vanessa comes to find him. Remembering that he is to announce her engagement, he starts to address the guests, but instead she sends him upstairs to fetch Erika and the Baroness, who have both refused to come down. Seeing her anger, Anatol advises her against too much brooding (duet: *Love has a bitter core*). The Doctor returns; Erika would not admit him. They all go into the ballroom, where the Doctor's voice is heard beginning his announcement, as Erika, pale and faltering, starts down the stairs and faints. Muttering that Anatol's child must not be born, she goes out into the night. The Baroness comes down too late to stop her.

ACT III A few hours later, as dawn approaches, Vanessa paces back and forth in Erika's room, complaining to the Doctor and Baroness that the girl has not yet been found (*Why must the greatest sorrows come from those we most love?*). Anatol and a group of peasants arrive; he is carrying the unconscious Erika, whom he found in a ravine (*On the path to the lake*). Suspecting that Erika and Anatol may have been lovers, Vanessa questions him. When he denies it, saying that Erika chose to judge him instead, Vanessa asks him to take her away from this house. The Doctor sees them out: reviving, Erika asks to be alone with her grandmother. When she tells the Baroness that her child will not be born, the old woman recoils in horror and refuses to speak to her, condemning her to endure the same silence that Vanessa endured for years.

§ Two weeks later, in the drawing room: Anatol and Vanessa are ready to leave for Paris, where they plan to live. The Doctor sadly contemplates his impending loneliness (*For every love there is a last farewell*). Alone with Erika for a moment, Vanessa tells the girl that she has willed her the house—unbeknownst to Anatol—and that she can live there as long as she likes.

Laconically, Erika replies she is ready to take Vanessa's place, evading direct questions about New Year's Eve by saying, "I thought I loved someone who did not love me." Vanessa and Anatol take a last look around the house; then, joined by Erika, the Doctor, and the Baroness, they muse about the sadness and elusiveness of love (quintet: *To leave, to break*). As the couple departs, Erika recognizes the wrench of her loss of the unworthy Anatol, wondering whether Vanessa believed her denial that there was anything between them. Then she orders the mirrors in the house covered again and the gate to the estate closed to visitors: "Now it is my turn to wait!"

BÉLA BARTÓK
1881–1945

hough Béla Bartók, Hungary's foremost composer after Liszt, wrote only one opera—and that a short one, seldom performed onstage—it has been extraordinarily influential, because of its original, evocative orchestral imagery. Influenced in turn by Debussy's *Pelléas et Mélisande,* it is a poetic, interior drama. Drawn from the myth of Bluebeard (one of whose wives Mélisande had been) and set in mythical times, *Duke Bluebeard's Castle* is a symbolic piece, whose actual location is the psyche of man. Like a theme with variations, it explores the various recesses of personality. It has also been called an allegory of the loneliness of the artist. The libretto is written in unrhymed alliterative trochaic verse, the same archaic form found in the Finnish epic *Kalevala* and used by Longfellow in *Hiawatha.*

Béla Balázs' symbolist text found a congenial interpreter in Bartók, a shy, temperamental man. Maintaining the same high, inflexible principles in life that he upheld in his music, he left an eminent career in Hungary—where his folk-song research in collaboration with Zoltán Kodály had earned him wider fame than his own compositions—because of the encroaching Nazis. He tried to begin a new life in America, but he was beset with poor health (culminating in fatal leukemia) and precarious finances. Friends who tried to help him often found he was too proud to accept their offers, so they had to find acceptable disguises: Serge Koussevitzky devised a commission for Bartók's most famous work, the Concerto for Orchestra, one of a series of late masterpieces that belied his failing health. As World War II neared its end, Bartók died in New York City, his eventual fame in the New World just beginning.

DUKE BLUEBEARD'S CASTLE

(A Kékszakállú Herceg Vára)

PROLOGUE AND ONE ACT
MUSIC: Béla Bartók
TEXT (Hungarian): Béla Balázs
WORLD PREMIERE: Budapest, National Opera, May 24, 1918
U.S. PREMIERE: Dallas (concert version, in English),
    January 8, 1946
METROPOLITAN OPERA PREMIERE: June 10, 1974 (in English)

CHARACTERS

Bard . . . . Speaking part
Duke Bluebeard . . . . Bass
Judith, *his wife* . . . . Mezzo-Soprano

PROLOGUE   A Bard appears before the curtain to introduce the story. Where does it really take place, he asks—in the outside world, or the world within? Inviting the audience to watch with him, he concludes, "Old the castle, old the legend."

§ In the windowless hall of a Gothic castle, "like a cave hewn in the heart of solid rock," seven closed doors are seen to one side. Through the main entrance Bluebeard arrives with his bride, Judith, whom he has taken from her protesting family. Once the entrance door is closed, Judith wonders at the darkness and gloom *(Milyen sötél a te várad!)*. She wants to let in the light, but Bluebeard says that nothing can lighten his castle. Seeing the seven doors, she wants to open them. Reluctantly, Bluebeard gives her the key to the first, which reveals a bloody chamber full of instruments of torture; Judith imagines that the castle itself is moaning and its walls are bleeding. Shaken but unafraid, she advances to the second door, which opens to reveal an armory of implements of war. She marvels at Bluebeard's power and asks to open the rest of the doors, but he, urging her to leave them unopened, at length gives her only the next three keys. The third door reveals a treasury filled with riches, but as Judith admires them, she notices they are smeared with blood. The fourth door more promisingly opens upon a garden, but the flowers are bloodstained. When Judith unlocks the fifth door, sunlight floods the room from a window overlooking Bluebeard's realm. Dazzled, she momentarily covers her eyes. Bluebeard says this realm is hers now and takes her in his arms, though she is apprehensive about blood-red clouds she sees gathering. He hopes she will proceed no farther, but her curiosity is too great, and she insists on opening the next door, behind which she finds a sea of mournful water *(Csendes fehér tavat tátok)*—these are tears, says Bluebeard. He embraces her, vowing that the last door will remain shut, but she begins to ask about the women he has loved before—what were they like? He asks her to love him unquestioningly. It strikes her, however, that he must be keeping the secret of the seventh door from her because of murders he committed *(Nyisd ki a hetedik ajtót!)*. With infinite sadness he relinquishes the final key, saying she will now see his other wives. This time she is hesitant, but at last she unlocks the door. Three pale, splendidly attired women file out silently as Bluebeard hails them *(Szépek, szászor szépek)*: the first was his bride of the morning, the second came at midday, the third in the evening. Judith is therefore his bride of the night. From the treasury he fetches a crown, a cloak, and some jewels, with which he adorns her. As if in a trance, she follows the other three women back into the seventh door, which closes. Alone, Bluebeard is engulfed in darkness, muttering that night has fallen forever *(Es mindég is éjjel lesz már)*.

LUDWIG VAN
BEETHOVEN
1770–1827

*L*udwig van Beethoven, the best-known symphonic composer in history, also longed for success as an opera composer. Having played the viola in theater orchestras as a youth, he had definite ideas about what opera should be—not frivolous Italian farces (he saw Mozart's comedies as immoral) but bourgeois German theater pieces bearing a message to mankind. In 1803 he accepted a commission from Emanuel Schikaneder, who had induced Mozart to write *Die Zauberflöte,* but Schikaneder soon went out of business, and his contract was taken up by the Vienna Hoftheater. To fit Beethoven's requirements, the theater's secretary, Josef Sonnleithner, adapted a text from a play by Jean Nicolas Bouilly, a standard rescue drama of the period, set during the Terror of the French Revolution. The same play had been put to music by Pierre Gaveaux and Ferdinando Paer. Because Vienna was occupied by Napoleon's troops, the locale had to be changed to Spain.

Performed as *Leonore* at the Theater an der Wien in 1805, the work was not successful—partly because of routine banalities in the text, partly because Beethoven's music (from the same period as his Fifth Symphony and Fourth Piano Concerto) rose so far beyond the usual operatic fare. Beethoven, not least for financial reasons, was so eager for the work to succeed that he gave in to the advice of friends and cut some of the music. This version, too, failed in 1806. It was not until 1814 that the work, rechristened *Fidelio* and further revised from three acts into two, struck the mark, this time at the Kärntnertor

11

Theater. Beethoven wrote no fewer than four versions of the overture, of which the fourth customarily precedes the opera and the third (*Leonore* No. 3) is often played between the scenes of Act II, following a precedent set in the later nineteenth century, when scenic changes could not be effected as rapidly as with modern machinery.

Fidelio, never out of the Metropolitan Opera repertory longer than nine years (and that because of World War I), was chosen to mark the centenary of the composer's birth with a new production in 1970.

FIDELIO

(or, Die Eheliche Liebe)

TWO ACTS

MUSIC: Ludwig van Beethoven

TEXT (German): Josef Sonnleithner, after Jean Nicolas Bouilly's French play *Léonore, ou L'Amour Conjugal*

WORLD PREMIERE: Vienna, Theater an der Wien, November 20, 1805; revised version, Vienna, Kärntnertor Theater, May 23, 1814

U.S. PREMIERE: New York, Park Theatre, September 9, 1839 (in English)

METROPOLITAN OPERA PREMIERE: November 19, 1884

CHARACTERS

Leonore, *wife of Florestan,* in male attire as Fidelio . . . . Soprano
Marzelline, *daughter of Rocco* . . . . Soprano
Florestan, *Spanish nobleman* . . . . Tenor
Jacquino, *assistant to Rocco* . . . . Tenor
Don Pizarro, *governor of the prison* . . . . Baritone
Don Fernando, *king's minister* . . . . Bass
Rocco, *chief jailer* . . . . Bass
Soldiers, prisoners, people

ACT I A prison near Seville, eighteenth century. In the warden Rocco's quarters, his daughter, Marzelline, is busy ironing. Jacquino, her father's assistant, presses her on the subject of marriage; she gives evasive replies, having recently become enamored of Fidelio, a young man her father has hired. Jacquino renews his pleas, and when Rocco calls the youth away, Marzelline muses that she feels sorry for him but that her thoughts are only for Fidelio, whom she would like to marry instead (*Oh wär' ich schon mit dir vereint*). Rocco and Jacquino enter, along with Fidelio, carrying supplies and dispatches; father and daughter both believe that Fidelio returns Marzelline's interest (quartet: *Mir ist so wunderbar*). To Fidelio's discomfort, Rocco encourages the supposed romance and even gives sound advice about the importance of setting aside some money as a basis for married life (*Hat man nicht auch Gold beineben*). Changing the subject, Fidelio asks to help Rocco on his rounds in the dungeons below the prison. At first Rocco says he is under strict orders to admit no one there; he soon relents but says there is one cell where he still may not take Fidelio, that of a certain prisoner who has been there two years and cannot last much longer. Fidelio persists, saying the sight would not be too much (trio: *Ich habe Mut*), and Rocco agrees to ask the prison's governor, Don Pizarro, for permission to take Fidelio along to help him. Pizarro himself appears and reads the dispatches that Fidelio brought earlier. Discovering that Don Fernando, a minister of state, plans to investigate charges of unjust imprisonment, Pizarro fears especially that his enemy Florestan—believed dead by the outside world—will be discovered in the dungeon. Pizarro resolves to kill Florestan before the minister can find him (*Ha! welch' ein Augenblick!*). He posts a sentry who will sound a trumpet signal when the minister's carriage is seen approaching. Then he asks Rocco to help him in the murder; Rocco refuses, saying it is not part of his duties, but reluctantly agrees to dig a grave in the dungeon area while Pizarro himself dispatches the victim. Both men leave. Fidelio—who is in reality Leonore, wife of the prisoner Florestan, in disguise—has overheard the plan and curses Pizarro's villainy, declaring that hope and divine providence will guide her in rescuing her husband (*Abscheulicher!*). Fidelio persuades Rocco to allow some prisoners into the courtyard; they are grateful to see daylight and to breathe fresh air once more, but afraid to express their feelings too openly (chorus: *Oh welche Lust*). Rocco tells Fidelio that Pizarro has agreed to his taking a helper into the dungeons, adding that their immediate job is to dig a grave for the luckless man in solitary confinement. Marzelline and Jacquino burst in, however, with more news of Pizarro: he is angry that the prisoners were allowed into the courtyard. Soon he himself appears, but Rocco deflects his fury by reminding him of their urgent business with Florestan, saying that it will do no harm to treat the other prisoners more leniently for a few minutes while they prepare for the crime. The four jailers herd the prisoners back to their cells. Jacquino wonders to himself what Rocco and Fidelio are up to.

ACT II In the underground dungeon, Florestan lies in chains. He stirs from sleep and cries out against the darkness of the prison. He knows he must accept his fate but imagines a vision of Leonore, leading him if not to freedom then to the kingdom of heaven *(Gott! welch' Dunkel hier!)*. He falls back to sleep as Fidelio and Rocco come down the stairs and set to work digging; Fidelio keeps trying to get a look at the prisoner, who eventually stirs again. His wife now recognizes him, but he does not recognize her. He asks who the governor of the prison is; learning that it is Pizarro, "the criminal I dared to expose," he knows that his situation is hopeless but asks for at least a drink of water. Rocco offers his flask to Florestan, who gives heartfelt thanks (trio: *Euch werde Lohn*). Fidelio produces a piece of bread, which Rocco feels it would be too risky to offer, but he gives in, as Florestan repeats his thanks. Rocco goes to the stairs and gives a signal that the grave is ready. Pizarro descends, orders Florestan unchained from the wall, and confronts the prisoner with his revenge; Florestan faces him without fear, but when Pizarro lunges with a dagger, Fidelio steps between the two men, delaying the blow and causing confusion. When Pizarro tries to strike again, Fidelio identifies "himself" as Leonore, crying, "First kill his wife!" Rocco, Pizarro, and Florestan are all thunderstruck by the discovery that Fidelio is Leonore, but Pizarro tells both husband and wife to prepare for death. At this point Leonore produces a pistol and holds the tyrant at bay. A distant trumpet call announces the arrival of the minister Don Fernando. As soldiers come to escort Pizarro upstairs, Florestan turns to Leonore and says, "What have you done for my sake?" She replies simply, "Nothing," and they sing of their rapture at being reunited *(O namenlose Freude!)*.

§ On the parade ground of the fortress, sentries escort Don Fernando, who tells the kneeling prisoners to rise as the assembled crowd of townspeople hails the day *(Heil sei dem Tag)*. Rocco leads in Florestan and Leonore, telling of the courageous wife who saved her husband. Fernando is astonished to find his friend Florestan still alive. Pizarro tries to defend himself, implicating Rocco as an accomplice, but the prisoners and townspeople cry out against their oppressor. Fernando tells Rocco to free Florestan from his chains, then suggests that it would be most appropriate for Leonore to do so; she takes the key and removes his fetters *(O Gott, welch' ein Augenblick!)*. Soldiers lead Pizarro off, under arrest, as the assemblage praises a wife's noble love and heroism *(Wer ein solches Weib errungen)*.

VINCENZO BELLINI
1801–35

Vincenzo Bellini, Sicily's most famous composer, was born in Catania to a musical family and began studies at age three, composing an aria at six. A municipal scholarship enabled him to go to Naples at seventeen; there his first opera was produced while he was still a student. His talent soon attracted the attention of the influential impresario Domenico Barbaia, who got him a commission to write *Il Pirata* for La Scala, and the young man was on his way.

After three more operas on tragic romantic subjects, Bellini turned to a lighter, sentimental story with *La Sonnambula,* his first widely performed opera, introduced at La Scala early in 1831. A simple tale of the opéra-comique type, *La Sonnambula* was a very popular work in the nineteenth century, until French grand opera, Wagner, and verismo came along. At one time every major soprano and several mezzo-sopranos (using lower keys) essayed the title role of this charming opus, written by Bellini in Milan in early 1831 for performance at the Teatro Carcano. His first cast starred Giuditta Pasta, a great tragic actress known more for purity of style than for purity of voice, and the reigning tenor of the day, Giovanni Battista Rubini, who sang very high and with great expression, though he too was not renowned for quality of voice.

Another famous exponent of *La Sonnambula,* Jenny Lind, sang it ninety-eight times, twenty-two of them in London, where it was said to be Queen Victoria's favorite opera. Chopin, who asked to hear *Ah, non credea mirarti,* from *La Sonnambula,* on his deathbed, characterized Lind in the role as "infallibly pure and true, and above all I admire her *piano* passages, the charm of which is indescribable." When Maria Malibran sang in the opera (in English) at Drury Lane in 1833, Bellini heard her for the first time and found her superbly expressive. (Two years later he died near Paris in his early thirties, and a year to the day after that, she fell from a horse while pregnant and died at Manchester, aged twenty-eight.)

By the end of 1831, Bellini had completed *Norma,* also for La Scala. This proved to be his most enduring success, remaining in the repertory even during the first half of the twentieth century, when enthusiasm for bel canto—the florid vocal style that prevailed in the early nineteenth century—was at its lowest ebb. In the decades after World War II, *Norma*'s popularity led to a revival of interest in Bellini's other operas. During the same period, Bellini's bel canto compatriots Rossini and Donizetti, who likewise had been remembered chiefly for one opera apiece, also enjoyed a revival. Singers capable of performing this intricate music with the requisite dramatic accent and expression—Maria Callas, Leyla Gencer, Joan Sutherland, Giulietta Simionato, Renata Scotto—played a key role in restoring bel canto operas to public favor.

Both *Norma* and Bellini's last opera, *I Puritani di Scozia* (The Puritans of Scotland), were based on French plays. *I Puritani* enjoyed an enormous success when it was introduced in 1835 at the Théâtre des Italiens in Paris. Whereas *Norma* is a tour de force built around its protagonist, who sings in virtually every scene, *I Puritani* is an ensemble opera, conceived for a quartet (even a quintet) of major singers. The tenor parts of Bellini's operas, especially *La Sonnambula* and *I Puritani,* lie extremely high, having been written for the light, agile voice of Rubini, who first sang them; modern tenors invariably have to use transposed versions. Sopranos with coloratura technique, including Marcella Sembrich and Lilli Lehmann of the early Metropolitan Opera years, were the principal forces in keeping Bellini's work alive at all until the resurgence of interest in bel canto after World War II.

Bellini's music had many admirers, including Verdi, Wagner, Liszt, and Schopenhauer; there is also a kinship with his long-phrased, expressively ornamented style evident in the piano pieces of his friend Chopin. Historically, Bellini is the link between the classically shaped operas of Gluck and Spontini on the one hand and the modern dramatic concepts of Verdi and Wagner on the other. The finale of Wagner's *Ring* cycle, for example, owes more than a little to the death of Norma.

LA SONNAMBULA

TWO ACTS
MUSIC: Vincenzo Bellini
TEXT (Italian): Felice Romani
WORLD PREMIERE: Milan, Teatro Carcano, March 6, 1831
U.S. PREMIERE: New York, Park Theatre, November 13, 1835
    (in English)
METROPOLITAN OPERA PREMIERE: November 14, 1883

CHARACTERS

Teresa, *owner of the mill* . . . . Mezzo-Soprano
Amina, *her foster daughter* . . . . Soprano
Lisa, *innkeeper* . . . . Soprano
Elvino, *young farmer* . . . . Tenor
Count Rodolfo, *lord of the castle* . . . . Bass
Alessio, *villager* . . . . Bass
Notary, villagers, etc.

ACT I   A village in the Swiss Alps early in the nineteenth century. The betrothal of Amina to Elvino is being celebrated by everyone except the local innkeeper, Lisa, a cast-off sweetheart of Elvino's *(Tutto e gioia)*. Lisa is bothered by another suitor, Alessio, who leads the villagers in praise of Amina *(In Elvezia non v'ha rosa)*. Amina expresses her gratitude to Teresa, owner of the mill, who brought her up as an orphaned girl; to the happy Amina, everything seems wonderful *(Come per me sereno)*. She thanks Alessio for serenading her and greets her fiancé, a well-to-do young farmer, who has just returned from a visit to his mother's grave. As a notary draws up the marriage contract, Elvino gives Amina his mother's engagement ring *(Prendi, l'anel ti dono)*; to Lisa's continued annoyance, the lovers express their rapture. An approaching carriage brings an unexpected visitor, Count Rodolfo, traveling incognito to his castle nearby. Because it is getting late, he decides to stay at the inn, meanwhile touring the surrounding countryside in which he grew up but which he has not seen in years *(Vi ravviso, o luoghi ameni)*. He compliments the charming bride and, in response to inquiries about what brings him there, explains that he was brought up by the lord of the castle, now dead. About the lord's son, presumed to have disappeared, he says evasively that the heir is alive and will return. As darkness approaches, Teresa speaks of a phantom that has been appearing in the neighborhood; the villagers elaborate, describing for Rodolfo's benefit a ghostly creature that walks by night *(A fosco cielo)*. Amused by their superstition, Rodolfo would like to see the phantom, but the villagers pray he may be spared. Elvino takes exception to the stranger's fond farewell to Amina and quarrels with her, then apologizes, saying the very breeze that caresses her arouses his jealousy *(Son geloso del zefiro errante)*. Reconciled, they bid each other good night.

§ In Rodolfo's room at the inn, he flirts with Lisa but regrets her discovery of his identity as count of the local castle—vouched for by the mayor—saying he prefers to remain incognito. A disturbance outside causes Lisa to hide in the closet, dropping her kerchief, which Rodolfo places on the bed. The French window opens to admit Amina, walking in her sleep. Rodolfo realizes she is the "apparition." Deciding not to wake her, he closes the window while Lisa—noting Amina's presence and assuming the worst—makes her exit. Touched by Amina's murmurs of fidelity to Elvino, Rodolfo resolves not to compromise her, though he still finds her attractive. She sinks on the couch as the villagers approach, bent on paying respects to the man they have learned is their count. So as not to be found with Amina, he leaves. As the villagers wonder at discovering a woman on the couch, Elvino's voice is heard: the vengeful Lisa has fetched him. Awakened by the commotion, Amina protests her innocence *(D'un pensiero e d'un accento)* to the outraged Elvino, who breaks their engagement and tears off her ring. Teresa tries to stop Elvino from making hasty conclusions; finding Lisa's kerchief on the bed, she assumes it is Amina's and ties it around the girl's neck. The villagers side with Elvino, declaring Amina an outcast.

ACT II   In a wooded spot en route to the castle, villagers pause to plan how they will ask the count to exonerate Amina if she is indeed innocent of dallying with him *(Qui la selva)*. As they move on, Amina enters, comforted by Teresa, and observes that they are near Elvino's farm. He appears and reviles her; he will not listen to her protestations of innocence *(Tutto è sciolto)*. When Elvino hears that the count is on his way, ready to attest to Amina's virtue, he refuses to see his "rival." With Amina about to collapse, however, he begins to soften, wondering why he cannot hate her *(Ah! perchè non posso odiarti)*. In despair Elvino goes back to his farm, while Teresa leads off the swooning Amina.

§ In the village, Alessio tries in vain to arouse Lisa's interest. Soon others arrive to congratulate her on being Elvino's second choice for his bride. Elvino enters, asks for her hand, and suggests they head for the church at once. Rodolfo interrupts to intercede with Elvino on Amina's behalf: by his honor he swears she is innocent. Elvino cannot believe this, but Rodolfo explains to the incredulous villagers that there are people who walk in their sleep, not knowing what they are doing *(V'han certuni che dormendo).* Teresa appears and asks them all to be quiet, since Amina has fallen into exhausted sleep. Seeing that Lisa intends to marry Elvino, Teresa accuses her of being a hussy: as proof she produces the kerchief, found in Rodolfo's room. Dumbfounded that Lisa too seems unfaithful, Elvino renounces love and turns for advice to the count, who will repeat only that Amina has been wronged. His word is presently borne out by the appearance of Amina, sleepwalking across a narrow footbridge above the mill wheel. Afraid of waking her, all watch in awe as she negotiates the bridge safely. Still asleep, Amina mourns and forgives her lost Elvino, taking the faded bouquet he gave her and bidding it farewell *(Ah, non credea mirarti).* Unable to see her suffer, Elvino, encouraged by Rodolfo, goes up to the sleeping girl and gives her back her ring. Pronouncing herself utterly happy, she embraces Teresa and suddenly awakens—at first embarrassed, then overjoyed. Aware that her dream has come true, Amina says human thoughts cannot encompass her joy and declares that heavenly love will come to earth in her union with Elvino *(Ah! non giunge).* Amid general rejoicing, the couple heads for the church.

NORMA

TWO ACTS
MUSIC: Vincenzo Bellini
TEXT (Italian): Felice Romani, after Alexandre Soumet's French
   play *Norma, ou L'Infanticide*
WORLD PREMIERE: Milan, La Scala, December 26, 1831
U.S. PREMIERE: New Orleans, April 1, 1836
METROPOLITAN OPERA PREMIERE: February 27, 1890 (in German)

CHARACTERS

Norma, *high priestess of the Druid temple* . . . . Soprano
Adalgisa, *virgin of the temple* . . . . Soprano
Clotilde, *Norma's confidante* . . . . Soprano
Pollione, *Roman proconsul in Gaul* . . . . Tenor
Flavio, *centurion* . . . . Tenor
Oroveso, *arch-Druid, father of Norma* . . . . Bass
   Priests, officers of the temple, Gallic warriors,
      priestesses, virgins of the temple

ACT I   Ancient Gaul, ca. 50 B.C. In the sacred grove of the Druids, Oroveso,
leader of the high priests, leads Gallic warriors and Druids by night to their
place of worship. They are waiting for Norma, Oroveso's daughter, who is the
high priestess, and invoke the god Irminsul to help them throw off the yoke
of Roman occupation. As they move to another part of the forest, the Roman
proconsul Pollione and his officer Flavio enter quietly. Pollione confides that
he no longer loves Norma, who has secretly been his mistress (in violation of
her vows) and is the mother of his two children. He has fallen in love with a
younger priestess, Adalgisa, and hopes to catch sight of her in the sacred
grove. He says that in a dream he imagined he was in Rome being married to
Adalgisa when Norma's vengeance struck (*Meco all'altar di Venere*). Sounds in
the distance indicate the beginning of the Druids' rites. Pollione curses their
plotting against Roman authority but declares that the power of love will
enable him to triumph (*Me protegge, me difende*). As the two soldiers withdraw,
Norma and her priestesses enter the grove. Hoping to protect her lover, Norma
counsels against insurrection, saying Rome will fall of its own vices, though
Oroveso and the other men are impatient to fight. With her sickle Norma
cuts the sacred mistletoe and invokes the goddess of the moon (*Casta Diva*);
she asks for peace but adds that if the Druid deities inspire her to do so, she
will tell her followers when to strike the Romans. Aside she prays that Pollione, whose love she has felt waning, will return (*Ah! bello a me ritorna*).
When she and her followers have left, Adalgisa enters the grove alone, preoccupied with Pollione's offer of love, which conflicts with her religious vows.
Pollione interrupts her prayer and urges her to accompany him to Rome at
daybreak (*Va, crudele*). She refuses but agrees to meet him at the same place
the following night, admitting that she returns his love.

§ At her dwelling in the forest, Norma confides to her friend Clotilde, who
helps her care for her two sons, that she both loves and hates the children,
who remind her of her broken vows. Pollione, she says, has been recalled to
Rome and seems likely to abandon her. Adalgisa appears, hesitantly wanting
to reveal to Norma her conflicting feelings about Pollione; she does not realize
that he has been Norma's lover. Norma at first listens sympathetically, recalling that she herself once felt the same way (*Io fui così rapita*). Not until Pollione enters the scene does it dawn on her that *he* is Adalgisa's lover. She turns
her full fury on Pollione (*Oh, non tremare, o perfido*), who stands his ground,
saying that they have both sinned but that Adalgisa is not involved in their
past and should be spared. Disgusted with his infidelity, Norma tells him to
leave with Adalgisa, but Adalgisa refuses to betray her friendship with Norma.
Recriminations continue until the bronze gong in the distance summons Norma
to her duties. Adalgisa now joins Norma in telling Pollione he must leave.

ACT II   Again at her dwelling, Norma looks upon her sleeping children and
resolves to kill them, so as to punish Pollione and spare them from life in

Rome. She tries to strike but cannot, then calls Clotilda and asks her to bring Adalgisa. When Adalgisa arrives, Norma asks her to promise to take the children to Pollione and be a mother to them; she intends to take her own life. Adalgisa refuses, appealing to Norma's motherly feelings and swearing friendship *(Mira, o Norma)*. Pollione, she says, no longer means anything to her: she will stay with Norma *(Sì, fino all'ore estreme)*.

§ Near the forest, Gallic warriors watch impatiently for Pollione's rumored departure. Oroveso tells them the Romans are sending a more tyrannical governor to replace Pollione. Though eager to fight, Oroveso says they have no choice but to feign docility until the time is right *(Ah! del Tebro)*.

§ At the temple of Irminsul, Norma believes that Adalgisa will persuade Pollione to come back to her, but Clotilda arrives to report the failure of Adalgisa's mission: Pollione still intends to carry Adalgisa off to Rome. Hearing this, Norma rages against the Romans, strikes the gong to summon her people, and tells them it is time for war (chorus: *Guerra, guerra!*). Oroveso asks her to complete the ritual and designate a victim. There is a disturbance outside: a Roman has been caught profaning the sacred precincts. When Pollione is led in, Norma prepares to stab him but cannot. Stalling for time, she says she must question the intruder and orders everyone else to leave. Alone with Pollione, she offers him safety if he will give up Adalgisa and return to her, but he declares he would sooner die. She threatens again to kill their children, adding she will sacrifice Adalgisa as well, but Pollione insists he alone should die, offering to kill himself. She calls back the crowd and announces that the victim will be a priestess who broke her vows. Unable to denounce the innocent Adalgisa, she tells the stunned followers that she herself is guilty and wants the sacrificial pyre prepared. She tells Pollione they now will die together *(Qual cor tradisti)*. Recognizing her worth at last, he announces that his love for her has been reborn in their last moments. Norma tells her father, Oroveso, about the children and asks him to protect them from the Romans *(Deh! non volerli vittime)*; moved by her plea, he agrees. Then Norma and Pollione mount the pyre, she bidding her father a last farewell, he looking toward a purer love beyond death.

I PURITANI

(The Puritans)

THREE ACTS
MUSIC: Vincenzo Bellini
TEXT: (Italian): Count Carlo Pepoli
WORLD PREMIERE: Paris, Théâtre des Italiens, January 25, 1835
U.S. PREMIERE: Philadelphia, November 22, 1843
METROPOLITAN OPERA PREMIERE: October 29, 1883

CHARACTERS

Elvira, *daughter of Lord Walton* . . . . Soprano
Queen Enrichetta, *widow of Charles I* . . . . Soprano
Lord Arturo Talbot, *of the Cavaliers* . . . . Tenor
Sir Bruno Robertson, *of the Puritans* . . . . Tenor
Sir Riccardo Forth, *of the Puritans* . . . . Baritone
Lord Gualtiero Walton, *of the Puritans* . . . . Bass
Sir Giorgio Walton, *his brother, of the Puritans* . . . . Bass
    Puritans, Commonwealth soldiers, men-at-arms, women, pages, etc.

ACT I A Puritan fortress in the south of England, near Plymouth, about
1650, during the Civil War, shortly after the execution of Charles I. Puritan
soldiers sing of their readiness to fight the Stuarts. They are interrupted by a
matins bell and the sound of voices offering prayers in the castle chapel: it is
the wedding day of Elvira, daughter of Lord Gualtiero Walton. Everyone is
happy except Riccardo, a colonel in the Puritan army, who had hoped to
marry Elvira himself *(O Elvira, o mio sospir soave)*. Efforts by a fellow officer,
Bruno, to console him are in vain, for Elvira's father has consented to her
marriage to Lord Arturo Talbot—a Cavalier (i.e., a royalist) but the man of
her heart's choice. Reminding him of his military duty, Bruno leads Riccardo
away.

§ In her apartments, Elvira greets Sir Giorgio, an uncle whom she regards as
a second father. When he hails her wedding day, she says she would rather
die than marry anyone but her beloved Arturo. Giorgio tells her it was he who
persuaded her father to allow her to marry Arturo *(Sorgea la notte folta)*, who
even now is approaching the castle. Voices are heard hailing his arrival.

I Puritani

§ In the main hall of the castle, Elvira's father and uncle lead her to meet her fiancé, who greets her happily *(A te, o cara)*. Walton, however, must excuse himself to speak privately with Enrichetta (actually the widow of the executed king), whom he has been ordered to escort to Parliament. Arturo overhears this and becomes interested in the mysterious woman's plight. Speaking to her a few moments later, he discovers her identity and pledges to save her from certain condemnation by the revolutionary Cromwell government. Elvira returns after putting on bridal attire and playfully places her veil on Enrichetta to see how it looks *(Son vergin vezzosa)*. When Elvira and her coterie step outside again, Arturo tells Enrichetta to keep the veil as a disguise for their escape. Riccardo interrupts them, burning with jealousy, and the two men are about to fight. Enrichetta, struggling to separate them, is recognized by Riccardo, who then coldly tells Arturo to go ahead and leave, realizing that his rival will be compromised. When Elvira returns, Riccardo tells the wedding party the would-be groom has fled with the female prisoner, believed to be a spy for the Stuarts. Soldiers give chase to the fugitives as Elvira, imagining she sees Arturo *(O vieni al tempio)*, succumbs to irrationality.

ACT II   In the castle, with the Stuart forces visible in the distance, Puritan retainers mourn Elvira's madness and heartbreak. Giorgio describes her forlorn wanderings and fantasies *(Cinta di fiori)*: she keeps imagining her wedding to Arturo. Riccardo enters to announce that Arturo has been condemned to the block by Parliament but adds that he is still at large and must be hunted down. Elvira comes in, recalling her abandonment by Arturo and calling upon him to return *(Qui la voce)*, while Riccardo and Giorgio advise her to forget her unworthy lover. At length she departs, leaving Giorgio alone with Riccardo, whom he tells to save Arturo, since that is the only way of saving Elvira. Riccardo refuses, but Giorgio paints a pitiful picture of Elvira following her lover in death and haunting the intractable Riccardo *(Se tra il buio un fantasma vedrai)*. Riccardo is moved, but both men agree that if the enemy should attack tomorrow, and if Arturo should be among them, he deserves to die *(Suoni la tromba)*.

ACT III   In a storm near the castle, Arturo takes refuge from his pursuers. In the distance he hears Elvira's voice repeating a love song they once shared *(A una fonte afflitto e solo)*. As if to reply, he repeats the refrain, but sounds of a search party force him into hiding. When they have passed, he takes up the song once more, and this time Elvira hears him. She comes in, her mind still straying, but the shock of recognition restores her reason, as Arturo begs forgiveness and pledges his love anew after three months of separation. He explains that the woman with whom he fled was not Elvira's rival but the former queen. This revelation further clears Elvira's mind, and the two sing of their happiness *(Vieni fra queste braccia)*. When military strains are heard, however, Elvira's disorientation and anxiety return. Attentive to her condition, Arturo scarcely notices the arrival of the soldiers and their leaders, who recognize and revile him. At the shock of the word "death," Elvira suddenly comes to her senses once more. Arturo takes the blame for her misfortune and asks only to die at her side *(Credeasi, misera)*. She in turn feels responsible for his capture and wants to marry him, so that, if he must die, he will die her husband. Riccardo and Giorgio, stirred by the lovers' devotion, plead with the soldiers for mercy. Elvira seems about to swoon and die of grief when an offstage fanfare announces the defeat of the Stuart forces and a general amnesty for prisoners. As the Puritans hail England's liberation, they also forgive Arturo and wish the lovers happiness.

ALBAN BERG
1885–1935

*A*lban Berg, his friend Anton von Webern, and their teacher Arnold Schoenberg make up the threesome that has come to be known as the Second Viennese School. Together they pursued, each in his own way, the development of dodecaphony, the so-called twelve-tone system, widely considered at the time a destructive rebellion against accepted principles of music. In retrospect it appears a logical extension of the atonality implied by the more chromatic, complicated forms of late-romantic harmony, emblematized by the ambivalent opening chord of Wagner's *Tristan und Isolde*. Today one may easily hear Berg's music, particularly his operas, as part of the aesthetic of Mahler and of the more adventurous scores of Richard Strauss.

Berg lived most of his life in Vienna, except for vacations in the Alps. The smug conservatism of Vienna was the milieu against which he and his contemporaries in all the arts had to fight. During World War I, which embodied the collapse of the old regime and its backward-looking values, Berg served in the Austrian army; because of uncertain health, he was assigned to guard duty and bureaucratic chores in Vienna. This experience, combined with his discovery of the play *Woyzeck*—the tragedy of a poor soldier—fueled his desire to write an opera. The play had been pieced together from sketches left by Georg Büchner, who died in 1837 at twenty-three without completing his psychological drama, based on a court case of the 1820s. Statements of the real-life Woyzeck, whose name was misspelled by the first editor, were incorporated from the courtroom transcript.

Berg organized his work according to strict formal precepts, joining the scenes, as Debussy had done in *Pelléas et Mélisande,* with symphonic interludes. Act I is expository, introducing the characters, and uses short, self-contained forms, like those of a suite. Act II, concerned with developing relations between the characters, is conceived as a symphony. Act III, the inevitable denouement, is spelled out as a series of inventions, each centered on a different ostinato element. Using this structure for his own guidance, like an architect with a blueprint, Berg insisted the public should be unaware of the musical structure, experiencing the drama directly.

Though considered avant-garde at its premiere under Erich Kleiber in 1925, *Wozzeck* had twenty-one performances in Berlin within seven years, reaching the stages of sixteen other German cities and eleven foreign ones. The music seemed difficult and unfamiliar to both audiences and performers, but the stageworthiness and emotional urgency of the work, which captured the disillusion of European life at the time, came through.

During what remained of the 1920s, Berg wrote his *Lyric Suite* for string quartet, a landmark of twentieth-century chamber music, and a concert song, *Der Wein,* with orchestra. Meanwhile, he was working on his second and last opera, *Lulu,* a conflation of two Frank Wedekind plays that had been banned in Germany. *Lulu,* with its phantasmagorical elements (both dramatic and musical), represented a new direction for Berg, beyond the Expressionist mood of *Wozzeck* and toward a sardonic, ironically modern feeling. Again, the musical organization parallels the action. Act I, based on sonata form, follows Dr. Schön's entanglement and losing battle with Lulu; Act II, a rondo, centers on the fixation of various lovers, each of whom sees Lulu as an extension of his own fantasy; Act III, theme and variations, follows Lulu's disintegration.

In some ways *Lulu* is an ultimate, grotesque Viennese operetta, parodying the world of carefree amorality but stripping away the sugar coating. Witty and learned, it makes allusions to characters and situations from familiar operas: the Schoolboy, for example recalls Cherubino in *Le Nozze di Figaro*, and Alwa behaves not unlike Offenbach's Hoffmann. As in *Don Giovanni*, the subject is often treated frivolously, but there is no mistaking the deadly earnest outcome. Because one of the main characters, Countess Geschwitz, is a lesbian (as Berg's own sister was), and because of the human degradation portrayed in the work, the composer's widow, Helene, delayed publication of the third act, which he had finished in short score but which remained to be fully orchestrated much later. Until her death, in 1976, Act III was available only in truncated form, its first scene missing, with a pantomime of Lulu's death accompanied by the passacaglia from the previously published *Lulu* Suite. As completed by Friedrich Cerha, the work finally had its first complete performances starting in 1979.

In the last year of his life, Berg managed to complete his Violin Concerto, which had a posthumous premiere. Though he was a "pure Aryan," Berg's closeness to Schoenberg and their joint "decadent modernism" guaranteed the eclipse of their music from Central Europe during the Hitler era, and some of his manuscripts survived the Second World War only because they had been buried in a hiding place. Despite her distaste for the subject matter of *Lulu,* Helene Berg remained devoted to her husband's music through the nightmare decade that followed his death, and did not destroy the pages she refused to have performed during her lifetime.

WOZZECK

THREE ACTS
MUSIC: Alban Berg
TEXT (German): adapted by the composer from Georg Büchner's
    German play *Woyzeck*
WORLD PREMIERE: Berlin Staatsoper, December 14, 1925
U.S. PREMIERE: Philadelphia, Opera Company, March 19, 1931
METROPOLITAN OPERA PREMIERE: March 5, 1959 (in English)

CHARACTERS

Franz Wozzeck, *soldier* . . . . Baritone
Marie, *his mistress* . . . . Soprano
Margret, *neighbor* . . . . Contralto
Marie's Child . . . . Treble
Drum Major. . . . . Tenor
Andres, *soldier* . . . . Tenor
Captain . . . . Tenor
Doctor . . . . Bass
Fool . . . . Tenor
        Soldiers, maids, servants, children, apprentices

ACT I   One morning in Leipzig in 1824, Franz Wozzeck is shaving his Captain, who harangues him with random, half-baked "philosophical" observations. When he reproaches Wozzeck for having no moral sense, the soldier replies that according to the Bible his illegitimate child is still acceptable to Jesus. Not accustomed to being answered back, the Captain flies into a rage, but Wozzeck explains he cannot help being ignorant—it comes from being poor *(Wir arme Leut)*. Calming down, the Captain calls Wozzeck a worthy man but says he shouldn't think so much: his thoughts are disconcerting.

§ In a field outside town, Wozzeck, cutting brushwood with another soldier, Andres, imagines that the place is accursed. Ignoring Wozzeck's twilight hallucinations, Andres sings a hunting song, suspecting all along that his buddy is crazy. Relieved to hear distant drums calling them to quarters, Andres says they must go back.

§ In her room, Marie, Wozzeck's common-law wife, holds their child up to see the marching regiment, admiring the handsome Drum Major in his uniform (*Soldaten, Soldaten*). She quarrels with a neighbor, Margret, who accuses her of looking at every man. Slamming the window in Margret's face, Marie settles down with the child and sings a lullaby (*Mädel, was fangst Du jetzt an?*) that refers sadly to her unwed state. As the child falls asleep, Wozzeck knocks at the window; he says he cannot stay but describes his vision at sunset of the world in flames. As he rushes off, distracted, Marie fears for their future: his fantasies seem to be getting the better of him (*Der Mann! So vergeistert!*).

§ In the office of a mad Doctor who pays him to participate in experiments, Wozzeck tries to explain his fears and visions, which the Doctor reduces to medical terms—an interesting case, making Wozzeck the more valuable as a guinea pig. Ordering Wozzeck to continue on an experimental diet, the Doctor dreams of immortality through his discoveries (*Oh! meine Theorie!*).

§ In front of Marie's dwelling, the vain Drum Major struts for her, then responds to her admiration by seizing her. She resists but soon yields to his advances.

ACT II   Inside her room, Marie looks in a piece of broken mirror, admiring earrings the Drum Major has given her. To make her child fall asleep, she offers a frightening song about abduction by Gypsies (*Mädel, mach's Lädel zu!*). If it were not for her poverty and ignorance, she reflects, she could be as attractive as any noble lady. When Wozzeck approaches, she takes off the earrings, but he sees them in her hand. Making the excuse that she found them, Marie flares up touchily. Placating her, he hands over the money he has earned from the Captain and the Doctor (*Da ist wieder Geld, Marie*). When he leaves, she feels guilty and unworthy.

§ On the street, the Captain accosts the Doctor, who is not anxious to stop and talk with him. Finally the Doctor, realizing he is trapped for the moment, starts describing medical phenomena: the Captain looks to him like a candidate for a stroke someday (*Und Sie selbst! Hm! Aufgedunsen*). Hearing the symptoms, the Captain turns hysterical. As Wozzeck passes, saluting the two, they detain him with veiled taunts about Marie's infidelity (*Ein langer Bart unter dem Kinn*). Shaken by their jokes over a serious matter, Wozzeck tries to explain that life can be hell for a simple man: only by hanging oneself can one end it and know where one is. Overcome by his outburst, he hurries away, leaving the others to wonder at his peculiarities. To assuage his own insecurities, as the Doctor tries to get away, the Captain congratulates himself on his moral superiority to Wozzeck.

§ Outside Marie's door, Wozzeck rushes up to her, his fantasies stirred by jealousy: was it on this spot that she saw the Drum Major? Standing her ground, Marie declares that anyone can walk by in the street, but when Wozzeck lunges at her, she says she would rather have a knife in her heart than have him lay a violent hand on her. As she goes inside, Wozzeck thinks of the knife and feels himself falling into an abyss.

§ At evening, apprentices, soldiers, and servant girls are dancing in a tavern garden. Wozzeck arrives and sees Marie waltzing with the Drum Major (*Immer zu!*); in his rage he is about to interrupt them, but the dance ends, to be replaced by a hunting song (*Ein Jäger aus der Pfalz*). After joining in, Andres sits with Wozzeck, whose irrationality makes him seem drunk, though he is not. An apprentice climbs on the table and delivers a disjointed but fervent mock sermon (*Warum ist der Mensch?*), concluding that even his soul has been corrupted by drink. A Fool remarks to Wozzeck that he smells blood. As the others dance again, Wozzeck moans that everything seems to be twisting in a red mist.

§ Lying in the barracks, Wozzeck is unable to sleep, tormented by visions of Marie and the Drum Major—and a knife. He tries reciting the Lord's Prayer. The Drum Major arrives, very drunk, boasting of his conquest of Marie and picking a fight with Wozzeck. The other soldiers rise in their bunks during the struggle, which ends with the defeated Wozzeck envisioning death for both Marie and himself.

ACT III   In her room, Marie reads from the Bible about the woman taken in adultery. Concerned because of her sadness, the child clings to her; she guiltily sends him away, then calls him back and embraces him. Continuing with the Bible, she finds a passage about Mary Magdalene that seems to indicate forgiveness for her sins. (*Heiland, Du hast Dich ihrer erbarmt*).

§ On a path near a pool outside town at nightfall, Wozzeck and Marie pause after walking in the woods. He asks how long they have known each other: three years, she recalls. Alarmed by his seriousness and disjointed remarks, she is anxious to get home, but he holds her back and kisses her. The moon rises, blood-red. Suddenly declaring no one else will have her if he cannot, he plunges a knife into her throat, rushing away as she falls dead.

§ In a tavern, Wozzeck starts a song about three horsemen, but it quickly refers to a girl lying dead (*Es ritten drei Reiter*). When he urges Margret to sing too (*In's Schwabenland*) and tries to pull her onto his lap, she notices blood on his hand. Saying he must have cut himself, Wozzeck rushes out, but the others suspect he has killed someone.

§ Wozzeck returns to the scene of the murder, where he sees Marie's body, marked with a "red necklace," and frantically searches for the incriminating knife, which he finds and throws in the pond. Afraid he did not throw it far enough, he wades in to retrieve it. Muttering that he must wash himself, he imagines that the water has turned to blood, bathed in red moonlight. Slipping, he sinks. The Captain and Doctor, happening to walk past, hear sounds of drowning. The eeriness of the place frightens them, and they move quickly on.

§ Outside Marie's door, children are playing ring-around-a-rosy *(Ringel, Ringel, Rosenkranz)*. Other children run in to tell Marie's child that his mother is dead, then run off again to investigate. Too young to understand, the child rides his hobbyhorse *(Hopp, hopp!)* until, noticing his playmates have left, he follows after them.

Lulu

PROLOGUE AND THREE ACTS
MUSIC: Alban Berg
TEXT (German): adapted by the composer from Frank Wedekind's
   plays *Erdgeist* and *Die Büchse der Pandora*
WORLD PREMIERE (unfinished): Zurich, Stadttheater, June 2, 1937
U.S. PREMIERE (unfinished): Santa Fe, August 7, 1963
METROPOLITAN PREMIERE (unfinished): March 18, 1977
WORLD PREMIERE (completed version): Paris Opera, February 24,
   1979
U.S. PREMIERE (completed version): Santa Fe, August 17, 1979
METROPOLITAN OPERA PREMIERE (completed version): December
   12, 1980

CHARACTERS

Lulu . . . . and . . . . Soprano
Countess Geschwitz . . . . Mezzo-Soprano
Wardrobe Mistress ⎫
Schoolboy   ⎬ . . . . Contralto
Groom   ⎭
Medical Professor ⎫
Banker   ⎬ . . . . Speaking Part

L U L U

Painter Black Man	. . . . Tenor
Alwa, *composter* . . . . Tenor	
African Prince Marquis Manservant	. . . . Tenor
Dr. Schön Jack the Ripper	. . . . Baritone
Athlete Ringmaster	. . . . Baritone
Schigolch, *old man* . . . . Bass	

PROLOGUE Somewhere in the German-speaking world, around 1871.* A Ringmaster, outside his circus tent, invites the audience to see some wild animals. He shows the wildest of the lot, the "serpent" Lulu, carried by a stagehand. We will soon see, he declares, how she snares people, begetting evil deeds.

ACT I In a Painter's studio, Lulu, an actress and dancer, is posing for her portrait. Married to Dr. Goll, an elderly Medical Professor, she is the mistress of Dr. Schön, an editor in chief, who rescued her from the gutter as a child. While Schön watches the work in progress, his son, the composer Alwa, enters, then excuses himself and leaves with his father. Alone with Lulu, the distracted Painter tries to make love to her, but she keeps escaping. A knock is heard. Knowing that it is Lulu's husband, the Painter hesitates to answer, so Dr. Goll breaks the door down. Horrified at finding the two alone together, he collapses and dies of a stroke. Lulu realizes she is now a rich widow. Frightened at the prospect of his apparent luck, the Painter questions her about her moral beliefs and finds she has none. He prays for strength.

§ In an elegant drawing room, the Painter—now married to Lulu—brings the morning mail, including commissions for his work. An announcement of Schön's engagement to a society girl disturbs Lulu. As the Painter looks lovingly at her, the doorbell rings. The caller turns out to be Schigolch, an old derelict who is somehow part of Lulu's past. Alone with her, he asks for money—a request she has heard often—and compliments her on her good fortune, but she reveals she is bored. When the bell rings again, he leaves, and Schön arrives, referring to the departing Schigolch as Lulu's father and asking her to remove herself from his life. The Painter, he points out, must sooner or later become aware of their continuing affair, but Lulu says that her

---

*The preface to the Universal Edition libretto notes, "Neither in the opera nor in the original plays is a time or place explicitly stated for the action. But Acts I and II are obviously set in a German city, and the 'revolution in Paris' referred to is presumably that of the Paris Commune, 1871. The third act clearly takes place in Paris (Scene 1) and London (Scene 2), where the 'Jack the Ripper' murders occurred in 1888–89."

husband is blinded by love. Schön reminds her how he helped her make two good marriages; now that he himself is engaged, he wants no scandal. Lulu replies that if she belongs to anyone it is to Schön, the only one who has given her real attention. When the Painter comes in, Lulu leaves him to learn some facts of life from Schön, who reminds him he has married a fortune (*Du hast eine halbe Million geheiratet*). Schön explains he has known Lulu since she was twelve and has tried to get her out of his life. Now, he says, the Painter must assert himself and make Lulu behave like a respectable wife. Deeply shocked, the Painter steps out and locks himself in another room. When Lulu and then Alwa appear, the three break down the door and find that the Painter has killed himself. Schön calls the police, and Lulu predicts he will end up marrying her.

§ Backstage at a theater, Alwa pours champagne for Lulu, who is changing costume. He recalls how he first met her, shortly before his mother's death, and wanted his father to marry her so she would always be around. An African Prince appears after Lulu leaves for her next cue; he hopes to marry her. There is a commotion: Lulu has pretended to faint onstage after seeing Schön in the audience with his fiancée. Schön promptly appears in her dressing room, indignantly ordering her back onstage (ensemble: *Das hättest du dir besser erspart!*). Alwa tells the theater director to go on with the next number, then leaves Schön with Lulu, who delivers an ultimatum: he must renounce his fiancée for her. She dictates the letter (*Sehr geehrtes Fräulein*), which Schön calls his death sentence. As the bell rings for her next number, Lulu calmly goes onstage.

ACT II Lulu, now married to Schön, is saying good-bye to a visitor, the lesbian Countess Geschwitz, who admires her. As the two women leave the sumptuous drawing room, Schön—irrational with jealousy of real and imagined rivals—laments the degradation of his final years of life (*Das mein Lebensabsend*). Complaining to him of his recent neglect, Lulu coaxes him into their bedroom. Geschwitz reenters and hides as several other hangers-on appear— Schigolch, an Athlete, a Schoolboy—to wait for Lulu, who comes in to make pleasantries with them. Schigolch denies he is Lulu's father, and she says she is a *Wunderkind*, a miraculous child of creation. A Manservant—himself infatuated with Lulu—announces Dr. Schön, so the Athlete and Schoolboy hide, but it turns out to be Alwa. Schön watches from a distance as Lulu and Alwa converse; at length Alwa passionately declares his love, though she murmurs she poisoned his mother. Schön escorts his son out of the room, then returns to look for the Athlete, who he knows is hiding. He is carrying a revolver, which he gives Lulu, telling her to use it on herself because of the shame she has brought both of them. Trying to calm him, Lulu calls herself blameless for whatever others may have done on her account (*Wenn sich die Menschen um meinetwillen umgebracht haben*); he turns the pistol in her hand toward herself and seems about to pull the trigger. When he is distracted by the emergence of the frightened Schoolboy from hiding, Lulu empties the revolver into Schön's back. The wounded man calls for water, but champagne is all she can find. He warns Alwa that he is her next victim, catches sight of Geschwitz, and dies. Though Lulu begs Alwa to let her escape, he bars her way until the police arrive.

§ After an interlude whose music traces Lulu's trial, conviction, imprisonment, and eventual escape,* the curtain rises on the same setting about a year later. Alwa, Geschwitz, and the Athlete, planning Lulu's escape, wait for Schigolch, who brings passports, then leaves with Geschwitz to rescue Lulu from prison. The Athlete, planning a marriage of expediency to Lulu as his show partner, complains of all the effort he has had to contribute toward her escape plans. The Schoolboy appears, having run away from reform school; to convince him that Lulu is dead, the Athlete shows a clipping that says she was hospitalized in prison with cholera, then throws him out. Lulu, leaning on Schigolch, appears wearing Geschwitz' clothes, her escape disguise. Angry at finding her wasted by illness, the Athlete threatens to go to the police. He leaves, as does Schigolch, who has to pick up train tickets. Geschwitz has traded places with Lulu in prison in order to get her out; Lulu tells Alwa how Geschwitz infected herself, then Lulu, with cholera so that the escape could be made through the prison hospital (O, *die Geschwitz hat das sehr klug eingerichtet*). Seductively she asks Alwa for a kiss, to be sure he will protect and accompany her. Though she remarks that they are lying on the sofa on which his father died, Alwa is carried away.

ACT III   Lulu and Alwa have escaped to Paris, trailed by the Athlete, who proposes a toast at a gambling party in their fashionable salon as the curtain rises. Guests are discussing the booming market in Jungfrau Railway stock. A Marquis, knowing Lulu is wanted for murder by the German police, blackmails her, meaning to sell her to a brothel in Cairo. Lulu protests she cannot sell herself—the only thing that is really hers. They are interrupted by people returning from the gaming tables, and as Lulu reads a note from the Athlete, threatening to inform on her unless she pays a large amount, the guests talk about their good luck at gambling (*Alle Welt gewinnt!*). When the Athlete reappears, she says that her money is gone; he replies that she and Alwa still own Jungfrau Railway shares, giving her until tomorrow evening to produce the money. As he moves away, a telegram arrives for the Banker: the market in Jungfrau shares has crashed. Schigolch appears, hoping to wheedle money out of Lulu, and learns of her predicament; he offers to push the Athlete out the window if Lulu can arrange for the latter to come to his apartment that evening. Since the Athlete has been bothering Countess Geschwitz with offers of his services as a gigolo, Lulu feels she can get him to Schigolch's place

---

*Berg specified that a silent film accompany this passage.

under the pretense of a meeting with the countess. As Schigolch and Lulu step out, the Athlete reappears and is questioned by the Marquis, who senses a competitor in his extortion scheme. He finds that his hunch is correct and leaves; Lulu then reenters to tell the Athlete that Geschwitz is waiting for him at a certain address; the countess, she adds, has promised to pay her for arranging the meeting, and this is the only way Lulu can get money for him. He agrees, leaving for the dining room, and Lulu calls Geschwitz to say that for her sake Geschwitz must submit to the Athlete, who reappears to escort her out. Lulu then arranges to change clothes with a young Groom. The gamblers come in, arguing, and the Banker reveals the worthlessness of the Jungfrau shares he has been offered in payment (*Alle Welt verliert!*). Shaken by their losses, they leave. Lulu hurriedly tells Alwa that the police are on their way and leads him out the servants' entrance as they arrive—to discover that "Lulu" is the Groom in her clothes.

§ Their funds gone, Lulu, Alwa, and Schigolch have taken refuge in a garret in London, where Lulu has been forced into prostitution. Schigolch hustles Alwa out of the room when Lulu returns with her first client, an eccentric professor afraid of being discovered. Next to arrive is the faithful Geschwitz, who has salvaged Lulu's portrait. Alwa, briefly inspired by the sight of Lulu's former beauty (*Warum nicht gar?*), hangs it on the wall, where the others join in admiring it. Lulu goes to find another client and returns with a Black Man, who says his father is emperor of an African country. Refusing to pay in advance, he tries to take Lulu by force and deals Alwa a fatal blow when the latter tries to restrain him. After Schigolch removes the corpse, Geschwitz contemplates suicide but recognizes that it would mean nothing to Lulu (*Nein, wenn sie mich heut in meinem Blut liegen sieht*). When Lulu returns with a third client, she says Geschwitz is her crazy sister. The client haggles over the price and is about to leave, but Lulu, feeling a desperate need for him, settles for less. As they go into her room, Geschwitz resolves to return to Germany and find a new life working for women's rights. Lulu's death shriek is heard, and when Geschwitz frantically tries to open the door, the murderer—Jack the Ripper—stabs her as well, then looks in irritation for a towel with which to wipe the blood from his hands. As he leaves, the dying Geschwitz murmurs that she will be near Lulu in death.

HECTOR BERLIOZ
1803–69

$\mathcal{J}$n 1832, when Wagner was still in his teens and Liszt two decades away from creating his tone poems, Hector Berlioz ushered in the romantic movement in music with the *Symphonie Fantastique*. His adventurous spirit and large-scale concepts earned him a reputation as an *enfant terrible*, but in retrospect Berlioz's works seem informed with a deep longing for the ordered world of classicism, a necessary counterforce to his impetuous imagination.

Les Troyens was his third dramatic work, if one includes the concert opera *La Damnation de Faust* in this category. Obsessed with the problems of creative artists, Berlioz then wrote an opera about one of them, but *Benvenuto Cellini* failed at its Paris Opera premiere in 1838. Thereafter, the doors of the French theaters were closed to him, and his monumental *Les Troyens* was written with no prospects for performance. Berlioz had fallen under the spell of Vergil as a boy, when his father tutored him in the classics. He recalled his childhood sorrow and empathy for Aeneas and the Trojans, for Dido and the inexorable fate that led to the founding of Rome. His libretto for *Les Troyens*, a model of clarity and precise epic-making, often comes directly from the Latin (Books I, II, and IV of the *Aeneid*). The composer made one major change: in Vergil, Aeneas tells of the fall of Troy in a flashback, but Berlioz made it the first part of his opera, with Cassandra as heroine.

Written during the same period as Wagner's *Tristan und Isolde,* which was likewise pronounced unperformable, only Part II of *Les Troyens* reached the stage during Berlioz' lifetime. The resurrection of the complete work began in the 1950s with cut performances by Boris Goldovsky in Boston and by the

Royal Opera, Covent Garden, followed by a complete edition published in 1969 and staged in the same year, again at Covent Garden. The Metropolitan Opera undertook it for the first time in 1973.

LES TROYENS

(The Trojans)

FIVE ACTS, NINE SCENES
MUSIC: Hector Berlioz
TEXT (French): by the composer, after Vergil's *Aeneid*
WORLD PREMIERE: Part II only: Paris, Théâtre Lyrique, November 4, 1863; entire work (in German): Karlsruhe, Hoftheater, December 5 and 6, 1890
U.S. PREMIERE: Part II (concert performance): New York, January 13, 1877 (in English)
METROPOLITAN OPERA PREMIERE: October 22, 1973

CHARACTERS

Part I: *La Prise de Troie* (The Capture of Troy; Acts I and II)
Cassandre, *Trojan prophetess* . . . . Soprano
Ascagne, *son of Enée* . . . . Soprano
Hécube, *wife of Priam* . . . . Mezzo-Soprano
Polyxène, *daughter of Priam* . . . . Soprano
Enée, *Trojan hero* . . . . Tenor
Chorèbe, *fiancé of Cassandre* . . . . Baritone
Panthée, *Trojan priest* . . . . Bass
Ghost of Hector . . . . Bass
Priam, *King of Troy* . . . . Bass
Andromaque, *Hector's widow* . . . . Mime
Astyanax, *her son* . . . . Mime
Soldiers of Greece and Troy, citizens, women, children

Part II: *Les Troyens à Carthage* (The Trojans at Carthage; Acts III–V)
Didon, *Queen of Carthage* . . . . Mezzo-Soprano
Anna, *her sister* . . . . Contralto
Ascagne . . . . Soprano
Enée . . . . Tenor
Iopas, *Carthaginian poet* . . . . Tenor
Hylas, *young Phrygian sailor* . . . . Tenor

Narbal, *Didon's minister* . . . . Bass
Panthée . . . . Bass
Ghost of Cassandre. . . . . Mezzo-Soprano
Ghost of Chorèbe . . . . Baritone
Ghost of Hector . . . . Bass
Ghost of Priam . . . . Bass
Mercury, *messenger of the gods*. . . . . Bass
*Trojan captains, courtiers, hunters, Carthaginians, invisible ghosts, work-
men, sailors, laborers, naiads, fauns, satyrs, wood nymphs*

ACT I   During the siege of Troy by the Greeks, in legendary times.* The
Trojans visit the seemingly abandoned camp of their enemy, the Greeks. They
rejoice at the prospect of peace after ten years of siege and marvel at the
gigantic wooden horse the Greeks left behind as an offering to Pallas Athena.
King Priam's daughter Cassandre (Cassandra), a prophetess, looks for the significance behind the Greeks' disappearance *(Les Grecs ont disparu!)*. In a moment
of revelation, she saw her brother Hector's ghost on the ramparts, and she has
tried to warn her father and Chorèbe (Coroebus), her fiancé, but they will not
listen. Chorèbe urges her to join the celebrations *(Reviens à toi, vierge adorée!)*;
she urges him to flee the city, because she foresees death for both of them.
Enée (Aeneas), leader of the Trojan army, enters with a group offering prayers
of thanks to the gods *(Dieux protecteurs de la ville éternelle)*; dances and public
games follow, but a somber note is introduced when Andromaque, Hector's
widow, brings her son Astyanax to King Priam and Queen Hécube (Hecuba).
Enée reports that a priest, Laocoön, suspecting that the wooden horse was
some kind of a trick, threw his spear at it and urged the crowd to set fire to
it, whereupon two sea serpents devoured him. Enée proposes that they make
amends to Athena by bringing the horse into the city as a holy object (octet:
Châtiment effroyable!). As the Trojan march sounds in the distance and the
horse is hauled closer, Cassandre realizes that it bears disaster. Unable to
prevent this, she runs off to prepare to meet death with her people, while the
horse is rolled within the city walls.

ACT II   Enée, asleep in his room, is visited by the ghost of Hector, who tells
him to escape, since his destiny is to found a mighty empire that will one day
rule the world. As the ghost disappears, Enée's friend Panthée rushes in,
wounded, to report that the Greek soldiers who emerged from the horse are
devastating Troy. Enée hastens to lead the defense forces.

§ In the King's palace, Trojan women pray for deliverance from the invaders.
Cassandre foretells that Enée and some of the Trojans will escape to Italy to
build Rome—a new Troy. Chorèbe is dead, and Cassandre prepares for her
own death, asking the women whether they will submit to rape and enslave-
ment. Some are afraid of death; driving these away, the others take up their

*Date given as 1183 B.C. in original edition of *Kobbé's Complete Opera Book*.

lyres and repeat their vow to die free *(Complices de sa gloire)*. Greek soldiers, entering in search of state treasure, are aghast at the sight of the women's mass suicide, while word reaches them that Enée has escaped with his men and the treasure.

ACT III   In a gallery of the palace of Didon (Dido), Queen of Carthage, her subjects hail her with an anthem *(Gloire à Didon)*. She reminds them that in only seven years, since they had to flee from Tyre, they have built a flourishing new kingdom. Celebrating the fruits of peace, groups of builders, sailors, and farmers file in to receive awards. Her sister, Anna, assures Didon, who is a widow, that one day she will be able to love again (duet: *Reine d'un jeune empire*). When Iopas, the court poet, announces visitors who have narrowly escaped shipwreck in a recent storm, Didon welcomes them, having once been in their situation herself. They are the remnants of the Trojan army, asking a few days' hospitality en route to Italy and offering Didon what is left of their treasure. When word reaches Didon that the Numidian ruler, Iarbas, is about to attack Carthage because she refused his offer of marriage, Enée steps from among the sailors' ranks, identifies himself, and offers to fight alongside the Carthaginians. Didon accepts his offer, admiring Enée as he rallies his forces to repel the invader *(C'est le dieu Mars qui nous rassemble)* and entrusts his son, Ascagne (Ascanius), to the queen's care.

ACT IV   Orchestral interlude: Royal Hunt and Storm.* Some days later in a forest, hunters pass across the scene as naiads run from their path. A storm breaks, and Didon and Enée seek shelter in a cave. Nymphs, satyrs, and fauns dance during the storm and disappear when it passes.

§ Evening has fallen in Didon's gardens by the sea. Anna asks Narbal, the queen's adviser, why he seems worried, now that the Numidians have been defeated. He replies that since Didon fell in love with Enée, she has been neglecting her duties, and that Enée's destiny is to go on to Italy, which means that no good can come of the romance. Narbal is afraid that in extending hospitality to the strangers, Carthage has invited its own doom (duet: *De quel revers*). As Didon and Enée enter with other courtiers, dancing girls and slaves perform for their entertainment; then Iopas sings a pastoral song *(O blonde Cérès)*. Didon asks Enée to tell her more about Troy's last days. When he says that Andromaque, Hector's widow, at length married Pyrrhus, one of the enemy, Didon sees a parallel to her own situation, excusing her to some extent from the weakness of loving *(Tout conspire à vaincre mes remords)*. All admire the enchantment of the peaceful night, and the the courtiers move off, leaving Didon and Enée to rhapsodize about their love *(O nuit d'ivresse)*, but at length the god Mercury appears in the moonlight and reminds Enée of his destination—Italy.

*In the original published edition, and in some productions, this interlude follows the next scene.

ACT V   By the shore at night, the Trojan ships moored near at hand, Hylas, a young sailor, sings a homesick ballad *(Vallon sonore)* and falls asleep. Enée's friend Panthée tells other Trojan leaders their delay is burdensome: daily omens and apparitions remind them of the gods' and the dead Hector's impatience with their failure to move on. Determined to leave the next day, they retire to their tents as two sentries pass, complaining they don't want to leave Carthage, where life treats them well. They make way for Enée, who struggles to banish misgivings and do what he must *(Inutiles regrets!)*, knowing that their departure will displease Didon. As he resolves to see her one more time, the ghosts of Priam, Hector, Chorèbe, and Cassandre appear, pressing their demands. Forced to give up Didon, he wakens the Trojans and tells them to sail before sunrise. Didon finds him, however, and rages at his desertion *(Errante sur tes pas)*. Though he protests that he loves her, she scorns a man who could treat her so cruelly, cursing him and his gods. As she storms off and the elements rumble in the distance, the distraught Enée boards his vessel.

§ In Didon's palace, as dawn breaks, the queen asks her sister to go to Enée. Now that her anger is spent, she will try to persuade him to stay a few more days. Too late: the Trojan ships are sighted on their way out to sea. Didon laments that she did not foresee Enée's treachery and burn his fleet. Instead, she will burn his gifts and trophies: she orders a pyre built. Telling everyone to leave her, she realizes that her life is over and bids farewell to Carthage *(Adieu, fière cité)*.

§ In the queen's gardens by the sea, a pyre has been set up, with relics of Enée, including the nuptial couch. Priests pray to the gods of the underworld to bring peace to Didon's heart, while Anna and Narbal curse Enée's venture to Italy. Didon predicts that her fate will be remembered, along with Enée's infamy: a future Carthaginian general, Hannibal, will avenge her against Italy one day *(Mon souvenir vivra parmi les âges)*. Seizing Enée's sword, she stabs herself and falls back on the couch. With her dying breath, Didon tells the shocked bystanders that fate is against Carthage: it will be destroyed, and Rome will rule eternal. A vision of the Roman capitol appears in the distance. Turning their backs on it, the survivors pronounce undying hatred on Enée and his descendants *(Haine eternelle à la race d'Enée!)*.

GEORGES BIZET
1838–75

*G*eorges Bizet, born in Paris to musician parents, entered the Paris Conservatory at the age of nine. There he eventually studied with Fromental Halévy, composer of *La Juive,* whose daughter Geneviève he later married. In 1857 Bizet won a Prix de Rome scholarship for study in Italy; from that same year dates his first opera, the one-act *Le Docteur Miracle.* In his thirty-seven-year life he wrote six operas that have been published, as well as eight unpublished or incomplete.

The first of Bizet's operas to reach the professional stage was *Les Pêcheurs de Perles* (The Pearl Fishers), which lasted eighteen performances after its premiere at the Théâtre Lyrique in 1863. Of the various opera projects on which he worked, two more were staged—*La Jolie Fille de Perth* in 1867, *Djamileh* in 1872—without establishing him as a major talent. Though discouraged by the indifference of theater managers and the public, he continued to pursue his natural métier. With *Carmen,* at the Opéra Comique in 1875, the tide of fortune started to turn, but Bizet died that year, thinking he had written another failure. The work caught on soon afterward and, together with the incidental music for Daudet's play *L'Arlésienne,* has carried Bizet's reputation.

Carmen was drawn from a popular short novel of the same title by Prosper Mérimée (1845), inspired in turn by the writing of George Henry Borrow, an Englishman who had lived among the Spanish Gypsies. Bizet's libretto, conventionalized and prettified for the conservative, bourgeois audience of the Opéra Comique, was the work of Ludovic Halévy (a cousin of his wife's) and Henri Meilhac. Since the opéra-comique genre called for spoken dialogue, sung recitatives had to be added if the work was ever to be performed at a grand-opera theater. This was done after Bizet's death by his friend Ernest Guiraud. The work's initially poor reception is attributable to the novelty and daring of presenting "low life" in this genre and allowing the heroine to die instead of contriving the customary happy ending. Gypsies smoking cigarettes onstage were another risqué element, as was the "immoral" character of the heroine. *Carmen* survived to become one of the most frequently performed operas everywhere in the world. At the Metropolitan, it has long held third place, after *Aida* and *La Bohème,* and several of its melodies are familiar to thousands who have never seen or heard an opera.

Carmen's eventual success aroused interest in Bizet's earlier operas, of which *Les Pêcheurs de Perles* has proved capable of holding the stage despite the flimsiness of Michel Carré's and Eugène Cormon's libretto. Since the work survived only in piano-vocal score, other hands had to orchestrate it anew. In doing so, they perpetrated various changes, especially in the final scene, for which a trio by Benjamin Godard was added for the 1893 revival; but the latest trend has been to return to what Bizet wrote. Because of his distinctive lyric gift, the exotic tale has been seen in a series of recent revivals, surpassing its most obvious spin-off, Delibes' *Lakmé* (1883), which once greatly exceeded it in public favor.

LES PÊCHEURS DE PERLES

(The Pearl Fishers)

THREE ACTS
MUSIC: Georges Bizet
TEXT (French): Eugène Cormon (Pierre Étienne Piestre) and
    Michel Carré
WORLD PREMIERE: Paris, Théâtre Lyrique, September 29, 1863
U.S. PREMIERE: Philadelphia, August 23, 1893 (in Italian)
METROPOLITAN OPERA PREMIERE: January 11, 1896 (two acts
    only); November 5, 1916 (complete)

CHARACTERS

Léila, *Brahman priestess* . . . . Soprano
Nadir, *hunter* . . . . Tenor
Zurga, *king of the fishermen* . . . . Baritone
Nourabad, *Brahman high priest* . . . . Bass
Pearl fishermen, priests, priestesses, natives, slaves, dancers

ACT I   On the island of Ceylon in olden times, pearl fishermen celebrate their skill and daring by singing and dancing on the beach. When Zurga arrives to remind them that it is time to choose a leader, they unanimously name him. Descending from the rocks is Nadir, a hunter, whom Zurga happily recognizes as his friend from youthful days. They reminisce about a trip they once took to Candi, where in the temple they were both smitten by a beautiful, goddess-like young woman (duet: *Au fond du temple saint*). For the sake of their friendship, they agreed to forget her, though neither has been able to do so. When a priestess, Léila, arrives to bless the pearl fishermen according to ancient custom, Zurga joins her in beginning the ceremony. Meanwhile, she and Nadir recognize each other from their chance meeting at Candi. As Zurga leads her up the embankment toward the temple, Nadir imagines once again the sound of her voice among the palm trees (*Je crois entendre encore*). Nourabad, the high priest, leads Léila back to the shore to begin the vigil required by the ceremony. As she leads prayers to Brahma and Shiva, Nadir is carried away by her beauty.

ACT II   Night is descending on the ruins of an old temple. Alluding to her strict vow of chastity, Nourabad tells Léila to spend the night there alone: sentries in the distance will protect her. She is courageous, she says, recalling an incident in her childhood when she sheltered a fugitive and refused to betray him; in gratitude he gave her a necklace (*J'étais encore enfant*). Left alone, she cannot sleep, disturbed by thoughts of Nadir (*Comme autrefois*). She hears Nadir's voice in the distance. He finds her, and they declare their love (duet: *Ton coeur n'a pas compris le mien*). As a storm threatens, she sends him away, promising that she will see him the next day. Scarcely has he left than Nourabad appears with a search party; they have spotted a stranger. They find Nadir and drag him back. Though Nourabad and the crowd insist that the punishment for this profanation is death to both lovers, Zurga rushes in, saying he alone will decide their fate. He tells the couple to flee, but when Nourabad rips off the girl's veil, Zurga recognizes her for the first time. In his jealousy and sense of betrayal, he now agrees that the two must be punished.

ACT III   Later that night, as the storm dissipates, Zurga sits by his tent and repents of his hasty action, determining to forgive Nadir and Léila. When the priestess appears before him, however, he is again disturbed by her beauty, and when she pleads for Nadir's life, his jealousy reawakens: he refuses to relent. Ready to die, Léila gives her necklace to a pearl fisherman and asks him to return it to her mother. Zurga recognizes the necklace as one he gave to a girl who saved his life. He runs off after Léila.

§   Waiting for the sunrise, natives celebrate the coming sacrifice by drinking and dancing. Nadir appears, looking for Léila; the lovers welcome death together (*O lumière sainte*), while Nourabad curses their blasphemy. As a glow lights the sky, the mob hails the dawn, but Zurga comes to tell them that it is the light of their burning village, struck by the fire of heaven *(Regardez, c'est le feu)*. As the natives run to save their homes, Zurga frees Nadir and Léila, showing her the necklace. The lovers make their escape, while Zurga waits stoically for his fate, since he has betrayed his own people by setting the fire (trio: *Plus de crainte*).

CARMEN

FOUR ACTS
MUSIC: Georges Bizet
TEXT (French): Henri Meilhac and Ludovic Halévy, based on the
  novel by Prosper Mérimée
WORLD PREMIERE: Paris, Opéra Comique, March 3, 1875
U.S. PREMIERE: New York, Academy of Music, October 23, 1879
METROPOLITAN OPERA PREMIERE: January 9, 1884 (in Italian)

CHARACTERS

Carmen, *cigarette girl and Gypsy* . . . . Soprano
Micaela, *peasant girl* . . . . Soprano
Frasquita⎫
Mercédès⎭ *Gypsies, friends of Carmen* . . . . Soprano
Don José, *corporal of dragoons* . . . . Tenor
Escamillo, *toreador* . . . . Baritone
Moralès, *corporal* . . . . Baritone
Zuniga, *lieutenant* . . . . Bass
  *Innkeeper, guide, officers, dragoons, boys, cigarette girls, Gypsies, smug-
    glers, mayor, vendors, spectators*

ACT I Spain around 1820. Dragoons of the Almanzar Regiment, serving on police duty in Seville, are standing in the square outside their guardhouse, watching the passing crowd. Their corporal, Moralès, spots a pretty girl, Micaela, and finds out she is looking for another corporal named Don José. Disappointed, Moralès tells her that Don José will be there soon. With the changing of the guard, children show up pretending to be soldiers *(Avec la garde montante)*, while Moralès tells the newly arrived Don José about his visitor. An officer, Zuniga, apparently new to this assignment, asks José whether it's true that there are lots of pretty girls among the workers at the cigarette factory across the square. Soon some young men appear, waiting for the factory girls to take their work break. The girls join them, singing the praises of relaxation and smoking *(Dans l'air, nous suivons des yeux la fumée)*. When the Gypsy girl Carmen comes out of the factory, she is immediately the center of attention and obliges her admirers with a song about the freedom and elusiveness of love (habanera: *L'amour est un oiseau rebelle*). The men vie for her attention, but she ignores them in favor of Don José, who has been ignoring *her*. When she goes back into the factory, she throws him a cassia flower from her bodice, and he mutters to himself that she must be a witch. His musings are cut short by Micaela with a message from his mother. Embarrassed, she also gives him a kiss from his mother. José is moved by reminiscences of home and sees his mother in his mind's eye (duet: *Ma mère, je la vois*). In the face of Micaela's simple goodness, he wonders how Carmen was able to distract him even momentarily. Micaela leaves him alone to read his mother's letter, which says he should marry Micaela; José agrees. Before Micaela has a chance to return, however, a commotion erupts in the factory, and several of the girls come running out to call for the police: Carmen and another girl have gotten into a fight. Amid arguments as to which struck the first blow, José takes a couple of soldiers into the factory and comes out with Carmen, whom he turns over to Zuniga for questioning. Carmen insolently refuses to answer and slaps one of her co-workers standing nearby. As soon as she is alone in José's custody, she tells him that he will help her escape, because he loves her: the flower she threw has worked its magic. José orders her not to talk, so she sings instead—a provocative song about taking her lover to Lillas Pastia's tavern on the outskirts of the city (seguidilla: *Près des remparts de Séville*). José's anger and confusion give way to Carmen's increasingly bold promises that he will be the lover in question, and she persuades him to let her escape. When Zuniga comes out of the guardhouse with a written order to take Carmen to jail, José starts to lead her away, but she pushes him off balance and runs away.

ACT II Two months later, at Lillas Pastia's inn. Carmen sings and dances with her friends Frasquita and Mercédès (Gypsy song: *Les tringles des sistres*) while waiting, as she promised, for Don José. Men appear, hailing the bullfighter Escamillo, who boasts of his prowess *(Toréador, en garde)* and takes an immediate liking to Carmen. She too is attracted but puts him off, along with other prospective lovers, since she expects José. When the inn closes for the night, Carmen tells her friends that she cannot join their latest smuggling expedition, because she is in love (quintet: *Nous avons en tête*). The minute José appears, these friends urge her to enlist him in their band. Carmen dances for him *(Je vais danser en votre honneur)* after he explains he had to spend two months in prison for letting her escape. When distant bugles sound the retreat, however, José says he has to get back to his barracks. Carmen makes fun of his schoolboy obedience, saying he cannot care much about her. He denies this, describing how he treasured the withered flower in prison and thought only of her *(La fleur que tu m'avais jetée)*. Trying to persuade him to run away, she plays hard to convince *(Là-bas dans la montagne)*. José says he cannot become a deserter for her sake; just as she tries to turn him out, Zuniga comes to see Carmen himself. Confronting José, who is already late for call to quarters, he orders him to leave, but José defies his superior. To prevent a fight, Carmen calls her Gypsy friends, who playfully hold Zuniga captive while José realizes that the die is cast: he is already a deserter. The Gypsies hail their free existence in the wide open spaces.

Act III   Border country, in the mountains. The smugglers, José among them, sing about the dangers and rewards of their life. Looking toward the valley where his mother lives, José regrets that he has betrayed her expectations. Carmen tells him he might as well leave—the sooner the better. Their relationship has cooled. Seeing his temper flare at her indifference, Carmen becomes aware that he is capable of killing her. Fatalistically, she reads tarot cards with Frasquita and Mercédès: where they find wealth and lovers, she finds only death, first for herself, then for him *(En vain pour éviter)*. José takes up watchman's duty, while the women talk about using their charms to disarm any civil guards who might find their hideout. After they leave, Micaela wanders in alone, having somehow found the smugglers' lair. Aware of Carmen's power over José and the dangers of the place, she declares that with God's help she will win José back *(Je dis que rien ne m'épouvante)*. She sees José on a promontory and calls to him, but just then he fires a warning shot challenging a trespasser, who turns out to be Escamillo in search of Carmen. Micaela hides as the two men confront each other, Escamillo quickly realizing from José's belligerent reception that he is Carmen's current lover. Challenged to a duel with knives, the bullfighter loses his footing, and only Carmen's reappearance saves his life. Escamillo tells José he will fight him again whenever José likes, but the smugglers want no violence. Escamillo leaves, inviting everyone to his next bullfight; José has to be restrained from going after him again with a knife. When Micaela is found hiding, José assures them all that she is not a spy. She pleads with him to come to his sick mother's bedside, and Carmen tells him to go. Swearing never to give her up, he does leave, while Escamillo's voice is heard in the distance, repeating his toreador song.

Act IV   In a square outside the bullring in Seville, crowds mill about in a festive mood, buying drinks and oranges.* Bullfighters parade in their regalia, hailed by children and the enthusiastic crowd. Following the picadors and banderilleros, Escamillo acknowledges the ovation, then—as everyone leaves to enter the arena—sees Carmen and draws her aside for a few tender words *(Si tu m'aimes)*. When he too has gone, accompanying the Alcalde (mayor) to

---

*In some productions, a ballet is added at this point.

the contest, Carmen receives a hasty warning from Frasquita and Mercédès that they have seen José in the shadows: wanted for desertion, he cannot show himself openly. Carmen declares she is not afraid and will speak with him alone. José comes forth and begins in a pleading tone *(C'est toi?)*, but Carmen's coldness gradually drives him to desperation. She declares that everything is over between them, that she will live free or die. When voices from the arena proclaim Escamillo's victory and Carmen tries to go inside, José blocks her way. Angrily she shouts that he should either let her go or kill her. With this she throws away a ring he once gave her, once more refusing José's demand to come with him. Wildly he stabs her, then falls on his knees beside her body as the crowd is heard taking up the toreador song. As horrified onlookers leave the arena and discover him, he surrenders, crying that he has killed his beloved Carmen.

Marc Blitzstein
1905–64

Of the relatively few American operas that have captured the public fancy, at least two have shown an affinity for the Broadway musical: *Porgy and Bess* and *Regina*. But whereas Gershwin set out to write a grand opera and ended up with a glorified musical, Marc Blitzstein set out to make a musical of Lillian Hellman's play *The Little Foxes* and ended up with a full-fledged opera. As a result, *Regina* has not had the number of performances it deserves as a landmark in the American musical theater.

Because of his activist views, heavily influenced by the Marxist playwright Bertolt Brecht and his various composer collaborators, Marc Blitzstein was a controversial figure during the 1930s. Following Hanns Eisler's decree that the artist "must transform himself from a parasite to a fighter," he gave up his quest for a contemporary-sounding, esoteric musical style and embraced more popular forms, as Kurt Weill had done, in a direct bid for audience acceptance. This, however, was slow in coming, perhaps because Blitzstein did not write escapist entertainment, which would have been welcome during the Depression years; instead he tackled abrasive social issues, such as the trade-union movement and the plight of the poor. Best remembered from this period in his work are the musicals *The Cradle Will Rock* (1937) and *No for an Answer* (1940).

In 1946 the Koussevitzky Foundation, which had commissioned Britten's *Peter Grimes,* asked Blitzstein for an opera, and he chose Lillian Hellman's play *The Little Foxes.* The resulting work, *Regina,* opened in New Haven to mixed notices and, after the usual last-minute cuts and adjustments, went to Broadway, where, as a hybrid work with grand-opera elements, it failed to hold its own against the standard musicals of the day. Reworked for the opera house, it fared distinctly better in its New York City Opera production, which placed the work in more favorable perspective. Miss Hellman, who had not been enthusiastic about having a musical adaptation made from her play, called it "the most original of American operas, the most daring."

It was not until 1960, when another commission came along—this time from the Ford Foundation—that Blitzstein again turned his thoughts to opera. He had been busy with several musical-theater projects, including a less than successful show called *Reuben, Reuben,* an adaptation of Sean O'Casey's *Juno and the Paycock,* and a still widely used English adaptation of the Brecht-Weill *Dreigroschenoper* (see p. 538). The Ford commission, channeled through the Metropolitan Opera, was to ensure the completion of an opera he had already started, based on the Sacco-Vanzetti case. Besides doing considerable work on this project, Blitzstein started to make musical settings of two short stories by Bernard Malamud, whom he met while serving as playwright in residence at Bennington College, 1962–63. While vacationing in Martinique in 1964, however, he was killed by sailors he had met at a bar. Appropriately for one whose social concerns had always been paramount, it was surmised to have been a political argument, though overtones of homosexuality somewhat clouded the issue at the time.

REGINA

PROLOGUE AND THREE ACTS

MUSIC: Marc Blitzstein

TEXT (English): by the composer, based on *The Little Foxes,* a play by Lillian Hellman

WORLD PREMIERE: New Haven, Shubert Theater, October 6, 1949

CHARACTERS

Regina Giddens	Soprano
Alexandra (Zan), *her daughter*	Soprano
Birdie Hubbard, *Oscar's wife*	Soprano
Addie, *housekeeper*	Contralto
Horace Giddens, *Regina's husband*	Bass
Benjamin Hubbard / Oscar Hubbard } *Regina's brothers*	Baritones
Leo Hubbard, *Birdie's son*	Tenor

Cal, *butler* . . . . Baritone
William Marshall, *visitor* . . . . Tenor
Townspeople, field workers

PROLOGUE.   Spring 1900, on the veranda of the Giddens house in Bowden, Alabama. Young Alexandra sits having breakfast and joins two black servants, Addie and Cal, in a hymn (*Stand where the angels stand*), which gradually changes to ragtime. Alexandra's mother, Regina, puts an end to this by reminding her that there will be company for supper: the girl should fix her hair.

ACT I   In the living room that evening, Birdie Hubbard, Regina's sister-in-law, talks to Cal about Mr. Marshall, the visitor, to whom she confided her love of music (*Music, music, music*). Her husband, Oscar, comes in and tells her to stop chattering. The others enter the room, having finished dinner, and after some small talk get down to business: Ben, Regina's other brother, wants to set up a cotton mill (*To bring the machine to the cotton, not the cotton to the machine*). The Hubbards have built a small cotton empire, in part by Oscar's marrying Birdie, who came from a landed family. Regina compliments Marshall by praising his courteous manners (*Gallantry, old-fashioned gallantry*). When he leaves, promising to return at the end of the week, Regina and her brothers relish the thought of getting rich from the partnership. One thing is lacking: the agreement of Horace, Regina's husband, who is convalescing at Johns Hopkins after a heart attack. Pretending that Horace, who built up his own bank, would drive a hard bargain (*I don't know*), Regina hints he would want more than a one-third share of the profits; her brothers recognize the greed as her own. Ben offers her a larger share, at the expense of the weaker Oscar, who balks angrily. If Oscar's son, Leo, were to marry Alexandra, that might improve the deal. When the two young people return from taking Marshall to the station, Regina tells her daughter to go to Baltimore next morning to fetch her father. When Alexandra wants to know why, Regina lures her with the excitement of the trip (*Just think, Alexandra*), then turns to Ben and lectures him on the necessity of fighting for what one wants (*You know, if you want something*). When she has gone upstairs, Birdie lingers to warn Alexandra that the others mean to make her marry Leo. Alexandra wonders what it will be like to meet the person she will really marry (*What will it be for me?*). Oscar, aware of what his wife has told Alexandra, slaps her across the face.

ACT II   In the living room a week later, preparations are being made for a party. Leo, arriving early, whiles away the time (*Deedle doodle*). Oscar catches the young man searching the room for cigars and finds out that Leo, through his job at the bank, has access to the safe-deposit box containing his uncle Horace's Union Pacific bonds. Oscar hints that since Horace never looks in the box, Leo could just take the bonds (*No, I don't guess he'd lend you the bonds*). Regina interrupts them, and soon Alexandra arrives with Horace (*Well, here we are at last*), who is greeted by his in-laws. After a quarrelsome beginning, Regina tries to be cordial to him (*Look at me, and let me look at you*), but this does not last. Seeing he does not want to talk business—though Marshall is expected that evening—she calls her brothers, who find he will not talk to them either. Aside, they discuss with Leo the possibility of his taking the bonds without Horace's or Regina's knowing it. Townspeople arrive, commenting drily on Regina's hypocritical hospitality (*Regina does a lovely party*). Annoyed at Horace's obstinacy about the Marshall deal, Regina flirts in front of him with an old beau (*Do you wish we had wed years ago?*). Leo slips the purloined bonds to his father, who hands them to Ben. As Marshall leaves, referring to the deal as settled, Regina does not understand how it could be so, without Horace's consent. As a dance—a gallop—commences for all the guests, Regina confronts Horace, gloating he has not long to live, hoping he dies soon.

ACT III The following afternoon, Horace sits in his wheelchair in the living room, while Birdie, Alexandra, and Addie drink elderberry wine and eat cookies (quartet: *Consider the rain*) and while field hands are heard in a spiritual *Certainly, Lord*). Birdie, who tends to drink too much, admits it and explains her unhappy life: Oscar married her to get the cotton on her parents' plantation (*Lionnet. Remember Lionnet*). When Alexandra walks her aunt home, Horace asks Addie to take the girl away from this environment, saying there is money in an envelope upstairs. Then he greets Regina with the news that her nephew stole $88,000 worth of bonds last night from his safe-deposit box. Denouncing her and her brothers, he says that he will "lend" the bonds to Ben and Oscar—and that the bonds will be Regina's only legacy from him (*I'm sick of you, I'm sick of this house*). She retorts that she has always held him in contempt. When he has a heart attack and accidentally breaks his bottle of medicine, she refuses to go upstairs for another but eventually calls for help. With Horace unconscious upstairs, she returns to confront her brothers with the theft of the bonds, blackmailing them into giving her a 75 percent interest in the Marshall deal. Ben reacts with frustrated fury (*Greedy girl*). Alexandra and Addie appear on the staircase: Horace has died. Regina cannot answer Alexandra's questions about his fatal attack; instead, she tells her brothers she will put them in jail if they don't go along with her terms (*Tomorrow I shall go straight to court*). Ben now accepts philosophically (*Well, I ask myself, what good will it do*) and leaves. When Alexandra tells her mother she is leaving, Regina makes a feeble effort to gain her sympathy but, seeing she cannot, goes upstairs. As Alexandra and Addie prepare to leave, the field hands' hymn is heard again in the background.

ARRIGO BOITO
1842–1918

*E*nrico (Arrigo) Boito, son of a miniatures painter and a Polish countess, fought with Garibaldi at twenty-five (just before composing *Mefistofele*) and in the richness of his intellectual life typifies the dilemma of Italy emerging from the Risorgimento. As a student in Milan he knew hardship, for his father abandoned his mother, who had to bring up two boys, Arrigo and his brother, Camillo, later a successful writer and architect. Though not a remarkable student at first, young Arrigo impressed teachers with his interest and studiousness. By the time he earned his diploma, he was something of a celebrity, having composed (in collaboration with Franco Faccio) two cantatas and earned a medal with a stipend for travel. He used the latter to visit his mother's native country and other European sites, notably Paris, where he met Victor Hugo, Rossini, Berlioz, and Verdi.

Returning to Milan, Boito won renown for his outspoken artistic liberalism, calling for a housecleaning of the Italian arts. Implying that Verdi was one of those who had "scrawled on the wall of the brothel"—degrading the temples of art with vulgar music—he antagonized the older composer, but years later they were reconciled through the offices of Giulio Ricordi, Verdi's publisher, who wanted Boito to write the libretto for *Otello*. This was followed by *Falstaff,* capping one of the great collaborations in the history of opera. Boito by then was middle-aged. He lived on through World War I, sinking gradually into reclusive eccentricity and working endlessly on his second opera, *Nerone,* for which Toscanini and Vincenzo Tommasini completed the orchestration after Boito's death. (Toscanini always believed that Boito, who despite a wonderful ear had technical trouble in orchestrating, had been helped by Faccio to score *Mefistofele.*)

Mefistofele is the work of an idealistic firebrand of twenty-six. Tame as it may seem today, it broke with many opera conventions and violently offended its first-night audience. The version we know is heavily cut, and Boito apparently destroyed what he took out, so that the nature of the original remains a matter of conjecture. Encompassing much more of Goethe's *Faust* (both parts) than Gounod's familiar opera does, *Mefistofele* marks the highest aspirations of the Italian lyric art. In his sense of the duality of man's nature, Boito belongs more to the twentieth century, yet in his willingness to drop Goethe's struggle of conscience in favor of a medieval miracle to save Faust's soul, he reverts to glib romanticism. With all its striving and searching, *Mefistofele* remains the testament of an artist whose ear for words was at one with his ear for music.

MEFISTOFELE

PROLOGUE, FOUR ACTS, AND EPILOGUE
MUSIC: Arrigo Boito
TEXT (Italian): by the composer, based on Goethe's *Faust*
WORLD PREMIERE: Milan, La Scala, March 5, 1868
U.S. PREMIERE: Boston, November 16, 1880 (in English)
METROPOLITAN OPERA PREMIERE: December 5, 1883

CHARACTERS

Mefistofele . . . . Bass
Faust, *philosopher* . . . . Tenor
Margherita, *young girl* . . . . Soprano
Marta, *her neighbor* . . . . Contralto
Wagner, *young student* . . . . Tenor
Elena (Helen of Troy) . . . . Soprano
    Mystic choir, celestial phalanxes, cherubs, penitents, wayfarers, men-at-arms, huntsmen, student, citizens, populace, townsmen, witches, wizards, Greek chorus, sirens, naiads, dancers, warriors

PROLOGUE In the heavens, angels and cherubim sing the praises of the Almighty. The fallen angel Mefistofele politely but sardonically greets the Deity from a distance, remarking that human beings, the lords of the earth, seem to him so feeble that he scarcely has the heart to tempt them. The mystic choir asks, "Do you know Faust?" Mefistofele replies that he does indeed know that strange madman, whose thirst for knowledge leads him past man's usual capacities. The mystic choir accepts his wager that he can lead Faust to damnation. Mefistofele remarks that he likes to visit with God, the "Old Man," occasionally and have him speak so humanly with the devil. The cherubim, who remind Mefistofele of a swarm of bees, start singing more songs of praise, and he retires. The chorus, augmented by the voices of earthly penitents and celestial phalanxes, swells in glorifying the Eternal.

ACT I   On Easter Sunday in Frankfurt, during the sixteenth century, groups of citizens gather in a festive mood. The old scholar Dr. Faust remarks to his pupil Wagner that spring has brought hope and beauty to the earth again, but Wagner tolerates the vulgar throng only for the sake of his master. Further celebration and wild dancing are stilled by the onset of darkness. Though apprehensive about spirits, Wagner thinks little of a gray friar who has been moving about them, but Faust notices that his steps leave traces of fire and that he seems to be tracing a circle or drawing a net around them. When they leave, the friar follows them.

§ At night in Faust's study, the friar enters unnoticed and conceals himself as Faust muses on the sleeping world and on what means most to him—the search for knowledge and good (*Dai campi, dai prati*). As he starts to read the Scriptures, the friar lets out a cry and shows himself to be Mefistofele, dressed like a gentleman of the world. Questioned as to his identity, he says he is the spirit that denies everything and answers the universe with a whistle of defiance (*Son lo spirito che nega*). He offers his services on earth in exchange for those of Faust in hell. Faust is less concerned about an afterlife than about achieving one perfect moment of contentment, a moment so beautiful that he would ask time to stop for it. Agreeing on this, the two make a contract.

ACT II   In the garden near Margherita's house, Faust walks with the girl while Mefistofele entertains and distracts her widowed neighbor, Marta. When Margherita asks Faust whether he believes in religion, he says he can neither affirm nor deny that he believes, having faith in nature, love, mystery, and life. She tries to leave, but he inquires whether they can ever be alone together, to which she replies that her mother shares her bed and is a very light sleeper. Faust gives her some sleeping medicine to make sure the old lady does not wake up, then woos Margherita ardently. Their declarations are interrupted by Marta and Mefistofele, returning from a stroll.

§ In the valley of Schirk, bounded by the heights of the Brocken, the witches' sabbath is about to take place. Mefistofele leads Faust toward the place, and they are greeted by will-o'-the-wisps, witches, and sorcerers, who hail Mefistofele as their ruler. They present him with a glass globe, which he proclaims is the world, capable of reflecting and continuing everything (*Ecco il mondo*). With scornful laughter he hurls the globe down and smashes it. Faust sees a vision of Margherita in chains, the mark of an executioner's ax on her neck. Mefistofele tries to disabuse him of the notion as the infernal orgy reaches its height.

ACT III   The delirious Margherita is in prison, imagining that her tormentors have made up stories, saying she drowned her baby and poisoned her mother, in order to drive her mad (*L'altra notte in fondo al mare*). Mefistofele helps Faust gain entrance to the cell to rescue her. Margherita greets Faust but sorrowfully notices that his love for her seems to have died. She says she cannot leave the prison, because of her crimes and her fear of the outside world, but he tries to calm her with visions of escape to a faraway island (*Lontano, lontano*). Mefistofele urges haste, because daybreak is at hand; seeing him, Margherita breaks into fearful fantasies about her approaching execution, then mourns the fact that today was to have been her wedding day (*Spunta l'aurora pallida*). Dying, she renounces Faust and prays for heavenly pardon. Mefistofele pronounces her damned, but heavenly voices declare her saved. As the two men make their escape, guards and the waiting headsman are seen, cheated of their victim.

ACT IV   In a valley of ancient Greece, the classical Sabbath is under way. Elena (Helen of Troy) summons sirens and nymphs to serenade her. In the distance, the voice of Faust is heard calling Elena as he dreams of her: he has asked Mefistofele to lead him to this legendary land, where the devil feels much less at ease than among his subjects of hell. Elena, carried away by a vision of the sack of Troy, cries out (*Notte cupa, truce*) and describes the horrible night of the vanquished. Faust enters and hails Elena as the ideal of classical beauty (*Forma ideal purissima*). Her courtiers retire, leaving the pair to join in a hymn to the mysterious power of love.

EPILOGUE   Faust, again an old man, is back in his study. Mefistofele stands behind him and reminds him death is near. Faust reflects on happy experiences but regrets that none of them ever struck him as so beautiful that he wanted to make time stand still. Though he has experienced everything—the love of a mortal maiden, the love of a goddess—reality has been grief, the ideal just a dream. Now at last he conceives of a higher dream, seeing himself as ruler of a peaceful realm, secure in wisdom and justice (*Giunto sul passo estremo*). Such a realm could create heaven on earth, and Mefistofele is shaken by it, fearing he may yet lose the wager for Faust's soul. As voices of heavenly cohorts are heard praising the Lord, Mefistofele tries desperate means to lure Faust away from his vision, conjuring up sirens to tempt him. But Faust kneels, grasping the Bible, aware that his vision is one of paradise and eternity. Recognizing it as the one fleeting vision he would wish to stay, he falls dead. Cherubim appear, showering roses on Faust—and on Mefistofele, who retreats in torment from them and from the dawning light. Whistling his last defiance, he returns to his own domain as heavenly forces claim the soul of the redeemed Faust.

ALEXANDER BORODIN
1833–87

Alexander Borodin was one of the Mighty Five of Russian nationalistic music, so named by the influential critic Vladimir Stasov—
the others being Balakirev, Cui, Mussorgsky, and Rimsky-Korsakov. The illegitimate son of a Georgian prince, Borodin received
an excellent liberal-arts education, including music; but after 1850, when he
entered the Academy of Medicine in his native St. Petersburg, most of his
energies were directed toward a career as a research chemist and professor.
Only in his spare time or when he was ill could he devote himself completely
to music. His one full-length opera, *Prince Igor,* had to be organized and its
orchestration completed after his death by Rimsky-Korsakov and the young
Alexander Glazunov, in order to make possible its world premiere in 1890.
(Act III was for the most part composed from memory by Glazunov, who had
often heard Borodin play it on the piano.)

Borodin's particular skill lay in evoking the colorful Orientalism of eastern
Russia and its adjoining, often hostile neighbors. The suite of Polovtsian dances
from *Prince Igor,* his most famous composition, was a concert favorite long
before its incorporation into *Kismet,* the Broadway musical comedy based on
Borodin melodies. His other best-known works are the Symphony No. 2, the
String Quartet No. 2, and the tone poem *In the Steppes of Central Asia.* A
repertory item in the U.S.S.R., *Prince Igor* makes occasional appearances in
the West, as in the New York City Opera production of 1969. Dramatically
discontinuous and sprawling, it shows its greatest strength in the unfolding
of epic tableaux.

PRINCE IGOR

PROLOGUE AND FOUR ACTS

MUSIC: Alexander Borodin; completed by Rimsky-Korsakov and
   Glazunov

TEXT (Russian): by the composer, after a play of Vladimir Stasov's
   based on the anonymous ninth-century poem *The Song of Igor*

WORLD PREMIERE: St. Petersburg, Maryinsky Theater, November
   4, 1890

U.S. PREMIERE: Metropolitan Opera House, December 30, 1915
   (in Italian)

CHARACTERS

Igor Sviatoslavich, *prince of Seversk* . . . . Baritone
Yaroslavna, *his wife* . . . . Soprano
Vladimir Igorevich, *Igor's son* . . . . Tenor
Prince Galitsky, *Yaroslavna's brother* . . . . Bass
Konchak⎫
Gzak⎩ *Polovtsian khans* . . . . Bass
Konchakovna, *Konchak's daughter* . . . . Mezzo-Soprano
Ovlur, *Polovtsian* . . . . Tenor
Skula⎫
Yeroshka⎩ *deserters* . . . . ⎧Bass
   ⎩Tenor
Russian princes and princesses, boyars and their wives, old men, Russian
warriors, young women, people, Polovtsian chiefs, Konchakovna's compan-
ions, slaves, prisoners, guards, soldiers

PROLOGUE   The Russian town of Putivl, 1185. In a public square, the people hail the leaders who are going to free them from the threat of invasion by
the barbaric Polovtsians (Tartars) from the east. But as Prince Igor summons
his fellow princes, an eclipse darkens the sky; the people, taking this as a bad
sign, beseech him to delay his departure. He replies that it is useless to resist
one's destiny; they will go *(Nam Bozhye znamenye ot Boga)*. As the troops get
ready to march, two good-for-nothing deserters, Skula and Yeroshka, sneak
off to find easier work in the court of the dissolute Prince Galitsky, Igor's
brother-in-law, who is staying behind as regent. Igor's wife, Princess Yaroslavna, pleads with him not to leave now *(Akh, lada, moy lada!)*. As farewells

are exchanged, Galitsky expresses his gratitude to Igor, who took him in when his father renounced him, and who later made peace within the family. Hailed again by the people, the army leaves.

ACT I.   The courtyard outside Galitsky's palace. As the crowd mills about, a story is circulated about a girl the prince kidnapped for his own pleasure. When Galitsky comes out, he declares that he is bored and would really enjoy himself if he were ruler (*Greshno tait, ya skuki ne lyublyu*). The kidnapped girl's companions plead for her release, but Galitsky refuses, assuring them that she is being treated well. When he returns indoors, Skula and Yeroshka and some of the other retainers predict that Yaroslvna will disapprove once more of what her brother has done—but they do not fear her, preferring the way they are treated by Galitsky, who keeps them supplied with plenty to drink. They even discuss the possibility of deposing Igor and installing Galitsky in his place (chorus: *Itak, narod na veche sozyvaite*).

§ Inside Igor's palace, Yaroslvna mourns her husband's absence, with never a word from the battlefront (*Akh, gde ty, prezhnaya pora*). The village girls enter, still trying to find their kidnapped friend, and tell Yaroslavna that Galitsky's revels are as bad as a Tartar invasion. Galitsky appears, sending them away and defying his sister's censure—until she threatens to have guards take him home to their father in Galich. At this he agrees to release the girl and leaves. The council of boyars comes to tell Yaroslavna of the army's defeat by superior forces: Igor, with his brother and son Vladimir, has been captured, and the enemy is advancing toward Putivl. An alarm bell sounds, and the edges of town are seen to be in flames.

ACT II   In the Polovtsian camp. Amid singing and dancing, Konchakovna, daughter of the Polovtsian leader Khan Konchak, looks forward to a rendez-vous with the captive Prince Vladimir, with whom she has fallen in love (*Merknet svet dnevnoy*). She tells the serving girls to give the Russian prisoners refreshment on their way back from work. Night begins to fall. Alone, Vla-dimir awaits his beloved (*Medlenno den ugasal*). When she arrives, they embrace ecstatically and talk of marriage, which her father would permit—but his would not, as long as they remain captives. Hearing Igor approach, they part. Unable to sleep, Igor reproaches himself for having failed to defeat the foe (*Ni sna, ni otdykha*). Ovlur, a Christian convert among the Polovtsians, who is on guard duty, proposes to help Igor escape. Though the idea of behaving dis-honorably angers him, Igor is tempted by the chance to return to combat; he will think it over. His captor, Khan Konchak, enters to see how Igor is doing: is anything lacking for his comfort? Respecting Igor as an adversary, Konchak treats him like an honored guest (*Vsyo plennikom sebya ty zdes schitayesh?*). Igor tells him that, if free, he could never promise not to fight the Polovtsians again. This frankness pleases Konchak, who says he would respond the same way himself; he orders entertainment (Polovtsian dances).

ACT III*   As Khan Gzak returns from a successful campaign (Polovtsian march), Konchak hails him, declaring they will soon conquer all Russia. They leave to hold a war council, while the captives, headed by Igor and Vladimir, lament the fate of their city at the hands of Khan Gzak. More prisoners are led in, and Polovtsian soldiers praise their leaders before going to sleep *(Slava! Slava!)*. Ovlur approaches Igor's tent, saying the escape is ready. Igor agrees and sends him off, but Konchakovna, having learned of the escape attempt, runs in to dissuade Vladimir from leaving. He is torn, but Igor reminds him of his duty (trio: *Vladimir, syn!*). In desperation the girl sounds an alarm; troops hold Vladimir but not Igor. As Konchakovna tries to protect Vladimir from being executed, her father arrives, praising Igor's courage and giving Vladimir the hand of Konchakovna in marriage, to discourage him from escaping too.

ACT IV   On the ramparts of Putivl, Yaroslavna again laments her husband's absence *(Akh, plachu ya)* while peasants mourn their devastated land. To her delight, Igor suddenly appears (duet: *On, moy sokol yasnyi!*), saying he escaped and will rally new troops. The deserters Yeroshka and Skula pass in the square, droning a lament about Igor's defeat. Aghast at seeing him alive, they save their skins by ringing the church bells to summon the people, denouncing Galitsky, and proclaiming Igor's return. Elders and boyars fetch Igor and Yaroslavna, who appear before the crowd amid a hymn of praise and welcome.

*Sometimes omitted in performance.

BENJAMIN BRITTEN
1913–76

*B*enjamin Britten, the most eminent and productive English composer of serious operas, was born in Lowestoft, Sussex, son of a dental surgeon and an amateur singer. He started composing at five, and his interest in the stage began soon afterward, when he took part in pageants and school plays. His early works showed prodigious talent, realized by the craftsmanship he achieved under Frank Bridge, his teacher from age eleven. Going on to the Royal College of Music in 1930, Britten perfected his skills as a pianist and studied composition further with John Ireland.

After hearing *Wozzeck* in 1934, when he was twenty-one, he wanted to study with Berg in Vienna but was advised not to do so, particularly by his mentor Ralph Vaughan Williams. While writing music for documentary films, Britten met W. H. Auden, whose poetry he set to music in works that demonstrated his pacifism and his opposition to the conventional mentality that was leading the world into war.

When Auden emigrated to the United States, Britten followed his example, coming in 1939 for an extended visit. Accompanying him was his lifelong friend the tenor Peter Pears, whose artistry helped shape Britten's talent for vocal writing and encouraged such works as *Les Illuminations* and the Serenade for Tenor, Horn, and Strings. Though a conscientious objector, Britten decided his place was at home and returned to England during the war years.

Shortly after the end of hostilities, he was fortunate to have his most ambitious work to date, the opera *Peter Grimes,* staged and enthusiastically received. (An earlier opera, to Auden's text, *Paul Bunyan,* had been tried out in New York but was withdrawn for revision.) *Grimes* was inspired by George Crabbe, a nineteenth-century English writer who dealt with small-town life. Britten's treatment shows the composer's humanitarian views and sympathy for the victimized, but it preserves the ambivalence of Crabbe's antihero—Grimes is neither entirely helpless nor especially "good," and the citizens of the Borough, while rich in human failings, are not totally "evil." Yet the theme of persecution plainly motivates the work, its secondary theme being that of man as his own worst enemy.

Because English opera was still a novelty at home, Britten occupied himself—while *Grimes* went on to success abroad—with a genre of chamber opera that would be easier to stage. The results were *The Rape of Lucretia* and *Albert Herring* in 1946 and 1947, respectively. The company formed to present these soon developed into the English Opera Group, which in turn led to the Aldeburgh Festival, launched in 1948 and still active. Britten never abandoned his interest in small-scale opera, producing works for children and amateurs (*The Little Sweep, Noye's Fludde*) as well as "parables for church performance" (*Curlew River, The Burning Fiery Furnace, The Prodigal Son*). At the same time, he continued writing works aimed at the opera house, starting with *Billy Budd* in 1951.

Compared with those in *Peter Grimes,* the forces of good and evil are more clearly arrayed in *Billy Budd,* drawn by E. M. Forster and Eric Crozier from the short novel by Herman Melville. Based on an incident of alleged mutiny aboard the U.S. naval brig *Somers* in 1843, witnessed by the author's cousin, the *Billy Budd* story broadened into a "crucifixion at sea," an allegory of the human condition.

Another American writer, Henry James, gave Britten the subject for *The Turn of the Screw* (1954). (*Gloriana,* written the preceding year, marked Britten's only essay in historical opera, dealing with Elizabeth I and Essex.) Like the comedy *Albert Herring* (1947), *The Turn of the Screw* focuses on intimate, everyday relationships, bringing chamber opera (with a small orchestra) into the world of larger theaters; but both works are informed by an element of fantasy that takes them beyond normal reality. In *Albert Herring* the flight of fancy begins with the quaint conceit (borrowed from a Maupassant story) that in default of any virtuous girls in a rural community, a young man could be chosen king (instead of queen) of the May. In Henry James's ghost story *The Turn of the Screw,* it is never clear whether the tempters—ghosts of former employees in the house—are real beings or figments of the Governess's repressed imagination. Britten made them actual, acknowledging a dimension beyond everyday reality. In musical form the opera is a theme with fifteen variations, each denoting a separate scene of the story.

Britten's later works, notably the monumental *War Requiem,* continue to reflect his concern for humanity's plight, but *A Midsummer Night's Dream*

(1960) offers no such explicit message, following its Shakespearean text in exploring the perplexities of human relationships in a lighthearted vein. Here, as in his final two operas, *Owen Wingrave* (written for television, 1970) and *Death in Venice* (after Thomas Mann's story, 1973), the composer used what might be called a large chamber orchestra.

Of Britten's nine major operas (not including the early *Paul Bunyan* or the adapted *The Beggar's Opera*), three are regularly performed on international stages, and two or three more are revived fairly regularly here and there—a figure that compares favorably with Verdi's, one opera out of three in standard repertory. Though certain concerns unite them, Britten succeeded in making his operas all quite different; each has its own emotional weight and temperature, its own distinctive musical language and instrumental color.

PETER GRIMES

PROLOGUE AND THREE ACTS
MUSIC: Benjamin Britten
TEXT (English): Montagu Slater, after the poem by George Crabbe
WORLD PREMIERE: London, Sadler's Wells, June 7, 1945
U.S. PREMIERE: Tanglewood, Berkshire Festival, August 6, 1946
METROPOLITAN OPERA PREMIERE: February 12, 1948

CHARACTERS

Peter Grimes, *fisherman* . . . . Tenor
John, *his apprentice* . . . . Silent
Ellen Orford, *widowed schoolmistress* . . . . Soprano
Mrs. Sedley, *widow* . . . . Mezzo-Soprano
Auntie, *landlady of the Boar* . . . . Contralto
Her two "Nieces," *main attractions of the Boar* . . . . Sopranos
Bob Boles, *fisherman and Methodist* . . . . Tenor
Reverend Horace Adams, *rector* . . . . Tenor
Captain Balstrode, *retired merchant skipper* . . . . Baritone
Ned Keene, *apothecary and quack* . . . . Baritone
Swallow, *lawyer* . . . . Bass
Hobson, *carter* . . . . Bass
Townspeople, fisherfolk

The action takes place in a fishing town on the East Coast of England, known simply as the Borough, around 1830.

PROLOGUE   In the Moot Hall (town hall), a fisherman, Peter Grimes, is called to testify at an investigation into the death of his boy apprentice the month before. Sworn in by the lawyer Swallow, who acts as coroner, Grimes describes how heavy weather and a large catch kept his boat at sea for three days, during which time the drinking water gave out and the boy died. There was excitement in the town at his return, and he "shouted abuse" at Mrs. Sedley, the town busybody, while the widowed schoolmistress, Ellen Orford, did what she could to help. Swallow rules the death accidental but warns Grimes not to get another boy apprentice—if he needs a helper, it must be an adult. When Peter protests that he cannot work without an apprentice, Swallow recommends that he find a woman to look after the boy. Grimes would like to marry but feels that he must clear his name first: people will continue to suspect him, regardless of the coroner's decision. As the court clears, Grimes is left alone with Ellen, who stands by him. (*The truth—the pity—and the truth*). She encourages him to look toward a better future, but he remains obsessed by the Borough's hostility.

ACT I   As morning rises several days later, fishermen and women tend to daily chores (chorus: *Oh hang at open doors the net and cork*). Several of the local characters exchange greetings and converse. When Grimes brings in his boat, no one will help him except Balstrode, a retired merchant captain, and the apothecary Ned Keene. Keene tells Grimes he can get him a new apprentice from the workhouse in another town. When the carter Hobson declines to fetch the boy on his next trip (*I have to go from pub to pub*), Ellen says she will go along to look after the passenger. The townspeople warn her, but she stands up to them (*Let her among you without fault cast the first stone*) and leaves with Hobson, while Mrs. Sedley, who is addicted to laudanum (morphine), quietly asks Keene for a fresh supply and learns she will have to return for it that night. Balstrode notes a storm coming and, as the crowd disperses, speaks to Grimes, suggesting he leave the Borough and try his hand at sailing the open seas. Still brooding on his ostracism, Grimes confides to Balstrode what it was like the day the apprentice died (*We strained into the wind*). He must stay and prove himself by building wealth (*They listen to money*) and marrying Ellen. Balstrode says Ellen would marry him now, but Grimes is too proud, and Balstrode grows angry, anticipating a repetition of the recent tragedy. Alone in the rising wind, Grimes repeats his dream of a better life with Ellen (*What harbour shelters peace?*).

§ Inside the Boar, Auntie's pub, Mrs. Sedley awaits Hobson's arrival with her medicine. Balstrode and several other fishermen enter. As the shutters bang in the storm, Auntie's "Nieces" (barmaids and presumed sometime prostitutes) scurry downstairs in a fright. Balstrode's joking annoys the nervous Auntie, who asks him to be more respectful (*A joke's a joke and fun is fun*). Bob Boles, drunk, waxes amorous toward one of the Nieces and has to be subdued by Balstrode (*We'll live and let live*), who says pub socializing requires a modicum of civility. Keene finally arrives, with word that there has been a rockslide on the cliff by Grimes' hut. Grimes himself bursts in, looking wild. Amid general silence, he raves in poetic terms about the disturbed elements and their relation to humanity (*Now the great Bear and Pleiades*). Boles lurches up to him in a belligerent mood, but Balstrode intervenes and urges everyone to start a song (round: *Old Joe has gone fishing*). At the height of the song, the door bursts open. Hobson's cart having made its way through the storm, Ellen arrives with the new apprentice and turns him over to Peter, who takes him home amid general disapproval.

ACT II   On a bright Sunday morning some weeks later, Ellen appears in the main square with John, the new apprentice. She speaks kindly to the silent boy but notices he shows signs of rough treatment—a rip in his clothes, a bruise on his neck. As churchgoers sing hymns in the background, Grimes appears, wanting to go fishing despite Ellen's insistence that the boy has earned a day of rest. Only by keeping up his tireless work, Grimes says, can he buy peace and respectability. She wonders whether her faith in Grimes has been too optimistic (duet: *Were we mistaken when we schemed to solve your life by lonely toil?*). Angered by Ellen's lack of faith and the Borough's continuing hostility, Grimes strikes her and runs off; she leaves in the other direction. This episode has been witnessed by Auntie, Keene, and Boles, who come forth and are soon joined by other townspeople, including Mrs. Sedley, who comments that Grimes is mistreating his new apprentice no less than the old one. The people are quick to assume the worst and condemn Grimes (ensemble: *Grimes is at his exercise*). Boles starts to address the crowd, speaking out against the apprentice system. Seeing Ellen return to the square, he asks her to explain. She starts to tell how she tried to help Grimes care for the boy, but the general consensus— little affected by Balstrode's attempts to calm everyone—is to go to Grimes's hut and confront him. Led by the self-righteous Boles, most of the crowd starts out. Ellen, Auntie, and the Nieces stay behind to lament the foolishness of men.

§ At Grimes' hut, the fisherman urges his apprentice to make ready to go to sea for a big catch. Feverishly, he describes his hopes (*I'll fish the sea dry. . . . I'll marry Ellen*), then calms down and reflects on a longer-range plan for a better life (*In dreams I've built myself some kindlier home*). He is still haunted, however, by the fate of the previous apprentice. In the distance the voices of the approaching villagers can be heard (chorus: *Now is gossip put on trial*). Seeing them, Grimes opens the rear door to the hut and tells the boy, whom he berates for gossiping about him with Ellen, to climb down to the boat. Someone knocks at the front door. Peter hears the boy cry out and rushes after him. The rector, Horace Adams, arrives with the lawyer Swallow to find the hut empty. Impressed by its orderly appearance, they wonder whether the Borough has judged Grimes too hastily. They leave, but Balstrode ruefully notices the back door open, facing the precipice.

ACT III.   A few days later, on a summer evening, a dance is in progress at the Moot Hall. Swallow pursues the Nieces into the square, trying to flirt with them. They evade him, and he enters the pub alone. Ned Keene also tries to chase them but is interrupted by Mrs. Sedley, who says Grimes and the boy have been missing for more than a day *(Murder most foul it is)*. He escapes from her into the pub as some older citizens pass, bidding each other good night. Ellen and Balstrode enter. Grimes' boat is back, but there has been no sign of him. Ellen found the boy's embroidered shirt by the shore; she remembers that embroidery once had a happier meaning for her *(Embroidery in childhood)*. Balstrode is still hopeful they can help Grimes, and they go off as Swallow sends for Hobson (the town's acting constable) when he sees Grimes' boat. The men decide to form a posse and go after Grimes in earnest.

§ Some hours later, Grimes stands alone by his boat, as voices call his name in the distance. His mind wanders in recollection of the death of his apprentices and his persecution by the villagers. When Ellen and Balstrode come to fetch him, he seems oblivious and continues his mad soliloquy *(What harbour shelters peace?)*. Balstrode helps Peter push his boat into the water and tells him to sink it as soon as he gets out of sight of land. Telling Peter good-bye, he leads the distraught Ellen away. The searchers wander back into town, and as dawn breaks, the daily life of the Borough resumes. When Swallow brings a coast-guard report of a boat sinking out at sea, a fisherman looks through a telescope but sees nothing, and the villages go about their business (chorus: *To those who pass the Borough sounds betray*).

ALBERT HERRING

THREE ACTS
MUSIC: Benjamin Britten
TEXT (English): Eric Crozier, based on Guy de Maupassant's *Le Rosier de Madame Husson*
WORLD PREMIERE: Glyndebourne, June 20, 1947
U.S. PREMIERE: Tanglewood, Berkshire Festival, August 8, 1949

CHARACTERS

Albert Herring, *greengrocer's son* .... Tenor
Lady Billows, *elderly autocrat* .... Soprano
Miss Wordsworth, *head teacher* .... Soprano

Nancy, *baker's daughter* . . . . Mezzo-Soprano
Mrs. Herring, *Albert's mother* . . . . Mezzo-Soprano
Florence Pike, *housekeeper* . . . . Contralto
Mr. Upfold, *mayor* . . . . Tenor
Mr. Gedge, *vicar* . . . . Baritone
Sid, *butcher's assistant* . . . . Baritone
Superintendent Budd . . . . Bass
Emmie⎫   ⎧Soprano
Cis   ⎬ *village children* . . . . ⎨Soprano
Harry ⎭   ⎩Treble

ACT I   Loxford, a small market town in East Suffolk, April 10, 1900. Lady Billows, doyenne of local society, has just finished breakfast and is issuing instructions to her housekeeper, Florence Pike, who has trouble writing everything down *(One lifetime, one brain)*. They are interrupted by a delegation of local worthies—Miss Wordsworth, the church-school teacher; Mr. Gedge, the vicar; Mr. Upfold, the mayor; and Police Superintendent Budd. They voice their concern about illegitimate births in the neighborhood, for they have an appointment with Lady Billows to choose a virtuous girl as queen of the May. Lady Billows recalls that in her youth all the girls vied for this honor *(All dressed in white)*, and she offers a prize of twenty-five pounds to "make virtue attractive." Local girls are discussed, but each has some mark against her for indiscreet behavior. Amid rising indignation, Superintendent Budd suggests that they choose a *king* of the May instead, naming Albert Herring, son of the widow greengrocer. All agree that Albert is a model youth, and after some initial resistance he is chosen with Lady Billows's approval.

§ Outside Mrs. Herring's shop, three children are playing ball *(Bounce me high, bounce me low)*. Sid, the butcher boy, happens by and catches one of the children trying to steal some apples. The children run off, and Albert appears, carrying a crate of turnips. Sid teases him about never having any fun because of his strict, teetotaling mother *(Girls mean spring six days a week)*. Nancy, the baker's daughter, appears at the door, and Sid makes a date with her for that evening. When they leave together for the butcher shop, Albert wonders whether Sid was right—there must be more to life than keeping track of every penny and waiting on customers. His reverie ends when one of the children reappears on an errand for her mother. Then Miss Pike arrives, asking for Albert's mother, who emerges from the back of the store. The other delegates now enter the shop, and Lady Billows proclaims Albert king of the May, to be crowned on May Day and awarded a cash prize, "to ensure virtue has its just reward." When they leave, Mrs. Herring orders the reluctant Albert to accept this honor, to the amusement of the three children, who overhear her threats.

ACT II   On May Day, a marquee has been put up in the garden of the vicarage. Nancy sets out refreshments while Miss Pike nervously awaits Albert, who finally arrives, having had a flat tire on his bicycle. Sid also arrives and tells Nancy he has a scheme, which he will explain outside. Miss Wordsworth, bringing her schoolchildren from church, rehearses them in a hymn *(Glory to our new May King!)*, then shepherds them out to await the ceremony. Sid returns with Nancy, who fills the glasses with lemonade while Sid surreptitiously spikes Albert's glass with rum. With the arrival of a crowd of townspeople, the children repeat their hymn, presenting flowers to Lady Billows, Albert, and his mother. The children can hardly wait to get at the food, but first Lady Billows gives a speech *(I'm full of happiness)*, exhorting them to admire Albert's example and scorn the ways of sin; she presents Albert with his prize, twenty-five sovereigns. The mayor follows, proclaiming Loxford a model town and giving Albert a savings-account book. Miss Wordsworth's turn is next: her presentation is a copy of Fox's *Book of Martyrs*. After Superintendent Budd has said a few words, Albert is called upon to speak but can barely manage "Thank you very much." When the vicar proposes a toast, Albert begins to feel the effects of the rum, but his hiccups are drowned in a sea of voices amid the excitement of eating.

§ Later that evening, Albert stumbles into the shop, cheerfully tipsy, having enjoyed his coronation hugely. Since his mother is not home yet, he tries unsuccessfully to light the gas lamp, then recollects the pleasures of the feast, especially the lemonade. Thinking of Nancy, however, he becomes less euphoric *(Girls don't care for chaps like me)*. Sid's whistle is heard outside, where Nancy joins him in the street; they pass the shop en route to their rendezvous, commenting on Albert's plight *(Poor kid! It does seem wrong to show him off to everyone)* and deciding to make the most of their short evening *(Hurry to work and hurry to play)*. After overhearing them, Albert sinks into a bog of self-pity as he realizes how drab his life is in comparison with theirs. Then he remembers his prize money and wonders whether to spend it on a spree: a flip of a coin decides in favor of the idea; so, imitating Sid's whistle, he takes a hat and jacket and heads off down the street. Soon Mrs. Herring comes home; assuming Albert has gone to bed, she retires.

ACT III The following afternoon, Nancy is unhappily doing some of Albert's chores in the shop. Emmie, one of the children, stops in to report that Albert is missing and presumed to have met with foul play. Nancy bitterly regrets the prank she and Sid played on Albert. Sid comes in, weary from searching for Albert, and protests he was only trying to help the boy when he spiked his drink. Superintendent Budd appears and asks for Mrs. Herring, who has to be roused from fitful rest; waiting for her, the police chief splutters in bewilderment at this case *(Give me a decent murder with a corpse!)*. He has no news for Mrs. Herring, who emerges in a state of grief, but he does request a photograph of Albert for identification. Nancy, confident of Albert's return, tries to cheer her, but two new arrivals, Miss Wordsworth and the vicar, can offer only consolation. Lady Billows appears, fuming about the police and calling for Scotland Yard. When Sid, the police chief, and the mayor appear with Albert's wreath, found crushed by a cart alongside the road near town, a pall falls over the gathering, and each muses on the ephemeral nature of life (threnody: *In the midst of life is death*). Just as they are intoning their epitaph for one who died so young, Albert pokes his head through the door, surprised at what is going on. The mood of the others turns at once to indignation, as they berate him for his unexplained disappearance. Questioned severely about his activities, Albert acknowledges that he went out with friends and still has twenty-two pounds of the prize money, then improvises a wild account of pub-crawling and brawling that leaves his hearers aghast (*I can't remember everything*), adding to his mother that her overprotectiveness was what drove him to it. Politely but firmly, he asks them all to leave, so he can catch up on his work; after they stalk out, he cuts his mother's reproaches short, causing her to go upstairs in near hysterics. Then he turns to Nancy and Sid (*I didn't lay it on too thick, did I?*), who laughingly welcome him back. When the three children appear outside, Albert offers them free peaches, and they agree with Nancy and Sid that "Albert's come back to stay, better for his holiday." When Sid picks up his crushed wreath, Albert happily tosses it away.

BILLY BUDD

PROLOGUE, TWO ACTS, AND EPILOGUE
MUSIC: Benjamin Britten
TEXT (English): E. M. Forster and Eric Crozier, based on a
    story by Herman Melville
WORLD PREMIERE: London, Covent Garden, December 1, 1951
U.S. PREMIERE: NBC–TV, October 19, 1952
METROPOLITAN OPERA PREMIERE: September 19, 1978

CHARACTERS

Billy Budd . . . . Baritone
Captain Vere, *in command of* H.M.S. Indomitable . . . . Tenor
Red Whiskers, *impressed man* . . . . Tenor
Novice . . . . Tenor
Squeak, *ship's corporal* . . . . Tenor
Mr. Redburn, *first lieutenant* . . . . Baritone
Mr. Flint, *sailing master* . . . . Baritone

Donald, *member of the crew* . . . . Baritone
Bosun . . . . Baritone
First and Second Mates . . . . Baritones
John Claggart, *master-at-arms* . . . . Bass
Lieutenant Ratcliffe . . . . Bass
Dansker, *old seaman* . . . . Bass

Officers, sailors, powder monkeys, drummers, marines

PROLOGUE   Middle of the nineteenth century. In his study, Edward Fairfax ("Starry") Vere, retired British navy captain, muses as an old man on his life experience. He has seen much good and much evil, but the good always had some flaw that made it vulnerable to evil. In the line of duty, he upheld the right, but one decision he had to make was so morally confusing that it still fills him with anguish. . . .

ACT I   Flashback to 1797, during the French wars, aboard Vere's ship, the frigate *H.M.S. Indomitable.* Early one morning, as a cutter is dispatched to board a passing merchant ship and "impress" (forcibly recruit) more sailors, the First Mate hectors his crew, busily scrubbing the deck *(O heave away, heave!)*. Donald, a sailor, grumbles resentfully about the young midshipmen (officers in training) who saunter past. The Bosun threatens a Novice, whose incompetence earns him twenty strokes of the whip. Second Lieutenant Ratcliffe, returning on the cutter, brings three recruits from the merchant ship. First Lieutenant Redburn and the master-at-arms John Claggart proceed to question the three. The first two, protesting, are assigned to posts. The third, William ("Billy") Budd, unlike the others, is a seaman by trade; illiterate, he does not even know his age, having been a foundling. Apart from his stammer, he appears able-bodied and willing. Claggart, recognizing him as "a find in a thousand," assigns Budd to the foretop. Billy cheerfully bids farewell to his former ship, the *Rights of Man,* whose name disturbs the officers because of its echoes of the French Revolution. Claggart orders Squeak, the ship's corporal, to test Billy's patience with covert sabotage. As they withdraw, the Novice is brought in, broken from his flogging—"lost forever on the endless sea," his shipmates note commiseratingly. Billy gets drawn into an altercation with several other sailors, sparked by the argumentative Red Whiskers, but it is broken up by the changing of the watch. Donald warns Billy about the treacherous Claggart, whom the men call Jemmy Legs, but has only praise for Captain Vere. The other sailors echo Donald's fear of the French: "They killed their king, and they'll kill ours." Billy says he would gladly give his life for a good leader like Vere.

§ A week later, the captain sits reading in his cabin at evening and sends for two of his fellow officers, Flint (the sailing master) and Redburn. They join him in a toast to the king, then in one to the defeat of the French, whose radical ideas they fear may inspire mutiny. They recall the incidents of Spithead and the Nore, where mutinous behavior broke out, and declare they must be vigilant. Ratcliffe brings news that Cape Finisterre has been sighted—the ship is in enemy waters. He and the other officers bid the captain good night, as he resumes his reading of history.

§ Below decks, the men relax around their hammocks, singing a chantey (*We're off to Samoa*). An old sailor, Dansker, wishes he had tobacco. When Billy goes to fetch some, he discovers Squeak meddling in his kit and drags him in front of the others. Squeak pulls a knife, and Billy floors him. Drawn by the noise, Claggart appears and orders Squeak put in irons, praising Billy for his action. The men climb into their hammocks.

§ Back on deck, Claggart muses alone in his element—darkness—on the fatefulness of his meeting with Billy, who represents a light and goodness unbearable to him (*To beauty, o handsomeness, goodness!*). He realizes that it is his nature and destiny to destroy Billy. When the Novice appears, begging not to be flogged again, Claggart offers to protect him if he will get false evidence against Billy as a potential mutineer. The Novice does not want to, but out of fear he agrees.

§ The Novice quietly wakens Billy, who says he dreamed of being fathoms under the sea. In a near whisper, the Novice says there is a group of shipmates who cannot stand conditions and want Billy to lead them. Billy admires the shining coins he is offered, but when he realizes that the purpose is mutiny, he angrily tries to denounce the Novice. Speechless because of his stammer, he raises his hand against the boy, who flees in a panic. Dansker comes near to see what is happening and warns Billy that Claggart has it in for him (*Jemmy Legs is down on you*). Billy cannot believe this, declaring that the life suits him and that he may even be promoted.

ACT II   On deck some days later, Vere worries about the mist that envelops the ship, while Redburn comments that the men are restless for action. Claggart appears and starts to tell the captain that there is a dangerous man on board, but the mist lifts to reveal a French frigate a few miles off, so Vere issues the order to give chase. Excitement seizes the crew (*This is our moment*) as the ship mobilizes. Several volunteers, including Billy, form a boarding party, and a round of cannon shot is fired, but the wind is weak and the other ship still too far away. When the mist descends again, Vere recognizes they must give up the chase. He turns to Claggart, who shows him a handful of coins allegedly offered by Billy to the Novice to induce him to mutiny. The captain refuses to believe it and warns Claggart that hanging awaits a false witness; when the master-at-arms persists, Vere sends for Billy.

§ In his cabin, Vere weighs his certainty that Billy is good, Claggart evil. Billy enters cheerfully, thinking he has been called about the promotion he longs for, but instead Claggart is summoned and confronts him with charges of treason and attempted mutiny. Billy starts to stammer helplessly, then almost involuntarily strikes Claggart, who falls dead from the force of his blow. The shocked Vere sees that he has no choice but to put Billy on trial; because of the dilemma of condemning innocence, it will really be Vere's trial. The three officers arrive, and Redburn presides over the inquiry, at which Billy and Vere testify as to what happened, Vere refusing to speculate on Claggart's motives. Under the articles of war, the officers are obliged to condemn Billy, and Vere says he cannot interfere with justice. When he is alone again, Vere ponders the contradiction of what he has seen—the defeat of evil by virtue, the condemnation of murder by earthly law. He himself is condemned by duty to carry out Claggart's destruction of Billy.

§ Shackled in the prisoners' bay *(Look! Through the port comes the moonshine astray!)*, Billy reflects that he will soon lie fathoms deep, as in his dream. Dansker, sneaking in with a drink for Billy, tells him the crew is furious and wants to rescue him. Billy insists they must not, or they will hang too. Bidding Dansker farewell, Billy says it was inevitable for him to kill Claggart and for Vere to let him go to his punishment—"We're both in sore trouble." Strong in his faith that his soul will find rest in a final port, Billy waits for the dawn.

§ At first daylight, all hands file on deck to hear Redburn read the sentence. Crying, "Starry Vere, God bless you!" Billy is hanged, as a murmur of anger and revulsion grows, then subsides, among the men. The execution over, the officers order everyone below.

EPILOGUE   As in the beginning, Vere appears as an old man, concluding his story. Still anguishing over his Pilate-like decision *(I could have saved him)*, he takes comfort in the thought that he himself was saved by Billy's blessing. Like Billy, he sees ahead to a calm port for the soul: "There's a land where she'll anchor forever."

THE TURN OF THE SCREW

PROLOGUE AND TWO ACTS
MUSIC: Benjamin Britten
TEXT (English): Myfanwy Piper, after the story by Henry James
WORLD PREMIERE: Venice, Teatro la Fenice, September 14, 1954
U.S. PREMIERE: New York College of Music, March 19, 1958
   (student performance); New York City Opera, March 25,
   1962

THE TURN OF THE SCREW

CHARACTERS

Prologue . . . . Tenor
Governess. . . . . Soprano
Miles ⎫ *children in her charge* . . . . ⎧ Treble
Flora ⎭   ⎩ Soprano
Mrs. Grose, *housekeeper* . . . . Soprano
Miss Jessel, *former governess* . . . . Soprano
Peter Quint, *former valet* . . . . Tenor

PROLOGUE An unidentified man in a contemporary business suit (or in the style of 1955, when the opera was introduced) steps before the curtain to explain that he has found the memoirs of a Governess, written "long ago." The memoirs, the man says, describe the Governess' meeting with an attractive employer who wanted someone to care for his two young wards in the country. Occupied with his own business in London, the employer asked that she not bother him with any problems but cope as best she could with the situation. Doubtful at first, she was charmed by his manner and accepted the post.

ACT I England, late nineteenth century. At Bly, the remote house in the Sussex countryside to which the Governess is being sent, Mrs. Grose, the elderly housekeeper, banters with the excited children, who wonder what their new Governess will be like. The young woman arrives and is much taken with the place; Mrs. Grose assures her that the children are bright and will benefit from her care. The children lead her off to show her around the premises.

§ On the porch, the Governess receives a letter: Miles, the boy, has been dismissed from school for something involving "an injury to his friends." She wonders whether there can be harm in so pleasant-seeming a child. When Mrs. Grose reassures her about Miles, she decides to let the matter pass.

§ Some time later, of a summer evening, the Governess wanders outside, wishing that the children's guardian could see how well they are doing (*How beautiful it is*). When she catches a glimpse of a man on the tower of the house, she thinks at first it is the guardian himself, come for a surprise visit. When she realizes that it is not, she wonders who it could have been.

§ In the main hall, Miles and his younger sister, Flora, are at play. The Governess sends them outside and is about to follow when she catches another glimpse of the man, this time looking through the window at her. Alarmed, she describes him to Mrs. Grose, who recognizes him as Peter Quint, the absent uncle's former valet. Quint, once left in charge of the house, had spent considerable time with Miles and carried on an affair with the former governess, Miss Jessel. Both of them died. Shaken by this brush with the supernatural, the Governess suspects that Quint's ghost has come in search of Miles, whom she must protect.

§ In a room used for tutoring, the Governess is teaching Miles his Latin lesson while Flora plays. Miles sings a song he says he found: *"Malo:* I would rather be / *Malo:* in an apple tree / *Malo:* than a naughty boy / *Malo:* in adversity."*

§ By a lake on the grounds, Flora sings to her doll *(Dolly must sleep wherever I choose).* When she sees Miss Jessel on the other side of the water, she turns away. The Governess then sees Miss Jessel, who disappears. Aware that Flora is also in danger, the Governess fears that both children are lost, that she can do nothing to save them.

§ By night, Quint appears on the tower and calls to Miles *(I am all things strange and bold),* while the boy, in his nightgown in the garden below, responds with hypnotized fascination. Soon Flora comes to her window, similarly responding to the apparition of Miss Jessel by the lake, who beckons her to a storybook land of dreams *(On the paths, in the woods).* The rapt exchange between children and ghosts is disrupted when the Governess and Mrs. Grose come after the children. Reentering the house, Miles asks, "I am bad, aren't I?"

ACT II   Quint and Miss Jessel are alone. She reproaches him for seducing and abandoning her; he retorts that she herself was to blame. Because of their failed relationship and separate fates, they cannot share each other's misery in death but must each find a young disciple among the living. Together they reiterate a line from a poem by W. B. Yeats, "The ceremony of innocence is drowned." Meanwhile, in a separate place, the Governess laments her own plight: innocent of the ways of evil, she is unable to deal with it.

§ In a churchyard near the house, en route to church, Miles and Flora are playing at being choirboys *(O sing unto them a new song),* while the Governess tries to explain to the good-hearted Mrs. Grose that the children are in terrible danger from the spirits who haunt them. Seeing she is alone with her dilemma, since Mrs. Grose does not understand, the Governess thinks only of getting away from this place.

§ Entering the tutoring room, the Governess finds Miss Jessel there and challenges her, but the ghost cannot or will not communicate with her, bemoaning only her own woe. Though Miss Jessel disappears when ordered out, the nearness of the apparition makes the Governess decide to disobey her instructions and write to her employer, saying she must meet with him at once.

§ In his room, Miles is getting ready for bed. Though he evades the Governess's solicitous questions, he implies he is quite aware of what she knows. When she talks of saving him, Quint is heard, reminding Miles of his presence. Miles lets out a shriek as the candle suddenly goes out, then tells the Governess that he himself blew it out.

---

*In the song, the same word is used with four different meanings, two related to *malus,* meaning "evil."

§ Quint's hovering presence persuades Miles to leave his room and steal the letter the Governess has written.

§ In the tutoring room, Miles plays the piano and Flora makes cat's cradles, while the Governess confides to Mrs. Grose that she has written the letter.

§ Near the lake, Mrs. Grose and the Governess search for Flora, who has wandered off. The Governess points to Miss Jessel, but Mrs. Grose cannot see her. Urged on by the ghost, Flora pretends not to see her either and turns against the Governess, crying that she hates her. As Mrs. Grose leads the child back to the house, the Governess admits that she has lost Flora (*Ah! my friend, you have forsaken me!*).

§ Having spent the night with the haunted Flora, Mrs. Grose now recognizes the danger and is preparing to take the child away. She informs the Governess that her letter never went out: Miles must have taken it. After the two have left, the Governess greets the returning Miles and asks whether he stole her letter. He seems eager to confide in her, but Quint's voice keeps calling from the tower, distracting him. Quint draws closer, insisting that Miles not betray him, but the Governess too insists—that Miles name his obsessor, thereby banishing him. At length Miles cries out, "Peter Quint, you devil!" and collapses in the Governess' arms. She believes she has saved him as Quint vanishes, but the boy is dead. She has saved his soul at the cost of his life. From his Latin verse, she repeats the word *malo*, a reference to the Lord's Prayer, *sed libera nos a malo*—"but deliver us from evil."

GUSTAVE
CHARPENTIER
1860–1956

One of the most colorful characters in the history of opera composition, Gustave Charpentier was born the son of a baker in the Moselle department of France, near Germany. When a scholarship raised by the town of Tourcoing, where his family moved in 1870, enabled him to study at the Paris Conservatory, he fell in love with Montmartre and the bohemian life it represented. For his independence he was expelled from the conservatory, but after a stint in the army he returned, studying in Massenet's composition class. It was a surprise to everyone, including Charpentier, when he won a Prix de Rome in 1887. In Rome he wrote his orchestral suite *Impressions d'Italie* and the first act of *Louise,* a realistic look at the life of Montmartre, to his own libretto. Advised by friends to make the opera more poetic, Charpentier (apparently with outside help) elaborated the text, completing the score in 1896. It reached the stage at the Opéra Comique in February 1900, providing the Scottish soprano Mary Garden with her identifying role when she stepped in and saved the production.

The director of the Comique, Albert Carré, took a calculated risk with *Louise,* which was shocking less because of its music than because of its text, extolling free love. Yet the portrayal of Louise's parents shows Charpentier's compassion for the poor and for the limitations of their working-class viewpoint. Dukas praised the opera for its human qualities and emotional truthfulness, but Debussy said only, "It's so bad it's touching." *Louise,* in the footsteps of *La Bohème,* enjoyed a world vogue, but Charpentier's sequel to it, *Julien,* made a poor showing.

There was something *louche* about the composer's reputation. Carré told the American tenor William Martin that Charpentier did not write Louise's celebrated *Depuis le jour* but appropriated it from a young man who had left the manuscript with him for an opinion and then died. Since the entire work is built on motifs from this song, Carré's is a serious allegation. Other sources question Charpentier's claim to authorship of the libretto, contending that his literary friends, notably Saint-Pol-Roux (pen name of Paul Pierre Roux, 1861–1940), contributed substantially more than helpful suggestions. Charpentier no doubt could not have cared less. Though already forty by the time of his first and only success, he lived to enjoy it amply. He died in 1956 in his beloved Paris.

LOUISE

FOUR ACTS
MUSIC: Gustave Charpentier
TEXT (French): by the composer
WORLD PREMIERE: Paris, Opéra Comique, February 2, 1900
U.S. PREMIERE: New York, Manhattan Opera House, January 3, 1908
METROPOLITAN OPERA PREMIERE: January 15, 1921

CHARACTERS

Louise . . . . Soprano
Her Mother . . . . Contralto
A Street Singer. . . . . Mezzo-Soprano
A Forewoman. . . . . Mezzo-Soprano
A Milk Woman . . . . Soprano
A Newspaper Girl . . . . Soprano
A Coal Gleaner . . . . Mezzo-Soprano
Julien, *young artist* . . . . Tenor
A Night Walker ("Noctambule") . . . . Tenor
Pope of Fools . . . . Tenor
Ragpicker . . . . Bass
Louise's Father . . . . Bass
Friends, seamstresses, street musicians, bohemians, townspeople, workmen

ACT I   In her parents' flat in a workingmen's quarter of Paris, around 1900, Louise, a young seamstress, leans out the window to talk with her beau,

Julien, an artist who lives across the alley. He has asked to marry her, but her parents have refused their consent; she tells him to write them another letter, adding that she will elope with him if they refuse again. Loving her parents as well as Julien, she is torn. He tells her how he first noticed her and fell in love with her *(Depuis longtemps j'habitais cette chambre)*. Louise's mother, overhearing, pulls the girl into the kitchen, then sticks her own head out and scolds Julien before slamming the window. She and Louise argue, but just as the Mother loses her temper, the Father is heard approaching. He sits down for supper, tired from his round of ceaseless toil. Though he finds life hard, he recognizes that wealth does not necessarily bring happiness, commenting that strong family ties are more important. Louise hands him Julien's most recent letter, which he reads. His mild reaction irritates the Mother, who rails against Julien as a good-for-nothing and slaps Louise when she protests. The Father tries to comfort her, saying her parents know best *(O mon enfant, ma Louise)*, but the Mother continues to mock Julien. The Father tells his daughter he could not go on living if she left home in disobedience. She reads to him from the newspaper and bursts into sobs at news of the brilliant spring season in Paris.

ACT II   At five in the morning, street characters populate the Montmartre section—a Ragpicker, a Coal Gleaner, a Newspaper Girl, a Night Walker, a Milk Woman. They exchange banter, and the Night Walker identifies himself as the Pleasure of Paris, "the procurer of the great city, your humble servant— or your master!" The street people trade sad anecdotes about losing their children to the lure of the city. For the lucky few, Paris is a paradise; for the likes of themselves, it leaves time only for hard work. Julien and his bohemian friends appear outside the factory where Louise works, preparing to abduct her if her parents have refused Julien's second request. A Street Singer offers a serenade, and the bohemians offer a theme song of their own *(Enfants de la Bohème)*. Seeing that it is near time for Louise to arrive, Julien asks his friends to withdraw. Working girls begin to arrive, including Louise, chaperoned by her still-irate Mother. As soon as the Mother leaves, Julien enters the workshop and brings Louise out. Not wanting to hurt her Father, she hesitates to run away from home, asking Julien to be patient a little longer. Then she goes inside.

§   In the sewing shop, the girls settle down to work. The Forewoman, looking in, puts a damper on their small talk, but this does not prevent several from commenting on how sad Louise has looked lately—perhaps she has troubles at home, perhaps she is in love. After a while, Julien's voice is heard outside in a serenade, which grows more impassioned with his frustration at Louise's failure to appear. The girls chatter about this new excitement. When other street musicians join in the playing, the girls start to dance around the room, and Louise says she does not feel well and is going home. The others watch from the window and note with glee that she is walking off with the young man who sang the serenade.

ACT III   On the heights of Montmartre, near twilight, with a view of the city beyond, Julien appears happily with Louise; evidently they have been living together. She rhapsodizes about the springlike beauty of life since she first gave herself to her lover (*Depuis le jour*). Though her parents are on her mind, she does not miss the restraints they put on her; every child, she says, has the right to find its own way to happiness. Julien expands this idea, proclaiming that every being has a right to freedom (*Tout être a le droit d'être libre!*). Together they hail the vitality and spirit of Paris (*Paris! Ville de force et de lumière!*) and sing of their love, then go inside. Bohemians and townspeople arrive, the former decorating Julien's and Louise's house with draperies and lanterns. The hippies of their generation, the bohemians attract a mixture of curiosity, mockery, and envy from their workaday compatriots. One thing all can agree on is the idea of a festival and a general good time (chorus: *Jour d'allégresse et jour d'amour*). Louise appears in her doorway, hailed by her friends as muse of the festival. The Pope of Fools presides over her coronation (*O jolie! Soeur choisie!*), and the crowd joins in a chorus of apotheosis. At its height, a hush falls as Louise's Mother approaches hesitantly through the crowd, the bohemians and Julien at first barring her path. Sensing trouble, the crowd backs off as the Mother quietly tells Julien she has come not to fight but to ask Louise's help for her Father, who is ailing. Though the parents resigned themselves to Louise's desertion, placing a cross on her door as if she were dead, the Father has been unable to get over it: sleepless and suffering, he keeps calling for Louise and looking for her return. If she will come back long enough to help him recover, they will not challenge her freedom. The Ragpicker, who lost his own daughter to the city, passes, singing a sad ditty: a girl in Paris is like a needle in a haystack. Julien agrees to let her go.

ACT IV   The house of Louise's parents on a summer evening. The building where Julien lived has been torn down, enlarging the view. The Father contemplates his old enemy—the city—with stoical sadness, wondering whether it is possible for poor people ever to have happiness (*Les pauvres gens peuvent-ils être heureux?*) under their double burden of fate and oppression. Waxing eloquent, he looks at Louise and reflects on the pain of parenthood, watching a child grow up, only to lose her (*Voir naître un enfant*). The Mother tells Louise they cannot let her go back to Julien and a disgraceful life of "free love," leaving the Father to suffer even more. Louise responds coolly to her Father's embraces, increasing his anguish. He recalls rocking her as a baby (*L'enfant dormira bientôt*), but she says that if he really loved her he would consider her needs as well as his own. An argument develops: the Mother declares they can give in to a marriage but not to an immoral liaison, Louise reminds her of her promise, the Father at first tries to be conciliatory. Louise's rhapsodic words about her newfound happiness, however, prove too much for his patience, and he rages at her, finally almost striking her, then opens the door for her to leave and practically throws her out. Now it is the Mother's turn to be conciliatory, but too late: Louise flies from her cage as the despairing Father, shaking his fist, curses Paris.

LUIGI CHERUBINI
1760–1842

*L*ike Rossini, Luigi Cherubini was a native Italian who died in Paris after spending much of his life in the City of Light, and who wrote operas in both countries. Although he lived over eighty years and exerted enormous influence over several generations of musicians, Cherubini won more respect than love—contemporary accounts draw him as a curmudgeon—and posterity has not dealt with him generously. Beethoven professed awe for this man who brought symphonic procedures into the opera orchestra. Best remembered as an educator, the Florentine-born Cherubini was named professor of composition at the Paris Conservatory in 1816 and became its director for two decades, 1821–41. He had first settled in Paris in 1788, but Napoleon's disfavor had dislodged him for a time.

The *New Grove Dictionary* credits Cherubini with thirty-eight operas, six of them pastiches (rewrites). *Médée* (1797) falls midway down the list. It is the only one remembered today, thanks largely to Maria Callas, for whom revivals were staged during the 1950s and early 1960s. In addition, his Symphony in D (revived by Toscanini with the NBC Symphony), several overtures, and two Requiems are heard with some frequency.

Médée, the fifth of Cherubini's French operas, was written as an opéra comique with spoken dialogue. More than half a century later, for the 1855 production in Frankfurt, the composer-conductor Franz Lachner added sung recitatives, performing the same service that Ernest Guiraud would later provide for *Carmen* and *Les Contes d'Hoffmann*. Though the work is today universally performed in Italian, it did not reach the Italian stage until 1909, using the Lachner musical adaptation with a translation by Carlo Zangarini, one of the librettists of Puccini's *La Fanciulla del West.* The present synopsis follows this version.

MEDEA

(Original French Title Médée*)*

THREE ACTS
MUSIC: Luigi Cherubini (recitatives added later by Franz Lachner)
TEXT (French): François Benoît Hoffmann, after Euripides' Greek
   play; Italian version by Carlo Zangarini
WORLD PREMIERE: Paris, Théâtre Feydeau, March 13, 1797
U.S. PREMIERE: New York, Town Hall, American Opera Society,
   November 8, 1955 (in Italian, concert version); San Francisco
   Opera, September 12, 1958 (in Italian)

CHARACTERS

Medea, *former wife of Giasone* . . . . Soprano
Glauce, *daughter of Creonte* . . . . Soprano
Neris, *maidservant of Medea* . . . . Mezzo-Soprano
Giasone, *leader of the Argonauts* . . . . Tenor
Captain of the Guard . . . . Baritone
Creonte, *King of Corinth* . . . . Bass
Two children of Medea, servants of Glauce, Argonauts, priests,
soldiers, people of Corinth

ACT I   The royal court of Corinth, in legendary antiquity. Maidservants try to cheer Glauce (Glaucis), daughter of Creonte (King Creon), on the eve of her wedding to Giasone (Jason), whose ship, the *Argo,* is visible in the harbor. Her mood clouded by forebodings, Glauce calls upon love to lighten her heart *(O Amore, vieni a me!).* Creonte enters with Giasone; at Glauce's urging, he promises to protect Giasone's two sons, whose lives are threatened by the mob because their mother, Medea—whom Giasone abandoned in Thessaly—is reputed to be a witch. Giasone, grateful for Creonte's hospitality, calls in his fellow Argonauts to present Glauce with the Golden Fleece, which they captured in Colchis. Frightened, Glauce recalls how Medea helped the Argonauts capture the fleece, adding that she will soon appear and threaten them all. Giasone tries to calm her with the assurance that he has left the danger of

Medea behind *(Or che più non vedrò quella sposa crudele),* and Creonte calls on the gods to ensure the safety of his daughter's marriage *(Pronube Dive, Dei custodi).* A Captain of the Guard intrudes to say that a strange, veiled woman is on her way. The woman appears and identifies herself as Medea, telling the people not to be afraid: she has come only for Giasone and his bride, who stand by without comment. Nevertheless, the people flee her in fear, leaving Creonte to threaten her with imprisonment if she stays. Medea retorts that if Glauce marries Giasone, she will destroy her. Angered rather than cautioned, Creonte says his power will stop her *(Qui tremar devi tu),* then leads Glauce away. Alone with Giasone, Medea reminds him how they met and fell in love, how she protected him with her spells and sacrificed everything for him *(Dei tuoi figli la madre),* but he rejects her entreaties. She swears vengeance, saying his wedding will never take place. Both ruefully recall that it was the unlucky Golden Fleece *(O fatal vello d'or)* that first brought them together.

ACT II   Outside Creonte's palace and the Temple of Hera, Medea bemoans the fact that the Corinthians want to turn her own children against her. Her confidante Neris warns her that the people are crying for her blood. Creonte appears, ordering Medea to leave while he can still protect her from the mob. Falling at his feet, she implores his mercy and vows she will live quietly as a private citizen if he lets her stay *(Date almen per pietà).* When he remains adamant, she accepts her fate, asking to stay only one more day *(Ecco, in esilio andrò)*; against his better judgment, he grants this, then leaves with his retinue. Seeing her collapse in deep brooding, Neris promises to share her fate, whatever sorrow it brings *(Solo un pianto con te versare).* As Medea rouses herself, intent on making use of the day that remains to her, Giasone enters. Finding out he still loves the children, she realizes they are her path to vengeance. In response to her pleas *(Figli miei, miei tesor),* Giasone says the children may stay with her during her last day in Corinth. Moved by her show of grief, Giasone admits to himself he cannot erase them from his memory, while she promises herself that he will pay for repudiating her. As he goes toward the temple, Medea tells Neris to bring the children. Priests invoke blessings on the wedding, provoking Medea's rage as she waits for the children to be brought.

ACT III   It is stormy nighttime outside Creonte's palace as Medea invokes infernal powers to aid her in sacrificing her children: Giasone will have to bear the sorrow and the blame. When she sees Neris with the boys, she steels herself and pulls a knife but drops it when they approach *(Del fiero duol).* As Neris tries to dissuade her from killing them, she embraces the children. Neris says she gave Glauce the robe and diadem that Medea sent—laden with curses—as a wedding gift. Deciding to spare the boys, she tells Neris to take them into the temple, then berates herself for her lack of resolve: she must take back the dagger and do the deed *(E che? Io son Medea!).* Voices, including Giasone's, are heard lamenting the horrible death of Glauce, whose robe burst into flames.

Rejoicing in her handiwork, Medea prepares to complete it *(Tu Glauce piangi sol)* and rushes into the temple as the throng approaches. In his desire to avenge Glauce's death with Medea's, Giasone has come in search of her. Neris runs to him, warning that Medea means to kill the children. Before he can pursue Medea into the temple, it bursts into flame, and the doors open to show Medea with the children's bodies at her feet. Crying to Giasone to admire what he has brought on himself, she says she will wait for him in the next world. As the temple starts to crumble, Medea picks up the children's bodies and walks into the flames. Giasone collapses, and the crowd recoils in horror (chorus: *Giusto ciel! O terror!*).

FRANCESCO CILÈA
1866–1950

*A*mong the minor masters of the so-called verismo movement, Francesco Cilèa earned a special place for creating, in *Adriana Lecouvreur,* a title role of compelling attraction. Because its main difficulty is interpretive rather than vocal, Adriana has always been a favorite role of experienced artists whose voices may be somewhat past their prime but whose acting skills are at a peak. In this respect it differs from such vehicles as Violetta in *La Traviata* and Amelia in *Un Ballo in Maschera,* dangerous for singers even in their best vocal estate.

Born in Calabria, in southern Italy, Cilèa was the son of a lawyer. Showing talent early, he was recommended at age nine for the Naples Conservatory, and all his life he remained closely associated with the academic world, teaching at and later directing conservatories. Unlike Mascagni, Puccini, and the other verists, Cilèa wrote extensively for piano, chamber ensembles, and orchestra. His reputation, however, rests entirely on the third and fourth of his five operas—*L'Arlesiana* (after Daudet, and seldom heard outside Italy) and *Adriana Lecouvreur.* Cilèa opted in the latter for a proven play by the French authors Scribe and Legouvé, based on the real-life character of Adrienne Lecouvreur (1692–1730) of the Comédie Française, one of the most famous actresses in history, who pioneered a simple, natural style of acting in defiance of the florid elocution then in vogue.

Because of the prolixity of the play, Cilèa's cuts sometimes left turns of plot unexplained. It is based on the attempt of Maurice, count of Saxony, one of 300-odd illegitimate offspring of Augustus II, elector of Saxony and king of Poland, to claim these thrones. Because he was the most important of Adrienne's lovers, and because she was the first actress accepted into polite society, she used her influence to help him. Though the Duchesse de Bouillon ("Princesse" in the stage version) was her rival and tried to poison her, the plot was detected. The actual cause of Adrienne's death remains a mystery and may be connected to her history of digestive disorders.

The world premiere of *Adriana Lecouvreur* drew a solid ovation at the Teatro Lirico, Milan, in 1902, and the work was soon produced all over Italy. It reached London in 1904 and opened the 1907–08 season of the Metropolitan Opera in New York, but despite the presence of Lina Cavalieri and Caruso in the cast, it did not take hold and had no revival there until 1962–63, when a new production was mounted for Renata Tebaldi.

ADRIANA LECOUVREUR

FOUR ACTS
MUSIC: Francesco Cilèa
TEXT (Italian): Arturo Colautti, from the French play by Eugène Scribe and Ernest Legouvé
WORLD PREMIERE: Milan, Teatro Lirico, November 26, 1902
U.S. PREMIERE: Metropolitan Opera, November 18, 1907

CHARACTERS

Adriana Lecouvreur	Soprano
Princess de Bouillon	Mezzo-Soprano
Mlle. Jouvenot ⎫ *members of the company* . . . . ⎧	Soprano
Mlle. Dangeville ⎭ ⎩	Mezzo-Soprano
Maurizio	Tenor
Abbé de Chazeuil	Tenor
Michonnet, *stage manager of the Comédie Française*	Baritone
Prince de Bouillon	Bass
Quinault ⎫ *members of the company* . . . . ⎧	Bass
Poisson ⎭ ⎩	Tenor

Ladies, gentlemen, servants

ACT I Backstage at the Comédie Française in Paris in 1730, actors and stagehands scramble to prepare for their current performance. The stage manager, Michonnet, grumbles amiably about the duties and errands he has to take care of. Two society gallants, the Prince de Bouillon and the Abbé de Chazeuil, come in search of the prince's mistress, the actress Duclos—a professional rival of Adriana Lecouvreur, who will appear with her on tonight's bill, sparking audience expectation. Duclos is not to be found, but Adriana comes in, costumed as Roxane in Racine's *Bajazet*. To the exaggerated compliments of the two visitors she replies she is just the handmaiden of the poet who created the play *(Io son l'umile ancella)*, her only mission being to seek the truth. For help in her work, she credits Michonnet, who is touched. Before leaving, the Prince tells the Abbé to get him a letter of Duclos's by whatever means necessary. Michonnet, alone for a moment with Adriana, tries to get up courage to declare his love for her, only to discover she is in love with Maurizio, an army officer. Forlorn, Michonnet leaves to oversee the raising of the curtain. Maurizio bursts in, declaring that Adriana is everything he holds dear *(La dolcissima effigie)*. Adriana offers to speak to the Count of Saxony about Maurizio's promised promotion. Then, realizing she must go onstage, she says she will deliver her lines for him alone. Handing him a bunch of violets from her bodice, she tells him to meet her at the stage door afterward. As they go their separate ways, the Prince and the Abbé return, the latter holding the coveted letter. It is addressed to Maurizio and asks him to come later that evening to a certain suburban villa, as Duclos has something important to discuss with him. The two men plan a late supper for the company at the same place, in order to catch the "lovers" by surprise *(Un gaio festino)*; the actors nearby, having overheard the elaborate plan, gossip among themselves that Duclos must be covering up for the Prince's wife, the Princess de Bouillon. Michonnet comes to alert them to their cues. Looking through the wings, he describes the hush in the theater and Adriana's superb reading of her monologue *(Ecco il monologo)*. As he rummages for a prop letter to be handed to Adriana in the next scene, Maurizio returns. He has received the Princess' message and wonders how to notify Adriana that he cannot meet her. It appears that the Princess has offered to help him realize his political ambitions. He uses the prop letter to write a message to Adriana onstage; Michonnet reports that she reacted to it with convincing emotion. The other members of the company come offstage, grumbling about the applause and attention Adriana receives. The Prince and the Abbé return in a good mood, however, anticipating their ambush. When they invite Adriana to the midnight party, she accepts in hopes of meeting the Count of Saxony, who she hopes will help Maurizio.

ACT II In Duclos's villa on the grounds of the Grange Batelière by the banks of the Seine, the Princess de Bouillon anxiously awaits Maurizio, calling on the stars to guide him safely to her *(O vagabonda stella d'Oriente)*. He arrives, saying he was trailed by two men. When she jealously spots his bouquet of violets, he says he brought it for her. She tells him that she has interceded on his behalf with the queen and the cardinal, who seem inclined to favor his claim to the Polish throne, but she warns of many enemies. Thanking her, Maurizio discreetly tries to extricate himself from her amorous advances. The Princess realizes he loves someone else, whom he refuses to identify, explaining he is weary at heart and preoccupied but wants to remain friends with her (*L'anima ho stanca*). When a carriage is heard approaching, Maurizio hides the Princess in a dressing room and awaits the Prince and the Abbé, expecting to be challenged to a duel. They seem jovial, however, and believe he was having a rendezvous with Duclos, of whom the Prince has tired. Adriana arrives and is astounded to learn that the Count of Saxony is Maurizio, whom she thought an ordinary soldier. As soon as they are alone, she forgives his deception, and he calls her his life's inspiration (duet: *No! Che giova?*). Michonnet comes in with the Abbé, saying he must speak with Duclos on urgent theater business, whereupon the Abbé assures him she will be there for dinner, since she had an earlier rendezvous—with Maurizio, he broadly hints, to Adriana's distress. Michonnet enters the dressing room while Maurizio hurriedly explains to Adriana that it was not Duclos he met, that his business was political, and that he is obligated to help the woman escape. Adriana agrees to help. Michonnet returns from the dressing room to say that the woman in there is not Duclos. When the curious Abbé determines to find out who she really is, Adriana bars his way. The Abbé hurries off to tell the Prince, thereby giving Adriana a chance to rescue the unknown woman. Sending Michonnet to guard the door, she calls for the woman to come out, then gives her a key to the garden gate. Neither recognizes the other, but the Princess senses a rival and lingers in order to challenge her (*Sì, con l'ansia, con l'impeto ardente*). No longer feeling obligated to help, Adriana does not care whether the Prince finds the woman there, but the latter slips out a hidden door, still unsure of Adriana's identity—though she knows she has heard the voice before. The Prince and the Abbé return with an entourage of actors, while Michonnet shows Adriana a bracelet he found on the ground.

ACT III In the salon of her palace, the Princess prepares for a reception, fuming about her rival, cursing Maurizio for his duplicity. She is no mood for the Abbé's foppish compliments (*Dite che il dio d'Amore*) but soon has to welcome her guests, among them Adriana, whose voice she recognizes. To test her suspicions, she lets Adriana overhear false news that Maurizio has been seriously wounded in a duel. Adriana almost faints, then shows joy when Maurizio arrives. As Maurizio speaks to the Princess, Adriana suspects *she* was the unknown woman at the villa. Maurizio regales the guests with an account of his exploits when a Russian general laid siege to his headquarters for three days (*Il russo Mèncikoff*). The curtain rises on an elaborate ballet, *The Judgment of Paris* by Champfleur, with its theme of a choice to be made among rival beauties. After it is over, the Princess and Adriana confront each other, each hinting heavily that the other is involved with Maurizio, finally pulling forth the bouquet and the lost bracelet, respectively. With feigned civility, the Princess invites Adriana to recite something for the guests—perhaps the monologue of *Ariadne Abandoned?* Stung by this blatant insult, Adriana chooses instead a monologue from Racine's *Phèdre* that denounces adulterous passion and shameless sinners, aiming it at the Princess, who pretends to dally with Maurizio instead of listening. Though the Princess orders Maurizio to stay, he manages to tell Adriana he will see her tomorrow.

ACT IV   Late afternoon in March at Adriana's house. Michonnet, coming to pay a call, tells his own heart to keep still *(Taci mio vecchio cuor!)*, while outwardly sympathizing with Adriana's disappointment in love. She greets him fondly but in obvious distraction: since that night at the Princess' soirée, she has been unable to return to the theater. Four actor colleagues come to try to cheer her with gifts and a skittish madrigal about a certain prince *(Una volta c'era un Principe)*. The maid brings a box marked as a gift from Maurizio; when Adriana opens it, she senses death in the package, which contains the violets she once gave him. She takes the bouquet and inhales its scent, imagining her own life wilting like that of the unfortunate flowers *(Poveri fiori)*. Michonnet says only a woman could have sent such a spiteful gift, adding he sent a message to Maurizio, who he is sure will come. Maurizio does arrive, begging Adriana's pardon and declaring he has come to know the Princess' wickedness and wants Adriana to marry him. When she replies she could never learn to wear a real-life crown *(No, la mia fronte)*, he calls her nobler than any queen. But she seems stricken; Maurizio and the returning Michonnet realize that the bouquet was poisoned and sent by the vengeful Princess. Adriana rises with her last strength, imagining herself Melpomene, the muse of tragedy. Drawn toward eternity by the light of love *(Ecco la luce)*, she collapses, dead.

DOMENICO CIMAROSA
1749–1801

*D*omenico Cimarosa was one of three prominent Neapolitan composers of opera buffa, the other two being Paisiello (whose *Il Barbiere
di Siviglia* was pushed off the boards by Rossini's later version) and
Piccinni. Cimarosa was Mozart's senior by seven years but outlived
him by a decade. That Mozart's achievements influenced him a great deal is
evident in Cimarosa's work; but he was writing for a general audience and,
being less of a creative adventurer, did not attempt finales as ambitiously
extended as Mozart's. His ensemble writing shows keen awareness of the variety possible within the opera-buffa format, and his lively characterizations
catch the essence of the genre, whose roots lie in commedia dell'arte. When
someone asked Rossini which of his operas was his favorite, he quipped, *"Il
Matrimonio Segreto."* There was no reason to make a secret of his indebtedness
to Cimarosa, whose most famous comedy (though he also wrote serious operas)
was a touchstone throughout the era. Berlioz, who visited Italy extensively,
grew so sick of the work that he wrote, "As for Cimarosa, I would pitch to
the devil his unique and everlasting *Il Matrimonio Segreto,* which is nearly as
tiresome as *Le Nozze di Figaro."*

The son of a stonemason, Cimarosa started his opera career in 1772 and
fifteen years later replaced Giuseppe Sarti in St. Petersburg as court composer
to Catherine the Great. After four years he began the voyage homeward, stopping in Vienna to write *Il Matrimonio Segreto,* which pleased Leopold II so
much that he ordered a repeat on the same day as the premiere. Cimarosa was

appointed Kappellmeister (music director) at the Viennese court, a post to which Mozart had earlier aspired in vain, but Leopold died almost immediately, whereupon the master politician Antonio Salieri regained the post. Returning to Naples, Cimarosa got into trouble with the authorities because of his sympathy with the French Revolution. Though he was pardoned from a death sentence, it was rumored after he died that he might have been murdered by agents of the Neapolitan government.

Il Matrimonio Segreto, with a libretto by Giovanni Bertati (who wrote the version of *Don Giovanni* on which Mozart's and Da Ponte's was modeled), derives from a London stage hit, *The Clandestine Marriage* (1766), by George Colman, Sr., and David Garrick, based in turn on Hogarth's satirical illustrations *Marriage à la Mode.* The score, more pre-Rossini than post-Mozart, is still prized for its chamber-music clarity and unaffected melodic appeal.

IL MATRIMONIO SEGRETO

(The Secret Marriage)

TWO ACTS
MUSIC: Domenico Cimarosa
TEXT (ITALIAN): Giovanni Bertati, after Colman's *The Clandestine Marriage*
WORLD PREMIERE: Vienna, Burgtheater, February 7, 1792
U.S. PREMIERE: New York, Italian Opera House, January 4, 1834
METROPOLITAN OPERA PREMIERE: February 25, 1937 (in English)

CHARACTERS

Elisetta, *Geronimo's daughter* . . . . Soprano
Carolina, *another daughter* . . . . Soprano
Fidalma, *Geronimo's sister* . . . . Mezzo-Soprano
Paolino, *young clerk* . . . . Tenor
Geronimo, *merchant* . . . . Buffo
Count Robinson, *English milord* . . . . Bass

ACT I   Mid-eighteenth-century Naples. In the salon of Geronimo, a prosperous merchant, his young clerk Paolino reassures Carolina, younger daughter of the household, that he will reveal in due time the secret of their marriage, and all will be well (duet: *Cara, non dubitar*). Hoping to ingratiate himself with his boss, Paolino has arranged a marriage contract between his protector, Count Robinson, and Elisetta, Geronimo's older daughter. Thinking they should not be seen alone together, Carolina leaves, and Geronimo embraces Paolino with delight over Count Robinson's letter expressing interest in the marriage (Elisetta has a substantial dowry). Calling his daughters and widowed sister, Fidalma, Geronimo announces that Elisetta will become a countess. She promptly puts on airs, annoying Carolina (duet: *Signora sorellina*), who leaves in a huff. Fidalma tells Elisetta to be more gracious, in view of her good fortune,and confides that she herself may soon be marrying too; she will not say to whom but admits to herself that she has her eye on Paolino. As they withdraw, Geronimo tells Carolina to cheer up, that he has found a husband of rank for her as well. This news upsets her, but before the discussion can proceed, Paolino introduces the Count, who makes himself at home, greeting father and daughters *(Senza tante ceremonie)*. When he learns that the attractive Carolina is not the proposed bride, he is disappointed *(Sento in petto un freddo gelo)*, while the sisters and their aunt wonder what will happen now.

§ Alone in the study, Paolino feels that the time is right to divulge the secret of his marriage, hailing Carolina as his true love *(Carolina, son tutto vostro)*. The Count seeks him out, saying he prefers the younger sister and will be content with a smaller dowry. Unwilling to hear arguments to the contrary, he sends Paolino to arrange it, then greets Carolina affectionately. She assures him she has no desire or qualification to become a countess *(Tanto onore e riservato)*, but he remains quite taken with her.

§ Geronimo, in turn, is distressed to learn from Elisetta and Fidalma that the Count treated them rudely. Paolino comes to fetch them all, saying the banquet is ready.

§ Carolina, still pursued by the Count, does not feel free to tell him she is married, though she says she does not have a lover, which only incites him further. Interrupting them, Elisetta accuses both of betraying her *(No, indegno, traditore)*. The commotion attracts Fidalma, who joins Carolina in trying to calm Elisetta. When Geronimo arrives with Paolino, an awkward silence hits the group (ensemble: *Che triste silenzio!*), followed by a babble in which everyone tries at once to explain his or her viewpoint to the confused, exasperated Geronimo.

ACT II   Having taken the Count off alone, Geronimo tries to get to the bottom of what has been happening. They argue, since the Count refuses to marry Elisetta, while Geronimo insists he must honor the contract. When the Count offers a substantial refund of dowry in exchange for marrying Carolina instead, Geronimo sees a way to save face *and* money, so he agrees, providing that Elisetta will consent. They leave as the distraught Paolino throws himself on the mercy of Fidalma. When he realizes she hopes to marry him herself, he faints, giving her the idea he returns her emotion. When Carolina enters, she too gets the impression that Paolino loves her aunt. As soon as Fidalma withdraws, she confronts him. To reassure her, he says they will leave before dawn and take refuge at the home of a relative (*Quel ch'è fatto è già fatto*).

§ Trying to get Elisetta to reject him, the Count tells her all his bad habits and physical and moral defects (*Sentite io ve li dico*), exaggerating and inventing wildly, but she feels that time will cure them all, and he finally says he cannot abide her. He leaves as Geronimo enters, also bent on persuading Elisetta to give up her claim on the Count. To spite her sister, she refuses. Fidalma, seeing Carolina as a source of trouble, wants her sent to a convent. Once free of these wrangling women, Geronimo is in no mood to listen to Carolina, who comes to tell him the truth; instead he orders her off to a convent and leaves. She bemoans the predicament in which she is caught (*Misera, in qual contrasto*). When the Count finds her, she asks him to help her, but they are pounced upon by Elisetta, Fidalma, and Geronimo, who again accuse her of flirting and will not listen to anything she says. Alone for a moment with Fidalma, Elisetta says it should be clear now that Carolina is not interested in Paolino, adding that once she is gone, the Count will be content to accept his marriage contract. Finding the Count wandering about after the others have gone to their rooms, Elisetta suspects he may be on his way to Carolina's room, but he bids her a polite good night and retires to his own room. Paolino and Carolina step furtively into the deserted hall, on their way to escape, but the sound of Elisetta's steps causes them to retreat to Carolina's room, where Elisetta—hearing voices—is now sure the Count must be. She calls Fidalma and Geronimo, who join her in calling forth the Count—only to see him emerge from his own room, across the hall. Amid general consternation, Paolino and Carolina come out, confessing they were married two months ago. Geronimo and Fidalma are furious, but the Count and Elisetta advise them to forgive the newlyweds, adding that they themselves will marry after all (ensemble: *Oh che gioia!*).

CLAUDE DEBUSSY
1862–1918

Though Claude Debussy is known as a leader of the impressionist movement, his music owes less to painting than to poetry. Mallarmé and the French symbolist poets supplied him with the congenial goals of "calculated vagueness," of mood and suggestion rather than emotion and statement. Virgil Thomson has ventured that Debussy's musical line is akin less to painting than to the evocative but precise strokes and shadings of a black-and-white sketch.

Since the Belgian playwright Maurice Maeterlinck, Debussy's exact contemporary, pursued many of the same aesthetic goals, the composer found himself drawn to *Pelléas et Mélisande*. Making few changes in the play but continually revising the music, he took nearly ten years to write his only complete opera. Because of its recitative style and emphasis on atmosphere, it was considered a revolutionary score at its 1902 premiere, where some of the Opéra Comique audience championed it and others ridiculed it. Though the music shows Debussy's fascination with Wagnerian sonorities, especially those of *Tristan* and *Parsifal,* it also shows his reaction against Wagnerian aesthetics: the lovers' avowal is accomplished not by symphonic climax but in virtual silence. Debussy's other guiding lights were Mussorgsky, whose *Boris Godunov* he discovered during a stay in Russia, and Rameau, whose plastic prosody mirrored the French taste for verbal nuance and clarity.

Pelléas did not immediately go on to other productions, but it earned the composer the Legion of Honor and thereby, for the first time, a steady income. The Italian premiere, under Toscanini in 1908, provoked disturbances, but soon the work gained favor, often with its first protagonist, Mary Garden, portraying the enigmatic heroine, as she did for the U.S. premiere, at the Manhattan Opera House in 1908. The Met waited until 1924–25 to mount the work, with Edward Johnson (later the company's general manager) and Lucrezia Bori as the lovers. *Pelléas* no longer sounds musically disturbing, but it remains extremely difficult to stage and perform with the required lightness, understatement, and pathos.

PELLÉAS ET MÉLISANDE

FIVE ACTS
MUSIC: Claude Debussy
TEXT (French): From Maurice Maeterlinck's play of the same name
WORLD PREMIERE: Paris, Opéra Comique, April 30, 1902
U.S. PREMIERE: New York, Manhattan Opera House, February 19, 1908
METROPOLITAN OPERA PREMIERE: March 21, 1925

CHARACTERS

Mélisande . . . . Soprano
Yniold, *Golaud's son by his first marriage* . . . . Soprano
Geneviève, *mother of Pelléas and Golaud* . . . . Alto
Pelléas ⎫ *King Arkel's grandsons* . . . . ⎧ Tenor
Golaud ⎭ ⎩ Baritone
Arkel, *King of Allemonde* . . . . Bass
A Physician . . . . Bass
Servants, beggars

ACT I   Time and place are unspecified, suggesting the Middle Ages, in the mythical country of Allemonde ("all the world"). In a forest, Prince Golaud has lost his way following the trace of an elusive quarry, which he wounded. Instead he finds a girl sitting at the edge of a pool, frightened. When she threatens to throw herself in the water if he touches her, Golaud reassures her and asks where she has come from. She answers vaguely, saying only that she has been mistreated and has run away, that she is originally from somewhere else.* She has dropped a crown she was given in the water; when Golaud offers to retrieve it, she says she would rather die than have it back. Saying that her name is Mélisande, the girl reluctantly agrees to accept Golaud's protection, though he admits he too is lost in the forest.

§ In a room of the castle of Golaud's family, his mother, Geneviève, reads to his grandfather, King Arkel, a letter written by Golaud to his younger half-brother, Pelléas (*Voici ce qu'il écrit*). It tells of finding a mysterious girl in the forest and marrying her. Golaud fears that his family will not accept the marriage and asks Pelléas to light a lamp in a tower overlooking the sea if it is safe for him to return. Arkel remarks that Golaud, a widower, was right to remarry. Pelléas enters, sad because he has heard from his friend Marcellus, who is dying and would like to see him once more. Arkel asks the youth not to leave before Golaud's return, and Geneviève reminds him to light the lamp in the tower.

§ Outside the castle, Geneviève is showing the newly arrived Mélisande around the premises when Pelléas comes up from the seaside to join them. The three watch a large ship, which brought Golaud and Mélisande, leave the harbor. Geneviève excuses herself to look after Yniold, Golaud's young son by his first marriage. Pelléas offers his arm to lead Mélisande back into the castle. When he says he will probably be leaving soon, she asks why.

ACT II   By a fountain in the park, Pelléas shows Mélisande a place where he often comes to sit by himself. He grows anxious as she leans over the water and reaches into it. When he asks how she and Golaud first met, she replies she remembers little about it. Playing with the ring Golaud gave her, tossing it and watching it shine in the sunlight, she accidentally drops it in the pool. The two discuss how they can retrieve it; Mélisande fears they cannot. Pelléas says it is time to go, since he heard the stroke of noon when she lost the ring. If Golaud asks what happened, he says, she should tell the truth.

§ Inside the castle, Golaud is lying in bed, injured. Just after the clock struck noon, his horse bolted in the forest, throwing him and landing on top of him. While Mélisande tends him, she reveals her malaise in this place, though she cannot attribute it to any specific cause. Golaud, aware that the castle is gloomy and that most of the people are older than Mélisande, sympathizes. As he takes her hands, he notices that her ring is missing. She says it fell when she was gathering shells for Yniold in a cave by the sea. Golaud insists she go at once and find it, taking Pelléas as a guide. Mélisande laments to herself that she is not happy.

§ Pelléas leads Mélisande to the cave, so that she can describe it if Golaud questions her. The girl is startled to discover three old vagrants sleeping in

---

*In Maeterlinck's *Ariane et Barbe-bleue* it is explained that she was one of Bluebeard's wives; evidently she escaped from his castle.

the cave; Pelléas remarks there is a famine in the land. The two young people leave.

ACT III   Leaning out of a tower in the castle, Mélisande sings a folklike song about how her hair reaches the ground from the window (Mes longs cheveux descendent). Pelléas hears her, approaches, and is struck by the beauty of her unbraided hair. He annoys her by saying he will leave the next day, then plays with her hair, tangling it in some branches. She begs to be let go, thinking she hears Golaud nearby. When Golaud does come by along the path, he tells them to stop playing like children and leads Pelléas away.

§ In a vault beneath the castle, Golaud shows Pelléas a chasm in the rock of the foundation. When he remarks on the scent of death, Pelléas feels himself stifling. They leave . . .

§ . . . to emerge on a terrace, where Pelléas welcomes the fresh sea air. When they catch sight of Mélisande and Geneviève in the distance, Golaud warns against further "children's games" with Mélisande, adding that she may be about to become a mother and that her delicate health must be protected. Without seeming obvious about it, Pelléas is to avoid her as much as possible.

§ Outside the castle at evening, Golaud asks his child, Yniold, whether Pelléas and Mélisande are often together. Yniold's replies could be interpreted to indicate either a budding romance or an innocent friendship. When a light appears in Mélisande's window, Golaud lifts the child so he can see in the window, then questions him. Both Pelléas and Mélisande are there, Yniold says; they are standing apart, looking at the lamp, saying nothing. Golaud wants to know more, but the child insists on being put down.

ACT IV   In a room in the castle, Pelléas asks Mélisande to meet him that evening by the fountain so they can talk alone. He has seen his father, who has been recovering from a long illness and who urged him to travel abroad. Pelléas intends to leave, despite Mélisande's protests. Arkel appears, telling Mélisande that since her arrival he has felt the time to be right for a new, more youthful atmosphere around the castle. Golaud enters to confirm the fact that Pelléas will leave that very evening. He speaks rudely to Mélisande, betraying his jealousy and mistrust; finally he pushes her to the floor and seizes her hair, swinging her from side to side. Muttering irrationally, he leaves, and Arkel says, "If I were God, I would have pity on the hearts of men."

§ In the park, Yniold sees a herd of sheep, apparently on their way to slaughter. Sensing their fate and fearing the approaching dark, he leaves. Pelléas appears; he realizes that matters have gotten out of hand in his burgeoning relationship with Mélisande. The time has come to make a break. When she arrives, he tells her he is leaving because he loves her. She replies she loves him too. Beside himself with joy, he says she was the first to bring beauty into his world. When they hear the castle gates closing, they understand that fate is decreeing they stay together, but they detect Golaud lurking in the distance. No longer caring whether they live or die, they embrace once more as Golaud runs forward and kills Pelléas with his sword.

ACT V   In a bedchamber in the castle, the slightly wounded Mélisande lies sleeping while a doctor tries to reassure the remorseful Golaud; Arkel, however, senses her impending death. When Mélisande awakens, Arkel tells her she has been delirious for several days. Golaud approaches hesitantly and, finding she bears him no malice, asks to speak with her alone. But when he asks whether her love for Pelléas was guilty or innocent, her vague replies neither confirm nor deny his suspicions, and he realizes they will both die without his really knowing. She feels cold—"Is it true that winter is beginning?"—she learns she has given birth to a baby girl. Unbidden, the household servants enter and stand along the walls as Arkel tells Golaud to leave Mélisande—"The human soul likes to go away alone." When the servants fall to their knees, it is evident that Mélisande has died. Arkel says her child must live—"Now it is the poor little one's turn."

LÉO DELIBES
1836–91

*L*éo Delibes, grandson of an opera baritone and nephew of an organist, studied with Adolphe Adam, composer of the ballet *Giselle*. While still in his teens, he sang in the chorus at the Opéra in Paris, played piano in a dance hall, became a church organist, and worked as a rehearsal accompanist at the Théâtre Lyrique. His career as composer began with ten operettas for the Théâtre des Folies Nouvelles and for Offenbach's Bouffes Parisiens. After collaborating with Ludwig Minkus on the ballet *La Source,* in which he somewhat upstaged his more famous colleague, he was asked to write a ballet on his own, *Coppélia* (1870), which became a success at the Opéra and remains a fixture in the world repertory to this day.

Delibes's first opera, *Le Roi l'a Dit,* fared less well at the Opéra Comique three years later, but the Opéra called on him for another full-length ballet, *Sylvia.* Determined to write more operas, he produced *Jean de Nivelle* (1880), given one hundred times at the Comique. The year 1883 saw the creation of his last and greatest success, *Lakmé,* also at the Comique. In keeping with the tradition of that theater, it is rather lightweight, a poetic rather than dramatic tragedy, its dialogue spoken rather than sung.

With the British colonizing abroad and the Japanese Exposition captivating Paris, *Lakmé* was contemporary, even topical. Edmond Gondinet and Philippe Gille based their libretto on *Le Mariage de Loti,* a recent novel by Pierre Loti (Louis Marie Julien Viaud), known for his atmospheric tales of faraway lands. Though *Lakmé* is best known for its bell song, this is actually one of the few flights of flashy coloratura in a basically lyric work, characterized by charm

97

and grace. Delibes wrote one more opera, *Kassya,* orchestrated after his death by Massenet, but it never approached the success of *Lakmé.*

LAKMÉ

THREE ACTS
MUSIC: Léo Delibes
TEXT (French): Edmond Gondinet and Philippe Gille, after Pierre Loti's *Le Mariage de Loti*
WORLD PREMIERE: Paris, Opéra Comique, April 14, 1883
U.S. PREMIERE: Chicago, Grand Opera House, October 4, 1883
METROPOLITAN OPERA PREMIERE: February 22, 1892

CHARACTERS

Lakmé, *priestess* . . . . Soprano
Mallika, *her servant* . . . . Mezzo-Soprano
Ellen $\Big\}$ *English ladies* . . . . $\Big\{$ Soprano
Rose $}$ Soprano
Miss Bentson, *their governess* . . . . Mezzo-Soprano
Gérald, *English officer* . . . . Tenor
Nilakantha, *Lakmé's father, a Brahman priest* . . . . Bass-Baritone
Frédéric, *English officer* . . . . Baritone
Hadji, *servant of Nilakantha* . . . . Tenor
Worshipers, merchants, people

ACT I At dawn in a garden in India, around 1880, worshipers pray to Brahma, guided by their priest, Nilakantha. He asks the god to strike down the British conquerors, who have forbidden him to practice his religion. In the background his daughter, Lakmé, a priestess, invokes Durga, Shiva, and Ganesh. Excusing his parishioners, Nilakantha welcomes the girl and tells her he must leave to preach in a nearby town, a dangerous pursuit. Lakmé and a servant, Mallika, decide to go by boat along the flowered river bank (duet: *Dôme épais de jasmin*), gathering blue lotus for the altar. When the place is deserted, a laughing group of five English people approach, curious to see something of native life. Looking over the fence, they inadvertently break it in. One of them, Frédéric, recognizes Nilakantha's garden and warns the others not to intrude. The two young ladies, Ellen and Rose, and their governess, Miss Bentson, are dubious about the alleged beauty of Lakmé, but the fifth, a young officer named Gérald, is intrigued to hear about her (quintet: *Quand une femme est si jolie*). Frédéric voices the romantic notion that Indian women are more carried away by love than Westerners are; Ellen, the governor's daughter and Gérald's fiancée, feels ordinary by comparison. When Frédéric repeats that it is dangerous to stay, the women become anxious to leave, but Gérald— seeing Lakmé's jewelry and wanting to sketch it, so Ellen can have it copied— decides to stay a few minutes longer, reflecting on the strange allure of the place (*Fantaisie aux divins mensonges*). Trying to imagine what Lakmé must be like, he is perturbed to hear her voice and hides as she returns with Mallika. Lakmé wonders why nature seems to affect her feelings so much today (*Pourquoi dans les grands bois*). Discovering Gérald, she lets out a cry, but when Mallika and the other servant, Hadji, respond, she sends them to wait for Nilakantha's return. Then she confronts the intruder (*D'où viens-tu?*), warning that his sacrilege could mean death. He admires her strength and loveliness; she is impressed by his courage and feels attracted to him, but hearing Nilakantha's approach, she insists that Gérald leave at once. Seeing the break in the fence, Nilakantha realizes a stranger has been there and swears he must die.

ACT II   In the town square, where merchants are hawking their wares, Miss Bentson is jostled and has her watch and handkerchief stolen. Dancing girls appear, their undulations greeted approvingly by the crowd (*Ah! pour nos yeux charmés*) but not by the prim Miss Bentson. Nilakantha and Lakmé appear, dressed as beggars. Rose confides to Frédéric that both young men are going to leave with their regiment tomorrow morning to put down an uprising. Nilakantha hopes to find the trespasser. When Lakmé asks why he cannot forget the incident, he says he must look out for her (*Lakmé, ton doux regard*). Then he tells her to sing, hoping the guilty man will give himself away. Lakmé entertains the crowd with her tale of a pariah girl who saves a stranger from wild animals with her magic bells (*Où va la jeune Hindoue*); the stranger turns out to be Vishnu, son of Brahma, and transports her to the heavens. Nilakantha spots Gérald as the young man recognizes Lakmé. Gérald, who wants to stay, is obliged to leave by his companions, but Nilakantha plots with some of the faithful to encircle him (*Au milieu des chants d'allégresse*). As they leave to find their victim, Hadji surmises that Lakmé loves Gérald and pledges to help her. Gérald, returning alone, addresses Lakmé impulsively, declaring himself completely taken with her. Though he is an enemy, she wants to save him and offers him a hiding place in the forest where she can visit him (*Dans la forêt près de nous*). She melts into the crowd as worshipers approach the temple, calling on the goddess Durga. Gérald's English companions find him but follow the procession out of curiosity; still in a dreamy state, he is singled out by Nilakantha, who strikes him with a dagger and leaves him for dead. Seeing that he is only unconscious, Lakmé declares he is now hers; Hadji carries him off.

ACT III   In her secret hut, Lakmé sings a lullaby to Gérald *(Sous le ciel tout étoilé),* who revives, hailing the forest seclusion where their love is safe *(Ah! viens dans la forêt profonde).* To a nearby spring, loving couples make a pilgrimage; not wanting them to see her with a foreigner, Lakmé says she will go alone. During her absence, Frédéric finds Gérald, having followed a trail of drops of blood. He understands Gérald's infatuation but nevertheless insists that his friend not become a deserter from the army. Confident of having persuaded Gérald, he leaves as Lakmé brings the holy water, which she tells Gérald will unite them forever. Hearing soldiers' voices in the distance, she sees his reaction and figures out what has happened. Unnoticed by him, she picks a poisonous datura flower and bites it. When she seems faint, Gérald embraces her with concern, and she murmurs he has given her a vision of rapture she never knew before *(Tu m'as donné le plus doux rêve).* Moved, he joins her in drinking the sacred draught that unites them in eternity. When Nilakantha storms in, determined to kill Gérald, he sees the dying Lakmé and turns his attention to her instead, exulting that she has escaped to immortality.

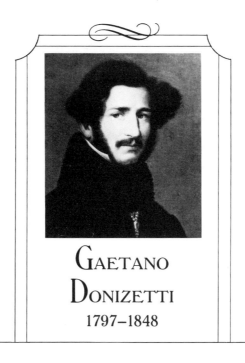

GAETANO DONIZETTI
1797–1848

*G*aetano Donizetti, son of a pawnshop caretaker and a seamstress, was born and died at Bergamo, like many of his opera characters, a victim of madness. To the older, baroque-based style known as bel canto (characterized by long, ornamented vocal lines), he added a dramatic urgency, especially in dialogue, that paved the way for Verdi and verismo. Like his colleagues Rossini and Bellini, Donizetti was primarily a melodist. Yet, out of his admiration for the classical masters Haydn and Mozart, he developed a sharp ear for orchestration—unobtrusive but sensitive—and for the dramatic shaping of concerted pieces along symphonic lines.

Extraordinarily prolific, Donizetti habitually overworked himself in the attempt to keep pace with demands from various opera houses. Though the total number of his operas has been estimated to be as high as seventy, the steadiness and the freshness of his lyric inspiration belie the fact that so much of it was created under hackwork conditions. Donizetti's construction of scenes relies on formula, but it is formula that works, and he imbues it with a pulsing inner life that often makes stock characters believable.

Until the bel canto revival that followed World War II, Donizetti was known chiefly as the composer of one tragedy, *Lucia di Lammermoor,* and one comedy, *L'Elisir d'Amore.* Today these are frequently accompanied in the repertory by other operas of his, both serious and comic. The former category tends toward the pseudo-historical subjects so much in vogue at the time, the remote country of England holding a particular fascination for him: *Anna*

101

Bolena, Maria Stuarda, and *Roberto Devereux* all portray English rulers, and Elizabeth I appears in two of them. *Lucrezia Borgia,* set in Italy, and *La Favorita,* set in Spain, further pursue the fictionalization of people who actually lived, a sport popularized by Sir Walter Scott, whose *Bride of Lammermoor* inspired *Lucia.*

If poignancy and lurid melodrama were Donizetti's to command, it was in his comedies that he showed his deftness of musical technique and gentle appreciation of human foibles. Amid the rollicking tunes of *L'Elisir d'Amore* we find the pensive *Una furtiva lagrima,* perhaps the most familiar of all Donizetti's airs. And in the lesson taught to Don Pasquale, an elderly suitor who needs to act his age, there is more than a touch of sympathy for the forlorn, foolish aspirations of all mankind.

ANNA BOLENA

TWO ACTS
MUSIC: Gaetano Donizetti
TEXT (Italian): Felice Romani
WORLD PREMIERE: Milan, Teatro Carcano, December 26, 1830
U.S. PREMIERE: New Orleans, December 12, 1839 (in French)

CHARACTERS

Anna Bolena, *second wife of Enrico VIII* . . . . Soprano
Giovanna Seymour, *her lady-in-waiting* . . . . Soprano
Smeton, *the queen's page* . . . . Contralto
Lord Riccardo Percy . . . . Tenor
Hervey, *official at the court* . . . . Tenor
Enrico VIII, *King of England* . . . . Bass
Lord Rochefort, *Anna's brother* . . . . Bass
Courtiers, officials, lords, huntsmen, soldiers, etc.

ACT I   England, 1536. At night in the queen's apartments in Windsor Castle, courtiers wait for the king's return, remarking he has found another love and left the queen brokenhearted. When they withdraw, Giovanna (Jane Seymour) comes in, lamenting that her own secret love for the king has filled her with remorse, since the queen is her friend. The queen, Anna Bolena (Anne Boleyn), appears with her retinue, including the court musician Smeton

(Smeaton), and calls for a song to relieve her sadness. Smeton, secretly in love with her himself, begins a serenade *(Cinta di nubi ancora)*, but when he reaches a line about "first love," Anna asks him to stop; to herself she admits that her own first love, which she gave up to marry the king, is rekindled by the song. Noting that dawn is near, she dismisses her followers, confiding to Giovanna that it is lonely and sad to be seduced by the glory of a throne. After both women have retired, Giovanna returns in great agitation, dreading discovery by the queen. Through a secret door, Enrico (Henry VIII) appears and says he wants to bring their love into the open. She retorts that she could never be his except in matrimony, causing him to suspect she is tempted by ambition rather than love (duet: *Vi preme il trono solo*). She denies this but worries about the fate of Anna, who Enrico declares is guilty of adultery.

§ At daybreak in Windsor Park, on the day of a hunt, Anna's brother, Rochefort, is surprised to recognize Anna's former suitor, Riccardo (Richard) Percy, whom the king sent into exile. Percy says he has been pardoned; though glad to return to English soil, he is bitter about the loss of Anna *(Da quel dì che, lei perduta)*. When the hunting party draws near, the king coolly greets Anna, ironically remarking that she is a subject of his constant attention. He greets Percy, who kisses his hand in thanks, but Enrico declares it was really Anna who secured his pardon. Struggling to keep her composure, Anna feels a surge of love as she sees Percy. Rochefort fears that Percy will betray both himself and Anna, for Enrico instructs his courtier Hervey to keep a close watch on Percy (quintet: *Io senti sulla mia mano*). Feigning friendliness toward Percy, Enrico returns to the hunt, hoping soon to catch his own prey.

§ In a chamber of the castle near the queen's apartments, Smeton tries to put back a portrait of her that he has taken, but he hides when Anna appears, arguing with her brother, who urges her—against her better judgment—to hear Percy for a few minutes. The latter enters, saying that he forgives Anna's breach of faith, because she has suffered so severely for it *(Io ti veggo infelice)*, and that he loves her as much as ever. She insists that her vows bind her, whereupon he threatens to take his own life. Stepping out of hiding, Smeton stops him, angering Percy, who wants to fight the intruder. The commotion brings Rochefort, who sees that the queen has fainted. Enrico, accompanied by Hervey, discovers the compromising scene and orders the disorderly men arrested *(Tace ognuno, è ognun tremante!)*. When Smeton protests his innocence and bares his breast to be stabbed, the portrait of Anna falls from his cloak. As Anna pleads, the enraged monarch says her tears only incriminate her further: Percy sees fate against him, Rochefort and Smeton deplore their contribution to Anna's downfall, and Giovanna blames herself (ensemble: *In quegli sguardi impresso*). When Anna realizes she will be placed on trial *(Giudici? ad Anna?)*, she fears that only in heaven will she be exonerated. Enrico retorts he will not hesitate to impose the death penalty on anyone who sullies his throne.

ACT II Outside the room where Anna is being held, her ladies-in-waiting comment that even Giovanna avoids the queen now that fate has turned against her. Anna enters, distraught, as Hervey comes to lead the ladies to Anna's hearing before the council of peers. Giovanna finds her at prayer and urges her to confess to adultery so that the king can divorce her instead of putting her to death. Anna refuses, since she is innocent, and curses her unknown rival. Overcome by the sorrow she has caused the queen, Giovanna falls at her feet and confesses she herself is the guilty one. Aware that her rival is punished by her own torment, Anna pardons her and bids her farewell (*Và, infelice, e teco reca il perdono*), as Giovanna recoils even more from her forgiveness.

§ Outside the council chamber where Anna's case is being tried, courtiers wonder what testimony Smeton will give. Hervey, sending for Percy and Anna, brings word that Smeton has confessed; this makes possible a charge of adultery against Anna. The courtiers withdraw when Enrico arrives, revealing in his conversation with Hervey that Smeton confessed because he had been led to believe he could save Anna's life and acquit himself. Enrico tries to avoid Anna when she and Percy arrive under guard, but she begs him to hear her declaration of innocence, seconded by Percy, who swears their love was never consummated. Enrico retorts that Smeton has confessed, whereupon Anna's indignation rises (*Io sfido tutta la tua potenza*) and Percy tries a new tack, declaring that since he and Anna were contracted to wed before she met Enrico, the royal marriage is invalid and should be annulled (*Fin dall'età più tenera*). Smarting from their defiance, Enrico swears that they will be punished regardless. When they are led off, Giovanna comes to beg Enrico to spare Anna's life; if she were the cause of Anna's death, she declares, she would go into exile. Though Enrico is annoyed by Anna's having caused this grief to his beloved, Giovanna persists in her pleading (*Per questa fiamma indomita*), interrupted only by the return of the courtiers and Hervey, who announces that the council has unanimously found Anna guilty, sentencing her and "any accomplice" to death.

§ In their prison cell, Rochefort blames himself for having spurred his sister's ambition for the throne, while Percy hopes their death will cause her to be spared (*Vivi tu*). Hervey comes to announce, however, that Anna will die. Learning that the king has pardoned them, both men scorn his mercy.

§ As the executioner awaits Anna, sympathetic courtiers watch her approach. Her wandering mind imagines she is about to be married to the king, but soon her image of him turns accusing, and she longs to return to the home of her youth (*Al dolce guidami castel natio*). When Hervey enters with guards, calling for the other condemned prisoners, she is surprised to see Rochefort and Percy again. Smeton throws himself at her feet, confessing he testified falsely in hopes of saving her. Anna imagines she hears Smeton's harp once more, accompanying her last prayer *(Cielo, a' miei lunghi spasimi concedi).* * The sounds of bells and cannon further confuse her, but when it comes time to go to her death, she draws herself up proudly, disdaining to condemn the guilty Enrico and Giovanna *(Coppia iniqua, l'estrema vendetta),* so she can meet God with forgiveness in her heart, hoping for His in return.

L'ELISIR D'AMORE

TWO ACTS
MUSIC: Gaetano Donizetti
TEXT (Italian): Felice Romani, based on Eugène Scribe's libretto
    Le Philtre
WORLD PREMIERE: Milan, Teatro della Canobbiana, May 12, 1832
U.S. PREMIERE: New York, June 18, 1838 (in English)
METROPOLITAN OPERA PREMIERE: January 23, 1904

CHARACTERS

Adina, *wealthy owner of a farm* .... Soprano
Giannetta, *peasant girl* .... Soprano
Nemorino, *young peasant* .... Tenor
Belcore, *sergeant* .... Baritone
Dulcamara, *quack doctor* .... Bass
        Villagers, soldiers, peasants, a notary

ACT I   Outside a Basque village around 1830. On the farm of Adina, a well-to-do local girl, workers are taking a rest from the noonday sun. As Adina sits reading, she is admired from a distance by Nemorino *(Quanto è bella),* who wonders how he could ever arouse her interest in him. Because the others cannot read, they ask Adina to relate the story. She reads a few verses from the legend of Tristan and Isolde, telling of an elixir that turned Isolde's hatred to love. Nemorino, Giannetta (another local girl), and the others are astonished. Adina's storytelling is cut short by the arrival of a troop of soldiers, headed by the fatuous Sergeant Belcore, who spots Adina as the prettiest of the girls and hands her a bouquet, just as Paris gave the golden apple to Helen

* A decorated version of *Home, Sweet Home* by Bishop, which was very popular at that time.

(Come Paride vezzoso). He woos Adina with allusions to classical literature, but she says she needs time to think it over. Nemorino fears he will lose her to the self-assured newcomer. Adina reminds everyone that the afternoon is progressing—time to get back to work. When he is finally alone with her, Nemorino awkwardly declares his love, but she reminds him he would be spending his time better by visiting his sick uncle, who might leave him some money. As for herself, she says, her affections are as fickle as the changing breeze *(Chiedi all'aura lusinghiera)*.

§ In the main square of the village, there is excitement at the arrival of a grandiose stranger, who sets up an array of bottles and addresses the populace. He is Dr. Dulcamara, sole purveyor of a marvelous elixir that cures all ills, even kills mice and bugs. As he describes the miracles his medicine has wrought, the gullible crowd, thinking it a bargain at only three lire, flocks to buy it up. While his young assistant hands out bottles, Nemorino draws the doctor aside and asks whether he also sells Isolde's love potion. Pretending he has heard of it, Dulcamara finds out how much money the boy has in his pocket and declares that is the exact price. Then he hands a bottle to the delighted Nemorino *(Obbligato! Son felice, son contento)*. The formula takes about a day to work, says Dulcamara—just long enough for him to finish selling and get out of town—while confiding to the audience that the bottle contains nothing but Bordeaux. As Dulcamara enters the tavern, Nemorino starts taking the potion and soon becomes rather tight, singing to himself and ignoring Adina when she appears. He is confident she will be infatuated with him by the next day and will regret her indifference *(Esulti pur la barbara)*. The arrival of Belcore gives her the opportunity to get back at Nemorino: she loudly promises to marry the sergeant at the end of a week. Nemorino remains convinced the elixir will vanquish her (trio: *Che cosa trova a ridere*). Giannetta and townspeople enter the square with news that Belcore's troop has been ordered to leave the next morning, so the sergeant asks Adina to marry him right away. Noting the effect on Nemorino, she agrees, but he abruptly changes his tone and pleads with her to wait at least until tomorrow *(Adina, credimi)*. While Belcore blusters at him, Nemorino calls out in despair for Dulcamara.

ACT II Indoors at Adina's farm, wedding festivities are under way, accompanied by the regimental band. Belcore proposes a toast to the glories of wine and womankind, while Dulcamara entertains the company with a new popular song about a girl who refuses to marry an old senator for his money *(Io son ricco, e tu sei bella)*. Adina joins in. When the notary arrives, Belcore observes Adina's reluctance to sign the contract: she feels her revenge will be incomplete unless Nemorino is there to see it. They leave to sign the papers, and Nemorino wanders in, surprised to find Dulcamara, whom he asks for help. Figuring he will leave soon, the doctor tells Nemorino to try some elixir—but the boy has no money. Belcore returns, perplexed that Adina now wants to postpone the contract until evening, and finds Nemorino bemoaning his lack of funds. Belcore tells the youth to enlist in the army and get twenty crowns right away (duet: *Venti scudi!*). Nemorino signs, takes the money, and rushes off to find Dulcamara.

§ In a nearby courtyard, Giannetta and a group of local girls discuss the latest news: Nemorino's rich uncle has died and left him a fortune. Not knowing this himself, he appears on the scene, having drunk his fill of elixir *(Dell'elisir mirabile)*. A drastic change in the attitude of the village girls, who start making up to him en masse, convinces him the elixir is working. When Adina and Dulcamara appear, the doctor cannot believe the potion had any effect, while Adina despairs of Nemorino's responding to her with real affection (ensemble: *Dottor, diceste il vero).* When Nemorino leaves, still surrounded by girls, Dulcamara tells Adina that Isolde's love potion is responsible, adding that Nemorino was in such anguish that he enlisted so as to buy the formula. Since Adina is taken aback by this news, Dulcamara tries to sell her the elixir too, but she says she knows an even more effective remedy—one of her own tender glances (duet: *Una tenera occhiatina*). After they have left, Nemorino returns alone, reflecting on a tear he saw on Adina's cheek and realizing she does love him *(Una furtiva lagrima)*. When she approaches, he feigns indifference, waiting to see what she will say. She tells him she bought back his enlistment papers *(Prendi; per me sei libero)*. Finding she has nothing further to say, he hands the paper back to her and says that if he cannot have her love, he wants to die a soldier. Adina now admits she loves him and asks him to forget her difficult behavior. As they embrace, Belcore marches in, followed by the populace. He readily accepts the loss of Adina, which is really *her* loss, he says: thousands of women are waiting for him. Dulcamara reminds everyone that his magic elixir cures all ills, and there is a rush of sales as he prepares to leave, hailed by Adina and Nemorino as the catalyst of their love.

LUCREZIA BORGIA

PROLOGUE AND TWO ACTS
MUSIC: Gaetano Donizetti
TEXT (Italian): Felice Romani, after Victor Hugo's French play
   Lucrèce Borgia
WORLD PREMIERE: Milan, La Scala, December 26, 1833
U.S. PREMIERE: New Orleans, May 11, 1843
METROPOLITAN OPERA PREMIERE: December 5, 1904

---

* Sometimes omitted.

CHARACTERS

Lucrezia Borgia . . . . Soprano
Maffio Orsini . . . . Contralto
Gennaro, *young nobleman* . . . . Tenor
Rustighello, *in the service of Alfonso* . . . . Tenor
Alfonso d'Este, *Duke of Ferrara* . . . . Baritone
Gubetta, *in the service of Lucrezia* . . . . Bass
Astolfo, *in the service of Princess Negroni* . . . . Bass
Gentlemen-at-arms, officers, nobles and ladies of the Venetian Republic;
same, attached to the court of Alfonso

PROLOGUE   Venice, 1519. At the Grimani Palace along the Giudecca Canal, evening festivities are in progress. A youth of noble family, Maffio Orsini, tells four of his friends how he was saved from death in battle by a fellow soldier of fortune, Gennaro, who is also present (*Nella fatal di Rimini*): a mysterious stranger they met on the battlefield, hearing them swear to stay together in life, had predicted they would also die together and warned them to avoid the notorious Borgias. Orsini makes light of the prophecy (ensemble: *Fede e fallaci oroscopi*) and goes inside, leaving Gennaro, who has dozed off. A gondola draws up bearing a masked woman—Lucrezia Borgia. She speaks to her spy, Gubetta, who has been mingling in the party. He warns her she will be insulted if recognized. Gazing at the sleeping Gennaro, she laments that fate has cast her as a villain when her heart is capable of such tender feelings (*Com'è bello!*). Awakening, Gennaro swears that no woman save his mother has moved him as much as the sight of this strange woman. He was raised as the son of a fisherman (*Di pescatore ignobile*), having been renounced by his mother out of fear for his safety. Lucrezia realizes that Gennaro is her own son, but she cannot let him know, since his birth was illegitimate and secret. She tells him always to revere his mother (duet: *Ama tua madre*). When the revelers return, Orsini recognizes her, and she is reviled with accusations of heinous crimes. Then the others, including the shocked Gennaro, flee her presence.

ACT I   Outside the Borgia Palace in Ferrara, Duke Alfonso, Lucrezia's husband, questions his henchman Rustighello about the young man whom he assumes to be his wife's lover and who has taken up residence across the square. He vows to do away with Gennaro (*Qualunque sia l'evento*). Alfonso exits as Gennaro and his friends appear. Orsini—who suspects the ubiquitous Gubetta of being a spy—is solicitous for his friend, whom he thinks Lucrezia has bewitched. Seeing the name BORGIA on the palace, Gennaro cuts away the first letter, leaving ORGIA (orgy), to the amusement of his friends. The group withdraws, and Rustighello, lurking in the square, encounters Astolfo, a servant of Princess Negroni, who has come to fetch Gennaro and his friends to a party. Rustighello sends Astolfo away and, with his men, forces his way into Gennaro's house.

§ In Alfonso's palace, Rustighello tells his master he has taken Gennaro prisoner. Asking for two pitchers, one of which contains the celebrated poisoned wine of the Borgias, Alfonso receives Lucrezia, who says she was publicly insulted in Venice and demands death for the one responsible. She is aghast to see Gennaro led in and charged with defacing the family crest; worse, he pleads guilty. Speaking to her husband alone, she pleads for the young man's life, but Alfonso is adamant, accusing her of loving the prisoner (duet: *Oh! a te bada*). She must decide whether he should die by poison or the sword. When Gennaro is brought back, Alfonso pretends to pardon him, offering him the rank of captain in his armed service. Gennaro accepts and Alfonso offers him wine. Gennaro wonders at this magnanimity, while Alfonso, in an aside, tells Lucrezia that she must serve the wine (trio: *Meco benigni tanto*). Satisfied that Gennaro will soon be dead, Alfonso leaves him with Lucrezia. With a hurried explanation and an antidote for the poison, she rushes him out a secret door.

ACT II Outside his house, Gennaro is preparing to leave Ferrara at Lucrezia's orders. In spite of himself, he cannot overcome the love he feels for her *(T'amo qual dama un angelo)*. He has no sooner entered his house than Rustighello appears with his henchmen, pleased to find that the duke's victim is still in town (chorus: *La fortuna al Duca è destra*). They disappear when Orsini comes and knocks at the door. Shocked to learn that Gennaro is leaving for Venice, Orsini reminds him of their sworn brotherhood; he suggests that Lucrezia is tricking him and urges him to stay at least until dawn, since Princess Negroni is having another party. After that, they can travel together (duet: *Sia qual vuolsi il tuo destino*). Rustighello restrains his followers, saying the party is a trap that Gennaro is walking into.

§ In the banquet hall of the Negroni Palace, Orsini leads his friends in praise of wine *(Io stimo quel che brilla)*. Making fun of his song, Lucrezia's spy Gubetta attempts to provoke a fight but is quieted by the others. When "wine of Syracuse" is offered, Gubetta pours it over his shoulder. Gennaro notices this, but Gubetta pretends friendliness, joining Orsini in the next drinking song *(Il segreto per esser felici)*. This is punctuated by the ominous tolling of a bell and voices outside proclaiming "The joy of the ungodly is like passing smoke." The torches have gone out, the doors are locked; the guests, their swords outside, are trapped. Lucrezia enters, saying she is returning the hospitality shown her in Venice. She is horrified when she sees Gennaro there, drinking. He still has the antidote, but since there is not enough for his friends, he will not save himself. In desperation, Lucrezia tells him he is a Borgia *(M'odi, io non t'imploro)*. When he still refuses to take the antidote, she admits she is his mother. Dying, he cries that death will unite the mother and son separated in life *(Tu! gran Dio! mi manca il core)*. Alfonso bursts in to find Gennaro and his friends dead, as Lucrezia, before fainting in her attendants' arms, confesses that the youth was her son and final hope *(Era desso il mio figlio)*.

MARIA STUARDA

THREE ACTS
MUSIC: Gaetano Donizetti
TEXT (Italian): Giuseppe Bardari, after Schiller's play *Maria Stuart*
WORLD PREMIERE: Naples, Teatro San Carlo, October 18, 1834,
    under the name *Buondelmonte,* with a revised libretto by Pietro
    Salatino and the composer; under its original title at Milan, La
    Scala, December 30, 1835
U.S. PREMIERE: New York (concert performance), Concert Opera
    Association, Carnegie Hall, November 16, 1964; New York
    City Opera, March 7, 1972

CHARACTERS

Maria Stuarda (Mary, Queen of Scots) . . . . Soprano
Elisabetta (Elizabeth, Queen of England) . . . . Soprano
Anna (Hannah Kennedy) . . . . Mezzo-Soprano
Roberto (Robert Dudley, Earl of Leicester) . . . . Tenor
Cecil (Lord Burleigh) . . . . Bass

ACT I   (Mary Stuart was beheaded in 1587; the action takes place during the period preceding this event.) Whitehall Palace, London. Her court welcomes Elisabetta (Queen Elizabeth I), who is considering marrying the king of France for reasons of state but who cannot forget her secret passion for Roberto, earl of Leicester *(Ah! quando all'ara scorgemi)*. Two of her advisers speak of Maria Stuarda (Mary, Queen of Scots)—Talbot to recommend clemency, Cecil to urge the death penalty. Her feelings in conflict, Elisabetta wishes she did not have to make the decision. She suspects, however, that Maria is her rival for the love of Leicester, who enters as she is musing on her dilemma. She gives him a ring to take to the French ambassador, saying she tentatively accepts the French king's proposal. To her chagrin, Leicester registers no emotion. The queen withdraws, leaving Leicester with Talbot, who gives him a letter from Maria. She is being kept confined at Fotheringhay because she is considered a possible threat to the throne of England. It is apparent that Leicester loves her *(Ah! rimiro il bel sembiante),* and he declares he will set her free or die in the attempt. Talbot departs, but when Leicester too starts to go, he meets Elisabetta, who notices his agitation and questions him: did Talbot give him a letter from Maria? Leicester at first evades the question but then decides to risk giving Elisabetta the letter, in which Maria begs for a meeting with her. The queen mistrusts Maria's arrogance and accuses Leicester of loving her; he protests that his concern for Maria is based only on pity for her plight. He persuades Elisabetta to come to a hunt near Fotheringhay, where a meeting can be arranged as if by chance. Elisabetta recalls, however, that Maria has offended her deeply *(Sul crin la rivale la man mi stendea).*

ACT II   On the grounds of Fotheringhay Castle, Maria walks with her companion Anna and reminisces about her happy youth in France *(O nube! che lieve per l'aria).* When huntsmen's voices sound in the nearby forest, Maria knows that Elisabetta is in the vicinity but no longer feels able to face her. Leicester arrives and entreats her to act humbly toward the queen; Maria, though, feels she cannot sacrifice her dignity. She leaves. Elisabetta arrives, nervous about the meeting, asking that the courtiers be sent off at a distance. Talbot escorts Maria back, and the two women contemplate each other from a distance, each privately musing on her resentments and grievances; finally, Maria steps forward reluctantly and kneels before Elisabetta, asking her pardon *(Morta al mondo).* When the queen disdains her, reminding her of her pride and past offenses, Maria at first tries to remain patient but soon loses her temper, calling Elisabetta the bastard daughter of Anne Boleyn *(Figlia impura di Bolena)* and asking how she dares talk of dishonor. Elisabetta retorts that death awaits this madwoman. Cecil reacts with satisfaction, Talbot and Leicester with chagrin.

ACT III   In a gallery at Westminster Palace, Cecil urges Elisabetta to sign Maria's death warrant. Though unrelenting toward her rival, Elisabetta is hesitant *(Quella vita a me funesta),* fearing criticism or reprisal. No sooner has she signed than Leicester comes to speak with her; seeing the warrant, he begs Elisabetta to delay. She retorts he has been a traitor and must witness the execution himself.

§ In Maria's apartment at Fotheringhay, Talbot arrives with Cecil, who tells her she is condemned. After Cecil's departure, Talbot adds that Leicester has been ordered to attend her execution. When she declares that her sins prevent her from being solaced by heaven, Talbot reveals the priestly vestments he is wearing and offers to absolve her. She recalls how she caused the death of her husband Henry Darnley *(Quando di luce rosea),* and Talbot prompts her to confess her involvement with the conspiracy of Babington, who lost his life for it. Talbot says God will forgive her and heaven bring her peace.

§ In a room adjoining the place of execution, Maria's coterie bemoans the horrid sight of the block. Anna comes in, asking them to be quiet because Maria is approaching. Maria, led in by Talbot, greets her friends and tells them not to weep—she is going to a better life *(Deh! non piangete!)*. She asks Anna to blindfold her when the time comes, and all join in prayer. When the first of three cannon shots is heard, Cecil comes to say that Elisabetta has ordered her last wishes granted; Maria asks that Anna accompany her to the block, then sends her forgiveness to Elisabetta, declaring she wants no remorse or rancor over her death *(D'un cor che muore)*. Leicester appears, angry and desperate, as the second shot is heard, but Maria tells him not to seal his own fate by trying to rescue her—instead he must lead her to death. At the third shot, she moves toward her doom as some of the observers proclaim their satisfaction at seeing justice done, while the others express their sorrow.

LUCIA DI LAMMERMOOR

THREE ACTS
MUSIC: Gaetano Donizetti
TEXT (Italian): Salvatore Commarano, after Sir Walter Scott's
　novel *The Bride of Lammermoor*
WORLD PREMIERE: Naples, Teatro San Carlo, September 26, 1835
U.S. PREMIERE: New Orleans, December 28, 1837
METROPOLITAN OPERA PREMIERE: October 24, 1883

CHARACTERS

Lucia, *Enrico's sister* . . . . Soprano
Alisa, *Lucia's companion* . . . . Mezzo-Soprano
Edgardo, *master of Ravenswood* . . . . Tenor
Arturo (Lord Arthur Bucklaw) . . . . Tenor
Normanno, *follower of Ashton* . . . . Tenor
Enrico (Lord Henry Ashton) of Lammermoor . . . . Baritone
Raimondo, *chaplain at Lammermoor* . . . . Bass
Relatives, retainers, and guests

ACT I　Seventeenth-century Scotland. The Ravenswood family has lost its lands to the politically ambitious Enrico (Henry Ashton). Enrico's sister Lucia

(Lucy), however, has fallen in love with one of the rival clan, Edgardo (Edgar of Ravenswood). As the opera begins, Normanno (Norman), an Ashton retainer, leads a hunting party in search of Edgardo, whom Enrico—his fortunes now on the wane—sees as a threat. Raimondo (Raymond Bide-the-Bent), Lucia's tutor, counsels Enrico against pushing the girl into a marriage of convenience, saying she is still grieving over her mother's death. Normanno retorts that she has a lover, whom she has been meeting in the park. When he adds that he thinks the lover is Edgardo, Enrico swears he will tolerate no such further insult to his family *(Cruda, funesta smania)*.

§ Elsewhere in the forest, at a park entrance before a fountain, Lucia waits for a glimpse of her beloved, though her companion, Alisa (Alice), cautions her against taking reckless chances. Lucia tells the legend of the fountain: once upon a time, a Ravenswood in mad jealousy stabbed his sweetheart there, and her ghost haunts the place *(Regnava nel silenzio)*. When Alisa declares this an ill omen, Lucia replies she has never known such happiness as her love has given her *(Quando, rapito in estasi)*. Alisa withdraws as Edgardo appears; he tells Lucia he is about to sail to France on affairs of state. Before he leaves, he intends to ask Enrico for permission to marry Lucia, even though Enrico killed his father. But the girl says their love must remain secret, though she exchanges rings with him and the two solemnly plight their troth. They forget their anxieties for a moment, imagining that their love will transcend the distance between them *(Verrano a te sull'aure)*.

ACT II   Some time later. In a chamber of his castle, Enrico waits for Lucia, whose wedding to Arturo (Lord Arthur Bucklaw) he has arranged for that very day. Normanno reassures him that since Lucia has heard nothing during Edgardo's absence—all his letters were intercepted—she will accept the match. To clinch matters, he hands Enrico a forged letter, supposedly from Edgardo, renouncing his pledge to Lucia. When the girl appears, Enrico tries to persuade her to marry Arturo for the family's sake, but she protests she is pledged to someone else *(Il pallor, funesto, orrendo)*. He then produces the forged letter. Though Lucia wants only to die, Enrico forces her to go through with the marriage *(Se tradirmi tu potrai)*. In a scene sometimes omitted, Raimondo tells Lucia that her dead mother would have wanted the match *(Ah! cedi, o più sciagure)*, adding that God will help her through her torment.

§ In the main hall, the guests look forward to the wedding celebration, and the prospective bridegroom offers Enrico his hand in friendship. When Lucia finally appears, shrinking from Arturo, her brother forces her to sign the marriage contract. But Edgardo, unexpectedly back from France, forces his way in and declares he still loves Lucia though she has betrayed him (sextet: *Chi mi frena in tal momento?*). Threatened by Enrico and Arturo, he says he will not give up without a fight; Raimondo steps between the angry men and orders them in God's name to shed no blood. Edgardo says that Lucia is betrothed to him, but Raimondo shows him the marriage contract, which Lucia in shame admits she signed. Edgardo gives back her ring and demands his own from her. Then he throws aside his sword and says his enemies might as well kill him, now that he has lost Lucia's love. Enrico tells him they will settle accounts later.

ACT III   In a scene sometimes omitted, Edgardo sits in a chamber at the foot of Wolf's Crag tower, deep in gloomy thought as a storm rages outside. Enrico rides there to confront him, and the flames of their enmity quickly flare as Edgardo realizes that Lucia is married to his rival. Since each man has sworn the death of the other, they agree to meet at dawn among the tombs of the Ravenswoods to fight (duet: *Ah! O sole, più ratto*).

§ In the main hall of Ashton's castle, festivities are still under way when the shaken Raimondo comes in to relate that Lucia has stabbed her bridegroom to death in the nuptial chamber *(Ah! Dalle stanze ove Lucia)*. Soon the disheveled girl appears, hallucinating about her marriage to Edgardo, which she imagines is about to take place (mad scene: *Il dolce suono*). Enrico enters and accosts her angrily but soon recognizes that it was he himself who pushed her into madness. Lucia begs the absent Edgardo's forgiveness for betraying him; she imagines herself dead, praying for him in heaven while bitter tears are shed on her grave *(Spargi d'amaro pianto)*. She swoons, Alisa leads her away, and Raimondo tries to blame the whole debacle on the scheming Normanno.

§ Among the Ravenswood tombs, Edgardo waits before dawn for Enrico. Life is unimaginable without Lucia, and he is prepared to die *(Fra poco a me ricovero)*. Instead of jubilation from the Ashton castle, however, he hears sounds of mourning as a procession approaches. He learns that Lucia is dying and has called for him. As he starts for the castle, Raimondo appears with the news that she is already dead. Edgardo now envisions her as an angel in heaven *(Tu che a Dio spiegasti l'ali)* and hopes to be united with her. At this he draws a dagger and stabs himself, as Raimondo and the bystanders pray that he be forgiven his rash act.

ROBERTO DEVEREUX

THREE ACTS
MUSIC: Gaetano Donizetti
TEXT (Italian): Salvatore Cammarano, after François Ancelot's
   Elisabeth d'Angleterre
WORLD PREMIERE: Naples, Teatro San Carlo, October 29, 1837
U.S. PREMIERE: New York, January 15, 1849

CHARACTERS

Elisabetta, *Queen of England* . . . . Soprano
Sara, *Duchess of Nottingham* . . . . Mezzo-Soprano
Roberto Devereux, *Earl of Essex* . . . . Tenor
Lord Cecil . . . . Tenor
Duke of Nottingham . . . . Baritone
Sir Walter Raleigh . . . . Bass
A Page . . . . Bass
Nottingham's servant . . . . Bass
Ladies of the royal court, courtiers, pages, royal guards,
Nottingham's attendants

ACT I   The great hall of Westminster Palace, 1598. Sara, Duchess of Nottingham, sits apart from other women of the court, reacting unhappily to a romantic story she has been reading. She cannot admit to her companions a love that consumes her own heart (*Ah! All'aflitto è dolce il pianto*). Enter Elisabetta (Queen Elizabeth I), who greets her affectionately and reveals that Roberto Devereux, Earl of Essex, is about to return from his campaign in Ireland. The queen adds she is worried about Roberto's loyalty—not to the throne but to her as a woman. When Sara realizes that Elisabetta too loves Roberto, she wants only to hide. Cecil, Sir Walter Raleigh, and other lords appear, and Cecil announces that Roberto is charged with treason. The queen declares that she requires further proof and wants to question the man in person; privately she hopes for a revival of their former love. Roberto is brought in and throws himself at her feet. Ordering him to rise, she asks whether he has betrayed her. He replies that his only offense was to show mercy toward the defeated Irish rebels. The queen, reminding him that she has not condemned him, points to his ring, a gift from her, and says she has been hoping for a return of their former feelings *(Ti porsi questo anello)*. Roberto ruefully admits to himself that the crown no longer tempts him. Pressed by Elisabetta, who suspects him of loving someone else, he denies it, increasing her anger. Resolving to crush her unknown rival and Roberto as well, she sweeps out. Roberto is left with the well-meaning Duke of Nottingham, but he recoils from his friend, who unsuspectingly tells him about the mysterious unhappiness of his wife, Sara *(Ieri, taceva il giorno)*. Cecil, eager to see Roberto executed, comes to fetch Nottingham for a meeting of the peers on this very subject. Nottingham alone wants to save Roberto, who guiltily asks to be left to his fate.

§ Sara realizes that Roberto is in even greater danger than she. He appears in her apartments, accusing her of playing him false; she explains that while he was away, her father died, and the queen made her marry Nottingham against her will. She urges Roberto to cultivate Elisabetta's favor for his own sake; when he says he cannot, she asks him to leave her forever and flee the country, though she admits she loves him. Seeing he has no choice, he agrees, and they bid each other an anguished farewell.

ACT II Back at Westminster, Parliament remains in session. Several lords, speculating on Roberto's likely condemnation, are silenced as Elisabetta approaches. Cecil reports to her that Nottingham's defense of Roberto was unsuccessful: she will shortly receive the warrant that seals his doom. All withdraw except Raleigh, whom Elisabetta questions about the arrest of Roberto that she ordered. Raleigh shows her a kerchief found next to Roberto's heart—a love token. Infuriated, she orders Nottingham admitted, sorrowfully bringing the condemnation paper. When he begs for mercy for his friend, Elisabetta refuses, saying she has new proof of Roberto's betrayal *(Il tradimento è orribile)*. Guards bring Roberto, and the queen confronts him with the kerchief. When Nottingham recognizes it as his wife's, he would like to kill Roberto himself, but Elisabetta signs the warrant (ensemble: *Va, la morte sul capo ti pende)*, while Roberto protests that he may be deprived of his life but not of his honor.

ACT III A servant hands Sara, still in her apartment, a letter from Roberto telling of his condemnation. He has left with her the ring Elisabetta once gave him, which may save his life if she takes it immediately to the queen. Before she can leave, however, Nottingham storms in, demanding vengeance *(Non sai che un nume vindice)* and ordering her confined to the house.

§ At the Tower of London, Roberto sits in his cell, hoping Sara will deliver the ring. He wants to live so that he can clear her name; he offers to die if necessary by Nottingham's sword but swears she was never an unfaithful wife *(Come uno spirto angelico)*. When Raleigh comes with guards to lead him to the block, Roberto realizes he can help Sara only by praying for her in heaven *(Ah! Bagnato il sen di lagrime)*.

§ Meanwhile, Elisabetta waits at Westminster, her anger spent, hoping Roberto will send the ring in order that she can pardon him, even if it means giving him up to her rival (*Vivi, ingrato, a lei d'accanto*). The disheveled Sara rushes in and presents the ring. Despite the shock of learning who her rival is, Elisabetta orders Roberto spared—only to hear from the gloating Nottingham that he is already dead. Elisabetta turns on both Nottinghams, who are led off under guard. In her misery she imagines Roberto's outraged spirit haunting the palace. Feeling that she is about to die, she mutters that James (the King of Scotland) should be her successor, then collapses, holding the fatal ring to her lips.

LA FILLE DU RÉGIMENT

TWO ACTS
MUSIC: Gaetano Donizetti
TEXT (French): Jules Henri Vernoy de Saint-Georges and Jean François Bayard
WORLD PREMIERE: Paris, Opéra Comique, February 11, 1840
U.S. PREMIERE: New Orleans, March 6, 1843
METROPOLITAN OPERA PREMIERE: January 6, 1902

CHARACTERS

Marie, *"Daughter of the Regiment"* .... Soprano
Marquise de Berkenfield .... Soprano
Duchesse de Krakentorp .... Soprano
Tonio, *Tyrolean peasant in love with Marie* .... Tenor
Sulpice, *sergeant of the French grenadiers* .... Bass
Hortensius, *steward to the Marquise* .... Bass
Soldiers, peasants, friends of the Marquise, etc.

ACT I In the mountains of the Swiss Tyrol about 1815, during the Napoleonic Wars. A skirmish has broken out, forcing the frightened Marquise de Berkenfield to stop on her journey home to her castle. There is a temporary lull in the fighting, and the Marquise thanks her ancestors for protecting her and the villagers from harm (ensemble: *Merci, mes aïeux*). Suddenly, a sergeant of the French army, Sulpice, enters, terrifying everyone anew, but he declares that he is a guardian of the peace. He is followed by Marie, "daughter," or mascot, of his regiment, the Twenty-first, which adopted her as an orphaned infant and has been a collective father to her. She and Sulpice reminisce, and she declares that military life exhilarates her (*Au bruit de la guerre*). Sulpice questions her about a young man with whom she has been seen. She replies that he is a Tyrolean who saved her life some time before, but before she can explain further, troops of the Twenty-first arrive with a prisoner suspected of spying; it is this same Tonio. He tells Marie that he was looking for her, and she intercedes on his behalf, explaining how he rescued her from falling into a ravine (*Un soir, au fond d'un précipice*). The soldiers befriend Tonio while Marie launches into a song glorifying the regiment (*Chacun le sait*). A drum roll brings everyone to attention as Sulpice enters to call the roll, asking Tonio to step aside: he is still a prisoner. When Tonio is told to follow the soldiers, however, he gives them the slip and returns to talk with Marie. Declaring he loves her (duet: *Depuis l'instant où, dans mes bras*), Tonio says he would forsake his home and follow her anywhere. She tells him not to risk his life: when in love, take care to preserve yourself for your beloved. Then she admits there is doubt and conflicting loyalty in her heart, for she returns his love (*Longtemps coquette*). Their embrace is interrupted by Sulpice, but the lovers pay no attention and wander off. The Marquise de Berkenfield asks Sulpice to help her return to her castle. When he hears the name Berkenfield, Sulpice is reminded of a certain Captain Robert, whom the Marquise allows she once knew: her sister, married to Captain Robert, bore a daughter and left the child in the Marquise's care, but the child was lost, and the Marquise believes she has died. Sulpice replies she is alive and well in the care of his regiment. Marie returns and is introduced to her new-found aunt, who tells her to leave the regiment and come to the castle for a proper upbringing. Marie at first balks but eventually agrees to come—if the whole regiment accompanies her on the way. Summoned by a drum, the soldiers hail the martial sound that calls them (*Rataplan!*). Tonio returns, having enlisted in the regiment, and welcomes the day he becomes one of them for the sake of the girl he loves (*Ah! mes amis, quel jour de fête!*). Jealously the regiment refuses permission for Marie to marry him, but when they realize she really wants to, they begin to relent—giving Tonio more cause to rejoice (*Pour mon âme quel destin!*). For the time being, Marie must go with her aunt. She comes to bid them farewell (*Il faut partir*) and learns of Tonio's enlistment, a further complication in her life. Now the soldiers argue whether they should let the Marquise take her away, while Tonio swears he will follow her, at whatever risk. When the Marquise arrives, they let Marie go, but Tonio tears the French insignia from his cap and tramples it underfoot in despair.

ACT II   In a salon of the castle, the Marquise reflects with satisfaction that she has arranged Marie's marriage to a German noble. Sulpice appears, summoned by the Marquise to persuade Marie to accept the match. When Marie joins them, the Marquise tries to start the girl's singing lesson, accompanying her at the piano, but Marie slips in phrases of the regimental song, joined by Sulpice. Finally, the women join in a duet *(En voyant Cypris aussi belle),* and Marie takes off in flights of coloratura, leaving her uncertain accompanist behind. Marie and Sulpice then take up the regimental song with a will. Though shocked, the Marquise finds the tune so catchy that she joins them. Regaining her composure, she asks Marie to act like a lady, since they are about to receive important guests. Sulpice leaves with the Marquise, and Marie muses on her unhappy lot, separated from the young man she loves. To her surprise, she hears the soldiers marching in the distance and breaks into a cheer for them *(Salut à la France!)* as they enter and join her. Tonio has been promoted for bravery, and Marie is overjoyed to see him among the ranks. Hortensius is scandalized to find common soldiers at the castle, but Marie orders him to serve them wine. As the troops file into the reception hall, Marie, Tonio, and Sulpice voice their happiness at being reunited (trio: *Tous les trois réunis*). When the Marquise appears and demands to know what Tonio is doing in her niece's company, he explains that he enlisted to be near her and fought bravely, inspired by her *(Pour me rapprocher de Marie).* The Marquise declares her niece engaged to another man and dismisses Tonio. Alone with Sulpice, she again asks his help, confessing that Marie is not her niece but her daughter, born out of wedlock. She is afraid of social ruin if her secret is discovered, but an advantageous marriage will give Marie a title, permitting the Marquise to leave everything to her without admitting parentage. Hortensius announces that the guests are arriving, headed by the intended groom's mother, the Duchesse de Krakentorp, who immediately protests Marie's absence. Meanwhile, Sulpice has told Marie that the Marquise is really her mother, and when the girl enters, moved by the discovery, she embraces the Marquise and says she is ready to do her bidding. A commotion outside stops the contract-signing ceremony as soldiers of the Twenty-first Regiment storm in to rescue their "daughter." The noble guests are horrified to learn that Marie was a canteen girl, but she still offers to go through with the arranged marriage if the Marquise wants it. The Marquise will not allow such a sacrifice: Marie can marry the man of her choice. The visiting Duchesse, scandalized, stalks out, amid the soldiers' and the lovers' rejoicing.

LA FAVORITA*

FOUR ACTS

MUSIC: Gaetano Donizetti

TEXT (French): Alphonse Royer, Gustave Vaëz, and Eugène
Scribe, based on Baculard d'Arnaud's play *Le Comte de Comminges*

WORLD PREMIERE: Paris Opera, December 2, 1840; Padua, June
1842 (in Italian as *Leonora di Guzman*)

U.S. PREMIERE: New Orleans, February 9, 1843; New York,
February 9, 1849 (in Italian)

METROPOLITAN OPERA PREMIERE: November 29, 1895 (in Italian)

CHARACTERS

Leonora di Guzman . . . . Soprano
Ines, *her confidante* . . . . Soprano
Fernando, *young novice of the Monastery of St. James
of Compostella* . . . . Tenor
Don Gasparo, *the king's minister* . . . . Tenor
Alfonso XI, *King of Castile* . . . . Baritone
Baldassare, *superior of the Monastery of St. James* . . . . Bass
Courtiers, guards, monks, ladies of the court, attendants

ACT I In fourteenth-century Spain, a group of monks passes through an
arcade in the Monastery of St. James of Compostella on the way to chapel for
morning prayers. The superior, Baldassare, stays outside to ask a young novice, Fernando, whether his faith is wavering. Fernando admits he has fallen in
love with a woman he has seen at prayer *(Una vergine, un'angel di Dio)*. Shocked
and disappointed, for he hoped Fernando would eventually succeed him, Baldassare tells the young man he is free to leave the order but warns him sternly
about dangers waiting in the outside world, especially since nothing is known
about the woman.

§ Some time later, on the shore of the Isle of León, a group of women, including Ines, a lady-in-waiting, welcomes Fernando, who has just landed, and

---

*Though written for France, this opera is almost invariably revived in its Italian version, by which the
characters and musical sections are here identified. The libretto retains some vestiges of the original version,
in which Fernando was Baldassare's son in the literal as well as the spiritual sense, hence the king's brother-
in-law.

removes a blindfold meant to keep him from knowing where he is. He asks Ines whether her mistress still refuses to reveal her identity, though he has visited her there before. Soon his beloved appears; she returns his love but cannot accept his proposal of marriage or reveal who she is. She holds a paper that she says will secure his future—but he must go away, which he declares he can never do (*Fia vero? Lasciarti!*). When Ines announces the arrival of the king of Castille, the unknown lady hands Fernando the document and bids him a hasty farewell. Suspecting that she is of noble birth, Fernando despairs of bridging the gap between their ranks, but since the document confers the title of captain on him, he interprets this as a means by which he can court her (*Gran Dio! Che degno io ne divenga*).

ACT II   The Alcazar Palace, in Seville, months later. King Alfonso XI learns with pleasure of the defeat of the Turks at the hands of Fernando, for whom he is waiting. His attendant, Don Gasparo, warns the king that his father-in-law (Baldassare) has arrived in an angry mood. Alfonso knows that this is because he has taken a mistress, Leonora di Guzman, whom he wants to marry. To protect his love for her, he will defy any opposition (*Vieni, amor! A'piedi tuoi*). Leonora enters; she is Fernando's unidentified beloved. Because of her sincere feeling for Fernando, she rebukes the king for having seduced her as a young girl and made her his mistress. Alfonso protests that his love is genuine, but Don Gasparo takes the king aside to reveal that Leonora has another lover. Angrily, Alfonso confronts her with a letter that proves this, asking the name of her lover, which she refuses to reveal. His threats are cut short by the intrusion of Baldassare, who warns Alfonso not to defy the laws of God (ensemble: *Ah, paventa il furor*), while the king declares he will replace his queen if he chooses. Baldassare retorts that the pope himself will excommunicate both Alfonso and Leonora if the king goes through with his plan. The courtiers, who disapprove of Alfonso's affair, side with the church and desire Leonora's banishment; she, in turn, prays for death to end her shame.

ACT III   Fernando arrives in a reception hall for his audience, still ignorant of Leonora's role at court, even of her name. Alfonso greets him heartily and promises any reward, so Fernando asks permission to marry the noble lady he loves. Just then Leonora enters the hall, and Alfonso realizes she is the one. Though seething with anger, he keeps his promise and offers her to Fernando; the wedding is to take place in an hour. The king promises Leonora he will be avenged. Then he leaves with Fernando. Alone, Leonora struggles to reconcile her shame with the fulfillment of her fondest wish: she fears that when Fernando learns the truth, he will spurn her love, though its intent is pure (*O mio Fernando*). Even heaven will not pardon her disgrace. When Ines enters, Leonora charges her with telling Fernando that she has been the king's mistress. As soon as Leonora leaves, however, Don Gasparo takes Ines into custody on the king's orders, thus preventing her from performing her mission. The courtiers, summoned for Fernando's wedding, enter in pleasant expectation but become resentful when Alfonso knights him as Marquis of Montreal. As Fernando reenters from the brief ceremony, the courtiers make insulting remarks about his loss of honor, quickly souring his happiness, and he demands satisfaction in a duel. Baldassare stops the threatened bloodshed, but as soon as Fernando learns that his wife is the king's former mistress, he again cries for revenge. When Alfonso appears, leading the bride, Fernando declares he owes all his good fortune to the king but at too high a price—that of his honor (ensemble: *Sire, io ti deggio mia fortuna*). Turning to the knights, he says he will renounce all titles, and he even breaks the sword the king sent him and throws it at his sovereign's feet. As he leaves with Baldassare, the knights stand aside and bow with respect.

ACT IV   Led by Baldassare *(Splendon più belle)*, the monks kneel before the Church of St. James. Monks and nuns enter the chapel, but Baldassare stays outside briefly to greet Fernando, who has returned as a novice. He reassures the young man that he will find faith again. Alone, Fernando recalls his illusory love for Leonora and begs her memory to leave his heart *(Spirto gentil)*. Baldassare returns to fetch him for prayer in the chapel. After they leave, Leonora appears, dressed as a supplicant. Mortally ill, she prays for Fernando's understanding and pardon before dying. When she hears prayers from inside the chapel asking divine retribution against a "guilty woman," however, she tries to leave. Strength fails her, and she collapses by the cross, to be discovered by Fernando, who offers help. When she identifies herself, begging him not to curse her, he orders her away *(Ah va, t'invola!)*. But she explains that she had sent Ines to tell him the truth before their wedding: she never meant to deceive him. Feeling his anger "wither like a leaf," Fernando now wants to revive their former love, but Leonora says it is too late: he must forget his past and come to terms with God's love, which will rejoin them in death. Feeling herself forgiven and blessed, she falls lifeless.

DON PASQUALE

THREE ACTS
MUSIC: Gaetano Donizetti
TEXT (Italian): Giovanni Ruffini and the composer
WORLD PREMIERE: Paris, Théâtre Italien, January 3, 1843
U.S. PREMIERE: New Orleans, January 7, 1845
METROPOLITAN OPERA PREMIERE: January 8, 1900

DON PASQUALE

CHARACTERS

Don Pasquale da Corneto, *old bachelor* .... Bass
Norina, *young widow* .... Soprano
Ernesto, *nephew of Don Pasquale* .... Tenor
Dr. Malatesta, *his friend* .... Baritone
A Notary .... Baritone

Servants, majordomo, hairdresser, dressmakers

ACT I Early nineteenth century. Don Pasquale da Corneto, a rich, eccentric bachelor in his sixties, has taken it into his head to disinherit his nephew, Ernesto, for refusing to marry according to the Don's wishes. Into his house comes his friend Dr. Malatesta, who reports on a recent interview with a lovely young woman whom Pasquale himself would like to marry *(Bella siccome un angelo)*. After describing her, Malatesta identifies her as his sister, increasing Pasquale's anticipation: he cannot wait to meet her. Malatesta says he will bring her later and leaves; Pasquale declares that the fires of youth seem to have been rekindled in his bosom *(Un foco insolito)*. Hoping to start a family and teach his dependent nephew a lesson, he welcomes the latter and asks him once again to do his bidding. Ernesto replies he cannot marry anyone else, because he is in love with a certain Norina, whom Pasquale dismisses sight unseen, because she has no dowry. Pasquale then declares that he is making good his threat to disinherit Ernesto, who must move out—Pasquale himself is taking a wife! As Ernesto voices disbelief, Pasquale assures him he means business *(L'ho detto e lo ripeto)*. When Ernesto advises consulting Malatesta, Pasquale retorts that the intended bride is Malatesta's own sister. Since Ernesto knows that this is none other than Norina, he feels betrayed and hopeless.

§ At home, Norina reads a knightly romance *(Quel guardo il cavaliere)*, adding that she too knows the wiles of courtship *(So anch'io la virtù magica)*. When her brother enters, Norina disclaims her part in the joke they are planning to play on Pasquale, giving Ernesto's despair as her reason. When she shows him Ernesto's letter of renunciation, Malatesta says not to worry—he will tell Ernesto their secret. He fills Norina in on the latest developments, saying he described her as his sister from the convent. Once the bogus marriage contract is signed, her job will be to drive Pasquale crazy. She looks forward to the assignment *(Pronta son)*, and the two hail their forthcoming success.

ACT II Ernesto, not yet having learned of his friends' plot, bids farewell to his uncle's house and declares he will go into exile *(Cercherò lontana terra)*. He wanders off, and Pasquale appears in his finest suit, impatiently awaiting Malatesta, who soon arrives with the modest "Sofronia." Her demure answers to his questions delight Pasquale, who pictures her as retiring and domestic. Acting as intermediary, Malatesta gets her to murmur her acceptance to a marriage. Then he summons the waiting "Notary" (his cousin Carlotto in disguise) to produce a contract. Malatesta dictates the terms, making it clear that half the Don's property will go to his wife. As Norina starts to sign, Ernesto bursts in, confronting Pasquale, who asks him to sign as a witness. Ernesto recognizes Norina, but Malatesta pulls him aside and tells him to keep quiet: the plot is for his benefit, and they will explain as soon as they have a chance. The Notary pronounces the couple legally married and slips out. Ernesto begins to catch on when Norina starts to behave shrewishly toward her new "husband." Without further ado, Norina declares she wants no disobedience or trouble from Pasquale, then orders extra servants, a new carriage, and furnishings, along with clothes and jewelry (*Ora attendete agli ordini*). Aghast, then enraged, Pasquale warns he will pay for none of this, but she tells him to keep quiet. He recognizes the extent of his mistake (*Son tradito*) while the others, including Ernesto, rejoice in their success.

Act III   Later that evening, Don Pasquale sits facing a stack of bills, as servants comment on their new mistress' extravagance. Realizing he will soon be ruined at this rate, Pasquale sees he must assert his rights. Norina enters, getting ready for an evening at the theater, and he accosts her, but she slaps him when he orders her to stay home. While Norina regrets to herself that she was so harsh, Pasquale bemoans his humiliation (*È finita, Don Pasquale*). He tells her to go ahead and leave—but not to come back. When she retorts she will be back in time to wake him the next morning, he declares he will get a divorce. On her way out, she "accidentally" drops a note, which Pasquale reads: it appears to be from a lover, setting a rendezvous in the garden that night. Sending for Malatesta, he storms off, leaving the servants in a state of commotion (*Che interminabile andirivieni!*). Ernesto comes in with Malatesta but makes a hasty exit as Pasquale reappears, admitting to Malatesta that he should never have tried to spite his nephew. Showing the letter, he plots with his crony to catch the lovers at their rendezvous and then to use the compromising situation to get rid of "Sofronia" (*Cheti, cheti immantinenti*).

§ As the evening wears on, Ernesto enters the garden, singing a serenade about the pleasant surroundings and his desire to meet his beloved (*Com'è gentil*). Norina approaches cautiously and joins him in an avowal of love (*Tornami a dir che m'ami*). When they hear Pasquale and Malatesta approaching, Ernesto ducks into the house while Pasquale confronts his "wife," who denies she has a lover and refuses to leave. Malatesta now plays his role, announcing to his sister that she ought to leave, because Ernesto's bride, Norina, will be there the next day. Pasquale welcomes the idea of Ernesto's marriage when he sees how "Sofronia" reacts against sharing the house with another woman. While she continues to object, Malatesta calls Ernesto and encourages Pasquale to give his blessing to the marriage at once. Pasquale is only too glad to settle an income on his nephew, whom he tells to send for Norina. He is flabbergasted, of course, to learn that "Sofronia" is in fact Norina, but matters are quickly explained: the real Sofronia is still at her convent school. Forgiveness is exchanged all around as Pasquale gives the couple his blessing and agrees to act his age.

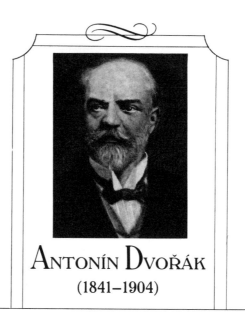

ANTONÍN DVOŘÁK
(1841–1904)

*A*ntonín Dvořák, the best-known composer of what is today Czechoslovakia, left home at sixteen to devote himself to music. Barely supporting himself as a violinist, he went on to play viola in the National Theater orchestra in Prague and became familiar with the staples of the repertory. Gradually his reputation as a composer grew, and he was invited several times to England to conduct, at length receiving an honorary doctorate in 1891 from Cambridge University. Befriended by Brahms, he built a following in the German-speaking countries and found a German publisher. In the years 1892–95 he served as director of the newly founded National Conservatory of Music in New York, visiting the Czech community at Spillville, Iowa, during the summer. From his stay in America, and the homesickness it inspired, came two of his most frequently heard compositions, the *New World* Symphony and the *American* Quartet.

Despite the success of his symphonic and chamber works, Dvořák remained devoted to large-scale choral composition and opera. In all he wrote nine operas, using Czech or Slavic subjects. In recent times, thanks to recordings, familiarity with some of them has spread outside Central Europe.

A few years after his American sojourn, and following immediately upon his successful comic opera *The Devil and Kate,* Dvořák began work on his next-to-last opera, *Rusalka.* The subject, as in a number of his other scores, was drawn from folklore and fairy tale. As musical spokesman for emergent Czech nationalism, Dvořák inherited the mantle of Bedřich Smetana; like Smetana, he felt that opera was a good way to reach the people. He did not place great importance on the exportability of his operas, with the result that they are

126

scarcely known outside his homeland—except for *Rusalka,* popular in Germany and periodically produced elsewhere. The world premiere took place in Prague in 1901, but in spite of Dvořák's popularity in America—where he left numerous pupils—*Rusalka* was not produced in the United States until 1935, and then not by a regular opera company but at Sokol Hall in Chicago.

Dvořák and his librettist, Jaroslav Kvapil, termed the work a "lyric fairy tale," hinting at its deliberate lack of epic or dramatic dimensions. The music reflects the influence of Wagner, whom Dvořák admired, though not without reservations. Leitmotifs and through-composed passages are evident in *Rusalka,* but its chief strength lies in its being what Otakar Šourek has called "one great song." Given a production that accepts and projects its mood, *Rusalka* can be a spellbinding experience.

RUSALKA

THREE ACTS
MUSIC: Antonín Dvořák
TEXT (Czech): Jaroslav Kvapil
WORLD PREMIERE: Prague, National Theater, March 31, 1901
U.S. PREMIERE: Chicago, Sokol Hall, March 10, 1935

CHARACTERS

Rusalka, *water nymph* . . . . Soprano
Foreign Princess . . . . Soprano
Ježibaba, *forest witch* . . . . Mezzo-Soprano
Turnspit . . . . Mezzo-Soprano
Prince . . . . Tenor
Gamekeeper . . . . Baritone
Water Gnome, *Rusalka's father* . . . . Bass
Wood nymphs, water nymphs, courtiers, wedding guests

ACT I By moonlight in a legendary time and place, the water nymph Rusalka sits in the lake near its shore, lost in thought as three wood sprites dance and sing nearby. When the Water Gnome climbs out of the lake, they flirt with him but run when he responds. His daughter, Rusalka, tells of her longing to be free from the world of water spirits: though human beings are merely mortal, she would like to become one of them, because she has fallen in love with a young man who comes to bathe in the lake. Warning her of the fatal consequences of such an infatuation, the Water Gnome returns to his element, leaving her in the domain of Ježibaba, the forest witch. Looking at the silver moon, Rusalka asks it to summon her lover (*Měsíčku na nebi hlubokém*): as if in reply, the moon disappears behind the clouds. Ježibaba emerges from her hut and, with a spell, enables Rusalka to leave the water. In answer to the girl's pleas (*Staletá moudrost tvá všechno ví*), Ježibaba agrees to make her human. If she loses her mortal love, she must return to the water, and her lover too will be doomed. An added condition is that Rusalka will be mute until her love is consummated. Retreating to the hut, Ježibaba brews a potion (*Čury mury fuk!*) as a group of hunters approaches. One of them, the Prince, tells how he sighted a lovely apparition on this spot, only to have her recede into the water (*Zde mihla se a zase zmizela!*). Deprived of speech but given human form, Rusalka comes toward him as he sits by the lake. Fascinated, he embraces her. Hearing her sister sprites and not wanting to rejoin them, Rusalka clings to the Prince, who calls her his dream come true.

ACT II Late in the afternoon a week later, in the park near the Prince's castle, a Gamekeeper and his nephew, the Turnspit, comment on the excitement of the forthcoming wedding. They fear that the Prince's strange sweetheart may be a water sprite, sent to lure him to his doom. They leave as the Prince approaches with Rusalka. He hopes her apparent coolness will melt when they are married (*Již týden dlíš mi po boku*). A foreign Princess, who hopes to marry the Prince herself, finds them and persuades him to lead her back to the ballroom, leaving Rusalka to ready herself for the ball. Dejected and abandoned, the girl wanders off as her father climbs out of a nearby pond to watch the festivities through a window, fearing the worst for her (*Ubohá Rusalko bledá*). Seeing the Prince's head turned by the Princess, Rusalka runs despairing from the hall and meets her father. Able to speak to one of her own kind, she says she already regrets having left her element: her lover has betrayed her, and now she is an outcast from both the mortal and the spirit worlds. They hide as the Prince and Princess come outdoors. Warmed by the Princess' mortal passion, he succumbs to her (duet: *Ó, teprve ted poznávám*). Running up to him, Rusalka throws herself into his arms, but he—now frightened of her—pushes her away. The Water Gnome, crying that the Prince will never escape Rusalka's love, draws her into the water. The Princess coldly tells him to follow his other beloved into damnation, then leaves him.

ACT III At sunset, Rusalka sits by the edge of the lake, wishing she could die of her sorrow. When Ježibaba finds her, Rusalka tells how she was betrayed. To rejoin the spirit world, the witch says, Rusalka herself must kill her betrayer. Offered a knife, Rusalka in horror admits she still loves the Prince. Ježibaba says she will have to suffer through the ages, then. As the witch leaves her, Rusalka slips back into the water, where her sister spirits shun her (*Odešla jsi do světa)* because of her contamination by mortals. As night nears, the Game-keeper and his nephew approach the witch's hut. Afraid to deliver the message with which he has been sent, the Turnspit hides behind his uncle as Ježibaba opens her door. Finally, he blurts out his story: the Princess has abandoned the Prince, who is now pining for the water nymph. Rusalka's father, rising from the lake, curses humankind for its treachery and frightens the two men away. As the moon rises, wood sprites come to dance. Spying the Water Gnome, they try to sport with him, but he is too sad and returns to the water. When the sprites have gone, the Prince appears in a daze, calling for his elusive Rusalka *(Bílá moje lani!)*, who appears above the water, calling back to him. He asks to join her, whether in death or in life; she replies she is neither dead nor alive but doomed to wander like a ghost, adding that it is now her destiny to bring him to his death. Saying he cannot live without her, he throws himself into her embrace and dies. She kisses him and hopes the strange passion of human love will win him God's mercy. Then she disappears into the lake.

FRIEDRICH VON FLOTOW
1812–83

*B*orn into a landed Prussian family, Friedrich von Flotow early showed a predilection for music. Though his parents wanted him to enter a "respectable" occupation, they were amateur musicians themselves and agreed to continue his study, sending him as a teenager to Paris. One of his teachers at the Paris Conservatory was Antonín Reicha, who also numbered Liszt and Berlioz among his pupils. Flotow was greatly impressed at the premiere of Rossini's *Guillaume Tell* in 1829 and aspired to write operas, of which his first, *Pierre et Cathérine,* was performed in Schwerin after the July Revolution of 1830 obliged the youth to return from France.

Since Paris was the opera capital of the time, Flotow went there again, but he never conquered its stage. He did, however, get a commission for a ballet, *Lady Henriette, ou La Servante de Greenwich,* which would eventually spawn his greatest success, *Martha,* an opera version of the same scenario. Introduced in the revolutionary year 1848, *Martha* quickly made the rounds of European opera houses and was given five hundred times in Vienna alone during the composer's lifetime. Except for *Alessandro Stradella,* a romantic melodrama based on the life of an Italian composer, none of Flotow's later works came anywhere near the success of *Martha,* which enabled him to live out his life in fame and comfort.

In no sense an innovator, Flotow owed his popularity to a gift for blending folklike directness of melody with the smoothness and vocal ingratiation of French opéra comique. Though *Martha* is a German singspiel (a musical play with spoken dialogue), its two most famous solos are associated with texts in other languages—the tenor air *Ach, so fromm,* universally known in Italian translation as *M'appari,* and the perennial *Last Rose of Summer,* adapted from an English ballad. (Actually the melody is Irish, *The Groves of Blarney,* and was fitted with its more familiar verses by Thomas Moore.)

MARTHA

FOUR ACTS

MUSIC: Friedrich von Flotow

TEXT (German): Wilhelm Friedrich Riese, after the ballet-panto-
mime *Lady Henriette, ou La Servante de Greenwich,* by J. H. Vernoy de Saint-Georges

WORLD PREMIERE: Vienna, Kärntnertor Theater, November 25,
1847

U.S. PREMIERE: New York, Niblo's Garden, November 1, 1852
(in English)

METROPOLITAN OPERA PREMIERE: March 14, 1884 (in Italian)

CHARACTERS

Lady Harriet Durham, *maid of honor to Queen Anne* . . . . Soprano
Nancy, *her friend* . . . . Contralto
Lionel, *young farmer, afterward earl of Derby* . . . . Tenor
Plunkett, *his foster brother* . . . . Bass
Sir Tristan, *Lady Harriet's cousin* . . . . Bass
Sheriff . . . . Bass
Servants, courtiers, pages, ladies, hunters, farmers

ACT I   The home of Lady Harriet Durham, maid of honor to Queen Anne of England (1702–14). A group of Lady Harriet's friends are concerned about their hostess' boredom. One of them, Nancy, thinks Harriet needs to have a romance, but this does not seem to be borne out by the events that follow: Harriet's cousin, Sir Tristan, who is madly in love with her, arrives and inundates her with invitations, which she refuses (trio: *Ha, der Narrheit ohne-gleichen!*). Harriet overhears the voices of maidservants on their way to the fair at Richmond. Despite Tristan's disapproval, she decides to dress up as one of them and go along. Calling herself "Martha," she persuades Nancy ("Julia") and Tristan ("Bob") to join her in the lark.

§ At the fair, farmers who want to hire servant girls greet the arrival of the aspiring maidservants. Plunkett and his foster brother Lionel, who are prospective employers, observe that until a man marries, he has to depend on hired help to run the house. Lionel recalls how his father, a nameless exile, left him with Plunkett's mother, then died; a ring that Lionel should show to the queen in case of trouble was his only souvenir (duet: *Ja! Seit früher Kindheit Tagen*). The Sheriff arrives and announces the rules: when a farmer hires a servant, she must remain in his employ for a year. He questions some of the girls on their domestic skills and finds employers willing to pay their wages. When the three masqueraders arrive, Harriet attracts the attention of Plunkett and Lionel, who decide to hire both girls (quartet: *Nun, fürwahr, das lass' ich gelten*). When Tristan returns surrounded by admiring servant girls, he tries to buy Harriet and Nancy out of the bargain, but the Sheriff backs up the employers.

ACT II   At Plunkett's farm, the girls feel that the joke is over, but their new bosses are serious and try to teach them their duties. Plunkett shows Nancy how to use the spinning wheel, which she knocks over. When she runs out, Plunkett pursues her. Lionel, in the meantime, tells Harriet how attracted he is to her; not knowing how to respond, she obliges with a song *(Letzte Rose, wie magst du)*. He blurts out a marriage proposal, but she knows she cannot encourage him, because of the difference in their station. His feelings are hurt *(Sie lacht zu meinen Leiden)*, while she regrets that she is not free to respond. Plunkett retrieves Nancy, and since it is getting late, the young men retire, bidding their new servants good night (quartet: *Schlafe wohl! Und mag dich reuen*). As soon as they have left, the girls admit to each other that they find the young men attractive; nevertheless, when they hear Tristan fumbling at the window, they leave with him. The sound of carriage wheels awakens Plunkett and Lionel, who summon neighbors and offer a reward for the return of their servants.

ACT III   At an inn in the woods, some time later. Plunkett sings the praises of English beer *(Lasst mich euch fragen)* to friends, who disperse as a hunting party is heard approaching. Among the party are Harriet and Nancy; when Plunkett comes back to the inn, he recognizes Nancy and threatens to call the Sheriff. When the girls ride off, Lionel muses alone on "Martha," whom he cannot drive from his thoughts *(Ach, so fromm)*. Unseen by him, Harriet wanders in with Tristan, whom she asks to leave her. She sings of her own feeling of lost love *(Hier in den stillen Schattengründen)*, but when Lionel overhears and recognizes her, she rejects him again and calls Tristan, who summons others from their party. The returning Plunkett joins Lionel in confronting the runaway servants, who deny they ever saw them before. Lionel wonders whether it was all just a dream (ensemble: *Mag der Himmel euch vergeben*), but when the queen's retinue is heard approaching, Plunkett remembers Lionel's father's ring and runs off with Nancy, hoping to show it to the queen. The hunters celebrate the joys of pursuing their quarry (chorus: *Keck und munter*).

ACT IV   Back at the farmhouse, Harriet admits to herself she really loves Lionel *(Den Teuren zu versöhnen)*. Nancy brings Plunkett, who describes the dejected Lionel sitting in his room, not saying or hearing anything. Sending them away, Harriet lures Lionel with another song *(Der Lenz ist gekommen)*. He comes in distrustfully, but she tells him that his father's ring revealed him to be the Earl of Derby. To her dismay, he refuses her offer of marriage. Though he loves her, he cannot forget her past rejection (duet: *O wehe mir! Sie war mein Stern*) and withdraws. She too departs, after calling back Nancy and Plunkett to ask their help. Pondering how to get Lionel and Harriet back together, Plunkett and Nancy banteringly decide they themselves might marry (duet: *Oh! Ich wüsste wohl schon Eine*), but Nancy is annoyed that he wants to help his friend first. They leave to work out their plan.

§ Outside the farmhouse, Nancy and Tristan direct the locals in making the place look as much as possible like the fairgrounds at Richmond. When the downcast Lionel approaches, Nancy leads a group of girls pretending to offer their services as maids, and the men pretend to consider hiring them. As Plunkett leads Lionel in, the latter sees Harriet once more as "Martha," and all is well. Everyone welcomes the happy ending for both couples.

CARLISLE FLOYD
b. 1926

*B*orn in South Carolina, Carlisle Floyd studied composition with Ernst Bacon and piano with Sidney Foster and Rudolf Firkušny. In 1947 he began a long teaching career at Florida State University in Tallahassee. Though he has composed in various other forms, his primary output has been a series of operas. Faithful to his instincts for the stage, he has been ruthlessly self-critical, not hesitating to rewrite an entire scene or act if need be. Having in college studied creative writing and music simultaneously, he found it natural and preferable to write his own librettos. In this respect, as in his willingness to communicate with a general audience in readily accessible musical terms, and to stage his own works, he has somewhat followed the example of Menotti.

An unqualified success at its premiere in 1955, *Susannah* has been in the repertory ever since—an astonishing track record for an American opera by a previously unknown composer. It is a recasting in the American South of the Biblical tale of Susannah and the Elders and owes something to Somerset Maugham's short story *Miss Thompson,* better known in its 1922 stage (later film) adaptation as *Rain.* The story is an elemental one, contrasting virtue among the fallen with falling among the virtuous; its theme is the devastation wrought by hypocrisy, among its victims as well as its practitioners. Of Floyd's other operas, *Of Mice and Men* (1970) has shown the most endurance, but of interest as well are *Wuthering Heights* (1958), *The Passion of Jonathan Wade* (1962), *Markheim* (1966), *Bilby's Doll* (1976), and *Willie Stark* (1981), of which the last in particular points toward an effective use of Broadway-musical-theater techniques within the opera framework.

Susannah

TWO ACTS
MUSIC: Carlisle Floyd
TEXT (English): the composer
WORLD PREMIERE: Tallahassee, Florida State University,
    February 24, 1955 (student performance); New York City
    Opera, September 27, 1956

CHARACTERS

Susannah Polk . . . . Soprano
Sam, *her brother* . . . . Baritone
Reverend Olin Blitch . . . . Bass
Little Bat McLean . . . . Tenor
Townspeople, elders and their wives

ACT I   New Hope Valley, Tennessee, time "the present," on a Monday night
in mid-July. A square dance is under way in the churchyard. Susannah Polk,
a beautiful young local girl, is enthusiastic about the dancing, but the elders'
wives are more concerned about the new minister they are getting: will he be
able to save enough sinners? One woman, Mrs. McLean, singles out Susannah
as an example of what she means *(She's a shameless girl, she is)*, adding that this
is only to be expected from an orphan who was raised by her drunken brother.
They are surprised when the minister, Olin Blitch, who is not expected until
tomorrow, appears in their midst (ensemble: *I am the Reverend Olin Blitch*),
declaring he brings the Lord's word to their valley. Noticing Susannah, Blitch
asks who she is, to which Mrs. McLean replies that both Susannah and her
brother, Sam, are evil. Saying he will pray for both of them that night, Blitch
asks Susannah to dance.

§ Later that evening, in front of the Polks' run-down farmhouse, Susannah
reminisces about the dance with Little Bat McLean, a somewhat retarded youth
whose parents, Elder and Mrs. McLean, don't like him to hang around the
Polks; infatuated with Susannah, he does anyway. Admiring the clear sky
(Ain't it a pretty night?), Susannah dreams of the day when she will see what
is beyond the mountains. Her brother, a misunderstood dreamer, arrives to
ask affectionately whether she had a good time. Before retiring, she asks him

to sing the song their father used to sing for them *(Oh, jaybird sittin' on a hick'ry limb)*.

§ Looking in the woods the next morning for a baptismal creek, the four elders of the church—Hayes, Ott, Gleaton, and McLean—catch sight of Susannah bathing nude. Outraged, they propose to tell Blitch *(This woman is of the devil)*.

§ That evening, at a church supper in the same location as the square dance, the four elders' wives—of whom Mrs. McLean is the most venomous, Mrs. Gleaton the most tolerant, and the other two somewhere in between—discuss Susannah's scandalous behavior and wait for the minister to arrive. Suspecting something is wrong but not realizing what, Susannah arrives and offers her contribution to the supper—freshly picked and cooked peas. When she is told that she is not welcome, the girl retreats in confusion.

§ At her house, looking for Sam, Susannah instead sees Little Bat, who explains why she has been ostracized *(My pa an' the other elders, they seen you bathin' this mornin')*. Susannah, who has always bathed there, cannot understand what she did wrong, but the boy goes on to say that she is being called a loose woman, that his mother made him say he too had been seduced by her *(I said you'd let me love you up)*. Incensed by his lie, she sends him away, telling him never to come back. When Sam returns home, he has heard the gossip and laments the streak in human nature that lets such a thing happen *(It's about the way people is made)*, adding there is nothing they can do but weather the storm.

ACT II   The following Friday morning, Sam informs his sister what the community wants: a public confession. She replies she has nothing to confess, though she is beginning to wonder whether maybe the devil is tempting her somehow, without her knowledge. The creek is now being used for baptisms *(I hear 'em singin' ev'ry evenin')*, and Blitch has asked her to come to a prayer meeting that evening; Sam thinks she should go to show that she is not afraid, but she feels unable to face public contempt. Sam says he has to leave for a while to empty his traps on the other side of the mountain but will be back the next day.

§ That evening, inside the church, Blitch takes up the collection while the congregation sings a hymn *(Free from sin, yes Lord!)*. Starting his sermon, Blitch stresses the need for personal salvation and calls on those who have not yet been baptized to come forward. Several candidates appear. Then Blitch singles out Susannah, as the others stare at her accusingly. Against her will, as if hypnotized, she comes down the aisle to receive the benediction, then runs out of the church crying, "No!"

§ An hour later, back at her house, Susannah recalls a folklike song that reflects her loneliness and sorrow *(The trees on the mountain are cold and bare)*.

The preacher surprises her, coming to pay a call: having failed to convert her at the meeting, he is determined to do so now. She defends herself vigorously, saying that the community has put her through hell all week. Feeling a conflict between his human understanding and his rigid religious convictions, Blitch finds himself drawn to her *(I'm a lonely man, Susannah)* and puts his arm around her. Her energy to resist is spent, and she allows him to lead her inside the house.

§ Saturday morning, Blitch kneels alone in the church, praying for forgiveness: his sin and its punishment are frighteningly real to him *(Hear me, o Lord)*. When the elders, their wives, and Susannah file in, he declares that the girl was innocent and should be forgiven. The elders, unimpressed, leave saying they will expect Blitch at the baptism. Alone with him in the church, Susannah starts to laugh bitterly. When Blitch begs her forgiveness, she says she has forgotten what the word means.

§ On the porch of the Polk house at sundown, Sam returns from his trip to learn what has happened to Susannah during his absence. When he asks why she yielded to the preacher, she says she had no more strength to resist—and besides, everybody believed the worst of her anyway. Furiously, Sam takes a gun and heads toward the baptism site at the creek. Not believing he would shoot Blitch, Susannah hears a shot ring out *(O Lord, I never meant him to do it!)*. Little Bat runs in with news of the assassination, followed by the elders and others, threatening to lynch Sam and demanding that Susannah leave the valley. Laughing at their attempts to make her feel guilty, she takes a gun and orders them off the property. Undefeated, they retreat *(There'll come a reckonin' time)*. Susannah gives Little Bat false encouragement *(Come an' love me up some)*, then slaps him with all her strength as he approaches. She laughs as he runs away. Then, aware of the loneliness of the exile she has created, she strengthens herself to face it.

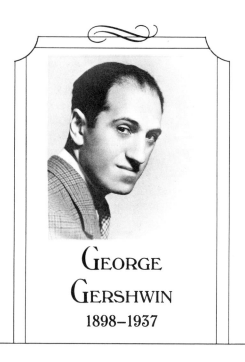

GEORGE
GERSHWIN
1898–1937

George Gershwin, the son of immigrant Russian Jewish parents, grew up on New York's Lower East Side. His musical talent was evident by the time he was in his teens, and he worked as a song plugger (demonstrating new songs on the piano) at music stores. Although his interest focused on Tin Pan Alley, he was curious about the entire range of music and pursued studies with several distinguished teachers, including Ernest Hutcheson in piano and Rubin Goldmark in composition. Later he studied with the noted composers Henry Cowell and Wallingford Riegger; in his late years he tried to systematize his composition scientifically under the tutelage of Joseph Schillinger, whose method helped him marshal the large forms required for his major work, *Porgy and Bess*.

Starting with the success of his song *Swanee,* when he was nineteen, Gershwin enjoyed a ready rapport with a broad public, which followed with interest if with some perplexity his ventures into more ambitious forms, notably the *Rhapsody in Blue* and the Concerto in F, wherein he used jazz rhythms and melodies as material for classically conceived concert music. While continuing to write concert works (*An American in Paris, Cuban Overture,* Three Preludes for piano), Gershwin earned great fame as one of America's most gifted songwriters. His experience with Broadway musicals fueled his greatest ambition—to write a real American grand opera, using the same folk and jazz elements that he had mastered with such inventive originality in his songs.

The result was *Porgy and Bess,* acclaimed for its individual tunes, though not at first as a theatrical entity. There were inevitable cavils that the opera elements, such as sung recitatives and big ensembles, were too pretentious for the Broadway-musical format, while on the other hand the hit tunes were too popular and simple for a "serious" opera. As a result, producers have often decided to present the dialogue in spoken form and omit some of the more complex music. In recent years, *Porgy and Bess* as Gershwin conceived it has seemed less problematic. The Broadway musical has become a more adventurous form, and popular operas, such as Menotti's, are no longer a rarity.

The original story was a novel (1925) by DuBose Heyward, a native of Charleston, who based the character of Porgy on a local figure, a cripple who got around by goat-drawn cart. Heyward and his wife adapted the novel for the stage two years later; in the meantime, Gershwin had expressed interest. During his most successful years as a Broadway composer (1927–33), Gershwin was too busy to start work on *Porgy*. He finally wrote it in 1934, stipulating an all-black cast for the first production the following year (blackface was still in use in the American theater at the time). The libretto, though written in dialect style, is not ethnically exact but aims for a regional flavor. Similarly the music, while it draws on spirituals and jazz (Gershwin spent time in South Carolina absorbing the locale and its sounds), unites show tunes with the orchestral sonorities of the big band and the concert hall.

PORGY AND BESS

THREE ACTS
MUSIC: George Gershwin
TEXT (English): DuBose Heyward and Ira Gershwin
WORLD PREMIERE: Boston, September 30, 1935
METROPOLITAN OPERA PREMIERE: Feburary 6, 1985

CHARACTERS

Porgy, *cripple* . . . . Bass-Baritone
Bess, *Crown's girl* . . . . Soprano
Crown, *tough stevedore* . . . . Baritone
Serena, *Robbins' wife* . . . . Soprano
Clara, *Jake's wife*. . . . . Soprano
Maria, *keeper of the cookshop* . . . . Contralto
Jake, *fisherman* . . . . Baritone

Sporting Life, *dope peddler* . . . . Tenor
Mingo . . . . Tenor
Robbins, *inhabitant of Catfish Row* . . . . Tenor
Peter, *honeyman* . . . . Tenor
Frazier, *self-styled lawyer* . . . . Baritone
Annie . . . . Mezzo-Soprano
Lily, *Peter's wife, strawberry woman* . . . . Mezzo-Soprano
Jim, *cotton picker* . . . . Baritone
Undertaker . . . . Baritone
Nelson . . . . Tenor
Crab Man . . . . Tenor
Mr. Archdale ⎫
Detective ⎪
Policeman ⎬ . . . . Speaking Parts
Coroner ⎪
Scipio, *small boy* ⎪
Jasbo Brown ⎭

ACT I In the courtyard square of Catfish Row, a black neighborhood on the Charleston waterfront, during the 1920s, Jasbo Brown plays the blues on the piano while couples dance slowly. Nearby, a young mother named Clara sings a lullaby to her baby *(Summertime)*. Several men are involved in a game of craps; Serena, another young woman, tries without success to persuade her husband, Robbins, not to join them. Jake, Clara's husband, takes the baby from her, continuing her lullaby with a warning about the chanciness of love *(A woman is a sometime thing)*. Porgy, a cripple, joins the game. The others tease him about liking Bess, Crown's easy-living girlfriend, but Porgy agrees with Jake's skeptical sentiments about women. Crown, a free-spending rough-neck, joins the game, and when he gets into a fight with Robbins over the latter's winning streak, Crown pulls out his cotton hook and kills Robbins. Knowing the police will soon be there, the crowd disperses, allowing Crown to escape. Bess says she will fend for herself, refusing an offer from Sporting Life, a pimp and drug dealer, to take her to New York, though she accepts some cocaine. As the police draw near, no one will open a door to Bess except Porgy.

§ In Serena's home, mourners pay their last respects to Robbins *(Gone, gone, gone)*, dropping money in a plate on the dead man's chest. Bess helps Porgy into the room; when Serena refuses Bess' contribution to the funeral expenses, Bess explains that it isn't Crown's money—Porgy is taking care of her now. Porgy pleads eloquently with everyone to help the widow. A white Detective, investigating Robbins' murder, learns that it was Crown who killed him. To put pressure on the community to help locate the killer, the Detective and a Policeman take away one of the citizens, old Peter, pretending they suspect him. Serena laments her husband's death *(My man's gone now)* and, when the Undertaker arrives, learns that the collection amounts to less than the cost of a burial, but the Undertaker says he will trust her for the rest. Bess leads a hymn about the journey to the Promised Land *(Oh, the train is at the station)*.

ACT II   Jake and some other fishermen are repairing nets *(Oh, I'm goin' out to de Blackfish banks)* when one of the local women, Annie, reminds them of the parade and church picnic scheduled for that day. Porgy cheerfully sings at his window *(I got plenty o' nuttin')*, impressing the neighbors with his improved disposition since Bess moved in. A shopkeeper, Maria, threatens Sporting Life for peddling "happy dust" (cocaine) near her place *(I hates yo' struttin' style)*, but attention soon turns to the lawyer Frazier, who tries to sell Porgy a "divorce" for Bess, so that she can live with him legally. A white man, Archdale, comes looking for Porgy, saying he knows old Peter and will post bail for him. Just then a low-flying buzzard is sighted. Afraid of bad luck, Porgy and his neighbors urge it on its way *(Buzzard, keep on flyin')*. The crowd disperses, leaving Bess with Sporting Life, who tries to persuade her to come to New York. Overhearing, Porgy threatens the pusher and drives him away, then joins Bess in expressing happiness (duet: *Bess, you is my woman now*). Dressed in their finery, the neighbors reappear, ready for the festivities. Bess means to stay behind, because Porgy cannot make the boat trip, but he tells her to go and have a good time.

§ On Kittiwah Island, with the picnic at its peak, Sporting Life tells everyone that there is more to the world than they learned in Sunday school *(It ain't necessarily so)*, but Serena scolds her neighbors for unbecoming behavior. As they board the steamboat for the trip home, Crown appears in the bushes and calls softly to Bess: he has been hiding on the island and wants her to stay. She tries to leave *(Oh, what you want wid Bess?)*, but he overpowers her.

§ More than a week later, at Catfish Row, Jake and the other fishermen are getting ready to set out in their boats, though a storm appears to be approaching. In Porgy's room, Bess mumbles deliriously: she was brought back a week ago, after being "lost" on Kittiwah Island for two days. Serena prays for her recovery *(Oh, Doctor Jesus)* as a strawberry woman hawks her wares. Peter, out on bail, sells honey, and a Crab Man offers deviled crabs. Bess revives and recognizes Porgy. She wants to stay with him but feels unworthy, confessing Crown's powerful hold over her. Porgy says she is free, but she asks his help *(I loves you, Porgy)*. Clara's fears of a hurricane are soon justified: the wind is rising, and an alarm sounds.

§ In Serena's room, as the storm rages, the citizens are huddled in dread, joining their voices in a spiritual *(Oh, Doctor Jesus)*. When knocking is heard at the door, they think it must be Death himself, but Crown forces his way in. He grabs Bess and knocks down Porgy, who tries to protect her. Then, laughing at the superstitious townspeople, he brags about his attraction for women *(A redheaded woman).* When Jake's overturned boat is sighted on the river, Clara rushes out into the storm, and Crown goes to bring her back.

ACT III   In the aftermath of the storm, women mourn their husbands lost in fishing boats, while Sporting Life bides his time, counting on a showdown between Bess' two lovers. As the square stands vacant, Crown steals in and crawls toward Porgy's door. Porgy, reaching through the shutter, stabs and strangles Crown to death.

§ The next day, the Detective arrives with the Coroner; they question Serena about the murder and order Porgy to come to the morgue and identify the body. Porgy believes, and Sporting Life confirms, that if Crown's murderer looks on the dead man's face, his wound will start to bleed. As Porgy is led away, Sporting Life renews his pitch to Bess *(There's a boat dat's leavin' soon for New York).* She is still indignant, but he is sure her hankering for drugs and high living will get the better of her.

§ A week later, neighbors greet one another *(How are you dis mornin'?),* then welcome Porgy as the patrol wagon brings him home. He happily announces that he kept his eyes closed and never looked at Crown's body. Jailed for contempt of court, he won money at craps and bought presents for several neighbors. Gradually he realizes that Bess is not coming to greet him: Maria breaks the news that Bess left. Learning she went to New York, which Maria says is "way up north pas' de custom house," Porgy calls for his goat and announces he will follow Bess—"Gawd help me to fin' her." Helped onto his cart, Porgy starts off *(Oh Lawd, I'm on my way).*

ALBERTO GINASTERA
(1916–83)

*B*orn in Buenos Aires, Alberto Ginastera was Argentina's most famous composer, his reputation resting equally on chamber works, symphonic scores, and operas. Though he wrote a ballet, *Panambí,* at the early age of twenty, he was nearly fifty before approaching the opera stage, waiting, he said, for the right libretto. The result was *Don Rodrigo,* which created a stir at the Teatro Colón in his native city in 1964; it came shortly afterward to the New York City Opera, where it featured the young Placido Domingo. *Don Rodrigo* employs the twelve-tone system in a lyrical, eminently vocal manner, using the chorus for sound effects as well as for singing a text.

In the same year that saw the premiere of *Don Rodrigo,* Ginastera introduced his cantata *Bomarzo* at the Library of Congress, on commission from the Coolidge Foundation. The opera of the same title is an expansion of this score, based on a text by Manuel Mujica Láinez. Ginastera and Mujica Láinez were awed and puzzled by the garden of huge stone-carved grotesques in the castle of Bomarzo in Italy; their opera is a fantasy about the origin of these. Banned by the mayor of Buenos Aires for its sex and violence, *Bomarzo* was given its world premiere by the Opera Society of Washington (which commissioned it) in 1967. Performances at the New York City Opera followed, and the work finally reached Buenos Aires in 1972.

A third opera, *Beatrix Cenci,* again on an Italian subject, inaugurated the Kennedy Center in Washington in 1972. Like its predecessors—and like many operas of the nineteenth century—it relies unabashedly on lust and mayhem. Yet the construction of Ginastera's operas shows exquisite craft—"The idea of strict construction combined with the essence of subjective feeling," notes Gilbert Chase in the *New Grove Dictionary,* adding that "The idioms are contemporary, but the tradition of grand opera is upheld. Penderecki may hover in the pit, but the spirit of Verdi watches in the wings."

Bomarzo

TWO ACTS
MUSIC: Alberto Ginastera
TEXT (Spanish): Manuel Mujica Láinez
WORLD PREMIERE: Opera Society of Washington, May 19, 1967
EUROPEAN PREMIERE (in German): Kiel, 1970

CHARACTERS

Pier Francesco Orsini, *Duke of Bomarzo* . . . . Tenor
Julia Farnese, *Florentine noblewoman* . . . . Soprano
Pantasilea, *Florentine courtesan* . . . . Mezzo-Soprano
Diana Orsini, *Pier Francesco's grandmother* . . . . Contralto
Nicolas Orsini, *nephew of Pier Francesco* . . . . Tenor
Silvio de Narni, *astrologer* . . . . Baritone
Girolamo⎫ *brothers of Pier Francesco* . . . . ⎧Baritone
Maerbale⎭ . . . . ⎩Baritone
Gian Corrado Orsini, *father of Pier Francesco* . . . . Bass
Messenger . . . . Baritone
Shepherd Boy . . . . Treble
Abul, *Gian Francesco's servant* . . . . Mime
Servants; *Pier Francesco, Girolamo, and Maerbale as children*

ACT I   In the park of the castle of Bomarzo, in the sixteenth century, stands a gaping sculpture of a monster's head, *The Mouth of Hell.* A Shepherd Boy's voice is heard singing that he would not change places with the Duke of Bomarzo, whose humped back is laden with the cares and sins of the world. The duke himself, Pier Francesco, arrives with his nephew, Nicolas, and his astrologer, Silvio de Narni. They come to fulfill Silvio's prophecy: the duke's immortality will be assured by his drinking a magic potion. Taking the chalice from the two, who withdraw, Pier Francesco steps inside *The Mouth of Hell,* where in a small chamber he prepares to drink the potion, reviewing his failures and desolation *(Estoy sólo contigo, mi destino).* As he drinks, a vision of his grandmother, Diana Orsini, appears, saying he has been betrayed and will die. Flashbacks follow as the duke recalls his life.

§ In childhood, Pier Francesco and his two older brothers, Girolamo and Maerbale, play in a castle storeroom with old clothes and ornaments. When Pier Francesco refuses to play the humiliating role of court jester, Girolamo forces him to dress as a duchess, then pierces his ear with a dagger to attach an earring. When their widowed father, Gian Corrado Orsini, surprises the boys, instead of taking pity on the tormented youngest, he abuses him for his effeminate dress, then throws him into a secret room that is said to be haunted. There Pier Francesco sees a skeleton rise up and dance, hurling itself on the terrified child.

§ In his study, Pier Francesco as a young man learns from Silvio de Narni of his horoscope, which indicates immortality *(La immortalidad, el viejo y terrible sueño del hombre).* Knowing his father's hatred, Pier Francesco doubts the prediction, but the astrologer draws a triangle and calls on spirits for protection. The cry of peacocks is heard from the gardens, though these birds—harbingers of ill—have been banished from Bomarzo. Pier Francesco's grandmother appears, and a Messenger announces the return of his father, wounded, from the siege of Florence.

§ In her sumptuous boudoir in Florence, the courtesan Pantasilea hails her city and her own beauty *(Ninguna ciudad del mundo)* as she awaits the prince, Pier Francesco Orsini, who is being sent to her. When the young man arrives, miserably nervous, she discovers he is not handsome but hunchbacked. Concealing her disappointment, she starts to seduce him, but he is distracted by mirror reflections all over the room, confronting him with his ugliness in mocking postures. Saying his father sent him as a joke, he offers a necklace and tries to retreat, but she repeats her seductive advances, offering him aphrodisiacs. Hearing again the cry of peacocks, Pier Francesco calls his servant Abul and hastens away. The laughing Pantasilea resumes her song to herself.

§ Beside the river Tiber in the Bomarzo countryside, Diana tells her favorite grandson that his father has never recovered from his wounds. When Pier Francesco replies that only with her does he feel at peace, she says she and the ancestral she-bear of the Orsinis will always guard him *(No temas, no).* Girolamo appears, preparing to dive into the river, and arrogantly mocks him. But the older brother's strutting causes him to lose his footing and fall, smashing his head on the rocks below. Impassively, Diana Orsini addresses Pier Francesco as "Duke of Bomarzo forever."

§ In the great hall of the castle, at ceremonies proclaiming him duke, Pier Francesco is introduced by his grandmother to Julia Farnese, daughter of another noble family, whom she wants him to marry. He is taken with her but notes with annoyance that his brother Maerbale is too. Then he is unnerved by the appearance of a figure resembling his father. Diana says there are no ghosts in Bomarzo, only his own glory as duke.

§ On the terrace outside, guests dance and gradually leave. Surveying the grounds, Pier Francesco muses on his affinity for their mysterious world, feeling akin to the landscape and rocks, which look hunchbacked to him (*Yo soy Bomarzo*). He imagines Julia Farnese, Pantasilea, and his servant Abul, each striving to take possession of him. When dancing guests reappear, he fancies he sees his own image in each of the men and feels pursued by them.

§ Back in his study, Pier Francesco looks at his idealized portrait, painted in Venice by Lorenzo Lotto, and admires the "hidden prince" it seems to reveal. Knowing that Abul is the only one who truly loves him, he confides to the servant that he wishes Julia Farnese could love him as well. When Abul leaves, Pier Francesco pulls a cover from another picture frame and discovers a mirror (*Este espejo infernal*), reminding him of his reality. Having banished mirrors from Bomarzo, he suspects his brother Maerbale of putting it there. When unseen voices remind him of immortality, he wishes he could be immortal in a pure form, not in a misshapen body.

ACT II   In the Farnese Palace in Rome, Julia sings a madrigal of courtly love as the adoring Maerbale listens, watched in torment by the hidden Pier Francesco. As Maerbale takes up the tune (*En el filtro del Amor*), Pier Francesco edges unseen down the stairs. Servants offer wine, which Maerbale passes to Julia, but Pier Francesco seizes the cup and offers it himself, spilling it and making a bloodlike splotch on her gown. He runs off, moaning that love only adds to his misery.

§ In a bridal chamber in Bomarzo, courtiers hail the newly married Pier Francesco and Julia, but both confess their sadness. After ladies-in-waiting remove the bride's finery, Pier Francesco cries that he sees a grinning devil in the corner, its face concealed among the mosaic family crests. Realizing he is pursued everywhere by his personal demon, he stares vacantly toward it as Julia falls to her knees, despairing, by his side.

§ Unable to consummate his marriage, Pier Francesco paces the chamber. Then he sits on the bed by the sleeping Julia, lamenting that love is unattainable to him (*Para qué mi grandeza*). He imagines that Pantasilea lies there instead of Julia. Then future sculptures of Bomarzo park appear to him, as writhing figures act out his erotic frustration. Remembering the dancing skeleton of his childhood, he thinks everything is a useless dream and asks God where truth and light can be found.

§ In the Bomarzo portrait gallery, busts of Roman emperors flank a statue of the mythical Minotaur, which Pier Francesco addresses as his brother in deformity (*Minotauro, hermano mio*), surrounded as he is by images of unattainable perfection. His presence startles a pair of lovers from the shadows, reminding Pier Francesco that the man-beast Minotaur is the only form his own desires can take; he kisses the statue. The idea of the garden of monsters takes shape in his mind during a villanella (*Si quieres saber de mi*) describing the rocks that take on their own life under the moonlight.

§ Some years later, Pier Francesco, restless with lingering doubts about his wife and Maerbale, brings Silvio de Narni at night to the garden, now peopled with stone monsters. As Pier Francesco and Abul hide, the astrologer greets Maerbale, inciting him toward the outside staircase to Julia's room. As Maerbale ascends, his son Nicolas Orsini sees him. Surprised, Julia puts off Maerbale's advances, but he kisses her ardently. Enraged, Pier Francesco sends Abul after Maerbale, who hears the sound and is sent off by Julia. Though Nicolas tries to save his father, Abul pursues and kills him, as Pier Francesco steps forward and embraces his wife with savage possessiveness.

§ In Silvio's laboratory, Pier Francesco wonders whether the garden of monsters is the immortality of which his horoscope speaks. Silvio addresses the various statues of astrologers of the past who watch over him as he prepares the potion of immortality. They descend from their pedestals and dance around as the work proceeds, watched by the hidden Nicolas. The potion complete, Pier Francesco dreams of remaining forever in his beloved Bomarzo (*Ay, quedar en Bomarzo para siempre*), but Nicolas swears that his father's murderer will not live.

§ At *The Mouth of Hell,* as in the first scene, Pier Francesco hears his grandmother's warning and calls upon monsters, ancestors, and God not to forsake him. As he falls dead, the Shepherd Boy wanders back in, singing again that he would not change places with the Duke of Bomarzo. Seeing the fallen man, wondering whether he is asleep, the youth lightly kisses his brow.

UMBERTO GIORDANO
1867–1948

*T*he story of the youthful years of Umberto Giordano reads like scenes from *La Bohème*. Supported by a meager advance from his publisher, he lived in Milan in a storage room for tombstones while working on his new opera, *Andrea Chénier*. Meanwhile, he courted Olga Spatz, daughter of the proprietor of the Hotel de Milan, where the elderly Verdi was living. Unimpressed by the young man's prospects, Spatz *père* took the manuscript of *Andrea Chénier* and, according to legend, showed it to Verdi for a candid opinion. "You needn't worry about entrusting your daughter to a man who could write this," Verdi allegedly replied. Verdi was right: the new opera enjoyed a triumph at La Scala in March 1896, amid a season of fiascos. It took the work only eight months to reach New York, where Mapleson's New Imperial Opera Company presented it at the Academy of Music. (The Metropolitan Opera premiere had to wait until March 1921, however.)

Giordano, born in Foggia, in southern Italy, had written three operas before, with indifferent success. When *Chénier* brought fame at last, he was qualified to appreciate the revenue that went with it, and for the rest of his life he lived well, neglecting the talent manifest in his early instrumental compositions. Of the several other operas he wrote, *Fedora* alone has endured, though *Madame Sans-Gêne, La Cena della Beffe,* and *Siberia* went the rounds in their time. Partly because it was written with such a keen desire to succeed, but largely because of its dramatically strong and poetic libretto, by Luigi Illica, *Chénier* remains effective both as theater and as a spontaneous outpouring of melody.

148

The opera's hero, André Chénier (1762–94), is still familiar to students of French poetry. He found the ideals of the French Revolution stirring in principle but appalling in practice. After writing articles that denounced the bloodthirsty Jacobins, he was thrown into St. Lazare Prison, where he wrote the verses that have secured his place in French literature. One of these, "La Jeune Captive," was addressed to a fellow prisoner, Aimée de Coigny, Duchesse de Fleury, who escaped the guillotine. Chénier was not so lucky: on July 25, 1794, two days before the end of the Reign of Terror, he and his friend Roucher, also a poet, were beheaded. Both Roucher and Mlle. de Coigny live again in the opera in fictionalized form. Chénier's own sentiments are reflected to some extent in the arias that Illica and Giordano devised for him.

ANDREA CHÉNIER

FOUR ACTS
MUSIC: Umberto Giordano
TEXT (Italian): Luigi Illica
WORLD PREMIERE: Milan, La Scala, March 28, 1896
U.S. PREMIERE: New York, Academy of Music, November 13, 1896
METROPOLITAN OPERA PREMIERE: March 7, 1921

CHARACTERS

Andrea Chénier, *poet* .... Tenor
Maddalena de Coigny............................ Soprano
Countess de Coigny, *her mother*................. Mezzo-Soprano
Bersi, *Maddalena's companion* .... Mezzo-Soprano
Madelon, *old woman* .... Mezzo-Soprano
The Abbé.. Tenor
L'Incredibile, *spy* .... Tenor
Carlo Gérard, *servant, later revolutionary* .... Baritone
Pietro Fléville, *cavalier ("romanziere")*................. Baritone
Mathieu, *sans-culotte*............................ Baritone
Dumas, *president of the tribunal* .... Baritone
Fouquier-Tinville, *attorney general* .... Baritone
Roucher, *friend of Chénier's* .... Bass
Fiorinelli, *musician* .... Mime
Courtiers and ladies, citizens of France, soldiers, servants, peasants, prisoners, revolutionary tribunal

ACT I At the château of the Countess de Coigny in the French provinces, in June 1789, servants are setting up the ballroom for a reception. One of them, Carlo Gérard, sarcastically addresses a sofa, imitating the vapid conversations that will take place on it *(Compiacente a'colloquii)*, then denounces the gilded house as a symbol of a doomed society. His mood turns pensive when the Countess' daughter, Maddalena, appears with her companion, Bersi, admiring the slow approach of dusk; Gérard has always secretly idealized and loved Maddalena. The Countess comes in, making sure her arrangements are taken care of, and Maddalena complains about the uncomfortable clothes currently in fashion. Among the guests who arrive is Pietro Fléville, a court poet, who introduces two young protégés—a musician, Fiorinelli, and a poet, Andrea Chénier. An Abbé, another of the Countess' circle, brings depressing news from Paris, but Fléville urges the aristocratic guests to forget their worries and enjoy a song by a group of "shepherdesses" *(O, pastorelle, addio!)*. The Countess asks Chénier to recite one of his poems; when he curtly begs off, she persuades Fiorinelli to play the harpsichord instead. Taking Chénier's diffidence as a challenge, Maddalena begs him to recite. He replies that the muse has a mind of its own and cannot be bidden. Maddalena mockingly turns from one guest to another, saying the muse will not favor them either. Aroused by her flippancy, Chénier declares that the word "love" deserves respect, and improvises a poem about the love he feels for his country and its people, adding that the clergy and aristocracy show none toward the poor and suffering *(Un dì all'azzurro spazio)*. The guests are shocked, but Maddalena recognizes the poet's sincerity and apologizes, while the servant Gérard, standing off to one side, is moved by Chénier's liberal sentiments. As a gavotte begins, Gérard steps outside, to return shortly with a group of ragged beggars, announcing "His Majesty Poverty." The horrified Countess orders him out. Taking with him his old father, who has also spent a lifetime in servitude, he tears off his livery and announces he is free. The Countess, momentarily stunned by his tirade, mutters that reading has ruined him. She quickly pulls herself together and asks the guests to resume dancing their gavotte, which now takes on a tone of fierce determination.

ACT II Four years later, the Revolution has come and gone, and France is in the grip of the Terror. Nervous gaiety is in the air outside the Café Hottot in Paris, with the Peronnet Bridge visible in the background. L'Incredibile, a spy for Robespierre's government, talks with Maddalena's former companion Bersi, now acting the part of a "merveilleuse" (streetwalker), and correctly suspects her of "nonspontaneous corruption," noting she has made eye contact with Chénier, who waits nearby, and has been seen in the company of a young woman (Maddalena) for whom he has been instructed to look. He steps out of sight as Chénier's friend Roucher, a fellow poet, enters from the Cours-la-Reine. He offers Chénier a passport and urges him to escape: intellectuals are fodder for the guillotine. Chénier declares he will not sully his name by acting like a coward: his calling is to be a poet, and he has nothing to hide (No! Credi al destino?). He adds a further reason for staying: he believes in an ideal of love, and an unknown woman, who has been writing to him, will come to meet him. Suspecting a trap, Roucher warns that the woman is most likely a "merveilleuse." Gérard, now a revolutionary leader, enters to the crowd's acclaim and takes L'Incredibile aside for a report on his findings. Gérard wants the spy to locate his beloved Maddalena, whom he glimpsed one day in a crowd. L'Incredibile is confident she will be there that evening. Seeing Bersi whisper to Roucher, he interrupts and leads her off, asking for a dance. Roucher reminds Chénier to leave Paris before dawn. Bersi, thinking she has shaken the spy— though he still observes her—seeks out Chénier and tells him an endangered woman will soon be there to see him. Soon the woman appears and cautiously addresses Chénier. When she removes her mantle and recites a few lines of his poem, he recognizes her as Maddalena; so does the spy, who hurries to fetch Gérard. Maddalena tells Chénier she has often seen him in Paris. Unlike him, she has had to live in semihiding, because of her aristocratic background. He is her only hope: will he protect her? Transported by love, he welcomes the moment that brought them together again (Ora soave! sublime ora d'amore!), and they vow to share their destiny, even unto death. Gérard bursts in as they embrace, trying to take Maddalena away, but Chénier pulls his sword. Roucher rescues Maddalena and aims a pistol at the spy, who backs off, enabling the two to escape. Gérard tries to duel with Chénier but quickly falls injured. He tells Chénier to save himself and care for Maddalena: his name has already been put on a list of political suspects. When the spy returns with guards, attracting a crowd, Gérard signals the spy to keep quiet and pretends he did not recognize his assailant.

ACT III   A year later, the sans-culotte Mathieu harangues a courtroom half full of people who have come to watch the revolutionary trials, telling them things are going badly—foreign countries are allying against France. Money is needed to outfit the troops, but no one in the indifferent audience will contribute a sou. Gérard comes in and pleads much more eloquently (Lacrime e sangue da la Francia!), drawing coins and jewelry into the collection pot. A blind old woman, Madelon, steps forward and offers the last of her family, her grandson, to die for his country (Son la vecchia Madelon). As a crowd outside sings a revolutionary song, the Carmagnole, and the courtroom emp-ties, L'Incredible comes to tell Gérard that Chénier is in prison: surely Mad-dalena will come out of hiding to find him (Donnina innamorata). He tells Gérard to write an indictment of Chénier for use at the trial. Realizing that Chénier is doomed anyway and that the trial will be a mere formality, the disgusted Gérard puts together a few clichés that make the poet seem an enemy of his country (Nemico della patria?), then stops writing to reflect on what is happening to him: once pure in heart, he has been corrupted by power, disillusioned by what he has seen. The only true, strong emotion that remains is his desire for Maddalena. As if in answer to his thought, she appears, and Gérard tells how he has always loved her. At first she recoils, but then it occurs to her to offer herself in exchange for Chénier's life. She describes how the Countess died to save her when the revolutionaries sacked their castle *(La mamma morta)*, how she lost everything except her love for Chénier. Recognizing the baseness of his own desire and overcome by admiration for her steadfastness, Gérard declares he will do anything to save Chénier. The crowd reconvenes, some accused prisoners are led in, and the prosecutor, Fouquier-Tinville, sits with Dumas, president of the tribunal. Chénier takes the stand to declare he was never a traitor: he always fought against falsehood and will do so now *(Sì, fui soldato)*. When witnesses are called, Gérard pushes his way through, admitting he testified falsely. The prosecutor, however, stands by the charges, and the crowd begins to suspect Gérard of being bought off. He pleads with them in vain, and the judges pronounce a death sentence.

ACT IV   In the courtyard of St. Lazare Prison, a month later, Roucher bribes the jailer to let him visit Chénier. The poet reads a verse he has just finished; it compares his life to the passing of a May morning *(Come un bel dì di maggio)*. Roucher embraces him and leaves as Gérard and Maddalena arrive. She tells the jailer she wants to take the place of another woman, whose name appears on the list of those to be executed, and who will go free. Gérard, crying in despair that she makes death seem enviable, rushes off to Robespierre for a last effort to save the lovers. Chénier greets her as the inspiration of his poetry and his life *(Vicino a te s'aqueta)*, and the two rejoice that they will be joined in death, never to be separated again. As dawn approaches, they hail the triumph of their love, walking to the guillotine when the jailer calls their names.

MIKHAIL GLINKA
1804–57

The creation of Russian national music, like that of opera itself by the Florentine Camerata, was primarily an act of will by a small intelligentsia. Mikhail Ivanovich Glinka, born in the environs of Smolensk, grew up on his family's estate, where he heard a wealth of folk melody sung and danced to by the peasants: it remained to incorporate this into art. Mostly self-taught until the age of twenty-seven, Glinka composed fashionable salon pieces, but friendship with writers, painters, and musicians stimulated him to ever more ambitious and serious projects. In 1829 he went to Italy for three years—partly for his health, partly to familiarize himself with the world of opera, which he then tried to translate into Russian form with *A Life for the Czar* (rechristened *Ivan Susanin* by the Soviets). Performed in 1836, the work was dismissed by its aristocratic audience as "coachmen's music," because a coachman's song appears in one of its early recitatives; the ensembles and vocal style, however, seem akin to those of Verdi's *Ernani,* which was not written until a few years later.

Glinka wanted to write another opera, one with even more Russian color, and responded to the suggestion that he adapt Pushkin's poem *Ruslan and Ludmila.* The poet apparently agreed and might have helped with the libretto had he not been killed in a duel. Instead, Glinka had to work from an outline by Konstantin Alexandrovich Bakhturin, writing some of the text himself and accepting contributions of verses by various friends. From a literary standpoint the result was a botch, but the score advanced the cause of Russian music. Despite a tepid reception at the premiere, in 1842, the work was given three hundred times in St. Petersburg within the next fifty years, and today it is a regular repertory item in the U.S.S.R.

RUSLAN AND LUDMILA

FIVE ACTS

MUSIC: Mikhail Glinka

TEXT (Russian): Valeryan Shirkov, K. A. Bakhturin, and the composer, after the poem by Alexander Pushkin

WORLD PREMIERE: St. Petersburg, Imperial Theatre, December 9, 1842

U.S. PREMIERE: New York, Town Hall, December 26, 1942 (concert version)

CHARACTERS

Ruslan, *knight* . . . . Baritone
Ludmila, *Svetozar's daughter* . . . . Soprano
Gorislava, *Ratmir's slave* . . . . Soprano
Naina, *bad fairy* . . . . Mezzo-Soprano
Ratmir, *Oriental prince* . . . . Contralto
Finn, *good fairy* . . . . Tenor
Bayan, *minstrel* . . . . Tenor
Svetozar, *Prince of Kiev* . . . . Bass
Farlaf, *warrior* . . . . Bass
Chernomor, *magician* . . . . Mime
Slave girls, knights, water nymphs

ACT I   In tenth-century Kiev, a wedding feast is under way at the palace of Svetozar, the ruling prince, for his daughter Ludmila and the knight Ruslan. Two other knights, the disappointed suitors Ratmir and Farlaf, sit at the banquet, listening to a baleful song by the minstrel Bayan, which seems to predict bad luck for the newlyweds (*Za blagom vsled idut pechali*). Chided for his gloomy tone, Bayan adds that an invisible power will protect the lovers; in the future, he predicts, another singer [Pushkin] will glorify the tale of Ruslan and Ludmila but will not live long, "for all the immortals are in heaven." The guests hail their prince (*Svetlomu kniazyu i zdravye*). To her father, Ludmila confesses sadness at leaving him; to Farlaf and Ratmir she offers kind words, trying to ease their grief at losing her. Svetozar blesses the pair, and Ratmir voices homesickness for his own country (*Breg daliokyi*), while Ruslan swears loyalty to Ludmila, but Farlaf mutters he will still capture Ludmila somehow. As the guests call upon the god of love to bless the couple (*Lel' tainstvennyhi!*), darkness and thunder descend, during which Ludmila is abducted by two strange creatures. Svetozar declares he will give her in marriage to the one who rescues her, and all three rivals set out to accomplish the task.

ACT II   In his cell, an old Finn welcomes Ruslan, telling him it was the magician Chernomor who took Ludmila. He tells Ruslan about himself (*Lyubeznyhi syhn!*): a herdsman from Finland, he loved Naina in his youth; she did not return his love, even after many exploits with which he tried to win her. Mastering the secrets of nature, he finally conjured her up, only to find her turned into an old witch, who has since pursued him and will now try to thwart Ruslan. The latter vows to pursue his quest without fear.

§ Elsewhere in the barren countryside, Farlaf stumbles upon an old woman who turns out to be Naina. She says she will help him win Ludmila and will lead Ruslan to perdition. When she disappears, Farlaf congratulates himself on his good fortune, rejoicing that Ludmila will be his (*O radost'!*).

§ Coming upon a deserted battlefield, Ruslan tries to find a weapon he can use (*O, poleh, poleh*). He prays to the god of love for a sword strong enough and remains confident he will prevail. As the mists lift, he finds an enormous head standing in the desert. From inside it, voices warn Ruslan not to disturb the battlefield, and by blowing up a wind, the head threatens him with a storm. But Ruslan strikes it with his spear, and it reveals a hidden sword— the very weapon he seeks. The head says the sword was a bone of contention between Chernomor and his giant brother; Chernomor beheaded the brother, leaving his head in the desert, and the sword must wreak vengeance on Chernomor in Ruslan's hand.

ACT III   In Naina's enchanted castle, Persian slave girls offer a welcome (*Lozhitsya v poleh*), while Naina looks forward to trapping the knights who hope to reach Chernomor's castle. Gorislava, once a member of Ratmir's harem, has wandered there in hopes of finding him (*Kakie sladostnyhye zvuki*). When Ratmir appears at the castle, however, he is longing for Ludmila (*I zhar, i znoi*) and quickly succumbs to the allure of the dancing girls. Next to arrive is Ruslan, moved by Gorislava's cry of anguish over the unresponsive Ratmir. The latter, however, is preoccupied with the slave girls, who rejoice in their triumph over the knights as Ruslan too begins to succumb to their charms. At the unexpected appearance of the old Finn, the girls vanish. He tells Ratmir to return to Gorislava, with whom his true happiness lies; fate has decreed that Ruslan will be reunited with Ludmila. At a sign from him, the enchanted castle turns into a forest. The three men and Gorislava set out to find Ludmila (quartet: *Teper Lyudmila*).

ACT IV   In Chernomor's magic gardens, with water in the background, Ludmila tries to drown herself but is stopped by water nymphs, who dance around her. She cannot see any reason to go on living (*Oh, shto mneh zhizn'?*). When unseen voices woo her on Chernomor's behalf, she defies them and falls in a swoon. A procession approaches, headed by Chernomor himself, an old gnome with an enormous beard, and Oriental dances are performed. Ruslan arrives, engages Chernomor in combat and kills him, cutting off his magic beard. But Ludmila now stays in a charmed sleep, unresponsive to her lover's pleas. With Gorislava and Ratmir, he takes her off in search of help.

ACT V   Standing guard in front of their camp, Ratmir sings the praises of Gorislava, who has returned his youth to him *(Oneh mneh zhizn')*. Terrified slaves run in to announce that Ruslan and Ludmila have disappeared from their tent. The Finn, urging calm, says this is Naina's last trick: fate will now turn against her. He gives Ratmir a magic ring: Ratmir must find Ruslan and use it to break Naina's spell (duet: *Stradan'yam nastupit kanetz*).

§ Back home in Svetozar's castle, Ludmila lies in an enchanted sleep, brought on by Farlaf, who hopes to claim her as his reward. To Farlaf's disgust, Ruslan arrives and revives Ludmila with the aid of the magic ring. Awakening from her terrible dream, she rejoices at finding her lover again *(Radost' v serdtze)*, and all the bystanders except Farlaf join in praise *(Slava velikim bogam)*.

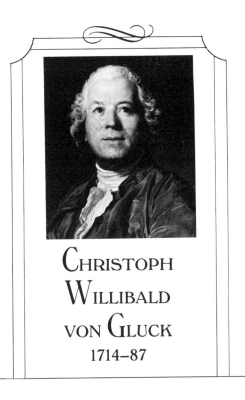

CHRISTOPH WILLIBALD VON GLUCK
1714–87

When Christoph Willibald von Gluck set about writing opera that did not conform to the prevailing styles, he was thoroughly prepared and knowledgeable on the subject. Trained in Milan by Giovanni Battista Sammartini, he had already composed a number of standard Italian operas in the static, florid style of the day. Gluck's real talent, however, lay in the direction of simplicity, to the extent that Handel is said to have snorted, "He knows no more counterpoint than my cook Walz." (Walz, besides being a cook, was a bass singer; Handel's opinion of singers as musicians cannot have been very high.) Entering into collaboration with the poet-diplomat Raniero de Calzabigi, whose theories greatly influenced his style, Gluck created in *Orfeo ed Euridice* an opera whose classical purity and directness of emotion recalled the ideals of the Florentine Camerata, in whose milieu the art form of opera had been born in order to fulfill those ideals. In an age ruled by virtuoso singers, Gluck became something of a renegade, and later composers, such as Berlioz and Wagner, could look upon him with veneration for pointing the way toward modern music drama.

Already forty-eight when he wrote *Orfeo ed Euridice,* Gluck was primarily a practical man of the theater. The son of a Bohemian forester in the employ of a Bavarian nobleman, he combined peasant common sense with the aristocratic benefits of education and (thanks to an advantageous marriage) travel.

The later period of his life was spent as court composer in Paris, where Marie Antoinette had arranged for his pension. He died in Vienna, the city in which *Orfeo* had had its premiere in 1762.

The role of Orfeo (Orpheus) was originally written for a male contralto. Gluck arranged it for tenor (Paris version) and for baritone (German version), but since nineteenth-century revivals in France it has usually been played by a female contralto or mezzo-soprano. Various editors, notably Berlioz and Alfred Dörffel, tried to reconcile the versions, keeping some musical improvements from each. (Having a better orchestra in Paris, Gluck had added embellishments to the instrumental parts.) Current productions tend toward the Berlioz version for low female voice, using the original Italian text and original keys, with further material sometimes added from later versions. As in Gluck's time, controversy persists between purists and eclectics, but the great reformer would doubtless be as happy with one edition as another, since they all started with him.

ORFEO ED EURIDICE

FOUR ACTS
MUSIC: Christoph Willibald von Gluck
TEXT (Italian): Rainiero de Calzabigi
WORLD PREMIERE: Vienna, Burgtheater, October 5, 1762
U.S. PREMIERE: Charleston, S.C., June 24, 1794
METROPOLITAN OPERA PREMIERE: December 30, 1891

CHARACTERS

Orfeo . . . . Contralto
Euridice, *shepherdess, his wife*. . . . . Soprano
Amore, *god of love* . . . . Soprano
Happy Shade . . . . Soprano
    Shepherds, shepherdesses, Furies, demons, heroes, heroines in Hades

ACT I   In a pleasant grove, shepherds and shepherdesses attend funeral rites for Euridice, wife of the bard Orfeo (Orpheus), who stands grief-stricken nearby and finally asks them all to leave. He calls upon the gods to give her back—or else let him join her in death. So eloquent is his pleading that Amore (Cupid), the god of love, comes to tell him that his request is granted: he will be allowed to enter the realm of death and return with Euridice. He is forbidden, however, to look upon her until they are on earth once more. Rejoicing in his good fortune, Orfeo calls upon the power of love to guide him on the journey (*La speme in sen ritorna*).

ACT II   In an austere landscape near the entrance to the underworld, Furies and monsters dance and guard the portals. Interrupted by the sound of Orfeo's lyre, they announce that whoever this mortal may be, he can go no farther. Orfeo pleads with them, but they refuse to let him pass. Eventually, however, Orfeo's repeated pleas soften their hearts: never have they heard such wondrously beautiful singing, which calms their fury and wins their sympathy. The gates of the underworld are opened to Orfeo, who walks fearlessly past the monsters and enters.

ACT III   The Elysian Fields are the domain of the Blessed Spirits, who sing of the timeless bliss they enjoy, with the cares of the world left behind. Orfeo wanders in and admires the beautiful realm of eternal peace (*Che puro ciel*). If he can just find Euridice now, his contentment will be complete. The Blessed Spirits reassure him he will soon find her, but he pleads with them to delay the moment no longer (*O larve che m'udite*). As they dance, Euridice is led in, her face veiled from sight. Keeping his gaze turned away, Orfeo takes her hand and prepares to lead her back to earth. The Blessed Spirits wonder at the power of love, strong enough to overcome the gulf between life and death (*Torna, o bella al tuo consorte*).

ACT IV   In a subterranean passage leading back to the world, Orfeo leads Euridice impatiently toward life. She expresses amazement at being reunited with him but soon notices he is not looking at her. This makes her wonder whether his love has faded. If he has rejected her in his heart, she would rather return to the realm of death. Each prays to the gods for relief from the sorrow they must endure (*Siate a me propizi, o Dei*). Aside, Euridice questions why she is being tested with Orfeo's indifference, as painful to her as the torments of hell. Orfeo in turn confesses he can hardly bear to conceal his true feelings any longer. When she begs for a glance, he almost weakens. When it seems she is about to fade back into the underworld, however, he defies his vow and looks at her, causing her to die at once. Having lost her a second time, Orfeo pours out his inconsolable grief: he asks how he will live without her (*Che farò senza Euridice*). Determined to take his own life and return to the underworld, he is stopped only by the intervention of Amore, who declares that Orfeo has proven his devotion to be stronger than even the bonds of death. As a reward, Amore revives Euridice and restores her to her husband's arms.

§ Back on earth, Orfeo and Euridice are joined by their friends and companions in a hymn to the triumph of love, accompanied by dances (*Di Pafo il Signor e di Gnido*).

CHARLES GOUNOD
1818–93

*C*harles François Gounod, a quintessentially Victorian composer in style and aspirations, was born and died in Paris, though for a time he lived in England to quiet a marital scandal. His father, a painter who won The Prix de Rome, died when Gounod was still a child, and he received his basic musical education from his mother, who also tutored him generally in the liberal arts. After studies at the Paris Conservatory with Halévy, Lesueur, and Paer, he won a Prix de Rome of his own in 1837 and another two years later. In Rome he studied church music, which was to become in later life his chief field of endeavor. Two youthful symphonies show boundless energy and invention, alongside the lyric fluency that made him a felicitous, though still largely neglected, song composer. It is for his operas that he is remembered today. Like Rossini, he was a trained singer, having what was described as a small but sweet tenor voice, and this training stood him in good stead as a composer for the voice.

Gounod's stage career began in 1851 with *Sapho* and reached its pinnacle with *Faust*, which began as an opéra comique with spoken dialogue in 1859 and grew into a grand opera ten years later. In his time he was considered a major opera composer, and his name was among those chosen to adorn the proscenium of the remodeled Metropolitan Opera House in 1903. Indeed, he was of special importance to the Met in its early years. *Faust*, fourth of his twelve operas, served to inaugurate the house in 1883. The ninth, *Roméo et Juliette*, rechristened it in 1891, after an interlude of seven seasons of opera in German only. The brothers Jean and Édouard de Reszke, who joined Emma Eames in that performance (a house debut for all three), had introduced the

160

work at the Paris Opera with Adelina Patti in 1878, eleven years after its world premiere at the Théâtre Lyrique, where it had starred Marie Miolhan-Carvalho.

Like Meyerbeer's, Gounod's popularity began to wane after the turn of the century, but *Faust* never left the international repertory, and *Roméo* is revived fairly often. Both have been scorned as sentimental glosses of the original dramas by Goethe and Shakespeare, but the texts—in both cases by Barbier and Carré—show them to be faithful, in both spirit and letter, to a greater extent than is usually supposed. Gounod may not have been a profound Shakespearean, in the sense that Berlioz or Verdi was, but he had a healthy respect for the classics as well as for the tastes of his own audience. A forerunner of Massenet, he aimed to please. If the seriousness of Wagnerism cast a pall on this aesthetic, the lyric felicity of Gounod's music has nonetheless survived.

FAUST

FIVE ACTS
MUSIC: Charles Gounod
TEXT (French): Jules Barbier and Michel Carré, from the play by Goethe
WORLD PREMIERE: Paris, Théâtre Lyrique, May 19, 1859
U.S. PREMIERE: New York, Academy of Music, November 26, 1863 (in Italian)
METROPOLITAN OPERA PREMIERE: October 22, 1883 (in Italian)

CHARACTERS

Faust, *learned doctor* . . . . Tenor
Méphistophélès . . . . Bass
Marguerite . . . . Soprano
Siébel, *village youth, in love with Marguerite* . . . . Mezzo-Soprano
Dame Marthe, *Marguerite's neighbor* . . . . Mezzo-Soprano
Valentin, *soldier, Marguerite's brother* . . . . Baritone
Wagner, *student* . . . . Baritone
Students, soldiers, villagers, angels, demons, etc.

ACT I   Sixteenth-century Germany; a village. After poring over his books all night, the aged scholar Dr. Faust protests that a lifetime in pursuit of wisdom has not granted him any answers to the meaning of life. He is tired of living and welcomes death; since it will not come for him, he prepares some poison, determined to be master of his own fate. As he is about to drink, voices singing outside his study remind him of spring and of life's simple pleasures. At first he tries to ignore them, but at the mention of God, he pauses. Reflecting that God will neither give him back his youth nor enlighten his old age, he calls on Satan in despair. The devil Méphistophélès appears, dressed as a man of the world, and assures the astonished Faust that he can be of service. Asked what he wants, Faust says he wishes to be young again. The devil tells him that this can be done but that Faust must sign away his soul in exchange. The aged scholar balks at this; however, when Méphistophélès conjures up a vision of the beautiful Marguerite at her spinning wheel, Faust is charmed and quickly complies. Méphistophélès prepares a youth potion for the doctor, who is transformed into a young man. Looking forward to adventure, the two rush off.

ACT II* At a kermis (village fair) nearby, students toast the pleasures of wine and beer. Soldiers, burghers and young girls join the throng, arousing the disapproval of older matrons. One of the soldiers, Valentin, a captain, holds a medal his sister has given him to protect him on the battlefield. He is the brother of Marguerite, and since their mother is dead, he worries that no one will look after his sister during his absence. Siébel, a young admirer of hers, says he will. Valentin offers a prayer to God—first for guidance in battle, then for Marguerite's safety *(Avant de quitter ces lieux)*. The serious mood is dispelled by a student, Wagner, who climbs on a table to offer a ditty about a rat who lived in a wine cellar. He has scarcely begun when Méphistophélès appears, proposing a song of his own. Making way for the stranger, the students hear his blasphemous ballad in praise of the legendary Golden Calf, worshiped by young and old as Satan calls the tune *(Le veau d'or)*. When he reads fortunes for some of the bystanders—Wagner will die in battle, Siébel will wither any flower he touches, Valentin will meet his death at the hands of a certain man—they begin to look on him with suspicion, and when he miraculously causes wine to flow from the sign in front of the inn, they know he has supernatural powers. Valentin fearlessly challenges him and—when Méphistophélès causes his sword to break—holds the handle up in the sign of the cross, momentarily cowing the devil. Left alone, Faust and Méphistophélès plan their next move. Faust wants to meet the girl of the vision, so Méphistophélès arranges for her to arrive with another group of townspeople, who enter to begin a waltz. As Méphistophélès chases Siébel away, Faust approaches Marguerite and offers her his arm, which she refuses. The waltz continues as Méphistophélès assures Faust that he does not have to take no for an answer.

---

*When, as is usual today, the opera is performed in four acts instead of the original five, this becomes Scene 2 of Act I.

ACT III   In the garden outside Marguerite's cottage that evening, Siébel decides to offer her a bouquet *(Faîtes-lui mes aveux)*, but thanks to Méphistophélès's spell, every flower withers when he picks it. Then he dips his fingers in a font of holy water where Marguerite prays every evening, and the spell is gone. Faust and Méphistophélès enter quietly and hide while Siébel makes the bouquet and leaves it. Méphistophélès declares he will fetch some precious gift for Marguerite. Left alone, Faust hails the dwelling place of the beautiful, innocent girl for whom he now feels such love *(Salut, demeure)*. Méphistophélès returns with a casket of jewels, and when Faust protests he feels unworthy of a girl of such virtue, the demon himself leaves the gift for Marguerite, then leads Faust back into hiding. Marguerite comes into the garden and sings to herself the ballad of the king of Thule, who remained faithful all his life to his bride who had died in youth *(Il était un roi de Thulé)*, interspersing in the verses remarks about the young man (Faust) who spoke to her at the fair. She finds the bouquet, then the jewel box, which for a moment she hesitates to open. Curiosity gets the better of her, and she tries on some of the jewels, looking in a hand mirror from the box and imagining herself as a great lady *(Ah! je ris de me voir si belle)*. A matronly neighbor, Dame Marthe, comes in and admires the jewels. Méphistophélès steps out of the shadows and draws Marthe aside, giving her news of her husband's death and pretending to court her himself, so that Faust can be alone with Marguerite. The girl removes the jewels and protests to Faust that she does not deserve such a gift; then she speaks of her brother's absence, her mother's death, and the loss of her younger sister. Though strongly attracted to her suitor, she tells him he must not stay. Seeing this, Méphistophélès stands apart and invokes a spell over the garden, calling on night and love to conceal and encourage the lovers *(O nuit, étends sur eux ton ombre!)*. Faust and Marguerite exchange tender words *(Laisse-moi contempler ton visage)*, and she plays a game of "he loves me, he loves me not" with a daisy. Having thus broached the subject of love, the two declare their feelings more passionately *(O nuit d'amour)*, but Marguerite still insists that Faust must leave. Respecting her purity, he is ready to go when Méphistophélès mocks his softheadedness and sends him back to the embrace of Marguerite, who has opened her window and expressed her impatience to see him the next day *(Il m'aime . . . quel trouble dans mon coeur)*.

ACT IV   Time has passed.* Marguerite sits spinning in her room while voices outside taunt her about the disappearance of her lover. She reflects sadly that Faust shows no signs of returning to her *(Il ne revient pas)*, whereupon Siébel, trying to share her misfortune, offers his faithful friendship *(Si le bonheur)*.

§ The dishonored Marguerite comes to church to ask forgiveness for her sin. She is haunted, however, by a vision of Méphistophélès, who says eternal damnation is her lot *(Souviens-toi du passé)*.

* This scene is often omitted.

§ In the public square, Valentin and his fellow soldiers return from the front in high spirits (*Gloire immortelle de nos aïeux*), but Siébel tries to keep him from entering his home. Perplexed by Siébel's evasive answers, Valentin goes in, and Faust enters the square with Méphistophélès. Faust calls Marguerite's name; when there is no reply, Méphistophélès launches into a mocking serenade, advising a girl who is being courted not to give her suitor any favors until she has a ring on her finger (*Vous qui faîtes l'endormie*). Valentin rushes angrily out of the house and smashes the devil's guitar with his sword, demanding to know which of the two newcomers will answer for Marguerite's shame. In the duel that follows, Faust, backed up by Méphistophélès, quickly dispatches Valentin and escapes as people approach. Valentin dies cursing his sister.

ACT V* Méphistophélès leads Faust to the Brocken, a peak in the Harz Mountains, where the Walpurgis Night is being celebrated. Spirits and phantoms gather, and celebrated beauties of the past appear amid the dancers and revelers, but Faust remains preoccupied with thoughts of Marguerite, whom he imagines he sees wearing a red ribbon—like the cut of an executioner's ax—around her neck. Finally he insists that Méphistophélès take him to her.

§ In prison, Marguerite lies condemned for the death of her illegitimate baby. Méphistophélès leads Faust to the sleeping girl and says he will wait outside. She appears happy to see him again (*Oui, c'est toi, je t'aime*), and they reminisce about the beginning of their romance, but Méphistophélès interrupts, saying they must escape. Seeing the evil one, Marguerite falls to her knees and prays for salvation as the two plead with her in vain to accompany them (trio: *Anges purs, anges radieux!*). With daybreak, Méphistophélès must drag away his supposed prize, Faust, whom Marguerite sees at last as an object of horror. The devil cries that she too is damned, but a heavenly choir proclaims her saved, and her soul ascends to heaven, as Faust and Méphistophélès watch in despair and impotence.

ROMÉO ET JULIETTE

PROLOGUE AND FIVE ACTS
MUSIC: Charles Gounod
TEXT (French): Jules Barbier and Michel Carré, after the tragedy
   by Shakespeare
WORLD PREMIERE: Paris, Théâtre Lyrique, April 27, 1867

* First scene sometimes omitted.

ROMÉO ET JULIETTE

U.S. PREMIERE: New York, Academy of Music, November 15, 1867

METROPOLITAN OPERA PREMIERE: December 14, 1891

CHARACTERS

Roméo, *a Montague* .... Tenor
Juliette, *a Capulet* .... Soprano
Gertrude, *her nurse* .... Mezzo-Soprano
Stéphano, *Roméo's page* .... Soprano
Tybalt, *Capulet's nephew* .... Tenor
Benvolio, *retainer to the Montagues* .... Tenor
Count Pâris .... Baritone
Mercutio, *Roméo's friend* .... Baritone
Grégorio, *Capulet retainer* .... Baritone
Frère Laurent .... Bass
Count Capulet, *Juliette's father* .... Bass
Duke of Verona .... Bass
Nobles and ladies of Verona, citizens, soldiers, monks, and pages

PROLOGUE   The chorus announces a tale of two noble families locked in a feud, and of the deathless love of two children of the opposing families, their lives sacrificed to their fathers' hatred.

ACT I   In the ballroom of the Capulets' house in fourteenth-century Verona, the beauty of Juliette, the sixteen-year-old daughter of the house, impresses her suitor Count Pâris, brought to the gathering by her cousin Tybalt. Capulet, Juliette's father, welcomes the guests *(Soyez les bienvenus, amis)* and exhorts them to dance; as they do, Mercutio and Roméo enter furtively. Both represent the rival Montague family, but whereas Roméo advises caution, the reckless Mercutio does not care, telling Roméo he dreamed last night of Queen Mab, maker of mischief and illusion *(Mab, la reine des mensonges)*. Shepherded by her nurse, Gertrude, Juliette rejects the idea of marrying Pâris, declaring she wants to enjoy her youth (waltz song: *Je veux vivre dans le rêve)*. Smitten with Juliette, Roméo offers his hand *(Ange adorable, ma main coupable)*. She responds with interest but is called away by Tybalt, who recognizes Roméo as an enemy. Juliette is shattered to learn the attractive young man's identity. Though Tybalt wants to fight, his hand is stayed by Capulet, who returns to say that his hospitality protects any guest, whoever it may be. The guests resume their merrymaking.

ACT II   In a garden outside Juliette's balcony later that night, Roméo catches sight of her and compares her beauty to that of the rising sun *(Ah, lève-toi, soleil)* that causes the stars to pale. He conceals himself as she steps on the balcony, confessing her love and wishing he were not Roméo; replying, he says he will renounce his name if it divides him from her. To this she replies that if he loves her, that is enough (*Cher Roméo, dis-moi loyalement: Je t'aime*). They withdraw when Grégorio, a guardsman, is heard searching the premises for the intruders—who, his retainers joke, must have come courting Gertrude. As they move on, Gertrude takes Juliette inside, and Roméo returns, fearing that his happiness is just a dream (*O nuit divine*). Juliette comes back to the balcony to say she will send word tomorrow: if his love is as serious as hers, they will find a way to marry. Ecstatically, they bid each other good night (*Adieu, de cet adieu si douce*), lamenting that parting is such sweet sorrow.

ACT III   In the cell of Frère Laurent (Friar Laurence), Roméo confesses his love for Juliette, who appears; both ask to be married. Despite the certain opposition of the parents, Laurent agrees and pronounces the ceremony (*Dieu qui fis l'homme à ton image*). When Gertrude enters, she joins in wishing happiness for the couple (quartet: *O pur bonheur*).

§ Outside the Capulet house, Roméo's page, Stéphano, sings a taunting serenade about a dove that managed to fly from the vultures' nest and join its sweetheart (*Que fais-tu, blanche tourterelle*). Grégorio comes out and threatens him, whereupon Stéphano draws his sword. As onlookers watch, Mercutio appears and interrupts, accusing Grégorio of fighting a mere boy. Tybalt in turn challenges Mercutio, then recognizes and challenges Roméo, who protests that he is unarmed and bears the Capulets no hatred. Seeing Roméo unwilling, Mercutio himself duels with Tybalt, as partisans of both sides cheer them on. Fatally wounded, Mercutio falls, pronouncing "a plague on both your houses!" for this murderous feud. Enraged by his friend's death, Roméo engages Tybalt and kills him, just as Capulet enters. The dying Tybalt calls for vengeance. Drawn by the disturbance, the Duke of Verona denounces both families for troublemaking, then orders Roméo banished for the death of Tybalt. Roméo laments the turn of fate that has put an end to his hopes, and the others echo his sentiments (*Ah! Jour de deuil et d'horreur et d'alarmes!*).

ACT IV   Roméo, who must leave Verona by daybreak, visits Juliette secretly in her chamber. Though Tybalt was her cousin, she knows he would have killed Roméo, so she does not mourn him. The lovers welcome the night as testimony to their everlasting love (*Nuit d'hyménée*), and when Roméo is afraid he hears the voice of the lark, signaling daybreak, Juliette replies that it is the nightingale. When she realizes that it *is* the lark, she tells him he must go (*Il faut partir, hélas*). He leaves by the balcony just as Gertrude, Capulet and Frère Laurent enter. Capulet tells the girl to get ready to marry Pâris, fulfilling the wish of the dying Tybalt (*L'autel est préparé*); Laurent will instruct her in her vows. Instead, as her father leaves, Laurent gives her a vial, saying it contains a draught that will make her appear dead (*Buvez donc ce breuvage*), after which she can rejoin Roméo. She takes the potion as Laurent leaves, and when Capulet returns, he finds his daughter apparently dying.

ACT V   In the tomb of the Capulets, Juliette lies motionless on a bier as Roméo, who found her before Laurent could reach him, cries out his anguish (*Salut, tombeau sombre et silencieux!*). Hailing his beloved for the last time, he takes poison, but no sooner has he swallowed it than she revives. Unable to believe his eyes and ears, Roméo embraces her ecstatically, only to realize that he himself is dying. Poignantly, she tells him that their love will survive death (*Console-toi, pauvre âme*). Seeing no poison left for her, she takes Roméo's dagger and stabs herself. The lovers die in a last embrace.

GEORGE FRIDERIC HANDEL
1685–1759

*G*eorge Frideric Handel arrived in London at the high tide of enthusiasm for Italian opera. He forthwith made his name a household word with *Rinaldo* (1711), a hastily engineered amplification of earlier pieces joined with new verses and recitatives. Though not remembered as such in modern times, Handel was primarily an opera composer. *Giulio Cesare* was the sixteenth of his forty-six operas. Along with *Rodelinda,* written a year later (1725), it ranks as his most successful in terms of the number and frequency of productions. After the middle of the eighteenth century, however, opera seria began to decline in popularity; Handel's current reemergence as an acknowledged master of opera did not begin until the 1920s, when there were a few revivals in Germany and *Giulio Cesare* bowed on the North American stage. It took the post–World War II resurgence of bel canto to provide the florid singing technique and stylized staging that a more widespread Handel revival required, and this was sparked in the United States by a much admired 1966 *Giulio Cesare* at the New York City Opera, with Beverly Sills and Norman Treigle. The movement has been carried energetically forward by the mezzo-soprano Marilyn Horne, whose technique and assertive delivery equip her for roles originally meant for male castrato singers.

GIULIO CESARE

THREE ACTS
MUSIC: George Frideric Handel
TEXT (Italian): Niccolò Haym
WORLD PREMIERE: London, Haymarket Theatre, March 2, 1724
U.S. PREMIERE: Northampton, Mass., Smith College, May 14,
    1927 (in English)

CHARACTERS

Giulio Cesare . . . . Contralto (Baritone)
Cleopatra, *Queen of Egypt* . . . . Soprano
Cornelia, *Pompeo's widow*. . . . . Contralto
Sesto, *Cornelia's son*. . . . . Soprano (Tenor)
Tolomeo, *King of Egypt*. . . . . Contralto (Bass)
Curio, *Roman tribune* . . . . Bass
Nireno, *Cleopatra's confidant* . . . . Contralto (Bass)
Achille, *Tolomeo's general*. . . . . Bass

ACT I Egypt, 48 B.C. Giulio Cesare (Julius Caesar) has defeated the forces of his rival and former son-in-law, Pompeo (Pompey), and arrives on the banks of the Nile in triumph. Cornelia, Pompeo's wife, begs for clemency for her husband, but Cesare says it will be granted only if the man comes to him in person. Scarcely has he said this than Achille (Achillas), the Egyptian military leader, brings in a casket containing Pompeo's head—a gift from Tolomeo (Ptolemy), the co-ruler, with Cleopatra, of Egypt. Cesare takes the gesture badly and leaves to remonstrate with Tolomeo. Cornelia faints, reviving in the arms of her son Sesto (Sextus). Curio, Cesare's aide, who wants to marry Cornelia, offers to help her avenge her husband's death, but she spurns him. She bemoans her sorrowful state, for which death offers no relief *(Priva son io d'ogni conforto)*. Sesto resolves to strike down the murderer of his father *(Vani sono i lamenti)*.

§ Cleopatra learns from her retinue of Pompeo's murder. Realizing that her brother Tolomeo arranged this in hopes of currying favor with Cesare, she decides she must see the Roman emperor herself to muster support for her position as queen. Tolomeo scoffs at her, but she is determined to use her charms on Cesare. Achille enters with the news that Cesare was angered by the murder of Pompeo, adding that he would gladly do away with Cesare in return for Cornelia's hand. Tolomeo welcomes the idea of being rid of the Roman conqueror (*L'empio, sleale, indegno*).

§ In his camp, the emperor muses on the fragility of life and fame as he stands before the urn containing Pompeo's remains (*Alma del gran Pompeo*). Curio introduces "Lidia"—actually Cleopatra in disguise as one of her ladies-in-waiting. As she tells of her tribulations at the hands of the tyrant Tolomeo (*Piangerò la sorte mia*), Cesare is amazed by her beauty. He excuses himself, leaving Cleopatra to hide as the grieving Cornelia appears and takes up her husband's sword. Sesto stops her, saying that *he* will avenge Pompeo. Cleopatra steps forth and offers the services of her adviser Nireno, who will lead the way to the guilty Tolomeo.

§ Tolomeo guardedly receives Cesare at his palace. He plans to have him ambushed, but Cesare suspects treachery (*Va tacito e nascosto*). When Achille introduces Cornelia, Tolomeo himself is smitten by her beauty, though he pretends to Achille that the latter may still hope to marry her. Sesto tries unsuccessfully to challenge Tolomeo to combat. When Cornelia scorns Achille's wooing (*Cornelia, se all'amor mio*), he sends Egyptian soldiers to arrest Sesto. As she bemoans this latest misfortune (*Son nata a sospirar*), Sesto bids her a dejected farewell.

ACT II   In her palace, Cleopatra tells Nireno to lure Cesare to her rooms by promising him news of "Lidia." She withdraws, and Cesare arrives in search of her. He is distracted by the sound of beautiful music, and when Cleopatra appears, singing the praises of Cupid's darts (*V'adoro, pupille*), Cesare is enchanted.

§ In the harem garden of Tolomeo's palace, Achille continues to plead with the adamant Cornelia (*Se a me non sei crudele*). When he leaves, Tolomeo also tries to court her, with the same results. Sesto enters, bent on avenging his father's death (*L'angue offeso mai riposa*).

§ In Cleopatra's quarters, meanwhile, her idyll with Cesare is disturbed by sounds of conspirators approaching. Revealing her identity, she urges him to flee, but he goes to face his enemies as she prays for his safety (*Se pietà di me non senti*).

§ In Tolomeo's harem, the king sits surrounded by his favorites, Cornelia among them. Sesto rushes in and attempts to stab Tolomeo, but he is subdued by Achille, who announces that his soldiers attacked Cesare, who jumped from a palace window into the sea and is undoubtedly dead. Achille now asks for the promised reward of Cornelia's hand in marriage and is sharply turned down by Tolomeo. Sesto tries to kill himself but is dissuaded by his mother;

he repeats his determination not to rest until the tyrant who murdered his father is punished *(Figlio non è, chi vendicar non cura)*.

ACT III   By the shores of the Mediterranean, sounds of battle denote the clash between Tolomeo's and Cleopatra's armies. Victorious, Tolomeo orders the still-defiant Cleopatra led off in chains. Cesare, having barely survived the fray, pulls himself from the water and prays for news of his beloved *(Aure, deh, per pietà)*. As he leaves, Sesto enters, guided by Nireno, in search of Tolomeo; instead he finds the wounded Achille. To avenge himself on Tolomeo for abducting Cornelia, Achillas hands Sesto a seal that will give him command over a hundred armed men in a nearby cave. As Achille dies, Cesare appears and demands the seal, declaring he will save both Cornelia and Cleopatra or die in the attempt *(Quel torrente, che cade dal monte)*.

§ Guarded by soldiers in Tolomeo's camp, Cleopatra fears that Cesare is dead, shattering her last hopes. She is astonished when he appears and embraces her *(Cara! Ti stringo al seno)*. As he leads his soldiers off to the conquest, she compares her joy to that of a person rescued from a shipwreck *(Da tempeste il legno infranto)*.

§ In the harem, Tolomeo continues to court Cornelia, but Sesto discovers them and kills him. Cornelia blesses her avenging son.

§ Cesare and Cleopatra enter Alexandria in triumph. Cornelia presents trophies of the slain Tolomeo to Cesare, who passes them on to Cleopatra, saying he will support her rule. As the two declare their love *(Un bel contento)*, the people welcome the return of peace.

Paul Hindemith
1895–1963

*M*ore than any other major twentieth-century composer, the German-born Paul Hindemith represents the voice of tradition, though in his earlier years he was considered a harsh modernist. The recent neglect of his work, in comparison with that of his contemporaries Stravinsky and Schoenberg, may be attributed to its basic conservatism—a trait that, with time, may provide its staying power.

Hindemith's three large-scale operas—*Cardillac, Mathis der Maler, Die Harmonie der Welt*—all deal with artists. Mathis (Matthias) Grünewald, a painter who worked in the first three decades of the sixteenth century, was aware not only of the emerging Renaissance but also of his roots in the medieval tradition. Like Bach (and Hindemith), he looked both forward and back, showing compassion for the woes that humanity was enduring in the turbulent period in which he lived. Toward the end of his life, Mathis embraced the Reformation, gave up painting, and died a millwright. The opera's other main character, Cardinal Albrecht, was a patron of the arts, brilliant but vacillating, about whom Hindemith noted, "A stronger man could have forced the next 100 years of Middle European history onto a different course."

Hindemith wrote his own libretto, basing it on history but informing it with his own literate, witty, philosophical turn of mind. The strength of the work is a result of its thoughtfulness as much as of its dramatic power, exemplified in the imaginative dream sequence that forms its climax. *Mathis der Maler* is one of those rare portrayals of an artist that ring true on every level. Though nourished by little of what usually sustains mass entertainment, it provokes and rewards thought and feeling as few operas do, elaborating like a choral prelude on the cantus firmus of faith that ties it to its period. Composed in 1932–34, in an atmosphere of political turbulence and change in Germany, it was first performed in Switzerland (Hindemith having been exiled for his "modernism") in 1938. After nearly thirty years of being respected but ignored, the opera began its gradual comeback with the Hamburg production of the mid-1960s. Meanwhile, *Mathis der Maler* gained considerable currency in the concert hall through the "symphony" that Hindemith arranged from three excerpts.

MATHIS DER MALER

SEVEN TABLEAUX
MUSIC: Paul Hindemith
TEXT (German): by the composer
WORLD PREMIERE: Zurich, Stadttheater, May 28, 1938
U.S. PREMIERE: Boston University, February 17, 1956 (in English)

CHARACTERS

Mathis, *painter* . . . . Baritone
Ursula Riedinger . . . . Soprano
Regina Schwalb . . . . Soprano
Countess Helfenstein . . . . Contralto
Cardinal Albrecht von Brandenburg, *Archbishop of Mainz* . . . Tenor
Wolfgang Capito, *cardinal's adviser* . . . . Tenor
Hans Schwalb, *leader of the peasants* . . . . Tenor
Sylvester von Schaumberg, *officer* . . . . Tenor
Lorenz von Pommersfelden, *Dean of Mainz* . . . . Bass
Riedinger, *rich Lutheran of Mainz* . . . . Bass
Count Helfenstein . . . . Silent
Soldiers, townspeople, etc.

TABLEAU I   A sunny spring day in 1524. Mathis the painter—ending a sabbatical granted by his patron, Cardinal Albrecht von Brandenburg, Archbishop of Mainz—wonders whether his work has become too enjoyable and easy to fulfill God's purpose. As monks of the Monastery of St. Anthony sing in the background, Mathis bids farewell to his year of independence. Suddenly a wounded man, Hans Schwalb, a leader of the Peasants' Revolt, stumbles in, supported by his daughter, Regina, and calls to the monks for help. Schwalb is persuaded by Mathis to rest as some monks go for bandages and medicine. Regina washes herself, repeating a ditty about a girl washing at a fountain when a knight discovers her and gives her a ribbon *(Es wollt ein Maidlein waschen gehn)*. Mathis finds a ribbon on his work table and gives it to her to tie her hair, saying it came by ship from a faraway land that has no winter. Regina replies she never heard of such a place *(Niemand hat mir gesagt)* and knows only her own part of the country, through which she and her father have wandered fitfully since her mother died and the fighting started. Schwalb revives; observing the scene around him, he expresses surprise that people are still painting when "so many hands are needed to make the world better," adding that art is of no use to ordinary people in their struggle to survive *(Darum haben sie keinen Sinn)*. Mathis insists he is much concerned with the peasants' cause. When Regina runs back to say that soldiers are coming, Mathis gives Schwalb his horse. Schwalb has scarcely ridden off when an officer, Sylvester von Schaumberg, arrives with a posse, demanding to know where the monks have hidden the fugitive. Mathis says he himself, not the monks, helped Schwalb escape. Sylvester threatens to denounce him to Cardinal Albrecht.

TABLEAU II Two days later, at his official residence in Mainz, Albrecht is expected back from a journey. Lutheran and Catholic factions among the burghers grumble in mutual distrust, but the cardinal's adviser, Wolfgang Capito, assures his adherents that heresy will be subdued, while students declare both factions too stubborn and benighted. As the squabble grows more heated, Albrecht arrives, presenting the city with a holy relic—the supposed remains of St. Martin, patron of the cathedral. Gradually the crowd disperses. Albrecht warmly greets Ursula, whose father, the burgher Riedinger, offers financial support for the cardinal's arts projects. Mathis, returning from his sabbatical, acknowledges Ursula's welcome. Infuriated to learn that the papal legate has ordered a book burning, Albrecht countermands the order, but when his dean, Lorenz von Pommersfelden, reminds him of the risks of disobedience, he signs the authorization. Albrecht then asks Mathis to design a shrine for the new relic, but Pommersfelden complains of growing opposition to Mathis's work, which portrays saintly characters as peasants. Albrecht defends the artist's right to his own view and addresses more pressing problems: the treasury is bare. Arriving with a message that asks Albrecht to assign cavalry for the war against the peasants, Sylvester spots Mathis and accuses him of helping the fugitive Schwalb. When Albrecht asks whether this is true, Mathis pleads with him not to take part in persecuting the peasants. Though Albrecht's humanistic instincts respond, he is bound by treaty obligations and tells Mathis to stick to art. The painter declares he cannot work while his fellow man suffers. Albrecht prevents his arrest, but when Mathis tries to speak with him further, he dismisses him too.

TABLEAU III   In Riedinger's house on the market square, the merchant and his fellow Lutherans are confident they can hide their books, but a group of mercenaries, led by Capito, finds the books and hauls them off. Capito shows the assemblage a letter from Martin Luther to the cardinal, urging him to marry, throw off churchly pomp, and set an example for other German priests. Thinking of the political advantages and money a marriage could bring, Capito believes that the idea is worth entertaining. When Ursula appears, her father asks whether she would sacrifice herself, for her faith, to a marriage not of her own choosing. As the others go out to watch the book burning, Ursula resents the lack of regard shown for her feelings. As darkness approaches, Mathis enters and embraces her. She confesses how much he means to her (*Wir sind im innersten Grund*), reminding him of the ribbon she gave him as a token to take on his sabbatical. He returns her love but says he is too old for her and cannot embrace personal happiness while the world is ruled by suffering: unable to work while the war is on, he must take part in it. They embrace again, he leaves, and the returning Riedinger is delighted to hear Ursula say she is ready to submit to her destiny.

TABLEAU IV   In the village square of Königshofen, peasants torment the captured Count Helfenstein, forcing his wife to wait on them as they carouse. After the count is dragged off for execution, Mathis enters the square, arguing with the peasants that such wrongdoing debases their cause. When they push him aside and set about looting, Mathis goes to the rescue of the countess, threatened with rape by some of the ruffians. He is getting the worst of it when Schwalb and Regina arrive. Warning that government troops are coming, Schwalb tries to whip his forces into resistance but recognizes that their cause is lost and commends his daughter to Mathis' care. The soldiers arrive and butcher the peasants who have not already fled. Schwalb is killed, and Mathis is about to meet the same fate when the countess intercedes, telling how he saved her from the mob. Left alone, Mathis dazedly realizes how presumptuous it was to imagine himself a redeemer: only Christ could be that (*Wagen wollen, was ein Wille nicht zu zwingen*). He finds the weeping Regina and carries her away.

TABLEAU V   In his study, Albrecht argues with Capito, who says it is not expedient to ignore the power of the Lutheran movement. Surprised to find that Ursula is the wife whom Capito has in mind for him, Albrecht receives her, asking why she submits to being bartered. The worthiness of the cause, she replies, makes it an honor to serve (*Handel? Seht ihr so mein Kommen an?*). Seeing his doubt, Ursula pleads with him to use his authority and lead his people (*Wie kein andrer Fürst die Macht und Weisheit*). Moved, he kisses her forehead and opens the door to Riedinger and Capito, telling them he has been convinced by Ursula—not to marry but to renounce worldly pomp and become a hermit. Capito wonders what his master's next whim will be; Riedinger is sorry to lose Albrecht's leadership. When Ursula pledges to help others, Albrecht blesses her for "raising yourself to God in your own way."

TABLEAU VI In a forest (the Odenwald), Mathis has difficulty keeping up with Regina. When he asks what she is fleeing from, she replies that she is haunted by her dead father *(Wie weisst du das?)*. Spreading his cloak so that she can rest on it, he comforts her by describing three angels making music; this prompts the girl to sing a chorale about them *(Es sungen drei Engel)*. The picture takes shape in Mathis's mind as he imagines music itself becoming prayer, transfiguring the dark doings of man. Regina falls asleep. Recalling that he once painted such a vision, Mathis disappears in the darkness, reappearing in dream guise as St. Anthony. Countess Helfenstein, costumed to represent luxury, accuses him of squandering his talent: if he had the wits to sell his paintings for their true worth, he could be rich and make a good life for Regina. Pommersfelden next appears as wealth, urging Mathis to seek not only money but also power. Then a beggar woman approaches, saying no matter how much she is given, it will not banish hunger and poverty; she throws off her cloak, showing herself to be Ursula, dressed as a seductive harlot. Mathis rejects her blandishments, saying physical gratification is only momentary. Transformed now into a martyr, she declares that anguish lasts longer and is more intense than pleasure. Capito, dressed as a scholar, offers a salvation of knowledge that Mathis sees only as misleading lies. Schwalb appears as a warlord, declaring that sensitivity is the enemy of action: to be a man, one must fight. The scene becomes a re-creation of Mathis's painting *The Temptation of St. Anthony,* the center panel of his Isenheim altarpiece. Monstrous figures surround him, tormenting him with figments of his artistic imagination *(Wir plagen dich mit deines eignen Abgrunds Bildern)*. The nightmare vision vanishes, to be replaced by another scene from the Isenheim altarpiece, *St. Anthony in the Hermitage of St. Paul.* Albrecht appears as St. Paul, explaining that Mathis has a talent too great to renounce *(Du bist zum Bilden übermenschlich begabt)*. As the city of Mainz appears, Mathis at last accepts his God-given gift and his duty as an artist.

TABLEAU VII In Mathis' studio in Mainz, surrounded by completed paintings and work in progress, Mathis lies asleep. Nearby, Ursula sits next to the sleeping, mortally ill Regina. Reflecting on the driven productivity of Mathis' life since his return, Ursula wonders at his exhaustion, so like death yet so unlike it *(Das ist der Kreuzweg, wo sie Tod und Leben scheiden)*. Regina awakens and describes how, in his painting *The Entombment,* Mathis caught the look in her dead father's eyes. She gives Ursula the ribbon and asks her to return it to Mathis. Ursula fetches Mathis, who joins her by the dying girl's bedside. After an orchestral interlude depicting *The Entombment,* the studio is seen again, this time by morning light, with all the paintings gone. Albrecht arrives, upset to learn that Mathis considers his work finished: body and spirit no longer have the strength to do it justice. Resigned, Albrecht embraces him in farewell and leaves. Mathis looks to the last stretch of his journey *(Auf denn zum letzten Stück des Weges)*, putting in a chest a few possessions—a scroll ("what I did well"), a ruler and compass ("what I strove for"), paints and brushes ("what I made"), a gold chain from Albrecht ("what brought me honor"), some books ("what troubled me")—and the ribbon ("what I loved").

ENGELBERT HUMPERDINCK
1854–1921

*T*he impact of Richard Wagner on opera was so great that it seemed for a time that no future composition could be unaffected by his work. One was either a Wagnerian or an anti-Wagnerian. The master himself urged young composers to find something new of their own rather than imitate him, but this was easier said than done.

One solution to the problem was a return to the German romanticism that had originally inspired Wagner—that is, to follow in the footsteps of Beethoven, Marschner, Lortzing, and Weber. This was the path chosen by Engelbert Humperdinck and adopted by his pupil Siegfried Wagner, Richard's son. Leaving the Wagner legacy to Richard Strauss, they evoked a less ambitious aesthetic, with roots in folklore and the popular theater.

Humperdinck's music, to be sure, often sounds Wagnerian, but his approach to mythology (in the form of folklore) is anything but monumental; in fact, it is not always especially serious. Born near Bonn, the composer started out to be an architect. Having taken up music, he was befriended by the Wagner family and invited to Bayreuth, where he assisted in preparing *Parsifal* for publication. Despite this immersion in the Wagner mystique, he was able to find an alternative to Wagnerism, and German-speaking audiences were delighted when *Hänsel und Gretel* was first performed, in 1893 in Weimar, with Strauss conducting.

Humperdinck visited the United States twice, supervising the Met's first *Hänsel* in November 1905 and returning in 1910 for the world premiere of

Königskinder. Though the latter was created to meet popular demand generated by *Hänsel,* audiences were disappointed, and the presence of Puccini, supervising the world premiere of *La Fanciulla del West,* cast a shadow over Humperdinck's last New York visit. With the advent of World War I and a period of general eclipse for German opera in America, his popularity suffered. After World War II, however, the Met management reported that it had more requests for a revival of *Hänsel und Gretel* than for that of any other opera. Ever since its premiere, which took place just before Christmas, *Hänsel* has been especially associated with the Christmas season, and despite its appeal to mature musical tastes it is still habitually considered a children's opera.

HÄNSEL UND GRETEL

THREE ACTS
MUSIC: Engelbert Humperdinck
TEXT (German): Adelheid Wette (the composer's sister),
    after a story by the Brothers Grimm
WORLD PREMIERE: Weimar, Hoftheater, December 23, 1893
U.S. PREMIERE: New York, Daly's Theater, October 8, 1895
    (in English)
METROPOLITAN OPERA PREMIERE: November 25, 1905

CHARACTERS

Hänsel . . . . Mezzo-Soprano
Gretel, *his sister* . . . . Soprano
The Witch . . . . Mezzo-Soprano
Gertrude, *mother of Hänsel and Gretel* . . . . Soprano
Peter, *their father, a broom maker* . . . . Baritone
Sandman . . . . Soprano
Dew Fairy . . . . Soprano
Angels, woodland voices, children

ACT I At some indeterminate time in the past, in a clearing in the Harz Mountains near the Ilsenstein peak, two children, Hänsel and Gretel, amuse themselves while they are supposed to be working at broom making; they sing nursery rhymes to each other *(Suse, liebe Suse).* Gretel feels hungry and wishes their mother would come home; to cheer Hänsel, she shows him a pitcher of fresh milk that a neighbor brought earlier in the day, daring him to taste it. Bored with work, the children enjoy themselves dancing (*Brüderchen, komm, tanz' mit mir*), ending up in a heap on the floor. At the height of their merrymaking, Gertrude, their mother, returns home, angry to find that the children have not been working. She accidentally knocks over and breaks the milk pitcher, scolding Hänsel when he dares to laugh. To chastise the children, she sends them into the woods with a basket, telling them to gather strawberries for supper. Then she sits down to lament their poverty: there is nothing in the house to feed the children. As she dozes in exhaustion, the voice of her husband, the broom maker Peter, is heard approaching. Happy with the day's broom sales, evidently having had a drink or two, he enters in a jovial mood. When he wakes his wife, she grumbles at his carefree attitude, but he shows he has brought food, going on to describe how a festival in town enabled him to find more customers than usual (*Drüben hinterm Herrenwald*). He asks where the children are, and when Gertrude says she sent them into the woods, he is shocked; he reminds her that there is a dreadful Witch who lives on the Ilsenstein, riding around on a broomstick and baking children into gingerbread. The mother rushes out to look for them, followed by her husband.

ACT II   As afternoon shadows lengthen, Gretel sits in the forest under a huge fir tree, making a garland of wildflowers while Hänsel looks for strawberries. Gretel sings a song about a "little man" who stands in the forest—in reality it is a wild mushroom with a black cap (*Ein Männlein steht im Walde*). Hänsel brings back a basket full of berries, but in their excitement—playing a game about a cuckoo ducking into a nest—the children eat them all. When Hänsel goes to pick more, he finds that it is getting too dark to see; this alarms them both, and their fear increases when they realize they cannot remember the way home. They imagine goblins in the surrounding woods, but a kindly Sandman appears, reassures them, and tells them it is time to sleep (*Der kleine Sandmann bin ich*). Drowsily, the children kneel and recite their evening prayer (*Abends, will ich schlafen gehn*), describing the fourteen angels that will guard them. As they fall asleep on the mossy ground, a stairway leading toward the sky appears, and the angels come down to keep watch.

ACT III   As morning mist shrouds the scene, the Dew Fairy appears, calling on nature to awaken (*Der kleine Taumann heiss' ich*). The children stir from their sleep and compare notes on the dream they both had, about angels surrounding them. The mist gradually lifts, revealing a candied house surrounded by a fence of gingerbread children. Dazzled by the sight and smell (*Wie duftet's von dorten*), Hänsel and Gretel approach it. When Hansel dares to break off a piece of cake from a corner of the house, a voice from within asks, "Who is nibbling at my house?" Pretending they heard nothing but the wind, the children continue to eat, but the Witch steals outside and ties Hänsel up.

When he struggles free, she hexes both children with a magic spell *(Hocus, pocus, Holderbusch!)* and locks Hänsel in the stable, ordering Gretel to help her in the house. When the Witch goes to get food to fatten Hänsel, he whispers to Gretel to pretend to cooperate with the Witch. Outside the house stands a large oven, into which the Witch plans to put Gretel *(Ja, Gretelchen, wirst bald ein Brätelchen!);* in wild delight she seizes a broomstick and rides about on it. Stopping in front of the stable, she asks Hänsel to poke his finger out so she can see whether he is getting fat enough to cook. He pokes a chicken bone out instead, convincing the nearsighted Witch he is still too scrawny. She sends Gretel to fetch more goodies for Hänsel. While the Witch is feeding them to him, Gretel sneaks behind her and repeats the words of the spell *(Hocus, pocus, Holderbusch!),* thereby breaking it. When the Witch asks Gretel to look in the oven, the girl—coached by Hänsel—pretends not to be able to see anything, causing the impatient Witch to lean in and look for herself. The children shove her into the oven and close the door, rejoicing that the Witch is no more *(Juchhei! Nun ist die Hexe tot).* They dance gaily and start to gather goodies to take home, but just then the oven makes ominous noises and explodes. As if by magic, the fence of gingerbread children comes to life. By touching each child, Gretel returns them to their normal state, while Hänsel repeats the Witch's spell to free them. All the children are dancing as Peter and Gertrude arrive on the scene. A gingerbread Witch is found in the oven, and all give thanks to God for their deliverance.

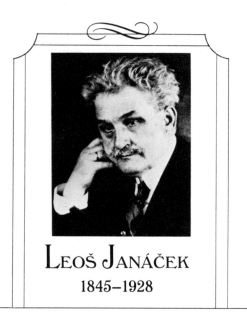

LEOŠ JANÁČEK
1845–1928

*L*eoš Janáček has often been described either as a romantic born too late or a modernist born too early. He did not carry on with the felicitous lyricism of Smetana and Dvořák, yet his style, more innovative than theirs, was too advanced to earn him the recognition later accorded to Bartók. As a result, he spent most of his life in relative obscurity, going about his business as an organist and pedagogue in his native city of Brno. Janáček was a Moravian, unlike Dvořák and Smetana, who were Bohemians, living in Prague, the cosmopolitan center of Czech musical life. Another cause of Janáček's not getting his due was undoubtedly his outspoken nature: a critic as well as a teacher and composer, he expressed himself all too frankly about his colleagues' work.

Janáček proved to be a late bloomer. A few years older than Strauss or Puccini, he wrote most of his operas late in life and was universally acclaimed for them only after World War II. Conceived around the turn of the century, *Jenůfa* was his first major opera. Like Mascagni's *Cavalleria Rusticana,* which created a wide stir at the time, *Jenůfa* is a veristic study of peasant life, but Janáček went beyond journalistic realism. Not content to accept death as a satisfactory conclusion to a drama, as the Italians had always been, he added the element of catharsis prized in Russian and other Slavic literature. The everyday credibility of his characters serves to further the emotional power of this transcendent conclusion.

Today, Janáček's laconic musical language and idiosyncratic, spare orchestration are in tune with the times, and several of his operas, including *The Makropoulos Case, The Cunning Little Vixen,* and *From the House of the Dead,* have made a place for themselves on international stages. Despite the composer's use of dialect and his emphasis on the nuances of conversational speech in shaping and accenting his vocal line, careful translators have found that these operas can be quite intelligible in foreign languages.

To the final decade of Janáček's life belongs *Kát'a Kabanová,* produced in Brno in 1921. Arguably the most passionate and fully realized of his operas, it reflects his pan-Slavic enthusiasms and his sympathy with youth in its struggle against rigid custom. *Wozzeck* had yet to be written by Alban Berg, but at least one scene in *Kát'a,* the interview between Kabanicha and the drunken Dikoy, anticipates it. Furthermore, a warmth of romanticism animates the opera and gives its story special poignancy. Unlike the late romanticism of Mahler or Strauss, it is not pervaded with fatigue, disillusion, or intimations of decadence. Anachronistically, it has the freshness of that second youth which was Janáček's remarkable old age.

A few months before his death, in 1928, Janáček attended the Prague premiere of his penultimate opera, *The Makropoulos Case.* His final opera, *From the House of the Dead,* after Dostoevsky's memoirs of Siberian prison life, was complete in manuscript but not yet copied out for performance when the seventy-four-year-old composer died of pneumonia.

The Makropoulos Case is a less than satisfactory translation of the title *Věc Makropulos,* literally "The Makropoulos Thing" (referring chiefly but not exclusively to the alchemist's formula around which the plot revolves). Only if the word *case* is read in a general way, meaning "instance," is the breadth of the Czech term suggested. The play, considered a comedy by its well-known author, Karel Čapek (1890–1938), contained much more dialogue than Janáček's expertly trimmed libretto, which enabled the composer to clothe with musical color and emotion the dry, ironic language of the original. The result is an opera of a serious, compassionate character, its climax achieved musically as well as dramatically. Čapek, who admired Janáček, allowed him a free hand with the text, though he could not see why it would appeal to a musician. Part of its fascination for Janáček, perhaps, was its reference to the cultural flowering of an earlier period (the turn of the sixteenth century to the seventeenth), when Rudolf II, last of the Prague-based Habsburg rulers, attracted artists and scientists to his court.

JENŮFA

THREE ACTS

MUSIC: Leoš Janáček

TEXT (Czech): by the composer, based on a story by Gabriela
Preissová

WORLD PREMIERE: Brno, Deutsches Nationaltheater, January 21,
1904

U.S. PREMIERE: Metropolitan Opera, December 6, 1924
(in German)

CHARACTERS

Jenůfa, *Kostelnička's stepdaughter* . . . . Soprano
Kostelnička Buryjovka, *Jenůfa's stepmother* . . . . Soprano
Grandmother Buryjovka, *owner of the mill* . . . . Contralto
Laca Klemeň⎫
Števa Buryja⎭ *grandsons of Grandmother Buryjovka* . . . . Tenors
Mill Foreman . . . . Baritone
The Mayor . . . . Bass
His Wife . . . . Mezzo-soprano
Karolka, *his daughter* . . . . Mezzo-soprano
Barena, *servant at the mill* . . . . Soprano
Jano, *shepherd boy* . . . . Soprano
Musicians, villagers

ACT I   Outside a rural mill in late-nineteenth-century Moravia on a spring afternoon. Jenůfa, a young woman who lives there with her grandmother, is looking anxiously into the distance, praying that her cousin Števa will soon return. She is engaged to him and is secretly carrying his child. He has gone to face the draft board, and Jenůfa fears that she will be ruined if he has to leave for military service without marrying her. While Grandmother Buryjovka chides her for not helping with the work, Jenůfa's stepcousin Laca comments bitterly that he is being treated like a mere hired hand. Jenůfa is uneasy around Laca, who seems to see right through her. The old Mill Foreman appears and sharpens Laca's knife to help him with his whittling; meanwhile, Laca needles Jenůfa about her preference for Števa. When she goes back into the house, the two men comment on her attractiveness. Laca admits he loves her and does not want her to marry Števa. When the Foreman reports that Števa was not drafted, Jenůfa's pleasure at hearing this further annoys Laca. Her spirits are dampened by the arrival of her stepmother, the stern Kostelnička, but the general mood picks up at the sound of happy voices in the distance. While the new army recruits look forward to getting away from home (*Všeci sa ženija*), Števa is delighted not to be going and joins in the merrymaking. Jenůfa is distressed to see that he has been drinking, because—as Kostelnička makes clear—unless Števa stays sober for a year, he will not receive permission to marry. Laca alone is grateful that Kostelnička is tough on the spoiled Števa. Grandmother Buryjovka comforts Jenůfa, assuring her that every couple has to go through trials (*Každý párek si musi svoje trápeni přestát*). Jenůfa tells Števa they must be married quickly, but he, unnerved by Kostelnička's hostility, makes excuses. He leaves, the others return to their chores, and Laca picks up a flower Števa dropped—given to him by one of the village girls—offering to pin it on Jenůfa's hat. He tries to embrace her, but she resists, and in the scuffle he cuts her cheek with the knife he has been holding. Grandmother Buryjovka and Barena, the maid, assume it was an accident, but the Foreman accuses Laca of doing it on purpose.

ACT II   In Kostelnička's house the following winter. Jenůfa has given birth to a son. Kostelnička has concealed Jenůfa and the baby in her house, pretending her stepdaughter went to Vienna to look for domestic work, but the situation cannot continue undetected for long, and the desperate woman wishes God would take the unwanted child (*Co jsem se namodlila*). Števa appears at the door: Kostelnička has sent for him. Still intimidated by her, and further put off by the scar on Jenůfa's cheek, he says he no longer loves Jenůfa—besides, he is engaged to Karolka, the Mayor's daughter. When Jenůfa calls out in her sleep, Števa makes a hasty exit. Kostelnička is next visited by Laca, who inquires about Jenůfa. Trusting in his love for the girl, Kostelnička blurts out the truth, but then—seeing Laca hesitant to accept Števa's child—she adds a lie, saying it died. She sends Laca to find out when Števa's wedding will take place. Determined to "carry the boy to God" (*Já Pánubohu chlapce zanesu*), Kostelnička takes the infant from Jenůfa's room and runs outdoors. When Jenůfa wakes, she is frightened to find her stepmother and baby gone. She prays to the Virgin to protect her child (*Zdrávas královno*), then jumps in terror when there is a knock at the window: Kostelnička, shaking too badly to unlock the door, passes in the key. Jenůfa, she says, has been delirious for two days, during which the baby died. When the shocked girl asks about Števa, Kostelnička tells her to think of Laca instead. Laca returns: while Jenůfa thanks him for his concern, she says she has been ruined and cannot think of marriage. Seeing his sincerity, she changes her mind, and Kostelnička gives them her blessing, still cursing Števa. When a gust of wind blows the window open, the older woman cries out that it is as though Death himself looked in.

ACT III   Three months later, the two women and Laca prepare for the wedding reception in the same room. The devout Kostelnička, tormented by her crime, has grown haggard and jumpy. She does her best to welcome the guests as they appear—the Mayor's Wife, first to arrive with her husband, comments on the austere wedding decorations, so contrary to local custom. Laca gives Jenůfa flowers and says he will spend the rest of his life making up for the harm he once did her. Števa arrives somewhat sheepishly with his fiancée. As the half-brothers shake hands, Jenůfa says each has his qualities: Števa is handsome, Laca good-hearted. Village girls arrive with a bouquet and a song for the bride *(Ej, mamko, maměnko moja!)*. Since it will soon be time to go to church, Grandmother Buryjovka proceeds with blessing the couple *(Tož já vám žehnám)*. As they kneel to receive Kostelnička's blessing, there is a commotion outside and Jano, the shepherd boy, runs in. He says that a drowned infant has been found under the ice in the river. Jenůfa recognizes one of the little garments that Jano is carrying and cries that it is her own baby. The outraged populace is ready to stone her until Kostelnička announces that the fault is hers—she got rid of the child for Jenůfa's sake *(Ještě jsem tu já!)*. Revolted at first, Jenůfa finally asks the praying Kostelnička to rise *(Vsaňte, pěstounko moja)*, saying that only God should judge her. Brokenhearted, Kostelnička says she realizes how selfish her act was. Forgiven by her stepdaughter, she is led away by the Mayor. When everyone else has gone, Jenůfa tells Laca he must go too *(Odešli . . . Jdi také!)*, adding he is the best man she ever knew—one who sinned, like her, only out of love. Laca insists that whatever fate holds in store, he wants to share her life. At last Jenůfa recognizes "that greater love in which God rejoices," as she and Laca look ahead to a new life.

KÁŤA KABANOVÁ

THREE ACTS
MUSIC: Leoš Janáček
TEXT (Czech): V. Červinka, based on Alexander Ostrovsky's play
   The Storm
WORLD PREMIERE: Brno, November 23, 1921
U.S. PREMIERE: Cleveland, Karamu House, November 26, 1957

CHARACTERS

Káťa Kabanová . . . . Soprano
Marfa Kabanová (Kabanicha), *rich widow* . . . . Contralto

KÁT'A KABANOVÁ

Varvara, *Kabanovs' foster child* . . . . Mezzo-Soprano
Boris Grigorjevič, *Dikoj's nephew* . . . . Tenor
Tichon Kabanov, *Kát'a's husband* . . . . Tenor
Váňa Kudrjáš, *Dikoj's clerk* . . . . Tenor
Kuligin, *friend of Váňa* . . . . Baritone
Savěl Dikoj, *rich merchant* . . . . Bass

Townspeople, servants

ACT I The small Russian town of Kalinově, sometime in the 1860s. The young clerk Váňa Kudrjáš rhapsodizes over the afternoon view of the Volga, to the amusement of the literal-minded housekeeper of the adjoining Kabanov home. They see two men approaching—the overbearing merchant Dikoj and his nephew, Boris Grigorjevič—and leave quickly as Dikoj continues his castigation of the young man. When they discover that Kabanicha, matriarch of the Kabanov family, is not at home, Dikoj stalks off, leaving Boris to explain to his friend Váňa why he puts up with such abuse: his parents are dead, and in order to collect his inheritance, he must treat his uncle with respect (*Rodiče nás v Moskvě dobře vychovali*). As members of the Kabanov household return from vespers, Boris confesses to Váňa that he is secretly in love with Kát'a, the young wife. The two men depart as old Kabanicha berates her son, Tichon, for his lack of attentiveness. He tries to please her, as does his wife, Kát'a, who tells the old woman that they love and respect her. At a sharp reply from Kabanicha, Kát'a enters the house, soon followed by her mother-in-law, when Tichon's temper snaps at being told he spoils his wife. Tichon complains to Varvara, the foster daughter of the family, who retorts he would rather drink and forget his troubles than stand up for Kát'a's rights.

§ Inside the house, Kát'a tells Varvara how free and happy she felt as a child (*Ach, byla jsem zcela jinši!*), constantly dreaming. Even now, she admits, she has dreamed of having a lover. Before she can say more about the man who attracts her, Tichon comes to say good-bye before a short trip to Kazan at his mother's behest. Kát'a begs him not to go or else to take her along, but he refuses. When she asks him to make her swear to speak to no strangers during his absence, he wonders what is wrong with her. Kabanicha announces that it is time to leave, adding that Tichon must tell his wife how to behave while he is gone. Tichon dutifully repeats that Kát'a must treat Kabanicha like her own mother and always act with propriety. Then he bows to his mother, kisses her and Kát'a and hurries away.

ACT II As the women work on embroidery, Kabanicha criticizes Kát'a for not making a display of grief over Tichon's absence. After she has left, Varvara shows Kát'a the key to the far part of the garden: she plans to meet her lover there and hints that Kát'a might want to do the same, pressing the key into her hand. Kát'a hestiates (*Vida! Neštěstí!*) but decides that fate has willed it: she is going to meet Boris. As darkness approaches, she steps outside. Kabanicha reenters with the drunken Dikoj, who says she is the only person he can talk to. He complains that people take advantage of his softheartedness: for example, a peasant recently angered him (*Kdysi—o velikém postě*), but he ended up on his knees to ask the man's forgiveness. As he demonstrates, blubbering, Kabanicha primly tells him to get hold of himself.

§ Waiting for Varvara in the garden, Váňa amuses himself with a song about an independent-minded young girl like her (*Poh zahrádce děvucha již*). To his surprise, Boris appears, having received a message to come there. Varvara arrives, cheerfully picking up Váňa's song, and they head for a walk by the river. When Kát'a appears, Boris proclaims his love. She is hesitant at first, seeing only sin and ruin, but finally her pent-up feelings pour out, and she embraces him. They, too, go for a walk as Váňa and Varvara return, Varvara explaining her precautions in case the old lady should look for any of them. As the rapturous voices of the second couple are heard, Váňa and Varvara call to them (through the verses of another folk song) that it's time to go home.

ACT III   Váňa and a friend, Kuligin, are walking near the river when an approaching storm drives them to shelter in a ruined building, where they are joined by other strollers. When Dikoj appears, Váňa tries to conciliate him by talking about a new invention, the lightning rod, but this only angers Dikoj, who insists that storms are not electricity but God's punishment (*Jak-ápak elektřina?*). When the rain lets up, people start to leave the shelter, and Váňa runs into Boris and Varvara. The girl reports that Tichon is back, and Kát'a seems very upset. The men retreat when they see Kabanicha approaching with Tichon and Kát'a. Bystanders at first assume that Kát'a is frightened by the returning storm, but she makes a confession to Tichon in front of everyone, saying she dallied with Boris during her husband's absence. Then she runs out into the tempest.

§ Later, as evening approaches and the storm has passed, Tichon looks frantically for Kát'a at another spot along the river bank. While they are helping him, Varvara and Váňa decide to escape to Moscow, where they can lead a life of their own. As the searchers move off, Kát'a appears, aware that her confession served only to dishonor her and humiliate Boris. Her life is a constant torment, and she longs to see her lover one last time. He wanders in, surprised to find her, and they embrace. He says his uncle is sending him away to another town—but what will become of Kát'a? Her mind wandering, she bids him farewell. As he walks off in sorrow, she thinks how nature will renew itself over her grave (*Ptáčci přiletí na mohylu*), then throws herself into the river. On the far bank, Kuligin sees her jump and calls for help. Tichon rushes back, followed by Kabanicha, whom he blames for Kát'a's self-destruction. Meanwhile, bystanders fetch a boat and try to help. When Dikoj brings Kát'a's body and lays it on the ground, Tichon flings himself down, sobbing. Coldly, Kabanicha bows to the bystanders, thanking them for their assistance.

THE MAKROPOULOS CASE

THREE ACTS
MUSIC: Leoš Janáček
TEXT (Czech): the composer, based on Karel Čapek's play
WORLD PREMIERE: Brno, December 18, 1926
U.S. PREMIERE: San Francisco, November 19, 1966

CHARACTERS

Emilia Marty, *singer* . . . . Dramatic Soprano
Krista, *Vítek's daughter* . . . . Mezzo-Soprano
Albert Gregor . . . . Tenor
Vítek, *clerk* . . . . Tenor
Janek . . . . Tenor
Count Hauk-Šendorf, *old man* . . . . Operetta Tenor
Jaroslav Prus, *Janek's father, nobleman* . . . . Baritone
Dr. Kolenatý, *lawyer* . . . . Bass-Baritone
A Cleaning Woman . . . . Contralto
A Stagehand . . . . Bass
Maid, doctor, servants

ACT I   The office of the lawyer Kolenatý, Prague, 1922. Vítek, a clerk, hunting through some old files, notes that the case of *Gregor* v. *Prus,* which has been revived, dates back almost a century. Albert Gregor, an interested party in the case, inquires how it is going: Kolenatý has taken it to the supreme court but has not yet returned. Vítek's daughter, Krista, a young singer, runs in, babbling enthusiastically about Emilia Marty, a soprano with whom she (in a bit part) has been rehearsing at the opera. To her surprise, Marty appears at the door, shown in by Kolenatý. The diva inquires about the Gregor case and, learning that Albert Gregor is one of the parties, says he might as well stay. In 1827, Kolenatý explains, Baron Ferdinand Josef Prus died without will or heirs, whereupon a certain Ferdinand Gregor laid claim to his estate, saying Prus had promised it to him verbally; Prus' cousin contested this. Marty interrupts to say that Ferdinand was really the baron's illegitimate son by an opera singer, Ellian MacGregor. When Kolenatý says that the current

Gregor is about to lose the case for lack of evidence, Marty asks what he would need to win. A will, says Kolenatý. Marty then describes a cupboard in the Prus house where this and other documents were kept. Kolenatý thinks she is making it up, but Gregor believes her and insists that Kolenatý investigate. Fascinated with Marty, Gregor converses with her after the lawyer leaves. He tells her that he has counted on the inheritance and would shoot himself if he lost the case. Though she brushes aside Gregor's infatuation, she nevertheless tries to enlist his help in getting certain documents that she feels sure will be found with the will. Kolenatý reappears, this time with his adversary, the aristocratic Jaroslav Prus. The will was found where Marty said it would be; Prus congratulates Gregor on the victory that will be his—if evidence can be found that the illegitimate Ferdinand was indisputably Ferdinand Gregor. Marty says she will provide this proof.

Act II   On the empty stage at the opera house, a Stagehand and Cleaning Woman discuss Marty's glamour and the success of her performance. Prus enters in search of Marty, followed by his son, Janek, and Krista. The diva enters, contemptuous of everyone—first of the tongue-tied Janek, who immediately falls under her spell, then of Gregor, who arrives with flowers that she reminds him he cannot afford. Her mood softens when a feebleminded old man, Hauk-Šendorf, wanders in, babbling about Eugenia, a gypsy he loved fifty years ago. Assuring him that Eugenia is not dead, Marty asks him in Spanish for a kiss, calling him by the nickname Maxi. When the others leave, Prus stays to question Marty about Ellian MacGregor, whose love letters he has read, and who he suspects may have been the "Elina Makropoulos" (same initials) specified on Ferdinand's birth certificate as the mother. Since illegitimate children bore the mother's name, a descendant of "Ferdinand Makropoulos" would have to be found; otherwise the estate would remain in Prus' hands. Marty offers to pay for an unopened envelope that Prus found with the other papers, but he refuses and leaves, feeling triumphant. Gregor reenters and tells the exhausted Marty he loves her desperately; her response is to doze off, at which he too leaves. She awakens to find Janek standing there and asks him, as a favor, to get her the envelope marked "To be handed to my son Ferdinand," which is in his father's house. Prus overhears and sends Janek away. Then he agrees to give Marty the envelope if she will spend the night with him.

Act III   The next morning, in Marty's hotel room, Prus gives her the envelope but feels cheated by her coldness as a lover. A maid announces there is a message for Prus downstairs, then starts to fix Marty's hair. When Prus returns, he says that Janek has just killed himself on account of his sudden hopeless infatuation with Marty. The diva's unconcerned response infuriates Prus, but they are interrupted by Hauk-Šendorf, who thinks he and Marty are about to leave for Spain. She humors him, really wanting to leave, but soon Gregor appears, accompanied by Kolenatý, Krista, and a doctor who leads Hauk-Šendorf away. Kolenatý has noticed the similarity between her autograph and the writing on a document signed "Ellian Magregor"; he suspects Marty of forgery. Since she is uncooperative, the others search her papers. When she pulls a revolver, Gregor knocks it from her hand. Changing her tack, Marty says she will talk to them after she gets dressed. While she is in the next room, they continue searching her effects, finding evidence of various pseudonyms, all with the initials "E.M." Prus confirms that Elina Makropoulos' writing is identical to Ellian Magregor's. Marty returns with a bottle and a glass and wearily confesses that she was born Elina Makropoulos in Crete in 1575—which she corrects to 1585, making her 337 years old. Her father, Hieronymos, was court physician to Rudolf II (who ruled in Bohemia 1576–1612). Ordered by his master to develop an elixir of eternal life, the alchemist tried it on his sixteen-year-old daughter; when she fell into a coma, he was imprisoned as a fraud, but shortly afterward the girl recovered and escaped. Some years later she gave the formula to her lover Baron Prus; she also bore him a son, which makes her Albert Gregor's grandmother several times over. Since the formula is good for only 300 years, she now needed to recover it in order to survive. Life having lost its meaning for her, however, she feels ready to die. At first no one believes her story, but little by little they realize that it must be true. Life should not last too long, she says—that way it keeps its value. She offers the formula (which was in the mysterious sealed envelope) to anyone who wants it, but no one will touch it—except Krista, who sets fire to it with a candle. Muttering "Pater hemon," the first words of the Lord's Prayer in Greek, Marty sinks lifeless to the floor.

SCOTT JOPLIN
1868–1917

*I*t is thought that Scott Joplin, the master of ragtime, was the first black American to write an opera. Using his command of popular piano music to create an ambitious stage work, he wrote *A Guest of Honor,* a "ragtime opera," in 1903, the manuscript of which appears to have been lost. Though he failed to interest any producers in his work, he went on to write *Treemonisha* against considerable odds, sacrificing his savings to have the piano scored printed. Though it is an accepted opinion today that the true road to American opera lies in the Broadway musical, Joplin was too far ahead of his time: *Treemonisha* could find no backers. Seriously ill, he died soon after it was finished.

In 1972, in the wake of Vera Brodsky Lawrence's collected edition of Joplin's music, *Treemonisha* was finally staged, in Atlanta, Georgia. In 1975 the famous Houston production followed, for which Gunther Schuller supplied an orchestration in keeping with the style of the period (Joplin's orchestration had been lost). Frank Corsaro, stage director for the Houston production, called *Treemonisha* "a sort of *Magic Flute,* American style."

TREEMONISHA

THREE ACTS
MUSIC: Scott Joplin
TEXT (English): the composer
WORLD PREMIERE: Atlanta, Morehouse College, January, 1972

CHARACTERS

Treemonisha	Soprano
Monisha, *her foster mother*	Soprano
Lucy, *Treemonisha's friend*	Soprano
Zodzetrick, *charlatan conjurer*	Tenor
Remus	Tenor
Andy	Tenor
Luddud, *partner to Zodzetrick*	Baritone
Ned, *Monisha's husband*	Bass-Baritone
Parson Alltalk	Bass

Simon, cornhuskers, conjurers

ACT I   A plantation in Arkansas, September 1884. Ned and his wife, Monisha, adopted a foundling girl eighteen years earlier. They named her Treemonisha and bartered their services with a white family to provide the growing girl with an education. Zodzetrick, a conjurer of old voodoo-style superstition, tries to sell Monisha a talisman, but Ned prevents the sale. Treemonisha also considers the conjurer a fraud and tactfully tries to reform him, but he threatens her with bad luck. When some cornhuskers appear, all form a circle for a lively dance *(We're goin' around)* before settling down to the task of husking. When she notices that the other girls are wearing wreaths on their heads, Treemonisha starts to pick leaves to make one for herself, but Monisha tells her not to take them from one particular tree: it is sacred to her, because under its branches she found the baby who grew up to be her daughter *(One autumn night)*. Everyone is surprised at this revelation, since Monisha never even hinted that the girl was adopted. Monisha goes on to tell how she and Ned concealed the circumstances of finding the baby, then raised her as their own *(We brought you up to believe)*. When Parson Alltalk arrives, everyone kneels in prayer, and he delivers an impromptu sermon on upright behavior *(Lis'en friends)*. After he leaves, Lucy—who went looking for leaves with Treemonisha—runs in to say that the two conjurers Zodzetrick and Luddud tried to kidnap both of them and succeeded in riding off with Treemonisha. The men leave in pursuit, urged on by the women.

ACT II   Deep in the woods, a huge wasps' nest hangs ominously in the background as the conjurers hold a meeting (*'Tis true, 'tis true*). Zodzetrick and Luddud enter with the captive Treemonisha. All the conjurers except one agree she should be punished for her disbelief. When they lead her off, eight bears enter the clearing and frolic, then lumber off when they hear voices. At Simon's suggestion, the returning conjurers prepare to throw Treemonisha into the wasps' nest, but they in turn are scared off by "de devil," whom Treemonisha alone recognizes as her family's friend Remus in disguise. He leads the girl away to safety.

§ In a cotton field, workers are taking a break (*We will rest awhile*) when Remus and Treemonisha happen upon them, ask directions, and proceed on their way. When the field hands hear the signal from their own plantation, indicating the end of the workday, they rejoice (*Aunt Dinah has blowed de horn*).

ACT III   At their cabin, Monisha worries about her missing daughter (*I want to see my child*) while Ned tries to comfort her. When Remus comes in with Treemonisha, they are overjoyed. Visitors soon arrive, including a posse with the captured Zodzetrick and Luddud. When the men prepare to beat the conjurers, Treemonisha stops them (*You will do evil for evil*), saying that a stern lecture is what the culprits need. This is delivered by Remus (*Wrong is never right*) and Ned (*When villains ramble far and near*). Treemonisha asks everyone to shake hands with the conjurers and forgive them for her sake. Then the neighbors urge Treemonisha to help them rise from ignorance to a better life (*We will trust you are our leader*). Doubtful at first, she agrees, and a dance of celebration follows (*A real slow drag*).

ERICH WOLFGANG KORNGOLD

1897–1957

*L*ike his contemporary Kurt Weill, Erich Wolfgang Korngold led a second life in the New World. From 1934 to 1947, beginning with Max Reinhardt's *A Midsummer Night's Dream,* the Viennese émigré scored some twenty films, mostly for Hollywood (including some Errol Flynn epics). His film work, for which he is remembered today, has inspired a revival of interest in his earlier "serious" music, most of it written in Europe, and in a few symphonic scores composed after he retired from films.

Before Hitler closed the door to Jewish musicians, the two most famous opera composers in the German-speaking world, next to Richard Strauss, were Franz Schreker and Korngold. Because their works are now largely forgotten, it is difficult to imagine the extent of their former popularity, which rivaled Puccini's. Erich, the son of Julius Korngold, an influential critic who succeeded Eduard Hanslick on *Die Neue Freie Presse,* was a true child prodigy: he was only about ten when Mahler recommended that he study with Alexander von Zemlinsky, who Korngold later said taught him everything. Though his music is freely eclectic—*Die Tote Stadt* borrows not only from the familiar Strauss but also from his very recent *Die Frau ohne Schatten*—Korngold was more than an imitator, for he possessed an inborn sense of theatrical timing and an extraordinary ear for orchestration.

DIE TOTE STADT

THREE ACTS

MUSIC: Erich Korngold

TEXT (German): Paul Schott (actually the composer and his father), from Georges Rodenbach's novel *Bruges la Morte*

WORLD PREMIERE: Hamburg, Stadttheater, and Cologne, Stadttheater, December 4, 1920

U.S. PREMIERE: Metropolitan Opera, November 19, 1921

CHARACTERS

Marietta, *dancer*
The Apparition of Marie } . . . . Soprano
Brigitta, *housekeeper* . . . . Mezzo-Soprano
Juliette and Lucienne, *dancers*. Sopranos
Paul, *painter* . . . . Tenor
Count Albert, *admirer of Marietta's* . . . . Tenor
Frank, *his friend* . . . . Baritone
Fritz, *actor* . . . . Baritone
Dancers, nuns, actors, and children

ACT I   The action takes place in Bruges, Belgium, late in the nineteenth century. As the curtain rises, the housekeeper Brigitta is explaining to Paul's friend Frank that her employer has created a shrine in his home to his wife, Marie, who died some years earlier. Paul has shut himself off from the world, but now he appears, excited at having met a woman who so closely resembles Marie that he feels she has been brought back to life (*Nein, nein, sie lebt!*). Though Frank warns of the danger of such fantasies, Paul, being an artist, insists on believing in his vision. He has invited the unknown woman to his house, and presently she arrives. She is Marietta—a dancer, cheerful and coquettish. When he puts Marie's shawl around her and hands her Marie's lute, which had been hanging on the wall, she obliges with a song about two lovers who will soon be parted by death (*Glück, das mir verblieb*). When the voices of some of her colleagues are heard in the street, Paul learns that Marietta is a dancer; she says dancing is her very life (*O Tanz, o Rausch!*). She is due at a rehearsal of *Robert le Diable*, in which she dances Hélène. Inadvertently, she uncovers the life-size portrait of Marie and is struck by its resemblance to her. After she has left, a vision of Marie steps out of the portrait to ask Paul whether he still loves her. She senses he is attracted by another woman—life beckons—and as she disappears, he imagines Marietta in her place, dancing seductively.

ACT II   As at the close of preceding act, Marie's voice is heard saying that life beckons to Paul. His vision continues, showing events that will happen in the future. On a canal in Bruges, a convent and Marietta's house are visible. Walking in the autumn mist at evening, Paul meets his housekeeper, Brigitta, who has joined the convent because of loyalty to her former mistress, though Paul protests he never broke faith with his departed wife. Frank appears, warning Paul that his attraction to Marietta is unhealthy; when it becomes apparent that Frank himself is attracted to Marietta, Paul breaks with him, snatching away the key to Marietta's house that Frank says she gave him. Paul steps into hiding as a boat approaches, carrying members of the theatrical troupe and Count Albert, another admirer of Marietta's. Fritz, who plays Pierrot, serenades the moon, likening Marietta to a fickle Columbine (*O Mond, vernimm die traurige Litanei*). Marietta appears from her house, flirts with the count and proposes a toast condemning Bruges (*Schach Brügge!*). Fritz obliges Marietta's request for a Rhenish serenade (*Mein Sehnen, mein Wähnen*). After a while, tiring of the attentions of the men, Marietta decides—having missed today's rehearsal—to dance her seduction scene from *Robert le Diable*. As she gets ready, nuns in the neighboring convent appear at their windows as spectators. Trying to stop her, Paul steps out of the shadows, but she begins her seductive dance; he seizes her and forces her to stop, whereupon the nuns disappear. Fritz and the count try to come to Marietta's aid, but she sends them away, saying she will deal with Paul alone. He curses her promiscuity, but she denies any liaison with Frank. Though it becomes obvious that Paul has been her lover, he says he was really making love only to the dead Marie. Using her wiles on him (*Paul, du leidest*), Marietta coaxes him into admitting that he really loves her. To confirm her triumph, she wants to make love with him in his own house. They rush off.

ACT III   In the cold morning light, Marietta confronts the portrait of Marie, asking it to allow the living to go on with their lives (*Dich such ich, Bild!*). Children's voices outside sing a religious song, reaffirming the power of life. Paul appears, having wandered off to hear the prayers in the streets. He seems to reject Marietta, who sings to herself, recalling Pierrot's serenade (*Mein Sehnen, mein Wähnen*) while Paul places lighted candles in the window, a local custom. He is increasingly involved in the ongoing procession outside, while she sulks, then insists on embracing him—at the very moment when he imagines the procession entering the room. Exasperated by his fixation on death and the past, she cries out that she is alive here and now (*Und wieder die Tote*), daring Paul to deny his attraction to her; she stands before the portrait and defies it. Seeing a braid of Marie's hair in a glass case, she holds it up, wraps it around her neck, and starts dancing *(Ich tanz)*. Outraged by this sacrilege, Paul strangles her with the braid, gasping that now she—in death—is just like Marie.

§ The scene reverts to the end of Act I, just after Marietta's departure from her first visit. Emerging from his reverie, Paul finds no body of Marietta, while the braid remains untouched in its reliquary. Brigitta comes to announce the lady's return: Marietta, having forgotten her umbrella and the roses Paul gave her, comes back. Despite her hints that she might stay, Paul lets her go. On her way out, she greets Frank, who tells Paul that the "miracle" appears to be over. Paul replies that though he will not see Marietta again, the dream of reality that she represented has shattered the hold that Marie's memory exerted over him *(O Freund, ich werde sie nicht wiedersehn)*. Realizing he must go on with his life, he will leave Bruges with Frank. He covers the portrait of Marie and, locking the door to her room, looks back in farewell.

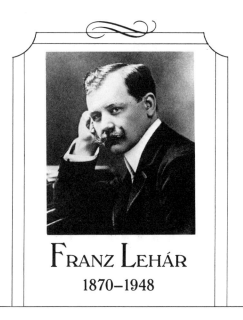

Franz Lehár
1870–1948

ntroduced at the end of 1905 at the Theater an der Wien, Vienna, by a management that felt sure it had a flop on its hands, *Die Lustige Witwe* turned out to be one of the legendary successes in the history of operetta. It made the fortune and reputation of its Hungarian-born composer, Franz (Ferenc) Lehár, who had trouble living up to this first hit in his later works, though several—especially those written for his friend the tenor Richard Tauber—remain.

The Merry Widow, as it is known in the English-speaking world, is a staple not only of summer repertory companies but of legitimate opera houses as well. Though often produced as a Broadway-style musical, it is written for trained operetta or opera voices. For reasons best known to the adaptors who have tampered with it, the mythical duchy of Pontevedro—a spoof on the little Balkan country of Montenegro, butt of endless jokes in Central Europe at the time—frequently has its name changed, and so do some of the principal characters, especially Hanna Glawari, the Merry Widow of the title, who is often called "Sonya" or "Anna," and Njegus, sometimes known as "Nitch."

DIE LUSTIGE WITWE

(The Merry Widow)

THREE ACTS

MUSIC: Franz Lehár

TEXT (German): Viktor Léon and Leo Stein

WORLD PREMIERE: Vienna, Theater an der Wien, December 30, 1905

U.S. PREMIERE: New York, New Amsterdam Theater, October 21, 1907

CHARACTERS

Hanna Glawari . . . . Soprano
Valencienne, *wife of Baron Zeta* . . . . Soprano
Count Danilo Danilovich . . . . Baritone
Camille de Rosillon, *diplomatic attaché* . . . . Tenor
Baron Mirko Zeta . . . . Baritone
Viscount Cascada . . . . Tenor
Raoul de St. Brioche . . . . Tenor
Njegus, *Zeta's aide* . . . . Buffo
Grisettes, *Parisian and Pontevedrian aristocracy, musicians,*
servants

ACT I   The action takes place in the Pontevedrian embassy, Paris, 1905. Baron Mirko Zeta leads his guests in a toast to the Pontevedrian chief of state in absentia. Meanwhile, Zeta's wife, Valencienne, speaks privately to Camille de Rosillon, a young attaché with whom she has been having a flirtation. Oblivious to this, Zeta is concerned only that Hanna Glawari—widow of the wealthiest man in Pontevedro—not marry a foreigner during her sojourn in Paris, since this would spell financial disaster for the tiny country. Camille protests the seriousness of his love to Valencienne, who reminds him she is a respectable wife (duet: *Ich bin eine anständ'ge Frau*). After they leave, Zeta welcomes the temperamental Hanna, who is quite aware of his interest in her money and reassures him that she is still a Pontevedrian at heart *(Bin noch Pontevedrinerin)*. Several men confess they have fallen under her spell; she leads them into the next room for the festivities. Next to arrive is Count Danilo Danilovich, who says that after a hard day's work on behalf of his country he likes nothing better than an evening at Maxim's *(Da geh' ich zu Maxim)*. Balking at the mention of Hanna, whom he evidently knows, he no sooner makes himself comfortable than Hanna herself walks in. It quickly develops that she and Danilo were once in love but that his uncle forbade the match. Danilo now swears that if saying "I love you" really means to Hanna "I love your money," he will never make such a declaration. Zeta, having seen them together, tells Danilo it is his patriotic duty to marry Hanna: since she is surrounded by suitors, danger to the national exchequer is imminent. Ladies' choice is announced for the next dance (ensemble: *(Damenwahl!)*, and both Cascada and St. Brioche hope Hanna will ask them to dance. Hanna is inclined to ask Danilo, who at first says he doesn't know how to dance, then offers to sell his turn as Hanna's partner for 10,000 francs, to be donated to charity. The mention of so much money scares the other men away. Alone with Hanna, Danilo offers to dance with her after all, but she refuses, so he dances by himself.

ACT II The evening of the next day, guests are gathered in the garden of Hanna's mansion, where she has promised a real Pontevedrian party. She interrupts the folksinging and dancing to sing the ballad of Vilja, a forest nymph who fell in love with a mortal *(Vilja, oh Vilja, du Waldmägdelein)*. When she tells Zeta she is importing dancing girls to entertain Danilo in the style of Maxim's cabaret, the baron gets his hopes up: Hanna seems interested in Danilo. The latter appears and joins Hanna in verses about a couple going for a romantic ride in a carriage—but the gentleman seems unwilling to get the lady's message of acceptance *(Heia, Mädel, aufgeschaut)*. Zeta asks his aide, Njegus, and Danilo to meet him in the summerhouse at eight for a conference. With some other men from the party, they reflect happily on how difficult it is to figure out women *(Ja, das Studium der Weiber ist schwer)*. Hanna tests Danilo's interest by asking whether she should feel free to marry the man of her choice. They wander off, leaving Valencienne with Camille; having decided to break off with him, she reluctantly means to persuade him to propose to Hanna. Camille asks why the flower of their romance must fade so soon *(Wie eine Rosenknospe)*. She replies that one evening remains before they must part, and they will spend it in the summerhouse *(Sieh dort den kleinen Pavillon)*. When Zeta appears for the conference, Njegus—having seen the lovers enter the summerhouse—rescues Valencienne through the back door. Zeta thinks he saw his wife in there; meanwhile, though, Hanna has taken her place—to the jealous Danilo's annoyance, since he assumes she is having a tryst with Camille. When Camille repeats his protestations of love to keep up the pretense, Valencienne is shocked by his fickleness. Enjoying the joke, Hanna announces her engagement to Camille. At first Danilo pretends nonchalance, saying marriage is a private matter, not subject to diplomatic opinion *(Die Ehe ist für mich privat)*, but as rage gets the better of him, he recites a warning fable about a princess who ruined herself to spite her lover *(Es waren zwei Königskinder),* then heads for Maxim's to forget his troubles.

ACT III   Later that night, Njegus has transformed Hanna's parlor into a replica of Maxim's, complete with dancing girls, including Valencienne. When Danilo is brought in, he accepts the illusion and is greeted by the girls *(Auf dem Boulevard am Abend).* Handed a telegram confirming the imminent ruin of the Pontevedrian treasury, Danilo bows to patriotic duty and officially forbids her marriage, then learns with joy that she never meant to marry Camille. Admitting his own love, he waltzes with her *(Lippen schweigen).* Meanwhile, Zeta figures out (with the help of a telltale fan) that it was really his wife in the summerhouse; announcing he will divorce her, he proposes to Hanna. Under her late husband's will, Hanna cautions, she will lose her fortune if she remarries. Delighted, Danilo wants to marry her, but she adds that she will lose it because it will pass to her new husband. Laughingly, he resigns himself to his fate, saving the fortunes of his country at the same time. Valencienne's standing with her husband is restored by her inscription on the fan—"I am a respectable wife"—and all ends with a recapitulation of the men's ode to the delightful enigma that is woman.

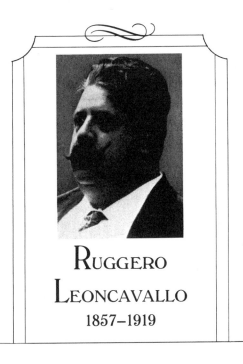

RUGGERO LEONCAVALLO
1857–1919

ate has bracketed two competitors, Pietro Mascagni and Ruggero Leoncavallo, as standard-bearers of the verismo (realism) movement, because their two short operas *Cavalleria Rusticana* and *Pagliacci* were conceived around the same time and today are usually performed as a double bill. Verismo actually had its roots in Verdi's *Rigoletto*, Bizet's *Carmen*, and Ponchielli's *La Gioconda;* what made verismo seem so novel was the brevity and topicality of the Mascagni/Leoncavallo operas, both of which are on contemporary, local subjects. Whereas Mascagni based *Cavalleria* on a popular short story that also became a play, Leoncavallo for *Pagliacci* chose a trial over which his magistrate father had presided. Both operas revolved around love triangles in which a jealous husband kills his wife's lover. In Leoncavallo's case, the perpetrator of the *crime passionelle*, after having served his prison term, was taken to see the opera.

Born in Naples, Leoncavallo was a few years older than Mascagni and one year older than the most famous of the verists, Giacomo Puccini. Except for the great and unexpected success of *Pagliacci*, Leoncavallo's career was a series of failures. Earning his living as a café pianist in his youth, he traveled extensively. Under the spell of Wagner's epic ideas, he planned a giant trilogy called *Crepusculum*, drawn from Italian Renaissance history, but completed only the first part. Of his numerous operas, the most interesting were *La Bohème* (1897), which suffered in comparison with Puccini's version, and *Zazà* (1900), an attractive lighter work that served as a vehicle for Geraldine Farrar's farewell to the Metropolitan Opera.

Apologists for Leoncavallo attribute his neglect in part to the fact that he chose the wrong publisher—Sonzogno, instead of the influential Ricordi—and in part to the relative earliness of his death (1919), which marked the end of the stipend that the Italian government paid to theaters presenting operas by living composers. The durable popularity of *Pagliacci*, however, would be the envy of any composer. Its most famous exponent, Enrico Caruso, sang the role of Canio eighty-three times at the Met and forty-three on tour, and his best-selling Victor record of *Vesti la giubba* resounded on thousands of phonographs around the world.

PAGLIACCI

PROLOGUE AND TWO ACTS
MUSIC: Ruggero Leoncavallo
TEXT (Italian): by the composer
WORLD PREMIERE: Milan, Teatro dal Verme, May 21, 1892
U.S. PREMIERE: New York, Grand Opera House, June 15, 1893
METROPOLITAN OPERA PREMIERE: December 11, 1893

CHARACTERS

Canio (*"Pagliaccio" in the play*), *head of a troupe of strolling players* . . . . Tenor
Nedda (*"Colombina" in the play*), *wife of Canio* . . . . Soprano
Beppe (*"Arlecchino" in the play*). . . . . Tenor
Tonio (*"Taddeo" in the play*), *clown* . . . . Baritone
Silvio, *villager* . . . . Baritone
Villagers

PROLOGUE   The hunchback Tonio, dressed as the clown Taddeo from commedia dell'arte, steps before the curtain to address the audience. The author of the drama, he says, wanted to revive the traditional masks and costumes, but with a difference. Instead of the commedia dell'arte tradition—"It's only a play, we're only acting"—the author and actors want to show that those onstage are human beings of flesh and blood. Do not be deceived by our costumes, says Tonio: underneath we are flesh and blood like you, and the play we bring you offers a "slice of life," a cross section of reality.

ACT I The curtain rises on an open space just outside Montalto, in Calabria, southern Italy, sometime around 1865–70. A troupe of traveling actors has arrived, and a chorus of citizens welcomes them, recognizing the familiar figures of Pagliaccio and Arlecchino (Harlequin). Canio, head of the troupe, thanks the townspeople and invites everyone to see the show that evening (*Un grande spettacolo*). When Tonio tries to help Canio's young wife, Nedda, down from the wagon, Canio boxes his ears and tells him to get away. Aside, Tonio promises to get even. When a villager jokes about Tonio's interest in Nedda, Canio announces he will not tolerate any fooling with his wife (*Un tal gioco*). The stage is one thing, he says—there one can joke—but real life is something else, and he loves his wife. Since it is the feast of the Assumption (mid-August), church bells call the locals away; they depart singing about the sound of the bells (*Din, don*). Canio, having changed from his costume into street clothes, heads for the tavern with Beppe and some local cronies, leaving Nedda alone. She muses on the fierceness of his jealousy and recognizes what it would mean if he knew her innermost dreams, for she feels trapped in the marriage. Banishing such thoughts, she responds to the sheer joy of the summer air, admiring the free, happy flight of birds overhead (ballatella: *Stridono lassù*). Not until her song is finished does she notice Tonio watching her. Clumsily the hunchback tries to declare his love for her, but she says he can play her lover only onstage—otherwise he had better keep away. When he persists in trying to kiss her, she hits him with a whip. As she denounces him in disgust, he snarls that she will pay for this. After he has left, Silvio, Nedda's erstwhile sweetheart from the town, appears. It is evident from their conversation that they have had trysts before and that Silvio is careful to avoid being found out. He declares his loneliness when she is away (*Decidi il mio destin*); she protests the fate that keeps them apart. As they talk lovingly, Tonio sneaks in unseen, gloating over the fact that he has caught Nedda in an act of indiscretion. He goes to fetch Canio. Silvio urges Nedda to come away with him for a life of happiness (*Tutto scordiam*). Tonio shows the guilty pair to Canio but restrains him until Silvio has slipped away. Nedda has promised to elope with him after the show that night. Then Canio rushes forward; Nedda stops him from following Silvio, who has escaped. To Tonio's glee, Canio demands that Nedda tell who her lover is. When the raging Canio pulls out a dagger, Beppe grabs his arm, reminding him that they have a show to give. It is time to put on their costumes, and Canio, alone, muses bitterly that a clown's face cannot mask his heartbreak (*Vesti la giubba*).

ACT II As people jostle for seats, Tonio beats the bass drum to publicize the spectacle. Silvio, unnoticed in the crowd, exchanges a quick word with Nedda, who is selling tickets: everything is set for their escape after the performance. The unruly audience clamors for the show to start, then hushes in expectation as the curtain of the little stage rises to reveal a commedia dell'arte setting.

Arlecchino (Beppe) serenades Colombina (Nedda), who, however, is taking advantage of the absence of her husband, Pagliaccio (Canio), to receive the foppish Taddeo (Tonio). Taddeo appears, carrying a basket with a chicken for their dinner. When Colombina distracts him, Arlecchino snatches the basket away, brings his own bottle of wine, and throws Taddeo out, meaning to dine with Colombina himself. As they start to eat, Arlecchino gives Colombina a drug to make Pagliaccio sleep soundly when he returns: then the two of them can run away. Pagliaccio enters in time to hear Nedda tell the departing Arlecchino that she will be his. Canio forgets the script and jealously insists on finding out the name of Nedda's lover. She improvises, trying to keep the play going, and he returns to the character of Pagliaccio for a few moments, finding the quaking Taddeo hiding in the closet. Goaded by the latter's pointed remarks about Colombina's innocence, Canio again drops his role and thunders that he has rights like any other man. Nedda tries to lead him back to the script, but Canio cries out he is not Pagliaccio any more *(No, Pagliaccio non son)*. The audience cheers Canio's "acting" as he denounces his wife for her betrayal, after all he has given her of himself. She asks why he does not send her away, then, and he replies that he will not give her up. After one more attempt to stay in character and show that her visitor was only the innocuous Arlecchino, Nedda finally defies her husband openly, enraging him further. Tonio stops Beppe from interfering, but when Silvio (in the audience) sees Canio grab a knife from the table, he rushes forward to protect Nedda, drawing his own dagger. As Nedda tries to escape, Canio stabs her, and when Silvio runs to her side, he stabs Silvio as well. Horrified by the double murder, the bystanders seize Canio and disarm him as Tonio ironically tells the audience, "The comedy is ended."*

---

*In some productions, contrary to the composer's intentions, this final line is delivered by Canio instead.

PIETRO MASCAGNI
1863–1945

*P*ietro Mascagni, born the son of a baker in Livorno (Leghorn), studied law but pursued a musical career despite parental disapproval. Enrolled at the Milan Conservatory (for a time he shared living quarters with Puccini), he dropped out when the lure of live performances beckoned in the form of an offer from a touring opera company. Though his career as a conductor never lived up to his expectations, it did teach him what does and does not work in the theater. His third opera, the first to be performed, was *Cavalleria Rusticana,* based on a popular short story and play by the Sicilian writer Giovanni Verga. It won the impoverished composer first prize in a contest sponsored by the publishing house of Sonzogno. The first performance, in the spring of 1890, was a clamorous success, and *Cavalleria* soon swept the world, inspiring many imitations. It reached the Metropolitan Opera stage on December 30, 1891, in a strange pairing with a truncated version of Gluck's *Orfeo.*

Mascagni never recaptured the glory of his youthful triumph. He did further his reputation with *L'Amico Fritz* (1891) and *Iris* (1898), though neither is seen often outside Italy today. *Parisina, Le Maschere,* and *Il Piccolo Marat* are among his other operas, each interesting for exploring new directions. Though Mascagni avoided the pitfall of repeating himself, he could not change the fact that his real, essential talent—a simple, limited, effective one—lay in the earthy communication of *Cavalleria Rusticana.*

The idea of a short opera proved widely attractive and spawned others in this genre, including even Strauss' *Salome* and *Elektra.* It also necessitated sharing the program with another work. To avoid unwelcome pairings, Puccini in *Il Trittico* wrote his own companion pieces, but to little avail, since his trilogy is often divided in practice. For better or for worse, Mascagni's *Cavalleria* drew a permanent mate in Leoncavallo's *Pagliacci*. Neither composer seems to have sought or approved the arrangement, but it has guaranteed their joint survival for decades on the stages of the world.

CAVALLERIA RUSTICANA

ONE ACT
MUSIC: Pietro Mascagni
TEXT (Italian): Giovanni Targioni-Tozzetti and Guido Menasci,
    based on a short story by Giovanni Verga
WORLD PREMIERE: Rome, Teatro Costanzi, May 17, 1890
U.S. PREMIERE: Philadelphia, September 9, 1891
METROPOLITAN OPERA PREMIERE: December 30, 1891

CHARACTERS

Santuzza, *village girl* . . . . Soprano
Lola, *Alfio's wife* . . . . Mezzo-Soprano
Mamma Lucia, *Turiddu's mother* . . . . Contralto
Turiddu, *young soldier* . . . . Tenor
Alfio, *village carter* . . . . Baritone
Villagers, peasants, boys

It is Easter morning in a Sicilian village around 1890. Before the curtain rises, a tenor voice is heard in the distance singing a siciliana—a stylized, popular song of the period *(O Lola)*. It is the local dandy Turiddu, serenading his former sweetheart, Lola, though she is now married to the town carter, Alfio. As the curtain rises on the town square, the local women sing about the arrival of springtime, while the men concern themselves with crops in the fields and contentment at home. Everyone is dressed for the holiday. Santuzza, a young woman of the parish, comes to question Mamma Lucia, proprietress of the inn that faces the church. Santuzza is looking for Mamma Lucia's son, Turiddu, who has been courting her until recently. Mamma Lucia doesn't want to hear Santuzza's problems and tries to take her inside, away from nosy neighbors, but Santuzza says she has been excommunicated as a result of her affair with Turiddu and is being ostracized. Before she can explain, Alfio appears with his horse and wagon, bragging about his life of travel and Lola, the pretty wife he comes home to *(Il cavallo scalpita)*. When he asks Mamma Lucia for wine, she says Turiddu has gone to nearby Francofonte to fetch some. Alfio thinks this is strange, since he saw Turiddu near his own house earlier that morning. Knowing that Turiddu is now courting Lola, Santuzza signals Mamma Lucia to say nothing more, and Alfio leaves to get ready for church. In response to a choir inside the church *(Regina coeli)*, the villagers, including the excommunicated Santuzza, sing an Easter hymn in the square *(Inneggiamo)*. As soon as the townspeople leave, Mamma Lucia asks Santuzza the reason for the secrecy about Turiddu's whereabouts. Santuzza reminds her *(Voi lo sapete)* that Turiddu, who used to be in love with Lola before he joined the army, returned home to find her married to Alfio, whereupon he took up with Santuzza and seduced her. Since then, however, he has resumed his affair with Lola—unbeknownst to her husband, whose business often takes him out of town. Mamma Lucia prays to the Virgin to help Santuzza, then goes into church, leaving the girl, who is not allowed to enter there, outside. Turiddu, on his way to church, is surprised to meet Santuzza (duet: *Tu qui, Santuzza?*). He tries to avoid a scene, but she is insistent: what was he doing near Lola's house when he was supposed to be in Francofonte? Turiddu accuses her of spying and of wanting Alfio to kill him if he finds out. Half-heartedly he denies loving Lola but insists he is free to do as he pleases. The argument is interrupted briefly as Lola breezes by on her way to church, glancing flirtatiously at Turiddu and needling Santuzza about her inability to go inside. Santuzza retorts that only those without sin are welcome in church, whereupon Lola thanks God that she is included and leaves. The angry Turiddu rejects Santuzza's increasingly hysterical pleas not to abandon her. As he storms off, she cries after him, "A bad Easter to you!"—the strongest malediction on a religious holiday. At this moment, the appearance of Alfio seems providential to the distraught Santuzza, who tells him plainly that Lola has been unfaithful to him with Turiddu. At first Alfio says he will kill Santuzza if she is lying, but she reminds him how badly Turiddu treated her *(Turiddu mi tolse l'onore)* and how truthful her character is. Alfio swears revenge, and Santuzza immediately regrets having told him: she has only hastened the inevitability of losing Turiddu. In the vain hope of calming Alfio, she follows him out of the square.

For a few minutes, the square remains empty as the church service proceeds unheard. In a short intermezzo, the orchestra depicts the mood of Santuzza's remorse and ruined love.

Then the people come out of church, eager to get to their homes for Easter dinner (chorus: *A casa, amici*). Turiddu tries to talk to Lola, but she says she must find Alfio, whom she has not seen since his return that morning. Turiddu says Alfio will soon be there, so she stays. Then Turiddu urges everyone to have wine *(Viva il vino spumeggiante)* and exchanges toasts with Lola. Alfio does appear, but when Turiddu offers him wine, the carter says it might be poisoned. Sensing trouble, the neighbors draw back as Turiddu and Alfio exchange the few words that constitute a challenge to a duel, and Turiddu gives Alfio the ritual bite on the ear. To Alfio, Turiddu admits he has been in the wrong, but he must fight to kill, for if he dies there will be no one to take care of Santuzza. Unmoved, Alfio says he will wait in back of a nearby garden. The contrite Turiddu now has a moment alone with his mother, who has missed the foregoing episode. He says he has had too much wine and is going for a walk, adding with rising emotion that she must look after Santuzza if anything happens to him *(Mamma, quel vino e generoso)*. Then he rushes away. The alarmed Mamma Lucia quickly realizes that something is wrong, but before she can follow Turiddu, neighbors rush in crying that he has been killed.

L'AMICO FRITZ

THREE ACTS
MUSIC: Pietro Mascagni
TEXT (Italian): P. Suardon (real name Nicolò Dispuro), based on a
    novel by Emile Erckmann and Alexandre Chatrian
WORLD PREMIERE: Rome, Teatro Costanzi, November 1, 1891
U.S. PREMIERE: Philadelphia, June 8, 1892
METROPOLITAN OPERA PREMIERE: January 10, 1894

CHARACTERS

Fritz Kobus, *rich bachelor landowner* . . . . Tenor
Suzel, *farmer's daughter* . . . . Soprano
Beppe, *Gypsy* . . . . Mezzo-Soprano
David, *rabbi* . . . . Baritone
Hanezò } *friends of Fritz* . . . . { Bass
Federico }   { Tenor
Caterina, *Fritz's housekeeper* . . . . Soprano

ACT I   Alsace, during the middle of the nineteenth century. Fritz Kobus, a young, wealthy bachelor, waits in his dining room for three friends to celebrate his birthday. The first to arrive, Rabbi David, greets him with what is evidently another in a series of requests for money for various good works— this time, to help a young couple who want to marry. Fritz agrees grudgingly, since marriage is not to his taste. The other friends, Hanezò and Federico, join them, and Fritz toasts bachelorhood. His housekeeper announces Suzel, the daughter of Fritz's caretaker farmer. The shy girl brings violets, and Fritz good-naturedly offers her a seat at the table. A violin outside announces the arrival of the Gypsy Beppe, who offers a song in praise of Fritz, the benefactor who rescued him from the threshold of death as a child (*Laceri, miseri, tanti bambini*). When Suzel excuses herself to return to her father, the matchmaker David vows to find her a husband. His friends make light of this, but he lectures them sternly for not taking marriage and fatherhood seriously (*Per voi, ghiottoni inutili*). He adds he will see even Fritz married. Fritz takes this as a wager and bets his vineyard in Clairefontaine that he will always remain single. As the town band draws near, saluting Fritz's birthday, he declares laughingly that the village children aré the only children he will have.

Act II   In the courtyard of Fritz's farm at Mésanges, Suzel picks flowers for his house and amuses herself with a song about a knight who falls in love with a plain girl like her (*Bel cavalier, che vai*). Fritz greets her, saying he mistook her song for a nightingale's. In addition to the bouquet, she has a surprise: cherries are ripe. As both admire the purple fruit (*Han della porpora vivo il colore*), she climbs into a tree and throws handfuls to the delighted Fritz. The song of the birds next draws their attention, and they marvel at the beauty of the still spring day (*Tutto tace*). Their idyll is interrupted by the arrival of a carriage with Fritz's friends. While Fritz shows the others around the farm, David stays behind to rest, wondering how serious Fritz is about Suzel (*Vediamo un po'*). Suzel brings a pitcher of water, reminding him of the Biblical tale of Rebecca, which he coaxes her to repeat: the first girl who offered Abraham's servant a drink should become the wife of his son Isaac. Embarrassed, she runs off when she hears Fritz's voice. David assures himself she will eventually marry Fritz. To move the plot along, he tells Fritz he has "just the right young man" for Suzel. This annoys Fritz, who argues with his friend about this incessant matchmaking. David leaves him to his thoughts, as Fritz realizes with alarm that he has been falling prey to the unfamiliar emotion of love (*Quale strano turbamento*). He decides not to let this happen and orders a carriage at once to take him into town. Returning, David is amused by Fritz's flight, but Suzel bursts into tears that she cannot explain.

Act III   Alone in his dining room, Fritz is unable to get Suzel out of his mind. Beppe stops by to see him, concerned about Fritz's dejection, and admits he too once knew the torments of love (*E l'ho provato anch'io*). Fritz sends him on his way, then muses that if Beppe was once in love, the problem must be universal (*O amore, o bella luce del core*)—in fact, life and love are synonymous. David wanders in with studied nonchalance, remarking he has arranged everything for Suzel's marriage, enjoying Fritz's distressed reaction. When both men leave the dining room, Suzel enters with a basket of fruit. Her mood is sorrowful, because she cannot muster the courage to tell her employer how she feels about him *(Non mi resta che il pianto)*. Fritz finds her and remarks bitterly that at least she might have invited him to her wedding. In tears, she says her father wants to impose an unwanted marriage on her. Fritz, she says, is the only one who can save her—he must plead with her father *(Ah! ditela per me)*. Sensing that she loves someone else, he demands to know who it is, saying that he will help her marry the one she wants. What, asks Fritz, if he were to tell her he loves her himself *(Io t'amo, dolce mio tesor)*? Naturally she is over-joyed, and they embrace. When David returns, declaring he has won, Fritz retorts it was love that won, but he gladly gives the vineyard to David, who turns it over to Suzel as a wedding present. Fritz's friends and housekeeper come with congratulations, but David warns he will soon marry them off too, as everyone hails the power of love.

JULES MASSENET
1842–1912

hough his operas, together with most of the nineteenth-century French repertory, passed from fashion in the mid-twentieth century, Jules Massenet was the most successful and prolific of Georges Bizet's successors. Like Gounod, he understood public taste and catered to it, writing music that did not strain the eardrums or the intellect. The stories he chose, like those favored by his Italian rival Puccini, stressed a discreet eroticism and plentiful local color.

Though Massenet has never been considered a one-opera composer, he is identified in most people's minds with his most important and durable score, *Manon*. Along with *Carmen* and *Faust* and the once perennial *Mignon*, it forms a quintessential nucleus of French opera, to which the connoisseur would add Debussy's *Pelléas*. Massenet, often frugal with his resources, lavished on *Manon* an outpouring of melody that has seduced audiences over the years, though there have always been musicians, such as Stravinsky and Milhaud, who dismissed it as mere confection. Spiced with touches of period color from France's musical past, the work is basically a sentimental overlay of the Abbé Prévost's cool, analytic *Histoire du Chevalier des Grieux et de Manon Lescaut* (1731), a semi-autobiographical book in memoir form, considered a direct forebear of the modern novel.

In *Werther* the composer turned again to a literary classic, this time of German origin. In the summer of 1772, just half a century after the time in which *Manon* takes place, Johann Wolfgang von Goethe visited the town of Wetzlar, where he became briefly infatuated with one Charlotte Buff, fiancée of Johann Christian Kestner. In the fall of that year, one Carl Wilhelm Jerusalem borrowed dueling pistols from Kestner, supposedly to take on a voyage—and used them to kill himself, because of his hopeless love for a married woman. When Kestner wrote to Goethe (by then no longer in Wetzlar) of the suicide, the poet identified his own luckless adventure with Jerusalem's and wrote *The Sorrows of Young Werther,* which appeared in 1774. The book enjoyed a vogue but was said to have encouraged such a rash of lovers' suicides throughout Europe that Goethe felt compelled to write a disavowal, saying he never meant to condone Werther's extreme behavior. Massenet's opera moves the action ahead a decade.

An example of Massenet's more exotic style is *Thaïs,* a perfumed, softened version of Anatole France's sharply satirical story about the excesses of religious fanaticism. Though the author snorted at this change in emphasis, he liked the luscious, piquant music in which Massenet clothed the tale.

In his use of the female voice throughout its registers, and in his prosody, Massenet holds a special place among French composers. His operas are not "great," nor are they meant to be: they are genre pieces, excelling within the limits he set for them, appealing to the general public because of their charm and frank sentiment.

MANON

FIVE ACTS
MUSIC: Jules Massenet
TEXT (French): Henri Meilhac and Philippe Gille, based on the
    novel by the Abbé Prévost
WORLD PREMIERE: Paris, Opéra Comique, January 19, 1884
U.S. PREMIERE: New York, Academy of Music, December 23,
    1885 (in Italian)
METROPOLITAN OPERA PREMIERE: January 16, 1895

CHARACTERS

Manon Lescaut . . . . Soprano
Chevalier des Grieux . . . . Tenor
Count des Grieux, *his father* . . . . Bass
Guillot de Morfontaine, *minister of finance, an old roué* . . . . . . Tenor
Brétigny, *nobleman* . . . . Baritone
Lescaut, *of the Royal Guard, Manon's cousin* . . . . Baritone

Sergeant . . . . Baritone
Pousette, Javotte, Rosette, *actresses* . . . . Sopranos
Students, soldiers, travelers, innkeepers, ladies, gentlemen

ACT I   France, 1721. The courtyard of an inn at Amiens is filled with an animated crowd. Two middle-aged roués, the finance minister Guillot de Morfontaine and the tax collector Brétigny, clamor for food and drink. Their dinner appears, and the innkeeper turns his attention to the coach from Arras, expected any minute. Lescaut, a soldier, enters to meet his cousin Manon, who has just arrived on the coach. The townspeople watch the passengers climbing out in various states of disarray and fatigue. Lescaut spots Manon, a girl of sixteen, who chatters about her first trip away from home (*Je suis encore tout étourdie*). Guillot spies Manon and tries to flirt with her, to the amusement of Brétigny and three actress acquaintances—Rosette, Pousette, and Javotte. Guillot says he will arrange for a carriage and take her away. Lescaut, preparing to rejoin his companions, advises Manon on proper behavior: she must avoid talking to strangers and must remember that he is guardian of the family reputation (*Ne bronchez pas, soyez gentille*). Musing that she will soon be at school in a convent, Manon bids farewell to her youthful dreams (*Voyons, Manon, plus de chimères*). The young Chevalier des Grieux passes by, intending to leave by the coach to meet his father at home, but the sight of Manon galvanizes him. Hesitantly he speaks to her, confessing himself smitten, and she replies kindly. He learns she is headed for a convent; when he says he will save her from such a fate, she suggests they commandeer the coach her admirer ordered. In no time they are dreaming of life in Paris together (*Nous vivrons à Paris*). When Guillot returns, charged by the tipsy Lescaut with trying to abduct Manon, both are stunned to learn that she has fled. Guillot swears revenge. Lescaut replies that he will find Manon eventually—and that Guillot will have to pay for her favors, if the "family honor" is to be served.

ACT II   A modest apartment in Paris. Manon looks over Des Grieux's shoulder as he writes to his father, describing her, hoping they will get permission to marry. Lescaut storms in with Brétigny, who is dressed as a guardsman, and acts indignant at Des Grieux's seduction of his cousin, while Brétigny pretends to restrain him. Des Grieux reassures Lescaut of his honorable intentions and shows him the letter. Meanwhile, from Brétigny's and Manon's asides it is evident that Brétigny has been trying to pay court to her and that so far she has refused him. He warns her that Des Grieux is to be taken away that evening at his father's orders. Brétigny adds that if she stays with Des Grieux, poverty will be her lot, but that if she lets him go, she can have the life she wants. While Lescaut finishes reading the letter, Manon agonizes over her decision. When the intruders leave—followed by Des Grieux, who goes to mail his letter—Manon vacillates between love and luxury but leans toward the latter. Sadly she bids farewell to the little table where they have shared meals *(Adieu, notre petite table)*. He returns, telling her of his dream of a country cottage *(En fermant les yeux)*. Knocking is heard. Manon tries to hold Des Grieux back, but he goes to see who it is. Sounds of a scuffle and a departing carriage reach Manon, who cries out, "My poor chevalier!"

ACT III A holiday in the Cours la Reine, a Parisian park. Peddlers and citizens sell and buy. Pousette, Javotte, and Rosette try to escape from their sometime keeper, Guillot. Lescaut enters, having done well at the gambling tables, and sings the praises of his current lady love, Rosalinde, as well as of Lady Luck *(O Rosalinde)*. Brétigny enters and teases Guillot about his womanizing, adding he hopes Guillot will not steal Manon from him. Guillot denies any such intention but asks whether the story he has heard is true—that Brétigny refused to bring the troupe of the Opéra to perform at his house, despite Manon's pleading. When Brétigny says it *is* true, Guillot gleefully sings a little ditty to himself about stealing Manon *(Dig et dig et don)*. The crowd admires Manon, who sings about how much she enjoys her life as reigning queen of the demimonde *(Je marche sur tous les chemins)*. Cheered for her bravado, she goes on with another song, a gavotte about taking advantage of youth while one has it *(Profitons bien de la jeunesse)*. Then she goes to shop at the stalls, and Brétigny recognizes Count des Grieux, father of the chevalier. The count remarks that his son is about to become an abbé at the seminary of St. Sulpice—thanks to an unfortunate love affair. Manon, who overhears, sends Brétigny to buy a certain bracelet she wants and questions the count about his son, who she pretends loved a friend of hers. The count replies that his son has learned to forget. As he excuses himself, Guillot brings the Paris Opera ballet to perform for Manon—a coup he hopes will win her—but she is so distraught that she hardly notices the performance.

§ At St. Sulpice, a group of women are leaving the chapel, impressed by the discourse they have just heard from the young abbé candidate. As he comes out, the count is waiting to congratulate him—and ask him not to rush into his vows but to marry some nice girl and settle down *(Épouse quelque brave fille)*. Seeing how serious his son seems to be, the count offers to send him 30,000 francs, his share of his mother's estate, to tide him over until he gets a religious appointment. After the count's departure, Des Grieux, alone at last, bids farewell to the tainted dream that bound him to worldly life *(Ah! fuyez, douce image)*. Then a porter calls him away: the service is beginning. Manon appears and asks to speak with Des Grieux. As the choir is heard from the chapel, Manon prays—for the return of her love. Des Grieux is upset to see Manon, but she speaks persuasively about her repentance, finally taking his hand and asking whether her touch doesn't bring back memories *(N'est-ce plus ma main?)*. He falters, though a bell calls him to prayers. At last he confesses that he still cannot resist her.

ACT IV At the Hôtel de Transylvanie in Paris, a group of gamblers are joined by card sharks, who say gambling is too serious to leave to chance. Lescaut, on a winning streak, sings the praises of a lady he loves—the queen of spades. Pousette, Jovette, and Rosette stroll in, followed by Guillot, whose jovial mood is quickly soured by the appearance of Manon with his rival Des Grieux. The latter, who has come unwillingly, recognizes that Manon's worldliness is the ruin of both of them *(Manon, sphinx étonnant)*. Since they have gone through his inheritance, he will have to win money. Lescaut has now lost, but he encourages Des Grieux to gamble on beginner's luck. Playing against Guillot, Des Grieux wins several rounds, and Manon's praise for her lover annoys Guillot to the point that he accuses them of cheating; he storms out. Manon thinks they should leave right away, but Des Grieux says that would make it look as if he really *were* cheating. When the police arrive, Lescaut and others make their escape, but Des Grieux is arrested and Manon named as his accomplice by Guillot, who mutters that he now has revenge. As Des Grieux threatens Guillot, he is restrained by his father, who has heard of the scandal and just arrived. Des Grieux pleads for forgiveness from his father, who says quietly he will arrange to get the young man out of the hands of the law. But Manon will be treated as an undesirable.

ACT V Beside the road to Le Havre, in a deserted countryside, Des Grieux imagines Manon on her way to be deported with other women of ill repute. Lescaut joins him with the news that their attempt to ambush the cart and to rescue Manon has failed: the soldiers scared their men off. Des Grieux favors a direct attack, but Lescaut convinces him that this is foolhardy and says he can arrange for Des Grieux to see Manon. Soon the guards appear, and Lescaut hails them as a colleague, asking the Sergeant a favor—to be allowed to see his relative, Manon—and bolstering the request with money. The Sergeant agrees to leave her for a while in Lescaut's custody. Manon falls exhausted in Des Grieux's arms, overjoyed to see him again. He declares that he will rescue her and that they will have a new life together, but she realizes that it is only a dream, admitting she brought about her own downfall. They reminisce, and she reassures Des Grieux of the sincerity of her love. Then, saying her story is ended, Manon dies in his arms.

WERTHER

FOUR ACTS
MUSIC: Jules Massenet
TEXT (French): Édouard Blau, Paul Milliet, and Georges Hart-
mann, based on the novel by Goethe
WORLD PREMIERE: Vienna, Imperial Opera, February 16, 1892
(in German)
METROPOLITAN OPERA PREMIERE: April 19, 1894

CHARACTERS

Werther, *young poet* . . . . Tenor
Charlotte, *Bailiff's daughter* . . . . Mezzo-Soprano
Sophie, *her sister* . . . . Bass
The Bailiff, *widower* . . . . Bass
Albert, *Charlotte's fiancé, later her husband* . . . . Baritone
Schmidt⎫ *friends of the Bailiff* . . . . ⎧Tenor
Johann ⎭ . . . . ⎩ Bass
Brühlmann⎫ *young couple* . . . . ⎧ Soprano
Kätchen ⎭ . . . . ⎩Baritone
Younger children of the Bailiff, servants, townspeople

ACT I   The German countryside near Wetzlar in the 1780s. Outside his
house, the Bailiff rehearses his young children in a Christmas carol. His friends
Johann and Schmidt stop by, remarking that July seems a strange time to be
practicing for Christmas, but the Bailiff says he wants them to get it right.
His daughter Sophie appears. She and her sister Charlotte, oldest of the family, are in charge of the young children since their mother died; but right now
Charlotte is getting dressed for a party. There is mention of Werther, a dreamy
young man who seems destined to do well. After Johann and Schmidt have
left and the Bailiff has herded his brood into the house, Werther appears,
marveling at the simple, natural surroundings (*O Nature, pleine de grâce*). Charlotte greets her father, saying she has just time to feed the children before
leaving. The Bailiff spies Werther and introduces him to Charlotte; they are
joined by a neighbor, Brühlmann, and his sweetheart, Kätchen, who will
accompany them to the party. Werther is much taken by Charlotte's way with
the children. Several other party guests have arrived, and together the group

sets out. Sophie insists that the Bailiff join his friends at the tavern; everything will be all right under her care. She is surprised to see Albert, Charlotte's fiancé, return unexpectedly after an absence of six months. Albert says he wanted to surprise Charlotte but, since she is not home, he'll come back the next morning. He pauses in the garden a moment, thinking gratefully of Charlotte's devotion to him *(Quelle prière de reconnaissance et d'amour)*. A little while later, Charlotte and Werther return from the party. Caught up in a romantic mood, Werther tells her he has fallen in love with her. Confused, she speaks of her sorrow over her mother's death. The Bailiff returns home and informs Charlotte that he has seen Albert. She tells Werther of her promise, at her mother's deathbed, to marry Albert. As she goes into the house, Werther cries out that this promise will be the death of him.

ACT II   That September, Johann and Schmidt are sitting in the main square of Wetzlar, drinking wine on a Sunday afternoon and watching townspeople gather for the pastor's fiftieth wedding anniversary. As the two go into the tavern, Albert and Charlotte pass on their way to church, Albert remarking on his contentment, she assuring him he is a model husband. Contemplating them from a distance, Werther bewails his loss of Charlotte *(Un autre est son époux!)*. Johann and Schmidt reappear briefly, consoling Brühlmann, who has lost Kätchen after a seven years' engagement. Albert returns to the square and, seeing Werther dejected on a bench, tactfully suggests that he understands Werther's suffering. Sophie brings flowers for the minister's party and extols the joyfulness of sunshine and fresh air *(Du gai soleil)*. As Albert leaves with her, Werther realizes he was lying when he told Albert he had gotten over his suffering. Resolving to leave Wetzlar, he is distracted by the appearance of Charlotte, who reminds him she is now Albert's wife. In effect, she tells him to go away, but seeing his anguish, she says that it will not, of course, be forever, that he will return to visit—at Christmas. As she leaves to join the party, Werther muses that the separation may kill him but that death will end his suffering. Questioning the wrongness of suicide, he reflects that God might accept him, as a father would welcome a child returning sooner than expected from a journey *(Lorsque l'enfant revient d'un voyage)*. Sophie, who had asked him for the first dance, returns to the square, but he says he is leaving for good. As he walks away, Charlotte finds Sophie in tears, and Albert realizes that Werther loves his wife.

ACT III   At Albert's house on Christmas Eve, Charlotte sits alone, rereading letters Werther has sent her *(Je vous écris de ma petite chambre)*. One of them mentions his return at Christmas, filling her with apprehension. Sophie comes in cheerfully, mentioning that Albert is away, noticing that Charlotte seems unhappy. Sophie calls laughter a blessing *(Ah! le rire est béni)*, but Charlotte bursts into tears, saying they will do her good *(Va! Laisse couler mes larmes)*. Sophie leaves, hoping Charlotte will follow her to the Bailiff's house. As

Charlotte prays for strength, Werther appears in the doorway, saying he had decided he would sooner die than see her again but, when Christmas drew near, had come in spite of himself. When she reminds him of the verses of Ossian that he once started to translate, he recites a doleful verse beginning, "Why awaken me, o breath of spring?" *(Pourquoi me réveiller)*, to Charlotte's accompaniment at the keyboard. He accuses her of not admitting she returns his love, and as he takes her in his arms, she tears away, saying she will not see him again, and locks herself in her room. Werther calls on nature to go into mourning for him *(Prends le deuil, o Nature!)*. Scarcely has he run out than Albert appears, having heard on the way home that Werther is back. He calls his wife and notices her extreme agitation. A servant brings a note from Werther, saying he is going on a journey and would like to borrow Albert's dueling pistols. Coldly, Albert tells Charlotte to give the pistols to the servant, who leaves with them. As Albert goes angrily to his room, Charlotte rushes out to find Werther.

Aст IV   Before the curtain rises, the orchestra depicts a Christmas Eve snowstorm that gradually obliterates Wetzlar from view.

§ In the study of Werther's apartment, where he has shot himself, Charlotte finds him lying wounded. He revives and asks her not to go for help, because it will do no good and because he wants to spend his last moments with her. She confesses her love and gives him the kiss he has longed for. As the children's voices are heard in the distance singing their Christmas carol, Werther imagines angels announcing his forgiveness. He asks to be buried by two linden trees at the end of the cemetery—or, if consecrated ground is forbidden him, near the road or in the lonesome valley, where she can visit his grave. As Werther dies, the Christmas carol and laughter that opened the opera resound once more.

Thaïs

THREE ACTS
MUSIC: Jules Massenet
TEXT (French): Louis Gallet, after the novel by Anatole France
WORLD PREMIERE: Paris Opera, March 16, 1894
U.S. PREMIERE: New York, November 25, 1907
METROPOLITAN OPERA PREMIERE: February 16, 1917

THAÏS

CHARACTERS

Thaïs, *courtesan* . . . . Soprano
Nicias, *young Alexandrian* . . . . Tenor
Athanaël, *young cenobitic monk* . . . . Baritone
Palémon, *old cenobitic monk* . . . . Bass
Crobyle⎫ *Nicias' slaves* . . . . ⎧ Soprano
Myrtale⎭ ⎩Mezzo-Soprano
Albine, *abbess* . . . . Contalto

Servants, monks, revelers, dancers

ACT I   Along the banks of the Nile outside Thebes, Egypt; during the late fourth century A.D., the old monk Palémon presides over the evening meal with his fellow cenobitic monks. They await the return of one of their number, Athanaël, who shortly joins them. Exhausted, he tells how he found Alexandria given over to sin, ruled by the courtesan Thaïs, whom he remembers seeing once *(Hélas! enfant encore)* before he joined the order. The other monks retreat, praying, to their huts as Athanaël lies down to sleep. In the darkness, a vision materializes—a troubled dream in which Thaïs is acclaimed for her portrayal of Aphrodite in a theater of Alexandria. As dawn breaks, Athanaël prays for strength *(Toi, qui mis la pitié dans nos âmes)* and wakens his brothers, saying he must return to the city and save Thaïs' soul. Since Alexandria is on the Mediterranean coast and Thebes along the southern Nile, this means another long journey. Palémon disapproves of mixing in the affairs of the secular world, but the brothers pray for Athanaël as he leaves.

§ On the terrace of the house of Nicias, a wealthy idler of Alexandria, a servant sees the ragged Athanaël approach and tries to send the "beggar" off, but Athanaël says he knows Nicias and asks the boy to fetch him. Meanwhile, he gazes upon the city of his birth, denouncing its worldliness and corruption *(Voilà donc la terrible cité!)*. Nicias appears, recognizing his old schoolmate. Athanaël makes it clear that this is not a social visit: he wants to convert Thaïs. She happens to be Nicias' mistress of the moment, though Nicias has run out of money and is about to lose her. Nicias laughingly warns that Venus will take revenge on Athanaël, but he agrees to introduce him to Thaïs and sets his slave girls, Crobyle and Myrtale, the task of making the monk look presentable (quartet: *Ne t'offense pas de leur raillerie*). Guests arrive singing the praises of Thaïs, who bids Nicias a tender adieu after their week of love (duet: *C'est Thaïs, l'idole fragile*). Athanaël confronts her and announces his mission, which she dismisses lightly, saying that only love has power and urging Athanaël to give in to it *(Qui te fait si sévère)*. Seeing that she is about to disrobe, he leaves in horror, declaring he will wait for her at her own palace.

ACT II   In Thaïs' home, she questions the superficiality of her companions and worries that time will end her beauty, looking into a mirror for reassurance (*Dis-moi que je suis belle*). Athanaël surprises her, praying to himself that her charms will not distract him. Saying that there is one kind of love she does not yet know, he exhorts her to prepare her soul for eternal life (*Ah! qui m'inspirera des discours embrasés*), in order to rise resurrected from the grave of sin. Thaïs hears Nicias' voice outside, pleading for her love. She rejects the world of luxury but tells Athanaël she rejects his God as well. He leaves, saying he will wait before her house till daybreak.

§ In the square outside, after an orchestral meditation that describes her soul-searching, Thaïs comes to tell Athanaël that she is ready to follow him. He says there is a convent to the west where she can join other women; their mother superior is Albine, whose name Thaïs recognizes as that of a daughter of the Caesars. Before leaving, he adds, Thaïs must destroy her past—put the place to the torch. She agrees but wants to save one keepsake, a little statue of Eros, representing love (*L'amour est une vertu rare*). Athanaël smashes the idol and leads her inside. Nicias enters the square happily with his friends: gambling, he has won back his money and can offer to keep Thaïs a while longer (*Suivez-moi tous, amis!*). He orders entertainment, led by the dancer La Charmeuse, accompanied by the singing of Crobyle and Myrtale (duet: *Celle qui vient est plus belle*). When Thaïs and Athanaël appear, the crowd turns against the monk for taking away their favorite, but Nicias throws gold coins around, permitting the two to escape as flames engulf Thaïs' palace.

ACT III   Nearing Albine's retreat in the desert, Thaïs and Athanaël pause at an oasis. She feels unable to go on. Sternly ordering her to force herself and deny her flesh, Athanaël relents when he sees her bleeding feet. He fetches water and fruit to revive her, as she pledges her life to God under Athanaël's guidance (duet: *Baigne d'eau mes mains et mes lèvres*). Albine comes from the convent with several of the sisters to welcome Thaïs, who bids farewell to Athanaël. Though she says they will meet in heaven, he gazes sadly as she goes toward the convent.

§ Back at the monks' retreat, the evening meal has concluded once more, as a desert storm gathers in the distance. Palémon remarks that Athanaël seems like a dead man since his return twenty days ago. Athanaël joins them, confessing to Palémon that in spite of all his fasting and prayer, Thaïs's image still haunts him with its profane, voluptuous beauty. Palémon laments the contaminating effect of the outside world and withdraws, leaving Athanaël to sleep—and to dream of Thaïs the temptress, followed by Thaïs about to die in the monastery. Waking, he cries he must go to her and runs toward the desert, despite the approaching storm.

§ At the monastery, Thaïs lies dying after three months of penance. Albine welcomes Athanaël, and Thaïs asks him whether he remembers converting her (*Te souvient-il du lumineux voyage*), but he replies that it is *she* who has converted *him*—to worldly love. No longer understanding his impassioned pleas, she rises, transfixed by a vision of heaven opening its gates. As she falls dead, Athanaël collapses in despair.

CENDRILLON

(Cinderella)

FAIRY TALE IN FOUR ACTS AND SIX TABLEAUX
MUSIC: Jules Massenet
TEXT (French): Henri Cain
WORLD PREMIERE: Paris, Opéra Comique, May 24, 1899
U.S. PREMIERE: New Orleans, December 23, 1902

CHARACTERS

Cendrillon (Lucette) . . . . Soprano
Noémie ⎫ *her stepsisters* . . . . ⎧ Soprano
Dorothée⎭   ⎩ Mezzo-Soprano
Mme. de la Haltière, *their mother* . . . . Contralto
Fairy . . . . Soprano
Prince Charming . . . . Soprano (Tenor)
The King . . . . Baritone
Pandolfe, *Cendrillon's father* . . . . Bass

ACT I   Sometime during the sixteenth or seventeenth century, in the salon of Mme. de la Haltière, her servants are kept going at a furious pace by her constant demands. Her amiable, henpecked husband, Pandolfe, wanders in, reflecting that all attempts to assert himself have proved useless *(Du côté de la barbe est la toute-puissance);* he is especially unhappy to see his daughter Lucette neglected while his wife's two daughters get preferential treatment. When he hears his wife approaching, he beats a hasty retreat. She lectures her daughters, Noémie and Dorothée, on the importance of looking their best at tonight's ball: they are going to be presented to the King *(Quel succès! Quel espoir!)*. Milliners, tailors, and hairdressers arrive to supervise their toilette. When they have finished, Pandolfe appears, dressed for the evening, and is obliged to admire the three women, who hustle him away without so much as a chance to kiss Lucette good-bye (trio: *De la race de la prestance)*. Lucette enters alone, thinking wistfully of what she is missing by having to stay home and do domestic work *(Reste au foyer, petit grillon)*. Once her chores are done, she dozes off and in her dream sees the Fairy, who rallies spirits and elves, hailing Lucette as Cendrillon (Cinderella) and promising to look out for her: they will produce a carriage and escort her to the ball. Insects are sent far and wide to find jewels and finery for her. The girl awakens to find herself beautifully gowned and the Fairy of her dreams standing there. Cautioning her to be home by midnight and giving her a magic slipper to prevent her stepmother and stepsisters from recognizing her, the Fairy sends Lucette—now transformed into Cendrillon—off to the ball.

ACT II   In the ballroom of Prince Charming's palace, musicians serenade him while courtiers discuss arrangements for the ball. Distracted, he pays no attention and sends them all away, reflecting on his loneliness and desire for love *(Si, me tendant les bras)*. His father, the King, enters with his court and tells Prince Charming to choose a bride from among the beauties who will attend the ball. To the sound of ballet music, elegantly dressed girls are introduced; Cendrillon appears last. Everyone admires Cendrillon except Mme. de la Haltière and her daughters, who do not recognize her but feel threatened. Seeing his son attracted to the stranger, the King leaves him alone with her. When the Prince asks her name, she says she must remain unknown and cannot stay, though she admits she would like to *(Vous êtes mon prince Charmant)*. Just as he is declaring his love, the hour strikes midnight, and the Fairy appears to take Cendrillon home, leaving the Prince distracted as dancing continues.

ACT III   The breathless Lucette arrives home, alarmed by her nocturnal flight through the streets and the loss of her glass slipper. As she realizes that it is all just a memory, her father, stepmother, and stepsisters arrive, in the midst of a spirited argument: Mme. de la Haltière is berating Pandolfe for gawking at the insolent stranger (Cendrillon) who crashed the party *(Fi donc! Monsieur)*. Mother and daughters indignantly describe to Lucette how the intruder caught the Prince's fancy and then ran away. When Pandolfe finally loses patience with them, mother and daughters storm out, leaving him to comfort Lucette with thoughts of taking her away from the city to a new, peaceful life *(Viens, nous quitterons cette ville)*. He goes to pack a few things for their escape, and Lucette sadly recalls the Prince, then says good-bye to her tame turtledoves and thinks back to her infancy, weeping over the memory of her mother. As a storm breaks outside, she runs off into the night, resolving to find the enchanted oak tree where the fairies gather and to meet her death there.

§ Beneath an oak near the seashore, fairies, sprites, and will-o'-the-wisps dance and sing at the behest of the Fairy herself. Lucette and the Prince approach from opposite directions without seeing each other and kneel, addressing their prayers to the Fairy. The Prince laments his loss of the mysterious girl at the ball *(Vous qui pouvez tout voir)*, then overhears (but does not recognize) her voice pleading that the Prince be spared suffering on her account. After he has declared that there is nothing he would not do to find the unknown girl, Lucette recognizes his voice and tells him her name. The Fairy appears among the branches and permits them to see each other. As they embrace, she invokes a spell causing them to fall asleep on the embankment, lulled by the voices of sprites.

ACT IV   Outside Pandolfe's house on a spring morning, he looks after the sleeping Lucette, who he says was found unconscious by a stream, months before. The convalescent awakens, and Pandolfe tells her that in her delirium she spoke of the ball and Prince Charming, of an enchanted oak, and of glass slippers. She is soon persuaded she only dreamt it all. Some girl friends come to visit her; though she is cheered by seeing them, she leaves sadly with her father at the sound of Mme. de la Haltière's voice. Mme. de la Haltière leads her daughters in, coaching them for their return appearance at court: the King has ordered girls from everywhere to come to the palace to try on the glass slipper that Cendrillon lost after the ball. As a herald's voice proclaims this in the street, Lucette hears it and realizes that her dream was true after all. She calls on the Fairy, who appears behind her.

§ At the palace, in a bright courtyard, the princesses appear before Prince Charming, who asks them to try the glass slipper but despairs of finding his true love *(Posez dans son écrin)*. The Fairy appears and tells the languishing Prince to look up: he immediately recognizes Lucette, who offers to heal his despair by returning his heart to him. Joyfully he tells her to keep it as the crowd acclaims its future queen. Pandolfe is stunned to discover that it is his own daughter, while—to the amusement of the courtiers—Mme. de la Haltière does a quick about-face, greeting Cendrillon affectionately as her own daughter as well. All say good-bye to the audience, hoping that the visit to fairyland was a pleasant one.

GIAN CARLO MENOTTI

b. 1911

With the premiere of *The Medium,* in May 1946 at Columbia University's Brander Matthews Theater, in New York, and its subsequent run as a successful Broadway show, history was made in American opera. Though Broadway adaptations had been shown, such as *Carmen Jones* and *My Darlin' Aida,* never before had a new serious opera made its own way on the commercial stage in this fashion. (The closest comparison would be to *Porgy and Bess,* a hybrid work that owes much to the Broadway musical.) Gian Carlo Menotti's name was already known: as early as 1937, a few years out of the Curtis Institute in Philadelphia, he had produced the delightful *Amelia Goes to the Ball,* which led to a commission from NBC for a radio opera, *The Old Maid and the Thief* (1939). Both were farces in the tradition of Italian opera buffa; an attempt at serious drama, *The Island God,* had little success at the Metropolitan Opera in 1942. With *The Medium* he achieved an amalgam of his talents as librettist and composer, building on the verismo style that had worked so effectively for his predecessors.

Menotti, a longtime resident of the United States, is an Italian citizen, born in Cadegliano. After his early years at the Milan Conservatory, he completed his studies in Philadelphia, where Samuel Barber, a fellow pupil at Curtis, became his lifelong friend. With a sense of humor, a penchant for theatrical timing, and an eye and ear for human quirks, Menotti from the first showed a natural talent for the stage. Not an innovator musically, he has used music as a means to an end—to convey theatrical content in terms immediately grasped. Often criticized for this facility, which brought ready success, he has reached a larger audience more consistently than any other contemporary serious composer. Of the works that followed *The Medium,* the most enduring have proved to be *The Consul* (1950) and *Amahl and the Night Visitors,* an annual television event of the Christmas season since 1951. His establishment of the Festival of Two Worlds in Spoleto, Italy, in 1958, followed by a sister festival in Charleston, South Carolina, in 1977, interfered with Menotti's composing career, but he saw *The Last Savage* staged by the Met in 1964, and *The Saint of Bleecker Street* makes an occasional reappearance. He has also been in demand as a stage director of other composers' operas, in addition to his own.

THE MEDIUM

TWO ACTS
MUSIC: Gian Carlo Menotti
TEXT (English): by the composer
WORLD PREMIERE: Columbia University, May 8, 1946 (student
    performance); New York, May 1, 1947 (professional staging)

CHARACTERS

Monica, *daughter of Mme. Flora* . . . . Soprano
Mme. Flora, *medium* . . . . Contralto
Mrs. Gobineau ⎫   ⎧   Soprano
Mr. Gobineau ⎬ *her clients* . . . . ⎨   Baritone
Mrs. Nolan ⎭   ⎩ Mezzo-Soprano
Toby, *mute* . . . . Dancer

ACT I The time is the present, or the period of the opera's composition (1947). In a shabby walk-up apartment somewhere in a large American city, Mme. Flora (Baba) ekes out an existence as a medium, assisted by her daughter, Monica, and a mute Gypsy youth named Toby. Waiting for Mme. Flora's return from an errand, Monica interrupts a ballad she is singing to remind Toby that they are supposed to be getting the apartment ready for the next séance. Entering in a discouraged mood, Mme. Flora lashes out at Toby for trying on her costumes instead of putting the place in order. While Monica

dresses in one of the costumes, Toby checks the machinery for causing apparitions and levitating the table. Soon three clients arrive—a middle-aged couple, Mr. and Mrs. Gobineau, and a lone woman, Mrs. Nolan, who is visiting
for the first time. Diffidently, she says that she wants to contact her daughter
Doodly, who died at sixteen the year before. To make her feel at ease, Mrs.
Gobineau tells her about their infant son, who drowned years ago while playing with a toy boat, and whom the medium has enabled them to hear. Mme.
Flora starts the session, dimming the light over the table and letting out a cry
of anguish, which fades as Monica appears behind a scrim, reassuring Mrs.
Nolan that she is her daughter (*Mummy dear, you must not cry for me*). Mrs.
Nolan wants to question her further, but the vision disappears. She sobs quietly as the Gobineaus call their son, whose childish laughter is simulated by
Monica. As that episode recedes, Mme. Flora appears suddenly disturbed:
Who touched her? Trembling, she looks around, insisting she felt a hand in
the dark. The clients reassure her—they have often felt the same thing—but
she orders them sharply to leave. Asking Monica to pour her a drink, she says
the séances must not go on: she surely felt a cold hand at her throat. She wants
to blame Toby, who cringes in fear, but Monica tries to calm her with a
doleful ballad (*O black swan*), which Toby accompanies on a tambourine. Mme.
Flora hears again the voices of her clients' children. Though Monica assures
her she is imagining, Mme. Flora, terribly shaken, makes the others kneel
with her as she prays.

ACT II   A few days later, Toby has given a puppet-theater performance to
amuse Monica, who sings for him while he dances around (*Monica, dance the
waltz*). Sensing Toby's attachment to her, Monica half-jokingly improvises a
dialogue in which he confesses his love. Mme. Flora, who has been drinking,
comes in and tries to cajole Toby into admitting it was he who touched her
during the séance (*Toby, you know that I love you as if you were my own son*). His
negative nods and obvious fear eventually arouse her anger; promises having
failed, she tries threats, then goes for a whip and starts beating him. Interrupted by the doorbell, she admits her three clients and asks them to sit down,
refunding their money and saying the séances were a fraud. To prove this, she
shows the machinery used to produce the illusions, asking Monica to repeat
her vocal effects. The clients, however, refuse to be convinced: for them the
séances were real (quartet: *Surely now, you won't let us down!*). Only when Mme.
Flora throws them out will they leave. She says Toby too must go. This angers
Monica, who retires to her room after Toby's frightened departure. Sitting
alone, Mme. Flora again hears a ghostly voice calling, "Mother, mother, are
you there?" Drinking more to calm her nerves, she sits at the table, wondering
how she, who has survived so much, can now be cracking (*Afraid, am I afraid?*).
As the liquor takes effect, she grows hysterical but calms herself and falls
asleep. Toby creeps back into the apartment, hoping to escape with Monica,
but he finds that Mme. Flora has locked the girl's door. When he accidentally

makes a noise that awakens Mme. Flora, he hides behind a curtain in terror. The terrified woman pulls a revolver from the drawer and fires, crying, "I've killed the ghost!" Toby's lifeless body falls to the floor as Mme. Flora unlock's Monica's door. The stunned girl runs crying for help as the medium tries to find the answer in Toby's unseeing eyes to her desperate question: "Was it you?"

AMAHL AND THE NIGHT VISITORS

MUSIC: Gian Carlo Menotti
TEXT (English): by the composer
WORLD PREMIERE: NBC Television, December 24, 1951;
    Bloomington, Ind., February 21, 1952 (staged premiere)

CHARACTERS

Amahl, *crippled boy of about twelve* . . . . Treble
His Mother . . . . Soprano
King Kaspar . . . . Tenor
King Melchior . . . . Baritone
King Balthazar . . . . Bass
The Page . . . . Baritone
Shepherds, villagers, dancers

Early in the year A.D. 1, Amahl, a crippled shepherd boy, is playing his pipe outside the hut where he lives with his widowed Mother. Because night has fallen, his Mother calls to him to come inside. When Amahl hesitates, she is annoyed, especially when he tells the unlikely story of having seen a comet. It soon develops that her irritability is sparked by anxiety about their poverty. Amahl tries to console her by saying he will go begging with her (*Don't cry, Mother dear*), but she puts him to bed and extinguishes the lamp. As they start to fall asleep, however, the singing of a small group of travelers is heard on the road outside (*From far away we come*). Looking out the window, Amahl sees a Page leading a procession of three kings bearing treasure. When they knock at the door, the Mother tells Amahl to see who it is. At first she does not believe his description, thinking he is making up stories again, but at length she goes to the door herself and bows in amazement before the strangers, who ask for a place to spend the night. She offers them what little comfort she can—a bed of straw. She steps outside to gather firewood, leaving Amahl to question the three—one of whom, Kaspar, is hard-of-hearing and somewhat absent-minded. Amahl tells the first king, Balthazar, that he used to be a shepherd but will have to go begging, now that his Mother was forced to sell the sheep (*I was a shepherd*). Kaspar shows the boy his tame parrot and a chest full of precious stones (*This is my box*), from which he offers Amahl a piece of licorice. The Mother returns and sends Amahl to the neighboring shepherds for whatever can be found to offer to the visitors. Then she looks in amazement at the treasure. The third king, Melchior, says they are taking these gifts to a child of whom they have heard, to whom a bright star is guiding them. But she can think only of her own child (ensemble: *Have you see a Child?*). Shepherds arrive, led by Amahl, and hesitantly enter the hut, awed by the kings, to whom they give presents of food. As some of the younger family members dance, Amahl and an old shepherd play their pipes (shepherds' dance). Balthazar thanks them all and bids them good night. After the shepherds have left, Amahl asks Kaspar whether one of his precious stones might cure a crippled boy, but the king's deafness prevents conversation. Everyone falls asleep except the Mother, who cannot take her thoughts off the treasure (*All that gold!*); she wonders whether rich people know what to do with their wealth, whether they realize what a little of it would mean to a destitute family. At length she decides she could take some: "They'll never miss it." When she touches the treasure, however, the Page awakens and seizes her, calling out to the kings that he caught her stealing. Amahl tries to attack the Page and pleads with the kings. Kaspar signals the Page to let go of the Mother, who falls to her knees, embracing Amahl. Melchior tells her to keep the gold she took, because the child they are going to visit will not need it: his kingdom will not be of this world, and he will bring new life. Realizing that this means the Messiah, the Mother says she has waited all her life for such a king, and insists that the others take back the gold for him. Amahl wants to send his homemade crutch, his only valued possession, as a gift: "He may need one." As he offers it to the kings, he finds he is healed and can walk. The kings hail this as a sign from God; Amahl gains confidence and dances around the room. The kings and the Page ask whether they may touch the child who has been blessed. Now Amahl wants to accompany the others on their journey, so that he can present the crutch himself, in thanks. Armed with motherly admonitions, he joins them as they set out, playing his pipe as he goes. Shepherds are heard outside, welcoming the dawn of a day of peace.

GIACOMO
MEYERBEER
1791–1864

A mastodon in the museum of music is Giacomo Meyerbeer, an extinct species from whom all later grand-opera elephants are descended. Without Meyerbeer's kind of French stage spectacle, with its gigantic sweep and unlimited resources, neither Wagner nor Verdi would have written as they did. "Like Liszt, another eclectic and highly influential composer, he will remain a problem child, difficult to categorize, easy to deride, fascinating to study," concludes music critic Alan Blyth.

Born in Berlin, the son of a banker, as Jakob Liebmann Beer, the composer incorporated into his name that of a grandfather, Meyer, who contributed to his expenses while he was studying, first in Darmstadt, where Weber was a classmate and friend, later in Italy, where he was advised to go by Salieri, Mozart's rival. He had great success with Italian-style operas until he left for Paris in 1825 and eventually settled there permanently, producing *Robert le Diable* in 1831 and *Les Huguenots* five years later.

The two decades 1830–50 were his period of glory. He favored the librettos of Eugène Scribe, a prolific craftsman whose atelier turned them out by the dozen, mixing strong emotional confrontations with a smattering of historical color. Like the Hollywood epics of a century later, these were meant more to entertain than to instruct. Wagner, who at first admired Meyerbeer and sought his help, later turned against him, citing his "effects without causes." Verdi more temperately saw what Meyerbeer had to offer and made it his own: *Un Ballo in Maschera, Don Carlos,* and *Aida* particularly reflect Meyerbeer's example and innovations.

Les Huguenots is a fictionalized account of events leading to the St. Bartholomew's Day Massacre of August 24, 1572, in which extremist elements of the French Catholic majority attacked their Huguenot (Protestant) countrymen. Marguerite de Valois married Henry of Navarre (later Henry IV of France) just a few days before the massacre, as part of a plan devised by her brother, Charles IX, to effect a rapprochement with the Huguenots. Though Henry was a Huguenot, he converted to Catholicism to save himself after the massacre and was held a virtual court prisoner until 1576, when he escaped and rejoined the Huguenots. Succeeding to the French throne in 1589, after more religious civil warfare in France, he eventually returned to the Catholic faith.

Religious struggle again fueled the "Scribe factory" for *Le Prophète,* a free account of the death of John of Leyden, who assumed leadership of the theocracy set up by the Anabaptists in Münster in 1534 and who was executed, with other leaders, the following year. In this "Kingdom of Zion," which abolished laws, marriage, and property, the Anabaptists showed their most extreme side. The gadflies of Protestantism, they represented the radical wing of those forces that brought on the Reformation. Their basic tenet, like that of the Baptists, an English sect, was that infant baptism was invalid—not being sanctioned by Scripture—and that only believers should receive baptism. Though the events of *Le Prophète* are mostly fictitious, its atmosphere of militant, distrustful commoners rising against their overlords is true to the period, which produced the abortive Peasants' War of the mid-1520s, vividly depicted in Hindemith's *Mathis der Maler.*

Because Meyerbeer's operas are seldom staged today, it is difficult to appreciate them for what they were in their time—namely, spectacular shows, tours de force of musical dramaturgy, conceived by a man with a singular instinct for the stage. It fell to his successors to develop his ideas. The grand marches in *Tannhäuser* and *Aida,* for example, make their immediate forebear, the coronation march of *Le Prophète,* seem simple by comparison. Yet they cannot eclipse the brilliant theatricality that made Meyerbeer the most celebrated entertainer of his day.

LES HUGUENOTS

FIVE ACTS
MUSIC: Giacomo Meyerbeer
TEXT (French): Eugène Scribe, after Émile Deschamps
WORLD PREMIERE: Paris Opera, February 29, 1836
U.S. PREMIERE: New Orleans, April 20, 1839
METROPOLITAN OPERA PREMIERE: March 19, 1884 (in Italian)

CHARACTERS

Valentine de Saint-Bris, *betrothed to Nevers* . . . . Soprano
Marguerite de Valois, *betrothed to Henry of Navarre* . . . . Soprano
Urbain, *Marguerite's page* . . . . Mezzo-Soprano
Raoul de Nangis, *Huguenot nobleman* . . . . Tenor
Count de Saint-Bris⎱ *Catholic gentlemen* . . . . Baritones
Count de Nevers ⎰
Marcel, *Huguenot soldier, Raoul's servant* . . . . Bass
      Catholic noblemen, gentlemen, Huguenots, servants, etc.

ACT I   The Château de Nevers, in the Touraine, 1572. Count de Nevers tells his companions that the king (Charles IX) wants to encourage friendship with the Huguenots, so Nevers has invited one Raoul de Nangis to join them. When Raoul arrives, Nevers, who is to be married the next day, proposes that they take turns confessing to some amorous adventure. Raoul begins, telling of an unknown woman he rescued from danger, and with whom he fell in love at first sight (*Plus blanche que la blanche hermine*). Camaraderie is strained by the arrival of Raoul's gruff old servant, Marcel, a fanatical Protestant who fought at La Rochelle and disapproves of the company his master is keeping. He launches into a Huguenot battle song (*Piff, paff, piff!*). A valet informs Nevers that a veiled lady is waiting in the chapel; intrigued, the count excuses himself. As the others gossip over her possible identity, Raoul recognizes her from the window as the unknown beauty of whom he spoke. Assuming the worst, he reviles her to himself as Nevers returns, obviously disturbed; the woman was his fiancée, requesting that they break their engagement. A young page, Urbain, arrives with a message for Raoul (*Nobles seigneurs, salut!*): he is bidden to a rendezvous but must be taken there blindfolded. Though assuming it to be a practical joke, he agrees to go. Since the others have recognized the seal of Marguerite de Valois on the note, they declare that he is on the brink of great fortune (ensemble: *Les plaisirs, les honneurs*).

ACT II On the grounds of the Château de Chenonceaux, near Amboise, Marguerite, the king's sister, admires the beautiful countryside (*O beau pays de la Touraine!*). Her maid of honor, Valentine de Saint-Bris, returns to say that Nevers has agreed to break their engagement. She admits that she is diffident about meeting Raoul, who rescued her from danger and aroused in her feelings of love, so Marguerite offers to talk to him first. The other maids of honor are swimming in the river (chorus: *Jeunes beautés, sous ce feuillage*); Urbain, overwhelmed at the sight of so many scantily clad beauties (*Non, non, non*), reports the approach of a blindfolded gentleman. Alone with Raoul, Marguerite captures his fancy when the blindfold is removed. To avenge himself on the faithless unknown woman, he pledges loyalty to Marguerite, whose aim, however, is to divert it in Valentine's favor. She tells Raoul he may remain in her court if he will marry the daughter of the Count de Saint-Bris, thereby encouraging peace between Catholics and Protestants. He agrees, and as other members of her entourage return, joined by Nevers and Saint-Bris himself, she announces the arrangement. When she presents the bride, Raoul and Nevers are both horrified—Raoul because she is the presumably faithless unknown beauty, Nevers because he gave up his fiancée to a rival (ensemble: *Trahison! perfidie!*). Valentine is hurt by at Raoul's negative reaction, an insult her father vows to avenge, but Marcel applauds his master's refusal to marry a Catholic.

ACT III On the Pré-aux-Clercs, a green stretching down toward the Seine in Paris, citizens enjoy the open air while Huguenot soldiers carouse in a nearby tavern (*Rataplan, rataplan*). Gypsy girls offer to read fortunes but are persuaded by some students to dance instead. Saint-Bris, who once again has promised his daughter's hand to Nevers, receives a message from Raoul, asking to meet him there later; Marcel, who delivered it, overhears Saint-Bris rejoice at the prospect of revenge. As worshipers enter the church for vespers, a constable enforces the curfew, moving people away from outside the church. Valentine appears, desperately wondering how to prevent her father and Raoul from confronting each other. Recognizing Marcel, concealed nearby, she enlists his help (duet: *Ah! tu ne peux éprouver ni comprendre*). She withdraws before Raoul and Saint-Bris arrive with their seconds, who fuss over the rules of combat (ensemble: *Quoi qu'il advienne ou qu'il arrive*) after Raoul brushes off Marcel's warning of a trap. Soon they all are caught up in a free-for-all between Catholic students and Protestant soldiers, the latter issuing from the tavern. At the height of the fracas, Marguerite appears, on her way back to the palace. Deploring the violence, she is further disturbed by the accusations flying between Raoul and Saint-Bris. Scarcely has she learned of Valentine's marriage to Nevers than the bridal procession comes into view, Nevers leading his bride

(*Noble dame, venez près d'un epoux*) as the others celebrate. In spite of Marguerite's order to keep the peace, the soldiers and students are still itching for a fight.

ACT IV   In Valentine's apartment in the Nevers town house, she grieves over Raoul, whom she cannot put from her thoughts (*Parmi les pleurs*). To her surprise, he appears at the door, saying he wanted to see her once more before dying. Though he refuses her advice to flee and save himself, he does hide when Saint-Bris, Nevers and several other Catholic nobles arrive. Interpreting the king's and Marguerite's desire for peace as a mandate to take matters into their own hands, they propose that Saint-Bris enact God's will by ambushing the Huguenots (*Pour cette cause sainte*). Nevers refuses to go along, saying he will fight for his king but not commit murder; Valentine thanks him. Ordering his son-in-law placed under guard, Saint-Bris tells the others to circulate with their men among the crowds, then strike when the Huguenot leaders meet with the king and Marguerite. The signal will be the bell of Saint-Germain followed by that of Auxerrois; the conspirators are to wear white scarves bearing the Cross of Lorraine. They all repeat that their mission is God's will (*Dieu le veut!*). When they have gone, Raoul emerges, and Valentine tries in vain to stop him from risking his life. Only when she declares her love does he agree to escape with her (*Tu m'aimes? Ah! quel éclair*). The sound of the first bell brings him back to his senses. He is held back by Valentine but drags her to the window at the second bell to see the massacre outside. As she swoons, he leaps from the balcony to the street.

ACT V   At the Hôtel de Nesle, Marguerite and the king entertain Protestant leaders. Raoul bursts in to warn of the ambush (*À la lueur de leurs torches funèbres*), calling his friends to arms.

§ Raoul finds the wounded Marcel outside a church, directing Huguenot civilians to shelter inside. Valentine in turn finds Raoul, offering him safe-conduct to the Louvre, where the queen will protect him—but he must take a white scarf, embracing Catholicism. When he learns that Nevers has died in combat, leaving her free, Raoul is torn, but Marcel calls him back to his duty. Crying that she cannot leave him to die (*Eh bien! tu connaîtras tout l'amour d'une femme!*), she renounces her religion and asks Marcel to marry them in the Protestant faith, which he does. A troupe of armed Catholics storms the church, massacring those inside, who die with Luther's hymn *A Mighty Fortress* on their lips. Inspired by Marcel, the lovers see a vision of heaven opening its gates (trio: *Délice suprème*). The assassins order them to recant or die. As the three try to get away, the assassins fire and leave them for dead. When Saint-Bris arrives with another group, the three wounded pronounce themselves Huguenots and are shot again. As Marguerite appears, trying in vain to stop the bloodshed, Saint-Bris realizes he ordered the death of his own daughter.

LE PROPHÈTE

FIVE ACTS
MUSIC: Giacomo Meyerbeer
TEXT (French): Eugène Scribe
WORLD PREMIERE: Paris Opera, April 16, 1849
U.S. PREMIERE: New Orleans, April 2, 1850
METROPOLITAN OPERA PREMIERE: March 21, 1884 (in Italian)

CHARACTERS

Jean de Leyde (John of Leyden) . . . . Tenor
Berthe, *his bride* . . . . Soprano
Fidès, *his mother* . . . . Mezzo-Soprano
Jonas ⎫
Mathisen ⎬ *Anabaptists* . . . . ⎰Tenor
Zacharie ⎭ ⎱Bass
                                                  Bass
Count Oberthal . . . . Baritone
Peasants, farmers, soldiers, citizens of Holland and Germany

ACT I Outside the castle of Count Oberthal, near Dordrecht and the River Meuse, Holland, 1534. An orphaned peasant girl, Berthe, appears amid rejoicing farmers and millers, bursting with expectation about her engagement to Jean de Leyde *(Mon coeur s'élance et palpite)*. She greets Jean's mother, Fidès, who brings the engagement ring and wants to take Berthe back to Leyden. Berthe explains she cannot leave without the consent of her feudal lord, Oberthal, so Berthe leads her toward the castle to ask him. Their errand is disturbed by three sinister-looking men in black, whom Berthe recognizes as itinerant preachers. They are Anabaptists—Jonas, Zacharie, and Mathisen. Addressing the crowd in Latin, they switch to the vernacular for their message, which is that peasants should rise against their masters. The credulous locals grab pitchforks and scythes for an assault on the castle (chorus: *O roi des cieux*) but quickly fall back when Oberthal appears at the door of the castle, surrounded by friends and retainers. He identifies the Anabaptists as troublemakers, recognizing Jonas as his former cellar master, dismissed for stealing. He tells soldiers to lead them away, then notices the attractive Berthe; she asks permission to marry Jean, who once rescued her from drowning in the river *(Un jour, dans les flots de la Meuse)*. Taken with her, Oberthal refuses to let her leave. This annoys the peasants anew, but when they advance as if to threaten him, he intimidates them (*Je l'ai dit, je le veux*) and has Berthe and Fidès taken to the castle. The Anabaptists return to bless the peasants and renew their attempts to spread their revolutionary doctrine.

Act II   At the inn operated by Fidès and Jean on the outskirts of Leyden, patrons dance and drink beer, while Jean impatiently awaits his mother's return with Berthe. The Anabaptists sit quietly to one side. Jonas remarks on Jean's resemblance to a portrait of King David at the Münster Cathedral. When the crowd leaves, the three approach Jean, who tells them of a disturbing dream he had in which he was hailed as a messiah but was threatened by the devil (*Sous les vastes arceaux d'un temple magnifique*). When the Anabaptists tell him that his dream is about to come true, he sends them away, saying he wants only to marry Berthe. A commotion outside signals the arrival of the breathless Berthe, with Oberthal in pursuit. Jean hides Berthe, but Oberthal tells him he must choose: either give her up or see Fidès put to death. Raging but helpless, Jean turns Berthe over to her captor. Fidès blesses Jean for saving her (*Ah! mon fils*). When he hears the Anabaptists' hymn, Jean asks whether he could conquer Oberthal by accepting their offer. They assure him he could, saying God calls him to lead the downtrodden (*Oui, c'est Dieu qui t'appelle*). Seeing his mother asleep, Jean hesitates, then follows them.

Act III   On a winter evening at the Anabaptist encampment in a Westphalian forest, sounds of a nearby conflict are heard, and Anabaptist soldiers drag in civilian prisoners. The crowd clamors for their execution, but Mathisen points out that these nobles can pay ransom. Zacharie hails a victory over tyranny, crying that their foes have been scattered like the sands of the desert (*Aussi nombreux que les étoiles*). Local farmers on skates bring provisions across the frozen pond for the famished soldiers (ballet).

§ By night in Zacharie's tent, Mathisen reports that Oberthal's father, the governor of Münster, refuses to surrender, that the emperor is sending reinforcements, and that the Anabaptists must thus act quickly. Zacharie tells Mathisen to take three hundred men for a night attack. As he goes out, Jonas and some soldiers appear with a man they have caught near the camp. It is Oberthal, who, unrecognized, pretends he was looking for the Anabaptists so that he could enlist with them. Jonas, Zacharie, and Oberthal drink together to their cause (*Verse, verse, frère*). When Jonas strikes a light, the fanatics recognize the intruder and order him executed. Jean, who has kept to himself for the past day, enters, saying he cannot bear to continue the slaughter. When the prisoner is led past, he orders him spared, then recognizes Oberthal and asks to be left alone with him. Oberthal says that Berthe tried to kill herself but has been reported safe in Münster. Jean resolves to find her, but Mathisen rushes in to report that his men met heavy resistance at Münster.

Jean demands to know who attacked without his knowledge, upbraiding Mathisen and Zacharie for taking matters into their own hands (*Perfides, que mon bras devrait punir!*), then leading his followers in prayer (*Seigneur, appaise ta colère!*). He has a vision in which angels tell him to conquer Münster. Outside, the fog over the pond clears and day dawns, showing the city in the distance as the Anabaptist forces prepare to march.

ACT IV   In the square in front of the Münster city hall, by orders of the conquering Anabaptists, citizens bring their silver and gold, hailing the conquerors out loud, cursing them under their breath. To prevent the identification of Jean as the Prophet, the Anabaptists have given out word that he died. Fidès, wandering like a lost soul in the square, believes her son dead and begs alms to have a mass said for him (*Donnez pour une pauvre âme*). Berthe, dressed as a pilgrim, wanders in; the two embrace, and Berthe tells how she threw herself into the ocean but was rescued by a fisherman (*Pour garder à ton fils*); Fidès lacks the heart to tell her of Jean's death but finally has to (duet: *Dernier espoir*). Both believe that the Prophet is responsible, and Berthe cries that God will lead her to vengeance.

§ Inside the cathedral, Jean, who is to be crowned king of the Anabaptists, walks in the procession that is slowly filing through. As Fidès comes in, trumpeters sound the coronation march. Fidès calls on God to punish the Prophet through Berthe. A children's chorus heralds the Prophet King, who supposedly was not born of mortal woman. When he reappears, wearing the crown, Fidès recognizes him as her son and cries out. Jean wants to go to her but is restrained by Mathisen, who says he must not acknowledge her if he wants her to live. Denied by her son, Fidès calls him an ingrate; he replies she must be mad. Questioning the Prophet's divine origin, the bystanders start a near-riot. When Jonas and other Anabaptists prepare to kill Fidès, however, Jean stops them and calls on God to cure her madness (*Que la sainte lumière*). Hypnotized by his gaze, she falls to her knees. He says the Anabaptists should run him through with their swords if he is her son. Faced with this, Fidès lies, saying he is not. The crowd believes it has seen a miracle. Fidès, prevented by the Anabaptists from following Jean, now wonders how to save him from the vengeance that Berthe is planning.

ACT V   The tides of battle have turned against the Anabaptists. In a basement dungeon of the palace of Münster, the three leaders agree to hand their plunder and the Prophet over to the emperor, who is preparing to attack, in exchange for their own safe-conduct out of the doomed city. Soldiers bring in Fidès, who curses the infidels that are keeping her from reaching Berthe and saving Jean (*O prêtres de Baal*). Though Jean's rejection torments her, she can forgive him. An officer tells her that the Prophet King is coming to see her; she waits with anxiety (*Il va venir!*). Entering, he tries to embrace her, but she upbraids him for denying her. He tells her he accepted the crown only in hopes of saving Berthe, admitting his remorse at the consequences (Ah! c'est mon seul amour). If he is truly repentant, says Fidès, he must renounce his power at once; otherwise heaven will be closed to him, and her heart as well (Ah! viens, il est temps). Happy in her forgiveness, he agrees. As they embrace, Berthe finds her way to the dungeon and tells Fidès she means to blow up the castle by igniting the munitions stored in its basement. Not knowing that Jean is the Prophet, she welcomes him, and the three briefly imagine their escape to a happier life (Loin de la ville). An officer comes to warn the Prophet of a conspiracy against his life. Learning his identity, Berthe recoils from him. Fidès says they must escape at once, but Jean wants to stay and meet death with Berthe as atonement for his crimes. Realizing she still loves the traitor, Berthe stabs herself. Jean has the soldiers lead Fidès to safety and carry Berthe away. Then he puts his crown back on and vows to punish those who led him into error. Going up the stairs, he takes note of the store of explosives Berthe mentioned.

§ In a hall of the palace, festivities are under way, with dining and dancing. All hail the Prophet's glory, but the three leaders mutter that his glory will not last long. Jean quietly tells his only faithful officers to wait for his signal, then to escape, locking everyone in and igniting the explosives. Feigning gaiety, he invites everyone to drink (Versez! que tout respire). Oberthal, leading imperial troops, bursts into the hall, and the three leaders turn against the Prophet. Jean declares that all will die with him. An explosion is heard, and the walls topple as smoke fills the hall. Fidès makes her way in to die with her son, who welcomes the divine flame of purification (Ah! viens, divine flamme).

ITALO
MONTEMEZZI
1875–1952

I ntroduced in 1913, *L'Amore dei Tre Re* illustrates several trends in Italian opera at the time. Italo Montemezzi's music, like Puccini's, emphasized vocal melody but also took into account "modern" trends exemplified by such bold spirits as Richard Strauss and Claude Debussy. The subject matter, a tragic medieval love story, seems straight out of *Tristan und Isolde,* its poetic language another trend of the time, led by the high-flown verse dramas of Gabriele D'Annunzio and Sem Benelli, author of *L'Amore dei Tre Re.*

The early success of Montemezzi's opera in the United States owed much to its interpreters: Arturo Toscanini conducted the American premiere at the Met in 1914, and among the sopranos who essayed the role of Fiora were Lucrezia Bori, Claudia Muzio, Rosa Ponselle, and Mary Garden. Scarcely less important is the nemesis role of King Archibaldo (a less benign version of Debussy's Arkel), on which Adamo Didur, Ezio Pinza, and Virgilio Lazzari left their mark. Revivals since World War II have been few, but—given soloists with the requisite vocal beauty and dramatic intensity—Montemezzi's opus, third of his five operas, seems ready to spring back to life.

The composer died in his native Verona in 1952. Neither he nor his contemporaries Pizzetti, Alfano, Zandonai, and Respighi achieved fame in opera comparable to that of Strauss or Puccini, but they all made important contributions during what many considered the dying era of the lyric stage.

L'AMORE DEI TRE RE

(The Love of Three Kings)

THREE ACTS
MUSIC: Italo Montemezzi
TEXT (Italian): Sem Benelli
WORLD PREMIERE: Milan, La Scala, April 19, 1913
U.S. PREMIERE: Metropolitan Opera, January 2, 1914

CHARACTERS

Archibaldo, *King of Altura* . . . . Bass
Baron Manfredo, *his son* . . . . Baritone
Avito, *former Prince of Altura* . . . . Tenor
Fiora, *Manfredo's wife* . . . . Soprano
Flaminio, *castle guard* . . . . Tenor
Children, young girl, old woman, people of Altura

ACT I   In tenth-century Italy, in a hall of King Archibaldo's castle opening onto a terrace, the blind old king asks the guard Flaminio whether dawn is approaching: he awaits the return of his son, Baron Manfredo, who has been away at battle. Some forty years earlier, Archibaldo invaded from the north and took Altura as his kingdom; later, to cement peace, the local people allowed their Princess Fiora, who was engaged to Prince Avito, to marry Manfredo instead. Fiora is now asleep in an adjoining chamber. Archibaldo recalls his lifelong love for Italy, the prize of his youth *(Son quarant'anni)*—to the discomfort of Flaminio, who belongs to the vanquished. When the guard describes dawn approaching, Archibaldo tells him to extinguish the signal lantern on the ramparts. Hearing a rustic flute in the distance, Flaminio, who knows its meaning, directs Archibaldo back toward his own apartments. The flute heralds the arrival of Avito, Fiora's former betrothed, who greets her as she emerges from her chamber. He is apprehensive, but her words of love turn his mind from danger (duet: *Dammi le labbra*) as they embrace passionately. The sound of Archibaldo's footsteps sends Avito hastily away. Sensing Fiora's presence and her agitation, the old king asks her who was with her. She was alone and could not sleep, she says. Despising her evasiveness, which apparently has galled him for some time, he mutters he could not bring himself to touch her, lest he kill her. Flaminio calls out that Manfredo has returned. Archibaldo sends Fiora to her room, then welcomes his son, who has taken a few days' leave from the siege; he genuinely loves Fiora and hopes she is learning to return his feeling. She comes out to greet him, needling Archibaldo by asking him to confirm that she was on the terrace, waiting for her husband at dawn. Embracing Fiora warmly (*Piccola fiore, vieni sul mio petto*), Manfredo voices happiness at being reunited with her, then leads her to her room. Archibaldo prays that since his eyesight has been taken, he may remain blind to what is happening.

ACT II   A few days later, as Manfredo prepares to return to the fray, he tries to convey to Fiora his sorrow at leaving her (*Suonata e l'ora della partenza*), asking her to wave her veil from the ramparts until he is out of sight. Sympathizing with the depth and sincerity of his emotion, she agrees, and he kisses her good-bye. As she ascends to the top of the castle wall, Avito appears, dressed as a castle guard: Flaminio has kept him in hiding. Fiora says their affair must end: her husband's goodness makes her guilt unbearable. When a maid brings the veil, she remembers her promise and waves it with effort, distracted by Avito's farewell pleading: if she will not give him a last kiss, he at least wants to kiss her garment. Stepping down from the wall, she yields to his arms and her own heart. Their embrace ends with the arrival of Archibaldo, who senses once more that someone has been there. As Avito slips away, Flaminio goes to meet Manfredo, whom he sees turning back toward the castle. Alone with Fiora, Archibaldo confronts her. Seeing his disbelief, she defies him at last: she admits she has a lover, saying she would sooner die than name him. Beside himself with rage and frustration, the old man throttles her, then steps back in horror from her mute body (*Silenzio! Notte fonda!*) as Manfredo returns: when he failed to see the waving veil, he feared that Fiora might have fallen from the wall. In horror and sadness he hears his father admit the murder and learns that Fiora was capable of such intense love—but not for him. Stunned, he reenters the castle, followed by Archibaldo, who carries Fiora's body over his shoulder.

ACT III   In the crypt of the castle chapel, mourners denounce the murder but are subdued by the sound of prayer (chorus: *Morte in gelido stupore*). As they leave, Avito approaches the body, crying out his grief. After a last kiss, he stumbles, overcome by a strange weakness. Manfredo enters the crypt and tells Avito that poison was placed on Fiora's lips to catch her lover. Avito acknowledges their love, telling Manfredo to avenge himself at once, since poison will soon claim its victim. Amazed at his inability to hate his rival, Manfredo catches the dying man and eases him to the ground, then kisses Fiora's lips himself. When Archibaldo feels his way into the crypt, he at first mistakes the dying Manfredo for the guilty lover. Then, realizing what has happened, he faces the darkness alone.

CLAUDIO MONTEVERDI
1567–1643

Opera is a relatively modern art form that evolved just before 1600. By staging a musical production that combined singing, drama, mime, and dance, the intellectuals who formed the Florentine Camerata were consciously seeking to imitate Greek drama as they understood it. A subject from classical mythology was considered indispensable, so that the figures onstage would already be as familiar to the educated audience as those of the commedia dell'arte were to a more general audience.

Claudio Monteverdi became the first great master of opera. A native of Mantua, Monteverdi was attached to the court of the Gonzaga family, dukes of Mantua.* His duties were to provide whatever music the court might need for religious services, parties, and household use. The court secretary Alessandro Striggio provided the text for Monteverdi's first opera, *Orfeo,* a "fable in music." Fittingly, it tells of Orpheus, the mythological figure who also happened to be a composer.

At the premiere, in 1607, the title role was sung by a male soprano; in modern productions it is usually assigned to a tenor. The instrumentation is partly optional, in the custom of the day, when the composer supplied a figured-bass line and vocal part and made suggestions for specific instruments in certain places. Though adaptations for modern instruments have been made, the practice today is to use period instruments or replicas that recapture the pungent tonal colors and delicate sonorities envisioned by the composer.

---

* By literary coincidence, this family included the Duke in Verdi's *Rigoletto.*

ORFEO

PROLOGUE AND FIVE ACTS
MUSIC: Claudio Monteverdi
TEXT (Italian): Alessandro Striggio
WORLD PREMIERE: Mantua, February 1607
U.S. PREMIERE: Metropolitan Opera, April 14, 1912
   (in concert form); Northampton, Mass., Smith College,
   May 12, 1929 (staged performance)

CHARACTERS

La Musica *(Prologue)* . . . . Soprano
Orfeo (Orpheus) . . . . Tenor or Baritone
Euridice, *his wife* . . . . Soprano
Sylvia, *Euridice's friend* . . . . Soprano
Speranza *(Hope)* . . . . Soprano
Proserpina, *Queen of the Underworld* . . . . Soprano
Apollone (Apollo), *Orfeo's father* . . . . Baritone
Caronte (Charon) . . . . Bass
Plutone (Pluto), *King of the Underworld* . . . . Bass
Nymphs, shepherds, spirits

PROLOGUE   La Musica appears, singing the praises of her art, with its power to move people to every emotion. She will present the story of Orfeo (Orpheus), who was able to charm the beasts, even the stern spirits of Hades, with his singing.

ACT I   In a rustic landscape of mythical antiquity, nymphs and shepherds hail the wedding of Orfeo and the nymph Euridice, who respond with a paean to their happiness (Orfeo: *Rosa del ciel, vita del mondo*). Orfeo had been unsuccessful in wooing Euridice at first, but his songs softened her heart and turned her indifference to love. Now his sorrow is banished and nature herself seems to celebrate the occasion.

ACT II   In a wooded glade, Orfeo recalls how sad he used to be. When the nymphs and shepherds ask him to sing for them, he hails the change in his fortunes brought about by Euridice's love *(Vi ricorda, o boschi ombrosi)*. His joy is short-lived: Sylvia, a companion of Euridice's, brings news that Orfeo's beloved was bitten by a poisonous snake while gathering flowers and died (*In un fiorito prato*). Orfeo wishes himself dead so that he can rejoin her (*Tu se' morta, mia vita*). The others lament the suddenness with which good fortune can change to ill, if heaven becomes envious of happy mortals.

ACT III   Orfeo entreats the goddess Speranza (Hope) to guide him to Euridice. She shows him to the river Styx, saying she can accompany him no farther, since the entrance to the underworld is marked, "Abandon all hope, ye who enter here." As Orfeo bids her an anxious farewell, the boatman Caronte (Charon) appears and tells Orfeo to turn back: only the dead can be ferried across. Orfeo replies that he is in effect dead, having been deprived of Euridice, who was his very life. Caronte remains adamant as Orfeo pleads even more eloquently, declaring he is denied both heaven and hell (*Ahi, sventurato amante*). Lulled by Orfeo's singing, Caronte falls asleep, whereupon the minstrel steps into the boat and drifts toward the underworld, calling upon the infernal spirits to give him back his Euridice. The spirits' voices are heard, expressing their surprise at his boldness (*Nulla impresa per uom si tenta invano*).

ACT IV   In the domain of hell, Proserpina, queen of the underworld, pleads Orfeo's cause with her husband, Plutone (Pluto), who rules there. He grants her wish but insists that Orfeo must never turn back to look at Euridice as he leads her back to earth, or he will lose her forever. Orfeo hails Plutone's mercy and starts to lead Euridice out, but soon he heeds the law of love rather than the powers of darkness and turns to look at her. As the infernal spirits force her to return to hell, Euridice bemoans the loss of her husband through too much love (*Ahi, vista troppo dolce*). Orfeo tries desperately to follow her but is held back by the spirits, who tell him he is undone by his failure to master his own emotions.

ACT V   Back on earth, Orfeo wanders through the Thracian woods, lamenting the loss of his wife. When an echo repeats the last word of each of his outpourings, he challenges the echo to repeat his whole lamentation. He then launches into an elegy for Euridice (*Ma tu, anima mia*). At this Apollone (Apollo), Orfeo's father, descends from a cloud, telling his son that since he has been so steadfast in overcoming every other hardship, he should also master his emotions and not give way to grief. Earthly pleasures are momentary (*Troppo gioisti di tua lieta ventura*): only in heaven can lasting happiness be found. In the sun and the stars Orfeo will see once again and forever the image of his beloved. Apollone leads Orfeo to the heavenly realm, as the chorus solemnly hails his triumph over sorrow and mortality (*Vanne, Orfeo, felice appieno*).

L'INCORONAZIONE DI POPPEA

(The Coronation of Poppea)

PROLOGUE AND THREE ACTS
MUSIC: Claudio Monteverdi
TEXT (Italian): Giovanni Francesco Busenello
WORLD PREMIERE: Venice, Teatro di Santi Giovanni e Paolo,
  autumn 1642
U.S. PREMIERE: Northampton, Mass., Smith College, April 27,
  1926

CHARACTERS

Poppea . . . . Soprano
Ottone, *Poppea's former lover* . . . . Soprano
Nerone, *Emperor of Rome* . . . . Soprano
Ottavia, *Empress of Rome* . . . . Mezzo-Soprano
Arnalta, *Poppea's old nurse* . . . . Contralto
Seneca, *philosopher, Nerone's former tutor* . . . . Bass
Goddesses of Fortune, Virtue, and Love . . . . Sopranos
Drusilla, *Ottavia's lady-in-waiting* . . . . Soprano
Maidservant, *in Ottavia's service* . . . . Soprano
Pallade, *goddess of wisdom* . . . . Soprano
Venus . . . . Soprano
Ottavia's Nurse . . . . Mezzo-Soprano
Two Soldiers of the emperor's bodyguard . . . . Tenor
Page, *Ottavia's young attendant* . . . . Tenor
Lucano, *Nero's friend* . . . . Tenor
Captain of the Guard . . . . Baritone
Lictor . . . . Bass
Mercurio . . . . Bass
Soldiers, disciples of Seneca, servants, consuls, tribunes, senators

PROLOGUE.* Three allegorical figures, representing Fortune, Virtue, and Love, argue about their preeminence: Fortune says Virtue has been reduced to the status of a beggar and should be banished. Virtue retorts that she alone,

*The opera telescopes historical time to combine the marriage of Nerone (the Roman Emperor Nero) in A.D. 62 with the suicide of the philosopher Seneca in A.D. 65.

unlike fickle Fortune, is constant. Amore (Love) chides them for quarreling and declares that she alone reigns supreme, as the story to follow will show . . .

ACT I   Outside Nerone's palace, Ottone (Otho), a nobleman, addresses a forlorn serenade to his beloved Poppea, who lies unhearing in the arms of Nerone in her own house nearby, having been chosen as his new mistress. Ottone sees two of Nerone's Soldiers asleep on guard duty and muses on the fragility of a ruler's safety (O salvezza di principe infelice) and the fickleness of Poppea's affections. His soliloquy awakens the Soldiers, who challenge him. As he leaves, the Soldiers exchange comments about their thankless job, brought on by Nerone's dalliance with Poppea and neglect of his duties. The emperor, they say, listens to no one except his tutor, Seneca, whom they consider a toady. Their remarks are cut short by the appearance of Poppea and Nerone. Bidding his mistress a reluctant farewell, Nerone says he wants to divorce his empress, Ottavia (Octavia), so that he can marry Poppea. He leaves, and Poppea thanks Hope and Fortune for guiding her. Her nurse, Arnalta, enters with a warning that Ottavia knows of the affair. Important men, she says, may bestow their love, only to withdraw it just as quickly (Il grande spira onor). Poppea, however, is confident.

§ Inside the palace, Ottavia tells her old Nurse how unjustly Nerone is treating her as both empress and wife. When the Nurse counsels finding a lover of her own, the virtuous Ottavia is indignant. The philosopher Seneca is shown in and assures Ottavia of his sympathy for her sad state. When he says her virtue will strengthen and reward her, she politely rejects his words as scant comfort, while the Page draws her aside and says Seneca is a humbug. Taking her leave, Ottavia tells Seneca to spread the word that Nerone means to divorce her and marry Poppea. Seneca muses on how uneasily rests the head that wears a crown (Le porpore regali), only to be surprised by a visit from the goddess Pallade (Pallas Athene), who tells him his death is near and will be signaled by Mercurio (Mercury); Seneca accepts this stoically. Nerone enters to advise the old man of his plans, saying he ranks next to Giove (Jove) and is not bound by the laws and morals of ordinary men. Seneca argues that a ruler must set an example, but Nerone dismisses him, welcoming Poppea. After an exchange of endearments, Poppea warns Nerone that Seneca may stand in their way. Nerone sends orders to Seneca to end his own life. After Nerone leaves, Ottone approaches Poppea and pleads with her to return his love, but she replies that she is going on to the throne. They go their separate ways, leaving Arnalta to comment on her mistress' lack of compassion.

§ Alone, Ottone bemoans his rejection by Poppea, but when Drusilla, lady-in-waiting to Ottavia, offers her own love, he pledges to return it (A te di quanto son).

ACT II At home, Seneca has a moment's respite from the deceits of the court, only to see Mercurio approach, welcoming him to immortality. Seneca sees death as a passage to a better life; to an officer who comes with Nerone's orders he therefore says that he will shortly comply. When some of his followers appear, he bids them farewell. Though they beg him not to take his own life *(Non morir, Seneca)*, he calmly tells them to prepare a bath, in which he intends to bleed to death.

§ In a moment of lighthearted contrast, illustrating the superficial hedonism of the court, the Page asks a Maidservant to identify the excitement he feels near her *(Sento un certo non so che)*. She replies that it is love, and they hasten off to enjoy more of it.

§ Relieved to learn of Seneca's death, Nerone bids his poet friend Lucano to join him in praises of Poppea *(Idolo mio, celebrarti io vorrei)*.

§ Unable to stay away from the palace, despite his avowal to Drusilla, Ottone sadly admits he still loves Poppea. Ottavia finds him and asks his aid in avenging her by killing Poppea. When he hesitates, she tells him it is an order: if he fails, she will denounce him to Nerone as having compromised her honor.

§ Drusilla rejoices in having regained Ottone's affections, and the Page asks the old Nurse whether she does not envy her. The Nurse muses on the brevity of a woman's day of glory *(Il giorno femminil)*, saying young people should make hay while the sun shines.

§ Ottone wonders what he has gotten himself into *(Io non so dov'io vada)*. When Drusilla appears, he asks her to lend him women's clothes in which to disguise himself for the murder he has been ordered to commit.

§ In the palace garden, Poppea rejoices at Seneca's death. Looking forward to marrying Nerone, she reassures Arnalta of a continuing place in her affections, and the old companion responds by singing a lullaby as her mistress rests *(Adagiati, Poppea)*. As she dozes, Amore sings a warning about the dangers that await careless mortals *(Siete rimasi)*. The disguised Ottone draws near, trying to bolster his courage by reminding himself of betrayal and duty. Amore stops him, awakening Poppea, who takes Ottone to be Drusilla. So do Arnalta and the servants, who rush in to give chase to the would-be assassin, as Amore declares he has saved Poppea and will now make her empress.

ACT III Drusilla looks forward to Ottone's return, but instead she finds herself accused by Arnalta and arrested by a Lictor (guard) for the attempted murder of Poppea. Faced with torture in which she might reveal Ottone's guilt, Drusilla decides to take the punishment in his stead. Nerone orders her executed, but Ottone enters and confesses his own guilt. Impressed by Drusilla's self-sacrifice and Ottone's frankness, Nerone orders them spared and exiled. He then announces his divorce from Ottavia and says she too must go into exile. Poppea arrives and learns that Nerone can marry her at once. With declarations of love (*Idolo del cor mio*), he leads her off.

§ On her way into exile, Ottavia bids farewell to her country (*Addio Roma*) and proclaims her innocence, saying she will live the rest of her life in sorrow.

§ In the palace, Arnalta looks forward to new respect as companion to the empress. Those who once scorned the old woman will now sue for her favor, and she can feel important, though at heart she knows her time is past.

§ In the throne room, Nerone hails his bride as consuls and tribunes present her with the crown, then withdraw. At Amore's urging, Venere (Venus) proclaims Poppea herself a goddess. Nerone and Poppea remain lost in each other's gaze, declaring anew their love (*Pur ti miro, pur ti stringo*).

DOUGLAS MOORE
1893–1969

*A*merican opera has made its greatest forward strides through works like Gershwin's *Porgy and Bess,* Blitzstein's *Regina,* and Douglas Moore's *Ballad of Baby Doe,* all of which have close relations to Broadway and demonstrate that opera can grow from native roots, independent of foreign graftings. All have appealed to audiences beyond the usual opera public, all derive from American subjects as described by American writers, and all use folklike melodies as an integral means of expression.

Douglas Moore, a native of Long Island, favored this grass-roots approach during his entire life but, like many American composers of his generation, received much of his training abroad. A graduate of Yale, he joined the navy during World War I and then gravitated toward Paris, where he studied with Nadia Boulanger, Vincent d'Indy, and Ernest Bloch. When he returned to the United States, he joined the Columbia University music faculty and succeeded Daniel Gregory Mason as its head in 1926. Moore remained a teacher until his retirement in 1962. Though his pupils included many avant-garde composers, he himself was always a plain-spoken conservative and a mischievous reteller of American tall tales.

Nine operas by Moore reached the stage, starting with *The Headless Horseman* (after Washington Irving) in 1936 and including *The Devil and Daniel Webster* (Stephen Vincent Benét) in 1939 and *Carrie Nation* in 1966. He also drew inspiration from novels—Rölvaag's *Giants in the Earth* (1951), Henry James' *Wings of the Dove* (1961). In the stories of Daniel Webster, Carrie Nation, and Baby Doe, he was guided by actual events. *The Ballad of Baby Doe* received its premiere in 1956 at Central City, Colorado, in the very countryside where Horace Tabor, his wife, Augusta, and Baby Doe pursued their destinies. The real Tabor died in 1899. Baby Doe, living out her years as an eccentric recluse, was found frozen to death in her cabin next to the Matchless Mine in March 1935.

THE BALLAD OF BABY DOE

TWO ACTS
MUSIC: Douglas Moore
TEXT (English): John Latouche
WORLD PREMIERE: Colorado, Central City Opera, July 7, 1956

CHARACTERS

Elizabeth ("Baby") Doe, *divorced wife of Harvey Doe,*
    miner . . . . Soprano
Augusta Tabor, *wife of Horace* . . . . Mezzo-Soprano
Mama McCourt, *Baby Doe's mother* . . . . Contralto
Horace Tabor, *wealthy miner* . . . . Baritone
William Jennings Bryan, *politician* . . . . Bass-Baritone
Father Chappelle, *priest* . . . . Tenor
President Chester A. Arthur . . . . Tenor
Miners, bartender, friends of Horace and Augusta, dance hall entertainers,
   hotel clerk and bellboy, dandies, Mayor of Leadville, citizens, a Denver
   politician, Effie and Silver Dollar (children of Tabor and Baby Doe),
                         stage doorman

ACT I   A summer evening in 1880 outside the Tabor Opera House in Leadville, Colorado. As an old miner is bounced from the saloon, he boasts that he has discovered the Matchless Mine, a bonanza of silver ore. He says that Horace Tabor, the local entrepreneur who "owns the whole damn town," has already tried to buy his mine. As he wanders off, the middle-aged Tabor emerges from the Opera House with four cronies. Though proud of the edifice—built at the behest of his wife, Augusta—Tabor seeks respite from the unremitting "culture" inside (an Adelina Patti recital). Teased by his miner friends, he recalls his beginnings in New England and his success in prospecting *(I came this way from Massachusetts)*. As his friends banter with girls from the saloon, Augusta and the cronies' wives come out of the Opera House during intermission. Augusta berates Horace for his uncouth behavior. As they start back into the theater, Horace pauses to give directions to a newcomer in town, a beautiful young woman who seems as impressed with him as he is with her.

§ Later that evening, lingering outside the Clarendon Hotel to finish a cigar, Tabor overhears jealous remarks by two saloon girls about the newcomer, Baby Doe. Soon she herself appears inside the hotel, accompanying herself at the piano in a song (*Willow, where we met together*). Startled by Tabor's applause, she comes to the window, and he confesses that her singing has reawakened longings from his earlier life (*Warm as the autumn light*). When Augusta leans out the window to call him upstairs to their apartment, he bids Baby Doe good night.

§ In the sitting room of the Tabor apartment, Augusta finds a pair of lace gloves while straightening her husband's desk. At first she thinks he meant to surprise her, but she finds a card addressed to Baby Doe. Augusta muses bitterly (*I suppose she's young and pretty*) on her own lack of glamour and warmth after years as Tabor's helpmate. Tabor comes in and looks for a check, his down payment on the Matchless Mine, but Augusta has taken it, meaning to discuss it with him. They argue, Tabor declaring it is his "foolishness" that has made them wealthy, against her better judgment. When she confronts him with the gloves, he admits his attraction to Baby Doe and says the marriage has grown cold. Augusta stalks out.

§ Several days later, in the hotel lobby, Baby Doe is about to check out—for a visit, she says, to her family back in Oshkosh. She pauses to write her mother (*Dearest Mama, I am writing*), explaining she came to Leadville after parting company with her husband, Harvey Doe, in Central City, only to meet someone she likes very much but could never marry. As she finishes, Augusta steps in to introduce herself, warning Baby Doe there will be trouble if she stays. Baby Doe says she is leaving and protests the innocence of her relationship (*I knew it was wrong*). Augusta replies that her husband is irresponsible in business and needs her too much to leave her. When she has said good-bye, Tabor himself enters, alerted by the hotel clerk to Baby Doe's departure. She has torn up the letter and decided to stay. He embraces her, declaring that the world may know of their love (duet: *You're not going, my heart*).

§ A short time later, Augusta is visited in her sitting room by the wives of Tabor's cronies. They tell her Tabor is living openly with Baby Doe, even heeding her business advice. Augusta becomes alarmed at rumors that he plans to divorce her. If he does, she will make him rue the day (ensemble: *Shout it from the housetops*).

§ In a private room in the Willard Hotel in Washington, Baby Doe's parents, sister, and brother are preparing a reception. Her mother, Mama McCourt, greets the guests, who, it soon appears, have just attended the wedding of Baby Doe and Tabor. The guests are all talking about protective tariffs and the controversy over whether the government should adopt a gold standard, a silver standard, or both. Baby Doe declares that silver is the finer, more poetic element, the stuff of dreams (*Gold is a fine thing*). As Tabor presents his bride with jewels, Mama McCourt says to Father Chappelle, the priest, that she wishes Baby Doe's ex-husband could see her now. The priest, not having been told that either party was previously married to someone still living, leaves in a state of shock, and the snobbish society guests start to leave as well. Just then President Chester A. Arthur is announced. He joins in a toast to the bride—and to silver.

ACT II   In the ballroom of the Windsor Hotel in Denver in 1893, during the Governor's Ball, Tabor's cronies argue with their wives about the latters' refusal to accept Baby Doe. When she enters with her mother, the ladies leave, reluctantly followed by their husbands. Baby Doe insists it is her genuine love for Tabor that arouses such jealousy (*The fine ladies walk*). After a butler announces Augusta, Baby Doe sends her mother to find Tabor, but Augusta has come in a conciliatory spirit to warn them that the president will soon sign a bill adopting the gold standard: Tabor's fortune, largely on paper, will be wiped out. When Tabor arrives, he turns a deaf ear to Augusta's predictions, then reassures Baby Doe that their fortunes will rise again. He makes her promise always to hold on to the Matchless Mine.

§ At a gaming table, Tabor's cronies play poker and speculate about his declining fortunes. He arrives and tries unsuccessfully to raise money on collateral or to rally their support for William Jennings Bryan, who will run against McKinley for the presidency in support of silver. When his friends back away, Tabor declares he will stand his ground alone (*Turn tail and run, then!*).

§ Outside the Matchless Mine in 1896, Baby Doe and her two little daughters help the miners' wives decorate a speaker's stand for the visiting Bryan. Tabor arrives with the candidate and exhorts all working people to vote for him (chorus: *We want Bryan!*). During a fervent address, Bryan christens the Tabors' younger child "Silver Dollar" and promises the voters a glorious future.

§ A few weeks later, at her home in California, Augusta learns of Bryan's defeat and receives a visit from Mama McCourt, who asks whether she will help the now ruined Tabors. Realizing that Tabor is too proud to come to her in person, Augusta says she will not help. Alone, she reflects that age and bitterness have cut her off from her feelings and prevented her from acting mercifully (*Augusta! How can you turn away?*).

§ In 1899, on the stage of his Opera House in Leadville, Tabor—old and dressed as a workman—recalls the past. His hallucinations frighten the stage doorman, who goes for help. In his mind's eye, Tabor sees his stern mother, then Augusta; he remembers his dream of marrying the boss' daughter, then his success as a prospector. Perplexed by his present failure *(The land was growing, and I grew with it),* he foresees a bleak future: one of his daughters will run away and repudiate her name, the other will sink in dissipation. As he struggles with these apparitions, Baby Doe comes to take him home, saying she will always stay by his side. He is weak, and she urges him to rest for a while on the stage. Her lullaby to the dying man *(Always through the changing of sun and shadow, time and space)* gradually turns to a soliloquy as she appears, years later and much older, outside the Matchless Mine. Snow begins to fall as she takes up her vigil near the mine entrance, true to her promise *(As our earthly eyes grow dim).*

Wolfgang Amadeus Mozart
1756–91

Wolfgang Amadeus Mozart, considered by many the greatest natural genius in the history of music, was Austrian-born, the son of a professional musician who trained the boy as a child prodigy. Taking up the harpsichord in his fourth year, Mozart was concertizing with his sister by the age of seven. At eleven he wrote his first opera, *Apollo et Hyacinthus*, quickly followed by *Bastien und Bastienne* and *La Finta Semplice*. On a trip to Italy, where he was honored by the pope, the fourteen-year-old conducted twenty performances of his *Mitridate* in Milan.

Mozart's circle included many singers, and throughout his short life he wrote generously for the voice, alongside his steady output of instrumental, chamber, and symphonic music. His operas fall into three distinct categories—the opera seria of his predecessors, Italian-style opera buffa, and the German-language singspiel or "song play," designed to appeal to bourgeois audiences. *Idomeneo,* which marked the emergence of his mature style at age twenty-five, falls into the first of these categories. Neglected for many years because of the supposed unwieldiness of the opera-seria format, *Idomeneo* was a favorite of Mozart's, and enough connoisseurs of his music have championed it over the years to bring about an eventual revival. The score shows the effects of Mozart's trips to Paris, where he discovered the extensive use of the chorus, and to Munich, where a rich orchestration was feasible. From the last year of his life dates *La Clemenza di Tito*—like *Idomeneo,* an opera seria, but one that shows Mozart again using the form innovatively, modifying it to suit his talent and contemporary tastes.

The years 1786–90 mark the production of Mozart's three famous Italian comedies, starting with *Le Nozze di Figaro,* whose premiere in Salzburg was almost scuttled by intriguing Italian singers loyal to their own composers. The work was especially well liked in Prague, for which Mozart wrote *Don Giovanni,* a darker comedy with strong undertones of serious melodrama. *Così Fan Tutte,* the most misunderstood of the three works, is an eighteenth-century morality play masquerading as a bedroom farce.

Of Mozart's singspiels, with their spoken dialogue and cosmopolitan style, mixing German folk elements with subtle French orchestration and raucous Italian wit, *Die Entführung aus dem Serail* is the earliest full-fledged example and *Die Zauberflöte* the last. Both show Mozart's curious blend of sophistication with coarse, earthy humor. Both feature "dangerous" Turkish characters—popular bugbears among the Austrians—accompanied by amusing pseudo-Turkish musical effects. *Die Entführung,* written just before Mozart's marriage to Constanze Weber, finds the composer experimenting, as usual, with an established style, bending it in the direction of greater dramatic expressiveness and sharper individualization of the characters. *Die Zauberflöte,* written when he was already dying, is suffused with his enthusiasm for the Masonic movement, its symbols, rituals, and meanings.

Mozart greatly expanded the horizons of music in his day, paving the way for the romantic movement. It was his humanization of dramatis personae that set him apart from other masters of post-baroque opera, such as Haydn, and that give his operas the warmth, spontaneity, and immediacy that have carried them onto the modern stage as the oldest yet freshest works in the regular repertory.

IDOMENEO, RE DI CRETA

(Idomeneus, King of Crete)

THREE ACTS
MUSIC: Wolfgang Amadeus Mozart
TEXT (Italian): Giovanni Battista (Giambattista) Varesco, after a
   French libretto by Antoine Danchet
WORLD PREMIERE: Munich, Hoftheater, January 29, 1781
U.S. PREMIERE: Tanglewood, Berkshire Festival, August 4, 1947
METROPOLITAN OPERA PREMIERE: October 14, 1982

IDOMENEO, RE DI CRETA

CHARACTERS

Idomeneo, *King of Crete* . . . . Tenor
Idamante, *his son* . . . . Soprano/Tenor
Ilia, *Trojan princess* . . . . Soprano
Elettra, *Greek princess* . . . . Soprano
Arbace, *confidant of Idomeneo* . . . . Tenor
High Priest of Neptune . . . . Tenor
Voice of Neptune . . . . Bass
People of Crete, Trojan prisoners, sailors, soldiers, priests, dancers

ACT I   The action takes place in Sidon, capital of the island of Crete. Idomeneo, king of Crete, has fought alongside the Greeks in the Trojan War, which is now ended. During his absence, his son, Idamante, has inspired the love of the Greek princess Elettra. Idamante does not return her love, being enamored of the Trojan princess Ilia, whom Idomeneo sent to Crete as a prisoner. The action begins in Idomeneo's palace, where Ilia reflects on the defeat of Troy, which she will never see again, and on her love for Idamante, which she hesitates to acknowledge. Soon Idamante comes to free the Trojan prisoners. Saddened by Ilia's rejection of his love, he tells her it is not his fault that their fathers were enemies (*Non ho colpa, e mi condanni*). Trojans and Cretans alike welcome the return of peace, but Elettra, jealous of Ilia, rushes in to protest Idamante's clemency toward the enemy prisoners. Arbace, the king's confidant, interrupts with the supposed news that Idomeneo has been lost at sea on his return voyage. Elettra, fearing that a Trojan will soon be Queen of Crete, feels the furies of Hades tormenting her (*Tutte nel cor vi sento*).

§ The scene shifts to the seashore, where Idomeneo's ship makes its way to safety through storm-tossed waves. Asking his followers to leave him, Idomeneo recalls the vow he foolishly made at sea—to sacrifice, if he were spared, the first person he meets on shore, as an offering to appease Neptune's wrath. The first person he sees is Idamante, but they do not recognize each other. Idamante declares he is mourning the king, lost at sea; Idomeneo reveals his identity but shuns his son's embrace, saying the young man must avoid him. Grief-stricken by his father's rejection, Idamante runs off. Cretan troops disembarking from Idomeneo's ship are met by their wives, and all sing the praises of Neptune, who will be honored with a sacrifice.

ACT II   At the palace, Idomeneo seeks counsel from Arbace in his dilemma: how to save his son's life without breaking his vow to Neptune. Arbace says a substitute could be sacrificed if Idamante went into exile immediately, so Idomeneo orders him sent to Argos, taking Elettra back to her native soil. Overhearing this, Ilia bids Idamante farewell, but he protests that he will never love anyone but her (*Non temer, amato bene*). Ilia then greets Idomeneo, whose kind words move her to declare that since she has lost everything, he will be her father and Crete her country (*Se il padre perdei*). As she leaves, Idomeneo realizes that she and Idamante are in love and foresees a triple sacrifice to Neptune—his son, Ilia, and then himself, fatally pierced by grief. Saved at sea, he now finds a tempest raging in his own bosom (*Fuor del mar*). Elettra welcomes the idea of going to Argos with Idamante, voicing her love for him (*Idol mio, se ritroso*). Sounds of a march announce that it is time to board ship for the voyage.

§ At the port of Sidon, Elettra calls on the winds to speed her journey. Idomeneo bids his son farewell and urges him to learn the art of ruling while he is away (trio: *Pria di partir, o Dio!*). Before the ship can sail, however, a storm breaks out, and a sea serpent appears among the waves. Recognizing it as a messenger from Neptune, the king offers himself as atonement for having defaulted in his bargain with the sea god. The population, seized with confusion and terror, flees (*Corriamo, fuggiamo*).

ACT III In the royal garden, Ilia asks the breezes to carry her love to Idamante (*Zeffiretti lusinghieri*). He himself appears, explaining that the serpent is wreaking havoc in the countryside and that he must go forth to fight it. When he says he may as well die as suffer the torments of unrequited love, Ilia confesses her love (duet: *Spiegarti non poss'io*). They are surprised by Elettra and Idomeneo. When Idamante asks his father why he shuns him and sends him away, Idomeneo can reply only that the youth simply must leave. Ilia asks for consolation from Elettra, who is preoccupied with revenge (quartet: *Andrò ramingo e solo*). Arbace comes with news that the people, led by the High Priest of Neptune, are clamoring for Idomeneo to speak. Arbace laments Crete's misfortune and offers his own life in sacrifice if this will appease Neptune (*Se colà ne'fati è scritto*).

§ Before the palace, the High Priest tells the king of the destruction wrought in the land by Neptune's monster. To put a stop to it, Idomeneo must come to the temple of Neptune and delay the promised sacrifice no longer. When Idomeneo confesses that his own son is the victim, the High Priest and populace react with horror.

§ Outside the temple, Idomeneo arrives with his retinue. The king and High Priest join with Neptune's priests in prayer that the god may be appeased. Arbace announces that Idamante has succeeded in killing the monster. As Idomeneo fears new reprisals from Neptune, Idamante enters in sacrificial robes, saying he at last understands his father's dilemma and is ready to die. After an agonizing farewell, Idomeneo is about to strike when Ilia intervenes, offering her own life instead, because the gods, she says, want to be rid of the "enemies of Greece"—the last of the Trojan royalty. As she kneels before the High Priest, however, an oracular Voice is heard, evidently sent by Neptune.

It announces that Idomeneo must yield the throne to Ilia and Idamante. Everyone is relieved except Elettra, who longs for her own death *(D'Oreste, d'Aiace).* Idomeneo presents Idamante and his bride to the people as their new rulers *(Torna la pace).* The people call upon the gods of love and marriage to bless the royal pair and bring peace.

DIE ENTFÜHRUNG AUS DEM SERAIL

(The Abduction from the Seraglio)

THREE ACTS
MUSIC: Wolfgang Amadeus Mozart
TEXT (German): Gottlob Stephanie, from a play by Christoph Friedrich Bretzner
WORLD PREMIERE: Vienna, Burgtheater, July 16, 1782
U.S. PREMIERE: Brooklyn, N.Y., Athenaeum, February 16, 1860 (in Italian as *Belmonte e Constanza*)
METROPOLITAN OPERA PREMIERE: November 29, 1946 (in English)

CHARACTERS

Constanze, *Spanish lady* .... Soprano
Blonde, *her English maid*...................... Soprano
Belmonte, *Spanish nobleman* .... Tenor
Pedrillo, *his servant*.......................... Tenor
Osmin, *overseer of the Pasha's harem* .... Bass
Pasha Selim .... Speaking Part
Turkish soldiers, guards, Turkish women

Count Belmonte, son of a noble Spaniard, has lost his beloved Constanze during an attack by pirates. He has sailed to Turkey, where Constanze—along with Blonde, her servant, and Pedrillo, Blonde's sweetheart (formerly Belmonte's servant)—has been sold into slavery to Pasha Selim. The time is the eighteenth century.

ACT I   When the newly arrived Belmonte walks into the Pasha's garden, he hopes he will find Constanze *(Hier soll ich dich denn sehen)* but meets instead the cantankerous Osmin, the Pasha's overseer, picking figs and singing about the joys of finding a sweetheart *(Wer ein Liebchen hat gefunden).* Belmonte's attempts to question Osmin get nowhere, and Osmin soon pushes him out. Pedrillo appears and likewise irritates Osmin, who grumbles about unwelcome competition for the available women *(Solche hergelaufne Laffen)*. When Osmin reenters the palace, Belmonte makes contact with Pedrillo and inquires after Constanze, only to learn that the Pasha has romantic designs on her. Pedrillo suggests introducing Belmonte to the Pasha as an architect, and Belmonte waxes rhapsodic over the idea of seeing his beloved *(O wie ängstlich)*. As the Pasha returns from a boat ride, his courtiers welcome him back. He asks Constanze why she still withholds her heart, and she explains that she cannot forget her betrothed *(Ach, ich liebte)*. She leaves, begging for more time to become reconciled with her sorrow, and Pedrillo introduces the "young architect" Belmonte, whom the Pasha engages into his service. This does not impress the returning Osmin, who asserts his authority over the two young men (trio: *Marsh! Trollt euch fort!*).

ACT II   Outside the Pasha's palace, Blonde puts off Osmin's wooing by telling him only gentle persuasion will win a girl *(Durch Zärtlichkeit und Schmeicheln)*. He reminds her that she is a slave, but she retorts that she is a freeborn Englishwoman and will not be cowed by threats. When he orders her to stay away from Pedrillo, she resists, and eventually he backs down, muttering threats (duet: *Ich gehe, doch rate ich dir*). Constanze appears, mourning her separation from Belmonte *(Traurigkeit ward mir zum Lose)*. When the Pasha asks whether she has made up her mind, she says she can never love him. He reminds her of his power over her and says that torture awaits her. She replies that no torture could be greater than the thought of unfaithfulness to her true love *(Martern aller Arten)*. When they have left, Pedrillo tells Blonde of an escape plan: at midnight he and Belmonte will rescue their sweethearts by ladder and leave on Belmonte's ship. As she takes a sleeping potion to give to the jealous Osmin, Blonde rejoices *(Welche Wonne, welche Lust)*. Pedrillo responds with reassurances *(Frisch zum Kampfe)*, only to be interrupted by Osmin, who suspects his good spirits. Pedrillo tries to get Osmin to drink wine, though it is against the Moslem religion; at length he succeeds, and the two enjoy a brief reconciliation in toasting the god of the grape *(Vivat Bacchus!)*. Pedrillo leads the tipsy Turk off to bed, then joins Belmonte to carry out their scheme. Belmonte at last meets Constanze again, greeting her with tears of joy *(Wenn der Freude Tränen fliessen)*. Both Belmonte and Pedrillo question whether their sweethearts have stayed faithful (quartet: *Ach, Belmonte! Ach, mein Leben!*). They are readily convinced, and all four hail their reunion.

ACT III   At midnight in front of the Pasha's palace, Belmonte counts on love to strengthen and inspire him *(Ich baue ganz auf deine Stärke)*.* Pedrillo joins him and sings a serenade about a maiden held captive by the Moors and

*Often omitted.

rescued by a foreign lover *(In Mohrenland gefangen war)*; by the time he reaches the end, the ladies have opened their windows. Osmin, however, has revived and finds the escape ladders. He orders the captives dragged off to the Pasha, exulting in his revenge *(Ha, wie will ich triumphieren)*: they will die like dogs.

§ In the Pasha's apartment, Osmin announces he caught the lovers trying to get away. Selim confronts them, and while Constanze offers to die to save her lover, Belmonte more realistically offers ransom: he is of a wealthy family. When the Pasha learns that Belmonte's father is his archenemy Lostados, commandant of Oran, he vows appropriate punishment. Belmonte and Constanze now bid each other a last farewell (duet: *Meinetwegen willst du sterben!*), but the Pasha announces he will repay evil with good: rather than stoop to the kind of treatment he suffered at the hands of Belmonte's father, he will let the lovers go free. Everyone is happy except Osmin, who protests the loss of Blonde to no avail, because the Pasha declares that love cannot be won by force. The grateful lovers praise their benefactor as they prepare to sail *(Nie werd' ich deine Huld verkennen)*.

LE NOZZE DI FIGARO

(The Marriage of Figaro)

FOUR ACTS
MUSIC: Wolfgang Amadeus Mozart
TEXT (Italian): Lorenzo da Ponte, after *Le Mariage de Figaro* by Beaumarchais (Pierre Auguste Caron)
WORLD PREMIERE: Vienna, Burgtheater, May 1, 1786
U.S. PREMIERE: New York, Park Theatre, May 10, 1824 (in English)
METROPOLITAN OPERA PREMIERE: January 31, 1894

CHARACTERS

Figaro, *barber, valet to Count Almaviva* . . . . Baritone
Rosina, Countess Almaviva . . . . Soprano
Susanna, *her personal maid, engaged to Figaro* . . . . Soprano
Cherubino, *page* . . . . Soprano
Marcellina, *duenna* . . . . Soprano
Barbarina, *Antonio's daughter* . . . . Soprano
Don Basilio, *music master* . . . . Tenor

Don Curzio, *lawyer* .... Tenor
Count Almaviva............................... Baritone
Doctor Bartolo................................ Bass
Antonio, *gardener* .... Bass

Peasants, townspeople, servants

ACT I   Spain, late eighteenth century. In the servants' quarter of the Alma-viva castle near Seville, Figaro—the town barber and sometime handyman to the Almaviva household—is measuring the room he and his fiancée, Susanna, will occupy after their marriage. Susanna, a maid in the household, dislikes the location of the room: it is too near that of the Count and Countess, and the Count has been making advances. She tells Figaro that the Count, tired of outside philandering, plans to exercise the ancient *droit du seigneur*—the right of a noble to take the bridegroom's place on the wedding night of his servants. The bell rings, and Susanna answers her mistress' summons, leaving Figaro to declare angrily that if the Count wants to lead them in a dance, Figaro will gladly teach him a few steps (*Se vuol ballare*). He leaves as the scheming Dr. Bartolo and Marcellina arrive, the former complaining that the latter has named him her attorney only on the day of Figaro's wedding, which Marcellina hopes to prevent. She wants to marry Figaro herself—something Figaro promised when he borrowed money from her. Bartolo in turn wants to get even with Figaro for having prevented him from marrying his ward, Rosina, who became the bride of the Count. Assuring Marcellina he will find a way to stop the wedding, Bartolo relishes the thought of vengeance (*La vendetta*). As he departs, Marcellina runs into Susanna, with whom she trades insults in the form of sarcastic, exaggerated compliments (*Via resti servita*). Angry at her younger rival, Marcellina storms out, leaving Susanna to greet the breathless page Cherubino, an adolescent boy whose romantic adventures are starting to get him in trouble. He has a crush on the Countess, who he realizes is unat-tainable, and has been caught alone with Barbarina, the gardener's daughter—an episode the Count intends to use as an excuse to dismiss the boy from his service. In return for one of the Countess' ribbons, Cherubino offers his latest love song, which praises love in general (*Non so più*). As he is leaving, Cher-ubino sees the Count approaching and hides behind an armchair. The Count, finding Susanna, urges her to make a rendezvous in the garden that evening. When Don Basilio, the music master, is heard approaching, the Count tries to hide from the old scandalmonger. As he heads for Cherubino's hiding place behind the chair, Susanna barely succeeds in shielding the page's escape to the seat of the chair, where she covers him with a cloth. Basilio comes in and hints that Susanna should be glad to have the attentions of a noble like the Count rather than those of a pipsqueak like Cherubino, who pants after every woman. The Count steps angrily out of hiding when he hears that Cherubino has eyes even for the Countess. The Count now wants more than ever to get rid of Cherubino and orders the gloating Basilio to fetch him (trio: *Cosa sento?*). Demonstrating how he came upon the page the day before at the gardener's cottage, the Count lifts the cloth from the chair—and discovers Cherubino once again. As the Count tries to sort out what has been happening, Figaro leads in a chorus of peasants, who strew flowers in front of the Count while singing his praises *(Giovani liete)*. Figaro pointedly explains that everyone appreciates the Count's progressiveness in abolishing the *droit du seigneur* when he married the Countess. The Count vows that he will outwit this upstart servant. Then he pretends to forgive Cherubino—by offering the youth a commission in his private regiment, which means leaving for Seville at once. Figaro, equally glad to see another of Susanna's admirers depart, joshes Cherubino about military life, which will put an end to his amorous wanderings *(Non più andrai)*.

ACT II   In the privacy of her room, the Countess calls on love to bring back her husband *(Porgi, amor)*. Susanna comes in, confirming that the Count has been making overtures to her, though he is still jealous of his wife where Cherubino is concerned. Figaro arrives with word that his master has been intriguing with Marcellina to stop the wedding if he cannot have his way with Susanna. To embroil the Count, Figaro proposes sending him a note that suggests the Countess herself has a lover, whom she wants to meet in the garden that evening. Cherubino will disguise himself as Susanna and go to a meeting with the Count, who will be eager to avenge his wife's supposed infidelity. Thus the Count will believe he is succeeding with Susanna and will no longer try to stop the wedding. When Figaro has left, Cherubino comes to say good-bye to the Countess and sings of his lovesickness *(Voi che sapete)*. Knowing of Figaro's scheme, Cherubino prepares to disguise himself as Susanna, who locks the door as a precaution. She arranges his hair so that it will not show from under his bonnet *(Venite, inginocchiatevi)*. Suddenly the Count is heard outside, angry because the door is locked. Cherubino ducks into the adjoining boudoir but in his haste knocks over a dressing table inside, which the Count hears as the Countess lets him in. Upset by Figaro's bogus letter, the Count suspects that a lover is hiding in the next room, but the Countess says that it is Susanna, who cannot come out just yet, because she is changing clothes. The Count insists that the Countess go with him while he fetches tools to force open the boudoir door. Susanna, unseen by the Count, has overheard this and calls to Cherubino to unlock the boudoir door so that she can take his place. Cherubino jumps out the window seconds before the Count and Countess reappear. As he starts to force the door, the Countess confesses that Cherubino is in the boudoir but insists that the escapade is harmless. The Count swears that Cherubino shall die, but to their consternation it is Susanna who steps out. Now the Count tries to make amends, but the Countess accuses him of neglecting her. She and Susanna confess that Figaro's letter was a trick.

Figaro comes to say that the wedding festivities are ready to begin; confronted with the letter, he at first denies knowing about it, then realizes that Susanna and the Countess have let the cat out of the bag. At this moment Antonio, the gardener, bursts in to complain that someone has jumped into his flower bed from the window. The Count suspects it was Cherubino after all, but Figaro says it was he, surprised in the act of visiting Susanna's room. He feigns injury and starts limping. Finally Marcellina enters with Bartolo to press her claims against Figaro. The confused Count sees a chance to reassert his authority and declares he will judge the case.

ACT III   In the main hall, decorated for the wedding, the Count wanders alone, puzzling over all the stange events. Susanna and the Countess enter unnoticed in the background: the Countess tells her maid to make an assignation with the Count for that evening. Susanna steps forward and—when the Count reminds her that Figaro may still have to marry Marcellina—says she will pay off Marcellina with the dowry the Count promised her. He replies that his promise was contingent on her responding to his affections. She goes along with his renewed invitation to meet that evening (*Crudel! perchè finora*). Momentarily pleased, the Count rages again when he hears Susanna reassure the returning Figaro, "We have won our case." As soon as the servants have left, the Count declares he will do whatever is necessary to win Susanna (*Vedrò, mentr'io sospiro*). Don Curzio, a lawyer, comes in with Figaro, Bartolo, and Marcellina to announce his decision: Figaro must repay Marcellina's loan or marry her. Figaro protests he is a foundling of noble birth and cannot marry without his parents' consent. A tattoo on his arm identifies him as the long-lost Rafaello, illegitimate son of Marcellina herself and Bartolo. When Susanna comes in with money to pay Figaro's debt, she is shocked to see her fiancé embracing Marcellina. But the older couple blesses the marriage, asking for a double wedding to set everything to rights. The Count appears to be the loser and is furious, but the happiness of the others knows no bounds. When they all leave, Barbarina, the gardener's daughter, sneaks Cherubino back into the castle, saying she will help him dress as a girl. The Countess comes in alone, having heard nothing from Susanna about the progress of their plan. She wonders what has become of the trust and intimacy she once shared with her husband (*Dove sono*). She goes, and Antonio, the gardener (who is also Susanna's uncle), enters with the Count, telling him Cherubino is being disguised as a girl in the gardener's cottage. They go to investigate, and the Countess returns with Susanna. To clinch Susanna's rendezvous with the Count, the Countess dictates a letter for Susanna to send him (*Che soave zefiretto*). In his disguise, Cherubino leads a chorus of country girls offering posies to the Countess. Barbarina introduces Cherubino as her cousin, come from Seville for the wedding. The Countess and Susanna both suspect that it is Cherubino—a suspicion confirmed by Antonio, who pulls off the page's wig. The Count enters and threatens Cherubino with punishment. Barbarina embarrasses the Count by reminding him that every time he kissed her, he promised to grant her any wish: now she wishes to marry Cherubino. As the Countess and Antonio both coldly face the Count, he wonders why every situation turns to his disadvantage. Figaro runs in, causing the Count to inquire about his sprained ankle. Figaro says it is better now and suggests they all get on with the dancing, but Antonio and the Count have more questions for him regarding Cherubino's whereabouts during the window-jumping episode: Cherubino's confession has made a liar of Figaro. When a wedding march is heard, Figaro extricates himself by saying the ceremony must start. The Countess persuades the Count to sit beside her on the thrones from which they are to welcome the bridal couples. Two country girls rub salt in the Count's wounds by again singing his praises for revoking the *droit du seigneur*. Susanna slips him the note, which is closed with her hatpin. When he starts to read the note, he accidentally pricks his finger and drops the pin, which Figaro retrieves as the Count invites everyone to celebrate the double wedding.

ACT IV   Later, in the same hall, Barbarina, sent by the Count to retrieve Susanna's hatpin, has been unable to find it *(L'ho perduta)*. Figaro comes in and learns the significance of the pin: the Count wants it given to Susanna as a sign that he will wait for her in the garden. Concealing his fury at Susanna's apparent duplicity, Figaro takes the pin from his lapel, pretends to find it on the floor and gives it to Barbarina, who runs off. Figaro turns to his mother for comfort, who feels there must be some explanation that vindicates Susanna; she comforts Figaro with a few homilies about how nature encourages fidelity in all creatures *(Il capro e la capretta).**

§ In the garden, Barbarina enters, hoping to find Cherubino, and hides when she sees a cloaked figure. It is Figaro, leading Basilio and Bartolo to witness the Count's revival of the *droit du seigneur*. When he moves away, Basilio tells Bartolo that Figaro is too headstrong: one must learn to take the bitter with the sweet *(In quegl'anni).** They wander off, and Figaro returns, outraged at the duplicity of womankind *(Aprite un po' quegli occhi)*. He hides as the Countess draws near with Marcellina and the disguised Susanna. Knowing that Figaro is listening, Susanna sings a serenade designed to pay him back for his suspicions: in melting tones she hopes for the arrival of her lover, not saying who he is *(Deh! vieni, non tardar)*. Cherubino arrives, and since the Countess and Susanna have switched clothes, he mistakes the former for the latter and addresses her. Afraid he will ruin her scheme, the Countess tries to shoo him off as the Count's voice is heard. Cherubino ducks into hiding with Barbarina, and the Count, mistaking Figaro for Cherubino in the dark, boxes his ears. Finally the Count makes out "Susanna" (actually the Countess) and starts to pay court to her, offering her a ring. Figaro, who by now understands the scheme, steps

---

* Often omitted in performance.

out and scares the Count away, saying people are coming. Then, pretending to mistake Susanna for the Countess, he proposes they get even with the Count by making love themselves. Stepping out of her assumed role, Susanna slaps him; he explains he knew it was she all along, and they resume their charade in order to infuriate the Count, who returns to find Figaro courting the supposed Countess. The Count wants to denounce his wife and calls everyone to witness, only to discover he himself has been gulled by the ladies' disguises. Kneeling to the Countess, he begs forgiveness, which she grants, as all hail the happy ending of a day of madness.

DON GIOVANNI

(Don Juan)

TWO ACTS

MUSIC: Wolfgang Amadeus Mozart

TEXT (Italian): Lorenzo da Ponte, after a libretto by Giovanni Bertati

WORLD PREMIERE: Prague, National Theater, October 29, 1787

U.S. PREMIERE: New York, Park Theatre, November 7, 1817 (in English as *The Libertine*)

METROPOLITAN OPERA PREMIERE: November 28, 1883

CHARACTERS

Don Giovanni, *nobleman of Seville* . . . . Baritone
Donna Anna, *noblewoman* . . . . Soprano
Donna Elvira, *lady of Burgos* . . . . Soprano
Zerlina, *country girl* . . . . Soprano
Don Ottavio, *Donna Anna's fiancé* . . . . Tenor
Masetto, *Zerlina's fiancé* . . . . Baritone
The Commendatore, *Donna Anna's father* . . . . Bass
Leporello, *Don Giovanni's servant* . . . . Bass

ACT I   In a street in eighteenth-century Seville, Leporello is standing watch outside the house of the Commendatore (Commandant of Ulloa) while his master, Don Giovanni (Don Juan Tenorio), is inside on his usual business of paying court to a woman. Leporello grumbles about the hours (*Notte e giorno faticar)* and the working conditions, saying he wants to quit and live like a gentleman. He moves out of sight when Donna Anna, the Commendatore's daughter, appears, hotly pursued by the masked Don Giovanni, who has been trying to seduce her, by force if necessary. Her cries for help soon draw her father into the street to challenge the arrogant Don, who does not want to fight an old man but, when forced to do so, quickly dispatches him. Don Giovanni calls Leporello and leaves just as Donna Anna returns with her fiancé, Don Ottavio, and some servants, in search of the attacker. Seeing her father's body, Donna Anna calls for vengeance, which Ottavio promises.

§ In a street not far away, Leporello catches up with his master and tries to quit his job, giving as reason the Don's scandalous behavior, but a few threatening gestures cow him into submission. Giovanni reminds Leporello he is supposed to be keeping the catalogue of his master's conquests up to date. Just then a woman passes nearby, and the Don steps into the shadows to observe her. Donna Elvira, a lady from Burgos, enters the square, looking for the faithless lover who abandoned her *(Ah! chi mi dice mai)*. Though the Don himself is the faithless lover, he does not recognize her and thinks he should offer consolation. As soon as he steps forward, they recognize each other, and as he tries to retreat, she heaps recriminations on him for having seduced her with promises of marriage, only to leave after three days. Saying Leporello will explain, the Don ducks out. Leporello breaks the news that Elvira is but one of a legion so deceived: from his catalogue he reads off all the kinds of women and the various places where his master enjoyed success with them *(Madamina! il catalogo è questo)*. Elvira vows to have revenge.

§ In the countryside near Don Giovanni's castle, two young peasants, Zerlina and Masetto, celebrate their betrothal with a group of friends. When the Don and Leporello happen upon the scene, Zerlina immediately catches the connoisseur's eye, and he invites the pair to his castle to celebrate, telling Leporello to distract Masetto. As Leporello leads him off, the balky youth declares that this "noble lord" is up to no good *(Ho capito, signor sì!)*. Alone with the girl, Don Giovanni tells her she should not marry such a bumpkin but come instead to his castle, where he will make her his wife *(Là ci darem la mano)*. Their idyll is punctuated by the arrival of Elvira, who rants at the would-be seducer and urges Zerlina to escape *(Ah! fuggi il traditor!)*. No sooner have the two women left than Anna and Ottavio appear. As Anna asks Giovanni's help in finding her unknown assailant, Elvira returns and advises Anna against trusting such a traitor *(Non ti fidar, o misera!)*. Anna and Ottavio are impressed by the strange woman's nobility and sincerity, but Giovanni tries to explain she is out of her mind. At length Elvira leaves, and Giovanni excuses himself to escort her. Right after he is out of sight, Anna declares she recognizes Giovanni as her father's murderer; she recapitulates the events of the evening before, describing the tone and bearing of the would-be seducer, then tells

Ottavio to avenge her *(Or sai chi l'onore)*. She withdraws, leaving Ottavio to declare he will not rest until he has satisfied her call for justice *(Dalla sua pace)*.

§ At the Don's castle, Leporello grumbles anew about his outrageous master, then tells him what happened when the peasants arrived at the castle: they started drinking and making merry, but Elvira burst in with Zerlina, and only after she had delivered a tirade was Leporello able to ease her out the back door and lock it. Preparing to enjoy the evening and augment his list of conquests, the Don toasts the revelry to come *(Finch'han dal vino)*.

§ Outside, Zerlina tries to conciliate the angry Masetto with a mixture of innocence and penitence *(Batti, batti, o bel Masetto)*. When Don Giovanni's voice is heard in the distance, calling everyone to celebrate, Masetto's suspicions flare up again. Zerlina tries to hide, but the Don finds her—and Masetto reminds him that he is there too. When all have moved back into the castle, three masked figures appear—Elvira, Anna, and Ottavio. Seeing them from a window, Leporello calls Don Giovanni, who tells him to invite them in.

§ In the ballroom, with the merriment under way, Masetto continues to warn Zerlina about the Don's advances. Leporello welcomes the trio of maskers, and their host toasts them, broadening his toast to include everyone's freedom to enjoy himself as he wishes *(Viva la libertà!)*. Three dances begin simultaneously, as Leporello distracts Masetto by forcing him to learn to dance. An offstage cry from Zerlina, however, interrupts the party, and the maskers move to protect her as she runs back into their midst, followed by Giovanni, who pretends it was Leporello who assaulted her. When the three intruders unmask, Giovanni recognizes the plot against him and defiantly dashes out.

ACT II   Back in the streets of Seville, Leporello decries his most recent endangerment at the Don's hands. The Don mollifies him with money and describes their next escapade: he will court Elvira's maid while Leporello, disguised in the Don's hat and cloak, walks Elvira away from the scene. Spotting Elvira at her window, the Don pretends to be repentant, but she declares she will not trust him. Soon she changes her mind and comes down to the street, to be welcomed by Leporello, whom she takes for Don Giovanni. The latter puts on Leporello's hat and cape to serenade the maid *(Deh vieni alla finestra)*, but as she appears at the window, Masetto and some other armed peasants enter in search of the culprit. Pretending to be Leporello, the Don tells them to divide into two groups; whichever finds a pair of lovers strolling should attack *(Metà di voi qua vadano)*. He makes Masetto stay behind to share a "secret," which turns out to be a thrashing, using the lad's own weapons. Zerlina comes in to find her sweetheart bruised and promises to nurse him back to health *(Vedrai, carino)*.

DON GIOVANNI

§ In the courtyard of Anna's house, Leporello hides Elvira and leaves her, on the pretext of reconnoitering and returning immediately. While she bemoans her state of perpetual abandonment (*Sola in buio loco*), he hides in another doorway. Anna and Ottavio approach, soon to be joined by Zerlina and Masetto, all bent on vengeance. When they discover Leporello, Elvira alone begs for mercy for the supposed Don, saying she is going to be his wife. The servant reveals his identity and begs them not to beat him (*Ah, pietà! Signori miei*). Then he escapes. Ottavio asks the others to stay with Anna while he searches out the real culprit for the sake of his beloved (*Il mio tesoro*). Elvira laments that her tormented heart still feels pity for the man who betrayed her (*Mi tradì quell'alma ingrata*).

§ Don Giovanni and Leporello jump over the wall into a cemetery. Comparing notes on their respective narrow escapes, they banter until a somber voice from behind announces that the Don's laughter will end before morning. Suspecting a joke, they discover the Commendatore's statue on his grave. The Don forces Leporello to invite the statue to dinner that same night: it nods in acceptance and, challenged by the Don, answers yes.

§ Ottavio reassures Anna in her house that Don Giovanni will pay for his crimes. She puts off their marriage plans by saying that mourning for her father has preempted her devotion (*Non mi dir*).

§ Preparing to enjoy dinner at his castle, Giovanni orders musicians to play. They offer selections from three popular operas of the day; when they reach the third, *Le Nozze di Figaro*, Leporello remarks that it has been heard too often. While both men are eating, Elvira rushes in, calling on Giovanni to save himself by repenting at once. Seeing from his jovial attitude that her mission is doomed, she leaves but screams in fright from the anteroom. Leporello says he hears the statue's approaching steps; refusing to open the door, he hides under the table. Giovanni himself admits the stone guest, who refuses food but invites the Don to his own table. Unafraid, the Don accepts and offers his hand, which the statue grips, demanding he repent or face damnation. The Don refuses, whereupon the statue disappears and Giovanni falls to the floor, gasping, as unseen spirits announce his consignment to hell. Amid rising smoke and flames, he sinks out of sight.

§ As day breaks over the city once more, Anna, Ottavio, Zerlina, and Masetto are still searching for Don Giovanni in the street, but Leporello tells them the most recent turn of events, which Elvira confirms by reporting that she saw the statue enter the Don's castle. Anna asks Ottavio to wait a year before marriage; Elvira will retire to a convent; Zerlina and Masetto head home for dinner; and Leporello looks forward to finding a better master at the tavern. They close with a refrain, "Such is an evildoer's end: death is the just reward for a misspent life."

COSÌ FAN TUTTE

(Women Are Like That)

TWO ACTS
MUSIC: Wolfgang Amadeus Mozart
TEXT (Italian): Lorenzo da Ponte
WORLD PREMIERE: Vienna, Burgtheater, January 26, 1790
U.S. PREMIERE: Metropolitan Opera House, March 24, 1922

CHARACTERS

Fiordiligi, *lady of Ferrara* . . . . Soprano
Dorabella, *her sister* . . . . Soprano
Despina, *their maid* . . . . Soprano
Ferrando, *Dorabella's fiancé* . . . . Tenor
Guglielmo, *engaged to Fiordiligi* . . . . Bass
Don Alfonso, *bachelor* . . . . Baritone
Townspeople, soldiers, musicians, servants

ACT I In Naples, toward the close of the eighteenth century, two young officers, Ferrando and Guglielmo, are having a lively discussion at a café with their friend Don Alfonso. Ferrando insists that his sweetheart, Dorabella, is trustworthy. Guglielmo, in love with Fiordiligi (Dorabella's sister), makes the same claim for *his* sweetheart. Alfonso, a graying bachelor, declares that from what he has seen of the world, trust in women is misplaced, and he offers to prove it. He persuades them to make a bet: for twenty-four hours they must do what he says, and if by then he has not proved his point, he loses. All three toast the idea.

§ In a seaside garden, the two sisters compare notes on Ferrando and Guglielmo, whose miniature portraits they admire in their lockets. Don Alfonso pays a call, bringing news: their lovers must leave with their regiment at once. The two arrive, dressed in traveling clothes, to bid an emotional farewell, with avowals of fidelity on all sides. Soldiers and villagers enter to the strains of a march as a boat draws up to the shore and the two young men board it, promising to write every day (quintet: *Di scrivermi ogni giorno*). As the boat disappears in the distance, the sisters and Don Alfonso pray for breezes to guide it (trio: *Soave sia il vento*). Left alone, Alfonso foresees no trouble in getting these ladies to forget their promises.

Così Fan Tutte

§ Inside the sisters' house, their maid, Despina, prepares to serve breakfast, grumbling about the trials of domestic service. She is surprised to see her mistresses enter in such a tragic mood, crying about ending their misery with poison or a dagger. Dorabella calls on misfortune and despair to martyr her (*Smanie implacabili*). At length Despina finds out what has happened and tells the sisters to forget their absent sweethearts. To expect fidelity in a man, she says—especially in a soldier—is wishful thinking, and women would be well advised to return men's fickle treatment in kind (*In uomini, in soldati*). Shocked, the girls leave, and Despina goes to her room. When Don Alfonso wanders in, wondering how to carry out his scheme without Despina's interference, he decides to make her his ally and knocks on her door, offering a bribe if she will help him introduce Fiordiligi and Dorabella to a couple of attractive foreigners who have come to visit him. In come Ferrando and Guglielmo, disguised so that not even the clever Despina recognizes them. When the girls return, they are outraged by this intrusion, and only fast talking by all three men prevents their being thrown out. Scarcely has Alfonso vouched for the visitors than they begin declaring in the most extravagant terms their admiration for each other's former sweethearts. The girls vacillate for a moment, but then Fiordiligi announces that her heart, like a fortress, will withstand any assault (*Come scoglio*). Alfonso begs them to be more hospitable, and Guglielmo also pleads the men's cause (*Non siate ritrosi*), but the girls withdraw before he is finished. The young men believe they have already won their bet, but Alfonso tells them there is another day to go. They are so happy that they don't mind waiting, and Ferrando sings the praises of love (*Un'aura amorosa*). Alfonso rejoins Despina, who tells him to bring the suitors to the garden.

§ The sisters, alone in the garden, again lament the loss of their lovers (duet: *Ah! che tutta in un momento*). They are interrupted by sounds of the suitors in the near distance, threatening to kill themselves in despair, while Alfonso tries to dissuade them. The young men enter the garden with bottles of "poison," which they drink, falling to the ground with exaggerated farewells to earthly life, blaming the women's heartlessness. The frantic girls call Despina, who says she will fetch help. She reappears shortly, dressed as a doctor, spouting Latin phrases and producing a magnet, with which she effects a "cure." The reviving swains protest their love, but the girls order them to leave.

ACT II In the sisters' room, Despina lectures them on their stubborn attitude. Any girl of fifteen or over, she says, should know how to handle men (*Una donna a quindici anni*). Though shocked by her boldness, the girls agree between themselves to give flirtation a try. Alfonso appears, inviting them to the garden for a serenade.

§ There Ferrando and Guglielmo, still in disguise, call upon the breezes to whisper their love to the young ladies (*Secondate, aurette amiche*). Coached by Alfonso, the hesitant suitors declare themselves again to the girls, who are now in a mood to listen. Despina in turn urges them to respond (quartet: *La mano a me date*); then she and Alfonso discreetly withdraw. Embarrassed at first, the couples quickly warm to each other as they stroll through the garden. Guglielmo presents Dorabella with a heart pendant (duet: *Il core vi dono*), attaching it in place of her locket, with its portrait of Ferrando; to himself he expresses pity for his friend. Ferrando has a harder time with Fiordiligi: after he has pleaded with her *(Ah! lo veggio quell'anima bella)** and excused himself, she wrestles with her inner conflict, resolving to return to her original sweetheart after this adventure *(Per pietà, ben mio)*. When she too has left, Ferrando happily tells Guglielmo that Fiordiligi is like the Rock of Gibraltar and has not broken faith. Guglielmo more soberly reveals that Dorabella has responded, even giving up Ferrando's portrait. When Ferrando takes it badly, his friend launches into a tirade against womankind *(Donne mie, la fate a tanti!)*. Then he leaves Ferrando, who declares himself brokenhearted but still faithful to Dorabella *(Tradito, schernito).** Alfonso and Guglielmo reason with their disillusioned friend: wouldn't he rather know the truth? Asking the young men to try one more stratagem, Alfonso declares he has not yet lost his wager.

§ In the house, Despina congratulates Dorabella on her good sense, but Fiordiligi storms in, cursing them and the others for causing her such torment. She admits that in her heart she has succumbed to the stranger, insisting nevertheless she will not yield to him. Dorabella tries to coax her, saying there is no point in resisting Cupid's wiles *(È amore un ladroncello)*.

§ Guglielmo happily overhears Fiordiligi resolving to herself that she will not receive her new suitor again. Calling Despina, she orders the maid to bring military outfits: the sisters will join their lovers at the front. The disguised Ferrando comes in as she is readying herself for the voyage; drawing his sword, he exhorts her to kill him then and there, since her cruelty has already pierced his heart. Now she starts to weaken. As Alfonso restrains Guglielmo from interrupting the scene, Fiordiligi at length pledges her heart to Ferrando.

§ Now it is Guglielmo's turn to be disillusioned. Ferrando and Alfonso offer words of common sense. There is no shortage of women in the world, but Alfonso gets the men to admit that they love their sweethearts in spite of the girls' fickleness. It is wrong, he declares *(Tutti accusan le donne)*, to blame them for being the way they are: "Così fan tutte!" (all women act like that). Despina rushes in to announce that the girls have decided to go ahead with a wedding to their new suitors.

§ In the festively decorated hall, a chorus hails the two couples, who exchange endearments, though Guglielmo mutters aside that the women deserve poison

* Often omitted in performance.

in their wine. Despina, disguised as a notary, appears and writes up the marriage contract between the girls and two "Albanian gentlemen," "Tizio" and "Sempronio." The girls sign, but before the men can do so, a march is heard: the original suitors have returned! Hiding their new fiancés in a side room, the girls, hysterical, do not know what to do, but Alfonso says he will save the situation. Soon Ferrando and Guglielmo come in, dressed in their uniforms. Greeting their sweethearts, they wonder why the nervousness and confusion. Then they discover the marriage contract. The sisters admit their duplicity and invite their former lovers to kill them, but they blame Alfonso and Despina for their predicament. Cheerfully admitting this, Alfonso takes the men out for a minute, then reintroduces them in "Albanian" disguise. His deception, he says, was undertaken to show the lovers that true happiness lies not in romantic illusion but in accepting things as they are. Agreeing that a trick can work both ways, the lovers reconcile joyously.

LA CLEMENZA DI TITO

(The Clemency of Titus)

TWO ACTS
MUSIC: Wolfgang Amadeus Mozart
TEXT (Italian): Caterino Mazzolà, based on a libretto by Pietro
   Metastasio
WORLD PREMIERE: Prague, National Theater, September 6, 1791
U.S. PREMIERE: Mutual Broadcasting System, June 22 and 29,
   1940 (radio performance); Tanglewood, Berkshire Festival,
   August 4, 1952 (in English)
METROPOLITAN OPERA PREMIERE: October 18, 1984

CHARACTERS

Tito *(Titus Vespasianius), Emperor of Rome* . . . . Tenor
Vitellia, *daughter of Aulus Vitellius, deposed Emperor of Rome* . Soprano
Servilia, *sister of Sesto* . . . . Soprano
Sesto ⎫ *young patricians* . . . . ⎧Mezzo-Soprano
Annio ⎭ . . . . ⎩Mezzo-Soprano
Publio, *captain of the Praetorian Guard* . . . . Bass
      Senators, guards, soldiers, envoys, Romans

Emperor Titus Flavius Sabinus Vespasianus (Tito) ruled Rome from A.D. 79 until his death in A.D. 81, having served as co-ruler since A.D. 71 with his father, Vespasian. Though he destroyed Jerusalem in the year 70, he was known at home as conciliatory and humane; hence the "clemency" of the opera's title.

ACT I Vitellia, daughter of the deposed emperor Vitellius, wants Tito assassinated because he has not returned her love and has chosen as his consort Berenice, daughter of the king of Judaea. Playing upon the devotion of her admirer Sesto (Sextus), she tries to overcome his scruples about committing treason for her sake (duet: *Come ti piace imponi*), threatening to replace him with a worthier champion. Sesto's friend Annio comes to fetch him for an audience with the emperor; he reveals that Berenice will not be consort after all but is returning to her homeland. At this news, Vitellia's ambitions for the throne revive, and she asks Sesto to hold off his plan, saying he should trust her *(Deh, se piacer mi vuoi)*. Annio reminds Sesto of his desire to marry Servilia and urges him to ask Tito for permission. The two men reaffirm their friendship.

§ In a square before the Capitol, the populace hails Tito, who declares that he will help the survivors of the recent eruption of Vesuvius at Pompeii. Annio learns that the emperor wishes to join his family with Sesto's by marrying Servilia. Diplomatically, Annio assures Tito that he welcomes the union, as the emperor offers him favor and advancement, declaring that the chief joy of power is in its opportunity to help others *(Del più sublime soglio)*. The crestfallen Sesto leaves for his audience with Tito. Annio, seeing Servilia enter the square, tells her the emperor wishes to marry her—a fact that takes her by surprise. She reaffirms her love for Annio, and he admits he returns it (duet: *Ah, perdona al primo affetto)*.

§ In the imperial palace, Publio, commander of the Praetorian Guard, shows Tito a list of those who have dared speak out against emperors past and present. Tito is inclined to forgive such offenses, but the discussion is interrupted by Servilia, who begs a private audience and confesses her prior commitment to Annio. Tito relinquishes his claim and remarks that kingdoms would be happier if rulers could trust all their subjects to be so frank *(Ah, se fosse intorno al trono)*. He leaves, followed shortly by Servilia. The angry Vitellia arrives, fuming to Sesto that now is the time to strike. Once more he declares that her wish is his command *(Parto, ma tu ben mio)*. Publio and Annio tell her, however, that Tito is looking for her. When she calls after Sesto to stop him, it is too late: he is out of earshot.

§ In front of the Capitol, Sesto, who has set fire to the building, trembles with remorse. Others appear on the scene—Annio, Servilia, Publio, Vitellia—voicing confusion at this turn of events (quintet: *Deh conservate, oh Dei)*.

Meanwhile, Sesto has reentered the Capitol. Believing he has succeeded in killing the emperor, he starts to confess but is hastily silenced by Vitellia.

ACT II   In the palace, Annio reassures Sesto that the emperor escaped harm during the abortive coup. When Sesto confesses his complicity and declares himself ready to go into exile, Annio urges him to tell Tito the truth—his remorse will earn him forgiveness (*Torna di Tito a lato*)—but Vitellia rushes in, telling him to flee for both their sakes. Publio enters, demanding Sesto's sword; the man Sesto struck by mistake in the flaming capitol was Lentulo, a fellow conspirator, who has survived. Before Publio leads Sesto off to a hearing before the senate, the latter bids a reproachful farewell to Vitellia, who fears disclosure of her crime (trio: *Se al volto mai ti senti*).

§ In a public hall, the people are relieved to know that Tito is safe; he, in turn, voices concern for his friend Sesto, who he fears was led into the conspiracy by Lentulo. Publio cautions the emperor against being too innocent in the face of betrayal. Annio pleads for Sesto, who has confessed his guilt before the senate and been sentenced, with his coconspirators, to be thrown to the wild beasts.* Only the emperor's signature is lacking on the decree. Annio, though he agrees that Sesto deserves punishment, asks Tito to consider his case compassionately (*Tu fosti tradito*). Tito, however, reacts angrily to Sesto's betrayal, hesitating to sign the document only until he has questioned him. When a guard brings Sesto, Tito marvels at his duplicity, while Publio notes to himself that Tito still seems to care for his former friend (trio: *Quello di Tito è il volto!*). Ordering Sesto to be left with him alone, Tito puts aside his regal manner and asks for the truth. Sesto says he did not want the throne for himself, yet he hesitates to implicate Vitellia. Unable to get a satisfactory explanation of Sesto's motive, Tito becomes exasperated again and orders him led to execution, refusing to listen as Sesto pleads to die forgiven (*Deh per questo istante solo*). Alone, Tito agonizes over his unwelcome choice between upholding the law and forgiving a man he values. Finally, he throws aside the writ of condemnation. To Publio, who comes looking for him, he says cryptically that Sesto's fate is decided and will be made known at the arena. Addressing the gods, he tells them that if they wanted a stern ruler, they ought not to have given him a human heart (*Se all'impero, amici Dei*). After he has gone, the distraught Vitellia finds Publio and says she must see the emperor. She believes Sesto has given away her part in the conspiracy. Servilia and Annio find her and beg her to save Sesto—as Tito's empress, she will be able to do so. From the news that Tito has just announced her as his choice, Vitellia knows that Sesto did not betray her secret. Servilia renews her pleas (*S'altro che lacrime*), then leaves Vitellia to realize that she cannot accept the throne at the price of Sesto's life (*Non più di fiori*): death is all that awaits her.

---

*Construction of the Colosseum was completed during the reign of the historical Titus.

§ At the Colosseum, the conspirators are led into the arena, and Tito asks to see Sesto one last time. As he faces him, Vitellia interrupts to declare her own guilt, confessing she used Sesto to further her ambitions. Seeing betrayal spread even to his intended wife, Tito feels almost driven to harden his heart but refuses to do so, pardoning the conspirators, whose repentance he values more than their fidelity (finale: *Tu, è ver, m'assolvi, Augusto*).

DIE ZAUBERFLÖTE

(The Magic Flute)

TWO ACTS

MUSIC: Wolfgang Amadeus Mozart

TEXT (German): Emanuel Schikaneder and Johann Georg Metzler (pseudonym of Karl Ludwig Giesecke)

WORLD PREMIERE: Vienna, Theater auf der Wieden, September 30, 1791

U.S. PREMIERE: New York, Park Theatre, April 17, 1833 (in English)

METROPOLITAN OPERA PREMIERE: March 30, 1900 (in Italian)

CHARACTERS

Queen of the Night . . . . Soprano
Pamina, *her daughter* . . . . Soprano
Papagena, *bird-woman* . . . . Soprano
Tamino, *Egyptian prince* . . . . Tenor
Monostatos, *Moor in the service of Sarastro* . . . . Tenor
Papageno, *bird catcher* . . . . Baritone
Sarastro, *high priest of Isis and Osiris* . . . . Bass
The Speaker . . . . Bass
Three Ladies, *in attendance on the*
   Queen of the Night . . . . Two Sopranos, Mezzo-Soprano
Three Genii . . . . Child trebles
Two Priests . . . . Tenor, Baritone
Two Men in Armor . . . . Tenor, Bass
Slaves, priests, people, etc.

ACT I   In mythological ancient Egypt, Prince Tamino has been overtaken by a giant serpent while wandering in a rocky wilderness. Unarmed and exhausted, he cries out for help and faints as the monster approaches to devour him. As if by magic, Three Ladies appear and kill the serpent with their lances. They admire the unconscious prince and argue about which of them will watch over him while the others report to their mistress, the Queen of the Night. Realizing they cannot all stay, they finally agree that all will leave. Tamino regains his senses and finds the serpent dead. As he wonders what miracle saved him, a feathered woodsman named Papageno wanders by, singing about his wish for a birdlike mate (*Der Vogelfänger bin ich ja*). Questioned by Tamino, he says he catches birds for the Queen of the Night but admits he has never seen her. He is in the process of taking credit for killing the serpent when the Three Ladies reappear, padlocking Papageno's mouth to keep him from telling any more lies. They turn to Tamino, tell him it was they who saved him, and give him a present from their Queen—a miniature portrait of her daughter, Pamina. He looks in wonder at her beauty and feels himself falling in love (*Dies Bildnis ist bezaubernd schön*). Rumbles of thunder announce the Queen herself. She assures the frightened Tamino that she has come only to ask his help: she has lost her daughter to evil forces (*Zum Leiden bin ich auserkoren*) and wants Tamino to win her back. Promising Pamina's hand as reward, the Queen vanishes as abruptly as she appeared. Papageno hums in protest against his padlock (quintet: *Hm! hm! hm! hm!*), and the Ladies remove it, making him promise to stop lying. They present him with a magic glockenspiel and Tamino with a magic flute, sending the men to Sarastro's temple to rescue the captive Pamina. The magic instruments are to be used in case of danger. Three Genii will guide the way, and no one's advice but theirs should be heeded.

§ In an elaborate chamber where Pamina has been held, three slaves compare notes about their mean overseer, the Moor Monostatos, and express hope that Pamina has escaped. It is soon apparent, however, that Pamina has not gotten far in her attempts to return to her mother: Monostatos drags the girl in and orders her tied up. Pleading for death, Pamina faints. Papageno, watching through the window, comes in to investigate. He and Monostatos, frightened by each other's outlandish appearance, mistake each other for the devil himself. Monostatos leaves to summon help. As Pamina revives, Papageno recognizes her as the Queen's daughter, comparing her face to the portrait. He tells her of Tamino's love and of their rescue mission. Cheered by the thought that someone loves her, Pamina joins Papageno is singing the praises of matrimony (*Bei Männern welche Liebe fühlen*).

§ In a grove by three temples, the Genii tell Tamino he is near the end of his search, but they cannot reveal whether he will find Pamina, advising him only to be stalwart. When they disappear, he approaches the first temple, and unseen voices warn him to get back; the same happens at the temple on the other side. He then approaches the middle temple and is confronted by a Priest, who opens the door to ask what he wants. When Tamino replies that he is seeking the realm of Sarastro, an evil tyrant, the Priest replies that

Tamino has been misinformed and should learn the truth. Admitting that Sarastro took Pamina from her mother, the Priest intimates that it was for the girl's own protection. After he has left, telling Tamino he will need holy teaching, the unseen chorus says that Pamina is still alive. Heartened, Tamino plays his magic flute in hopes of making Pamina appear. She is nearby, attempting to escape with Papageno, who replies to the flute with a whistle on his bird-luring pipe. Before she can reach Tamino, however, Monostatos appears with his search party of slaves and orders the escaping pair tied up. Papageno resorts to his glockenspiel, which enchants Monostatos and the slaves into harmless dancing. Voices are heard singing Sarastro's praises, terrifying the fugitives anew as the high priest himself comes to question them. Pamina admits she was trying to escape but says it was for her mother's sake, not her own. Sarastro reassures her that she will come to no harm and that he approves of her love for Tamino; still, her mother is dangerous, and he cannot yet let Pamina go free. Monostatos drags in Tamino and prevents him from embracing Pamina. When Monostatos asks a reward from Sarastro, however, he learns it will be seventy-seven lashes with a switch. As the chorus praises Sarastro's justice, two Priests blindfold Tamino and Papageno and lead them off as Sarastro reenters the main temple with Pamina.

ACT II In a palm grove, Sarastro tells a procession of priests that Tamino is to be initiated and helped. He will not be able to win Pamina until he has proved himself strong in wisdom through a series of tests. Sarastro then calls on the gods to favor Tamino and Papageno as they face these tests *(O Isis und Osiris)*.

§ By night in the temple courtyard, Tamino and Papageno wonder at their strange predicament as thunder rumbles, terrifying the chicken-hearted bird-man. They are met by a Speaker (spokesman) and Priest, who question Tamino and find him steadfast. Papageno, however, confides that something to eat and drink and a wife of his own are really all he wants, asking what the trials will consist of. When he learns that Sarastro has already found him a bird-woman bride named Papagena, he becomes more interested in persevering. As a first test, the initiates are sworn to silence, even if they should meet their sweethearts. As soon as their mentors have left, the Three Ladies appear, urging Tamino and Papageno to escape. Reminding his companion they are sworn to silence, Tamino refuses to respond, and the Ladies leave in consternation. Speaker and Priest return with veils and torches and lead off their respective charges.

§ Monostatos finds Pamina sleeping in a garden and exults that finally he will be able to make love to her *(Alles fühlt der Liebe Freuden)*. As he approaches, however, the Queen of the Night appears and orders him away, then gives the wakening Pamina a dagger with which to kill Sarastro. When Pamina demurs, her mother declares she must perform the deed or be disowned as a daughter

(Der Hölle Rache). As soon as the Queen vanishes, Monostatos resumes his attempt to win Pamina, saying he is the only one who can save her and her mother. When she refuses, he threatens her with a dagger, only to be stopped by Sarastro, who orders him out. Monostatos resolves to side with the Queen and leaves. Pamina begs Sarastro not to punish her mother, and he replies that love is the only answer to revenge *(In diesen heil'gen Hallen)*.

§ In a temple hallway, Tamino and Papageno receive further instructions: they are to remain silent and to proceed in a certain direction when they hear trumpets. When the priests have left, Papageno tries to talk to Tamino, who hushes him. Complaining that not even a drink of water can be had, Papageno is approached by an old hag carrying a cup. He banters with her about her sweetheart and thinks, when she says she is eighteen, that she means "eighty." At the sound of thunder, she vanishes and the Three Genii reappear, conjuring up food and drink and giving back the flute and glockenspiel. Pamina comes in and, when Tamino cannot reply, complains that her grief is worse than death *(Ach, ich fühl's)*, then leaves in total dejection. Papageno is attacked by wild animals, which Tamino tames by playing his flute. Trumpets announce the priestly chorus, joined by Sarastro in praise of Tamino's progress during the trials. Summoning Pamina, the high priest tells her she can meet her prince for a last farewell before Tamino proceeds for the rest of his testing. As for Papageno, heaven means nothing to him, and he would like nothing better than a glass of wine. When this wish is granted by the Speaker, Papageno— now alone—revives a little and speculates on his promised wife *(Ein Mädchen oder Weibchen)*. At this point the old hag returns to offer herself as a bride, saying he will never escape the place if he refuses. He agrees, saying aside, "Until I find someone prettier," but just as she is transformed into a pretty young Papagena, the Speaker returns to whisk her away, declaring Papageno not yet worthy.

§ In a palm garden, the Three Genii say that the sunlight will soon be at hand, but as they withdraw, Pamina approaches, intending to use her mother's dagger to take her own life. The Genii return and snatch away the dagger, then reassure her of Tamino's love.

§ Rocky caves, with fire at one side and a waterfall at the other, representing the elements. Two Men in Armor sing severely of the trials of fire and water that one must overcome to reach the enlightenment of heaven (chorale: *Der, welcher wandert*). Tamino, led in by two Priests, declares he is ready to face the trials. He is permitted an unexpected reunion with Pamina, and this time the lovers embrace. She will join him in the trials of fire and water, to which the Men in Armor direct them. As a solemn march sounds, Tamino plays his magic flute. The couple passes through the cave of fire, then through the waterfall.

§ Outside the temple, the lovers rejoice that they have finally earned each other. Sarastro leads them inside.

§ In a garden, Papageno whistles happily for Papagena, but she is nowhere to be found. Abruptly discouraged, he decides to hang himself from a tree but is stayed by the Three Genii, who remind him to play his glockenspiel. When he does, his sweetheart appears, and the two sing rapturously about all the bird-children they hope to have (*Pa, pa, pa, pa*).

§ In darkness in a rocky wilderness, the Queen, her Three Ladies, and Monostatos get ready to storm the temple. The Queen promises Monostatos her daughter in marriage, but thunder proclaims the end of her might, and the defeated group sinks into the earth.

§ At the temple, Sarastro says day has triumphed over the powers of darkness. He joins Tamino and Pamina as the chorus hails Isis and Osiris, the triumph of courage, virtue, and wisdom.

THEA MUSGRAVE
b. 1928

hea Musgrave was not the first woman to write an opera, but she is certainly the first Scottish woman to compose one about her most famous countrywoman. A notable predecessor in dealing with the subject, Gaetano Donizetti, based his *Maria Stuarda* on a play by Schiller. Musgrave based her libretto on a play by Amalia Elguera, who had supplied the text for Musgrave's first stage work, *The Voice of Ariadne*. These two scores were followed by an opera version of Dickens' *A Christmas Carol*. Born in the district known as Midlothian—Sir Walter Scott country—Musgrave began to enjoy a certain prominence by the mid-1950s. Her operas are characterized by their special mood and atmosphere, created by instrumental and vocal writing that does not strive for modernity or novelty but achieves instead a timeless, communicative quality. In *Mary, Queen of Scots*, the composer is able to view the subject with immediacy as well as with long-term perspective, telescoping and combining events of actual history. Unlike Donizetti's opera, the Musgrave work deals not with Mary's death but with the events between her return from France and her exile in England.

MARY, QUEEN OF SCOTS

THREE ACTS
MUSIC: Thea Musgrave
TEXT (English): by the composer, based on *Moray,* a play
    by Amalia Elguera
WORLD PREMIERE: Edinburgh Festival, Scottish Opera,
    September 6, 1977
U.S. PREMIERE: Norfolk, Virginia, March 29, 1978

CHARACTERS

Mary, *Queen of Scots* . . . . Soprano
James Hepburn, *Earl of Bothwell* . . . . Tenor
Henry Stuart, *Lord Darnley* . . . . Tenor
Earl of Ruthven . . . . Tenor
James Stewart, *Earl of Moray* . . . . Baritone
Earl of Morton . . . . Baritone
Cardinal Beaton . . . . Baritone
David Riccio . . . . Bass-Baritone
Lord Gordon . . . . Bass
The Four Marys . . . . Two Sopranos, Mezzo, Contralto
    Monks, soldiers, courtiers, Lords of the Congregation,
                people of Edinburgh

ACT I   In Cardinal Beaton's house in Edinburgh, 1561, the old man is rob-
ing himself for mass when James Stewart, Earl of Moray, breaks in unexpectedly. From his hostile tone and from Beaton's reproaches it is evident that
James has left the Catholic church to follow the Protestant leader John Knox.
When he says he never wanted the crown, Beaton challenges him: why else
did he give up the chance to become cardinal himself? Ordering Beaton
imprisoned, James destroys a letter the cardinal had intended for Mary, James'
sister, telling her not to trust her brother's counsel but to rely on the military
leader James Hepburn, Earl of Bothwell.

§ By the quayside of the port of Leith, shrouded in fog, Mary arrives in
Scotland from France, of which she is the widowed queen. Though a Catholic,
she has been invited by the Protestant lords to assume the Scottish throne.
Sadly she bids adieu to the happiness she knew in France, receiving no wel-

come in her new kingdom (*No one and no one and no one*). Bothwell, standing in the mist to observe her, steps forward to introduce himself and offer protection: she may have to fear imprisonment by her ambitious brother. James appears, confronts Bothwell, and accuses him of trying to create a gulf between Mary and himself. James' cold logic and his blood relationship to the queen force Bothwell to stand back. A crowd materializes as the people recognize and hail their new ruler (*Welcome, Mary, our queen!*). Their plea for a peaceful reign is disrupted by Lord Gordon's message that Beaton has died in prison. Though Gordon exhorts the people not to trust James, they walk away unheeding, while the Earl of Morton—a supporter of James—warns him against speaking treason.

§ In the ballroom at Holyrood Castle, dancing is in progress. To the annoyance of James and Bothwell, Mary has taken a fancy to the foppish Henry, Lord Darnley—cousin to both her and Elizabeth of England—who pays obvious court to her (*What precious stone has shape more perfect than the oval of your face?*). Seeing that James is unsure how to deal with this threat, Bothwell provocatively leads his men in a roistering song (*Sir John Sinclair began to dance*). When Mary returns, she surprises the men by taking part in the dance herself, relieving the tension. Then, resting from this exertion, she lets her Italian-born secretary, David Riccio, sing a gentler song (*In ancient Thrace*) while she muses about the three men in her life. Bothwell mutters that only he has the strength to protect her. Seeing Darnley paying court to her again, James interrupts, warning of Darnley's unsuitability as a consort, of his divisive effect on her court. Defiantly, she says she alone will choose her associates. The surly Bothwell picks a quarrel with Darnley and draws his sword, whereupon Mary restores peace and orders Bothwell back to the frontier until further notice. Bothwell is confident that the time will come when Mary cannot do without him (*So she has chosen*).

ACT II   The following winter. The Lords, waiting for an audience with the queen, complain about her weak, dissolute husband, Darnley, with whom she appears. Annoyed by the Lords' coldness, Darnley presses Mary to make him king, accusing her of still being under her brother's thumb (*What queen? Where is she?*). As she goes into the adjacent council chamber to meet with the Lords, Darnley—already somewhat drunk—pours more wine. The Earls of Morton and Ruthven, waiting to see him alone, step out of the shadows; pretending they wish him to be king, they insinuate that the queen's pregnancy might have been caused by Riccio, whom they describe as a schemer. Darnley vows to kill his former friend Riccio (*I am born to be king*). In the meantime, however, the voices of the Lords have been raised in the next room, proclaiming their stubborn opposition to Darnley as king. James, who has been waiting unseen, steps forward as the two earls usher Darnley out. He is confident that things will go his way (*Now I shall rule!*), but when Mary appears, she realizes he will not stand by her, since he is ambitious for himself alone. With growing resolution, she refuses to give him power, finally telling him to leave. Afraid she cannot trust Bothwell either, she resolves to rule by herself (*Alone, I stand alone*)—it is her right.

§ In Mary's supper room, her four attendants—all named Mary—join Riccio in a reprise of his song. When the queen appears, they continue the song in hopes of cheering her. Darnley, backed by Morton and Ruthven, stumbles in, accuses Riccio of being Mary's lover, and stabs him to death. James comes in, feigning concern for Mary, who withdraws with her entourage. The scene fades to . . .

§ . . . the council chamber, where Lords loyal to Mary argue with a dissident faction (spurred on by Morton) that wants to make James regent. Ruthven bursts in to say the queen is nowhere to be found. As the crowd outside clamors for a word from her, James goes to the window to announce Riccio's murder and the queen's apparent flight. Gordon, appearing amid the crowd, calls James a liar and suggests he is holding Mary prisoner. James cries he must take power to preserve the peace, but Mary appears from the crowd, denounces James for putting Darnley up to Riccio's murder, and banishes him for trying to usurp her power. The people back Mary as the hostile Lords are forced into banishment.

ACT III   Some months later, after the birth of Mary's son,* sounds of battle fade into a lullaby as Mary laments her husband's lack of interest, then joins the nurse, Mary Seton, in pinning her hopes on the child (*Sleep, little child*). Gordon arrives with news that James has raised an army, regained popular support, and started to march on Edinburgh. He urges her to take refuge at Stirling Castle, but she says she has sent for Bothwell. Gordon, knowing the people's mistrust of Bothwell, fears that the queen will be overpowered, but she says she intends to keep control. After Gordon has gone, she receives Bothwell, telling him she needs his protection against her brother. Taking advantage of her weakened condition, he embraces her and declares she will be his. When he leads her into an adjoining room, James enters by a secret door, confident that since Mary is now compromised, she will have to give him power. He enters the chambers and confronts Bothwell, who defies him. When Gordon arrives with news that Darnley has been found murdered, the two rivals trade accusations and start fighting. Wounded, Bothwell makes his escape. Mary realizes that no one will believe her to be innocent of enticing Bothwell (*Oh, dark treacherous night*). Gordon reports that James has swayed the people, who call on her to abdicate. Her son has been taken to safety; though she protests (*Who will comfort him?*), Gordon says she has no choice

---

*Eventually King James VI of Scotland and James I of England.

but to seek asylum across the English border, since Bothwell, her only protector, has disappeared. Gordon resolves to kill the traitor James. When Mary tries to address the people from her window, she is shouted down. Fearing Bothwell, the people call for James to rule. Unnoticed, as when she arrived in Scotland, Mary crosses the border, and a portcullis separates her from her child and people. She watches as Gordon fatally stabs James and as Morton—the future regent—takes custody of the child.

MODEST MUSSORGSKY
1839–81

hough *Boris Godunov* is today considered the Russian national opera, it made its way onto the world's stages quite slowly. The work was saved from oblivion by two powerful personalities: Nikolai Rimsky-Korsakov, who edited the version generally used, and Feodor Chaliapin, whose charismatic portrayal of the title role spanned the first three decades of the twentieth century.

Modest Mussorgsky embarked on a military career and became seriously interested in composition only in 1857, after meeting the prime movers in the Russian nationalist movement. The critic Vladimir Stasov considered Mussorgsky one of the Five (the others being Balakirev, Borodin, Cui, and Rimsky), an avant-garde group that would give Russian music a distinctive character independent of European models. Hampered by lack of formal training, Mussorgsky relied on colleagues for help in dealing with harmony and orchestration, but the sheer novelty and boldness of his talent often confounded them. Today the well-meaning posthumous ministrations of Rimsky-Korsakov are frequently set aside for a reassessment of Mussorgsky's originals, which possess a directness and vitality often lost or weakened by revisions.

Mussorgsky called his adaptation of Pushkin's verse drama *Boris Godunov* a "musical folk drama," and a large portion of its thematic material stems from two sources close to the grass roots—folk song and liturgy. The composer's concern with the rise and fall of speech resulted in a continuous, plastic amalgam of recitative and song, flowing in and out of each other. A vital force in

Boris Godunov is the chorus, representing not only the voice of the people but also an articulate body of factions, often at odds with each other.

In its original form, *Boris* was a series of tableaux. The committee of the Maryinsky Theater in St. Petersburg rejected the work in February 1871, despite Mussorgsky's efforts to make it acceptable for conventional opera production. Two years later, three scenes were given as part of a benefit program, and in February 1874, largely at the insistence of the prima donna Yulia Platonova, the world premiere of the complete work took place. Critics were generally unfriendly, but youthful supporters helped sell enough tickets for twenty performances. Arturo Toscanini conducted the American premiere at the Metropolitan Opera, using an Italian translation of the Rimsky-Korsakov version, which had appeared in 1896.

Dogged by epilepsy and alcoholism, Mussorgsky suffered from disorganized work habits. Of the several operas he undertook, *Boris* was the only one he completed. Another epic of Russian history, *Khovanshchina,* was finished and orchestrated by Rimsky-Korsakov, and various composers have made performing versions of other Mussorgsky operas.

The historical Boris, a contemporary of England's Elizabeth I, was an important ruler who led Russia in its first steps out of the Middle Ages. Though judged a "Russian Macbeth" in an era of routine bloodshed, he has been exonerated by history of the crime around which Pushkin's plot revolves— the murder of the Czarevitch Dimitri. Boris died in 1605, after only seven years of reign. Like him, his successor the False Dimitri was soon brought down by the conniving of Prince Shuisky, who himself then briefly ruled.

BORIS GODUNOV

PROLOGUE AND FOUR ACTS

MUSIC: Modest Mussorgsky

TEXT (Russian): the composer, based on Alexander Pushkin's play of the same name and on *History of the Russian State* by Nikolai M. Karamzin

WORLD PREMIERE: St. Petersburg, Maryinsky Theater, February 8, 1874

U.S. PREMIERE: Metropolitan Opera, March 19, 1913 (in Italian)

MODEST MUSSORGSKY

CHARACTERS

Boris Godunov, *Czar of Russia* . . . . Bass
Xenia, *his daughter* . . . . Soprano
Fyodor, *his son* . . . . Mezzo-Soprano
Nurse . . . . Contralto
Prince Vassili Shuisky . . . . Tenor
Grigori, *later the pretender Dimitri* . . . . Tenor
Simpleton . . . . Tenor
Andrei Shchelkalov, *clerk of the Duma* . . . . Baritone
Pimen, *old monk* . . . . Bass
Marina Mnishek, *Polish princess* . . . . Soprano
Rangoni, *Jesuit* . . . . Bass
Varlaam ⎫ *wandering monks* . . . . ⎧ Bass
Missail ⎭ . . . . ⎩ Tenor
Innkeeper . . . . Mezzo-Soprano
Khrushchov, *boyar* . . . . Tenor
Lavitsky ⎫ *two Jesuits* . . . . Bass
Chernikovsky ⎭

Soldiers, boyars, pilgrims, children, people

PROLOGUE   Russia, February 1598. Fyodor, the youthful heir to the throne of Ivan the Terrible, has just died. The throne is vacant, and the candidate favored by the boyars (nobles), the regent Boris Godunov, seems reluctant. As the opera opens, a crowd of people is being herded into position by guards outside the monastery near Moscow where Boris is in seclusion. Shchelkalov, secretary of the Duma (council), addresses the peasants, telling them that Boris still refuses the throne and urging them to pray for his change of heart. As pilgrims arrive, the crowd welcomes them reverently, but enthusiasm for Boris is not spontaneous. By the end of the scene, word has filtered through that Boris will be the new czar.

§ In the Kremlin square, a clangor of bells hails Boris' ascent to the throne. The wily Prince Vassili Shuisky, one of Boris' most powerful advisers, leads the multitude in calling for the czar. When Boris appears, he is in a dark, introspective mood *(Skorbit dusha!)*, praying for God's guidance. Shuisky and others of his retinue accompany him into the cathedral to be crowned, as the crowd repeats its cries of "Glory to the czar!"

ACT I   Five years later, in a monastery in the Russian countryside, the old monk Pimen sits laboring over a chronicle he is writing: the history of Russia as he has known it in his lifetime. Grigori, a novice who has been asleep in Pimen's cell, awakens suddenly from a recurrent dream he has been having, in which he climbs a tower and sees the Muscovites crawling below like ants, laughing at him. Musing on the vanities of youthful adventure and earthly glory, Pimen reminds him that many men, even czars, gave up everything to enter a monastic order. Pimen recalls his own youth and, questioned by Grigori, describes the day the young Czarevitch Dimitri, heir to the late Fyodor, was murdered at Uglich by servants, who said Czar Boris ordered them to do it (Okh, pomnyu!). Grigori asks how old the czarevitch would be. "As old as you are," Pimen replies. The old man leaves for matins while Grigori, pausing on the doorstep, swears that Boris will pay for his crimes.

§ In a country inn near the Lithuanian border, the good-natured Innkeeper sits plucking a goose, lightening her work with a folklike song about the bird. She is interrupted by two disreputable-looking wandering monks, Varlaam and Missail, who try to get free food and wine. Right behind them, scarcely noticed, comes Grigori, who has escaped from the monastery and now hopes to impersonate the Czarevitch Dimitri and overthrow the czar. Wanting to escape to Poland, he has followed Varlaam and Missail as far as the border. The sight of wine encourages Varlaam to burst into a lusty song about the siege of Kazan, where 40,000 Tartars were slaughtered by the czar's defenders (Kak vo gorodye bylo vo Kazanye). Grigori, drinking nothing himself, realizes he is about to lose his guide as Varlaam lapses into a stupor. He asks the Innkeeper's help in finding the border; she says the police are watching the road for some fugitive, but she knows a back way. Just as Grigori is about to make his escape, two policemen appear at the door, carrying a warrant for the fugitive's arrest and trying to find someone who can read it. Grigori offers his services and changes the wording so that it describes Varlaam. The latter protests and starts to decipher the document himself, laboriously stumbling through it. As the description of Grigori emerges, the young man makes his escape through a window.

ACT II   In the library of the czar's palace in the Kremlin, Boris' daughter, Xenia, intones a lament for her recently dead fiancé. Her brother, Fyodor, and their Nurse try to comfort her—the Nurse first with a song about a gnat, then Fyodor with a nonsense song about barnyard animals. Boris enters and also tries to console Xenia. Fyodor turns to a map of Russia and identifies some places on it, earning his father's praise and a reminder that he will be czar himself one day. After his children and their Nurse have left, Boris muses on his power. He feels that the death of his daughter's fiancé is an ill omen. The sorrows of his country—discontent and poverty among the people, tales of an uprising in Lithuania—he perceives as God's punishment directed at him for ordering the czarevitch murdered. He has had nightmares in which the wounded child cried out to him. His musings are disturbed by a boyar announcing Shuisky, and by a commotion among the servants caused by a parrot. Boris listens to Fyodor's description of the event, praising the boy for being observant and warning him not to trust Shuisky. Boris greets Shuisky roughly, calling him a hypocrite. Shuisky says he has come to warn of a rebellion led by the pretender "Dimitri." Fyodor wants to hear this too, but Boris sends him away, then turns to Shuisky and demands to know whether the young Czarevitch Dimitri was killed beyond any shadow of a doubt. Shuisky recalls that he saw the dead child with an unearthly smile on his face. Boris orders him out, then cries to himself that he is suffocating with guilt. As a clock strikes, he imagines seeing the child (clock scene: *Ouf! Tyazhelo!*), then cries out to God for mercy and collapses.

ACT III   At a castle in Sandomierz,* Poland, Grigori, masquerading as the Czarevitch Dimitri, is trying to play upon the enmity of the Polish nobility toward Russia, to get their help in putting him on the throne. He also seeks the hand of the vain, ambitious Princess Marina Mnishek, daughter of the local governor. Marina listens to praises from her handmaidens, but she is bored and dismisses them. Alone, she reflects on the superficiality of court life and welcomes the attentions of Dimitri, seeing herself on the Russian throne *(Skuchno Marinye)*. She receives the scheming monk Rangoni, who tells her to ensnare Dimitri by whatever means necessary, because Russia must be brought under the dominion of the Roman church.

§ Near a fountain, Grigori waits impatiently for a rendezvous with Marina. Instead he meets Rangoni, who warns him against being discovered there and spirits him away. To the strains of a polonaise, the guests enter. Marina scoffs at an admirer's protestations, then leads a toast to her own ambitions. When they all have left, Grigori returns, more resolved than ever to win Marina and the throne. She appears, telling him she is not interested in hearing how much he loves her, only in what he is prepared to do because of it *(Znayu, vsyo znayu!)*. Assured that his ambition equals hers, she admits she returns his love, as the gloating Rangoni watches from the shadows.

ACT IV   The square outside the church of St. Basil the Blessed in Moscow.† A crowd of poor people discuss the pretender Grishka Otrepyev (Grigori), whose name has been cursed during the church service; they believe, however, that Dimitri is genuine and will save them from Russia's misfortunes. Attention turns to a Simpleton, teased by a group of boys who snatch a kopek from him. Boris and some boyars emerge from the church, distributing alms to the poor. The Simpleton tells Boris about the boys who stole his coin, adding, "Why don't you have them killed, the way you did our czarevitch?" Shuisky wants the Simpleton arrested, but Boris, remembering the almost sacred status of madmen, asks the Simpleton instead to pray for him. The Simpleton says he cannot, because "Our Lady ordered me, 'Don't pray for Herod.' "

---

*Pushkin's verse play gives the location as Sambor, somewhat to the southeast of Sandomierz and now part of the U.S.S.R. Both towns are near Lvov.
†This scene is omitted from some productions.

BORIS GODUNOV

§ In the Great Hall of the Kremlin,* the Duma convenes, awaiting the czar. Shchelkalov, secretary of the Duma, recites a decree from Boris and the Holy Patriarch denouncing the usurper Dimitri and asking the boyars to decide his punishment. The council agrees that Dimitri, when caught, should be put to death, along with his followers. Shuisky appears and tells the boyars how he saw Boris having a hallucinatory fit, crying out to the dead Dimitri. The boyars are disinclined to believe him, but his story is interrupted by Boris himself, crying, "Go, my child!" Coming to his senses, the czar takes the throne and addresses his nobles. Shuisky asks audience for an old pilgrim, who turns out to be the monk Pimen. The pilgrim tells about a blind shepherd whose sight was restored when he visited Uglich and prayed at the grave of the Czarevitch Dimitri (*Odnazhdy, v vecherni chas*). Overwhelmed, Boris feels himself choking and sends for his son as Pimen is led off. Cautioning the boy against the boyars' treachery, Boris prays to God for guidance for his children. He cries, "I am still czar!" but realizes that he is dying. He names Fyodor his successor, falling to the ground with a last prayer for forgiveness.

§ In a forest near Kromy, insurgent peasants have caught a boyar, Khrushchov, whom they plan to lynch "like any decent thief." Their attention is diverted by the arrival of Varlaam and Missail, expediently singing the praises of Dimitri. Less fortunate are two Jesuits, Lavitsky and Chernikovsky, who wander in chanting Latin and are quickly tied up. Attempts to hang the scapegoats come to nothing as the pretender rides in, praised by everyone, including the Jesuits and Khrushchov. Declaring clemency and salvation for the downtrodden Russian people, Grigori rallies his followers and leads them away. Only the Simpleton is left, singing quietly about the tears that must flow for Russia's continuing misfortune (*Lyeytes, lyeytes slyozy gorkiye*).

---

*The order of the last two scenes is sometimes reversed, so that the opera ends with the death of Boris, which took place in the year 1605.

OTTO NICOLAI
1810–49

German comic opera, unlike the French and Italian varieties, has always held no more than a limited appeal for foreign audiences, perhaps because of its deliberate simplicity and its reliance on regional language and humor. Mozart, in his desire to reach a larger German-speaking public, introduced cosmopolitan elements into his singspiels. But after his death, the genre declined sharply in popularity, only partially relieved by some of the works of Gustav Albert Lortzing and by *Die Lustigen Weiber von Windsor* of Otto Nicolai.

Nicolai, like Meyerbeer before him, studied in his native Germany but went to Italy to enlarge his horizons, hoping to write for the theater. He wrote two operas there, *Il Templario* and *Il Proscritto,* which were brought back to Germany, where he translated and adapted them. After a not very fruitful stay in Vienna, he moved to Berlin, serving as music director at the Hofoper. *Die Lustigen Weiber* was conceived for Vienna, but the impresario Balachino rejected it on the grounds that it was submitted too late in the season, and the opera was first staged in Berlin in 1849, two months before the composer's death. In its first sixty years, it received 250 performances there, an average of about four a year.

Since *Die Lustigen Weiber* is based on Shakespeare's *Merry Wives of Windsor,* comparisons with Verdi's *Falstaff* of half a century later are inevitable. But *Die Lustigen Weiber* is a completely different kind of work—a German romantic opera in singspiel form, reflecting the tradition of Weber, Schubert, and Mendelssohn—making such comparisons unfair and irrelevant. In its own genre it remains a minor masterpiece, and Wagner paid it the compliment of borrowing one of its themes for *Die Meistersinger.*

DIE LUSTIGEN WEIBER VON WINDSOR

(The Merry Wives of Windsor)

THREE ACTS
MUSIC: Otto Nicolai
TEXT (German): Hermann von Mosenthal, after Shakespeare's play
WORLD PREMIERE: Berlin, Hofoper, March 9, 1849
U.S. PREMIERE: Philadelphia, Academy of Music, March 16, 1863
METROPOLITAN OPERA PREMIERE: March 9, 1900

CHARACTERS

Frau Fluth (Mistress Ford) . . . . Soprano
Frau Reich (Mistress Page) . . . . Mezzo-Soprano
Anna Reich (Anne Page) . . . . Soprano
Fenton . . . . Tenor
Spärlich (Slender) . . . . Tenor
Herr Fluth (Mr. Ford) . . . . Baritone
Herr Reich (Mr. Page) . . . . Bass
Sir John Falstaff . . . . Bass
Dr. Cajus . . . . Bass
Townspeople, children, servants

ACT I   The courtyard of the Fluth house in Windsor, England, sometime during the first quarter of the fifteenth century. Frau Fluth is amused at the presumption of Sir John Falstaff in writing her a love letter *(O schönste Frau)*. Her neighbor Frau Reich comes to see her, having received an identical letter. They resolve to trick Falstaff and teach him a lesson. As they enter the house, their husbands arrive, accompanied by Spärlich (Reich's choice among his daughter Anna's suitors) and Fenton (Anna's own choice). While Cajus, a pedant with a thick French accent, rants that he will marry Anna himself, Reich ignores him, listening impatiently to Fenton *(Wenn eure Seele je empfunden)* and declaring the well-to-do Spärlich a better choice.

§ Inside, Frau Fluth devises a clever plan to deal with Falstaff, to whom she has written, inviting him to visit her *(Nun eilt herbei)*. Frau Reich has told Fluth of the rendezvous, because Frau Fluth also wishes to teach her jealous husband a lesson. When Falstaff appears, protesting his love, Frau Fluth reacts coyly. At the sound of knocking, she hides him behind a screen before admitting Frau Reich, who says the jealous Fluth is on his way. Pretending to be surprised at Falstaff's presence—didn't he swear he loved *her?*—Frau Reich helps him into a laundry hamper, where the ladies cover him with dirty linen. As Fluth arrives, they have the servants carry out the basket and empty it into the Thames. Fluth calls on his friends and the townspeople to witness his outrage *(Herein! Kommt all' herein)*, as he frantically searches the house in vain. Led by Frau Reich, the others reproach Fluth for his jealousy, and Frau Fluth proclaims her innocence *(Ach, einst in jenen Tagen)*. Apologizing, he says he was told Falstaff would be there, but she pretends indignation at the very idea and threatens to leave him.

ACT II   At the Garter Inn, Falstaff, recovering from a soaking, orders his "usual breakfast," beginning with wine. He is cheered by another note from Frau Fluth, asking him to call on her again. When two townsmen challenge him to a drinking bout, he jovially accepts, declaring that a jug of sack has always been his best friend *(Als Büblein an der Mutter Brust)*. He holds his own against the challengers, and they depart unsteadily, leaving him alone to receive Fluth disguised as "Bach," who offers money for the fat knight's help in an amorous venture. It seems he too loves Frau Fluth; Falstaff confides that he has begun an intimate dalliance with her. As Fluth struggles to conceal his rage on learning that a second tryst has been set, Falstaff predicts they will both succeed in winning Frau Fluth *(Ja, ein Sieg ist leichte Mühe)*.

§ In the garden behind the Reich house, Spärlich waits in hopes of wooing Anna *(Nein, nicht länger will ich warten)* but hides when his rival Cajus appears, bent on the same mission. When the third rival, Fenton, is heard approaching, Cajus too steps out of sight. As Fenton serenades at Anna's window with an apostrophe to the wood lark *(Horch, die Lerche)*, the young lady emerges from the house, sad because of her parents' conflicting demands but firm in her love for Fenton *(Kannst du zweifeln?)*. When mention is made of the other two suitors, these poke their heads out of the bushes to mutter and grumble. Eventually, beside themselves with frustration, they step into the open, but the lovers pay them no attention.

§ Falstaff returns to the Fluth house, only to learn that Fluth is on the rampage again. Frau Fluth sends him into another room with Frau Reich, instructing him to put on a huge gown belonging to her maid's aunt, Frau Klatsch, the "fat woman of Brainford." Fluth arrives and argues with his wife, threatening her and her lover with mayhem (duet: *So! jetzt hätt' ich ihn gefangen!*). When servants again pass through with the laundry hamper, Fluth searches it, even thrusts his sword into it, to his wife's amusement. When his cronies arrive, he insists on searching the house, so Frau Fluth calls to Frau Reich to take the "fat woman of Brainford" outside. Having forbidden his house to the fat woman, whom he considers a gossip and a witch, Fluth attacks and beats "her" on the way out, then tears the rest of the place apart.

ACT III In their parlor, Reich, his wife, and his daughter sit at lunch with the Fluths. Fluth endorses the plan suggested by Frau Reich, who describes the haunted oak of Herne the Hunter in Windsor Forest (*Vom Jäger Herne die Mähr' ist alt*): they will invite Falstaff there at night and lie in wait for him, dressed as elves. Each of Anna's parents speaks to her aside, saying she will marry their respective choices that same night. Seeing how they hope to deceive each other, she means to deceive both and marry Fenton (*Wohl denn! gefasst ist der Entschluss*).

§ As midnight strikes in Windsor Forest, Falstaff enters, costumed as Herne the Hunter with antlers on his head. When he recognizes Frau Fluth and Frau Reich, he is reassured by the seeming loyalty of his two intended sweethearts, paying court by turns to each (*Nun mag es blitzen*). Fear gets the better of him, however, when he thinks fairies are approaching: whoever sees them is as good as dead (chorus: *Ihr Elfen, weiss und rot und grau*). Anna steps forward, dressed as the fairy queen, Titania, and welcomes her lover Oberon (the disguised Fenton). Reich joins them, disguised as Herne, and discovers the impostor Falstaff, calling a plague of insects on him until he confesses his sins (*Was trieb dich, frecher Menschensohn*). As "elves" pinch and poke the terrified Falstaff, Cajus and Spärlich enter in costume, looking for Anna. Hearing no confession from Falstaff, the gathering attacks him in earnest (*Fasst ihn, Geister, nach der Reih'*), causing him to give up. Laughing, Reich says their victim has been punished enough: now it's time to settle everything among themselves amiably. Reich even takes it gracefully when he sees Cajus accidentally "married" to Spärlich, and gives Anna and Fenton his blessing, in which his wife joins. Frau Fluth invites Falstaff to the wedding feast as everyone rejoices (ensemble: *So hat der Schwank der fröhlichen Nacht*).

JACQUES OFFENBACH
1819–80

acques Offenbach was born in Germany, son of the cantor of the Cologne synagogue, who had adopted the name of his family's hometown, Offenbach am Main. Like Meyerbeer before him, he was destined to make his career in France. Offenbach first caught the attention of the Parisians with his cello playing. In addition to being a salon virtuoso, he earned a steady income as cellist in the Opéra Comique orchestra, eventually achieving the post of conductor at the Théâtre Français. It was as manager of his own theater, the Bouffes Parisiens (1855–66), that he became king of the light musical stage, for which he wrote *Orphée aux Enfers, La Belle Hélène, La Vie Parisienne,* and others.

All told, he produced over one hundred stage works, of which *Les Contes d'Hoffmann* was the only serious opera. It was also his swan song. The idea for it had come during an 1876 visit to America, when the composer was reminded of a play by Jules Barbier and Michel Carré. The rights took time to arrange, and since theater management and operetta composition continued to demand most of his time, work went slowly. Meanwhile, his health began to fail.

On May 18, 1879, there was a private reading of *Hoffmann* at his home. Offenbach had given the Opéra Comique performance rights, and he was able to attend some rehearsals. Unfortunately, he died four months before the premiere and therefore could not make changes that might have affected the length, order, and contents of the various scenes. He had completed a piano score and orchestrated the prologue and first act, sketching the orchestration of the rest. The work was finished by Ernest Guiraud, who also composed the recitatives—a service he had performed for *Carmen*. For the premiere, one of the acts was omitted altogether. The published edition that has been used most often since then (and in the story that follows) is based on the first Vienna production. A recent complete edition offers producing companies more options—and more problems, since the uncut score is too long for practical use.

Hoffmann, actually three short operas, is drawn from a play based on stories by E. T. A. Hoffmann (1776–1822), often considered the archetypical romantic artist, whose talents included painting and musical composition. The macabre, fanciful nature of the tales makes for a feverish, concentrated mood, to which Offenbach's light touch brings elegant irony as well as passion. There is real terror in the music portraying Dr. Miracle, who hounds the singer Antonia into a premature grave. Since the composer was dying as he wrote this, his valedictory took on particular urgency and authenticity.

It has become traditional, though not mandatory, to cast the three soprano leads with the same singer; because the vocal requirements differ, a versatile artist is required. To a lesser extent this is true of Hoffmann's nemeses, who dog him throughout the opera; these roles too are often assigned to one singer.

LES CONTES D'HOFFMANN

(The Tales of Hoffmann)

PROLOGUE, THREE ACTS, AND EPILOGUE
MUSIC: Jacques Offenbach
TEXT (French): Jules Barbier and Michel Carré, based on stories
by E. T. A. Hoffmann
WORLD PREMIERE: Paris, Opéra Comique, February 10, 1881
U.S. PREMIERE: New York, Fifth Avenue Theater, October 16,
1882
METROPOLITAN OPERA PREMIERE: January 11, 1913

CHARACTERS

Hoffmann, *poet* . . . . Tenor
Nicklausse, *his companion* . . . . Mezzo-Soprano
Olympia, *mechanical doll*⎫
Antonia, *singer*　　　　　⎬ . . . . Soprano
Giulietta, *courtesan*　　⎭

Lindorf, *councilor of Nuremberg*
Dr. Coppélius, *scientist*
Dappertutto, *sorcerer* .... Baritone
Dr. Miracle, *doctor*
Stella, *opera singer* .... Soprano
The Voice of Antonia's Mother .... Mezzo-Soprano
Andrès, *Stella's servant* .... Tenor
Nathanael, *student* .... Tenor
Spalanzani, *inventor* .... Tenor
Cochenille, *his servant* .... Tenor
Pitichinaccio, *Giulietta's admirer* .... Tenor
Frantz, *Crespel's servant* .... Tenor
Hermann, *student* .... Baritone
Crespel, *Antonia's father* .... Baritone
Luther, *innkeeper* .... Bass
Schlémil, *Giulietta's lover* .... Bass

Students, guests, servants

PROLOGUE Nineteenth-century Nuremberg. In Luther's tavern, unseen voices—the Spirits of Wine and Beer—sing of how they drive men's cares away. Councilor Lindorf enters with Andrès, a servant of the Milanese prima donna Stella, and bribes him to give up a letter from Stella to the poet Hoffmann, setting a rendezvous for later that evening. Remarking that he himself is a very devil with women, Lindorf vows that he, not the drunkard Hoffmann, will keep the appointment. Luther leads his waiters in, ordering them to get ready for the after-theater crowd. Soon a group of students arrives, praising Luther's drinks (*Drig! drig! drig!*) and Stella's performance in *Don Giovanni*; they miss Hoffmann, who should be there to praise her too. He appears shortly with his companion and watchdog, Nicklausse. Hoffmann is in a bad mood and admits that the performance aroused painful memories for him. To banish these, he launches into a ballad about a grotesque dwarf, Kleinzach (*Il était une fois à la cour d'Eisenach*), but drifts off into a reverie about a beautiful woman before returning to Kleinzach. Deciding that the beer is flat, Hoffmann and his cronies call for a punch bowl and serenade Luther anew (*Luther est un brave homme*). Hoffmann scoffs at the suggestion that he must be in love, but the sight of Lindorf unnerves him—he recognizes the latter as a nemesis, and the two trade mock compliments until Nicklausse prevents them from coming to blows. At length, Hoffmann privately admits he is in love with Stella, who is three women in one: artist, maiden, courtesan. To the others he declares he has had three loves and will tell the story of each. Ignoring the fact that another act of *Don Giovanni* is about to begin next door, Hoffmann's audience settles down for the tale of Olympia, first of the three.

ACT I The house of the inventor Spalanzani in Paris. Hoffmann enters: he has been studying science with Spalanzani, who greets him and says he will introduce him to his daughter, Olympia. Hoffmann catches a glimpse of the sleeping girl and rhapsodizes about her (Laisse, laisse ma flamme). Nicklausse appears and teases Hoffmann with a song about a life-size doll that could inspire love. They are interrupted by Coppélius, a fellow inventor of Spalanzani's, who specializes in magic eyeglasses and persuades Hoffmann to try a pair. The glasses make Olympia look lovelier than ever. Spalanzani returns to the room and argues with Coppélius about their joint invention, Olympia. Coppélius insists that because he created her eyes, he is entitled to a share in the riches Spalanzani will shortly earn when he unveils the doll. The wily Spalanzani agrees but writes a bank draft on the house of Elias, which recently went bankrupt. Coppélius urges him to marry Olympia off to the love-struck Hoffmann, then leaves to deposit his bank draft. Spalanzani's stammering servant, Cochenille, admits guests for the unveiling of Olympia. The inventor goes to fetch his "daughter" and introduces her. Sending for a harp, he declares she will sing, and she begins a chirping song about birds in the springtime (Les oiseaux dans la charmille), pausing for rewinding between stanzas. Hoffmann, still wearing his rose-colored glasses, is carried away with enchantment. When the others go to dinner, he stays with Olympia and declares his love; when he touches her shoulder, she mechanically replies, "Yes." When he presses her hand, she stands up and hurries back to her room. Convinced that she returns his love, Hoffmann refuses to listen to Nicklausse and rushes after her. Coppélius storms in, having discovered Spalanzani's trickery, and steals into Olympia's room, where he hides as Hoffmann returns with the girl, inviting her to dance. Waltzing faster and faster, Olympia leads Hoffmann on an exhausting round until Spalanzani takes her to her room for a rest. Noises of breaking machinery are heard: the vengeful Coppélius has destroyed the doll and comes out, gloating, to confront Spalanzani as it dawns on Hoffmann that the object of his love was not real.

ACT II   In a sumptuous palace by the Grand Canal in Venice, Nicklausse and the courtesan Giulietta sing a barcarole as gondolas drift past (Belle nuit, o nuit d'amour). Hoffmann proclaims that idle romance is futile: only wild passion is worthy of the name of love. Giulietta's lover Schlémil appears and is introduced to Hoffmann. The two dislike each other at once, but Hoffmann confides to Nicklausse that he doesn't care about Giulietta's other admirers if he can just have a rendezvous with her that evening. Nicklausse, however, wants to leave Venice and has horses waiting on the far shore. The demonic Dappertutto, another incarnation of Lindorf and Spalanzani, displays a diamond with which he hopes to ensnare Giulietta (Scintille, diamant). When she appears, magnetized by the stone, he gives her his orders: just as she has secured the shadow of Schlémil, now she is to get the reflection of Hoffmann. Hoffmann comes from the gambling table, where he has lost, and prepares to leave. Feigning deep interest in him, Giulietta says it is dangerous for him there—Schlémil would kill him—but promises to meet him the next day.

Her words evoke a passionate declaration of love from Hoffmann (*O Dieu! de quelle ivresse*), whom she then asks for his reflection—something to remember him by. She holds up a mirror to catch his image. Schlémil, Dappertutto, and the other guests find them together, and Schlémil scornfully holds up a mirror of his own, whereupon Hoffmann realizes he no longer has a reflection. Nicklausse, seeing Hoffmann in danger of losing his soul, urges flight, but Hoffmann cannot extricate himself from the courtesan's spell (septet: *Hélas! mon coeur s'égare encore*). He challenges Schlémil for the key to Giulietta's boudoir. Schlémil says he will give up the key only with his life, whereupon Dappertutto hands Hoffmann a sword. The two men duel, and Hoffmann quickly dispatches Schlémil, then runs off to Giulietta's room with the key. Dappertutto withdraws. As distant voices repeat the barcarole, Hoffmann returns, having found no one. Suddenly, he spies Giulietta in a gondola with another admirer, Pitichinaccio. The police are on their way, and this time Nicklausse succeeds in getting Hoffmann to escape.

ACT III   Crespel's house in Munich. Sitting at the spinet, his daughter, Antonia, sings a ballad about a dove who has flown (*Elle a fui, la tourterelle*). Crespel comes in to remind her that though she inherited a beautiful voice from her dead mother, it is dangerous for her health to sing. Crespel blames the girl's suitor, Hoffmann, for having aroused her desire to sing. It was to escape his influence that Crespel spirited his daughter away to Munich. He tells the hard-of-hearing servant, Frantz, to admit no one. Briefly alone, Frantz delivers a ditty about how he likes to sing and dance, though he is not much good at either. Hoffmann arrives, having found out where Crespel and Antonia are living. Sitting at the spinet, he plays a love song (*C'est un chanson d'amour*) that draws Antonia; embracing him happily, she joins in the song. The effort strains her heart, and she seems about to faint but revives when she hears her father coming. As she goes out, Hoffmann hides. Crespel learns from Frantz that Dr. Miracle is at the door—another incarnation of Hoffmann's nemesis. Crespel wants him kept out, but Miracle enters anyway, insisting he can cure Antonia of the disease that took her mother's life. Crespel retorts that Miracle wants to kill the girl as he killed her mother. Miracle diagnoses Antonia's illness in absentia: when he calls on her to sing, over Crespel's protests, the girl's voice is heard from her room. Miracle produces medicine, and when Crespel forces him out the door, he reappears through the wall. Crespel drags him out again. Antonia comes to ask Hoffmann what happened. He says they must go off and have their own life together: he will come back for her tomorrow. Alone, Antonia is tormented by apparitions of Dr. Miracle, urging her not to listen to Hoffmann, to be true to her beauty and talent. At first she refuses to listen, but Miracle makes the portrait of her mother come to life, urging the girl to sing (trio: *Cher enfant*). Antonia collapses on a sofa; as Miracle gloats, Crespel rushes in to find his daughter breathing her last. In a fury he blames and attacks the returning Hoffmann, but Nicklausse intervenes. When Hoffmann tells Nicklausse to fetch a doctor, Miracle reappears, pronouncing Antonia dead.

EPILOGUE   Back at Luther's tavern, Hoffmann concludes his tales as voices in the theater next door hail Stella, his present love. Nicklausse recognizes the allegory of the three tales—Stella is all three women in one—but Hoffmann wants no more of it and proposes they drown their sorrows in another bowl of punch. After one more drinking song, the students straggle homeward. Stella appears on the arm of Lindorf, but Hoffmann, lost in thought and an alcoholic haze, does not respond to Nicklausse's call. Seeing him in this condition, Stella leaves on the arm of the triumphant Lindorf.

GIOVANNI
BATTISTA
PERGOLESI
1710–36

*B*ecause of its popularity throughout Europe in the middle of the eighteenth century, *La Serva Padrona* is often cited as the earliest example of opera buffa as we know it through the works of Mozart, Rossini, and Donizetti. It comes as a surprise to find that so influential a score is actually a graceful and ingenious trifle. Drawing on the traditions of commedia dell'arte, *La Serva Padrona* presents two stock types—the bossy servant and the crotchety bachelor—in a domestic contretemps. The joke, as in so much comedy of the period, revolves around a reversal of roles—the servant is mistress of the situation, while the master is at her service.

Little is known about Giovanni Battista Pergolesi, dead at twenty-six of tuberculosis, which had made him a cripple. Trained in Naples, he introduced his first operas there at twenty-one and went on to write several more, experiencing both success and failure. The Italian stage at that time was in the grip of opera seria, and to relieve its lengthy solemnity, the custom arose of performing skits, called intermezzos, during the evening. *La Serva Padrona,* written to be performed between the acts of Pergolesi's own *Il Prigioniero Superbo* (1733), quickly assumed a life of its own. In German translation it swept the stages of the German-speaking cities, and when introduced in Paris in 1752, getting nearly 200 performances that year and the next at the Opéra, it sparked the Querelle des Bouffons, a feud between partisans of French and

Italian opera. Scored simply for strings and continuo, with only three characters (one of whom is a mime), *La Serva Padrona* is a chamber opera, perfectly suited to student workshop performances.

LA SERVA PADRONA

(The Maid Mistress)

TWO ACTS
MUSIC: Giovanni Battista Pergolesi
TEXT (Italian): Gennaro Antonio Federico
WORLD PREMIERE: Naples, Teatro di San Bartolomeo, August 28,
    1733
U.S. PREMIERE: Baltimore, New Theatre, June 12, 1790 (in
    French)
METROPOLITAN OPERA PREMIERE: February 23, 1935

CHARACTERS

Serpina, *servant* . . . . Soprano
Uberto, *her master* . . . . Bass
Vespone, *another servant* . . . . Mute

ACT I   Somewhere in early-eighteenth-century Italy, the bachelor Uberto is preparing his morning toilette, assisted by his valet, Vespone, and fuming because the maid, Serpina, who has a mind of her own, chooses not to bring his breakfast on time *(Aspettare e non venire)*. Sending Vespone to find her, Uberto complains that after bringing the girl up as if she were his own daughter, he is repaid with such ingratitude. She appears shortly, boxing Vespone's ears for bothering her with their master's requests. Turning to Uberto, she announces she wants to be treated as though she herself were mistress *(Adunque perchè io son serva)*. As for his breakfast, since it's nearly lunchtime, he'll have to go without. Uberto retorts that her behavior is a constant trial *(Sempre in contrasti)*. Insisting that she has his best interests at heart, she tells him not to go out, adding that if he were more obedient there would be less trouble *(Stizzoso, mio stizzoso)*. Kissing her hand in mock obedience, Uberto turns to Vespone and orders him to find him a wife—that will teach the insolent girl a lesson. Serpina encourages this plan but says he must marry *her*. Though indignant, Uberto privately feels it will be hard to refuse (duet: *Lo conosco a quegli occhietti*).

ACT II   A while later, Serpina coaches the disguised Vespone in her scheme, but when Uberto enters, hopeful at last of going out, she hides Vespone. She tells Uberto that since he is getting married, she has decided to do the same: her fiancé is Captain Tempesta, a terrible-tempered army officer. Getting Uberto worried about her safety as the wife of such a brute, Serpina asks him to remember her now and then *(A Serpina penserete)*. As she leaves to fetch Vespone, disguised as her intended, Uberto admits he is fond of her *(Son imbrogliato io già)*. The wild-eyed Tempesta confirms his fears for her future by stamping his foot in rage and demanding (through Serpina) that Uberto furnish a dowry—otherwise he will not marry her. Furthermore, if Tempesta does not marry Serpina, Uberto will have to—or risk being cut to pieces. Uberto takes her hand and agrees, whereupon Vespone unmasks. The trick only momentarily annoys Uberto, who is delighted with his decision and with Serpina's assurances that she loves him and will make him happy (duet: *Contento tu sarai*).

AMILCARE PONCHIELLI
1834–86

"A real gentleman, a simple, honest man, an artist who obeyed his heart"—such was Pietro Mascagni's recollection of his teacher Amilcare Ponchielli. Mild-mannered and absent-minded, Ponchielli seems an unlikely composer for so bloody and exclamatory an opera as *La Gioconda*, and indeed he had reservations about the libretto, but *La Gioconda* proved to be his one lasting success. Like that of *Il Trovatore*, the score provides singers with a field day, each of five stars having a chance to shine. Its heritage is the French grand opera of Meyerbeer, but its progeny is the verismo movement, encouraged by the intensity and vitality of Ponchielli's outspoken melodies.

The librettist for this thunderous opus was Arrigo Boito, who eight years earlier had composed his own *Mefistofele*. Boito, using the pseudonym "Tobia Gorrio," based his text on a play by Victor Hugo, *Angelo, Tyran de Padoue* (1835), and captured some of Hugo's romantic fustian. The idea of a French-style ballet, the Dance of the Hours, proved to be an inspired one: the opera is remembered as much for this as for its string of vocal gems.

Born in Cremona, Ponchielli became town bandmaster there after graduating from the Milan Conservatory, to which he returned as professor in the last three years of his life. Though he wrote other kinds of music, it was opera that persistently lured him. A major reputation always seemed just around the corner. Beyond the authentic success of *La Gioconda* (Milan, 1876), he did enjoy varying degrees of acceptance with *I Promessi Sposi* (after Manzoni's novel, Cremona, 1856; revised version Milan, 1972), *I Lituani* (Milan, 1874), and *Marion Delorme* (Milan, 1885). Many forgotten Italian operas briefly reached the footlights during the period 1871–87, when the volcano named Verdi was dormant, but *La Gioconda* is the only one that has survived. Its first performance at the Metropolitan, during the inaugural season, had the audience (according to Henry Krehbiel in the *Tribune*) "in a state of almost painful excitement," and—given a proper cast—that is the impact it has usually had ever since.

La Gioconda

FOUR ACTS

MUSIC: Amilcare Ponchielli

TEXT (Italian): Arrigo Boito, based on Victor Hugo's *Angelo, Tyran de Padoue*

WORLD PREMIERE: Milan, La Scala, April 8, 1876

U.S. PREMIERE: Metropolitan Opera, December 20, 1883

CHARACTERS

Gioconda, *street singer* . . . . Soprano
La Cieca, *her blind mother* . . . . Contralto
Laura, *wife of Alvise Badoero* . . . . Mezzo-Soprano
Enzo Grimaldo, *Genoese nobleman* . . . . Tenor
Isèpo, *public letter writer* . . . . Tenor
Barnaba, *spy of the Inquisition* . . . . Baritone
Alvise Badoero, *chief of the Inquisition* . . . . Bass
Zuane, *boatman* . . . . Bass
  Monks, senators, sailors, ladies, gentlemen, Venetians, guards

ACT I In seventeenth-century Venice, citizens crowd the courtyard of the Doge's Palace in anticipation of a holiday. As they leave for the regatta, Barnaba, a street singer, observes that they are dancing on their own tombs—there is a state prison under the courtyard. He himself is a spy and intriguer, who uses his songs and street-wise ways to gather information. But he has been unable to catch the object of his desire, a fellow street singer called Gioconda. He steps out of sight as the girl enters with her blind mother, La

Cieca (the Blind Woman), and stops on the church steps of San Marco. Gioconda excuses herself for a short while, promising to return with her lover, Enzo, but Barnaba tries to bar her way, combining threats with protestations of love. When she evades him, he determines to snare her through her mother. The crowd returns, and a popular favorite among the sailors, Zuane, disgruntled at losing the race, hears Barnaba say that the Blind Woman put a curse on his boat. The nosy town scribe, Isèpo, overhears, and soon other citizens are talking about her witchcraft, surrounding and threatening her. Enzo, dressed as a Dalmatian sailor, enters with Gioconda and tries to rescue the old woman; when the mob resists him, he calls for help from other sailors. Alvise Badoero, chief of the Inquisition, appears on the steps of the palace with his wife, Laura, a Genoese noblewoman, and asks about the cause of the commotion. If La Cieca is charged with witchcraft, he says, she should have a trial. Gioconda, Laura, and Enzo plead with him to pardon her. Meanwhile, Barnaba notices a look of recognition that passes between Laura and Enzo. To Barnaba's annoyance, Alvise pardons La Cieca, who thanks Laura for interceding on her behalf and gives her a rosary (*Voce di donna*) as the fickle crowd decides that the old woman is under heavenly protection. All enter the church except Enzo and Barnaba, who addresses him by his proper name—Enzo Grimaldo, prince of Santafior—despite his protests that he is a Dalmatian ship's captain, "Enzo Giordan." Barnaba assures Enzo that he knows the risk the latter runs in returning to Venice, where he has been banned. Barnaba knows Enzo is there because of his love for Laura, whom he knew in Genoa, and that he has only brotherly feelings for Gioconda. When Barnaba offers to arrange for Laura to come to Enzo's ship that evening, Enzo privately rejoices (*O grido di quest' anima*), even though he realizes that Barnaba must have an ulterior motive. Unable to resist the idea of seeing Laura, Enzo agrees, and Barnaba calls Isèpo to write a note to Alvise, warning him of his wife's imminent flight with Enzo. The returning Gioconda overhears the message and goes back inside the church, jealous and hurt. Alone, Barnaba addresses the palace as a symbol of oppressive rule (*O monumento!*), noting that above the doge, a mere figurehead, the Inquisition rules. He deposits his note in the Lion's Mouth, official receptacle for such denunciations. Merrymakers invade the courtyard, dancing a furlana, while voices inside the church intone hymns. A monk tells the crowd to kneel for vespers, and Gioconda confides her anguish to her mother.

ACT II Near the Fusina lagoon, Enzo's ship, the *Hecate,* lies moored. Beneath the rising moon the crew attend to their chores, observed by Barnaba (disguised as a fisherman), who sends Isèpo to make sure that sentries are in place for a later assault. He then sings a barcarole about fishing with a net to catch a mermaid (*Pescator, affonda l'esca*). He steps out of sight when Enzo appears on deck, telling his crew to get some rest before they set sail later that night. Standing watch alone, Enzo admires the calm sea and ocean, anticipating

Laura's arrival *(Cielo e mar!)*. Barnaba helps Laura board the *Hecate* and sar-castically wishes the lovers luck before disappearing. In a rapturous embrace, Enzo and Laura think of their flight across the waves *(Laggiù nelle nebbie remote)*. Enzo leaves for a few moments to alert his crew, and Laura kneels in prayers to the Virgin, guiding star of sailors *(Stella del marinar!)*, only to be faced by the irate Gioconda. Each claims herself unrivaled in intensity of love for Enzo *(L'amo come il fulgor del creato!)*, but as Gioconda is about to stab Laura, she thinks it would be even sweeter revenge to send her back to the sadistic Alvise, whose boat is seen approaching in pursuit. As Barnaba joins forces with Alvise's men, Gioconda—suddenly seeing Laura's rosary and realizing that the woman has her mother's blessing—helps Laura escape. When Enzo reappears, Gio-conda points out the fleeing Laura, whom he declares he will rescue. To frus-trate the men who are about to take his ship, he sets fire to it, then disappears in the direction of the ocean, leaving Gioconda to watch the vessel sink.

ACT III   In the Ca' d'Oro, Alvise decides that his wife must die to assuage his offended honor. In the midst of festivities about to take place, he intends to poison her *(Sì! morir ella de'!)*. When she appears, he accuses her of having a lover and tells her she must pay with her life. She vehemently protests *(Morir! è troppo orribile!)*, but his reply is to show her a bier and hand her a vial of poison with orders to take it at once. As offstage voices raise a cheerful song, he storms out. Suddenly Gioconda appears, substituting a different vial, which she says will cause only deathlike sleep. The startled Laura does as she is told and goes to lie on the bier. As the offstage barcarole ends, Alvise returns to assure himself that his wife is dead. Bitterly, Gioconda cries out that for her mother's sake she is giving up Enzo and helping her rival.

§ In the main hall of the palace, Alvise greets his guests and announces the Dance of the Hours. Dancers appear and enact the times of day from dawn to night. When they have finished, Barnaba appears, dragging La Cieca, whom he has discovered praying; to Enzo, who has mingled with the guests, Barnaba confides that she was praying for the dead Laura. Enzo confronts Alvise, tear-ing off his mask and identifying himself as the proscribed Enzo Grimaldo, defying the Inquisitor to kill him. As the guests look on in horror *(D'un vampiro fatal)*, Alvise orders Enzo imprisoned. La Cieca blames Barnaba for Laura's death, while Barnaba vows that he will use the old woman to wreak his revenge on Gioconda. In desperation, Gioconda offers herself to Barnaba if he will save Enzo. The gloating Alvise displays Laura's body stretched on a bier. Guards drag Enzo off when he tries to attack Alvise, and Barnaba spirits La Cieca away.

ACT IV   In a ruined palace by the Orfana Canal, where Gioconda makes her home, she admits two other street singers carrying the inert Laura. They refuse payment, and she asks a further test of friendship: Can they find the missing La Cieca? If so, she will meet them the next day at Cannaregio, since she means to flee her present lodgings. Left alone, she grimly contemplates a dagger then the poison originally intended for Laura, and realizes that her end is at hand *(Suicidio!)*. She briefly considers killing her unconscious rival instead, but Enzo's arrival puts an end to such thoughts. He asks why Gioconda saved him, declaring that without Laura he no longer wants to live. Aware that he can never be hers, Gioconda reveals she has made off with Laura's body. Calling her a hyena, Enzo is about to stab her—an outcome she welcomes—when Laura's awakening voice is heard calling from the alcove. The reunited lovers now overwhelm Gioconda with gratitude. She says her friends are coming in a boat to take them to safety in Dalmatia. Wistfully, she recalls how her mother prayed for Laura's happiness. The boat arrives, and the couple leaves Gioconda with more words of thanks. As she prays to the Virgin to protect her from Barnaba, he appears, anticipating the rapture of possessing her at last *(Ebbrezza! Delirio!)*. Pretending she has to beautify herself for him, she reaches for the dagger among her jewels and kills herself. Barnaba shouts that he strangled her mother the day before, but seeing that Gioconda is past hearing, he rushes out, raging.

Francis Poulenc
1899–1963

$\mathcal{F}$rancis Poulenc came of age as a composer and pianist in the years after World War I, a period of frenetic musical activity whose center was Paris. Early on, he associated himself with the principles of Erik Satie, an eccentric who ridiculed the cumbersome apparatus of romanticism. Though never avant-garde or experimental, Poulenc embodied a peculiarly modern spirit, one that placed a high value on wit, facility, and cultivated eclecticism. His gifts as a songwriter led him inevitably to opera, where his projects, sharply different from each other, run the gamut from the bitingly ridiculous to the spiritually sublime.

Of the group known as Les Six (Honegger, Milhaud, Durey, and Tailleferre being the others), Poulenc and Georges Auric maintained the most direct style. Poulenc was nearing fifty when he began to write operas, choosing (in the shadow of World War II) a World War I subject, *Les Mamelles de Tirésias,* from the pen of the surrealist poet Guillaume Apollinaire. Operas that invite the audience to "be fruitful and multiply" are few. The best-known, Mascagni's *L'Amico Fritz,* Strauss's *Die Frau ohne Schatten,* and Poulenc's *Les Mamelles,* make strange bedfellows. Perhaps they reflect the sober awareness that World War I was not "the war to end all wars," that more cannon fodder would be needed for conflicts to come; perhaps they reflect only the European nations' need to return to peaceful productivity. In any event, to Poulenc alone belongs the distinction of treating the subject lightly. His satiric tone lessens neither the serious nor the touching side of his subject, which includes the emerging question of women's rights.

For his only full-length opera, Poulenc fulfilled a commission from the publisher Ricordi in Milan, where *Dialogues des Carmélites* had its premiere (in Italian) at the Teatro alla Scala, a decade after *Les Mamelles*. The text of *Dialogues* was a shortened version of a play by Georges Bernanos, a conservative French Catholic writer, based on a German novella by Gertrud von Le Fort, drawn in turn from a historical incident: on July 17, 1794, a group of Carmelite nuns was guillotined during the Reign of Terror. Both play and opera are conceived as a series of dialogues. The French Revolution is not the subject but the setting. The story, which could take place anywhere, centers on faith and the conquest over fear.

Poulenc's last opera, *La Voix Humaine,* is a monologue conceived for the soprano Denise Duval, one of the composer's favorite interpreters. The original text, by Jean Cocteau, dates back to 1930. Though Cocteau meant his work as a play, he praised Poulenc's setting for raising the work to a level "where a truth greater than truth transcends life," showing a connection with *Dialogues des Carmélites* despite the dissimilarity in subject and treatment.

LES MAMELLES DE TIRÉSIAS

(The Breasts of Tiresias)

PROLOGUE AND TWO ACTS
MUSIC: Francis Poulenc
TEXT (French): Guillaume Apollinaire
WORLD PREMIERE: Paris, Opéra Comique, June 3, 1947
U.S. PREMIERE: Waltham, Mass., Brandeis University,
   June 13, 1953
METROPOLITAN OPERA PREMIERE: February 20, 1981

CHARACTERS

Thérèse/Card Reader . . . . Soprano
Newspaper Seller/Fat Lady . . . . Soprano
Husband . . . . Tenor
Lacouf . . . . Tenor
A Journalist . . . . Tenor
The Theater Manager . . . . Baritone
Presto . . . . Baritone
The Gendarme . . . . Baritone
People of Zanzibar

PROLOGUE   Dressed in evening clothes, the Theater Manager steps before the curtain to announce "a play whose aim is to reform manners." Besides amusing the audience, the show is meant to encourage people to have children, he adds.

ACT I   The year 1910, a town called Zanzibar, in southern France. A young woman, Thérèse, announces to no one in particular that she is sick of housework and domesticity and wants to go to war for her rights. Ignoring calls from her Husband, an "idiot" who "thinks only of love," she proclaims her independence by opening her blouse and getting rid of her breasts, which float upward in the form of balloons before she pops them with a cigarette lighter. When her Husband emerges to find her sporting a beard, he panics and cannot prevent her from proclaiming her new name, Tirésias, or from moving out of their house.

§ Presto and Lacouf, habitués of the bar across the way, arguing drunkenly as to whether they are in Zanzibar or Paris, decide to fight a duel. As the now clean-shaven Tirésias comes out of the house with her Husband (dressed as a woman), the two men shoot each other dead. The incident is described by a group of citizens coming out of the café (*Comme il perdait au Zanzibar*). As they carry away the corpses, Tirésias contemplates a grandiose career as town councilor. A Gendarme strolls in and tries to flirt with the Husband, who suddenly realizes both he and his wife have changed sex. The people of Zanzibar hail Tirésias as a general and a congressman. Casting off his female clothes, the Husband tells the Gendarme that Zanzibar will soon be in a bad way, since the women are giving up having children. As a Newspaper Seller proclaims a hoax, the people begin to worry about the consequences of sex changes and no more children (*Vous qui pleurez*). The Husband reassures them: he himself will provide children. Joined by the resurrected Presto and Lacouf, the people hail this news with a song praising the remarkable baker's wife who changed her skin every seven years.

ENTR'ACTE   Four singing and dancing couples come out before the curtain to serenade the audience with a reprise (*Vous qui pleurez*), punctuated by cries from newborn infants in the orchestra pit.

ACT II   Later the same day, the Husband proudly displays some of the 40,049 children he has managed to bring into the world in a scant few hours. A Journalist arrives from Paris to find out how he did it: willpower, declares the Husband, adding that he expects his new progeny to make him rich. The Husband considers which occupations to teach his children. One of his sons, already full-grown, appears and threatens to blackmail him but leaves empty-handed. The Gendarme brings news that Zanzibar is starving: the town cannot feed so many. The Husband recommends food cards, available from the Card Reader, who now appears, offering to tell fortunes. She banters with spectators and with the Gendarme, who starts to arrest her, whereupon she attacks and kills him. The Husband tries to seize her, only to discover she is really Thérèse in another disguise. As the Gendarme revives, the couple rejoices in their reunion, the Husband shedding his smock to reveal evening clothes. They dance, and he offers her new balloons, but she sets them loose. Joined by the rest of the citizenry, they confront the audience: "Listen, O Frenchmen, to the lessons of war and make children, you who were making hardly any" (*Ecoutez, ô Français*).

DIALOGUES DES CARMÉLITES

THREE ACTS
MUSIC: Francis Poulenc
TEXT (French): Emmet Lavery, based on the drama by Georges
    Bernanos
WORLD PREMIERE: Milan, La Scala, January 26, 1957 (in Italian)
U.S. PREMIERE: San Francisco, September 20, 1957
METROPOLITAN OPERA PREMIERE: February 5, 1977 (in English)

CHARACTERS

Blanche de la Force . . . . Soprano
Sister Constance of St. Denis, *young novice* . . . . Soprano
Mme. Lidoine, *new prioress* . . . . Soprano
Mother Marie of the Incarnation, *assisant prioress* . . . Mezzo-Soprano
Mme. de Croissy, *prioress* . . . . Contralto
Mother Jeanne, *dean* . . . . Contralto
Chevalier de la Force, *Blanche's brother* . . . . Tenor
The Chaplain . . . . Tenor
The Commissioner . . . . Tenor
Marquis de la Force, *Blanche's father* . . . . Baritone
Thierry, *footman* . . . . Baritone
M. Javelinot, *doctor* . . . . Baritone
        Officers, Carmelites, policemen, prisoners, guards, townspeople

ACT I   In Paris, April 1789, the first rumblings of the French Revolution are starting to shake the Old Regime. In his library, the Marquis de la Force is resting when his son, the Chevalier, bursts in, looking for his sister, Blanche.

Her carriage was last seen surrounded by rioting peasants. With a shudder, the Marquis recalls a similar incident years before, which brought about his wife's death in childbirth when Blanche was born. The Chevalier is worried less about Blanche's safe return than about the effect of the turmoil on her sensitive, apprehensive temperament. Midway in the conversation Blanche appears. Admitting her fright at the incident in the carriage, she excuses herself, and the Chevalier also leaves, but Blanche is soon back, startled by a shadow when a footman lit candles in her room. She blurts out to her father that she wishes to become a nun, deeming it the life for which she was meant—unlike that of the world she knows. Reluctantly the Marquis says she must do what she thinks right.

§ Several weeks later, in the receiving room of the Carmelite convent at Compiègne, Blanche speaks with Mme. de Croissy, the mother superior, who apologizes for her luxurious armchair: she is incapacitated by a serious illness, to which she barely refers. She warns Blanche against illusions about the heroism of a religious life, declaring, "We are nothing but a house of prayer." When Blanche says that God will give her strength, Mme. de Croissy replies that God wishes to test her weakness, not her strength. To be a nun, she adds, is not to have a refuge: "It is not the order that protects us, but we who protect the order." When she asks what name the prospective novice has chosen, Blanche replies, "Sister Blanche of the Agony of Christ."

§ Blanche, having been accepted by the order, is working with another young nun, Sister Constance, sorting groceries and discussing death, since Mme. de Croissy's illness has grown worse. Blanche scolds Constance for her seemingly immature cheerfulness. Constance says she has always felt she would die young, adding she is sure she and Blanche will die together.

§ On her deathbed, Mme. de Croissy struggles to keep her composure. Wracked by pain, she admits to Mother Marie that she feels God is not helping her. She expresses concern for Blanche, whose chosen name—Sister Blanche of the Agony of Christ—is the same one she chose as a novice many years earlier. She charges Mother Marie with Blanche's spiritual development. When Blanche arrives, Mother Marie leaves her alone with Mme. de Croissy, who admonishes and blesses her. Blanche withdraws as Mother Marie returns with the physician. Mme. de Croissy asks for medicine to ease her pain so that she can say good-bye to the other nuns. Denied this, she enters her final delirium, rousing herself to describe a vision of their convent profaned and devastated. She cries that God has forsaken them. Mother Marie does not want any of the sisters to see or hear Mme. de Croissy when she is no longer herself. Blanche nevertheless returns and, as the older woman falls back dead, kneels beside the bed, sobbing.

ACT II   In the convent chapel that night, the mother superior lies in state, with Blanche and Constance standing watch. As Constance goes to fetch their replacements, Blanche is overcome by fear of being left alone in the presence of death. She starts to leave as Mother Marie arrives. Seeing that the girl is genuinely afraid, Mother Marie tries to reassure her.

§ Blanche and Constance carry a cross made of flowers—too large, perhaps, for the mother superior's simple grave. When Constance wonders whether Mother Marie will be named the new prioress, Blanche chides her for wanting God to grant her own wishes. Constance ventures, "What we call chance is perhaps the logic of God," remarking that the mother superior's hard death did not suit her and must have been meant for someone else, who one day will find death surprisingly simple.

§ In the chapter room, the nuns are gathered for the ceremony of obedience to the new prioress, Mme. Lidoine. She addresses them *(Mes chères filles)*, reminding them that martyrdom is not a goal but a reward: they must not lose sight of their central purpose, which consists of humility and prayer.

§ From Sister Constance, Mme. Lidoine learns that a man at the gate is asking for her. Mother Marie finds out that it is Blanche's brother, the Chevalier, now known simply as Monsieur de la Force, who wants to see Blanche before he leaves France. Mme. Lidoine says the urgency of the situation justifies breaking the rules, but she asks Mother Marie to be present at the interview.

§ The Chevalier enters the parlor to urge Blanche to leave the convent: their father is afraid for her. Blanche refuses. As her brother leaves, she asks him to accept her in her new life as a "companion in battle." Afterward she feels ashamed of the pride in her words.

§ In the sacristy, the Chaplain tells the nuns that the Mass he just performed will be his last: the civil authorities have forbidden him to officiate any longer. When Blanche asks the Chaplain what he will do, he replies he has been ordered by his superiors to disguise himself. As he goes out, the sisters discuss the epidemic of fear that has left France unable to defend its priests. This gives Mother Marie the idea of the Carmelites' offering their lives to the cause, but Mme. Lidoine reminds her one cannot choose to be a martyr. The Chaplain returns, saying that his departure was blocked and that he must leave by another route; he escapes as the mob starts knocking at the main entrance. Mother Marie tells Constance to open the door, through which four commissioners enter, telling the nuns that the revolutionary government has voted to confiscate all religious retreats. The first commissioner, whispering to Mother Marie that he used to be a sacristan, sends away the patrol and the crowd. Seeing Blanche desolate, Mother Jeanne hands her a figurine of the Christ Child as a keepsake, but in her nervousness Blanche drops and breaks it; this she takes as a terrifying omen.

ACT III As the nuns prepare to leave their devastated convent, the Chaplain, in civilian clothes, asks Mother Marie to address them in the absence of Mme.

Lidoine. Mother Marie proposes they all take the vow of martyrdom, which must be unanimous. One by one the nuns pass behind the altar and give the Chaplain their votes. He tells Mother Marie that there was one vote against, and the others immediately suspect that it was cast by Blanche, but Constance steps forward to claim it was hers, asking permission to change it. The Chaplain administers the vow to the nuns in pairs, starting with Blanche and Constance, who offer their lives for the salvation of the Carmelites and of France.

§ As the nuns, in civilian clothes, are leaving, an officer of the revolutionary army cautions them against maintaining their organization or engaging in suspicious activities. As he goes, Mme. Lidoine asks that the Chaplain be notified not to celebrate Mass once more with them—this would be dangerous for all concerned. Mother Marie feels that such caution does not accord with the vow of martyrdom, but Mme. Lidoine replies that it would be irresponsible to subject the community to needless risk.

§ Back in the library of the Marquis de la Force, Blanche is working as a servant for revolutionaries who have taken over the mansion. She is found by Mother Marie, who says it is time to rejoin the other sisters. Blanche confesses she is still dogged by fear: her father was guillotined the week before. Though Blanche protests she is not ready, Mother Marie gives her an address, telling her to report there within twenty-four hours.

§ In a street near the Bastille, Blanche learns from an old woman from Compiègne that the nuns have been arrested.

§ In a cell in the Conciergerie prison, Mme. Lidoine tells the Carmelites she will join in their vow of martyrdom—made during her absence—and continue to take responsibility for them. When Constance says she dreamed of Blanche's return, the others laugh. A jailer reads the death sentence pronounced earlier by the Revolutionary Tribunal: the nuns have been judged guilty of illegal assembly and conspiracy against the republic. Mme. Lidoine calmly bids farewell to her daughters.

§ The Chaplain meets with Mother Marie and tells her the nuns have been condemned. Though she desperately wants to join them, the Chaplain reminds her she cannot make a martyr of herself: that is for God to choose.

§ In the Place de la Révolution, the Carmelites are delivered to the guillotine, chanting the *Salve Regina*. Beginning with the mother superior, each is led to death, as their numbers and their voices are cut off one at a time. The Chaplain, disguised in the crowd, secretly gives each absolution. Finally, only Constance remains. On her way to the scaffold, she sees Blanche step from the crowd, take up the chant, and follow her. The crowd, now quiet, disperses.

LA VOIX HUMAINE

ONE ACT
MUSIC: Francis Poulenc
TEXT (French): Jean Cocteau
WORLD PREMIERE: Paris, Opéra Comique, February 6, 1959
U.S. PREMIERE: New York, Carnegie Hall, February 23, 1960

CHARACTER

Elle (She) . . . . Soprano

A woman has been abandoned by her lover, who is marrying someone else. Alone in her bedroom, she makes a last attempt to maintain contact with the man who has been the focus of her life, knowing that he is lost to her beyond recovery. He has called her on the telephone, but they were cut off. With some difficulty, since she is on a party line, she succeeds in reestablishing the connection. She tries to seem brave and nonchalant, admitting she has used sleeping pills to get to sleep but praising her friend Marthe, who has been very helpful. She has been out with Marthe; she describes what she wore.

From her remarks, it is apparent that the man suspects her of putting up a front. Evidently, he feels guilty about his treatment of her and wants to find out how seriously hurt she is. Her responses are fragmentary and shift abruptly from one subject to another, betraying her stressed state of mind. Trying to appear practical and worldly, she takes part of the blame for their rift—perhaps she was too impulsive, too demanding. Realizing he intends to marry the next day, she is startled but arranges for his belongings to be picked up.

The call is cut off again, but she manages to reestablish contact. They discuss what he is wearing; she imagines how he looks. She admits she is not ready to deal with the idea of living alone. She senses he is being kind to her because he loves her. They are cut off again. She says she was not telling the whole truth earlier: she did not dress, she did not go out with Marthe, she has been waiting all evening for him to call. She thought of taking a taxi and wandering outside his house.

Finally she admits she took an overdose of sleeping pills the night before and had to call Marthe, because "I didn't have the courage to die alone." Marthe came at four in the morning, bringing a doctor. She knows that it is a trial for him to have this conversation, but she desperately needs to talk with him, since she cannot bear the loneliness of her own company. Even her dog seems to have turned against her since her lover left.

After another intrusion by a nosy woman on the party line, she promises she will not repeat her suicide attempt. As it becomes apparent that the conversation will end soon, never to be resumed, she grows more and more emotional. Trying to be brave, she gasps a last farewell and an avowal of love, then collapses on her bed, letting the telephone "drop like a stone."

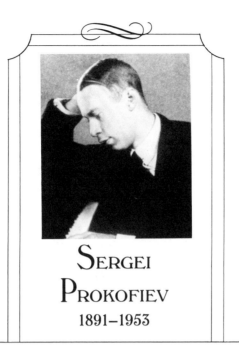

SERGEI PROKOFIEV
1891–1953

*B*orn in the Ukraine, the only child of parents in comfortable circumstances, Sergei Prokofiev studied piano with his mother and showed signs of being a child prodigy. At the Conservatory of St. Petersburg, he was disappointed in the composition teaching of Liadov and Rimsky-Korsakov and much more responsive to the ideas of a classmate, Nikolai Myaskovsky, who remained a lifetime friend. Meanwhile, Prokofiev developed his talents as a pianist, and eventually it was a piano teacher, Anna Esipova, who brought to his work the discipline that composition teachers had been unable to instill. A further influence was the professor of conducting, Nikolai Tcherepnin, who sympathized with Prokofiev's interest in avant-garde experimentation.

Because he is remembered today for compositions that are not especially "modern"—*Peter and the Wolf,* the *Classical* Symphony, the *Lieutenant Kije* Suite, and certain of the concertos—it is easy to forget that Prokofiev passed his early decades as an *enfant terrible,* writing "ironic, willful, unconventional" music, often as a vehicle for his own use in piano recitals. In his capacity as a touring soloist, he was introduced to the world outside Russia. In London in 1914 he met the impresario Sergei Diaghilev, who commissioned two ballets from him; though the first was not performed by the Ballets Russes, Diaghilev's company, and the second was staged only after World War I, Diaghilev's encouragement was a milestone in Prokofiev's creative life.

The turbulent conditions in Russia in the wake of World War I and the

Bolshevik Revolution minimized interest in new music there, so Prokofiev, looking for new worlds to conquer, came to the United States in 1918, using the long voyage to work on a libretto for a projected opera, *The Love for Three Oranges*. Following his initial success as a recitalist in New York, the Chicago Opera commissioned the new work; Prokofiev readied it for a 1919 premiere, but the death of the Chicago impresario Cleofonte Campanini forced postponement until 1921, when it was presented under the aegis of the company's new director, Mary Garden. The composer's own French text was used, based on Meyerhold's Russian adaptation of a commedia dell'arte satire by the eighteenth-century Venetian playwright Carlo Gozzi. Prokofiev saw in it a chance to launch a good-natured but devastating lampoon against romantic grand opera, particularly the fairy tales set onstage by Glinka (in *Ruslan and Ludmila*) and Rimsky-Korsakov. After the premiere, which Prokofiev himself conducted, the march tune caught on, but one critic grumbled that most of the music sounded as if a shotgun had been fired at sheets of manuscript paper. The work was not really a success until the Leningrad production, which coincided with Prokofiev's first visit to his homeland since the Revolution.

After his three-month concert tour of the U.S.S.R. in 1927, Prokofiev had another of his operas produced—*The Gambler,* after Dostoevsky—in Brussels in 1929. Though he took up residence in the U.S.S.R. in 1936 and spent most of the rest of his life there, his countrymen were reluctant to produce his operas. Even when he turned to "socialist realism" or patriotic subjects—*Semyon Kotko, War and Peace, The Story of a Real Man*—he faced ideological criticism, culminating in the denunciation by the Soviet government's Committee on the Arts in 1948, which cited "formalist perversions . . . alien to the Soviet people" in the works of Prokofiev, Shostakovich, and several less illustrious colleagues. Prokofiev, who died on the same day as Stalin, never lived to see himself fully rehabilitated, but one of his operas—*Betrothal in a Monastery,* after Sheridan's *The Duenna* (Leningrad 1946)—escaped controversy and enjoyed success on Russian stages.

In all, Prokofiev projected and at least partially completed no fewer than fourteen operas, from a youthful effort called *The Giant* in 1900 to *Distant Seas,* in progress at the time of his death. *The Love for Three Oranges* was preceded and followed by *The Gambler* and *The Flaming Angel,* the latter unperformed until a Paris production of 1954. Though he habitually revised his scores and often reused materials from them, probably no opera proved as difficult for Prokofiev as *War and Peace,* begun during the war years as a group of scenes depicting the more intimate, personal chapters of Tolstoy's vast novel. The Committee on the Arts advised Prokofiev to fill out the patriotic scenes as well, and a projected premiere at the Bolshoi in 1943 was canceled. After enlarging the opera, Prokofiev found it too long for a single evening; with help from the stage director Boris Pokrovsky, he began to reshape it, a process that continued through his last years.

In opera and ballet, Prokofiev showed a natural inclination for the stage, for character delineation and dramatic events. In his work, diverse elements appear side by side—innocent lyricism and fierce, mechanized rhythms and dissonances; poetry and irony. When in later years his style achieved a calmer, more humanistic unity, he kept the distinctive profile that makes his music instantly recognizable. Though he was doomed to disappointment as an opera composer during his lifetime, the decades since his death have seen the emergence of his full stature in that capacity.

THE LOVE FOR THREE ORANGES

(Lyubov k Trem Apelsinam)

PROLOGUE AND FOUR ACTS
MUSIC: Sergei Prokofiev
TEXT (Russian): the composer, based on a comedy by Carolo Gozzi

WORLD PREMIERE: Chicago, Opera House, December 30, 1921 (in French)

CHARACTERS

The King	Bass
The Prince, *his son*	Tenor
Princess Clarissa, *King's niece*	Contralto
Fata Morgana, *witch*	Soprano
Linetta	Contralto
Nicoletta } *princesses hidden in the oranges* {	Mezzo-Soprano
Ninetta	Soprano
Smeraldina, *Fata Morgana's servant*	Mezzo-Soprano
Leandro, *prime minister*	Baritone
Pantaloon, *King's friend*	Baritone
Truffaldino, *court jester*	Tenor
Celio, *magician*	Bass
Cook	Bass
Farfarello, *devil*	Bass

Monsters, drunkards, gluttons, guards, servants,
soldiers, jokers, members of the audience

PROLOGUE   A performance is about to take place, but the audience cannot agree on what it wants to see. As proponents of tragedy and comedy shout each other down, the Romanticists call for a love story, the Empty Heads for slapstick. The argument is stilled by ten Eccentrics armed with shovels, who force the others to their seats, then announce something superb—*The Love for Three Oranges*. A herald steps forward to begin by saying the Prince is hopelessly ill with hypochondria, to the despair of his father, the King of Clubs . . .

ACT I   The curtain rises on a fairytale setting inside the palace, where physicians try to diagnose the Prince's illness. The King dismisses them and tells his crony, Pantaloon, that he fears that the Prince's wicked cousin Clarissa may inherit the throne. (Eccentrics among the audience, meanwhile, express anxiety that the King may be overacting.) Since the physicians have prescribed laughter as the only cure for the Prince, the two men plan how they can amuse him. When the court jester, Truffaldino, appears, they order a festival of merriment. The King sends for Leandro, his prime minister, whose treachery he does not suspect, and repeats the order.

§ In dark, mysterious surroundings, the magician Celio (guardian spirit of the King) and the witch Fata Morgana (guardian spirit of Leandro) contend at cards, egged on by Eccentrics in the audience. As little devils dance around, Celio loses, cursing his luck.

§ In the palace, Clarissa asks Leandro, whom she has promised to marry if he gets her the throne, what he has been doing to undermine the Prince's health. Leandro replies he has been feeding the youth tragic prose and heavy verse. (This occasions a scuffle at the edge of the stage between those favoring tragedy and the Eccentrics.) Clarissa urges more direct action—poison or a bullet. Smeraldina, Fata Morgana's accomplice, is discovered hiding under the table. Threatened for spying, she promises that Fata Morgana will intervene at tomorrow's festival and prevent the Prince from laughing.

ACT II   In the Prince's sickroom, Truffaldino tries to amuse him, but the Prince manages only to cough up some "old, rotten, and disagreeable rhymes." (Proponents of comedy try to intervene but are driven off by the Eccentrics, who declare that Truffaldino must handle the problem alone.) At the distant sound of a march, Truffaldino throws the Prince's medicines out the window, wraps the young man in a cloak, and drags him off.

§ Truffaldino brings the Prince to the palace courtyard, ordering the amusements to begin. A fight between two "monsters," and the sight of gluttons crowding around fountains of oil and wine, merely disgusts the Prince. Fata Morgana enters disguised as an old woman, whispering to Leandro that the Prince will not laugh while she is there. When Truffaldino chases the "old woman" and she falls with her feet in the air, however, the Prince does burst out laughing. Furiously the witch retorts with a curse: he will fall hopelessly in love with three oranges *(Vlyubis v tri apelsina!)*. Immediately the Prince betrays his obsession, calling for armor to rescue his beloved oranges from another witch, Creonta, who holds them captive. No one can stop him; he leaves with Truffaldino, fanned by a bellows in the hands of Farfarello, a devil.

ACT III   In the desert, Farfarello pauses while leading the two men to Creonta's castle. Celio appears and tries to stop him with threats, but the devil is unafraid of a magician who cannot even win at cards. Seeing the Prince and Truffaldino, Celio warns them of a dreadful Cook who guards the oranges and will kill any intruder with a giant spoon. Since the two still insist on going, Celio arms them with a magic ribbon to divert the Cook, warning that the oranges must be opened only near water. Farfarello brings his bellows, fanning the two on their way.

§ After an interlude, Farfarello delivers his charges to Creonta's castle, where they fall down in exhaustion. Truffaldino wants to escape, but the Prince insists on investigating the kitchen, where they rouse the monstrous Cook *(Kto tut pishchit?)*. Truffaldino pulls out the ribbon, which exercises a hypnotic fascination over the Cook, enabling the Prince to find the oranges and run off with Truffaldino.

§ In the desert that night, the two grow weary of carrying the oranges, which have been growing steadily larger. When the Prince falls asleep, Truffaldino—dying of thirst *(Kak mogu ya spat)*—yields to temptation and cuts open one of the oranges. Instead of orange juice, he finds inside Princess Linetta, who says she too is dying of thirst. Unable to wake the Prince, Truffaldino desperately opens another orange, only to find Princess Nicoletta, who is in the same condition. When both princesses fall dead, the terrified Truffaldino runs away, leaving the Prince to awaken in puzzlement. A group of soldiers, marching by, removes the corpses, and the Prince, eager to find his happiness inside the third orange, cuts it open. He finds Princess Ninetta, who falls dying of thirst in his arms but is rescued by the Eccentrics, who troop onstage with a bucket of water. The princess voices her gratitude to the smitten Prince, who vows his love in romantic terms *(Sil ne bylo)*, prompting the Romanticists in the audience to cheer them on. The Prince wants to take her to the palace, but she says he must go first and bring royal robes. As she happily waits alone, Smeraldina sneaks up and pricks her with a pin, changing her into a rat. Fata Morgana appears, telling Smeraldina to disguise herself as the princess. When the Prince returns with his father, he recognizes the deception, but the King tells him he must keep his promise to wed the girl.

ACT IV   Celio and Fata Morgana again confront each other, each calling the other a fraud. When Fata Morgana appears to be gaining the upper hand, the Eccentrics come onstage and trick her into a tower, where they lock her up, leaving Celio free to rescue his protégés.

§ In the throne room, the royal procession (chorus: *Slava korolyu!*) is horrified to discover a huge rat on the princess' throne, but Celio turns her back into Ninetta. Truffaldino suddenly appears and identifies the imposter Smeraldina. The King orders her and Clarissa hanged, but Fata Morgana breaks out of her tower, and, along with Leandro, they all disappear in a puff of smoke. Eccentrics join the court in hailing the King and the happy couple.

WAR AND PEACE

(Voina y Mir)

EPIGRAPH AND TWO PARTS
MUSIC: Sergei Prokofiev
TEXT (Russian): the composer and Mira Mendelson, after Tolstoy
WORLD PREMIERE: Moscow, June 7, 1945
U.S. PREMIERE: NBC–TV, 1957 (in English)

CHARACTERS

Natasha Rostova . . . . Soprano
Sonya, *Natasha's cousin* . . . . Mezzo-Soprano
Hélène Bezukhova, *Pierre's wife* . . . . Mezzo-Soprano
Princess Maria Bolkonskaya, *Andrei's sister* . . . . Mezzo-Soprano
Maria Akhrosimova, *Natasha's godmother* . . . . Contralto
Count Pierre Bezukhov . . . . Tenor
Count Anatol Kuragin, *Hélène's brother* . . . . Tenor
Platon Karatayev, *farmer turned soldier* . . . . Tenor
Prince Andrei Bolkonsky . . . . Baritone
Lieutenant Colonel Vasska Denisov . . . . Baritone
Lieutenant Dolokhov . . . . Baritone
Napoleon Bonaparte . . . . Baritone
Count Ilya Rostov, *Natasha's father* . . . . Bass
Prince Nikolai Bolkonsky, *Andrei's father* . . . . Bass
Field Marshal Prince Mikhail Kutuzov . . . . Bass
Officers, servants, soldiers, peasants

EPIGRAPH Hailing the greatness of the Russian land, the chorus declares that many nations have tried to invade her but that all have been driven back.

WAR AND PEACE

PART I Outside the country home of Count Rostov at Otradnoye on a spring evening in 1809. A guest, Prince Andrei Bolkonsky, is seen looking from his window, wondering whether the romantic promise of spring is an illusion. At an upstairs window the Rostovs' daughter, Natasha, unable to sleep, muses with her cousin Sonya on the beauties of nature. Aware that someone is listening, she closes the window, leaving Andrei to realize that his life is not over at thirty-one after all: this girl has revived his interest in living *(I dela net do moyevo)*.

§ The following New Year's Eve, at a fashionable ball in St. Petersburg, Maria Akhrosimova welcomes her goddaughter Natasha, her cousin Sonya, and Count Rostov. They immediately notice the glamorous Hélène, wife of Pierre Bezukhov, and her dashing brother, Count Anatol Kuragin. Prince Andrei asks Natasha to dance and tells her that he heard her "dreaming aloud" the preceding spring; Rostov invites him to call the following Sunday.

§ Two years later, in February 1812, Rostov brings Natasha, now engaged to Andrei, to the Bolkonsky town house in Moscow to meet Andrei's formidable father. The old man does not want to receive them, and Andrei's sister, Princess Maria, handles the situation instead. As the latter makes awkward conversation, mentioning the threat of war, the old Prince intrudes, not aware that the callers are there. Insultingly, he mumbles that Andrei can do as he pleases. Maria is upset by her father's behavior, but Natasha realizes he sent Andrei away for a year in hopes of discouraging the marriage. To herself she fumes that Andrei's family has no right to reject her, that she wants him back right away *(Kakoye pravo oni imeyut)*.

§ In May at the Bezukhov house, Hélène congratulates Natasha on her engagement but confides that her brother Anatol is lovesick over her. Impressed by Hélène's beauty and friendliness, Natasha thinks there can be no harm in such a person *(Chudo, kak khorosha one)*. Anatol appears, declares his love, and thrusts a letter into her hand, kissing her before leaving. Flustered, she reads the letter *("Reshite moyu uchast")*, couched in extravagant romantic terms, saying she alone must decide his fate. Because she misses Andrei and is vulnerable in his absence, she is swept off her feet by Anatol. Sonya notices her reaction and warns that Anatol is a scoundrel. Count Rostov, disapproving of the free-and-easy atmosphere, takes the girls home.

§ At the home of his comrade-in-arms, Lieutenant Dolokhov, Anatol boasts that Natasha has agreed to elope with him. Though Dolokhov wrote Anatol's love letter for him, he disapproves of the elopement, pointing out that there is sure to be trouble, not least because Anatol is already married. Infatuated, Anatol cannot think of the future. When a coachman arrives to take him to his rendezvous, he and Dolokhov rush off into the snowstorm.

§ Meanwhile, at Maria Akhrosimova's house, Natasha learns from a maid that Sonya has revealed her elopement plans. When Anatol arrives, the footman is under orders to bring him to the lady of the house, but Anatol—warned by Dolokhov of a trap—makes his exit. The older woman confronts Natasha with her disgraceful behavior, the result of associating with Hélène (*Ghorosha, ochen' ghorosha!*). Natasha is defiant. With relief Maria Akhrosimova welcomes Pierre, whom she considers ineffectual but kindhearted, and tells what has happened; he promises to get Anatol out of Moscow before there is a scandal or a duel. Alone, Pierre admits he too has found Natasha disturbingly attractive (*Ya izbegal yeyo*). Natasha, who trusts Pierre, hears him confirm what she has just learned from her godmother: Anatol is already married. Upset by his own feelings toward the girl, Pierre leaves hurriedly. Believing her life ruined, Natasha takes poison in an adjoining room, then calls to Sonya for help.

§ In his study Pierre confronts Anatol and demands that he leave Moscow, even offering him money. Disgusted with his wife, brother-in-law, and their like, Pierre wishes he could live according to his humanitarian instincts (*Uyehat' kuda-nibud'*). Lieutenant Colonel Denisov enters with news that Napoleon's troops are gathering at the frontier: war is inevitable.

PART II On August 25, 1812, before the Battle of Borodino, soldiers dig entrenchments as Denisov enters, looking for Prince Andrei. The soldiers talk of Marshal Kutuzov, who has rallied them by the thousands (*Kak prishyol k narodu nash Kutuzov*). Alone for a moment, Andrei reflects on the love he felt for Natasha and how foolishly things turned out (*I ya lyubil yeyo*). Spying Pierre, who has come as a civilian observer, he tells him of his contempt for the German military advisers, who reduce everything to tactics, ignoring the people. Andrei embraces Pierre, saying he fears they will not meet again. Pierre leaves as the marshal arrives, greeted by his soldiers. Though Kutuzov asks Andrei to join his staff, Andrei declines, saying he has to lead his own regiment. Opening shots of the battle are heard.

§ That afternoon, Napoleon surveys the scene, looking forward to conquest as adjutants run in with urgent communiqués. To one of his generals he confides that things have not been going as usual: it is a very hard victory (*Ne to, sovsem ne to*).

§ Two evenings later, Kutuzov sits in council at a peasant hut with his advisers. After hearing their opinions, he makes the decision to retreat from Moscow (*Itak, gospoda, stalo byt' mne platit' za perebitye gorshki*), thereby ensuring eventual victory. When he is alone, he muses on what Moscow means to the people; he knows they will rise to the occasion (*Kogda zhe*).

§ A month or so later, during the French occupation of Moscow, Pierre has a fantasy of assassinating Napoleon. From servants in the street he learns that

Natasha has been nursing the wounded at her family's country home, and that—unknown to her as yet—Andrei is among them. French soldiers and officers, dispirited by the natives' continued resistance, take Pierre into custody as a suspicious character. In a gaggle of prisoners he meets Platon Karatayev, a farmer whose stoical attitude symbolizes the people's resolution *(Kak ne skuchno, sokolik)*. The prisoners are led off, and Napoleon arrives with his officers, appalled to see Moscow burning at the hands of its own citizens.

§ Andrei lies wounded in a hut on the outskirts of the city, wishing he could see Natasha once more. She comes in, and he regrets having discovered the real meaning of his life only at the end of it (duet: *Ja dumal, mne otkrylas' istina zhizni*). She stays at his bedside as he dies.

§ During a blizzard in November, the French retreat along the Smolensk road with the prisoners they have taken, including Pierre and Karatayev. When a guard shoots the latter, a partisan ambushes the guard and the French soldiers are overpowered by his comrades. Pierre learns from Denisov that life is beginning to return to Moscow. Kutuzov appears and pronounces Russia saved. He thanks the troops, who cheer him and their victory *(Ura! za otechestvo shli my v smertnyi boi)*.

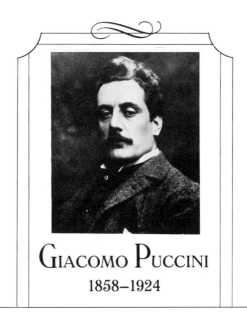

GIACOMO PUCCINI
1858–1924

$\mathcal{U}$ nlike the other major opera composers—Mozart, Wagner, Rossini, Verdi—Puccini is totally unknown in the symphonic concert hall. Because his is a talent purely of the theater, critics and academics, especially in his native land, have always tried to deny him his proper place in the pantheon of serious composers. The public, however, feels differently, and Puccini remains one of its favorites.

Born in Lucca, Puccini was descended from several generations of professional musicians. Initially little interested in carrying on the family tradition, he was compelled by his mother to study music. As a teenager he had acquired proficiency enough to hold down two jobs as a church organist. Drawn to gadgets and machinery, he was intrigued by the organ and by the mechanics of music, doodling and improvising during services. Several factors combined to push him into his career: some church pieces and a cantata he wrote enjoyed a favorable reception; he heard *Aida,* the latest novelty from Verdi's pen; finally, stipends from a great-uncle and Queen Margherita of Savoy enabled him to study at the Milan Conservatory, 1880–83, where his teachers were Bazzini and Ponchielli.

Big-city life never really agreed with Puccini, but it stimulated him. His bohemian existence as a poor student later found expression in *La Bohème.* In 1884 he entered a one-act opera, *Le Villi,* in a competition sponsored by the publisher Sonzogno. Though it did not win, it attracted the attention of Sonzogno's rival, Ricordi, who thenceforth played a large role in advancing Puccini's career. A first commission produced *Edgar* (1889), whose shortcomings prompted the composer to be extremely selective about his librettos from then on. For this reason his next operas, *Manon Lescaut* and *La Bohème,* underwent difficult birth pangs but were rewarded with public enthusiasm. Though loosely associated with the verismo movement, a drive toward more natural and believable opera theater, Puccini did not hesitate to write period pieces or to exploit exotic locales. In *Tosca* he wrote an intense melodrama set in Rome during Napoleonic times. For *Madama Butterfly* he chose an American story set in Japan.

Having enjoyed consistent and gradually expanding acceptance up to that point in his career, Puccini was totally unprepared for the total failure of *Madama Butterfly* when it was first presented, in 1904. But he had faith in the work and revised it until it was accepted. The travail over *Butterfly* delayed him in beginning his next work and undermined his confidence, but during a visit to New York he agreed to write *La Fanciulla del West,* based on David Belasco's popular play *The Girl of the Golden West,* and returned for its world premiere at the Met in 1910. Though reluctant to embrace "modernisms"— Strauss' *Elektra* confused and repelled him—Puccini cautiously adapted to changing times in *La Fanciulla,* absorbing the influence of Debussy's *Pelléas,* which he admired.

The next major hiatus in Puccini's creative life was brought about by World War I. Hostilities found him in the midst of negotiations to write an operetta for Vienna, which was now enemy territory. The operetta became instead a light opera, *La Rondine,* produced at Monte Carlo and welcomed coolly at the Met as "the afternoon off of a genius." Puccini never regained his youthful eminence and romantic spontaneity, but he continued to work seriously, broadening his horizons. Experimenting with the one-act format, he created the trilogy *Il Trittico,* a second world premiere for the Met (1918).

A chain smoker, Puccini developed throat cancer and was taken to Brussels in 1924 for treatment by a specialist. Though the surgery was successful, Puccini's heart failed, and he died shortly afterward. At the time of his death, he had been working on the most ambitious of his operas, *Turandot,* based on Schiller's romantic adaptation of a fantasy by Carlo Gozzi, the eighteenth-century Venetian satirist. In *Turandot* for the first time he wrote extensively for the chorus, and he provided an enlarged, enriched orchestral tapestry that showed an awareness of Stravinsky's *Petrouchka* and other contemporary scores.

Sadly, he could not summon strength to write the difficult final scene (dissatisfaction with the text had caused delays), which would have been quite unlike anything he had previously attempted. After his death a diffident colleague, Franco Alfano, was persuaded by Ricordi to complete the opera, using Puccini's sketches. The world premiere, at La Scala in 1926, conducted by Toscanini, ended as Puccini had requested, without the final scene. Toscanini found Alfano's conclusion too lengthy and insisted it be cut by 30 percent, after which he conducted it at future performances. Though Alfano's music makes *Turandot* performable, it is anticlimactic. Like Süssmayr's completion of the Mozart Requiem, it serves only to emphasize a dying composer's inability to complete his life work with a worthy testament.

MANON LESCAUT

FOUR ACTS
MUSIC: Giacomo Puccini
TEXT (Italian): Luigi Illica and others, based on the novel by the Abbé Prévost
WORLD PREMIERE: Turin, Teatro Regio, February 1, 1893
U.S. PREMIERE: Philadelphia, Grand Opera House, August 29, 1894
METROPOLITAN OPERA PREMIERE: January 18, 1907

CHARACTERS

Manon Lescaut . . . . Soprano
Chevalier des Grieux . . . . Tenor
Edmondo, *student* . . . . Tenor
Lescaut, *sergeant of the King's Guards* . . . . Baritone
Geronte di Ravoir, *treasurer general* . . . . Bass
Innkeeper, servants, dancing master, musicians, etc.

ACT I   In a square at Amiens, 1721, Edmondo and some fellow students sing in praise of youth. One of them, Des Grieux, jokingly addresses a group of girls, asking which will be his sweetheart *(Tra voi, belle, brune e bionde)*. Merrymaking is disrupted by the arrival of a coach from Arras, from which three travelers alight—Manon, a girl of eighteen; Lescaut, her brother; and Geronte di Ravoir, a treasury official. Des Grieux cannot take his eyes off the pretty Manon and speaks to her, learning she is to leave for a convent school the next morning. Pleased by his sincerity, she agrees to talk with him later, then enters the inn. Des Grieux exclaims at her beauty and charm *(Donna non vidi mai)*, ignoring the jokes of his companions, who are amused to see him smitten. Lescaut reappears with Geronte, who is also interested in Manon and tries to ingratiate himself with her brother. When Lescaut joins the students at cards, Geronte calls the innkeeper and, while Edmondo eavesdrops, arranges for a carriage and horses with which to spirit Manon off to Paris. Des Grieux reenters and learns from Edmondo about the elderly roué's scheme. Manon comes from the inn to keep her rendezvous with Des Grieux *(Vedete? io son fedele)*, who tells her he loves her and warns her of Geronte's plan. Impulsively insisting that she elope with him instead, he persuades her, and they leave. Geronte comes to fetch Manon and Lescaut, only to find her gone. Lescaut reassures Geronte that her affection for a poor student cannot last long in Paris: they will be able to get her back through her love of luxury. With this the two go to dinner, as the students laugh at Geronte.

ACT II   True to Lescaut's prediction, Manon has tired of poverty and is living as Geronte's mistress in a sumptuous town house. Lescaut visits while she is having her hair and makeup done. He congratulates her on taking his advice and finding such fortune, though he acknowledges that Des Grieux is a fine fellow. This prompts Manon to recall wistfully how happy she was with him before leaving, without a word or a kiss. Now, in these luxurious surroundings, she feels a silence and a chill that make her long for the love she left behind *(In quelle trine morbide)*. Lescaut tells her he has remained friendly with Des Grieux and has taught him gambling, in hopes the youth will win enough to get Manon back. A group of madrigalists enters to serenade Manon with one of Geronte's own compositions *(Sulla vetta tu del monte)*, which bores her. When it finishes, Geronte appears with friends and arranges for Manon to have a dancing lesson as musicians strike up a minuet; then he dances with her himself. At length he has to leave, and Des Grieux appears, brought by Lescaut. She greets him in agitation *(Tu? amore, tu?)* and fears he no longer cares for her, since she abandoned him. He says he has suffered cruelly, but when she asks forgiveness, he is once again bewitched by her *(O tentatrice!)*. At the height of their impassioned declarations, Geronte returns unexpectedly. He coldly reminds Manon that she is under his protection. When she makes him look at himself in a hand mirror, he is angered and leaves, remarking tersely that he knows what to do. Des Grieux urges Manon to escape at once. Lescaut bursts in with news that Geronte has denounced Manon to the police, who are on their way to arrest her. The three try to escape, but precious time is lost as Manon gathers her jewels, and a police sergeant enters. The furious Des Grieux wants to fight, but Lescaut restrains him, saying he must stay out of trouble in order to save Manon.

ACT III   At the harbor of Le Havre. Des Grieux and Lescaut have a plan to free Manon from the guardhouse where she is being held for deportation. Manon comes to the barred window; though happy to see Des Grieux, she fears that the plan will end badly. A lamplighter passes, singing a ditty. A commotion is heard nearby, and Lescaut rushes in to say their plot has miscarried. He drags Des Grieux to safety. A crowd gathers, drawn by the excitement, and soldiers come to escort the women condemned as "undesirables" to the ship for deportation. A sergeant calls the roll as onlookers appraise the prisoners. Forlornly, Manon bids farewell to Des Grieux, who threatens the sergeant who tries to lead her away. Sympathy for the young lovers is fanned among the crowd by Lescaut. Des Grieux sees the ship's captain and falls on his knees before him, begging to be taken on board in any capacity *(No! pazzo son! guardate!)*. Touched by his pleas, the captain says he can come along.

ACT IV   In a wilderness in the French territory of New Orleans, Manon and Des Grieux, exhausted from wandering, come to a resting place. Manon is too faint to go any farther, so Des Grieux tries to make her comfortable. Thinking she has fallen asleep, he wanders off in search of water or any nearby habitation. She awakens alone and fears he has left her *(Sola, perduta, abbandonata!)*. She briefly refers to events that forced them into flight after their arrival in New Orleans—troubles brought on by her attractiveness and Des Grieux's jealousy. As she cries out that she does not want to die, Des Grieux rushes back, saying he has found nothing. While she declares her love once more, he realizes she is dying, and he falls, wracked with sobs, upon her body. With her last breath she murmurs that her love will never die.

LA BOHÈME

FOUR ACTS
MUSIC: Giacomo Puccini
TEXT (Italian): Giuseppe Giacosa and Luigi Illica, based on Henry
    Murger's novel *Scènes de la Vie de Bohème*
WORLD PREMIERE: Turin, Teatro Regio, February 1, 1896
U.S. PREMIERE: Los Angeles, October 14, 1897
METROPOLITAN OPERA PREMIERE: December 26, 1900

CHARACTERS

Rodolfo, *poet* . . . . Tenor
Marcello, *painter* . . . . Baritone
Colline, *philosopher* . . . . Bass
Schaunard, *musician* . . . . Baritone
Mimi, *seamstress* . . . . Soprano
Musetta, *coquette* . . . . Soprano
Parpignol, *toy vendor* . . . . Tenor
Benoit, *landlord* . . . . Bass
Alcindoro, *admirer of Musetta's* . . . . Bass
Students, working girls, citizens, shopkeepers,
soldiers, waiters, etc.

La Bohème

Act I Christmas Eve, ca. 1830. In the Parisian garret they share with two other artists, the painter Marcello and writer Rodolfo try to make light of the fact that the cold keeps them from working. Rodolfo stops his friend from breaking up a chair for fuel, offering to sacrifice instead the manuscript of his drama. A third roommate, the philosopher Colline, enters, complaining that pawnshops are closed for the holiday, so he could not pawn his books. As the fire dies in the stove, the three are surprised by a delivery of firewood and provisions, heralding the return of the musician Schaunard, who recently got a job working for an eccentric Englishman. Schaunard had to play continuously until a bothersome parrot in a neighboring apartment died of annoyance; he accelerated the bird's demise by feeding it a poisonous herb. Just as the four decide to go out for dinner, they are interrupted by the landlord, Benoit, who reminds them they owe three months' rent. Plying him with wine and toasts, they take his mind off the rent, teasing him about his philandering, then pretending to be shocked at his infidelity to his wife. Dividing the money Schaunard brought, they all leave except Rodolfo, who wants to finish an article before joining the others. He has barely started work when there is a knock on the door. A young woman appears, explaining that her candle blew out on the stairs. Momentarily faint, she is eased into a chair by Rodolfo, who notes her sickly appearance and offers her wine. She gets ready to leave but cannot find her key. As they look for it, Rodolfo finds and pockets it so as to keep her there a little longer. Touching her by chance as they continue the search, Rodolfo remarks on the coldness of her hand, then asks her to sit down as he tells about his work, fashioning rhymes out of daydreams *(Che gelida manina)*. When he asks her to tell about herself, she says her nickname is Mimì and she does sewing and embroidery but prefers the real flowers of spring to the ones she makes *(Mi chiamano Mimì)*. Hearing his friends call from outside, he turns to Mimì and declares her his dream of love come true *(O soave fanciulla)*. Flustered, she suggests they join his friends at the restaurant, whereupon they leave, speaking of their new found love.

Act II Outside the Café Momus, vendors and shoppers set up a din in the street as the bohemians approach and Colline buys a used overcoat, while Rodolfo buys Mimì a pink bonnet. As they take seats at an outside table, Rodolfo introduces Mimì to his friends and improvises a brief lyric, saying she is his inspiration *(Dal mio cervel)*. During their conversation a pretty, flirtatious young woman approaches in the company of an older man; Marcello recognizes her as Musetta, a love from his past, and describes her to Mimì as a heartless siren. Musetta tries to attract Marcello's attention; when he ignores her, she behaves more and more outrageously, complaining about the food and service, to the embarrassment of her escort, Alcindoro, a state councilor. Finally she begins a popular waltz, bragging about how men admire her wherever she goes *(Quando me'n vo)*. This evokes the expected response from Marcello. To get rid of Alcindoro, Musetta pretends that her shoe is pinching and sends him to find another; as soon as he leaves, she and Marcello embrace. Trouble looms when the waiter brings the check, because Schaunard's pocket has apparently been picked, but Musetta simply asks the waiter to add the check to hers, then leaves it for Alcindoro. As soldiers of the Garde Republicaine march past, followed by excited children, the group hails Musetta as queen of the Latin Quarter and heads home, leaving Alcindoro with the bill.

ACT III   On the outskirts of Paris, Marcello and Musetta have taken up residence at a tavern earning their keep by painting and giving voice lessons. Customs officers open the gates to let street cleaners enter, as voices inside the tavern toast youth and love. Farm women arrive, en route to market with produce. Mimi appears, looking for the tavern where Marcello works. He comes out and greets her with surprise. Though Rodolfo has come to the tavern, Marcello is unaware of what Mimi tells him—that her lover's incessant jealousy is destroying their relationship. Regretfully, Marcello advises Mimi not to stay with Rodolfo any longer. When the latter appears, telling Marcello he intends to break with Mimi, she overhears the conversation. At first he calls Mimi an incorrigible flirt, but Rodolfo finally admits his real worry: her tuberculosis can only get worse in their life of poverty *(Mimi è tanta malata!)* Mimi's coughing and sobbing betray her presence. As the lovers embrace, Marcello is drawn away by Musetta's flirtatious laughter inside the tavern. Mimi tells Rodolfo she will send for her belongings, offering her bonnet as a keepsake *(Donde lieta uscì)* and saying they should part without bitterness. Their reminiscences prompt them, however, to postpone their separation until they can share one more spring. Meanwhile, Musetta and Marcello come outside, in the heat of an argument, and part company on much less congenial terms (quartet: *Addio, dolce svegliare*).

ACT IV   Some months later, in the garret, Marcello and Rodolfo are once again trying unsuccessfully to work. This time the problem is preoccupation with their lost sweethearts, who they admit inspired them *(O Mimi, tu più non torni)*. Schaunard enters with a few rolls and Colline with a herring, which the four pretend is a banquet, acting the roles of noblemen, dancing, and staging a mock duel. At the height of their merriment, Musetta opens the door, saying she has brought Mimi, weak and sick. As Rodolfo tries to make her comfortable, Musetta explains to the others that Mimi left her current admirer, the viscount, so as to die near Rodolfo. Musetta gives Marcello her earrings to pawn for medicine and a doctor, while Colline bids farewell to his overcoat, which he will sell for the same purpose *(Vecchia zimarra)*. Mimi reassures Rodolfo of her undying love and reminisces about their first meeting *(Sono andati?)*. After a while Marcello returns with brandy, saying a doctor is on his way; Musetta mutters a prayer. Schaunard is the first to realize that Mimi, who seems to have dozed off, is dead. In desolation Rodolfo cries out her name.

TOSCA

THREE ACTS
MUSIC: Giacomo Puccini
TEXT (Italian): Giuseppe Giacosa and Luigi Illica, based on the
  play by Victorien Sardou
WORLD PREMIERE: Rome, Teatro Costanzi, January 14, 1900
U.S. PREMIERE: Metropolitan Opera, February 4, 1901

CHARACTERS

Floria Tosca, *celebrated singer*	Soprano
Mario Cavaradossi, *painter*	Tenor
Baron Scarpia, *chief of police*	Baritone
Sacristan	Baritone
Cesare Angelotti, *political prisoner*	Bass
Sciarrone, *gendarme*	Bass
A Shepherd Boy	Contralto
Spoletta, *police agent*	Tenor
A Jailer	Bass

Soldiers, officers, police agents, ladies, nobles,
priests, choir boys, citizens, artisans

ACT I   June 1800. Rome is suffering under a reactionary, repressive monarchy, made even harsher by Napoleon's advances to the north. As the curtain rises, Cesare Angelotti—consul of the defunct Roman republic, now an escaped political prisoner—arrives, haggard and frightened, at his sister's private chapel in the Church of Sant'Andrea della Valle. His sister, the Marchesa Attavanti, has gotten word to him that he will find a key to the chapel at the feet of the Madonna's statue. He finds it and enters, just in time to avoid the nosy Sacristan searching for the painter Mario Cavaradossi, whose brushes he has cleaned. Snooping in Mario's untouched lunch basket, the Sacristan ascertains that the painter has not come back yet. As he kneels to pray, Mario does appear and climbs the scaffold he has placed there so that he can paint a Magdalen using the Marchesa Attavanti, when she prays at her chapel, as an unwitting model. The Sacristan takes note of the painting's resemblance to the chapel's proprietress, muttering about the godless worldliness of people like this Cavaradossi. Mario marvels at the contrasting beauty of the blond Attavanti and the brunette Floria Tosca, his lover *(Recondita armonia)*. The Sacristan, further shocked, hints at his interest in Mario's lunch basket if the latter is fasting, but Mario tells him to leave. As the painter resumes work, Angelotti unlocks the gate from inside and comes out. He quickly recognizes Mario, who for a moment does not know him, then rejoices to see him. Angelotti explains he has just escaped from Castel Sant'Angelo, nearby. Mario has to send Angelotti back into hiding, with the basket of provisions, when he hears Tosca's voice calling him. As Tosca enters, Mario acts as if nothing unusual had happened, but she questions him: was there another woman here? With whom was he whispering? Mario makes light of her suspicions, and she explains she has to sing that evening but will meet him afterward at the stage exit and go with him to his villa, not far away. Tosca asks why he is not more enthusiastic *(Non la sospiri),* but he assures her of his love, only to have her revive the subject of the portrait: isn't that Attavanti? Is he involved with her? Tosca notes the intensity of the eyes in the painting. Mario thereupon praises Tosca's own incomparable eyes *(Qual'occhio al mondo)*. He insists fervently on his love, making her self-conscious, since they are in church. Finally she leaves with a kiss— and orders him to make the eyes in the portrait dark like hers. Mario opens the grate for Angelotti, explaining it would be best to keep Tosca in ignorance, because she tells her confessor everything. Angelotti says his sister has hidden female clothing there so he can disguise himself and get to her house, escaping the chief of police, Scarpia. At the mention of this name, Mario characterizes Scarpia as a lecher who uses his power to serve his own ends. "If it costs me my life, I'll save you!" he declares, inviting Angelotti to hide at his own villa, across a field from the chapel. He gives him the key to the villa and says that a disguise is unnecessary, as the path is deserted; he adds that there is a hiding place halfway down the well in the garden. At that moment a cannon shot sounds from Castel Sant'Angelo, signaling the escape of a prisoner, so Angelotti rushes off, followed by Mario. When the Sacristan returns with the news, he is startled to find Mario no longer there but is quickly occupied by a sudden influx of priests and choristers to celebrate a special Mass in thanks for Napoleon's newly reported defeat at Marengo. The mood of lightness is dispelled by the appearance of Scarpia, an ominous figure, in search of his missing prisoner, who he assumes has come to the Attavanti chapel. Ordering his flunkies to search everywhere, he discovers the unlocked gate and two clues—a woman's fan and the empty lunch basket. He notes that Attavanti crest on the fan and the face of Attavanti on the painting. Learning from the Sacristan that Mario is the painter, he puts two and two together: Mario is already under suspicion for libertarian leanings. Tosca reappears, looking for Mario, and Scarpia, knowing of their liaison, plays upon her jealousy to get more information. Unable to conceal how upset she is at the discovery of Attavanti's fan, she vows she will catch Mario with her rival at his villa and leaves. Scarpia sends agents to follow her, swearing to use the situation to his advantage and possess the diva himself. Hearing the *Te Deum* of the chorus, he kneels in hypocritical devotion.

ACT II   Scarpia's headquarters at the Farnese Palace. Relaxing at his supper table, he muses on his strategy: Tosca will serve as a decoy to find the hidden Angelotti, Mario will be convicted for shielding the fugitive, and Scarpia can enjoy Tosca himself. He sends for her, knowing she will come if Mario is in danger, and toasts his philosophy: God has created different women, different wines, and Scarpia will taste them all, preferring forceful conquest to romantic courtship *(Ha più forte sapore)*. Spoletta, one of his men, arrives nervously with news that Angelotti was not to be found at Mario's villa. During the search, Mario was so defiant that Spoletta arrested him and brought him here. Scarpia asks to see him and sends for two more men—a torturer and a judge to take testimony. Mario is brought in, still defiant but distracted by the sound of Tosca's voice singing in the courtyard outside. Angered at Mario's pretended ignorance about Angelotti's whereabouts, Scarpia shuts the window to the courtyard and presses his questioning, but Mario defies him. Tosca's arrival disrupts the session, and after a brief greeting in which Mario softly tells her not to reveal anything, Scarpia orders Mario taken for questioning. Addressing Tosca, he gets nowhere with her until she hears Mario's screams from the torture chamber; then she reveals Angelotti's hiding place in the garden well. Scarpia orders the questioning stopped, and Mario is brought out, fainting. When Scarpia pointedly orders his men to the well, Mario curses Tosca. A report arrives that the earlier word of Napoleon's defeat was premature: he won at Marengo, putting General Melas to flight. Mario rouses himself to denounce Scarpia *(Vittoria! Vittoria!)* but is dragged off. Alone with Scarpia, Tosca asks the price of her lover's freedom, and Scarpia—explaining he cannot be bought with money *(Già mi dicon venal)*—says that the price is Tosca herself. Drums are heard, marking Mario's removal for execution. In desperation Tosca raises a prayer to God, saying she has lived only for art and love and does not deserve such a fate *(Vissi d'arte)*. Trapped, she agrees to the odious bargain, and Scarpia agrees to free Mario, but not openly. He will give orders for a mock execution, "like Palmieri's;" she will be allowed to tell Mario about it in person. He gives instructions to Spoletta, then turns to Tosca, who demands a safe-conduct so that she can escape with Mario. Scarpia writes it, then rushes to embrace his conquest, who meanwhile has taken a sharp knife from the table and stabs him, crying, "This is Tosca's kiss!" He falls dying. Before she leaves, Tosca places a candle on either side of the corpse, a crucifix on his chest, muttering, "And before him all Rome trembled!"

ACT III   On the roof of Castel Sant'Angelo, night begins to wane as a Shepherd's voice is heard in the distance, singing a sad love song. Bells of different churches are heard from various directions. A Jailer offers Mario the last offices of a priest. Mario refuses, but he does present a ring in exchange for delivery of a last note to Tosca. Trying to write, Mario is overcome by memories of romantic meetings with her *(E lucevan le stelle)*. Suddenly Tosca appears, carrying the safe-conduct from Scarpia. Mario cannot believe it: Scarpia has never shown clemency. Tosca explains hurriedly what happened a short time before, and Mario wonders at the fact that her gentle hands committed murder *(O dolci mani)*. They wax ecstatic over the idea of freedom, and she explains how he should pretend to fall when shot. The firing squad files in, and Tosca stands aside as the order is given to fire. Mario falls; Spoletta prevents the sergeant from delivering the coup de grace, then covers Mario with a cloak. Tosca, at first afraid her lover will stir too soon, finally tells him all is clear, only to realize Scarpia's final treachery: the bullets were real. Spoletta and the other henchmen rush in, having discovered their chief's murder, but Tosca leaps off the parapet with a cry to Scarpia to meet her before God.

MADAMA BUTTERFLY

THREE ACTS
MUSIC: Giacomo Puccini
TEXT (Italian): Giuseppe Giacosa and Luigi Illica, based on David
    Belasco's play
WORLD PREMIERE: Milan, La Scala, February 17, 1904
U.S. PREMIERE: Washington, D.C., October 15, 1906 (in English)
METROPOLITAN OPERA PREMIERE: February 22, 1907

CHARACTERS

Cio-Cio-San, Madama Butterfly . . . . Soprano
Suzuki, *her servant* . . . . Mezzo-Soprano
Kate Pinkerton, *Pinkerton's American wife* . . . . Mezzo-Soprano
B. F. Pinkerton, *lieutenant, U.S. Navy* . . . . Tenor
Goro, *marriage broker* . . . . Tenor
Sharpless, *U.S. consul at Nagasaki* . . . . Baritone
Prince Yamadori, *rich Japanese* . . . . Baritone
The Imperial Commissioner . . . . Bass
The Bonze, *Cio-Cio-San's uncle* . . . . Bass
        Cio-Cio-San's relations and friends

ACT I   Nagasaki in the early years of the twentieth century. On a hill overlooking the harbor, U.S. Navy Lieutenant Benjamin Franklin Pinkerton inspects a Japanese house with Goro, a sharp local marriage broker who has arranged for him to have it when he marries Madama Butterfly (Cio-Cio-San). Pinkerton is introduced to Suzuki, who has been hired as his bride's chambermaid, and to a cook and a kitchen maid. Goro explains that official guests and some relatives of the bride will be there shortly for the ceremony. The consul, a middle-aged gentleman named Sharpless, is first to arrive, wheezing from the steep ascent. The carefree Pinkerton explains to Sharpless that he has signed a 999-year marriage contract, which he can cancel any time he likes. Boasting of the venturesome Yankee spirit, he offers Sharpless a drink *(Dovunque al mondo)*. Sharpless, saddened by this free-and-easy doctrine, joins Pinkerton when he toasts "America forever!"—and the day when he will marry a "real American wife" in a "real wedding." Sharpless feels concern for the Japanese girl, who may take her vows more seriously. Their discussion is broken by the sound of the approaching bridal party, headed by Cio-Cio-San, whose voice rises above the others *(Spira sul mare)*. She greets Pinkerton and the consul, to whose polite questions she replies with information about her background: the family having lost its money, she became a geisha, which she points out is a respectable profession. Her mother is still living, her father—dead (at the mention of this, her friends show embarrassment). She playfully asks Sharpless to guess her age; he starts at twenty, but fifteen turns out to be the answer. Goro summons the servants and announces the latest arrivals, the Imperial Commissioner and a registry official. Though Cio-Cio-San's mother politely praises the groom, relatives and friends vary in their opinions, some predicting an early divorce. Sharpless hopes Pinkerton appreciates the bride *(O amico fortunato)*. When Pinkerton asks Butterfly what she is carrying in her full sleeves, she shows toilet articles, then a sheathed knife, which she does not want to discuss. Goro quietly explains that Cio-Cio-San's father committed hara-kiri on orders from the emperor. The girl tells Pinkerton she visited the consulate to see about adopting his religion. Goro claps for attention, and the Commissioner reads the marriage contract, which the parties sign. Sharpless leaves with the Commissioner, and Pinkerton, impatient to get rid of the relatives, proposes a drink all around, but the party is interrupted by strange cries: an uncle of Cio-Cio-San's, a bonze (Buddhist monk), has found out about her conversion and bursts upon the scene. He stirs up the others to denounce her, and they all leave. Pinkerton comforts Cio-Cio-San, who calls Suzuki to help her change into her bridal nightgown. As evening falls, Pinkerton speaks lovingly to his bride, and they embrace before entering the house *(Dolce notte!)*.

ACT II   Three years later. In the same house, Butterfly is waiting patiently for her husband's return. Suzuki, noting they are almost out of money, doubts that Pinkerton will come back "when the robins build their nests," as he had promised. Butterfly describes how his ship will arrive in Nagasaki harbor *(Un bel dì vedremo)*. Goro appears with Sharpless, who fears that Butterfly may not remember him, but she welcomes the consul, assuring him that hers is an American household. Pinkerton has written him, asking him to seek her out. Overjoyed, Butterfly asks how often the robins nest in America—perhaps less often than in Japan, which would explain why he has not been back for three years. Goro laughs from outside, prompting Butterfly to explain that he has been plaguing her with proposals on behalf of other suitors. Goro now introduces one of these, Prince Yamadori, whom she haughtily informs that she is already married. Goro, Yamadori, and Sharpless privately share the information that Pinkerton's ship will soon arrive but that he does not want to see Butterfly. When Goro and his client leave, Sharpless starts to read the letter aloud, interrupting to ask what Butterfly would do if her husband never returned. She could go back to being a geisha, she says—or, better, die. Sharpless advises her to marry Yamadori, at which the indignant Butterfly introduces her child, Dolore (Trouble), saying Pinkerton will surely come when he knows about him. Lugubriously she imagines having to go begging with her child if she were abandoned *(Che tua madre dovra)*. After Sharpless leaves, lacking the heart to deliver his entire message, Suzuki drags Goro in and scolds him for spreading rumors about Butterfly's "illegitimate" child. The two women indignantly throw him out. A cannon shot is heard, announcing a ship in the harbor; Butterfly recognizes it as Pinkerton's. Beside herself with joy, she makes Suzuki join her in gathering flowers and strewing them around the house *(Gettiamo a mani piene)*. Readying herself, Butterfly reflects sadly on the changes the years of waiting have wrought in her. Once more she has Suzuki bring her bridal gown. Then the two women and child sit by the drawn shoji, poking holes through which to watch for Pinkerton's return.

ACT III   As night wanes, amid harbor sounds and voices in the distance, the exhausted Butterfly finally goes to her room to sleep for a while with Suzuki's promise to wake her when Pinkerton comes. Scarcely has she gone than Pinkerton does arrive, accompanied by Sharpless, telling Suzuki not to wake Butterfly. Suzuki spots a woman in the garden, Pinkerton's "real American wife." Sharpless has told Pinkerton about the child, and the two men want Suzuki's help in persuading Butterfly to relinquish it (trio: *Io so che alle sue pene*). Distressed by this house full of reminders, Pinkerton asks Sharpless to do whatever is necessary for Butterfly, then leaves, bidding farewell to the house *(Addio fiorito asil)*. Pinkerton's wife, Kate, comes in with Suzuki, asking her to reassure Butterfly that Kate can be trusted with the child. Butterfly is heard calling; she returns, wondering where Pinkerton may be, quickly guessing that Kate is his wife. Butterfly says Pinkerton can take the boy if he will come for him in person. When the visitors have gone, she orders Suzuki to leave her alone, then takes her father's dagger, reading its inscription, "He dies with honor who can no longer live with honor." She is about to stab herself when the child runs in unexpectedly. Butterfly embraces him in an impassioned farewell *(Tu, piccolo Iddio!)*, hands him a miniature American flag and a doll, and bandages his eyes, then goes behind a screen and runs herself through with the knife. Dragging herself back to embrace her son, she dies as the distraught Pinkerton, calling her name, returns with Sharpless.

LA FANCIULLA DEL WEST

(The Girl of the Golden West)

THREE ACTS
MUSIC: Giacomo Puccini
TEXT (Italian): Carlo Zangarini and Guelfo Civinini, after David
   Belasco's English play
WORLD PREMIERE: Metropolitan Opera, December 10, 1910

CHARACTERS

Minnie, *keeper of the Polka* . . . . Soprano
Dick Johnson, *bandit* . . . . Tenor
Nick, *bartender at the Polka* . . . . Tenor
Jack Rance, *sheriff* . . . . Baritone
Jake Wallace, *traveling minstrel* . . . . Baritone
Ashby, *agent of the Wells Fargo Company* . . . . Bass
Billy Jackrabbit, *Indian* . . . . Bass
Wowkle, *his squaw* . . . . Mezzo-Soprano
José Castro, *"greaser" from Ramerrez' band* . . . . Bass
   Miners: Sonora, Trin, Sid, Handsome, Harry, Joe, Happy, Larkens

ACT I   A mining camp in California during the gold rush (1849–50). In the Polka saloon, miners' voices are heard in nostalgic refrains. Handsome inquires about Minnie—a sort of den mother for the community—and learns from Nick, the bartender, that she is fine. A card game starts. Larkens is plagued with homesickness. When Sonora and Trin ask Nick whether Minnie seems to favor them, he diplomatically answers yes to each. As Trin jubilantly orders whiskey for everybody, the voice of the camp minstrel, Jake Wallace, is heard approaching. His nostalgic song about the old folks at home (*Che faranno i vecchi miei*) casts a pensive silence over the group and proves too much for Larkens, who breaks down in sobs. The men take up a collection to send him home. In the game that resumes, Handsome catches Sid cheating, and Sonora draws his revolver. The ensuing commotion brings the sheriff, Jack Rance, who pins the offending card on Sid's chest and says he will hang if he takes it off. The others throw Sid out of the bar. Rance turns to welcome Mr. Ashby of the Wells Fargo agency, who has just arrived, and asks news of the bandit who has been plaguing him. Ashby replies that the man has eluded capture for three months but is known to be nearby: his gang of Mexican highwaymen will stop at nothing. Nick announces a round of drinks on Minnie, whom everyone cheers. Rance says she will soon be his wife, but Sonora, somewhat drunk, ridicules the idea and provokes Rance to draw his revolver. Sonora draws too, but Trin grabs his arm, and the shot goes wild. Minnie arrives, demanding to know what the trouble is. She scolds Sonora and threatens not to teach the miners any longer: they try to make up to her, and Joe shyly offers a bunch of flowers he has picked by the river, while Sonora proffers a ribbon and Harry a silk handkerchief. Placated, she offers a cigar to Mr. Ashby and, noticing Rance, greets him. Seeing Sonora pay his bar bill with a bag of nuggets, Ashby tells Rance it is crazy to keep gold in the saloon with bandits around. Minnie pulls a Bible from a drawer and starts to read to the attentive miners, starting with the fifty-first Psalm, asking who remembers who King David was and explaining the moral: "There is no sinner in the world whose way to salvation is barred." As the lesson draws to a close, the pony express arrives, the rider remarking he saw a sinister-looking man en route. Ashby, receiving a dispatch, asks whether anyone knows a certain Nina Micheltorena, whom Minnie refers to as a "siren." Ashby says this woman knows the where- abouts of the bandit chief and has asked Ashby to meet her at the Palmas saloon late that night. Happy, Handsome, Harry, and Joe read letters from home. A stranger is reported outside the bar, asking for whiskey and water, an unheard-of mixture. As the miners go to investigate, Rance tells Minnie he loves her. She reminds him he has a wife, but he declares he will get a divorce; she says she lives alone by preference and trusts in her revolver. He replies bitterly that he has had a loveless life; a gambler at heart, he was drawn to California by the gold and would wager everything for Minnie's love *(Min- nie, dalla mia casa son partito)*. Minnie says true love is different: she grew up in a bar-restaurant in Soledad, and her parents loved each other very much *(Laggiù nel Soledad)*. When Nick brings in the stranger, Rance roughly tells the newcomer that he must have lost his way and that he is not welcome. Asking his name, he learns that it is "Johnson" from Sacramento. Johnson and Minnie recognize each other: they met once on the trail to Monterey. Annoyed, Rance calls the miners to say the stranger won't state his business. When they come in, Minnie vouches for Johnson, satisfying everyone except Rance. Harry suggests a dance in the adjoining hall, and though Minnie protests she has never danced, Johnson leads her off in a waltz. Ashby and some miners come in, having caught a suspicious character, Castro, hanging around outside. Castro throws them off the scent by pretending to despise his leader and offering to show where he can be found. As Rance and the others form a posse, Johnson comes in and Castro whispers that the other bandits are hidden outside the camp, waiting for a whistled signal. The miners go off, and Nick closes the bar. Minnie wanders in from the dance hall and talks with Johnson, saying she has yet to give her first kiss. She adds that she trusts him, though she doesn't know who he is. He replies that he himself is unsure of his own identity, adding that he is aware of her feelings even if she has trouble finding words for them (*Quello che tacete*). Nick reappears to warn that another suspicious-looking man has been seen outside, and Johnson hears the whistled signal. Minnie tells Johnson that the miners leave their gold in her care: anyone who tries to steal it will have to kill her first. Saying he has to go, Johnson accepts Minnie's invitation to stop and see her at her cabin halfway up the mountain. She bursts into tears at her sense of worthlessness, but Johnson says she has a pure heart and the face of an angel, then quickly leaves.

ACT II   A short time later, in Minnie's log cabin, an Indian couple, Wowkle and Billy Jackrabbit, discuss how they will soon be married—at their mistress' urging, since they already have a papoose. Minnie arrives and tells Wowkle there will be a guest for dinner. Johnson soon appears, at first trying to embrace Minnie, who stops him. He makes amends for his forwardness and sits down, admiring her cabin. She waxes enthusiastic about her life there (*Oh, se sapeste come il vivere è allegro!*). Johnson offers to send books for her miners' school and tries again to kiss her. She sends Wowkle to the shed and finally yields to Johnson's embrace. When he declares he has loved her ever since they first met, she admits to similar feelings, but he says he must leave. Heavy snow is falling; shots sound in the distance. Minnie says he should stay and offers to give up her bed: she will sleep by the fire. Voices are heard calling outside: Nick and Sonora come to the door to warn that the bandit Ramerrez has been seen near her cabin. Because of the sheriff's jealousy, she hides Johnson behind a curtain, then opens the door to admit the two men with Ashby and Rance. They tell her they feared for her life, because Johnson is actually the notorious Ramerrez. Nick, seeing Johnson's cigar butt, realizes he is in the cabin but tries to help Minnie by saying they may have mistaken the trail. Rance sneeringly tells Minnie it was Nina Micheltorena who showed them a picture of her lover, Ramerrez, revealing he was really Johnson. Minnie pretends to make light of it and shows the men out, but as soon as they leave, she orders her visitor out of hiding. He denies nothing but insists he would never have robbed her. Six months ago, he explains, his bandit father died, leaving him no means of support but a band of highwaymen (*Or son sei mesi*). Upset that she gave her first kiss to such a man, she orders him out. He goes, but a shot rings out, and his body falls against the door. She helps him inside and pushes him up the ladder to the loft. Rance returns, convinced that Ramerrez is in the cabin, but his search reveals nothing. He again expresses his love for Minnie and declares no one else will have her. As she defies him, a drop of blood from the loft lands on Rance's hand. Shoving Minnie aside, Rance orders Ramerrez down from the loft; painfully the bandit drags himself down, slumping into a chair in a faint. In desperation Minnie offers to gamble with Rance—a game of poker. If he wins, Minnie and Ramerrez are his; if he loses, Minnie keeps her lover. Furtively, she conceals something in her stocking while Rance shuffles. Minnie wins the first hand, Rance the second. When Rance is about to win the third, Minnie asks him to fetch her a drink—she feels faint—and pulls concealed cards from her stocking, giving her a winning hand: three aces and a pair. Stunned by her unlikely win, Rance stalks out.

ACT III   A clearing in the forest. At dawn a week later, the posse is waiting for Johnson to come out of Minnie's cabin. A group of miners appears, having spotted Ramerrez trying to make his escape on the other side of the mountain. Rance gloats that now it is Minnie's turn to suffer (Or piangi tu, o Minnie). Miners run in with various reports—their quarry has escaped on horseback— and finally Sonora reports his capture. Ashby and his Wells Fargo men bring in the bandit, whom Rance taunts; everyone is ready to hang him from a tree. Ramerrez asks them to get it over quickly, admitting the robberies but denying the murders his captors charge him with. As a last favor he asks that Minnie not be told how he died: she should believe he got away to a life of redemption (Ch'ella mi creda libero). As the miners prepare to string him up, Minnie's call is heard. She rides in, jumps off her horse, and throws herself in front of Johnson, pulling her revolver. As Rance orders the hanging to proceed, the miners hesitate; Sonora is the first to take her side. She tells the men they never objected when she mothered, helped, and taught them—now, she says, this man is hers from God (Non vi fu mai chi disse 'Basta!'), adding he is a bandit no longer. When they still resist, she reminds them individually how she looked after them. As Rance leaves in disgust, the miners give Minnie what she asks: they owe her no less. With sadness on both sides, they bid farewell to Minnie and Ramerrez, who ride off to a new life across the far mountains.

LA RONDINE

(The Swallow)

THREE ACTS

MUSIC: Giacomo Puccini

TEXT (Italian): Giuseppe Adami, from a German libretto by Alfred Maria Willner and Heinrich Reichert

WORLD PREMIERE: Monte Carlo, Théâtre du Casino, March 27, 1917

U.S. PREMIERE: Metropolitan Opera, March 10, 1928

CHARACTERS

Magda, *Rambaldo's mistress* . . . . Soprano
Lisette, *her maid* . . . . Soprano
Yvette ⎫
Bianca ⎬ *friends of Magda's* . . . . ⎧ Soprano / Soprano
Suzy ⎭ . . . . ⎩ Mezzo-Soprano
Ruggero, *young man* . . . . Tenor
Prunier, *poet* . . . . Tenor
Rambaldo, *wealthy Parisian* . . . . Baritone
Perichaud ⎫
Gobin ⎬ *his friends* . . . . ⎧ Bass-Baritone / Tenor
Crébillon ⎭ . . . . ⎩ Bass-Baritone
Students, artists, demi-mondaines

ACT I Near the Tuileries in Paris, sometime during the Second Empire (1852–70). Rambaldo and his mistress, Magda, are entertaining theatrical and literary friends at her salon. Prunier, a poet (and the lover of Magda's maid, Lisette), declares that romantic love is back in fashion, a veritable epidemic *(La malattia—diciamo epidemia)*. He has written a ballad about a girl named Doretta, who discovers love in a student's ardent kiss; he begins the song, intriguing the romantically minded Magda, who sits at the piano and finishes it *(Chi il bel sogno di Doretta)*. Rambaldo presents her with a pearl necklace, which she accepts without changing her opinion that true love is unrelated to wealth. As the guests wander toward another room, Lisette tells Rambaldo that a young man has been waiting outside to see him on business. As Rambaldo excuses himself, Magda recalls to her friends the days of her own youth, when romance still seemed fresh *(Ore dolci e divine)* and she fled, frightened, from her first flirtation. Prunier offers to read Magda's palm as Rambaldo greets Ruggero, son of a childhood friend. Prunier predicts that Magda may take off in pursuit of her romantic dream, but his reading is disrupted by Rambaldo's call for the group's advice: young Ruggero is new to Paris and wants to know where to spend the evening. Various nightclubs are suggested, the most popular being Bullier, endorsed by Lisette *(Amore è la, gioia e piacer)*. He leaves to go there, and the other guests also bid Magda adieu, leaving her alone with Lisette, who says it is her evening off. As Magda goes to her room, thinking nostalgically about Bullier, Prunier comes to escort Lisette, declaring his love while she responds in a bantering tone (duet: *No! Tu sapessi a quale prezzo*). As they depart, Magda comes out of her room dressed as a shop girl, confident no one will recognize her.

ACT II   At Bullier, students and grisettes are joking as flower vendors and streetwalkers pass. Several of the girls teasingly approach the solitary Ruggero *(Su via! Come ti chiami?)*, who waves them off. Students offer to escort the arriving Magda; to avoid them, she says she already has a date and joins the seated Ruggero. She is about to excuse herself (duet: *Scusate, ma fu per liberarmi*), but he is taken with her and asks her to stay and dance. Meanwhile, Prunier and Lisette arrive, sparring archly (duet: *Ti voglio bene*); they dance, while Magda and Ruggero return to their table, she introducing herself as "Paulette," not wanting to give more details *(Perchè mai cercate di saper)*, he responding to her mystery with growing infatuation. Prunier, recognizing Ruggero, sits down with him as Lisette marvels at the resemblance between "Paulette" and Magda (quartet: *È il mio sogno che s'averra!*). When Rambaldo arrives, Prunier drops the pretense of not recognizing Magda and takes her aside, sending Ruggero out with Lisette. Rambaldo goes to Magda through the crowd and asks her to abandon this "escapade." Replying that she has found true love, she says she will stay, whereupon Rambaldo steps out gracefully, hoping she will not regret it. When Ruggero returns, she leaves on his arm, fearful for the fragility of her happiness.

ACT III   On the terrace of a villa on the Riviera on a spring afternoon, Magda and Ruggero are enjoying an idyllic life, which cannot go on much longer unless he is able to get money from his family. When Magda reacts with surprise to his having written asking his parents' permission to marry, he urges her to think how happy they will be *(Dimmi che vuoi seguirmi)*. Prunier and Lisette discover the place. They quarrel as Magda appears from the villa, surprised to meet them, telling Lisette she would be glad to have her back. Prunier cannot imagine Magda continuing this fantasy life and intimates that Rambaldo would have *her* back. He leaves as Ruggero comes out with a letter from his mother, giving her blessing to the marriage—if the girl is virtuous. Magda has to confess she has been a kept woman: she can be his mistress but not his wife. Though he insists he loves her anyway, she says she cannot ruin things for him. Begging him to remember her, she turns sadly away from the heartbroken young man to return to her old life.

IL TRITTICO

Trittico means "triptych"—originally three writing tablets joined together, later a group of three paintings, here a trilogy of one-act operas whose common themes are death and escape from confinement.

IL TABARRO

(The Cloak)

ONE ACT
MUSIC: Giacomo Puccini
TEXT (Italian): Giuseppe Adami, from Didier Gold's play
   La Houppelande
WORLD PREMIERE: Metropolitan Opera, December 14,
   1918

CHARACTERS

Giorgetta, *Michele's wife, age twenty-five* . . . . Soprano
Frugola, *Talpa's wife, age fifty* . . . . Mezzo-Soprano
Michele, *owner of the barge, age fifty* . . . . Baritone
Luigi, *stevedore, age twenty* . . . . Tenor
Tinca, *stevedore, age thirty-five* . . . . Tenor
Talpa, *stevedore, age fifty-five* . . . . Bass
                    Organ-grinder, song peddler, two lovers

Paris, at the beginning of the twentieth century. On board Michele's barge, tied up along the banks of the Seine, stevedores sing a chantey to accompany their work. Michele's wife, Giorgetta, younger than he, suggests offering the stevedores a glass of wine. Disappointed at her coolness when he tries to kiss her, Michele goes below. The stevedores Tinca, Talpa, and Luigi toast their benefactress, and Tinca tries clumsily to dance with her to the music of a passing organ-grinder. They go back to work, and when Michele returns, Giorgetta asks him whether they will be leaving soon with another cargo and keeping Luigi on as a helper; Michele replies that Luigi doesn't seem especially reliable. A song peddler passes, hawking his wares, and Frugola, Talpa's wife, draws near. Michele asks Giorgetta why she seems so withdrawn, and she replies that he too is undemonstrative. When Frugola comes on board, he retires to the cabin. Frugola, who has spent the day scavenging, presents Giorgetta with her prize find, a good-as-new comb. She has also found a beef heart for her cat, Caporale *(E il più bel gatto)*. As Tinca quits work and heads for a saloon to drown his disappointment with the world, Luigi declares that Tinca is right: there is no future for them but backbreaking work *(Hai ben ragione)*. Frugola dreams of a cottage where she and Talpa can spend their declining years *(Ho sognato una casetta)*, but Giorgetta says she is tired of the drab life on the barge and would like the excitement of the city *(E ben altro il mio sogno!)*. It is apparent that she and Luigi are strongly attracted; as soon as the older couple leaves, they declare their love and their need to escape this stifling environment. Michele reappears, and Luigi inquires whether he could get off at Rouen on the next trip; Michele replies there would be no work for him there, then returns to the cabin. Giorgetta asks Luigi why he wants to quit, and the stevedore replies he cannot bear sharing her with her husband. She begs him to come back later, after dark, when she will give the all-clear signal with a lighted match. He leaves, promising to return, and Michele steps on deck, trying once more without success to elicit warmth from his wife. When he mentions their infant child, who died within the past year, she turns away in pain. He reminds her of how he used to hold her enfolded in his *tabarro* (cloak), but she evades him, saying she wants to sleep. Alone on deck as two lovers stroll by, Michele grimly contemplates the dark, mysterious river, which has carried so many to their fate *(Nulla! silenzio!)*.* When he lights his pipe, Luigi, mistaking the match for Giorgetta's signal, slips on board, only to be seized by the startled Michele, who forces him to admit he loves Giorgetta. Strangling Luigi, Michele wraps his cloak around the corpse, then sits down again to appear calm as Giorgetta comes on deck, nervous and sleepless. She tries to make up to him, even saying she would join him again under his cloak. Abruptly, Michele throws open the cloak, revealing Luigi's body, and roughly pushes Giorgetta toward her lifeless lover.

---

* The alternative monologue *Scorri, fiume eterno!* is sometimes substituted.

SUOR ANGELICA

(Sister Angelica)

ONE ACT
MUSIC: Giacomo Puccini
TEXT (Italian): Giovacchino Forzano
WORLD PREMIERE: Metropolitan Opera, December 14, 1918

CHARACTERS

Suor Angelica.................................. Soprano
Alms Collector .... Soprano
Suor Genovieffa .... Soprano
Suor Osmina .... Soprano
Abbess...................................... Mezzo-Soprano
Monitor .... Mezzo-Soprano
Mistress of Novices .... Mezzo-Soprano
Suor Dolcina .... Mezzo-Soprano
The Princess, *Suor Angelica's aunt* .... Contralto
Novices, sisters

A convent outside Florence in the late seventeenth century. A Monitor assigns penance to two novices who have neglected their prayers, then tells the other sisters they may have a recreation period. Sister Genovieffa and a few others notice the spring sunshine finding its way into their courtyard. The Mistress of Novices notes that on three evenings of the year, in May, the sun turns the water in the fountain golden—a sign of divine grace. Sister Genovieffa suggests that when the water turns golden, they take some to sprinkle on the grave of Sister Bianca Rosa, who died during the past year. Though the monitor warns that personal wishes are earthly vanity, Genovieffa confesses she has one: as a former shepherdess, she would like to hold a lamb once more. Sister Dolcina, known for her sweet tooth, is headed off by the other sisters from expressing her own wish—doubtless for something to eat. When Sister Angelica denies that she wishes anything for herself, the others say she is not admitting that she has heard nothing from her family in over seven years and would like news of them. Of noble birth, she was sent to the convent for some offense. The nursing sister runs in breathless to ask for help for Sister Chiara, stung by wasps in the garden; Angelica, who is familiar with herbs, offers a remedy. Alms Collectors enter with a donkey cart bearing provisions they have solicited around the countryside. One remarks that he saw a fine carriage draw up outside the convent. Angelica reacts anxiously, and the other sisters hope the visit will be for her. The Abbess calls Angelica to say the visitor is her aunt, the Princess. Angelica, alone with the Princess, kneels before her as she enters, but the old woman avoids her imploring glances and announces she has come on business. Angelica's sister Anna Viola is to be married, and the inheritance left by her parents, dead twenty years, has to be divided *(Il Principe Gualtiero vostro padre)*. Angelica's signature is needed on a document. The Princess alludes to Angelica's sin, which stained the family honor, and rebukes the young woman for calling her harsh and unbending. When the girl says she cannot forget the child she bore out of wedlock and begs for news of him, the Princess says he died two years ago. Angelica nearly faints but regains control as the old woman sends for the Abbess and places the document in front of her niece to sign, then leaves with no further word. Evening has fallen, and the other sisters go about their duties, lighting candles in the cemetery. Alone, Angelica thinks of her child dying motherless; as an angel in heaven he can see her at last, and she longs to see him too *(Senza mamma)*. The sisters return to find her in a near-visionary state, declaring she has glimpsed the Virgin's grace and heard angelic singing. It is time for all to retire, but after they have gone, Angelica returns alone to brew some herbs—oleander, laurel, nightshade, hemlock—to help her join her son in heaven. She addresses a simple farewell to the convent where her sisters are sleeping *(Addio, buone sorelle)* and embraces the cross, then takes the poison. Coming out of her exaltation, she realizes that her suicide is a sin and prays despairingly for pardon, declaring that mother love was her motive. As she dies, she sees a miracle: the chapel glows with light, and the door opens, through which the Virgin steps, gently pushing toward her a child in white.

GIANNI SCHICCHI

ONE ACT

MUSIC: Giacomo Puccini

TEXT (Italian): Giovacchino Forzano, from an episode in Dante's *Inferno*

WORLD PREMIERE: Metropolitan Opera, December 14, 1918

GIANNI SCHICCHI

CHARACTERS

Gianni Schicchi, *age fifty* .... Baritone
Lauretta, *his daughter* .... Soprano
Buoso Donati's relatives:
    Zita, *called La Vecchia, Buoso's cousin* .... Contralto
    Rinuccio, *Zita's nephew*.......................... Tenor
    Gherardo, *Buoso's nephew* .... Tenor
    Nella, *his wife* .... Soprano
    Gherardino, *their son* .... Alto
    Betto di Signa, *Buoso's brother-in-law* .... Bass
    Simone, *Buoso's cousin*.......................... Bass
    Marco, *Simone's son* .... Baritone
    La Ciesca, *Marco's wife* .... Mezzo-Soprano
Maestro Spinelloccio, *doctor* .... Bass
Ser Amantio di Nicolao, *notary* .... Baritone
Pinelli, *cobbler* ⎫
Guccio, *painter* ⎭ .... Bass

Florence, 1299. The wealthy Buoso Donati lies on his deathbed, surrounded by greedy, anxious relatives. One of them, Betto, whispers in Nella's ear what is rumored in nearby Signa — that Buoso meant to leave most of his property to an order of monks. Simone says that if the will is already filed in the town hall, they are out of luck. They ransack the room, and young Rinuccio finds the document, hoping he will receive enough to marry his sweetheart, Lauretta. His old aunt Zita starts to decipher the will, as everyone clusters around for a look. The news is bad: Buoso did leave everything to the monks. Eyes turn toward Simone, oldest of the tribe, but he can think of no way around it. Rinuccio suggests that one man—Lauretta's father, the canny bourgeois Gianni Schicchi—might be able to help. Distrustful of this upstart, the relatives argue they should have nothing to do with him, but the boy Gherardino announces that Schicchi is on his way, having been summoned by Rinuccio, who sings his praises as a resourceful, self-made man *(Avete torto!)* comparable to Arnolfo, Giotto, and the Medicis—outsiders who have given Florence new life. Schicchi arrives and sizes up the situation. As he locks horns with Zita, who refuses to let her nephew marry a parvenu's daughter unless there is a dowry, the lovers bid farewell to their hopes of an early marriage *(Addio, speranza bella)*. The relatives stay out of it, wanting only to do something about Buoso's will. Rinuccio tries to stop Schicchi from leaving, but it takes Lauretta's pleas to soften his heart: she begs him on behalf of her love for Rinuccio *(O mio babbino caro)*. He reads the will, sends Lauretta out on the terrace "to feed the birdie," and addresses himself to Buoso's relatives. Does anyone outside know of Buoso's death? Good, no one should know. They are to carry the body into the next room and ask no questions. An emergency arises when Buoso's doctor, Spinelloccio, is heard outside inquiring about the patient. Betto draws the window curtain, darkening the room, and Schicchi hurriedly gets into the bed, impersonating Buoso and asking the old physician to come back later. Schicchi is amazed that the relatives still do not grasp his plan: he will dictate a new will to a notary *(Che zucconi!)*. They flatter Schicchi, each pressing his own special requests regarding the will. Quarrels develop as conflicting greeds emerge, but the hubbub is cut short by the pealing of the city's funeral bell. All seems lost, but Gherardo runs out to the street and learns that the bell is for the mayor's Moorish majordomo, not for Buoso Donati. Simone favors letting Schicchi use his own judgment about a fair division, but other relatives try to bribe Schicchi privately to serve their interests. As he dresses in Buoso's nightshirt and cap, Zita, Nella, and Ciesca serenade him cajolingly *(Spogliati, bambolino)*. Before climbing into bed, Schicchi warns that falsification of a will is punishable by loss of a hand and banishment from Florence. To drive home his point, he waves farewell to the city with a make-believe handless arm *(Addio Firenze)*. Amantio, the notary, arrives with two witnesses and hears Schicchi's deposition. The monks are to get only a token sum. Ready cash, investments, and smaller properties are divided among the various relatives. The valuable properties, however—the house in Florence, the sawmill in Signa—he leaves to his "devoted friend Gianni Schicchi." The relatives seethe with fury, but Schicchi hums a reminder of his farewell to Florence: if caught, they would all be accomplices. He then orders Zita to pay the notary and witnesses, who leave. The relatives fall upon Schicchi and pillage the house as he tries to drive them out with Buoso's walking stick. Finally they leave, carrying all they can, and Lauretta and Rinuccio share a moment of happiness, surveying Florence and Fiesole from the terrace of their future house. Schicchi asks the audience whether he was not justified in tricking the relatives and condemning his own soul (a reference to the appearance of his name in Dante's *Divine Comedy*) for the sake of the young lovers. He asks for applause and interprets it as a verdict of "not guilty."

TURANDOT

THREE ACTS

MUSIC: Giacomo Puccini

TEXT (Italian): Giuseppe Adami and Renato Simoni, based on Carlo Gozzi's fairy tale

WORLD PREMIERE: Milan, La Scala, April 25, 1926

U.S. PREMIERE: Metropolitan Opera, November 16, 1926

CHARACTERS

Princess Turandot .... Soprano
Liù, *slave girl* .... Soprano
Emperor Altoum .... Tenor
Calaf, *Unknown Prince*........................ Tenor
Pang, *Lord of Provisions*....................... Tenor
Pong, *Lord of the Imperial Kitchen* .... Tenor
Ping, *Chancellor of China* .... Baritone
Mandarin .... Baritone
Timur, *exiled King of Tartary* .... Bass
Executioner, slaves, soldiers, dancers, populace

ACT I   Peking in legendary times. A Mandarin appears on a parapet to read a proclamation to the crowd in the square below: Princess Turandot will marry any noble suitor who can answer three riddles she poses. All who fail must pay with their heads. Today it the Prince of Persia's turn to die. The bloodthirsty crowd, pushed back by guards, clamors for the executioner. In the turmoil a blind old man is knocked down and helped up by his faithful slave girl. An Unknown Prince pushes through the crowd and recognizes the old man as his father, Timur, driven from their realm by a usurper. Each had thought the other dead. Timur identifies the slave as Liù, the only one willing to accompany him into exile. As the crowd turns its attention to the honing of the executioner's ax, the prince asks why the girl has been so kind. She replies that one day at the palace he smiled at her, and she has felt loving devotion ever since. As the hour of moonrise approaches, the crowd gives way to hushed anticipation, exhorting the moon—"O severed head"—to show itself. Boys' voices are heard singing a refrain like a folk song *(Là sui monti dell'Est)* as executioner, priests, and dignitaries file past, followed by the Prince of Persia, whose youthful face arouses sympathy. The populace now calls on Turandot to spare the young man's life. At length she shows herself on a balcony and gives the sign that her suitor must die. She withdraws, leaving the Unknown Prince dazzled by her beauty. He rushes toward the big gong with which suitors signal their acceptance of her challenge, but Liù tries to hold him back. The Prince of Persia is heard calling Turandot's name as he goes to his death. The Unknown Prince reaches the gong but is stopped by a trio of officials, Ping, Pang, and Pong, who tell him he is a fool and will surely die. Ping's advice is to leave women alone or else marry a harem *(Lascia le donne!)*. Turandot's handmaidens call down for silence. One more time the three ministers try to persuade the stranger that the riddles are impossible to solve. As if in agreement, the ghosts of executed suitors appear on the ramparts, moaning of their love for Turandot. As the executioner passes with the latest victim's head, Timur asks whether his son will leave him alone in the world, and Liù pleads in the name of love *(Signore, ascolta!)*. The young man replies that if Liù really loves him, she should look after his father (Non piangere, Liù). The ministers, Timur, and Liù join in one last effort to stop him (Ah! Per l'ultima volta!), but this only increases his determination. He tears himself away, strikes the gong three times, and cries out Turandot's name.

ACT II   In a pavilion, the three ministers think about the extra work the stranger's challenge will mean for them, whether he wins or loses. They will have to arrange a wedding or, much more likely, a funeral. Ping recalls the old days, when China was peaceful and orderly (O China, O China). Nowadays it is just a steady round of executions—thirteen in the present year alone. Ping longs for his country house in Hunan, where he can look at his pond instead of racking his brains over sacred books (Ho una casa nell'Honan). The others agree they may as well bid farewell to their divine heritage (Addio, amore, addio, razza!). If only Turandot yielded to love, there would no longer be any unreasonable women in China (Non v'è in China, per nostra fortuna). But they are dreaming: here comes the next execution.

In a square before the imperial palace, the crowd hails Emperor Altoum, a venerable man who tells the new challenger to go away—there has been enough bloodshed. But the youth begs to confront the riddles. The Mandarin once more reads the decree. Turandot, exquisite in regal dress, appears and declares she is the reincarnation of an ancestor, Princess Lou-Ling, who was ravished by the Tartar King when he conquered China centuries before (In questa Reggia). Hatred toward men lives in her heart, and she takes revenge on them, swearing none shall possess her (Mai nessun m'avrà). Her advice to the stranger is that the riddles are three but death is one. He replies life is one. She asks the first riddle: What phantom is born every night and dies every morning in the human heart? His reply—"Hope"—turns out to be correct, but she warns him his hope is false. The second riddle: What flickers and warms like a flame, yet is not flame? He replies, "Love"—again correctly. Shaken by his success, she confronts him with the last riddle: What is like ice yet generates fire, enslaving you if you go free, making you a king if it takes you as slave? Confident his own ardor will thaw her, he correctly answers, "Turandot." A poor loser, she begs the emperor to protect her. The stranger offers a riddle of his own: if she can discover his name before dawn, he will forfeit his life. The crowd hails the generous stranger and the holy emperor.

ACT III   As night shrouds the city, heralds read Turandot's decree: on penalty of death, no one shall sleep, because the name of the Unknown Prince must be known by dawn. Repeating the edict, he declares no one shall know his name until he himself tells it to Turandot when she yields to his love (Nessun dorma). Ping, Pang, and Pong appear among the shadows, trying to buy him off with women, riches, glory—whatever he wants. They themselves fear torture if they cannot discover his name before dawn. Suddenly soldiers enter, dragging Timur and Liù, whom they suspect of knowing the prince's identity. Liù says she alone knows it, and she resists torture until Turandot appears, demanding to know what gives Liù such courage. The girl replies it is love for the Unknown Prince *(Tanto amore segreto, inconfessato)*, whom she now offers to Turandot. Faced with more torture, Liù says that Turandot will lose her icy composure and learn to love him too *(Tu che di gel sei cinta)*. The girl seizes a knife from a soldier and kills herself. Timur declares that her offended spirit will seek revenge; the crowd that has gathered prays superstitiously that she have mercy on them. Following the procession carrying her body, everyone leaves except Turandot and the prince. He tears off her veil, demanding she look on the innocent blood shed for her sake *(Principessa di gelo)*. Haughtily, she warns him not to touch her, but he embraces her passionately and kisses her. Nearly swooning, she confesses that of all her suitors he was the first she feared, and it is he who has drawn her first tears *(Del primo pianto)*. Now that he has won, she begs him to leave without demanding more. He makes her a gift of his life: his name is Calaf, son of Timur. She too has won, he says, as she summons him before the emperor and the populace.

Outside the imperial palace, Turandot brings Calaf in triumph. For a moment it appears she might announce his name and demand his death. Instead she says his name is Love. The crowd hails love as the light of the world.

HENRY PURCELL
1659–95

*H*enry Purcell, one of the most inventive and gifted of English composers, wrote only one opera, since the preference of his time was for plays with incidental music or interpolated masques, of which he wrote several. His natural talent for the stage is apparent in *Dido and Aeneas,* written in 1689, when he was thirty, for a girls' boarding school in Chelsea. Students sang the chorus and female roles, presumably with guest artists or faculty members in the more demanding and/or male roles and probably with Purcell at the harpsichord. Because of the modest circumstances of the performance, the orchestration otherwise consists only of four string parts. As Jack Westrup notes in the *New Grove Dictionary,* "Everywhere the music triumphs over a prosaic libretto." Best known for its climactic soprano lament *When I am laid in earth,* a passacaglia over a chromatic ground bass, *Dido and Aeneas* shares with Benjamin Britten's operas the honor of having spread English music to the lyric stages of the world.

DIDO AND AENEAS

THREE ACTS
MUSIC: Henry Purcell
TEXT (English): Nahum Tate
WORLD PREMIERE: London, December 1689
U.S. PREMIERE: New York, Town Hall, January 13, 1924

CHARACTERS

Dido, *Queen of Carthage* . . . . Mezzo-Soprano
Aeneas, *Trojan prince* . . . . Tenor
Belinda, *lady-in-waiting* . . . . Soprano
Sorceress . . . . Mezzo-Soprano
Courtiers, people, witches, sailors

ACT I   The Trojan War having ended, the hero Aeneas has wandered with his followers to Carthage. His eventual destiny, as decreed by the gods, is to found Italy, but he has meanwhile fallen in love with the Carthaginian queen, Dido. Her handmaiden Belinda and other courtiers urge her to enjoy her good fortune, but Dido confesses uneasiness *(Ah! Belinda, I am pressed with torment)*. Belinda replies there is no reason for her not to return Aeneas' love, but Dido fears that it will be her undoing, despite reassurances that Aeneas is sincere *(Fear no danger to ensue)*. Aeneas enters and asks the queen, evidently not for the first time, to respond to his wooing: vanquished at home, he wants to be victorious abroad. As he leads Dido away, Belinda notes that her mistress seems to be capitulating *(Pursue thy conquest, Love)*, as the courtiers hail love's triumph with a song and dance.

§ In a witches' cave, the Sorceress summons her cohorts to make trouble in Carthage (chorus: *Harm's our delight*), declaring Dido will be ruined before sunset. Knowing of Aeneas's destiny to move on to Italy, the Sorceress will send a Spirit in the guise of Mercury to tell the hero he must depart at once. Since Dido and Aeneas are out on a hunt, the witches decide to conjure up a storm, spoiling the lovers' outing and driving them back to court. Eerily the witches plan their spell (echo chorus: *In our deep-vaulted cell)*, whereupon Furies appear and dance to an accompaniment of thunder and lightning.

HENRY PURCELL

ACT II   In a grove, the royal party rests, noting that Diana and Actaeon themselves might have hunted in such a place. Aeneas admires a boar he has killed, but Dido feels the approaching storm, so all agree they must leave *(Haste, haste to town)*. Aeneas, the last to go, is accosted by the Spirit posing as Mercury with Jove's command: Aeneas must stay in Carthage no longer. He accepts his orders but wonders how to break the news to Dido, who has given herself to him during the hunt.

ACT III   Aeneas' men prepare to weigh anchor *(Come away, fellow sailors)* and dance happily. Watching them from a distance, the Sorceress and her witches gleefully note that their plot is working, referring to Dido by their own name for her, "Elissa." Once Aeneas has sailed, they will not only see Carthage ruined but also cause a storm on the ocean *(Destruction's our delight)*. They dance to celebrate their mischief, then disappear.

§ In her palace, Dido has learned of Aeneas' impending departure. When he draws near, she scorns his grief as hypocrisy and even spurns his impulsive offer to stay. After sending him off, she faces the inevitability of death, her mood turning from wrath to sad tenderness as she asks Belinda to remember her but to forget her fate *(When I am laid in earth)*. As she goes to her funeral pyre, her courtiers pray quietly for Cupids to scatter roses on her tomb *(With drooping wings)*.

MAURICE RAVEL
1875–1937

hough Maurice Ravel wrote only two short operas, he loved the stage and motion pictures. In 1906, at the age of thirty-one, he was thinking of writing a full-length opera, possibly on Gerhart Hauptmann's play *The Sunken Bell* (eventually set to music by Respighi) or Maurice Maeterlinck's *Intérieur*. Perhaps because Ravel was a hesitant, painstaking worker, these major projects came to nothing. But he was also capable of acting on impulse, and meanwhile a short comedy—a great success at the Odéon—captured his imagination. This was *L'Heure Espagnole,* by Franc-Nohain (pseudonym of Ernest Legrand), a cheerfully amoral little farce. Such plays were frequently the basis of operettas, such as Offenbach's *Un Mari à la Porte,* but that is not the genre in which Ravel meant to write: he wanted to capture the spirit of Italian opera buffa without imitating its forms, and he was attracted by the "picturesque rhythms" of a Spanish setting. He had also been impressed by *The Marriage,* Mussorgsky's unfinished one-act opera after Gogol.

The title *L'Heure Espagnole* is a play on words, since *l'heure* means both "the hour" and "the time" as told by a clock. Therefore the work is referred to in English as *The Spanish Hour* or *Spanish Time,* but each version gives only half the meaning. The husband of the heroine is a clockmaker by profession, but in a colloquial sense he doesn't know the time of day. An hour is all his wife needs for a rendezvous with a lover more aware of her needs and nature.

Albert Carré, director of the Opéra Comique, accepted the work with some hesitation and delayed its premiere until 1911, when it was well received. Ravel's other opera, *L'Enfant et les Sortilèges,* did not follow until 1925. Though its mood is quite different, it too involves a grandfather clock. Ravel, whose father was a Swiss engineer, was fascinated by mechanical devices.

All his life, Ravel lived in a world of children and animals, suffering from the discrepancy between his own small physical stature and that of the rest of mankind. For *L'Enfant et les Sortilèges,* Ravel worked with the popular French author Colette: "Imagine an enchantress collaborating with an illusionist," remarked Ravel's pupil and biographer Alexis Roland-Manuel. Colette celebrated the natural world, Ravel the imaginary.

In her memoirs, the novelist recalled the origin of the project, suggested by Jacques Rouché, director of the Paris Opera, in 1917. She readily agreed to write the text and asked who would do the music. Rouché mentioned several composers, to whose names she responded politely, but when he came to Ravel, she could not restrain her enthusiasm. Rouché warned that Ravel was a slow worker. World War I, in which the composer volunteered as an ambulance driver, interrupted the opera's progress, and only a deadline from the impresario Raoul Gunsbourg of Monte Carlo, "the Diaghilev of opera," finally coaxed *L'Enfant* onto the stage in 1925.

Sortilège means "witchcraft, charm, spell," making this title as hard to translate as *L'Heure Espagnole. The Child and the Sorcerers* is a version often given, but there are no sorcerers in the story, only manifestations of sorcery—the transformation of reality through the imagination of the Child, who is the central character. Furniture and toys come to life, animals converse, and only a desperate call for his Mother puts the Child back in touch with the "real" world. "In this work," writes another biographer, H. H. Stuckenschmidt, "Ravel truly found his way back to all mothers, and therefore without doubt *L'Enfant et les Sortilèges* is his *summum opus.* It embraces all the characteristics of his personality, psychological as well as musical."

L'HEURE ESPAGNOLE

(Spanish Time)

ONE ACT
MUSIC: Maurice Ravel
TEXT (French): Franc-Nohain (Maurice Étienne Legrand)
WORLD PREMIERE: Paris, Opéra Comique, May 19, 1911
U.S. PREMIERE: Chicago, January 5, 1920
METROPOLITAN OPERA PREMIERE: November 7, 1925

L'HEURE ESPAGNOLE

CHARACTERS

Concepción, *Torquemada's wife* .... Soprano
Torquemada, *clockmaker* .... Tenor
Gonzalve, *poet* .... Tenor
Ramiro, *mule driver* .... Baritone
Don Inigo Gomez, *banker* .... Bass

The story takes place in a Spanish town at some indeterminate time in the past, perhaps as far back as the time of Boccaccio, whose moral is cited at the close. In his shop, the clockmaker Torquemada sits at his worktable, surrounded by timepieces. Ramiro, a mule driver in government service, arrives with a problem: his work requires him to be punctual, but his watch has stopped. Torquemada prescribes a complete overhaul, just as his pretty young wife, Concepción, comes to remind him he is supposed to wind the town clocks today. Excusing himself to attend to this regular chore, Torquemada asks Ramiro to remain there, saying, "Official time cannot wait." At first Concepción is annoyed: her hour alone out of the week seems interrupted. Ramiro in turn wonders how to make conversation. Showing him two grandfather clocks, she asks whether it would be hard to move one—she would like it upstairs—and he offers to carry it. As he leaves, Concepción welcomes her lover Gonzalve, a poet; but instead of using the fleeting moments to make love, he waxes poetic about clocks and the idea of time, declaring he will compose a sonnet *(Cette image est très poétique!)*. When Ramiro returns from his errand, Concepción asks him to bring the clock back and take the other one up instead. She tells Gonzalve to hide inside the second clock: that way he will be transported to her room *(Oui, c'est fou, je te le concède)*. Still spouting poetry, he complies. The banker Don Inigo Gomez drops in, hinting he arranged Torquemada's appointment as town clockwinder so he could visit Concepción *(Dieu m'en garde!)*. Nervous about the hidden Gonzalve, she puts off these advances. Ramiro reappears and lifts the second clock without difficulty. Excusing herself from her new visitor, Concepción explains, "The mechanism is very delicate," and she must accompany Ramiro when he takes it upstairs. Alone, Inigo feels momentarily rejected *(Evidement, elle me congédie)* but decides she is intimidated by his age and rank: to woo her, he will be more playful and hide in the first clock, so he does as soon as Ramiro comes back down. Ramiro, who is beginning to like Concepción, cheerfully accepts her charge to look after the shop for a while *(Voilà ce que j'appelle une femme charmante)*. He is soon asked again, however, by the apologetic Concepción to bring down the second clock: it doesn't keep correct time. When he obligingly goes to fetch it, Inigo makes cuckoo noises inside the first clock, trying to woo Concepción. She shuts him back in when Ramiro returns, then asks Ramiro to take *that* clock upstairs again, whispering to Inigo that it's a game. Ramiro takes the clock containing Inigo, and Concepción releases Gonzalve, who recites more verses *(Je veux graver ici nos chiffres enlacés).* Annoyed with his babbling, she takes leave of him, but he decides to stay inside the clock as Ramiro returns, once again prepared to watch the shop. Concepción reappears; seeing her flustered, and assuming that she is still not satisfied with her choice of clocks, Ramiro goes once more to change them. Concepción fumes about the ineptitude of her lovers *(Oh! la pitoyable aventure!),* the banker being so prosaic, the poet so flighty. In frustration she beats her fists against the remaining clock, causing Gonzalve to step out, still reciting. When Ramiro brings the second clock (which contains Inigo), she begins to admire his simple strength and obliging nature. Saying she wants neither clock in her room, she leads Ramiro there as the two other suitors stay behind. Inigo laments his imprisonment, ducking back inside when Gonzalve emerges, bidding farewell to his confinement—but trying to regain it when he sees the husband, Torquemada, approach. In his haste the poet tries the wrong clock, but Torquemada suspects nothing and thinks he is lucky to have clients waiting for his return. As the "clients" admire the clocks, pretending they are interested in buying, Torquemada and Gonzalve help the portly Inigo out, aided by the returning Concepción and Ramiro. Since it develops that Ramiro passes the house regularly every day, Torquemada innocently asks him to give his wife the time regularly. Then the characters step out of their roles to tell the audience Boccaccio's moral: among lovers there's a place and time for the one who's able to do the job.

L'ENFANT ET LES SORTILÈGES

(The Child and the Enchantments)

TWO ACTS
MUSIC: Maurice Ravel
TEXT (French): Colette
WORLD PREMIERE: Monte Carlo, Théâtre du Casino, March 21, 1925
U.S. PREMIERE: San Francisco, September 19, 1930
METROPOLITAN OPERA PREMIERE: February 20, 1981

CHARACTERS

Child . . . . Mezzo-Soprano
His Mother . . . . Contralto
Louis XV Chair . . . . Soprano

Fire ⎫
Princess ⎬ .... Soprano
Nightingale ⎭

Bat .... Soprano
Little Owl .... Soprano
Shepherd Girl........................... Soprano
Cat .... Mezzo-Soprano
Dragonfly .... Mezzo-Soprano
Squirrel .... Mezzo-Soprano
Chinese Cup..................... Mezzo contralto
Shepherd .... Contralto
Teapot .... Tenor

Little Old Man ⎫
Frog   ⎬ .... Tenor

Tom Cat................................ Baritone
Grandfather Clock .... Baritone
Armchair .... Bass
Tree .... Bass

Other articles of furniture, numbers, shepherds, frogs, animals, trees

ACT I   At a country house in Normandy, around 1917, a boy of six or seven sits in front of his homework and declares he would rather be naughty than work. When his Mother appears and reprimands him, he sticks his tongue out. Leaving him an austere lunch of butterless bread and sugarless tea, she tells him to stay in his room until dinner, then leaves. In a tantrum the Child knocks down and breaks the teapot and cup. Then he opens the Squirrel's cage and jabs the animal with his pen; it escapes out the window. When the Child pulls the Black Cat's tail, it hides under an armchair. Then the Child grabs the poker, stirs up the Fire in the fireplace and defaces the figures printed on the wallpaper, tearing it. Next he tears his books. Finally he swings on the pendulum of the Grandfather's Clock, loosening it. When he goes to collapse in the Armchair, however, it moves away from him and invites a Louis XV Bergère (a small chair) to dance. Other pieces of furniture join in declaring they have had enough of this naughty Child. Racing without its pendulum, the Grandfather Clock talks and starts to move, frightening the Child; ashamed of no longer being able to count time correctly, it hides its face against a wall. A black Wedgwood Teapot and a Chinese Cup begin a dialogue in mock-English and mock-Chinese gibberish. Afraid and cold as the sun starts to set, the Child draws near the Fire, which spits a spark at him and comes to life, chasing him and threatening to melt him for his misdeeds. A gray figure representing the Cinders, however, subdues the Fire. Soon other figures appear, a Shepherd and Shepherdess from the wallpaper, lamenting the Child's destruction of their fairy-tale world. The Child begins to weep, and the Princess from the torn pages of one of his storybooks appears to him, then recedes from reach as he laments her loss (*Toi, le coeur de la rose*). Looking for the last pages of the fairy tale, he finds instead pages of mathematics, from which a Little Old Man appears, representing Arithmetic. Other figures, representing numbers, join him and lead the Child in a bewildering dance. The Black Cat comes out of hiding and scorns the Child, joining instead in a meowing duet with a visiting White Cat outside. This draws the Child's attention to the garden, where he finds himself transported.

ACT II Relieved at first to be outside, the Child is soon surrounded by complaints from a Tree, a Dragonfly, a Bat, and the Squirrel, all of whom he has wronged. Only a Frog has yet to be caught or hurt by the Child. Now the Child is afraid and calls for his Mother, but the animals surround him, declaring he should be punished for mistreating them. Scrambling to get at their victim, the animals begin to inflict injuries among themselves. Seeing a Squirrel that has been hurt, the Child takes a ribbon from his neck and bandages its paw. Now the animals recognize his repentance and his power to do them good as well as harm. Again they surround the Child, who seems to have fainted, and decide to carry him to his "nest"—back to the house—where his Mother will care for him. Imitating the Child's cry of "Mama," they try to call her, then leave him, revived and standing again, at the door, gently observing that now he is a good Child.

NIKOLAI RIMSKY KORSAKOV
1844–1908

*T*hough folk songs and dances and liturgical music were always plentiful in Russia, concert music and opera had a late start. Audiences for such entertainment were mostly aristocratic, and fashion decreed an imported product. It was Mikhail Ivanovich Glinka, himself an aristocrat, who inspired a new movement toward nationalism in Russian music. His most illustrious successors, Tchaikovsky and Rimsky-Korsakov, were rivals with different ideals. Though most of their works sound Russian to the outsider, Tchaikovsky was more inclined toward cosmopolitanism, caring for the world audience, while Rimsky-Korsakov remained something of a chauvinist. Of his fourteen operas (he himself wrote the texts for eight), only one, *Le Coq d'Or,* is produced abroad with any regularity.

Born near Novgorod, Nikolai Rimsky-Korsakov entered the naval academy at St. Petersburg in 1856 and spent most of the rest of his life in that city. Graduating in 1862, he embarked on a two-and-a-half-year cruise on a naval ship, making visits to exotic ports that helped develop his interest in musical coloration. (In his opera *Sadko,* visitors from various parts of the globe describe their countries.) Resigning from active duty in 1873, he remained inspector of naval bands for another decade and wrote a treatise on orchestration, which is considered one of the standard textbooks on the subject to this day. He was the first Russian to write a symphony, but in spite of his innovative turn of mind, Rimsky-Korsakov remained an academic and a conservative. From 1871 until his death, he taught at the St. Petersburg Conservatory, where his pupils included Alexander Glazunov, Anatol Liadov, Mikhail Ippolitov-Ivanov, Nikolai Tcherepnin, and Nikolai Myaskovsky. His most illustrious pupil, Igor Stravinsky, studied with him privately from 1903 until Rimsky-Korsakov's death, five years later.

The composer's fatal heart attack may have been aggravated by quarrels over the government's attempts to censor the text of his last opera, *Le Coq d'Or*. Though no revolutionary, Rimsky-Korsakov was impatient with bureaucratic inefficiency and stolidity, committed as he was to doing everything in as professional a way as possible. Usually known by its French title, the opera is in fact a satire on inept monarchy; but the original text was by Pushkin, not Rimsky-Korsakov, and the composer did not want it violated. His work was staged in Moscow the year after his death and reached the United States in March 1918 via the Metropolitan Opera.

Apart from his compositions and theoretical writing, Rimsky-Korsakov is remembered for his editions of Mussorgsky's music, notably *Boris Godunov*—a labor of love criticized by many for its extensive meddling, but one that made Mussorgsky available to a much wider public than would otherwise have known about him.

LE COQ D'OR

(Zolotoy Pyetushok) (The Golden Cockerel)

PROLOGUE, THREE ACTS AND EPILOGUE
MUSIC: Nikolai Rimsky-Korsakov
TEXT (Russian): Vladimir Bielsky, from a story by Alexander Pushkin
WORLD PREMIERE: Moscow, Solodovnikov Theater, October 7, 1909
U.S. PREMIERE: Metropolitan Opera, March 6, 1918 (in French)

CHARACTERS

Golden Cockerel	Soprano
Queen of Shemakha	Soprano
Amelfa, *royal housekeeper*	Contralto
Prince Guidon	Tenor
Astrologer	Tenor
Prince Afron	Baritone

LE COQ D'OR (ZOLOTOY PYETUSHOK)

King Dodon . . . . Bass
General Polkan . . . . Bass

Sevants, soldiers, populace

PROLOGUE An Astrologer announces that through his magic powers he is about to bring to life an old tale, containing a moral for the observant.

ACT I   On the steppes of southern Russia, in the palace of the mythical King Dodon, the ruler has called his courtiers and advisers together, along with his two sons, to tell them the country is in peril. When Prince Guidon suggests they outwit their enemies by seeming to retreat, the better to prepare a counteroffensive, there is general approval except from General Polkan, who considers it foolishness. Prince Afron, trying to appear as brilliant as his brother, offers an alternative plan: demobilize the army and pretend to disarm, then surprise the enemy. When Polkan tries to talk sense, the king and courtiers berate him. Volunteering advice of their own, the courtiers fall to arguing about the best method of divining the future. At the height of their argument, the Astrologer bows to Dodon (*Slavenbud, velikii tsar!*) and offers the services of a Golden Cockerel that will crow in case of danger. Delighted, the king asks the price, to which the Astrologer replies that he will name his reward later. Dismissing his entourage, Dodon relaxes a moment with the Cockerel, enjoying refreshments brought by his housekeeper, Amelfa. She also brings a parrot, interpreting its squawks as praise of Dodon, then urging him to take a nap. This he does, accompanied by reassuring words from the watchful Cockerel. Lulled by the noonday sun, the palace guards and Amelfa start to doze too, but the Cockerel awakens them by warning of danger. Its cries also arouse the citizenry, who do not understand what is going on, though General Polkan quickly sizes up the situation: the enemy has them surrounded. The flustered king declares war and levies emergency taxes, sending his reluctant sons to military duty. After everyone has left, Dodon hears from the Cockerel that the nation's safety has been restored, prompting the king to resume his nap. Struggling to remember his dream so that he can pick up where it left off, he settles back, only to be roused by the Cockerel's renewed call of alarm. Polkan enters, telling Dodon the two of them must leave for the front, since the army is already gone. Cheered on by his people, Dodon struggles into battle garb and sets out.

ACT II   In a mountain pass, Dodon and the remnants of his army stumble in confusion upon the bodies of their cohorts, including the king's two sons. The soldiers notice a silken tent and prepare to attack it, but a glamorous woman appears from the tent and hails the rising sun (*Otvyet mnye, zorkoye svyetilo, svostokaknam prokhodish ty*). Awed by the sight of her, Dodon approaches and learns she is the Queen of Shemakha, who has come to conquer him—but not, she says suggestively, by military means. She invites Dodon and Polkan to sit down; conversation is strained, so she offers a few bars of a song, then asks Dodon to do likewise. He awkwardly begins a ditty, but she cuts him short, saying his sons, who arrived earlier and quarreled over her, were much better wooers. When he asks where she has come from, she describes a miragelike palace in the far Orient *(Da, dodesh do vostoka)*, ending in tears of unhappiness because it is only a dream now. Dodon tries to console her, and her mood abruptly brightens: she suggests dancing, at which Dodon proves inept. Winded, he stops and offers his kingdom to her if she will marry him. Dubious for a moment, she decides that it would be a lark and joins Dodon in a procession back to his palace.

ACT III   In the city, the populace waits apprehensively for news from the front. Amelfa tells of the death of the two princes, adding that Dodon has found a bride. Soon the royal procession approaches (march), and Dodon greets the Astrologer, who now asks payment for the Golden Cockerel: he names the Queen as his price. Dodon offers some other reward, then grows impatient and strikes the Astrologer, who falls dead. The Queen is unmoved, saying the Astrologer was properly repaid for his impertinence; but she also rejects Dodon, saying she is disgusted with the celebration. The Cockerel flies from its perch and pecks Dodon on the head, killing him. The Astrologer reappears, seeming to hold the Queen under a spell, and they leave together. The people mourn the loss of their bumbling monarch.

EPILOGUE   Once more the Astrologer steps before the curtain, this time to tell the audience that all the figures in the drama were imaginary except the Queen and himself.

GIOACCHINO ROSSINI
1792–1868

*T*he composer of over thirty operas, plus numerous pastiches and alternative versions, Gioacchino Rossini was one of the giants of his age. This stature was achieved during the first half of his life: though he lived to be seventy-six, he stopped composing operas at thirty-seven. His musical retirement marked the end of an era. Despite a kinship with Donizetti and Bellini, the other masters of the bel canto age, Rossini belonged to an earlier time in his tastes and loyalties, perhaps because as a boy he had been trained in the older school of singing. His colleagues could adapt to changing times, but he, though he outlived them by decades, chose not to try. Once he had written the paradigmatic French grand opera *Guillaume Tell* in 1829, he could go no farther along the path he had chosen; within a few years he saw even *Guillaume Tell* pushed aside as old-fashioned. Given also his serious health problems, and the sheer fatigue of a youth spent in constant work, one can understand Rossini's decision. He had had his day.

Born in Pesaro, Rossini was the son of small-time musicians. His father played trumpet and horn, while his mother, whom he adored, sang secondary roles with touring opera companies. Known for the purity of his voice as a choirboy, Rossini went on to the Liceo in Bologna and wrote his first opera, *La Cambiale di Matrimonio,* at eighteen. Working to order for theaters in various Italian cities, he tailored his operas to the singers and public tastes prevailing in each place, making changes to adapt these scores if they were later mounted elsewhere. His early works were predominantly comedies, for which he showed a special aptitude, but when he was asked for serious dramas, he gladly obliged.

L'Italiana in Algeri took Venice by storm in 1813. Written in twenty-seven days (some say eighteen), the work raised Rossini to the first rank among the musicians of his day. That this position was not secure, however, is indicated by the reception given *Il Barbiere di Siviglia* in Rome three years later. After the first performance, the opera caught on; but the premiere was disrupted, not only by onstage mishaps but also by partisans of Giovanni Paisiello, who had written an opera on the same subject. Another year elapsed before he wrote *La Cenerentola*, a comedic setting of the traditional Cinderella story. Less outrageously funny than the preceding two, it shows a greater warmth of human portrayal, and Cenerentola's final scene of forgiveness verges on *comédie larmoyante*.

In that same year, 1817, Rossini launched a series of serious operas, of which *Mosè in Egitto* and *Semiramide* proved especially notable. Though it seems long-winded and dramatically disjointed in comparison with, say, Donizetti's *Lucia di Lammermoor* or Verdi's *Rigoletto*—works of a more modern temper— *Semiramide* abounds in glorious music and shows how much could still be accomplished within the old opera-seria format. Rossini wrote only three more operas, all for Paris. The second of them, the delightful *Le Comte Ory*, uses music from the first, *Il Viaggio a Reims*, which failed in a run of only three performances. Finally, with *Guillaume Tell*, he bid farewell to the stage, writing only piano pieces, songs, and his *Petite Messe Solennelle* in the many years that remained to him.

L'ITALIANA IN ALGERI

(The Italian Girl in Algiers)

TWO ACTS
MUSIC: Gioacchino Rossini
TEXT (Italian): Angelo Anelli
WORLD PREMIERE: Venice, Teatro San Benedetto, May 22, 1813
U.S. PREMIERE: New York, Richmond Hill Theatre, November 5, 1832
METROPOLITAN OPERA PREMIERE: December 5, 1919

L'ITALIANA IN ALGERI

CHARACTERS

Isabella, *Italian woman* . . . . Mezzo-Soprano
Elvira, *wife of the pasha* . . . . Soprano
Zulma, *woman of the court* . . . . Mezzo-Soprano
Lindoro, *Isabella's Italian lover* . . . . Tenor
Taddeo, *her admirer* . . . . Baritone
Mustafà, *Bey of Algiers* . . . . Bass
Haly, *pirate chief* . . . . Baritone

ACT I   In early nineteenth-century Algiers, at the seaside palace of the Bey Mustafà, his wife, Elvira, complains that her husband no longer loves her; her attendants reply there is nothing she can do. Mustafà himself bursts in. Asserting he will not let women get the better of him (*Delle donne l'arroganza*), he sends Elvira away when she complains. Mustafà says he has tired of his wife and will give her to Lindoro, a young Italian at the court, to marry. Then he orders Haly (Ali), a pirate captain, to provide an Italian woman for himself—someone more interesting than the girls in his harem, all of whom bore him. Lindoro longs for his own sweetheart, Isabella, whom he lost when pirates captured him (*Languir per una bella*). Mustafà tells him he can have Elvira, insisting she possesses every virtue that Lindoro, in his attempt to stall, can enumerate (duet: *Se inclinassi a prender moglie*).

§ Elsewhere along the shore, a shipwreck is spotted in the distance, and Haly's pirates exult in the catch. Isabella arrives on shore, lamenting the cruelty of a fate that has interrupted her quest for her lost fiancé, Lindoro (*Cruda sorte*). Though in danger, she is confident of her skill in taming men. The pirates seize Taddeo, an aging admirer of Isabella's, and attempt to sell him into slavery, but he claims he is Isabella's uncle and cannot leave her. When the Turks learn that both captives are Italian, they rejoice in having found the new star for their leader's harem. Taddeo is aghast at the aplomb with which Isabella takes his news (duet: *Ai capricci della sorte*), but after a quarrel about his jealousy, they decide they had better face their predicament together.

§ Elvira's slave, Zulma, tries to reconcile Lindoro and her mistress to the fact that Mustafà has ordered them to marry. Mustafà promises Lindoro he may return to Italy—if he will take Elvira. Seeing no other way, Lindoro accepts, making it clear he might not marry Elvira until after they reach Italy. Elvira, however, loves her husband and sees no advantage in aiding Lindoro's escape. When Haly announces the capture of an Italian woman, Mustafà gloats in anticipation of conquest (*Già d'insolito ardore*), then leaves to meet her. Lindoro tries to tell Elvira she has no choice but to leave her heartless husband.

§ In the main hall of his palace, hailed by eunuchs as "the scourge of women," Mustafà welcomes Isabella with ceremony. Aside, she remarks that he looks ridiculous *(Oh! che muso)* and feels sure that she will be able to deal with him; he, on the other hand, finds her enchanting. As she seemingly throws herself on his mercy, the jealous Taddeo starts to make a scene and is saved only when she declares that he is her "uncle." Elvira and Lindoro, about to leave for Italy, come to say good-bye to the bey, and Lindoro and Isabella are stunned to recognize each other. To prevent Lindoro's departure, Isabella insists that Mustafà cannot banish his wife, adding that Lindoro must stay as her own personal servant. Between the frustration of Mustafà's plans and the happy but confused excitement of the lovers, everyone's head reels (ensemble: *Va sossopra il mio cervell*).

ACT II   Elvira and various members of the court are discussing how easily the Italian woman has cowed Mustafà, giving Elvira hope of regaining his love. When Mustafà enters, however, it is to declare he will visit Isabella in her room for coffee. She comes out of her room, upset because Lindoro apparently broke faith with her by agreeing to escape with Elvira. Lindoro appears and reassures her of his loyalty. Promising a scheme for their freedom, Isabella leaves him to his rapturous feelings *(Ah, come il cor di giubilo).* * After he too leaves, Mustafà reappears, followed by attendants with the terrified Taddeo, who is to be honored as the bey's Kaimakan, or personal bodyguard (chorus: *Vive il grande Kaimakan*), in exchange for helping secure Isabella's affections. Dressed in Turkish garb, he sees no choice but to accept the compulsory honor *(Ho un gran peso sulla testa).*

§ In her apartment, Isabella dons Turkish clothes herself and prepares for Mustafà's visit, telling Elvira that the way to keep her husband is to be more assertive. As she completes her toilette, Isabella, knowing she is overheard by Mustafà in the background, sings a half-mocking invocation to Venus to help conquer her victim *(Per lui che adoro)*. To make him impatient, she keeps him waiting, as her "servant" Lindoro acts as go-between. At length she presents herself to the bey, who introduces Taddeo as his Kaimakan. Mustafà sneezes— a signal for Taddeo to leave—but Taddeo stays, and Isabella invites Elvira too for coffee, to Mustafà's displeasure. When Isabella insists that he treat his wife gently, Mustafà bursts out in annoyance *(Andate alla malora)*, while the others wonder what to make of his fulminations.

§ Elsewhere in the palace, Haly predicts that his master is no match for an Italian woman *(Le femmine d'Italia)*. As Lindoro and Taddeo plan their escape, Taddeo says he is Isabella's true love. Lindoro is amused but realizes he needs Taddeo's help in dealing with Mustafà, who enters, still furious. Lindoro says Isabella actually cares very much for the bey and wants him to prove his worthiness by entering the Italian order of Pappataci (Silent Sufferer). Believing this an honor *(Pappataci! che mai sento!)*, Mustafà asks what he has to do.

*Often omitted.

Simple, says Lindoro: eat, drink, and sleep all you like, oblivious to anything around you *(Fra gli amori e le bellezze)*. Aside, Haly and Zulma wonder what Isabella is up to.

§ In Isabella's apartment, she readies a feast of initiation for the bey, exhorting her fellow Italians to be confident *(Pensa alla patria)*. Mustafà arrives, and Lindoro reminds him of the initiation procedure *(Di veder e non veder)*. After he is pronounced a Pappataci, food is brought in, and he is tested by Isabella and Lindoro, who pretend to make love while Taddeo reminds Mustafà to ignore them. A ship draws up in the background, and the lovers prepare to embark with other Italian captives, but Taddeo realizes that he too is being tricked and tries to rally Mustafà, who persists in keeping his vow of paying no attention. When Mustafà finally responds, the Italians have the situation under control and bid a courteous farewell. Mustafà, his lesson learned, takes Elvira back, and everyone sings the praises of the resourceful Italian woman *(La bella Italiana venuta in Algeri)*.

Il Barbiere di Siviglia

(The Barber of Seville)

TWO ACTS
MUSIC: Gioacchino Rossini
TEXT (Italian): Cesare Sterbini, after the play *Le Barbier de Séville*
    by Beaumarchais (Pierre Auguste Caron)
WORLD PREMIERE: Rome, Teatro Argentina, February 2, 1816
U.S. PREMIERE: New York, Park Theatre, May 17, 1819
METROPOLITAN OPERA PREMIERE: November 23, 1883

CHARACTERS

Rosina, *ward of Dr. Bartolo* . . . . Soprano or Mezzo-Soprano
Berta, *Bartolo's maid* . . . . Soprano
Count Almaviva, *alias "Lindoro"* . . . . Tenor
Figaro, *barber* . . . . Baritone
Dr. Bartolo, *physician* . . . . Bass
Don Basilio, *music teacher* . . . . Bass
Fiorello, *servant of the count* . . . . Bass
                Servants, policemen, soldiers, notary

ACT I In a square in seventeenth-century Seville, the young Count Almaviva arrives by the early morning light with his servant Fiorello and some musicians to serenade a girl who has caught his fancy. Almaviva offers a song (*Ecco ridente*) but sees no sign of his beloved. The town barber, Figaro, soon arrives on the scene, telling how his trade keeps him running everywhere (*Largo al factotum*). When Almaviva says he wants to woo a girl he has seen in the Prado, Figaro identifies her as Rosina, ward of a crotchety doctor, Dr. Bartolo, and offers to help, since he has access to the household. Rosina at last shows herself on a balcony. She has a letter for her unknown admirer, which Bartolo discovers when he comes to see what she is doing. She drops the letter "accidentally" and asks Bartolo to go down and retrieve it. He cannot find it, because Almaviva and Figaro have it. They read Rosina's description of her predicament with her jealous guardian and her request that her suitor identify himself. When Bartolo is overheard saying he will marry his ward himself, Figaro realizes there is no time to lose. The musicians have left, so he fetches his guitar to accompany Almaviva in another serenade (*Se il mio nome*), in which the count identifies himself as "Lindoro," but Rosina disappears suddenly from her window. When Figaro seems hesitant about how to further the count's courtship, Almaviva promises payment; the idea of gold, Figaro says, stimulates his genius (*All'idea di quel metallo*). His first plan is to disguise Almaviva as a soldier in order to get him inside Bartolo's house. The two agree to meet at Figaro's barbershop and there set the scheme in motion.

§ Inside the house, Rosina resolves that Lindoro will be hers (*Una voce poco fa*). She is confident of Figaro's help, but his attempts to talk with her are frustrated by Bartolo's appearance. He is trying to get to the bottom of the intrigue that he feels sure is afoot. His first solid clue comes from the music master Don Basilio, who enters with news that Almaviva is courting Rosina. Basilio suggests slander as the means for ruining the count's plans and reputation (*La calunnia*). Bartolo likes the idea but thinks it would settle matters even faster to have a marriage contract drawn up as soon as possible between Rosina and himself. Figaro, hiding, overhears this and, as soon as the two men leave, informs Rosina. When she asks about her suitor, Figaro says he is his cousin, Lindoro (duet: *Dunque io son*). When Figaro suggests that Rosina send a note to Lindoro, Rosina gives him one she has already written. Bartolo reappears, accusing her of writing to her admirer; when she denies it, he warns her that a learned man is not so easily fooled (*A un dottor della mia sorte*). Though he threatens to lock her in, she defies him. When both have left the room, the maid, Berta, admits Almaviva, disguised as an army officer. Bartolo reappears, suspicious; Almaviva, acting drunk, says he has been assigned to board there. Bartolo claims he has a certificate of exemption from housing the military; as he looks for it, the count slips Rosina a note. Bartolo sees this byplay and demands that she surrender the note, but she substitutes a laundry list; meanwhile, Almaviva turns belligerent, threatening to fight Bartolo. Hearing the commotion, Figaro comes in and tries to get Almaviva to quiet down (*Che cosa accadde*). Soon the civil-guard patrol comes to the door and starts to arrest Almaviva, who privately identifies himself to the officer in charge. Dumbfounded by all these goings-on, Bartolo stands as if petrified, to the amusement of the others (ensemble: *Freddo ed immobile*).

Act II In his study, Bartolo wonders whether the drunken soldier was a spy for Almaviva. The latter returns, disguised as a music master, Don Alonso (*Pace e gioia*), sent to replace the ailing Basilio for Rosina's voice lesson. To throw Bartolo off the scent and earn his confidence, "Alonso" shows him a letter from Rosina to Count Almaviva, saying he found it at Almaviva's lodgings. Bartolo fetches Rosina and sits down to hear her lesson, an air from the popular opera *The Useless Precaution*, proclaiming that love will surmount all obstacles (*Contro un cor*). Bartolo dislikes the song and sings one from his own youth (*Quando mi sei vicina*), addressing it to Rosina. Figaro arrives to shave Bartolo, insisting that he cannot perform the chore any other time. When the annoyed Bartolo sends him to fetch a towel, Figaro breaks some crockery down the hallway, complaining that the house is too dark with the shutters closed; he slips "Alonso" the key to the balcony, then starts to shave Bartolo. Basilio unexpectedly appears, but a bribe persuades him to go home and take care of his "fever." Figaro covers Bartolo with lather, so that the lovers can resume their lesson and whisper their escape plans: Figaro and the count will come for Rosina at midnight. Bartolo overhears enough to accuse them of scheming (*Bricconi! birbanti!*). The three others try to convince him he is having a seizure, then leave him. He tells his servants to fetch Basilio, then withdraws. The maid, Berta, reflects on the madness that love inspires in people of all ages (*Il vecchiotto cerca moglie*). Bartolo returns with Basilio, whom he questions about "Alonso." When Basilio says the impostor must have been Almaviva, Bartolo sees that it is more urgent than ever to draw up a marriage contract. Basilio goes to find a notary, though it is raining, and Bartolo calls for Rosina, triumphantly telling her that Lindoro and Figaro are just hirelings of Count Almaviva. As proof of Lindoro's insincerity, Bartolo produces her letter to him, saying Lindoro left it at a girl friend's house as a joke. Disillusioned and furious, Rosina agrees to marry Bartolo that very night and gives away the escape plan. Bartolo says he will have Figaro and Lindoro arrested as burglars. The two go to their rooms as a thunderstorm breaks. When it subsides, Almaviva and Figaro gain the balcony by a ladder. Rosina denounces her suitor, but when he explains that he himself is Almaviva, her rage turns to delight (trio: *Ah! qual colpo inaspettato!*), as Figaro reminds the lovers to hurry. When they finally go to the balcony, they find that the ladder has been removed. Almaviva and Rosina hide as Basilio enters with a notary, with whom Figaro pretending to be Bartolo, makes arrangements to marry

Almaviva to his "niece." Once again Almaviva bribes Basilio, who witnesses the document, along with Figaro, as the lovers are pronounced man and wife. Bartolo bursts in with the civil guard, but again Almaviva reveals his identity, and Bartolo is faced with a fait accompli. When he learns that no dowry is expected, he accepts the situation and gives his blessing. All express their relief at the happy outcome (Figaro: *Di sì felice innesto*).

LA CENERENTOLA

(Cinderella)

TWO ACTS
MUSIC: Gioacchino Rossini
TEXT (Italian): Jacopo Ferretti, after *Cendrillon,* a French libretto
  by Charles Guillaume Étienne
WORLD PREMIERE: Rome, Teatro Valle, January 25, 1817
U.S. PREMIERE: New York, Park Theatre, June 27, 1826

CHARACTERS

Angelina (Cenerentola)........................ Mezzo-Soprano
Clorinda ⎫ *her stepsisters* .... ⎧ Soprano
Tisbe ⎭   ⎩ Mezzo-Soprano
Don Magnifico, *their father* .... Bass
Don Ramiro, *prince* .... Tenor
Dandini, *his valet* .... Baritone
Alidoro, *his tutor* .... Bass
        Servants, ball guests, courtiers

ACT I The action takes place in the late eighteenth or early nineteenth century. In the run-down mansion of Don Magnifico, baron of Montefiascone, his two daughters, Clorinda and Tisbe, try on finery while Cenerentola (Cinderella), his stepdaughter, who serves as the family maid, sings a forlorn ditty about a king who found a wife among the common folk *(Una volta c'era un re)*. When a beggar appears, the stepsisters want to send him away, but Cenerentola offers him bread and coffee. While he stands by the door, several courtiers arrive to announce that Prince Ramiro will soon pay a visit: he is looking for the most beautiful girl in the land to be his bride. The sisters order Cenerentola to fetch them more jewels. Magnifico, awakened by the commotion, comes to investigate, scolding the girls *(Miei rampolli femminini)* for interrupting his dream of a donkey that sprouted wings. When he learns of the prince's visit, he exhorts the girls to save the family fortunes by capturing the young man's fancy. All retire to their rooms, and Prince Ramiro—disguised as his own valet—arrives alone, so as to see the women of the household without their knowing who he is. Cenerentola is startled by the handsome stranger, and each admires the other (duet: *Una grazia, un certo incanto*). Asked who she is, Cenerentola gives a flustered explanation about her mother's death and her own servile position, then excuses herself to respond to her stepsisters' call. When Magnifico enters, Ramiro says the prince will be along shortly. Magnifico fetches Clorinda and Tisbe, and they greet Dandini—the prince's valet, disguised as the prince himself—playing his role to the hilt as he searches for the fairest in the realm *(Come un'ape ne' giorni d'aprile)*. The sisters fawn over Dandini, who invites them to a ball. Don Magnifico also prepares to leave, arguing with Cenerentola, who does not want to be left behind (quintet: *Signor, una parola*). Ramiro notes how badly Cenerentola is treated. His tutor, Alidoro, still dressed as the beggar who came earlier, reads from a census list and asks for the third daughter of the household. Magnifico denies that she is still alive. Once Dandini has left with Magnifico, Alidoro tells Cenerentola that she is to accompany him to the ball. Casting off his rags, he identifies himself as a member of the court and assures the girl that heaven will reward her purity of heart *(Là del ciel nell' arcano profondo)*.

§ Dandini, still posing as the prince, escorts the two sisters into the royal country house and offers Magnifico a tour of the wine cellar, hoping to get him drunk. Dandini disentangles himself from the sisters and says he will see them later.

§ In a drawing room of the palace, Magnifico is hailed as the prince's new wine counselor. No one, he decrees, shall mix a drop of water with any wine for the next fifteen years. Looking forward to the feast, he and his attendants leave. Dandini reports to the prince with his negative opinion of the two sisters. This confuses Ramiro, who has heard Alidoro speak well of one of Magnifico's daughters. Clorinda and Tisbe rejoin Dandini; when he offers Ramiro as an escort for one of them, they turn their noses up at a mere groom. Alidoro announces the arrival of an unknown, veiled lady. Ramiro recognizes something in her voice. When she lifts her veil, he and Dandini, as well as the sisters, sense there is something familiar about her appearance. Their confusion is shared by Magnifico, who comes to announce supper and notices the newcomer's resemblance to Cenerentola. All feel they are in a dream but on the verge of being awakened by some rude shock *(Mi par d'essere sognando)*.

ACT II   In a room of the palace, Magnifico stews over this new threat to his daughters' eligibility, telling them not to forget his importance when either of them ascends the throne *(Sia qualunque delle figlie)*. He leaves with the girls, whereupon Ramiro wanders in, smitten with the newly arrived guest because of her resemblance to the girl he met that morning. He conceals himself as Dandini arrives with the magnificently attired Cenerentola, courting her. She politely declines, saying she is in love with someone else—his groom. At this the delighted Ramiro steps forth. To test his sincerity, she gives him one of a pair of matching bracelets, saying that if he really cares for her, he will find her. After she leaves, Ramiro, with Alidoro's encouragement, calls his men together, so that the search can begin.

§ Once again the prince's valet, Dandini, faces Magnifico, who still believes he is the prince and insists that he decide which daughter to marry. Dandini assures him that he is a valet (duet: *Un segreto d'importanza*). When Magnifico turns indignant, Dandini orders him out of the palace.

§ At Magnifico's house, Cenerentola, once more in rags, tends the fire and sings her ballad *(Una volta c'era un re)*. Magnifico and the sisters return, all in a vile mood, and order Cenerentola to prepare supper. She obeys, as a thunderstorm rages. Dandini appears at the door, saying the prince's carriage has overturned outside. Cenerentola, bringing a chair for the prince, realizes he is Ramiro; he in turn recognizes her bracelet. Confusion reigns as Magnifico and his daughters smart from their defeat; angered by such meanness, Ramiro threatens them, but Cenerentola asks him to show mercy (sextet: *Siete voi?*). Her family still against her, Cenerentola leaves with the prince, while Alidoro gives thanks to heaven for this happy outcome.

§ In the throne room of Ramiro's palace, Magnifico curries favor with the newly created princess, but she asks only to be acknowledged at last as his daughter. Secure in her happiness, she asks the prince to forgive Magnifico and the two girls: born to misfortune, she has seen her fortunes change *(nacqui all'affanno)*. Chastened, her father and stepsisters embrace her as she declares that her days of sitting by the fire are over *(Non più mesta accanto al fuoco)*.

SEMIRAMIDE

(Semiramis)

TWO ACTS
MUSIC: Gioacchino Rossini
TEXT (Italian): Gaetano Rossi, from the French play *Sémiramis* by Voltaire
WORLD PREMIERE: Venice, Teatro La Fenice, February 3, 1823

U.S. PREMIERE: New Orleans, February 1, 1837
METROPOLITAN OPERA PREMIERE: January 12, 1894

CHARACTERS

Semiramide, *Queen of Babylon* . . . . Soprano
Azema, *Princess, beloved of Arsace* . . . . Soprano
Arsace, *Assyrian army captain* . . . . Mezzo-Soprano
Idreno, *suitor of Azema* . . . . Tenor
Assur, *Assyrian prince* . . . . Baritone
Oroe, *high priest of Baal* . . . . Bass
Ghost of Nino, *Semiramide's husband* . . . . Bass
Populace, soldiers, priests

ACT I   Babylon, several centuries before the birth of Christ.* The high priest Oroe opens the doors of the temple of Baal, as Idreno, an Indian prince, pays homage *(La dal Gange)* and Assur, a prince descended from Baal, brings offerings *(Si, sperate)* in hopes that the queen will choose him as successor to her late husband. Queen Semiramide (Semiramis) enters, hesitant, and there is a flash of lightning, whereupon the sacred flame on the altar goes out—an omen, according to Oroe, that the ceremony should not proceed. Arsace, captain of the Assyrian army, then arrives from the Caucasus in answer to a summons from the queen. He warmly recalls his beloved Azema, whom he once rescued from barbarians *(Ah! quel giorno)*. To Oroe, who welcomes him, he entrusts a casket from his dying father, containing royal documents and relics. Oroe hints darkly that Arsace's father did not die a natural death and must be avenged. Learning that Assur is suspect, Arsace faces the older man, who is not pleased to see him. When Arsace says he will ask Semiramide for Azema's hand in reward for his bravery, Assur warns that Azema is of royal blood, betrothed since birth to Ninia (Ninias), the missing crown prince; but Arsace only reiterates that his love will bow to no obstacles *(Bella imago degli dei)*. Assur admits his own desire for Azema, of whom Arsace calls him unworthy (duet: *D'un tenero amore)*. The two part, exchanging threats. Azema appears, rejoicing in the news of Arsace's return. Idreno, who also aspires to marry her, hears her say the queen will decide whom she will wed. Anxious about the outcome, Idreno asks her to believe the sincerity of his love *(E, se ancor libero è tuo bel core)*.

§ In the Hanging Gardens, the queen looks forward to seeing Arsace, whom she herself hopes to wed *(Bel raggio lusinghier)*. A message is delivered from an oracle, saying she will regain peace of mind with a new marriage; she inter-

*Historians have surmised that the figure of Semiramis may be based on the regent Sammuramat, who reigned 810–805 B.C.

prets this to mean her own. When Arsace enters, she says she is aware of Assur's ambitions for the throne and will not permit his marriage to Azema. Arsace believes that the queen knows he loves Azema, but the queen takes Arsace's protestations of love as being meant for herself.

§ In the throne room, Semiramide prepares to announce to the people her choice for their new king and her husband—Arsace. This comes as a blow not only to Arsace but also to Oroe and Assur, especially when Semiramide goes on to promise Azema's hand to Idreno. Lightning and subterranean rumblings indicate the gods' displeasure, while groans emanate from the tomb of Semiramide's husband, Nino (ensemble: *Qual mesto gemito*). Stepping from the tomb, Nino's Ghost announces that Arsace will reign, but only after certain crimes have been expiated and a victim sacrificed. Fearlessly, Arsace offers his services, but the apparition goes away, warning Semiramide not to follow until her time has come. The crowd wonders what guilty person has incurred the gods' displeasure (*Ah!Sconvolta nell'ordine eterno*).

ACT II In a hall in the palace, Assur reminds Semiramide that it was in order to save the throne for her that he arranged Nino's death fifteen years before (*Quella, ricordati, notte di morte*). In return she promised Assur he would become her consort—a promise she repudiates, saying that if her son were alive, he would help her. Assur is determined to be avenged, though her downfall will ruin him too.

§ In the sanctuary of the palace, Oroe tells Arsace he is actually the crown prince Ninia, believed to have died in infancy but saved by order of the dying Nino, who left a scroll identifying Assur and Semiramide as his assassins. Taking his father's sword, Arsace accepts the duty of avenging him (*Sacro acciar del genitore*). He will kill Assur, but to kill his own mother is unthinkable: perhaps the Ghost of Nino will spare her.

§ In Semiramide's apartments, Azema mourns the loss of Arsace, but when Idreno entreats her (*E tu, ingrata*), she realizes that her beloved is not yet married to the queen. Idreno hopes that Azema will eventually accept his love (*Si, sperar voglio contento*). Semiramide and Arsace enter, but he says the marriage cannot take place, showing her the fatal scroll left by Nino. Guilt-stricken, she bids her newly rediscovered son to kill her and avenge his father, but Arsace still hopes the gods will spare his mother (duet: *Giorno d'orrore!*).

§ Outside Nino's tomb, Assur learns from satraps loyal to him that their chance to seize the throne is lost: Oroe has frightened the people with omens. Assur plans to hide in the tomb and ambush Arsace, but the vision of an iron hand, brandishing a sword, terrifies him (*Ah! che miro?*). Fearing he has gone mad, his cohorts are relieved when the apparition fades and he regains his composure.

SEMIRAMIDE

§ In the vault beneath the tomb, a group of Magi awaits the traitor who will try to violate its precincts. Guided by Oroe, Arsace descends into the vault and conceals himself to await Assur, who appears with like intent *(Fra questi orrori)*. Semiramide in turn descends, armed, in hopes of saving Arsace from his rival. Wandering about in the dark, all three feel faint with fear (trio: *L'usato ardir)*. When Oroe says that the time is at hand to strike Assur, Arsace fells Semiramide, who has stepped between them. Oroe orders the arrest of Assur, who is horrified to discover that Arsace is actually heir to the throne. Arsace, in despair at having unintentionally killed his mother, is stopped from committing suicide by Oroe, and the people tell Arsace that it is the gods' will that he rule.

CAMILLE
SAINT-SAËNS
1835–1921

Charles Camille Saint-Saëns began life, musically speaking, as a nationalistic insurgent and ended it, at eighty-six, as an archconservative who looked askance at Debussy and snorted at Stravinsky. A child prodigy, he made his debut as a pianist at eleven. After studies with Halévy at the Paris Conservatory, he earned praise from Gounod, who wrote to him of the "obligation to become a great master." Saint-Saëns also earned fame as a church organist in his native Paris and briefly as a teacher, numbering Fauré among his pupils.

Writing with facility in most of the traditional forms, he remains best known for his concertos (piano, violin, cello), Third Symphony (with piano and organ), and a musical joke, *Carnival of the Animals,* which includes the famous "Swan." In the opera house *Samson et Dalila* has been more a recurrent than an established favorite, though by the time of his death it had received nearly five hundred performances in the French capital.

At first Paris was reluctant to hear *Samson.* Saint-Saëns was a recognized figure, but there was prejudice against the staging of Biblical subjects. Franz Liszt, to whom he was indebted for the invention of the symphonic poem (a form used by Saint-Saëns in *Le Rouet d'Omphale* and in *Danse Macabre*), was the first to do something about getting *Samson* produced—at Weimar, where he directed the court opera. In that same year (1877) the composer Auber had persuaded the Paris Opera to stage the first of Saint-Saëns' operas, *Le Timbre d'Argent,* which enjoyed no great success. "If they won't come to us in the

382

opera house, we must go to them in the concert hall" was Saint-Saëns' resigned reaction, but he never stopped loving the lyric stage, and his last opera, *Déjanire* (1911), was his twelfth. In recent years his *Henry VIII* (1883) has had occasional revivals.

Paris did not see *Samson* until 1890, at the Théâtre Eden, and the Opéra did not capitulate until 1892. In the latter year a concert version reached New York, and in January 1893 a staged version was given in New Orleans. The Metropolitan Opera first tried the work on February 8, 1895, with Francesco Tamagno (the first Otello) and Eugenia Mantelli as the protagonists. Absent from the Met repertory from 1908 to 1915, *Samson et Dalila* became a popular vehicle for such singers as Caruso, Martinelli, Homer, and Matzenauer.

SAMSON ET DALILA

(Samson and Delilah)

THREE ACTS
MUSIC: Charles Camille Saint-Saëns
TEXT (French): Ferdinand Lemaire, after the Old Testament story (Judges 13–16)
WORLD PREMIERE: Weimar, December 2, 1877 (concert form, in German); Paris, Opéra, November 23, 1892 (stage premiere)
U.S. PREMIERE: New York, Carnegie Hall, March 25, 1892 (concert form, in English); New Orleans, French Opera House, January 4, 1893
METROPOLITAN OPERA PREMIERE: February 8, 1895

CHARACTERS

Dalila, *Philistine woman* . . . . Mezzo-Soprano
Samson, *leader of the Hebrews* . . . . Tenor
High Priest of Dagon . . . . Baritone
Abimélech, *Philistine satrap of Gaza* . . . . Bass
Old Hebrew . . . . Bass
Hebrews, Philistines, priestesses, dancers, boy, messenger

ACT I In Gaza, Palestine, during Old Testament times. Hebrews gather around Samson, their leader, under the portals of the heathen Temple of Dagon, erected by their oppressors, the Philistines. Praying, they ask God why he has abandoned them, but Samson criticizes the weakness of their faith *(Arrêtez, ô mes frères!)*, saying they should never cease to trust and glorify the Lord. Abimélech, satrap (provincial governor) of Gaza, upbraids the Hebrews for refusing to recognize Dagon as their god and the Philistines as their rulers. Samson replies with fiery words, exhorting Israel to regain her freedom *(Israël! romps ta chaîne!)*, whereupon Abimélech attacks him. Samson grabs the satrap's sword and kills him, holding his retainers at bay while the other Hebrews leave. The temple portals open, and the High Priest of Dagon appears, shocked at the sight of Abimélech's body and the evidence of open revolt. Philistine soldiers explain lamely that their strength deserted them and that they could not give chase. Calling them cowards, the High Priest curses the Jews *(Maudite à jamais soit la race)*, but the other Philistines, awed by Samson's legendary strength, are in favor of giving back the land they are occupying. As they retreat, the High Priest reluctantly joins them. Some Israelites reenter, and an Old Hebrew leads them in giving thanks to God. Dalila appears with other Philistine women, gently hailing the return of spring. She greets the victorious Samson *(Je viens célébrer la victoire)*, reminding him that he has already conquered her heart and inviting him to visit her in the valley of Sorek. Finding her hard to resist, he prays to God for guidance, while the Old Hebrew warns against yielding to the foreign woman's allure. As her compatriots dance sinuously, Dalila sings the praises of spring *(Printemps qui commence)*, repeating to Samson that she eagerly awaits the renewal of their relationship.

ACT II   Night is approaching as Dalila waits for Samson in her valley dwelling. She hopes to use his infatuation to defeat him, avenging her people. As distant lightning flashes, the High Priest visits her, reminding her that Samson has struck terror into the Philistine forces and must be vanquished. She explains that during her past affair with Samson she tried unsuccessfully to coax from him the secret of his gigantic strength; tonight she feels confident that she will succeed, since absence has made him desire her more than ever. The High Priest calls on Dagon to bless her endeavor (duet: *Il faut, pour assouvir ma haine*) and leaves, saying he will return later. Samson arrives and admits he still loves Dalila. At first he tries to break off the affair, saying his religion and his people call him, but she says love is just as powerful a faith, one that opens her heart to his words like a flower to the dawn *(Mon coeur s'ouvre à ta voix)*. Once sure of her conquest, Dalila expresses doubts: he left her once before. If he truly loves her, he will share the secret of his strength. When he balks, fearing that the thunder and lightning are a warning from God, she spurns him and runs into her house. Unable to resist, he follows her as the storm breaks. Not long afterward, having finally learned that the secret of his strength is his long hair, she calls to hidden Philistine soldiers, who rush in and take Samson captive.

ACT III   Blinded and shorn of his hair by his captors, Samson is chained to a millstone and forced to grind wheat in a dungeon in Gaza. He declares his remorse and asks God's mercy for his sins *(Vois ma misère, hélas!)*, while other captive Hebrews accuse him of betrayal. Philistine soldiers take him away.

§ At dawn in the Temple of Dagon, the High Priest and Dalila lead the Philistines in hailing their deliverance from Samson. They sing the praises of love and dance a bacchanal. Silence falls over the gathering as the blind Samson is led in by a child. Dalila mockingly toasts him with reminders of love—and revenge *(Laisse-moi prendre ta main)*—while the High Priest taunts him, saying Jehovah should restore his sight. As Samson quietly prays for the power to vanquish them, the High Priest leads his followers in praises of Dagon *(Gloire à Dagon vainqueur!)* and tells Samson to kneel at the altar of the pagan god. As if to approach the altar, Samson whispers to the child to lead him between two pillars that support the roof. With the congregation preoccupied by another hymn *(Dagon se révèle)*, Samson tries his strength against the pillars, crying to God for a return of his strength. With a superhuman effort he pushes the pillars, bringing the temple down to bury himself and his enemies.

ARNOLD SCHOENBERG
1874–1951

*T*hough his name is now synonymous with the so-called twelve-tone system (serialism), Arnold Schoenberg did not invent it single-handedly, as many suppose, and many of his compositions are not written in it. Born in Vienna, Schoenberg felt the overwhelming influence of late German romanticism, notably Brahms, the Wagner of *Tristan und Isolde,* and Gustav Mahler, who became a supporter of his youthful compositions. Among these, the string sextet *Verklärte Nacht* and the giant cantata *Gurre-Lieder,* dating from 1899 and the early 1900s, exemplify the crisis of overwrought romanticism, which was about to surge into the Expressionism of the pre-World War I period. Unlike Richard Strauss, who in *Elektra* stepped to the brink of atonality, only to retreat afterward, Schoenberg followed his chosen path. Though in consequence he lost both audience and press, he gained the support of avant-garde colleagues, enhanced his influence by teaching, and wrote one of the definitive textbooks on traditional harmony, in which he pointed toward serialism as the next logical development.

Schoenberg's first two operas, the monodrama *Erwartung* and the symbolic *Die Glückliche Hand,* make use of atonality but antedate the composer's first fully serial work, the Suite for Piano (1924), in which all twelve notes of the scale are treated as having equal weight and are considered only in relation to one another, rather than in relation to a base tonality. This "system" is evident in such diverse works as *Von Heute auf Morgen* (1928), a comedy of almost operetta-like tone, and in the earnest Old Testament epic *Moses und Aron.*

The composer wrote the complete text but never supplied music for the last act of *Moses und Aron,* leaving the first two acts unperformed at his death, in California in 1951. A citizen of the United States for the last decade of his life, Schoenberg had converted to Protestantism in his earlier years but had formally reembraced Judaism in 1933, after his expulsion from a teaching post in Berlin and subsequent exile. His Protestant experience left him familiar with Martin Luther's translation of the Old Testament and broadened his perspective on religious and philosophical history. This is reflected in *Moses und Aron,* where the dialogue of two brothers focuses on the difficulty of expressing one's perception of God. Where Freud had suggested that Moses was really more than one person, Schoenberg suggests that Moses (speaking role) and Aaron (cantorial coloratura tenor) are two facets of one and the same person, each needing the other yet never able to resolve their differences, those between absolute theory and practical application.

Oratorio-like in concept, *Moses und Aron* is built on a foundation of traditional grand opera. For all the theoretical nature of the score's construction, it works well as pure theater. Hans Rosbaud led the world premiere concert performance in Hamburg in 1954; the stage premiere, also under Rosbaud, took place in Zurich in 1957. Though unlikely ever to become a repertory opera, *Moses und Aron* is recognized as one of the major musical testaments of the twentieth century.

MOSES UND ARON

(Moses and Aaron)

TWO ACTS (third act never set to music)
MUSIC: Arnold Schoenberg
TEXT (German): the composer, after Old Testament texts
WORLD PREMIERE: Hamburg, March 12, 1954 (concert); Zurich,
   Stadttheater, June 6, 1957 (staged)
U.S. PREMIERE: Opera Company of Boston, November 30, 1966

CHARACTERS

Young Girl . . . . Soprano
Invalid Woman . . . . Contralto
Moses . . . . Speaking Role
Aron . . . . Tenor

Young Man . . . . Tenor
Naked Youth . . . . Tenor
Another Man . . . . Baritone
Ephraimite . . . . Baritone
Priest . . . . Bass
Naked virgins, voice from the Burning Bush, beggars, elders, tribal leaders, populace

ACT I   Thirteenth century B.C. In the desert, Moses calls upon God and is answered by voices from the Burning Bush, asking the reluctant man to become a prophet. It is God's intention to free the Jews from bondage in Egypt, and Moses has been chosen to lead them. Moses greets his brother Aron (Aaron), who will have to serve as his spokesman, explaining his difficult ideas in terms the people can understand. Moses worries that the human imagination cannot grasp the unimaginable, but Aron assures him that love is the key to unlocking this mystery. When Aron praises God for hearing prayers and receiving offerings, Moses cautions that the purification of one's own thinking is the only reward to be expected from paying such tributes.

A young couple discusses Moses' having been chosen to lead the Jews. Because he killed an Egyptian guard, bringing retribution on his people, they are afraid he will get them into further trouble. One man expresses hope that the new idea of a single God will prove stronger than Egypt's multiple gods, stronger than Pharaoh's hold. The people reiterate this hope (chorus: *Ein lieblicher Gott!*), looking toward the arriving Moses and Aron, who keep changing roles, so that it is difficult to distinguish one from the other. Trying to explain how God can be perceived only within oneself, Moses grows frustrated by Aron's glibness, which seems to weaken his idea. Aron defies Moses, seizing his rod and throwing it down, whereupon it turns into a serpent; this, says Aron, shows how the rigid idea can be made flexible. The people wonder how this new God can help them against Pharaoh. Aron shows them another wonder: Moses' hand, which appears leprous, is healed when he places it over his heart, wherein God dwells. The people now believe God will strengthen their own hands: they will throw off their shackles and escape into the wilderness, where Moses says purity of thought will provide the only sustenance they need. Pouring Nile water, which appears to change into blood, Aron interprets the sign, saying they will no longer sweat blood for the Egyptians but will be free. When the water appears clear again, Aron says Pharaoh will drown in it. Promised a land of milk and honey, the people pledge their allegiance to this new God (*Er hat uns auserwählt*).

INTERLUDE   Moses has been gone for forty days. Unnerved by his long absence, the people wonder whether God and Moses have abandoned them (*Wo ist Moses?*).

MOSES UND ARON

ACT II At the foot of the mountain, Aron, a Priest, and a group of elders wonder why Moses is gone so long, as license and disorder prevail among the people. Aron assures them that once Moses has assimilated God's intent, he will present it in a form the people can grasp. To the anxious people who flock to him for advice, however, he admits that Moses may have defected or be in danger. Seeing them unruly and ready to kill their priests, Aron tries to calm them by giving them back their other gods: he will let them have an image they can worship (chorus: *Götter, Bilder unsres Auges*). A golden calf is set up, and offerings are brought, including self-sacrifices at the altar. An emaciated youth who protests the false image is killed by tribal leaders. Priests sacrifice four maidens, and the people, who have been drinking and dancing, turn wild and orgiastic. When they have worn themselves out, and many have fallen asleep, a lookout sees Moses. Destroying the golden calf as the people slink away from him, Moses demands an accounting from Aron, who justifies his indulgence of the people by saying that no word had come from Moses. While Moses' love is entirely for his idea of God, Aron says, the people too need his love and cannot survive without it. In despair Moses smashes the tablets of laws he has brought from the mountain. Aron denounces him as fainthearted, saying he himself keeps Moses' idea alive by trying to explain it. Led by a pillar of fire in the darkness, which turns to a pillar of cloud by day, the people come forth, encouraged once more to follow God's sign to the Promised Land. Moses distrusts the pillar as another vain image, but Aron says it guides them truly. As Aron joins the people in their exodus, Moses feels defeated (*Unvorstellbarer Gott!*). By putting words and images to what cannot be expressed, Aron has falsified Moses' absolute perception of God. "O word, thou word that I lack!" he cries, sinking in despair.

[ACT III (Schoenberg wrote no music for this act.) Moses puts Aron under arrest, accusing him of fostering idle hopes with his imagery, such as that of the Promised Land. Aron insists that Moses' word would mean nothing to the people unless interpreted in terms they can understand. Moses declares that such sophistry has won the people's allegiance to Aron rather than to God: "Images lead and rule this people you have freed, and strange wishes are their gods." By misrepresenting the true nature of God, Aron keeps leading his people back into the wilderness. When Moses tells the soldiers to let Aron go free, Aron falls dead. Even in the wilderness, Moses says, the people will reach their destined goal—unity with God.]

Bedřich Smetana
1824–84

*B*edřich Smetana, the son of a Bohemian brewmaster, showed an early talent for the piano but was discouraged by his father, an amateur musician himself, from pursuing an artistic career. Known for his interpretations of Chopin, young Smetana harbored ambitions as a composer. After the financial failure of his first recital tour, he sought the advice of Liszt, who helped him establish a piano school, and for a time it was successful. Finally, in 1856, he was offered the musical directorship of the Göteborg Philharmonic, in southern Sweden, where he remained for five years.

It was in Sweden that Smetana began his compositional career in earnest, showing Liszt's influence in the choice of historical subjects for tone poems. It was not until after his return to Bohemia, which had been granted a measure of autonomy by the Austrian Empire in the 1860s, that his historical subjects began to be nationalistic and patriotic. During his youth, the language of education and culture in his homeland had been German; it required a conscious shift in orientation for Smetana to devote himself to the emergent Czech culture. His sympathies had always been with national independence, and once he became involved, he gave himself to it heart and soul—not without conflict, for those were times when the mark of success for a provincial composer was to develop a cosmopolitan style.

In the first stirrings of Czech opera, the language barrier had to be breached. Operas were customarily performed in German or Italian, though there had been some attempts earlier in the century to launch operas with Czech texts. Smetana went beyond language to make his music sound Czech as well, mining a rich vein of folklore, less for its actual material than for its feeling and inspiration. Like Dvořák, he was able to invent melodies that sounded like folk tunes.

While waiting for the production of his first opera, *The Brandenburgers in Bohemia* (1863), Smetana tried a more direct path to public affection by writing a comedy, *The Bartered Bride.* There are popular dances in it—a polka, a furiant—and instead of heroic figures from history, ordinary people. The work enjoyed great success after a tentative initial reception in Prague; the composer, however, was frustrated, since he esteemed his serious works more highly and sought recognition for them.

Like Mascagni and Leoncavallo after him, Smetana had cause to lament being considered a one-opera man. His next stage work after *The Bartered Bride* was the quasi-historical *Dalibor,* a sort of Czech *Fidelio* with an unhappy ending. Smetana realized, however, that the public really wanted more comedy, so he wrote three—*Two Widows, The Kiss,* and *The Secret*—before moving on to one more historical epic, *Libuše,* in 1881 and a final folk comedy, *The Devil's Wall,* the year after. Cursed with deafness in his later years, the composer died insane. Meanwhile, the one opera that he considered overrated, *The Bartered Bride,* proved to be the right one at the right time—a voice for the Czech nation, heard round the world.

THE BARTERED BRIDE

(Prodaná Nevěsta)

THREE ACTS
MUSIC: Bedřich Smetana
TEXT (Czech): Karel Sabina
WORLD PREMIERE: Prague, National Theater, May 30, 1866
U.S. PREMIERE: Chicago, Haymarket Theater, August 20, 1893
METROPOLITAN OPERA PREMIERE: February 19, 1909 (in German)

CHARACTERS

Mařenka . . . . Soprano
Esmeralda, *circus girl* . . . . Soprano

Ludmila, *Mařenka's mother* .... Soprano
Háta, *Micha's wife* .... Mezzo-Soprano
Jeník, *Mařenka's sweetheart* .... Tenor
Vašek, *Micha's son* .... Tenor
Kečal, *marriage broker* .... Bass
Krušina, *farmer, Mařenka's father* .... Baritone
Micha, *landowner* .... Bass
Circus Barker .... Tenor
"Red Indian," *circus performer* .... Bass
Villagers, members of the circus troupe

ACT I On a village green in mid-nineteenth-century Bohemia, a fair is in progress. Mařenka tells her sweetheart, Jeník, that her parents have been arranging for her to marry someone else. She is determined to resist but fears that Jeník is not so steadfast as she and perhaps loves another girl (*Kdybych se cos takového*). When she asks about his past, a subject of speculation in the village, he confides that he is the eldest son of a well-to-do farmer but left home after his mother died and his father remarried (duet: *Jako matka požehnáním*). The two renew their promises of fidelity, then leave as they see the marriage broker Kečal approaching with Mařenka's parents, Krušina and Ludmila. Kečal insists that the proposed groom—son of Micha, a prosperous farmer—is a prize catch. Ludmila notes that Micha had two sons, one by his first wife and one by his second, but she is hesitant, because she has never met either one. Kečal reminds her that some years ago, to satisfy a debt to Micha, she and her husband promised their daughter's hand to Micha's son. Which son? The only one, Vašek, since the elder was a good-for-nothing and disappeared. Kečal sways the couple with praises of Vašek (trio: *Mladík slušný a mravů víc tichých*), but they still want to consider Mařenka's feelings. When the girl appears, Kečal asks whether she has a sweetheart—if not, he would like her to meet one. The parents assure her she can refuse. When she says she does have a sweetheart, Kečal says this obstacle is easily removed (quartet: *Tu ji máme*). Mařenka refuses to acknowledge the contract between her father and Micha, though Kečal shows her that it is already signed. The parents say they want Mařenka to meet the proposed groom, who Kečal says is very shy. The villagers reappear and break into a polka.

ACT II At a village inn, Jeník and some other farmhands are drinking beer (chorus: *To pivečko*). Kečal, watching from another table, remarks that wit and money are the only real forces in the world, despite Jeník's tributes to love. The young people dance a furiant and leave. Into the deserted inn wanders Vašek, who stammeringly reflects that his mother has ordered him to marry (*Má ma-ma-matička*). Mařenka asks whether he is Mařenka Krušinová's fiancé; if so, the whole village pities him, because Mařenka loves someone else and would deceive or even poison him after the wedding. She adds there is another girl in town who loves Vašek and would treat him much better (duet: *Známt' já jednu dívčinu*)—but Vašek must take an oath renouncing Mařenka, which he does. After they leave, Kečal reappears with Jeník, for whom he is trying to arrange a marriage with another girl. Jeník refuses to give up Mařenka, but Kečal urges him to be practical, offering him 300 gulden to get out of the way; Jeník accepts on the condition that Mařenka not marry anyone but Tobias, Micha's son (duet: *Nuže, milý chasníku*)—and that when the marriage takes place, the debt Mařenka's father owes to Micha shall be canceled. Kečal agrees and leaves Jeník to muse on his love for Mařenka, whom he would not really give up for anything (*Jak možná věřit*). Kečal brings witnesses for the agreement, including Krušina, who at first thanks Jeník for his generosity but turns against him, as do the other villagers, on learning that he did it for money.

ACT III   Back on the village green, Vašek fears that Mařenka might try to do away with him (*To-to mi v hlavě leží*). A Circus Barker announces a performance by a traveling troupe, starring the tightrope dancer Esmeralda, a "real East Indian," and a bear from America. Vašek is taken with the glamorous Esmeralda; when the Indian informs the Barker that the man who usually plays the bear has gotten drunk, the Barker entices Vašek to wear the bear costume (duet: *Milost-né zvířátiko*). When the players leave to prepare for their act, Vašek's parents find him and ask him to sign the marriage contract, but Vašek balks, saying a pretty girl warned that Mařenka might try to poison him (quartet: *Aj! Jakže? Nechce ji?*). He wanders off, and Mařenka enters with her parents. When she learns that Jeník apparently sold out for 300 gulden, she is heartbroken. Vašek is brought back and identifies her as the girl who warned him, adding he really likes her. Mařenka asks for time to decide what to do, and everyone urges her to decide sensibly (sextet: *Rozmysli si*). Alone, she pours out her grief and disillusion (*Ten lásky sen*). When Jeník appears, she refuses to hear any excuses (duet: *Tak tvrdošíjná, divko, jsi*). Her horror increases when Kečal enters to promise the cash reward and Jeník offers to persuade her to marry Micha's son (trio: *Utiš se divko*). The men send for all the villagers so that Mařenka can announce her decision. Thinking Jeník has betrayed her, she says she will do as he asks and marry Micha's son. Jeník presents himself to Micha and his wife, Háta, who recognize him with surprise as Micha's elder son: since there are now two sons, Mařenka must choose one. Understanding Jeník's strategy at last, she joyfully chooses him, while Kečal grumbles in defeat. When boys run in to warn that the circus bear has gotten loose, Vašek appears in the bear suit and is quickly led off by his embarrassed mother. Mařenka's mother urges Micha to welcome his son back and to realize that Vašek is not yet grown up. Seeing she is right, he gives his blessing to the marriage, and everyone celebrates.

JOHANN
STRAUSS, II
1825–99

*J*ohann Strauss, II, Vienna's Waltz King, made his reputation as a composer and conductor of dance music, as did his father and brothers. It was inevitable, after he had established his supremacy in that field, that he would be lured into the theater. During a visit to Vienna, Jacques Offenbach urged Strauss to write operettas. Eventually he produced sixteen of them, but the coaxing to get started came from Max Steiner, director of the Theater an der Wien. After producing Strauss's first two stage works with encouraging success, Steiner stumbled upon a property—a farce called *Le Réveillon,* by Meilhac and Halévy—that was to result in the all-time operetta masterpiece. Seeing it in a Viennese setting with Strauss's music, he hatched *Die Fledermaus.*

Meilhac and Halévy were librettists by profession, having supplied texts for Offenbach and for Bizet's *Carmen,* but this particular piece was a play, so Steiner turned it over to the Austrian versifiers Richard Genée and Carl Haffner, who tailored their text to Strauss's talent. Strauss retired to his suburban villa in Hietzing and wrote the score nonstop in forty-three days.

Die Fledermaus made its debut at the Theater an der Wien in 1874, a relatively sober year in Viennese history, following a stock market slump. Eduard Hanslick, the critic who served as the model for Beckmesser in *Die Meistersinger,* dismissed it as commonplace, and not until after a successful Berlin production did *Die Fledermaus* really take hold in its native city. It reached New York six months after the premiere and has been a favorite ever since.

DIE FLEDERMAUS
(The Bat)

THREE ACTS

MUSIC: Johann Strauss, II.

TEXT (German): Carl Haffner and Richard Genée, after the French
   play *Le Réveillon* by Henri Meilhac and Ludovic Halévy, based on
   the German comedy *Das Gefängnis* by Roderich Benedix

WORLD PREMIERE: Vienna, Theater an der Wien, April 5, 1874

U.S. PREMIERE: New York, Stadt Theater, November 21, 1874

METROPOLITAN OPERA PREMIERE: February 16, 1905

CHARACTERS

Rosalinde von Eisenstein . . . . Soprano
Adele, *her maid* . . . . Soprano
Ida, *Adele's sister* . . . . Speaking Role
Prince Orlofsky, *wealthy young Russian eccentric* . . . . . Mezzo-Soprano
Alfred, *singer* . . . . Tenor
Gabriel von Eisenstein, *Rosalinde's husband* . . . . Tenor
Dr. Falke, *alias "The Bat"* . . . . Baritone
Frank, *warden of the prison* . . . . Baritone
Dr. Blind, *lawyer* . . . . Tenor
Frosch, *turnkey at the prison* . . . . Speaking role
Dancers, servants, party guests

ACT I   Belle Epoque Vienna, around the middle of the nineteenth century.
A tenor voice is heard *(Täubchen, das entflattert ist)* outside the home of Gabriel
von Eisenstein, a well-to-do citizen, whose wife, Rosalinde, is the object of
the serenade. Rosalinde's maid, Adele, comes into the salon, reading a letter
from her sister, asking whether she can get the evening free to come to a party
at the home of Prince Orlofsky, a wealthy eccentric. When Rosalinde appears,
Adele invents a sick aunt and asks for the evening off. Rosalinde says no,
because her husband is due to start a five-day prison sentence for an altercation
with a policeman, and she doesn't want to be left alone (duet: *Ach, ich darf
nicht hin zu dir!*). Having recognized the voice of Alfred, who once courted her
at a spa in Bohemia, Rosalinde is startled by his audacity in entering her
home, now that she is married. Quickly she sends him off; he leaves, on the

condition that he be allowed to return while her husband is in jail. Eisenstein arrives home, arguing with his lawyer, Dr. Blind, whose bungling has gotten him a prolonged sentence of eight days. Since neither can get the other to talk reasonably, Rosalinde advises Blind to leave (trio: *Ach, mit solchen Advokaten*). She looks forward to a last meal with her husband, but their solitude lasts barely a moment: Dr. Falke, a friend of Eisenstein's, arrives, and while Rosalinde goes in search of some old clothes for her husband to wear to jail, he invites Eisenstein to the Orlofsky party—he can begin his sentence the next morning. Falke suggests that Eisenstein bring along his repeater stopwatch, which charms all the ladies *(Komm mit mir zum Souper)*. When Rosalinde returns, she is mystified that her husband seems cheerful and prefers to dress formally, in order to show his jailers with whom they are dealing. Meanwhile, in order to be sure of seeing Alfred alone, she tells Adele to take the evening off after all, then bids Eisenstein, a sorrowful farewell (trio: *So muss allein ich bleiben*). No sooner is she alone than Alfred returns; he sees that the table is set for two and opens the wine with another serenade *(Trinke, Liebchen, trinke schnell)*. Rosalinde resigns herself to her fate—which shortly appears in the person of Frank, warden of the jail. When Rosalinde pretends that Alfred is her husband (trio: *Mein Herr, was dächten Sie von mir*), Frank reassures him that going to jail is as pleasant as being a bird in a cage, and Alfred has no choice but to accompany him.

ACT II   At Prince Orlofsky's villa, the guests rejoice in the lavish hospitality (chorus: *Ein Souper heut uns winkt*). Adele is surprised to learn that her sister, Ida, did not send the letter inviting her. Orlofsky hopes for some amusement from a prank—"The Bat's Revenge"—that Falke is planning. It was Falke who wrote the letter to Adele, supposedly from Ida, who introduces her as the actress "Mlle. Olga." A "Marquis Renard," who turns out to be Eisenstein, is announced, and Orlofsy explains to him that though bored himself, he will not tolerate boredom in his guests and expects them to match him drink for drink *(Ich lade gern mir Gäste ein)*. His motto is "Chacun à son goût" and he too does exactly as he pleases. Eisenstein recognizes Adele in his wife's evening dress, but she laughs this off as a faux pas and subtly challenges his own alias *(Mein Herr Marquis)*. Frank, the prison warden, arrives disguised as "Chevalier Chagrin," thickening Falke's plot. Now Rosalinde, also summoned by Falke, appears masked as a Hungarian countess. When she sees her husband flirting with her maid, she nearly drops her disguise, but Falke restrains her. He introduces her to Eisenstein who lures her with his famous repeater watch (duet: *Dieser Anstand, so manierlich*). Asking him to take her pulse, she pockets the watch, then—to prove she is Hungarian—launches into a csárdás in praise of her native land *(Die Klänge meiner Heimat!)*. Falke tells the guests the story of his adventure as Die Fledermaus, "The Bat": three years ago, when he and the "Marquis" shared a bachelor existence, they went to a costume ball, after which the latter abandoned him, quite drunk and still wearing his bat cos-

tume, in the middle of a park. He was awakened the next morning by pas-
sersby who laughingly christened him "Dr. Bat." Orlofsky proposes a toast to
champagne, the king of wines *(Im Feuerstrom der Reben)*. As Eisenstein tipsily
befriends Frank *(Herr Chevalier, ich grüsse Sie!)*, Falke urges everyone to address
one another with the familiar "du" and share a spirit of affection *(Brüderlein
und Schwesterlein)*. A waltz follows, and Eisenstein tries to unmask the countess, but when a clock strikes six, he realizes he must hurry to jail.

ACT III   In jail, Alfred persists in singing, to the annoyance of the jailer
Frosch, who has taken advantage of his boss's absence to get drunk. When
Frank arrives, none too steady himself, reminiscing about the party, he can
find nothing but water to slake his thirst. Falling asleep over a newspaper, he
is awakened by Frosch, who opens the door to two unexpected callers, Ida and
Adele. Reminding Frank of his earlier attentions, Adele says she would like
his help to go on the stage. To prove she would be a good actress, she offers
impersonations of a farm girl, a queen, and a Parisian lady *(Spiel' ich die Unschuld
vom Lande)*. When "Marquis Renard" is announced, Frank shows the girls to
a waiting room. Eisenstein appears, and the men admit their identity—Frank
savoring the joke, since he personally arrested the supposed Eisenstein last
night and had him locked up. When Rosalinde is announced, Frank excuses
himself, and the real Eisenstein greets his lawyer, Blind, with whom he hastily changes clothes. Blind has been summoned by Alfred, who comes out of
his cell to meet him but finds Eisenstein instead, disguised as a lawyer. Rosalinde enters, not recognizing her husband and wondering what sort of explanation to make so as not to compromise herself (trio: *Ich stehe voll Zagen*).
Learning of Alfred's supper with his wife the evening before, Eisenstein becomes
more and more outraged. Rosalinde says that her husband was out on the
town himself *(Es scheint mir fast, als empfinden Sie)* and that she should divorce
him, whereupon Eisenstein sheds his disguise *(Ja, ich bin's, den ihr betrogen)*.
When she produces the watch, however, he realizes she was the "Hungarian
countess." Checkmated, he looks up to see Falke arriving with guests from
the party, jovially hailing "The Bat's Revenge" (ensemble: *So rächt sich die
Fledermaus!*). Eisenstein now believes his wife's tête-à-tête with Alfred was
part of the prank, so he can forgive her, asking her forgiveness as well. Orlofsky declares he will underwrite Adele's career, and everyone repeats the joyous
toast to King Champagne.

RICHARD STRAUSS
1864–1949

he son of a horn player, Richard Strauss grew up in a musical atmosphere. Though he showed talent early and was considered a *Wunderkind,* his youthful compositions reflect the ethos of romanticism and give little indication of the originality to come. When he was seventeen, his first symphony was performed; he was only twenty when his second had its premiere, in the United States under Theodore Thomas. A brief apprenticeship under Hans von Bülow in Meiningen seems to have introduced him to the ideals of Wagner, whom Strauss' father considered a fraud. After a trip to Italy, Strauss joined the conducting staff at the Munich Hoftheater in 1886 and wrote his first important tone poems, influenced by the aesthetics of Wagner and Liszt. These works, with their literary programs and dramatic depiction of events, led him toward the theater, and he wrote his first opera, *Guntram,* in 1894. Neither it nor *Feuersnot* (1901) matched his symphonic works in success, but by the turn of the century Strauss had reached the end of his tone-poem period and was ready to devote himself more and more to the stage.

It was with *Salome* (1905), a setting of Oscar Wilde's play, that Strauss emerged as an apostle of decadence and modernism. The work was banned after one performance at the Met in 1907, and when Strauss followed it with *Elektra* (1909), the critics swore he had achieved the impossible—a work even noisier, more violent, and more depraved than *Salome.* The presence of Freudian psychology in these operas, combined with their brevity and musical impact, made them not only shocking but timely, and they exerted a broad influence. Strauss showed no further interest in this genre, however, and went on to a romantic period comedy, his most popular opera, *Der Rosenkavalier* (1911), which offended some with its racy sexuality but conciliated most with its sugary waltzes.

In *Elektra* Strauss had begun his long collaboration with the poet-dramatist Hugo von Hofmannsthal. Whereas *Elektra* was an adaptation from Sophocles, *Der Rosenkavalier* was all original, vintage Hofmannsthal, as was *Ariadne auf Naxos* (1912). With *Die Frau ohne Schatten* (1919), both librettist and composer overreached their sense of proportion, but the public loved the gigantic, symbol-fraught work. It was Strauss's last major stage success. Yet *Arabella* (1933), their final collaboration (Hofmannsthal did not live to see it onstage), despite accusations of "arterioscle*Rosenkavalier*" from irreverent critics, proved substantially more than a backward look: in the context of rising Nazism, Strauss' ironic nostalgia had something to say about the vanishing past of the German-speaking world.

Strauss continued to write operas during World War II. The final one, *Capriccio* — really a chamber work — was meant to appeal only to the connoisseur, which it does with great success. Clemens Krauss' brilliant libretto, made to order for the composer's talents and concerns, explores the relationship of the artist with his art. As a retrospective on Strauss' life work, *Capriccio* shows him drawn back more and more not only into the preceding century (whose ideals had nurtured him) but to the age of Mozart, whose operas he had championed as a conductor in Berlin and Vienna. Though Strauss wrote other valedictories, notably his *Metamorphosen* for strings and *Four Last Songs, Capriccio* was his farewell to the stage, not by coincidence but by intent.

SALOME

ONE ACT

MUSIC: Richard Strauss

TEXT (German): Hedwig Lachmann's translation of Oscar Wilde's French play *Salomé*

WORLD PREMIERE: Dresden, Hofoper, December 9, 1905

U.S. PREMIERE: Metropolitan Opera, January 22, 1907 (semipublic dress rehearsal, withdrawn); New York, Manhattan Opera, January 28, 1909 (in French)

METROPOLITAN OPERA PREMIERE: January 13, 1934 (first repertory performance)

RICHARD STRAUSS

CHARACTERS

Salome, *Princess of Judea* . . . . Soprano
Herodias, *her mother* . . . . Mezzo-Soprano
Page . . . . Contralto
Herodes, *Tetrarch of Judea, Herodias' husband* . . . . Tenor
Narraboth, *young Syrian, captain of the palace guard* . . . . Tenor
Jochanaan, *prophet* . . . . Baritone
Slaves, soldiers, Jews, Nazarenes, Cappadocians, executioner

Galilee, ca. A.D. 28–30, outside the palace of Herodes (Herod Antipas, son of Herod the Great), ruler of Judea. Looking toward the palace from the terrace, Narraboth, a young Syrian captain of the guard, admires the princess Salome from a distance while a Page describes the moon with various poetic images. The page warns Narraboth that it is dangerous to look so fixedly at Salome. From a cistern in the middle of the terrace resounds a voice prophesying the coming of a great spiritual leader. A Cappadocian asks whose voice it is and learns from a soldier that Jochanaan (John the Baptist), a gentle man who came from the desert and had a great following, is imprisoned there for criticizing Herodes' marriage to Herodias, who is his own niece as well as the widow of his brother. Salome, annoyed by the noisy company and by Herodes' lecherous glances, comes outside for air and is struck by the moon's virginal whiteness. Hearing Jochanaan's voice, she is fascinated by his cryptic utterances and wheedles Narraboth to bring him up, though Herodes has strictly forbidden it. When the prophet appears, he calls for the man and woman who have perpetrated so many abominations; though he does not mention their names, it is clear to Salome that he means Herodes and her mother. Jochanaan orders the girl from his sight. When she identifies herself, he denounces Herodias again and tells Salome to go into the desert to find the Son of Man, for he hears the wings of death beating in the palace. Salome responds by praising Jochanaan's beautiful body and by announcing herself enamored of him. She goes on to praise his black hair and finally his mouth, saying she wants to kiss him. His revulsion stirs her to plead more passionately, so that she does not even notice when the distraught Narraboth, mad with jealousy, kills himself. Pronouncing her accursed, Jochanaan refuses to look at her and goes back down into the cistern. Herodes comes outside, rebuked by Herodias for looking longingly at Salome. He slips in Narraboth's blood and recoils when he sees the corpse, which he takes as a bad omen. Then he tries to tempt Salome with wine and fruit, which she refuses, to her mother's satisfaction. When Herodias hears the prophet's voice, she wants him silenced, but Herodes says he is a great man who has seen God. A group of Jews ask that the prophet be turned over to them, but they quickly fall to arguing as to whether he *could* have seen God (ensemble: *Das kann nicht sein*). Jochanaan is heard again, proclaiming the Savior of the world, whereupon renewed argument breaks out, this time joined by two Nazarenes, who describe some of the miracles attributed to this Messiah, including raising the dead; Herodes says this must not be allowed. When Jochanaan denounces the "daughter of Babylon," Herodias protests that she is being insulted, but Herodes reminds her that the prophet did not mention her name. He tries to change the subject, inviting Salome to dance for him, which she does not want to do. Recklessly he promises her anything, up to half his kingdom. Though her mother disapproves, the girl agrees to dance if she can name her own reward. She takes seven veils and dances, shedding them one by one and falling at Herodes' feet. When the delighted ruler asks what she wants, Salome says the head of Jochanaan on a silver platter. Pleased, Herodias reminds her husband he swore an oath. In vain he tries to dissuade the girl, offering rich jewels, but Salome remains adamant, and finally he orders that she be given what she asks. Herodias takes the ring of death from her husband's finger and hands it to a soldier, who gives it to Naaman, the executioner, who descends into the cistern. In a tense silence, Salome listens at the grate but hears no struggle, only a sound like that of the executioner dropping his sword to the ground in fear. She entreats the Page and soldiers to bring the head to her, but none will move. At length the executioner's arm rises from the cistern, bearing the platter with Jochanaan's head. Salome seizes her prize and, oblivious to those around her, addresses it *(Ah! Du wolltest mich nicht deinen Mund küssen lassen, Jochanaan!)*. His eyes, once filled with rage and scorn, are closed; his tongue, which lashed out at her, is silent; he is in her power. With extravagant words she praises the strange fascination that was his and wonders why he would not look at her *(Ah! Warum hast du mich nicht angesehen, Jochanaan?)*. If he had looked at her, surely he would have loved her, and the mystery of love is greater than the mystery of death. The terrified Herodes tries to get Herodias to come inside the palace. He orders the torches put out, and clouds cover the moon. Salome, lost in her obsession, finally kisses Jochanaan's lips and says love has a bitter taste. Herodes orders her killed, and the soldiers crush her beneath their shields.

ELEKTRA

ONE ACT
MUSIC: Richard Strauss
TEXT (German): Hugo von Hofmannsthal, after Greek tragedies by
   Sophocles, Euripides, and Aeschylus
WORLD PREMIERE: Dresden, Hofoper, January 25, 1909

U.S. PREMIERE: New York, Manhattan Opera, February 1, 1910
(in French)
METROPOLITAN OPERA PREMIERE: December 3, 1932

CHARACTERS

Elektra . . . . Soprano
Chrysothemis, *her sister* . . . . Soprano
Klytämnestra, *their mother* . . . . Mezzo-Soprano
Aegisth, *her consort* . . . . Tenor
Orest, *brother of Elektra and Chrysothemis* . . . . Baritone
Tutor of Orest . . . . Bass
Old Servant . . . . Bass
Confidante, Trainbearer, Overseer, servants

In Greek mythology, King Agamemnon, the leader of the Greek forces in the Trojan War, was killed in his bath by his wife, Clytemnestra, and her lover, Aegisthus, whom she subsequently married. Intent on avenging this outrage, Agamemnon's daughter Electra (sister of the late Iphigenia and of Chrysothemis) lives only for the day when her brother, Orestes, will return from exile, so that they can punish their mother in kind.

As the opera begins, servants of the royal palace of the House of Atreus at Mycenae stand in the courtyard discussing Elektra's strange behavior: she calls out her father's name, crawls and moans, disdains food and company. One of the maids, a young girl, reminds the others that Elektra is a princess and deserves better than to be fed with the animals, but the Overseer, an older woman, sends her into the palace, remarking that for all her degraded appearance Elektra calls the servants dogs and talks constantly of the "uncleanness" of the palace—never cleansed of her father's blood. When the maids return to work, Elektra enters, calling her father's name (*Agamemnon! Wo bist du, Vater?*) and reciting the details of his murder. When he is avenged, she says, she and her brother, Orest (Orestes), and sister Chrysothemis will dance solemnly around his tomb. Chrysothemis interrupts her brooding to warn that their mother, Klytämnestra (Clytemnestra), and her new husband, Aegisth (Aegisthus), are planning to imprison Elektra in a dark tower. Chrysothemis' own wish is to escape to a normal life (*Ich hab's wie Feuer in der Brust*); she accuses Elektra of keeping her bound to her old life, crying that she would like to have children of her own. In mounting exultation she pleads with Elektra to join her in putting this place behind them, but Elektra scorns her sister's lack of defiance. Chrysothemis warns her again: Klytämnestra has had a dream about Orest. Even now, beasts are being driven to sacrifice inside the palace. Elektra says she wants to speak to her their mother, but Chrysothemis does not wish to stay. The queen, bloated and drugged, approaches, hung with talismans to ward off evil. She starts at the sight of Elektra, whose words she does not understand, but seeing her daughter apparently less ferocious today, she comes forth, sending away her sycophantic Confidante and Trainbearer. Admitting that she would welcome a more understanding relationship with her daugher, she says her nights are riddled with bad dreams *(Ich habe keine guten Nächte)* and asks what sacrifice will dispel them. Elektra replies that her mother's nightmares will stop when the right sacrifice falls under the ax. Questioned about the identity of the sacrificial victim, Elektra says it is an impure woman, to be killed by an outsider. When Elektra asks whether Orest would be allowed to return, Klytämnestra betrays her fear of him, then berates Elektra for talking in riddles. At this Elektra speaks directly *(Was bluten muss?)*, declaring Klytämnestra herself is the one who must be slaughtered; she describes the deed in the same terms as her father's murder. Klytämnestra is speechless until her Confidante returns to whisper something reassuring in her ear; then she draws herself up and enters the palace. Elektra learns from Chrysothemis that Orest has been reported dead. Elektra refuses to believe it, but when she sees a servant hastening to fetch Aegisth, she tells her sister they must prepare to act in case it turns out to be true. They must use the very ax with which Agamemnon was struck down; Elektra has kept it buried. When Chrysothemis recoils, Elektra resorts to flattery, telling her sister how strong she is, how easy it will be. After the deed is done, she will wait on Chrysothemis hand and foot in a joyful new life. Chrysothemis, still horrified, runs off, and Elektra realizes she will have to act alone. As she gropes along the castle walls, looking for the spot where she buried the ax, a strange man approaches, saying he must wait there until summoned into the palace. He and a companion have brought the message that Orest died under the hoofs of his own horses. From the way she grieves for Orest, the man guesses her to be a member of the family: she admits she is Elektra. He then confides that Orest is not really dead. "The dogs of the courtyard know me, and my sister does not?" he says— and with a wild cry she recognizes him *(Orest! Es rührt sich niemand!)*. She gazes upon him in rapture, but when he tries to embrace her, she draws away, ashamed of the estate to which she has fallen, and describes the anguish of her long vigil. Orest senses the moment is at hand to take action, and she hails him as the redeemer of their family honor *(Der ist selig, der seine Tat zu tun kommt)*. Orest's old Tutor comes to warn them against giving themselves away, saying Klytämnestra is ready to receive him and Orest as messengers. A servant lights the men's way as Elektra waits in feverish anxiety, realizing too late that she failed to give Orest the fatal ax. Two screams are heard from inside: the deed is done. Amid confusion among the servants, Aegisth arrives, annoyed to find no one with a torch. With sarcastic obsequiousness Elektra offers her own services, leading him to his doom. After entering the palace, Aegisth appears at a window, calling for help as his assassin strikes. "Agamemnon hears you!" Elektra cries. Chrysothemis rushes out to announce that Orest has been recognized, loyal servants have risen against those faithful to the usur-pers, and blood flows everywhere. Elektra savors her triumph privately, unable to join in outward jubilation *(Ob ich nicht höre?)*. Chrysothemis' pleas cannot draw her away from her need to perform a ceremonial dance *(Schweig, und tanze)*, which she does alone. Suddenly, Elektra collapses dead upon the ground, as Chrysothemis cries for Orest's help.

DER ROSENKAVALIER

(The Cavalier of the Rose)

THREE ACTS
MUSIC: Richard Strauss
TEXT (German): Hugo von Hofmannsthal
WORLD PREMIERE: Dresden, Hofoper, January 26, 1911
U.S. PREMIERE: Metropolitan Opera, December 9, 1913

CHARACTERS

Octavian Rofrano, *young count* . . . . Mezzo-Soprano
Princess von Werdenberg, *Marschallin* . . . . Soprano
Sophie von Faninal, *young bourgeoise* . . . . Soprano
Marianne Leitmetzerin, *her nurse* . . . . Soprano
Annina, *Italian intriguer* . . . . Mezzo-Soprano
Baron Ochs von Lerchenau,
    Marschallin's country cousin . . . . Bass
Faninal, *Sophie's father, wealthy merchant*
    recently admitted to the nobility . . . . Baritone
Valzacchi, *Annina's accomplice* . . . . Tenor
Italian Singer . . . . Tenor
    Majordomo, innkeeper, servants, merchants, children, doctor, police

ACT I   During the early 1740s, the start of Maria Theresa's reign as empress of Austria, in the bedroom of the Princess von Werdenberg (the Marschallin, or field marshal's wife) in Vienna, morning sunlight shows Octavian Rofrano, a nobleman barely past adolescence, embracing the Marschallin after a night of lovemaking. The Marschallin, who is approaching thirty, indulgently accepts his extravagant declarations but says he must leave soon, since people will be coming for her levée. He ducks behind a screen when Mohammed, a Moorish servant boy, enters with a pot of hot chocolate. After the boy goes, the Marschallin scolds Octavian for leaving his sword in plain sight, then invites him to join her for breakfast and describes a dream she had the preceding night in which her husband returned home from hunting in the wilds of Croatia. As Octavian reacts with anxiety and jealousy, noise is heard in the hallway outside. Both lovers assume it is the Marschallin's husband, so she quickly hides the youth in the bed curtains. The unexpected visitor, however, turns out to be a country cousin of the Marschallin's, Baron Ochs von Lerchenau, who pushes his way past the servants unannounced. Though he greets her in courtly style, his manners are only skin-deep, and he turns his ill-disguised attention toward Octavian, who has slipped into women's clothing and poses as a chambermaid. The purpose of his visit, the baron says, is to formalize his engagement to Sophie von Faninal, daughter of a prosperous bourgeois in the city: someone has to deliver a silver rose to her, according to the custom in noble families. As the majordomo enters to announce visitors, the Marschallin says they will have to wait a few minutes; the baron continues his obvious attempts to make a date with "Mariandel," the disguised Octavian. Excusing himself to his cousin, the baron explains that while he is still single he sees no harm in pursuing the joys of Cupid as he is used to doing *(Macht das einen lahmen Esel aus mir?)*. The Marschallin suggests that Octavian would be a suitable bearer of the silver rose. When she shows a miniature portrait of the young man, Ochs notes the resemblance to Mariandel and suspects that the maid is a product of some nobleman's household indiscretion. His continued attentions to "her," however, are cut short by the arrival of a servant to help the Marschallin dress, followed by servants, merchants, and other visitors. Three nobly born children, supervised by their widowed mother, ask for money while a milliner and an animal vendor regale the Marschallin with their wares. An intriguer, Valzacchi, tries to sell her a scandal sheet. While a hairdresser prepares to work on the Marschallin's coiffure, a flute player begins his cadenza, and an Italian Singer launches into a tenor romance *(Di rigori armato il seno)*, punctuated by outcries from the baron, who is arguing with an attorney about his proposed bride's dowry. After this hubbub dies down and the visitors begin to leave, the baron looks in vain for Mariandel. He is drawn aside by Valzacchi and the latter's wife, Annina, who offer to set up a rendezvous. The Marschallin accepts the silver rose from the baron for safekeeping and bids him withdraw. Alone at last, she mutters good riddance to her boorish cousin *(Da geht er hin)* and comments on her advancing years, visualizing her next stage in life as an old lady. One cannot resist the inevitable, she concludes—but one's way of accepting it can make all the difference. Octavian, back in his regular clothes, enters quietly and is struck by her pensive mood, which he interprets as a wavering in her love for him. She asks him not to behave as most men do—more and more callously, as experience toughens them—and warns that time waits for no one *(Die Zeit im Grund, Quinquin)*. Sooner or later he will give her up for a younger woman. This he heatedly denies, but she says it is time for him to leave: she has to go to church, then visit her old uncle. Perhaps later they can meet again for a ride in the park. Hurt by her stoicism, he goes. She has a second thought about dismissing him so abruptly, but when she dispatches footmen to bring him back, he has left the palace. She sends for Mohammed and gives him the case containing the silver rose, with instructions to deliver it to Count Rofrano.

ACT II   In a reception hall of Herr von Faninal's pretentious mansion, the family governess, Marianne, stands by as Faninal takes his leave, since by custom the bride's father should not be home when the silver rose is delivered. When he returns, he will be escorting the groom, whom none of them have met. His daughter, Sophie, prays with naïve confidence that her marriage will be blessed by heaven *(In dieser feierlichen Stunde);* her mother is dead, and she feels alone amid the confusion and vanity of the world. Footmen are heard announcing the name Rofrano, and Octavian enters, ceremonially dressed in silver with a white powdered wig. Meeting Sophie for the first time, he recites his mission of delivering the rose *(Mir ist die Ehre widerfahren).* Entranced with each other, the two young people attribute their exhilaration to the beauty of the rose, which has been perfumed to smell real. Regaining their composure, they exchange family information and get acquainted. Their visit is terminated by the arrival of the baron, presented by the obsequious Faninal. Sophie is quickly disillusioned by his coarse behavior and innuendos about wild oats sown by the nobility; when he tries to kiss her, she protests that they have just met. He sings a maudlin waltz song *(Mit mir keine Kammer dir zu klein),* ending vulgarly, "With me, no night will be too long for you." When he leaves with Faninal and a notary to look over the marriage agreement, Octavian finally voices his indignation to Sophie, who agrees she could never marry such a lout. After a fracas has broken out backstairs, caused by the baron's servants chasing Faninal's maids, Sophie asks Octavian to save her from the marriage. As he promises to help, impetuously kissing her *(Mit Ihren Augen voller Tränen),* Valzacchi and Annina surprise the pair and summon Baron Ochs, who asks what they are up to. Octavian retorts that the young lady will not accept her suitor. Not taking this seriously, Ochs tries to lead Sophie off to sign the marriage contract, but Octavian stands in his way, calling him a dowry hunter and drawing his sword. When he sees that Octavian really means to fight, Ochs pulls his own sword and lunges clumsily. He receives a scratch on the arm and drops his weapon, screaming bloody murder. Amid further household tumult, Faninal wrings his hands in despair at the disgrace. He will not hear Octavian's and Sophie's explanation and insists that his daughter go through with the marriage or be banished to a convent for life. The baron, resting on a chaise, is approached by Annina *(Herr Kavalier),* bearing a note from the supposed chambermaid Mariandel, setting a rendezvous for the next evening. In better spirits, he repeats his waltz song but refuses to tip Annina, causing her to vow she will get even.

ACT III   In a private room at a rather disreputable inn, the innkeeper annoys Baron Ochs with his solicitousness. Eager to be alone with Mariandel, the baron—assisted by Valzacchi—shoos out the inn staff and tries to ply Mariandel with wine, which "she" demurely refuses at first, reminding the baron he is engaged. The baron starts to kiss Mariandel but recoils at "her" close resemblance to Octavian, whose memory haunts him. In the dim light he glimpses a face from behind a trap door—a spy planted by Octavian, in collusion with Valzacchi—and is further unnerved. As his servant brings supper and a small band in the next room plays maudlin waltzes, he regains his composure and renews the assault on Mariandel, who pretends to be getting drunk. Ochs starts to relax and removes his wig, but he sees another hidden face and rings for help. Now Annina bursts in, dressed in mourning, and accuses him of being the husband who abandoned her. She produces a troop of children, who call him "Papa." The innkeeper and his staff come to see what is the matter. Realizing he is the victim of a cabal, Ochs calls for help from the authorities, who appear in the form of a police commisioner with two constables. The commissioner, however, is unsympathetic and even questions Ochs' identity, about which Valzacchi pretends ignorance. Faninal, sent for by the schemers, arrives and indignantly denies that Mariandel is his daughter, as Ochs had tried to claim. He sends for Sophie, who comes in from her sedan chair to see Faninal threatening Ochs. Octavian takes the commissioner aside and identifies himself, then goes into the alcove to change into his usual clothes, poking his head out as the Marschallin enters. The commissioner, having been her husband's orderly, recognizes her. Though she has not seen Sophie before, she sizes up the situation and notes Octavian's attachment to the girl. Sophie tells the baron that their engagement is broken. Confidentially, the Marschallin advises him it is time to go home with what is left of his dignity. To the commissioner she explains that the whole affair is a joke, so he leaves. The baron realizes he should follow suit, especially when the innkeeper and waiters appear with a bill, but Annina blocks his escape and forces him to face the reckoning. Angry at Octavian for fulfilling her prediction so soon, the Marschallin tells him to go to Sophie. To herself she admits that her vow to love Octavian was made in the knowledge that it could not last (trio: *Hab' mir's gelobt*), while the two young people become aware of the depth of their attachment. Unnoticed by them, the Marschallin steps into the next room, where she joins Faninal and goes to her carriage with him, leaving Octavian with Sophie to wonder at their new-found love (duet: *Ist ein Traum*). They kiss and depart, but Sophie drops her handkerchief. A moment later, Mohammed, the Marschallin's servant, is sent in to retrieve it as the curtain falls.

ARIADNE AUF NAXOS

(Ariadne on Naxos)

TWO ACTS (PROLOGUE AND OPERA PROPER)
MUSIC: Richard Strauss
TEXT (German): Hugo von Hofmannsthal
WORLD PREMIERE: Stuttgart, October 25, 1912; Vienna, October 4, 1916 (revision)
U.S. PREMIERE: Philadelphia, Academy of Music, November 1, 1928
METROPOLITAN OPERA PREMIERE: December 19, 1962 (prologue in English)

CHARACTERS

PROLOGUE:

Composer	Soprano
Prima Donna	Soprano
Zerbinetta, *comedienne*	Soprano
Harlekin ⎫	Baritone
Scaramuccio ⎪ *her fellow troupers*	Tenor
Truffaldin ⎬	Bass
Brighella ⎭	Tenor
Music Master	Baritone
Dancing Master	Tenor
Tenor	Tenor
Majordomo	Speaking Role
Officer	Tenor
Lackey	Baritone
Wigmaker	Bass

OPERA:

Ariadne	Soprano
Najade ⎫	Soprano
Dryade ⎬ *her companions*	Contralto
Echo ⎭	Soprano
Zerbinetta	Soprano
Harlekin	Baritone
Scaramuccio	Tenor
Truffaldin	Bass

Brighella .... Tenor
Bacchus .... Tenor
Musicians, servants, party guests

PROLOGUE In Paris around 1670, a pretentious *nouveau riche* (in Molière's original play, *Le Bourgeois Gentilhomme,* he is Monsieur Jourdain) has commissioned an opera from a young Composer in order to entertain his guests after dinner. Amid backstage preparations the Music Master accosts the haughty Majordomo to confirm alarming news: a commedia dell'arte entertainment by a group of clowns, plus a fireworks display, will follow the opera seria *Ariadne.* The Music Master leaves, worried about breaking the news to his pupil, the Composer, who meanwhile enters from another direction, naïvely hoping to assemble the musicians for a last-minute rehearsal—but learning they have to play dinner music. He then hopes to rehearse with the Prima Donna but gets no answer when he knocks at the dressing room, which unbeknownst to him is occupied by Zerbinetta, chief of the clown troupe, and an admirer of hers. When a lackey laughs at him, the Composer bursts into a nervous tirade *(Eselsgesicht!)* but is calmed by a quick inspiration for a melody, which he expands with delight. A quarrel explodes between the Tenor and the Wig-maker, who burst out of the dressing room, soon followed by Zerbinetta and her admirer, then the Prima Donna and the Music Master. As the Composer wonders who Zerbinetta is, the Dancing Master assures her that *Ariadne* is a bore, adding that the usual routines will suffice to amuse the audience. When the Composer learns of the "low entertainment" to follow his exalted work, he is outraged, though the thought of his new melody still comforts him. As he jots it down *(Du, Venus' Sohn),* the comedians assemble, and the Composer turns accusingly to his Music Master, who counsels a stoical approach. Zer-binetta and the Dancing Master further plot how to amuse an audience sated with food and lulled to sleep by an opera seria, while the Music Master soothes the Prima Donna, saying her appearance is the event of the evening. In the midst of this the Majordomo delivers another thunderbolt: his master has decided to have the comic and serious shows performed *simultaneously.* Deem-ing the desert-island setting for *Ariadne* barren and tedious, he has decided that the comedians should enliven it. In shock, the Composer is ready to leave, but the Music Master reminds him of the fee they will lose, which would keep the Composer in comfort for six months. The Dancing Master takes a practical stance, suggesting cuts that would permit the experienced comedians to improvise. As the Tenor and Prima Donna each try to persuade the Music Master to shorten the other's part, the Dancing Master briefs Zerbinetta on the plot of Ariadne: the heroine has been abandoned on an island by her lover and yearns for death. Zerbinetta assumes she is ready for a new lover, while the Composer tries to explain her high-mindedness: Ariadne mistakes the newcomer, Bacchus, for the god of death. Zerbinetta tells her colleagues their job will be to amuse the grieving princess until her next wooer arrives. To assuage the Composer's fears, Zerbinetta flirts with him, pretending to have a deeper side to her character and to long, like Ariadne, for one love more serious than the others. As everyone prepares to go onstage, the Music Master tells the Prima Donna that the comedians' shallowness will set her art in favorable relief. The Composer, wishing to be friends with his teacher once again, says he has found courage to face the unexpected, thanks to the holy art of music *(Seien wir wieder gut!)*. But as he sees the comedians taking their place, he wishes he had chosen starvation rather than let this happen.

OPERA   In the period of classical mythology, Ariadne waits for death on her desert island. A trio of nature spirits—Najade (Naiad), Dryade (Dryad), and Echo—comments on her dejection. When she rouses herself, it is to wonder why she is still alive. She waxes poetic at the recollection of her love for Theseus *(Ein Schönes war)* and exalted at the thought of deliverance through death. Watching from the wings, the comedians think she is out of her mind and impossible to comfort, but they try, Harlekin offering a song about the resiliency of the human heart *(Lieben, Hassen, Hoffen, Zagen)*. Ignoring them, Ariadne describes the realm of death *(Es gibt ein Reich)*, where the burden of living will be lifted from her and she will be free, transfigured. The others of the comedy troupe—Brighella, Scaramuccio, Truffaldin—join Harlekin and Zerbinetta in offering a dance to cheer her. Zerbinetta decides to address her woman to woman *(Grossmächtige Prinzessin)* and sends the others off, but Ariadne retreats into her cave. Undaunted, Zerbinetta goes on at length about the fickleness of men and the failure of her own romances, concluding it was the thrill of finding a new love that made it worthwhile each time. Harlekin returns and flirts with Zerbinetta, while the others, unsuccessful suitors for her attention, lose sight of the lovers and search for them in disguises. The search eventually takes them offstage, and music is heard heralding the approach of Bacchus' ship. Najade, Dryade, and Echo run in, excitedly discussing his approach. Bacchus' voice is heard declaring that he has escaped the enchantment of Circe's island, where men are transformed into beasts. Ariadne comes out of her cave, believing that her deliverer has arrived, while the three spirits hail his voice in hymnlike tones *(Töne, töne, süsse Stimme)*. Bacchus climbs over the rocks and greets Ariadne, asking whether she is queen of this island, whether she is a sorceress like Circe. She replies she has been waiting for him. Perplexed by her talk of death and deliverance, Bacchus admits he is a god and the captain of a ship but says that her life is just beginning, that he will protect her from death. She imagines that this is his way of transfiguring her, a process she both hopes for and fears. Hailing him as a magician, she is told the magic is hers: he is the one transfigured, by his new-found love for her. They embrace and enter the cave. Zerbinetta tiptoes out to tell the audience she was right: a new lover is what it takes to bring about a happy end. The voice of the unseen Bacchus heralds the couple's immortality as their constellation appears in the heavens, symbol of their transformation into eternal form.

DIE FRAU OHNE SCHATTEN
(The Woman Without a Shadow)

THREE ACTS
MUSIC: Richard Strauss
TEXT (German): Hugo von Hofmannsthal
WORLD PREMIERE: Vienna, Staatsoper, October 10, 1919
U.S. PREMIERE: San Francisco, September 18, 1959
METROPOLITAN OPERA PREMIERE: October 2, 1966

CHARACTERS

Empress . . . . Soprano
Dyer's Wife . . . . Soprano
Nurse . . . . Mezzo-Soprano
Falcon's Voice . . . . Soprano
Temple Guardian . . . . Soprano
Voice . . . . Contralto
Emperor of the Southeastern Islands . . . . Tenor
Barak, *dyer* . . . . Baritone
Vision of a Young Man . . . . Tenor
Spirit Messenger . . . . Baritone
Barak's brothers, servants, beggars, spirits, voices of watchmen,
unborn children

The opera takes place in a mythical time and place. While hunting with a Falcon (a son of the spirit ruler Keikobad in disguise), the Emperor of the Southeastern Islands wounded a gazelle (Keikobad's daughter in disguise). She turned into a beautiful woman, whom the Emperor married. Keikobad has decreed, however, that unless she gains a shadow—that is, the ability to bear children—within a year, she must return to her father, and the Emperor will be turned to stone. Because a shadow is the mark of humanity, Keikobad permits a negative spirit, in the form of the Nurse, to interfere. Her function is to test the other characters, pushing them to realize their human potential.

ACT I At dawn outside the imperial apartments, the Nurse, keeping watch, is visited by the twelfth of Keikobad's monthly messengers: a year has almost passed, yet the Empress still casts no shadow. The Messenger warns again that if she does not do so within the three days remaining, her father will reclaim her and turn the Emperor to stone (*Nicht der Gebieter*). After the Messenger disappears, the Emperor comes to tell the Nurse that he is going hunting. He hopes to recover his Falcon, who flew away after the gazelle was wounded, but whom the Emperor now wishes to thank for leading him to his bride. No sooner has he left than the Empress appears and spots the Falcon, who repeats Keikobad's warning. The Empress begs the Nurse to help her find a shadow; this means descending to the world of mortals, which the Nurse regards with horror. When the Empress insists (*Amme, um alles*), the two begin their trip.

§ In the house of Barak, a dyer, his three deformed brothers are fighting among themselves. When the Dyer's Wife disgustedly throws a bucket of water on them, they turn on her instead. Barak appears and orders his brothers back to work. Though he speaks kindly to his Wife, he is disappointed that they have no children. She in turn is disillusioned: after two and a half years of marriage, she has not become pregnant, and in any case—considering his brothers' behavior—she takes a dim view of family life. As he leaves with a load of fabrics to be dyed, the Nurse and the Empress enter, dressed in servants' clothes. The Nurse quickly comes to the point: the Dyer's Wife could get a high price for her shadow. The Nurse conjures up a vision of luxury (*Ach! Schönheit ohnegleichen!*), and offers herself and her "daughter" (the Empress) as servants for three days if the Dyer's Wife will forswear motherhood, denying her husband her bed. In a manifestation of supernatural symbolism, five fish fly through the air and land in a pan on the stove, while the double bed breaks in half. The Nurse and Empress vanish, and from the fish in the pan the Dyer's Wife hears the voices of unborn children begging to be brought into the world. When Barak reenters, she tells him to eat—she is not hungry—and sleep alone, adding that two cousins will be staying there as of the next day. Unhappily, Barak listens to the voices of Watchmen outside (*Ihr Gatten in den Häusern dieser Stadt*), praising the sacredness of parenthood: "You husbands and wives . . . you are the bridge across the gulf over which the dead come back to life."

ACT II The next day, as soon as Barak has left, the Nurse (disguised as a servant) conjures up a Vision of a Young Man to tempt the Dyer's Wife. When the Empress senses Barak's return, the Nurse makes the vision disappear. Barak comes in with his brothers and some beggar children, all clamoring for a meal (*Schlag ab, du Schlächter*), but the distracted Dyer's Wife refuses to wait on them, so they have to shift for themselves.

§ Outside the imperial hunting lodge, the Emperor stands in the woods by moonlight, calling out to his Falcon, who has led him there (*Falke, du wie-*

dergefundener). The Empress has sent him a message to explain her absence, saying she will seclude herself in the lodge for three days with only the Nurse for company. When he sees the two women furtively enter the lodge, he realizes that his wife has lied about her seclusion and has visited mankind; he thinks of killing her. But he cannot do it and escapes to a more remote part of the woods, where he can lament alone.

§ At the dyer's house, Barak is slow about getting ready to take his goods to market. When he asks for a drink, the Nurse gives him one containing a sleeping potion. She causes the Vision of a Young Man to reappear. As the Young Man speaks of his longing, the Nurse urges the Dyer's Wife to enjoy the delight that puts one in touch with eternity, banishing fear of death. But by confessing her desire for a lover, the Dyer's Wife causes the Young Man to fall in a swoon (trio: *Bin ich dir ferne*). The Nurse causes him once again to disappear, as the Dyer's Wife wakes Barak and tells him he should be looking after her *(Hierher! Zu mir!)*, warning that if he does not pay attention to her emotional needs she may leave one day and not come back.

§ Sleeping fitfully at the hunting lodge, the Empress mutters that she has sinned against Barak (by helping divide him from his wife), then dreams of the Emperor standing before a cavern as the Falcon's voice repeats, "The woman casts no shadow—the Emperor must turn to stone!" As he seems to disappear into the cave, she wakes up, aware that she is responsible for the downfall of both Barak and her own husband *(Da und dort, alles ist meine Schuld).*

§ Mysterious darkness shrouds the dyer's house, frightening Barak and his brothers, while the Empress, who has learned from Barak what it means to be human, resolves to acknowledge her own humanity and accept mankind's lot (septet: *Wie ertrag ich dies Haus*). Telling Barak of her growing estrangement from him in the past three days, the Dyer's Wife admits she has foresaken her shadow and renounced childbearing, for a fine price—pleasure, attention to her own needs. When the brothers stir up the fire, its light reveals that she casts no shadow, and the Nurse tells the Empress to seize the shadow at once, while the woman is still of a mind to part with it. The Empress, however, does not want to take it (sextet: *Der Schatten ist abgefallen*). Furious at his wife, Barak threatens to kill her. Though she repents, saying she has not yet actually given up the shadow *(Barak! Ich hab' es nicht getan!),* he seizes a sword that mysteriously appears in his hand. When he attempts to strike her, the sword disappears from his grasp and the earth opens, swallowing him and his wife. The Nurse realizes that Keikobad has intervened.

ACT III   In an underground vault, Barak and his Wife are—unbeknownst to each other—imprisoned in separate, adjoining chambers. Tormented by the recollection of the unborn children's voices *(Schweight doch, ihr Stimmen!),* the Dyer's Wife cries out that she did want to leave Barak but has come to value his qualities as a human being. For his part, Barak regrets his anger, recalling his vow to care for her *(Mir anvertraut)*. Both wish they could see each other once more to explain their real feelings. A voice bids them ascend a staircase.

§ On a rocky terrace before a bronze portal, Keikobad's Messenger stands waiting with attendant spirits for a boat carrying the Nurse and the sleeping Empress. When she learns where the boat has brought them—to Keikobad's domain—the Nurse can think only of escape, but the awakening Empress says she is not afraid to face her father once again and must find her husband *(Hier ist ein Tor!)*. The Nurse warns of Keikobad's wrath: he will not tolerate any dallying with the world of mortals. The Empress retorts that her Nurse does not understand the real nature of humanity. The portal swings open, admitting the Empress. Barak and his Wife stumble in separately, trying to find each other; the Nurse gives them misleading directions, hoping to revive their animosity. Thinking she can still save the Empress, the Nurse calls on Keikobad, but his Messenger forces her back into the boat and sets it adrift, condemning her to end her days in the detested world of mankind. Barak and his Wife are heard calling out in despair and fear.

§ In a temple-like hall within the grotto, spirits welcome the Empress, who asks her unseen father *(Vater, bist du's?)* to recognize her humanity by allowing her to cast a shadow. A spring of water appears, and a Guardian of the Threshold tells her to drink of the water of life so as to cast the shadow of the Dyer's Wife. The latter and Barak are still calling for each other, and when she hears them, the Empress refuses to drink, saying the water is tainted with blood. The fountain subsides. The Empress declares herself part of the human world, ready to take her punishment. At this moment her husband is revealed, turned to stone except for his eyes, which look pleadingly toward her. Spirit voices tempt her once more to drink of the fountain, which springs up again: she can have the shadow of the Dyer's Wife *and* save the Emperor. Torn by agony, she nevertheless refuses *(Ich—will—nicht!)*, whereupon the fountain vanishes and she casts a shadow of her own. The Emperor, restored to life, embraces her and hails the voices of the unborn children, for whom both now long *(Engel sind's, die von sich sagen!)*.

§ By a waterfall, Barak finds his wife and sees that she casts her shadow once more. A bridge appears across the waterfall—"the bridge across the gulf over which the dead come back to life"—enabling them to be reunited. The Emperor and Empress appear above the waterfall, and both couples hail their discovery of their own humanity (quartet: *Schatten zu beide in prüfenden Flammen gestählt!*), to cries of approval from the unborn children that will be theirs.

ARABELLA

THREE ACTS
MUSIC: Richard Strauss
TEXT (German): Hugo von Hofmannsthal
WORLD PREMIERE: Dresden, Staatsoper, July 1, 1933
U.S. PREMIERE: Metropolitan Opera, February 10, 1955
   (in English)

CHARACTERS

Arabella . . . . Soprano
Zdenka, *her sister* . . . . Soprano
Countess Adelaide Waldner, *their mother* . . . . Mezzo-Soprano
Fortuneteller . . . . Mezzo-Soprano
Fiakermilli, *music-hall singer* . . . . Soprano
Mandryka, *landowner from Slavonia* . . . . Bass-Baritone
Count Theodor Waldner, *retired military captain,*
   father of Arabella and Zdenka . . . . Baritone
Matteo, *young officer, suitor of Arabella* . . . . Tenor
Elemer ⎫   ⎧ Baritone
Dominik ⎬ *counts, suitors of Arabella* . . . . ⎨ Tenor
Lamoral ⎭   ⎩ Tenor
   Hussars, servants, hotel and party guests, gamblers, physician

ACT I   In a hotel in Vienna in the 1860s, Adelaide, wife of Count Waldner, consults a Fortuneteller, who says the family fortunes will improve—but not right away, for the count is still gambling and losing heavily. Zdenka, the younger of their two daughters, has been raised as a boy to save the expense of a girl's wardrobe and education. She is now occupied with warding off creditors and keeping track of unpaid bills. The Fortuneteller, however, sees a wealthy stranger coming to marry the older daughter, Arabella, on whom Adelaide has pinned her hopes. As she takes the Fortuneteller into the next room to try to clarify some confusing predictions, Zdenka muses on the family's precarious finances *(Sie Wollen alle Geld!)*. She is secretly in love with one of Arabella's suitors, the officer Matteo, but would renounce him in favor of her sister. Matteo, who takes Zdenka for a boy, "Zdenko," and treats "him" as a confidant, appears at the door asking for Arabella, who is out for a walk. He asks for help in wooing Arabella, who has other suitors—Counts Elemer,

Dominik, and Lamoral. Zdenka, who has written him love letters in Arabella's name, wonders how she can help him, since he seems almost suicidal. He leaves, and Arabella returns from her walk, annoyed to find more flowers from Matteo. Zdenka pleads on the officer's behalf, but Arabella says her interest in him has waned. Perhaps this is a fault of hers, she admits, but when the right man comes along, she will no longer have any doubts (*Aber der Richtige*). This is the end of the Carnival season, and Arabella will have to decide which suitor to accept before the evening is over. As she waits for Elemer to pick her up for a sleigh ride, she confides to Zdenka that she was much taken by the looks of a stranger who visited their suite when she was leaving for her walk: if the flowers had come from him, they would have meant something. When Elemer arrives, Arabella is not amused to discover that the three counts drew lots to see which one would take her out. Elemer in turn is disappointed that Arabella means to bring her "brother" along. Looking out the window, Arabella glimpses the mysterious stranger. When the bedraggled Waldner comes home, his wife sends the girls to their rooms to dress. Waldner has lost more money and confesses he even sent Arabella's photograph to an old friend, a certain Mandryka, whom he remembers as wealthy and reckless. The two contemplate their future: they could always keep house for their wealthy aunt Jadwiga in her castle. All the family jewels have been pawned. When Waldner rings for a cognac, he learns he will no longer be served except for cash. A visitor is announced; he assumes it is another creditor but then reads the calling card, "Mandryka." It turns out to be the nephew of the Mandryka whom Waldner once knew, now deceased. Entranced by the picture Waldner sent his uncle, Mandryka asks whether Arabella is still single, adding that he has inherited his uncle's estates and wants to marry. Arabella's image has been on his mind: may he meet her? Waldner, though surprised, has the presence of mind to borrow money before the visitor leaves. Zdenka returns, still worried that they will have to leave Vienna and that she will never see Matteo again. Matteo returns, hoping to find Arabella, but Zdenka sends him away, saying he should attend the Coachmen's Ball that night. Arabella comes back and, waiting for Zdenka to get ready, muses on the men in her life (*Mein Elemer!*), all of whom seem unimportant since she has seen the stranger. Tonight, however, she will be queen of the Coachmen's Ball. As Zdenka returns with coat and hat, the two leave for their sleigh ride.

ACT II   At the ball that evening, Mandryka nervously awaits his introduction to the girl of his dreams, who shortly appears. Though her other suitors periodically interrupt, asking for a dance, Mandryka tells her of his background: he is from Slavonia, "really half a peasant" and a widower. Though they have just met, he summons the courage to propose, and she reminds herself of her earlier words—that she would know immediately when the right man came along (*Der Richtige—so hab' ich still zu mir gesagt*). He tells her of the Slavonian custom of marking a betrothal with a glass of water. She accepts but asks to stay at the ball and say farewell to the girl she has been up till now. Fiakermilli, a pretty girl chosen by the coachmen to be their hostess, bounces up to Arabella and names her queen of the ball as the merrymaking gets under way. Mandryka stays on the sidelines with Arabella's parents and orders champagne and flowers, while Matteo, still desperate for a word with Arabella, waits on the sidelines with Zdenka. Arabella enters from the dance floor and bids adieu to Dominik, Elemer, and Lamoral, each unhappy to lose her. Zdenka, trying to calm Matteo, gives him a forged note in which Arabella supposedly suggests a rendezvous with him in her room a short while later; the key is enclosed. Seeing this, Mandryka is violently upset, the more so when he observes that Arabella has left. A message delivered to him, saying that tomorrow she will be his, does not assuage his wrath. Recklessly he drinks and celebrates, flirting with Fiakermilli and singing her a folk song (*Ging durch einen Wald*). Arabella's distraught parents, not knowing where she is, leave for the hotel to find her, while Mandryka, quite drunk, urges that the festivities continue at his expense.

ACT III   In the hotel waiting room later that evening, Matteo is glimpsed outside the Waldners' apartment upstairs. Arabella comes and pauses in the lobby, musing on her forthcoming engagement, but Matteo reappears and interrupts her. Believing he has just been with her in her room, he cannot understand her coolness. As he blocks her from climbing the stairs, her parents return from the ball with Mandryka, who sees Matteo and angrily announces he is going home in the morning. Arabella realizes that Mandryka believes she has compromised herself; in the ensuing confusion, Waldner challenges Mandryka but finds he has pawned his dueling pistols, while Adelaide upbraids Matteo for seeking a disappointed suitor's revenge. Attracted by the commotion, other hotel guests gather. Mandryka calms down enough to ask Arabella to admit that Matteo has been her lover. Offended, she walks away, leaving him to challenge Matteo to a duel with sabers. Only the appearance of Zdenka, dressed for the first time as a girl, resolves the situation. Zdenka confesses she was so worried about Matteo, and loved him so much, that she kept a rendezvous with him in the darkened room upstairs. Recognizing her as the "boy" he saw giving Matteo the key, Mandryka declares himself unworthy of Arabella, who turns her attention to comforting her sister (ensemble: *Wie steh' ich vor Ihnen, Arabella?*). Though Matteo is overjoyed to discover Zdenka, the girl thinks her parents will disown her. Arabella rather coolly forgives Mandryka, who now pleads Matteo's cause with the Waldners. They allow themselves to be persuaded. The curious crowd drifts off, and Adelaide takes Zdenka upstairs, leaving Arabella alone with Mandryka. She asks him to have his servant bring a drink of water to her room. She too goes upstairs, and Mandryka assumes, dejectedly, that he has lost out (*Sie gibt mir keinen Blick*). But soon she reappears, carrying the glass and offering it to him as the symbolic "drink that none has touched" (*Das war sehr gut, Mandryka*). He drinks the water and breaks the glass, signifying his own commitment, and they embrace before Arabella runs back to her room, followed by Mandryka's adoring gaze.

CAPRICCIO

ONE ACT
MUSIC: Richard Strauss
TEXT (German): Clemens Krauss
WORLD PREMIERE: Munich, National Theater, October 28, 1942
U.S. PREMIERE: Santa Fe, August 1, 1958

CHARACTERS

Countess Madeleine . . . . Soprano
Clairon, *actress* . . . . Contralto
Flamand, *composer* . . . . Tenor
Monsieur Taupe, *prompter* . . . . Tenor
The Count, *Madeleine's brother* . . . . Baritone
Olivier, *poet* . . . . Baritone
La Roche, *theater director* . . . . Bass
Majordomo . . . . Bass
Two Italian singers, young dancer, servants, musicians

At the château of Countess Madeleine near Paris during the 1780s. During a performance of Flamand's string sextet in the adjoining room, La Roche has fallen asleep in his chair. Discussing the Countess' rapt attention to the music, Flamand and Olivier discover they are rivals for her affection: which takes first place, the music or the words? Applause awakens La Roche, who tells both men that their contribution takes second place to his scenic effects—the real reason for theater. Without him, their work would be lifeless paper. As the argument goes on, La Roche, defending his box-office-oriented pragmatism, reminds Olivier of his recent infatuation with the actress Clairon. The Countess, a young, attractive widow, enters from the salon with her brother, remarking that Rameau's bad manners spoiled her enjoyment of his music: she cannot separate the man from his art, any more than she can bring intellect to bear on the emotions aroused in her by music. The Count, more of an intellectual, prefers poetry—perhaps because Clairon, whom he admires, is coming to the château to act with him in Olivier's play. When the Count, who lives for the moment, teases his sister about her two suitors, she says perhaps she will choose neither, since choosing one means losing the other (duet: *Leicht zu verlieren*). La Roche returns to announce that everyone should start rehearsing for the Countess' birthday celebration, which will pit the talent of the composer against that of the poet, culminating in an *azione teatrale* (production number) by his own company. Again Olivier and Flamand twit the impresario about his vulgar taste, but their banter is interrupted by the sound of Clairon's carriage. The Count introduces Clairon as priestess to the tragic muse, seconded by pompous praise from La Roche. Clairon fears that her offstage conversation will come as an anticlimax after her dramatic readings. She asks Olivier whether he has finished the love scene of his play. Glancing meaningfully at the Countess, Olivier says he has just found the inspiration to write the remaining verses. The Count and Clairon read through the scene *(Ihr geht. Entliess Euch schon die Macht)*—a flowery exchange for parting lovers, culminating in the Count's pledge of fidelity to his beloved *(Kein Andres, das mir so im Herzen loht)*. Clairon tactfully calls a halt to his overzealous reading by saying she likes his acting and looks forward to working with him. She hands the script to La Roche, asking him to direct the rehearsal. He leads them into the theater, asking the author to stay behind. The latter tells the Countess that his lines were really meant for her; as he recites more, Flamand sits at the harpsichord and improvises a setting of the verses, which he then rushes off to transfer to paper. Olivier is upset, not wanting his poetry "disfigured" by music, but the Countess points out that music too must have its inspiration. She adds that true love thrives on hope and fancy, not necessarily on fulfillment. Olivier, fearing she is more partial to music—and to Flamand's attractive looks—than to wit and poetry, wishes she would make up her mind. Flamand rushes in with his composition and plays it, singing Olivier's words. The Countess feels that it enhances the emotional appeal of the lines, but Olivier feels that it competes with and detracts from them (trio: *Des Dichters Worte*). Is the poem still his own, or has Flamand appropriated it? Though the Countess realizes that her suitors will not like this, she is happy to have both their feelings joined in one work of art, one that will outlast them all. La Roche returns to ask for the author, saying he needs his permission for some judicious cuts to improve the play's effectiveness. Alone with the Countess, Flamand waxes eloquent in declaring his love *(. . . dass ich Euch liebe!)*. She reproves him for abandoning music and resorting to words. He too presses her to make up her mind: Which suitor has won her heart? She says she will give her answer the next morning at eleven in the library. After he rushes out, she sinks briefly into contemplation, broken by the sounds of rehearsal and laughter in the theater hall. The Count, in fine spirits, enters from the rehearsal, captivated by Clairon. His sister warns of the dangers of infatuation, then states her own dilemma: the blend of Olivier's verses with Flamand's music moved her more than either ingredient separately, and she finds a choice impossible. The result of the conflict, she jokes, could lead to an opera. The Count says his own commitment is to poetry. When Clairon and La Roche reappear, Clairon pronounces the Count a promising actor and politely declines the Countess' invitation to stay for dinner: she must study. As chocolate is served, La Roche introduces a ballerina from his troupe; while she dances a passepied, a gigue, and a gavotte, the Count watches admiringly, and Olivier tries to thank Clairon for coming to the rehearsal. Recalling the end of their relationship, she reacts angrily. In fugal counterpoint, La Roche and Flamand, joined by the others, debate the importance of music to the other arts, Flamand insisting it is the prime mover *(Tanz und Musik)*. The argument turns to opera, which the Count calls an absurd form, but the Countess says Gluck's genius has proved otherwise. La Roche summons an Italian tenor and soprano from his troupe to sing a duet on a text by Metastasio *(Addio, mia vita)*, forcing the Count and Olivier to admit the persuasive charm of music, which overrides their intellectual reservations. The Count offers to escort Clairon back to Paris; she agrees, provided he is willing to read cues for her to practice her part in Voltaire's *Tancred*. La Roche outlines to the Countess his grand design for her birthday pageant, beginning with an allegory of the birth of Pallas Athene, but the humorous comments of the others make his description difficult. While the Italian singers haggle, La Roche tries to finish his description of the scenario, ending with the fall of Carthage, amid the others' comments (octet: *Sie lachen ihn aus*), which gradually turn quarrelsome. Challenged by Flamand and Olivier as a theatrical charlatan, La Roche finally bursts out *(Hola, ihr Streiter in Apoll!)*, again insisting that their talents would amount to nothing without the impresario's genius in presenting the result. The Countess asks poet and musician to collaborate with La Roche for her birthday celebration. In a moment of rare accord, the two men praise the descent of the goddess of harmony to earth *(Die Göttin Harmonie)*, graciously implying that this goddess is the Countess, who will lead their dispute to a resolution. Talk turns to a subject for their opera: *Ariadne auf Naxos?* Done too often. *Daphne?* The transformation into a tree is too difficult. The Count suggests they write about themselves, the events of that very afternoon. At first astonished, the collaborators agree it is an exciting challenge. As the party disperses, however, Flamand and Olivier each clings to the conviction that his art takes precedence over the other's. La Roche, finding their rivalry irrelevant, reminds them that practical considerations of the theater will make or break the piece, and that they had better heed his advice. In the wake of the gathering, eight servants come to straighten up the salon, gossiping about what they have overheard. Their own preference in entertainment is for acrobats and clowns. When the Majordomo tells them they may have the evening free after supper, since there are no guests tonight, the servants rejoice together (ensemble: *Welch Vergnügen*), then leave. As the Majordomo lights the chandeliers, Monsieur Taupe, having emerged like a mole from the prompter's box, comes in search of La Roche. He identifies himself to the Majordomo, who recognizes his role as unseen but important. Since La Roche and the troupe have left without him, the Majordomo offers to get him some supper and a carriage.

§ As evening and candlelight transform the room, an interlude sets the stage for the Countess' reappearance. Since her brother has escorted Clairon to Paris, she will dine alone (*Wo ist mein Bruder?*). Olivier has left word that he will wait in the library next morning at eleven, to learn what ending the Countess has chosen for the opera. Flamand already has made an appointment for the same place and time: he will be disappointed to meet his collaborator instead of the Countess. Going over the song they wrote together, the Countess declares that it is a single creation: she cannot make the choice that will give the opera its ending. The question is left unanswered as she goes in for supper.

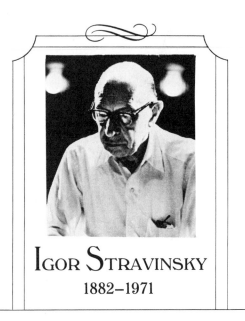

IGOR STRAVINSKY
1882–1971

The career of Igor Stravinsky spans several stylistic phases, encapsulating the broad spectrum of twentieth-century music. Born in Russia, the son of a distinguished bass opera singer of Polish descent, Stravinsky early formed a lifelong attachment to the theater. His roots were anchored in Russian folklore, myths, and fairy tales, with their bizarre events and characters underpinned by earthy peasant practicality. At eleven, the boy caught a glimpse of Tchaikovsky; he always cherished this recollection of the man whose nationalistically based cosmopolitanism he admired and emulated. When Stravinsky was twenty, his father—to whom he had never felt close—died, and the guiding role model for his musical youth became his teacher Rimsky-Korsakov. For six years, until Rimsky-Korsakov's death, the young man was practically an adoptive member of his family.

A turning point came in the years 1908–10, when the impresario Diaghilev first heard Stravinsky's music in St. Petersburg and invited him to compose something for the Ballets Russes to perform in Paris. From 1910 until World War I, Sravinsky lived in Paris, where he not only wrote for Diaghilev his celebrated trio of ballets—*L'Oiseau de Feu, Petrouchka,* and *Le Sacre du Printemps*—but also completed for the impresario his earlier opera *Le Rossignol,* begun in Russia. Diaghilev, whose interests included opera as well as ballet, was instrumental in encouraging Stravinsky to write his second opera, *Mavra* (1922), after a Pushkin tale.

His ballets were the subject of immediate attention and many performances, but his operas did not enjoy comparable acceptance. Spending the World War I years in Switzerland, Stravinsky had begun to experiment with alternative forms of theater, producing *L'Histoire du Soldat,* a chamber work with dancer and narrator. Soon afterward, in 1920, he wrote *Pulcinella,* a ballet with songs in the style of an eighteenth-century intermezzo. He was now embarked on a period of neoclassicism, which confounded the music world because of his earlier reputation as an aggressive modernist. The ballet *Les Noces,* which again combined singing roles (this time adding a chorus) with dancing, marked Stravinsky's last major work with a Russian subject. Still cautiously flirting with opera, he wrote *Oedipus Rex* four years later, in 1927, calling it an opera-oratorio. But critics from the first sensed that the work needed a full stage production in order to make its dramatic effect. Next, Stravinsky wrote *Perséphone* (1934), a melodrama—a concert piece with spoken narration against a choral-orchestral background.

Altogether Stravinsky wrote ten works that included some elements of opera, but the only full-length, fully operatic one is *The Rake's Progress,* a product of his years in America starting with World War II. It is in fact the longest of all of Stravinsky's compositions. Though it dates from the late 1940s and early 1950s, *The Rake's Progress* shows Stravinsky's continuing loyalty to neoclassic principles. Soon afterward, in the remaining two decades of his life, he began to explore the possibilities of serialism, but from a classical orientation, just as Schoenberg proceeded from a late-romantic orientation.

Since *The Rake's Progress* was not written on commission, it is evident that the composer really wanted to do this project. At the Art Institute of Chicago in 1947, he had seen the series of engravings by Hogarth of the same title, and had been struck by their presentation of scenes that are almost operatic, akin in feeling to a work like *Don Giovanni.* Stravinsky discussed this with the poet W. H. Auden, and the two agreed on the importance of formal coherence as an antidote for the tumult and confusion of the twentieth century, which the poet had termed the Age of Anxiety.

Auden and his literary collaborator Chester Kallman invoked the conventions of the eighteenth-century theater, as did Stravinsky in his music. The composer used recitative (both *secco* and *accompagnato),* arias, ensembles, and recapitulations to reinforce the shape of the verses, explore their emotional implications, and fill out the characterizations, which are more moralistic and symbolic than realistic. The result is an opera unlike any other—one whose actual subject is form itself. Though nothing about it sounds Russian, it is linked with *L'Histoire du Soldat,* a Russian folktale about the struggle of good and evil for the possession of a man's soul.

Stravinsky bade farewell to the theater with *The Flood,* written for CBS Television (1962). Once more he created a mixed-media work, as he had done several times before *The Rake's Progress,* combining elements of opera with those of dance, mime, and the spoken theater. As in *Rake,* the subject was a morality play.

THE RAKE'S PROGRESS

THREE ACTS AND AN EPILOGUE
MUSIC: Igor Stravinsky
TEXT (English): W. H. Auden, Chester Kallman
WORLD PREMIERE: Venice, Teatro La Fenice, September 11, 1951
U.S. PREMIERE: Metropolitan Opera, February 14, 1953

CHARACTERS

Anne Trulove . . . . Soprano
Baba the Turk, *bearded lady* . . . . Mezzo-Soprano
Mother Goose, *madam of a brothel* . . . . Mezzo-Soprano
Tom Rakewell, *libertine* . . . . Tenor
Nick Shadow . . . . Baritone
Trulove, *Anne's father* . . . . Bass
Sellem, *auctioneer* . . . . Tenor
Keeper of the Madhouse . . . . Bass
Libertines, whores, servants, citizens, madmen

ACT I Eighteenth-century England. In the garden of her father's country house, Anne Trulove sits with her suitor, Tom Rakewell, admiring the springtime. Sending Anne into the house, Trulove tells Tom he has arranged an accountant's job for him in London. Tom courteously refuses, but as soon as the older man has left him, he declares his determination to live by his wits and enjoy life *(Since it is not by merit)*. As soon as he says the words "I wish I had money," a stranger appears at the gate. Introducing himself as Nick Shadow, "at your service," he tells Tom that a forgotten rich uncle has died, leaving the young man a fortune. Anne and Trulove return to hear the news, the latter urging Tom to accompany Shadow to London to settle the estate. As Tom leaves, promising to send for Anne as soon as everything is arranged, Shadow turns to the audience to announce, "The Progress of a Rake begins."

§ At a brothel in London, whores entertain a group of "roaring boys," dissolute young playboys; together they toast Venus and Mars. Shadow coaxes Tom to recite for the madam, Mother Goose, the catechism he has taught him: to follow nature rather than doctrine, to seek beauty (which is perishable) and pleasure (which means different things to different people). Tom refuses, however, to define love. Turning back the clock when he sees Tom restless to escape, Shadow commends him to the pursuit of hedonism with these companions. Tom replies with a sad song (*Love, too frequently betrayed*) that shows he is still thinking of Anne. When the whores offer to console him, Mother Goose claims him for herself and leads him off (chorus: *The sun is bright, the grass is green*).

§ As evening falls, Anne leaves her father's house, determined to find Tom, since she has heard nothing from him (*Quietly, night, O find him and caress*).

ACT II   In the morning room of the house that Tom has acquired in London, he is beginning to tire of city pleasures (*Vary the song, O London, change!*) and no longer dares think of Anne. When he says, "I wish I were happy," Shadow appears, showing a poster for Baba the Turk, a bearded lady whom he urges Tom to marry (*In youth the panting slave pursues*), because only when one is obligated to neither passion nor reason can one be truly free. Amused by the idea, Tom gets ready to go out (duet: *My tale shall be told*).

§ Outside Tom's house, Anne approaches, hesitant to knock. As darkness falls, she sees servants enter with strangely shaped packages. Tom, startled to see her, says she must forget him: he cannot go back to her (*Leave pretenses, Anne*). A sedan chair appears, and Baba sticks her head out, whereupon Tom admits he has married her. Hurried along by Baba's impatient remarks, Anne faces the bitter realities (*Could it then have been known*), while Tom repeats that it is too late to turn back. Anne takes her leave. As Tom assists Baba from the sedan chair, a curious crowd gathers.

§ In his morning room, Tom sits sulking amid Baba's curios as she chatters about the origin of each. When he refuses to respond to her gestures of affection, she complains bitterly (*Scorned! Abused! Neglected! Baited!*). Tom pulls her wig down over her head; she remains silent and motionless as Tom lies down to sleep. Shadow wheels in a strange contraption, and when Tom wakens, saying, "O I wish it were true," the machine turns out to be his dream: an invention for making stones into bread (*O Nick, I've had the strangest dream*). Seeing it as a means of redemption for his misdeeds, Tom wonders whether he might again deserve Anne. Shadow points out the device's usefulness in gulling potential investors.

ACT III   On a spring afternoon, the same scene (including the stationary Baba) is covered with dust and cobwebs. Auction customers examine the various objects: Tom's business venture has ended in ruin. Amid rumors as to what has become of Tom, Anne enters in search of him. An auctioneer, Sellem, begins to hawk various objects (*Who hears me, knows me*)—including Baba, who resumes her chatter as soon as the wig is lifted from her head.

Indignant at finding her own belongings up for sale, she tries to order everyone out. She draws Anne aside, saying the girl should try to save Tom, who still loves her. Disappointed, Sellem calls a halt to the auction. Anne, hearing Tom and Shadow singing in the street, runs out.

§ Starless night in a churchyard, with a freshly dug grave. Shadow leads in the breathless Tom, reminding him that a year and a day have passed since he promised to serve him: now the servant claims his wage. Tom must end his life by any means he chooses, before the stroke of twelve. Suddenly, Shadow offers a reprieve: they will gamble for Tom's soul. When Tom, placing his trust in the Queen of Hearts, calls upon Anne, and her voice is heard, Shadow realizes he has lost. In retaliation he condemns Tom to insanity. As Shadow disappears and dawn rises, Tom—gone mad—imagines himself Adonis, waiting for Venus.

§ In Bedlam, the London insane asylum, Tom declares that Venus will visit him. Fellow inmates mock the idea *(Leave all love and hope behind)*, but when the Keeper admits Anne, they disperse. Believing her to be Venus, Tom confesses his sins: "I hunted shadows, disdaining thy true love." Briefly they imagine timeless love in Elysium. With his head upon her breast, Tom asks her to sing him to sleep. As she does *(Gently, little boat)*, her voice moves the other inmates, who hear from their cells *(O sacred music of the spheres!)*. Trulove comes to fetch his daughter, who bids the sleeping Tom farewell. When he wakens to find her gone, he cries out for Venus, then collapses, dying, as the other patients gather around him *(Mourn for Adonis)*.

EPILOGUE Before the curtain, the principals gather to tell the moral that each finds in the story. Anne warns that not every man can hope for someone like her to save him; Baba warns that men are all mad; Tom warns against self-delusion, to Trulove's agreement; Shadow mourns his role as man's alter ego; and all concur that the devil finds work for idle hands.

Piotr Ilyich Tchaikovsky
1840–93

ashion in music is a fickle jade, especially where opera is concerned, but Piotr Ilyich Tchaikovsky has never lost his hold on the public. Admittedly, his reputation is based almost entirely on ballet and symphonic works: his songs are largely neglected, and his operas have had a fluctuating acceptance. Perhaps Tchaikovsky the composer of *Eugene Onegin* and *Pique Dame* will never achieve the secure status of Tchaikovsky the composer of *Romeo and Juliet* and the *Pathétique* Symphony. Nevertheless, the operas have proved themselves not only on the Russian stage, where several are standard repertory, but increasingly abroad, where in recent years the trend has been toward performing them in the original language.

Born the son of a mining inspector in the Urals, Tchaikovsky received a good education but showed no early predilection for music. When he was ten, his family moved to St. Petersburg; four years later, his mother died of cholera. The young man studied law and prepared for a career in the civil service. At twenty-one he was smitten with music, entering the new conservatory opened by Anton Rubinstein. Making up for lost time, he applied himself strenuously to composition and at twenty-six was teaching it at the Moscow Conservatory, run by Anton's brother Nikolai. Tchaikovsky was nearly thirty, however, when he produced his first lasting work, the *Romeo and Juliet* Overture, and this he revised a decade later.

Constantly tormented in personal life, in part because he could not accept his own homosexuality, Tchaikovsky was nevertheless able to go on working.

In this he was greatly helped for many years by an admirer of his music, the widow Nadezhda von Meck, whom he never sought to meet in person. He maintained a certain aloofness toward the nationalist movement, exemplified by the so-called Five: though fairly friendly with them, he went his own way artistically, his cosmopolitan tastes reflecting frequent travel abroad. In his choice of opera subjects, however, Tchaikovsky was profoundly Russian. *Eugene Onegin,* the fourth of his nine operas, and *Pique Dame,* the eighth, were both based (very freely) on poems by Alexander Pushkin (1799–1837), the first great author of modern Russia. In both cases, Pushkin's rather cynical, detached tone has been replaced by an intense concern for the characters. What was conceived as social satire has become romantic drama. Tchaikovsky himself wrote or adapted the texts of five of his operas, rewriting Pushkin's *Onegin* on his own but entrusting *Pique Dame* to his brother Modest.

When *Onegin* was pronounced undramatic, the composer retorted that such was his intention: he rejected the apparatus of grand opera, with its exterior effects. (This did not prevent him, in *The Maid of Orleans* two years later, from attempting a European-style grand opera.) For the poignancy of its personal statement, *Onegin* remains in a class by itself. *Pique Dame,* which more clearly reflects the composer's fatalism, expands the theme of a vulnerable, romantic girl wounded by a driven, egotistical man—in *Onegin* by rejection, in *Pique Dame* by seduction. Both operas contain genre scenes that give them a vivid sense of time and place. Gustav Mahler thought highly enough of *Pique Dame* to introduce it at the Metropolitan Opera in March 1910. It lasted only four performances but returned to the semiregular repertory during the mid-1960s.

EUGENE ONEGIN

(Yevgeni Onegin)

THREE ACTS
MUSIC: Piotr Ilyich Tchaikovsky
TEXT (Russian): adapted by the composer from the poem by
    Alexander Pushkin
WORLD PREMIERE: Moscow, Imperial College of Music, January
    23, 1881
U.S. PREMIERE: New York, Carnegie Hall, February 1, 1908
    (concert performance in English); Metropolitan Opera,
    March 24, 1920 (in Italian)

E U G E N E   O N E G I N

CHARACTERS

Tatyana, *girl of the provincial petty nobility* . . . . Soprano
Olga, *her sister* . . . . Mezzo-Soprano
Mme. Larina, *their mother* . . . . Mezzo-Soprano
Filippyevna, *their nurse* . . . . Contralto
Vladimir Lensky, *poet, Olga's suitor* . . . . Tenor
Monsieur Triquet, *French tutor* . . . . Tenor
Eugene Onegin, *Lensky's friend* . . . . Baritone
Prince Gremin, *Onegin's cousin* . . . . Bass
Zaretsky, *friend of Lensky* . . . . Bass
Captain . . . . Bass

Peasants, servants, party guests

ACT I At her house in the Russian countryside, during the 1820s, Mme. Larina sits outdoors with her servant Filippyevna, making preserves. Through the open door of the house are heard the voices of Tatyana and her younger sister, Olga, Mme. Larina's daughters. They are singing a love song that Larina remembers from her youth (duet: *Slikhali l vi za roschei),* when she was fond of romantic fiction and found herself married to a man chosen by her parents. Joined by Filippyevna, Mme. Larina ventures the opinion that life's routines offer a secure refuge from unhappiness and uncertainty (duet: *Privichka svishe nam dana).* A group of reapers appear, singing about their hard day's work *(Bolyat moi skori nozhenki),* and present Mme. Larina with a decorated sheaf of wheat. Tatyana and Olga come outside, the latter praising an uncomplicated, extroverted life *(Oozh kak po mostoo).* Larina sends the field hands indoors, asking Flippyevna to give them wine. Then she and Olga remark how pale Tatyana looks; the girl replies she has been moved by a love story she is reading. Arriving early for an expected visit, a neighbor, the young poet Vladimir Lensky, brings along a friend, Eugene Onegin, who has just inherited property nearby. Onegin remarks to his friend that he finds Tatyana the more attractive of the two girls, expressing surprise that Lensky is in love with Olga. Tatyana sees the poised Onegin, with his city manners, as the man of whom she has dreamed, while Olga reflects with amusement on the gossip that his arrival will occasion in this quiet province (quartet: *Skazhi, kotoraya Tatyana).* When Lensky walks off with Olga, Onegin — amused by Tatyana's rustic simplicity—engages the girl in conversation, in which she says she reads and dreams a great deal. As they walk into the garden, the other couple appears, Lensky declaring his love for Olga *(Ya lyublyu vas).* Larina announces supper and sends Filippyevna to fetch Tatyana. As they enter the house, Onegin tells Tatyana about the aged uncle from whom he inherited his country place *(Moi dyadya).* Filippyevna notices that the girl seems smitten by the newcomer.

§ Later, in Tatyana's room, Filippyevna tries to say good night, but the restless Tatyana asks her to stay. Questioned about her own youth, Filippyevna confesses she was never in love but had to accept a marriage arranged by her family. Tatyana admits she is in love and asks Filippyevna to leave her alone. Determined to write to Onegin, she has trouble getting started, then begins (letter scene: *Pooskai pogibnoo ya*), declaring that heaven has decreed her love for Onegin, whom she imagined in her dreams before he came to visit. In him she confides her hopes: will he encourage or scorn her? As dawn breaks, she seals the letter without daring to reread it. When Filippyevna comes to wake her early for Mass, Tatyana asks the old woman to have the envelope delivered by her grandson to Onegin's estate.

§ In the garden, peasant girls are gathering berries and singing. They withdraw when Tatyana comes in, anxious and embarrassed because Onegin's visit has been announced. He greets her, praising the honesty of her letter and asking her to hear an equally frank admission from him: he is not cut out for a life of dull domesticity in the provinces and can offer only "a brother's love." He adds a warning: if she is not more guarded with her feelings, someone less scrupulous may take advantage of her. Seeing the girl at a loss for words, he leads her toward the house.

ACT II   Some months later, Tatyana's name day is the occasion for a ball at Larina's house. When she dances with Onegin, local gossips comment disapprovingly on his reputation. Out of boredom, and wanting to annoy Lensky for having insisted he attend, Onegin flirts with Olga and invites her to dance. Lensky challenges Olga's behavior, only to be told he is making a fuss over nothing. Out of spite, Olga agrees to dance again with Onegin. Before she can, the guests make way for Monsieur Triquet, an elderly French tutor, who recites French verses he has composed in Tatyana's honor. Onegin joins Olga in a mazurka, then teases Lensky, who takes his mocking seriously and insists on a duel, while Larina begs them not to create a scandal. Privately, Onegin regrets his behavior; Tatyana is disturbed by the side of his character that it has shown; Lensky feels he placed too much faith in Olga; she in turn complains of the quarrelsome nature of men, a sentiment shared by her mother (ensemble: *No syevodnya uznal ya drugoye*). In the face of Lensky's continuing anger, Onegin loses patience and resolves to teach him a lesson, accepting the challenge to a duel at dawn, as other guests keep the two apart.

§ Near an old mill the next morning, Lensky and his second, Zaretsky, arrive to await the duel. Lensky muses on the passing of his youthful life and wonders, should he be killed, whether Olga will ever think of him *(Kuda vi udalilis)*. Onegin arrives; his valet, Gillot, will serve as his second. While the seconds prepare pistols, Onegin and Lensky murmur regrets to themselves: they ought to part as friends, but pride forbids it. Instructed by Zaretsky, they stand back to back, take four strides and turn. Onegin shoots, and Lensky falls. To Onegin's horror, Zaretsky pronounces him dead.

ACT III Several years later, in a fashionable house in St. Petersburg, guests dance a polonaise. Onegin appears among them, observing that neither his aimless travels nor the social whirl offers relief from guilt over Lensky's death and from boredom with his own existence *(I zdyes mnye skuchno!)*. Suddenly he notices the resemblance of the party's hostess, Princess Gremin, to the simple country girl Tatyana. He questions Prince Gremin, an older cousin of his, who explains how love for Tatyana has enriched his life *(Lyubvi vsye vozrasti pokorni)*; then he introduces Onegin to her. Masking her anxiety, she politely recalls their former acquaintance, then excuses herself. Alone, Onegin wonders at her transformation *(Uzhel ta samaya Tatyana)* and feels a surge of passionate love. Upset by it, he leaves the party.

§ A day or two later, Tatyana sits in a drawing room of her house, reading a letter from Onegin, who has asked to see her. He appears at the door and throws himself at her feet. She reminds him how he rejected her when she was young and vulnerable *(Onegin, ya togda molozhe)*. Now that she has risen in society, would he want to dishonor her? He pleads desperately, and she weeps to think that happiness was once within their grasp. He says he cannot possibly go, now that he has found her again and recognized his true feelings and need for her. Though torn, she stands by her marriage vows: there is no room for Onegin in her life. Overwhelmed by despair, he rushes out as she collapses in tears.

PIQUE DAME

(Pikovaya Dama) (The Queen of Spades)

THREE ACTS
MUSIC: Piotr Ilyich Tchaikovsky
TEXT (Russian): Modest Ilyich Tchaikovsky, after the story by
    Alexander Pushkin
WORLD PREMIERE: St. Petersburg, Imperial Opera, December 19,
    1890
U.S. PREMIERE: Metropolitan Opera, March 5, 1910 (in German)

CHARACTERS

Lisa . . . . Soprano
Pauline, *her companion* . . . . Contralto
Old Countess, *her grandmother* . . . . Mezzo-Soprano
Masha, *maid* . . . . Soprano
Governess . . . . Mezzo-Soprano
Gherman, *young officer* . . . . Tenor
Count Tomsky, *Gherman's friend* . . . . Baritone
Prince Yeletsky, *officer, Lisa's fiancé* . . . . Baritone
Tsurin ⎫   ⎧ Bass
Chekalinsky ⎬ *officers* . . . . ⎨ Tenor
Narumov ⎭   ⎩ Bass
Chaplitsky, *proprietor of gambling parlor* . . . . Tenor
*Majordomo, servants, maskers, party guests, children, St. Petersburg
citizens, soldiers, gamblers*

ACT I   During the reign of Catherine the Great (1762–96), children are at play in a St. Petersburg summer park while their nurses watch. As the little boys pretend to be soldiers, two real officers enter—Tsurin and Chekalinsky, the former complaining about his bad luck at gambling. They remark that one of their number, Gherman, seems obsessed with the gaming table but never bets, since he is frugal and methodical. Gherman appears on the scene with Tomsky, who says Gherman hardly seems like his old self: is anything bothering him? Gherman admits he is in love from afar with a girl above his station, whose name he does not even know (*Ya imeni yeyo ne znayu*). When Prince Yeletsky, an officer, strolls into the park, Chekalinsky congratulates him on his recent engagement. Yeletsky declares his happiness while Gherman, aside, curses him enviously (duet: *Schastlivyi den Tebya*). Yeletsky points out his fiancée, Lisa, who has just appeared with her grandmother, the Old Countess, once known as the Venus of Moscow. Catching sight of Gherman, the two women note they have seen him before, staring at them with frightening intensity (quintet: *Mne strashno!*). Gherman realizes that Lisa is his unknown beloved. When Yeletsky and the women leave, Gherman is sunk in thought as the other officers discuss the Countess: known as the Queen of Spades, she succeeded at gambling in her youth by trading her favors for the winning formula of Count St. Germain in Paris. Tomsky says (*O, tak poslushaite!*) that only two men, one of them her husband, ever learned her secret, because she was warned by an apparition to beware a "third suitor" who would try to force it from her. Musing on the magical three cards (*Tri karty*), the others lightly suggest that such a combination would solve Gherman's problems. Threatened by approaching thunder, all leave except Gherman, who vows to learn the Countess's secret (*Poluchish smertelnyi udar*).

§ At home, Lisa plays the spinet as she and her friend Pauline sing a duet about evening in the countryside (*Uzh vecher*). Their girlfriends ask to hear more, so Pauline launches into a sad ballad *(Podugi milye),* followed by a dancelike song. As the merriment increases, Lisa remains pensively apart. A Governess appears at the door to chide the girls for indulging in folk dancing, unfit for their ladylike station, and to ask the visitors to leave. Pauline, the last to go, urges Lisa to cheer up; Lisa replies that after the storm there is a beautiful night, and asks the maid, Masha, not to close the French windows to the balcony. Alone, Lisa voices her sadness *(Otkuda eti slyozy),* confessing she is not happy with her engagement and has been stirred by the romantic look of the young man in the park. To her shock, Gherman appears on the balcony. Claiming he is about to shoot himself over her betrothal to another, he begs her to take pity on a dying man *(Krasav-itsa! Boginya! Angel!).* When the Countess is heard knocking, Lisa hides Gherman and opens the door to the old woman, who tells her to shut the window and go to bed. After the Countess retires, Lisa asks Gherman to leave but is betrayed by her feelings and falls into his embrace.

ACT II   Not long afterward, at a masked ball in a dignitary's mansion, Gherman's comrades comment on his obsession with the secret of the winning cards. Yeletsky passes with Lisa, noting her sadness and declaring his love *(Postoite, na odno mgnovenye!).* Gherman receives a note from Lisa, asking him to meet her later. Tsurin and Chekalinsky sneak up behind, muttering he is the "third suitor" who will learn the Countess' secret, then melt into the crowd as Gherman wonders whether he is hearing things. The master of ceremonies announces a tableau of shepherdesses (chorus: *Pod teniyu gustoi),* during which a girl rejects the entreaties of a rich suitor in favor of her rustic sweetheart; Cupid and Hymen appear, giving the lovers their blessing. Lisa slips Gherman the key to her grandmother's room, saying the old lady will not be there the next day, but Gherman insists on coming that very night. Thinking fate is handing him the Countess' secret, he leaves. The guests' attention turns to the imminent arrival of Catherine the Great, for which a polonaise by O. Kozlovsky (1757–1831) is played and sung in greeting.

§ Gherman slips into the Countess' room and looks in fascination at her portrait as a young woman. Their fates, he feels, are linked: one of them will die because of the other. He conceals himself as the old lady approaches, escorted by servants and hangers-on. Exhausted, the Countess sends them off, declaring she wants to rest. Alone, she deplores the manners of today and reminisces about her youth, singing an air from Grétry's *Richard Coeur-de-lion;** the French words deal with nameless fear when one is confronted by a lover *(Je crains de lui parler la nuit).* As she dozes off, Gherman stands before her. She awakens in horror as he pleads with her to tell him her secret *(Yesli kogda-nibud znali).* When she remains speechless, he grows desperate and threatens her with a pistol—at which she dies of fright. Lisa rushes in, only to learn that the lover

---

*An opera of 1784, about the time of the present action rather than of the Countess' youth.

to whom she gave her heart was more interested in the Old Countess' secret. She orders him out and falls sobbing.

Act III In his room at the barracks, as the winter wind howls, Gherman reads a letter from Lisa, who wants him to meet her at midnight by the river bank. He imagines he hears the chorus chanting at the Old Countess' funeral, then is startled by a knock at the window. The old woman's ghost appears, announcing that against her will she must tell him the secret so that he can marry and save Lisa *(Ya prishla k tebe protiv voli)*. Dazed, Gherman repeats the three cards—three, seven, ace *(Troika, semyorka, tuz!)*.

§ By the Winter Canal, Lisa waits for Gherman: it is already near midnight *(Uzh polnoch blizitsya)*, and though she clings to a forlorn hope that he still loves her, she sees her youth and happiness swallowed in darkness. At last he appears, but after uttering words of reassurance (duet: *Zabyty stenanya i slyozy!)*, he starts to babble wildly about the Countess and her secret. No longer even recognizing Lisa, he rushes away. She realizes that all is lost and throws herself into the icy waters.

§ At a gambling house, Gherman's fellow officers are finishing supper and getting ready to play faro. Yeletsky, who has not gambled before, joins the group because his engagement has been broken: "unlucky in love, lucky at cards." Tomsky entertains the others with a song: if girls were birds, he would like to be a tree and hold them in his branches *(Yesli b milye devitsky)*. Then Chekalinsky leads a traditional gamblers' song (chorus: *Tak v nenastnye dni,* words by Pushkin). Settling down to play, they are surprised to see Gherman arrive, wild and distracted. Yeletsky senses a confrontation and asks Tomsky to be his second if a duel should result. Gherman, intent only on betting, starts with 40,000 rubles, a recklessly large stake. He bets the three and wins, upsetting the others with his maniacal expression. Next he bets the seven and wins again. At this he takes a wine glass and declares that life is but a game *(Chto nasha zhizn?)*. Yeletsky accepts his challenge to bet on the next round. Gherman bets the ace but is confronted by Yeletsky with the winning card— the queen of spades. Seeing the Countess' ghost, Gherman takes his own life, asking Yeletsky's forgiveness *(Knyaz, prosti menya!)* and Lisa's as well. The others pray for his tormented soul.

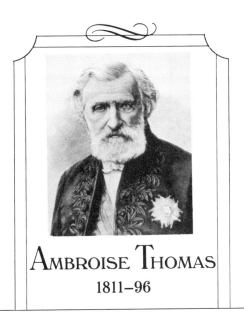

AMBROISE THOMAS
1811–96

A number of composers might be forgotten today were it not for the continuing popularity of a single opera. One is tempted to believe this would apply to Bizet, and it is surely true of Ponchielli, Boito, and Nicolai. Ambroise Thomas, a hardy survivor of a generally undistinguished period in French music, was a contemporary of Gounod, with whom he shared the goal of pleasing the public by not burdening it with undue demands. What distinguished both men was their fluent melodic gift, enhanced in Thomas's case by a piquant sense of rhythm, often derived from dance. Though he seems a minor figure in retrospect, in his day he was an important fixture of Parisian musical life. Honors and appointments were heaped upon him, starting with the Grand Prix de Rome in 1832, which entitled him to a sojourn at the Villa Medici under the watchful eye of its supervisor, the painter Ingres. In 1851 Thomas was named to the Institut of the Académie Française, filling the vacancy left by the death of Spontini. In 1871 he succeeded Auber as director of the Paris Conservatory, and in 1894, to mark the 1,000th performance of *Mignon* at the Opéra Comique, he received the Cross of the Legion of Honor.

Thomas first gained prominence with *Le Caïd* (1849), fifth of his eleven operas, an opéra bouffe akin to those of Offenbach, for whose frivolity Thomas had little use. His *Le Songe d'une Nuit d'Été* (1850), which sounds like a setting of *A Midsummer Night's Dream,* is actually a Hoffmannesque tale about Shakespeare, with Elizabeth I standing in for his muse. *Raymond,* introduced the following year and remembered today only for its overture, shows Thomas veering toward subjects from literature, in this case Dumas' *The Man in the*

Iron Mask. This trend served Thomas well, for his ninth and tenth operas, *Mignon* (after Goethe's *Wilhelm Meister,* with Shakespeare again lurking in the wings) and *Hamlet.* The latter was hailed in his lifetime as a masterpiece, but it was *Mignon* that rivaled *Carmen* in public favor and at one time formed part of the standard repertory. Its first protagonist was Célestine Galli-Marié, who also sang the first Carmen, and in less than a century *Mignon* had been performed 2,000 times at the Opéra Comique alone, meanwhile conquering the New World as well as England and the rest of Europe.

MIGNON

THREE ACTS
MUSIC: Charles Louis Ambroise Thomas
TEXT (French): Jules Barbier and Michel Carré, after Goethe's novel
    Wilhelm Meisters Lehrjahre
WORLD PREMIERE: Paris, Opéra Comique, November 17, 1866
U.S. PREMIERE: New Orleans, French Opera House, May 9, 1871
METROPOLITAN OPERA PREMIERE: October 31, 1883 (in Italian)

CHARACTERS

Mignon, *kidnaped and brought up by Gypsies* . . . . Mezzo-Soprano
Philine, *actress* . . . . Soprano
Frédéric, *student, in love with Philine* . . . . Mezzo-Soprano
Wilhelm Meister, *student on a tour of study* . . . . Tenor
Lothario, *minstrel of noble birth* . . . . Bass
Laërte, *actor* . . . . Tenor
Jarno, *leader of a Gypsy troupe* . . . . Bass
Antonio, *servant* . . . . Bass
    Townspeople, Gypsies, actors, servants, party guests

ACT I In the courtyard of an inn in Germany, middle of the eighteenth century. Lothario, an old minstrel, appears, hopeful of someday finding his lost daughter, Sperata. The townspeople offer him a drink. A troupe of Gypsies bursts upon the scene, bent on entertaining them for money. At the same time, a traveling actress named Philine, staying at the inn, calls her colleague Laërte to watch the show. She extends a gracious welcome to the Gypsies *(O filles de Bohème).* Their leader, Jarno, announces that Mignon, a youngster attached to the troupe, will next perform a dance on eggs without breaking them. Rudely awakened from a brief nap on the wagon, Mignon refuses, whereupon Jarno threatens her. Lothario tries to protect Mignon, but Jarno backs off only when threatened with a pistol by Wilhelm Meister, a new arrival. To pacify Jarno, Philine tosses him a purse, while the grateful Mignon offers flowers to her protectors. Philine admires the newcomer and wonders who he is. Eventually all leave except Wilhelm and Laërte, who volunteers that he and Philine are survivors of a ruined theatrical troupe. Meister offers to buy him a drink and says he is a refugee from law study in Vienna, twenty years old and eager to see the world (*Oui, je veux par le monde promener librement*). Laërte confides that he was once unhappily married; Philine he describes as silly and fickle but good company. At her approach, Wilhelm compliments her; in turn, she tries to charm him (*Essayons de nos charmes*). When the actors leave, Mignon comes in search of Wilhelm. She thanks him again and tells him she remembers little of her childhood except being kidnaped and sold to the Gypsies. When Wilhelm asks where her home was, she asks whether he knows a land where orange blossoms and roses bloom in an eternal spring (*Connais-tu le pays*); he guesses she means Italy. Jarno appears and offers to sell Mignon. The two men go off to discuss this, and Lothario reappears to say good-bye to Mignon before resuming his wandering. He means to head south, following the swallows. She wishes she could go too (duet: *Légères hirondelles*). They leave as Philine appears with a new admirer, Frédéric, whom she introduces to Wilhelm when he returns with the news that he has ransomed Mignon. Laërte brings a letter inviting Philine and her friends to visit the nearby castle of one Baron Rosenberg, but Frédéric, recognizing the baron as his own uncle—and a rival—is unhappy at the idea. Wilhelm, on the other hand, would like to go. Mignon appears, asking what he will do with her now that he has bought her freedom: she had thought she would repay his kindness by becoming his servant. Sensing he is embarrassed to have her stay with him, she is about to leave with Lothario instead, but Wilhelm recognizes his responsibility and asks her not to go. The actors and their colleagues leave the inn, ready to perform at the baron's castle (*En route, amis, plions bagages*), where Wilhelm says he will join them later for supper. Philine appropriates the bouquet Mignon had given Wilhelm, to the girl's chagrin. Resigned to following Wilhelm even in his foolish pursuit of the actress, Mignon says farewell to the Gypsies, and everyone gets ready to depart.

ACT II   In a dressing room at the castle, Philine, enjoying the elegance of the place, banters with Laërte, who makes up a madrigal in her praise (*Belle, ayez pitié de nous!*), then leaves to prepare for that evening's performance. It is to be *A Midsummer Night's Dream*, in which Philine will play Titania. Wilhelm arrives, accompanied by Mignon, dressed as his page. Satisfied to be near him, she tolerates Philine's jokes and Wilhelm's apparent infatuation (*Je crois entendre),* pretending to sleep until they leave. Alone, she regrets Wilhelm's indifference *(Il était un pauvre enfant)* but decides to experiment with Philine's makeup and make herself attractive. She goes into the wardrobe in search of a dress, as Frédéric comes through the window, hopeful of winning Philine's attention (gavotte: *Me voici dans son boudoir*). He is soon confronted by Wilhelm, and the two are about to cross swords when Mignon, in one of Philine's dresses, comes out of the wardrobe and throws herself between them. As Frédéric leaves, Wilhelm, realizing he cannot keep a "page" who is really an attractive young girl, thinks he should send her to a family of his acquaintance *(Adieu, Mignon! Courage!).* Refusing Wilhelm's offer of money, she declares she would rather return to the Gypsies. Philine, coming back with Frédéric, airily tells Mignon she may keep the dress, at which the girl tears the lace off in anger. For the first time, Wilhelm senses that Mignon is fond of him and jealous of Philine. Still under Philine's spell, however, he escorts her out as Frédéric and Mignon give voice to their frustration.

§ Near a lake in the castle park, Mignon wanders about dejectedly. Lothario, still looking for his daughter, draws near and commiserates with Mignon (duet: *As-tu souffert?*). Hearing distant applause for Philine's performance, Mignon wishes that flames would consume the place; this gives Lothario the notion to set fire to the castle. Philine and her troupe appear, surrounded by their admiring audience, and the actress declares she is queen of the fairies for that night (polonaise: *Je suis Titania*). Wilhelm arrives late, having searched for Mignon. They wander off as Lothario comes back with the girl, telling her he started a fire in the building. Wilhelm returns with Philine and asks Mignon to retrieve Philine's bouquet (originally Mignon's gift to Wilhelm) from the boudoir. As the girl leaves on her errand, Laërte and some of the guests warn the assembled visitors about the fire. Wilhelm runs in search of Mignon while th others exclaim over the sudden disaster, punctuated by Lothario's fixated refrain about his lost daughter. As the castle walls collapse, Wilhelm carries in Mignon, unconscious but still clutching the bouquet.

ACT III   Lothario has brought the delirious Mignon to an abandoned estate in Italy, where boatsmen's voices are heard in the distance (chorus: *Ah! Au souffle leger du vent*). Lothario sings a lullaby for the exhausted girl *(De son coeur j'ai calmé la fièvre!).* A retainer, Antonio, leads Wilhelm into the castle, and they discuss the legend of a child and mother who were lost in the lake years before, causing the father to lose his reason and wander away; soon the place will be for sale, if Wilhelm fancies to buy it. Saying he will decide tomorrow, Wilhelm thinks he should buy the place for Mignon, who seems to be reviving in her native land. He now returns her love, and wonders at her devotion to him *(Elle ne croyait pas).* Antonio brings a message from Laërte that Philine has followed Wilhelm there and should be avoided. The fully revived Mignon comes in from the other room, happy to be reunited with Wilhelm *(Je suis heureuse!*), who greets her tenderly. When Mignon reminds him of Philine, however, the latter's voice is heard in the distance. Despite Wilhelm's reassurances (duet: *Mignon, je n'entends que ta voix*), the girl suffers a relapse and calls for Lothario, who appears dressed in fine clothes, carrying a small box. Saying he has recognized the castle as his own, he gives her the box, which contains mementos of her childhood: when she sees these she realizes she is Sperata, his lost daughter. (trio: *O Dieu, je te bénis!*). Mignon feels she is about to die of happiness; she joins Lothario and Wilhelm in thanking God for this blessing (trio: *C'est là que je voulais vivre*).

[In this version, Philine does not reappear. An alternative ending exists, in which Philine hails the lovers' union and announces she will marry Frédéric.]

VIRGIL THOMSON
b. 1896

*I*f Charles Ives represents the spirit of the Yankee tinkerer in American music, Virgil Thomson exemplifies the independence implicit in the statement "I'm from Missouri." Born in Kansas City, Thomson served as church organist in his youth, absorbing revivalist hymn tunes, parlor songs, and band concerts. He did not start to compose until after he entered Harvard, in 1919. In 1921, at the end of a European tour with the Harvard Glee Club, for which he served as accompanist and sometimes as conductor, he chose to stay in Paris for a while to study organ and composition with Nadia Boulanger, who eventually taught a whole generation of American musicians. Thomson graduated from Harvard in 1923 and studied for a short time in New York, but in 1925 he returned to Paris, where he lived for most of the next fifteen years.

Although influenced by French musical aesthetics, notably the ideas of Erik Satie, Thomson never lost touch with his American roots, and it was in collaboration with another well-known expatriate, Gertrude Stein, that he produced his first two operas, *Four Saints in Three Acts* (Hartford, 1934) and *The Mother of Us All* (New York, 1947). To the uninitiated these texts may look like errant nonsense, but to the aficionado they are inspired nonsense; Thomson's music does much to enhance their allusive meaning and suggestive power. To help in this process, Maurice Grosser, a painter friend of the composer, drew up scenarios to guide the staging of both operas. Though Miss Stein, in Thomson's words, "hadn't an ear for music the way she had an eye for painting," she liked the grandness of opera and the prominence his settings gave her words. For the subject of *The Mother of Us All* she chose a quintessentially

American figure of fact and legend, Susan B. Anthony (1820–1906), who fought against slavery and for women's rights.

Thomson's third opera, *Lord Byron* (New York, 1972), again deals with a legendary figure who actually lived, but it does so in a more cosmopolitan way. *The Mother of Us All,* which became unexpectedly timely three decades after it was written, is Thomson's all-American opera. Though rooted in the ideals of Monteverdi and the Florentine Camerata, it is equally redolent of filibusters and apple pie. Instead of plot line in the conventional sense, there is a string of free associations, bearing out Thomson's determination to consider opera only as "poetic theater."

THE MOTHER OF US ALL

TWO ACTS
MUSIC: Virgil Thomson
TEXT (English): Gertrude Stein
WORLD PREMIERE: New York, Columbia University, May 7, 1947

CHARACTERS

Susan B. Anthony, *suffragette leader* . . . . Soprano
Anne, *her companion* . . . . Mezzo-Soprano
Indiana Elliot . . . . Soprano
Angel More . . . . Soprano
Constance Fletcher . . . . Mezzo-Soprano
Anna Hope . . . . Soprano
Lillian Russell . . . . Soprano
Jo the Loiterer . . . . Tenor
Chris the Citizen . . . . Tenor
John Adams . . . . Tenor
Thaddeus Stevens . . . . Tenor
Ulysses S. Grant . . . . Baritone
Daniel Webster . . . . Bass
Gertrude S., Virgil T., Henrietta M., Henry B., Anthony
Comstock, Gloster Heming, Isabel Wentworth, Jenny Reefer, Herman
Atlan, Donald Gallup, Andrew J., Indiana Elliot's Brother, two Postilions, Negro Man, Negro Woman

ACT I In Susan B. Anthony's house, she and her companion, Anne, converse, while two narrators—Gertrude S. and Virgil T.—comment. The politically active Susan laments, "Men are so conservative, so selfish, so boresome," adding "It is useful to be right." The battle she is fighting on women's behalf may be futile, given men's intransigence, but at least she makes them listen.

§ At a political meeting, a crowd watches the entering dignitaries, led by Daniel Webster, who chants a lugubrious jingle (He digged a pit, he digged it deep). Bystanders play with the name Daniel—its associations of a beard, bearding the lion in its lair, Daniel in the lions' den. Chris the Citizen and Jo the Loiterer discuss the eccentricity of Chris' wife, and others converse until Susan and Daniel begin their debate, in which he refers to his opponent with parliamentary correctness as "sir." Though she is impatient in pursuing her cause, Susan says she is also patient, in the sense that she never gives up. Amid Webster's rhetorical irrelevancies, which make it clear that he is paying no attention, she makes it equally clear that her protests will continue. As the debate dissolves, Jo the Loiterer teases Angel More about her fear of mice.

§ On the village green in front of Susan's house, Andrew Johnson complains about the cold weather he finds everywhere, and argues with his habitual opponent Thaddeus Stevens. Constance Fletcher appears, interpreting their argument as a form of friendship (Antagonizes is a pleasant name) and welcoming her own perpetual adversary John Adams, who insists on paying flowery court to her but is too proper to go further. Lillian Russell complains that men are always quarreling, and everyone starts to waltz, agreeing with her (chorus: Naughty men they quarrel so). Jo asks whether everyone has forgotten Isabel Wentworth, to which Chris replies, "Why shouldn't everyone forget Isabel Wentworth?"

§ Later, Susan sits on her porch half-asleep, as in a daydream she meets a Negro Man, who she knows will use his right to vote—which she fought to help him get—but who cannot help her get the vote for women too. Donald Gallup, appearing as a college professor, cannot help either, though he is more enlightened and has more power. Finally she sees Johnson, Stevens, and Webster, too preoccupied with their own importance to take an interest in her cause (We are the chorus of the V.I.P.). As Jo and Chris discuss the difference between rich and poor, Jo asks Susan to define it. The rich, she replies, no longer listen, while the poor can still listen, but that is all they can do. For herself, if her pen still has ink to write, she does not feel deprived. Jo reminds her that even a pen is fallible.

§ In the same place, later, Susan, prompted by the wedding of Jo and Indiana Elliot, wonders if women realize how alone they are in life, whether married or not. As the couple enters, it occurs to her—and she tells Jenny Reefer, who is against marriage—that perhaps there is some purpose in marriage after all, since men are so helpless without women to guide them. Adams again defers to Constance, who greets him euphorically *(So beautiful)*, and Webster pays tribute to Angel More. General Grant pounds his chair on the porch for silence, but the Brother of Indiana Elliot intrudes, trying to forbid her marriage to Jo. No one pays attention, and Susan explains why she never tried marriage herself: "I have had to do what I have had to do, I have had to be what I have had to be, I could never be one of two." When Adams and Webster again court their idols, the others ask why *they* don't get married. Webster likes the idea of giving his blessing to marriage in general, and when Indiana's Brother again tries to intrude, he is thrown out. Susan B. imagines that it may take another generation but that the children of today's marriages will have universal suffrage.

ACT II   In Susan's house, Jenny begs her to come outside and give a speech. Jo appears, saying his new wife will not take his name; she follows, asking Susan to come and speak. Susan is reluctant. Paying lip service to her, Johnson and Stevens plead in the name of humanity, but she replies,"There is no humanity in humans, there is only law, and . . . you will not vote my laws." Other men ask her to speak, and she reminds them that they always make exceptions and water down her demands *(Yes but I work for you I do)*. The only honest one, who admits he will not vote for her laws, is Jo—who cannot vote, because he is a loiterer. Giving in, Susan gets ready to speak; Stevens hopes to use her presence in support of his own causes.

§ Returning from the rally, Anne calls the speech a success, but Susan realizes she has frightened the men into adding the word "male" to their suffrage amendment to the Constitution *(Yes but, what is man, what are men, what are they)*. Women have less to lose and are not so afraid as men, she declares. When women do get the vote, "It will do them no good because having the vote they will become like men, they will be afraid." Jenny and the suffragettes arrive, proclaiming they have converted Lillian Russell, who greets them rhetorically *(Dear friends, it is so beautiful)*, as Adams resumes his praise of Constance. Webster reproaches Susan for her impatience *(What what is it)*, saying that the addition of the word *male* is a minor detail in the nation's glorious progress. Jo says Indiana has finally agreed to take his name, but she insists that he take hers in return. The crowd hails Susan for her persistence.

§ Some years later, a statue of Susan is being unveiled in the halls of Congress. Susan crosses the scene as a ghost. Anne reflects that at long last, women have the vote. Adams, Johnson, Stevens, and Webster arrive, the last calling for Angel More, who replies, as does the nearly blind Constance to her still adoring Adams. Indiana Elliot tries to take the floor to lecture on marriage, but Susan's voice interrupts, pointing out that marriage is an evil necessary to the continuance of the race. Several others speak without saying much of anything, and Lillian Russell's blowsy entrance stirs attention. The fact of women's suffrage seems to have stunned the illustrious individuals in the group, but the chorus accepts it nonchalantly *(To vote the vote)*. The American flag veiling the statue is lifted, and Susan's voice is heard *(We cannot retrace our steps)*. As the others pay tribute to her image and depart, she reflects on her lifelong struggle, hoping her goal will not lose value now that it is won.

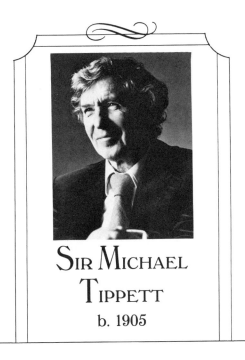

SIR MICHAEL
TIPPETT
b. 1905

Though Benjamin Britten seems to have overshadowed other British opera composers, several have made their mark since World War II, notably Michael (now Sir Michael) Tippett. Born in London eight years before Britten, Tippett did not begin studying music until the age of eighteen and did not write the first piece he would allow performed until he was thirty. Not until ten years later did he gain general public approval, with the oratorio *A Child of Our Time,* a work that showed his concern about man's inhumanity to man.

Coming from an unpretentious background, Tippett owes the freshness of his musical approach in part to a rejection of establishment values. Of leftist persuasion as a young man, he saw the realities of fascism and communism as threats to individual expression and became a Trotskyite pacifist, serving two months in prison in 1942 for refusing to aid the war effort except through music.

Tippett, who had done odd jobs before the war, including the teaching of French in school, was able to devote himself full-time to music thereafter. He headed the Bath Festival in the years 1969–74 and worked hard at composition. His first full-length opera (he had previously written ballad and folk-song operas), *The Midsummer Marriage,* provoked admiration for its lyric impulse but puzzlement over its quasi-mythic text, which goes beyond storytelling to probe symbolism and inner meaning. Tippett had spent seven years writing *The Midsummer Marriage,* which deals with a couple that elopes, separates, and is rejoined. It suggests that people's difficulties with relationships begin and end with their difficulty in understanding themselves. Tippett espouses the Jungian notion that each person must recognize the light and dark sides within his own nature; failure to do so causes alienation, conflict, and self-destruction (ultimately war). Because his lovers undergo trials and deal with priestlike figures, *The Midsummer Marriage* has been compared to Mozart's *Die Zauberflöte* and Strauss' *Die Frau ohne Schatten*. It also bears comparison to *Die Meistersinger*, in which youth struggles against entrenched values and wins the right to go its own way.

Sir Colin Davis, who conducted the work on records, says it "has the ambiguity of great art," while the composer calls it "a collective imaginative experience, dealing with the interaction of two worlds, the natural and the supernatural." Tippett's subsequent operas include *King Priam*, a sharply different, austere, and direct work, as well as *The Knot Garden* and *The Ice Break*, both of which tackle the myriad problems of modern man.

THE MIDSUMMER MARRIAGE

THREE ACTS
MUSIC: Michael Tippett
TEST (English): the composer
WORLD PREMIERE: London, Royal Opera (Covent Garden), January 27, 1955
U.S. PREMIERE: San Francisco Opera, October 15, 1983

CHARACTERS

Jenifer, *King Fisher's daughter* . . . . Soprano
Bella, *his secretary* . . . . Soprano
Sosostris, *clairvoyant* . . . . Contralto
Mark, *Jenifer's fiancé* . . . . Tenor
Jack, *mechanic, Bella's fiancé* . . . . Tenor
King Fisher, *businessman* . . . . Baritone
The Ancients (Priest, Priestess) . . . . Bass, Mezzo-Soprano
Strephon . . . . Dancer
Half-tipsy man, dancing man, friends of Mark and Jenifer, attendants upon the Ancients, dancers

ACT I   The time is the present, but the scene is timeless. A clearing in the woods, with a building like a Greek temple in the background. Before daybreak on Midsummer Day, longest day of the year, a group of people arrive, recognizing the spot as the meeting place chosen by their friends Mark and Jenifer. They hail the dawning light (*Ah! the sun, midsummer morning!*) but retreat when strange sounds precede the arrival of dancers led by Strephon and two Ancients from the temple. Mark, a young man in modern dress, enters and, seeing them dancing, tells them to stop: for his wedding day he wants a new dance, something different. The Ancients warn that to meddle with tradition may be dangerous and may destroy the beauty of the past. The Ancients retire, leaving Mark to tell his friends, as they arrive, that he has seen these strange figures on summer evenings since childhood (*I don't know who they really are*) and believes they know the secret of his birth. Since they would not perform a new dance, he hails his wedding day with a new song (*Ah, the summer morning dances in my heart*). But when Jenifer appears, she is wearing travel clothes instead of a wedding dress. She announces that she has left her father and must leave Mark as well (*It isn't love I want, but truth*). Finding a flight of stone steps, she begins to climb them (*O magic staircase that I've always known in dreams*), choosing the light above and saying that the shadow below is for Mark. He enters a cave, whose gates clang shut behind him as King Fisher, Jenifer's businessman father, enters in search of her. Thinking Jenifer must have followed Mark into the cave, he calls Bella, his secretary, who tries to persuade the Ancients to open the gates. Failing, she goes to fetch her boyfriend, Jack, a mechanic, to force open the gates. King Fisher asks Mark's friends to scout the area, throwing them money (*So you are Mark's fine brood of friends*), but when he tries the same with Jenifer's friends, they refuse to be bribed. Jack arrives and tries to force the gates, but a voice within (the seer Sosostris) warns against it. An argument ensues between King Fisher, who wants to proceed; Bella and the friends, who think it wrong to tamper with the gates; and Jack, torn between employer and girl friend. At the height of this contretemps, Jenifer reappears at the head of the stairs (partially transformed so as to suggest Athena). A moment later, Mark emerges from below (transfigured to suggest Dionysus). Jenifer sings, "I am a child of the starry heaven," and he shouts back, "I am a child of the fruitful earth." The He-Ancient and She-Ancient come forth to monitor "the contest that you now begin." Jenifer praises the loftiness to which her soul aspires. When King Fisher tries to talk sense to her, the He-Ancient stops him from intervening. Mark replies with praise for "common children of the earth." When Jenifer raises a mirror for Mark to see his beastlike image, he causes it to fall and break. Seeing herself cast as a saint and Mark as a demon, she resolves to complete the process of self-discovery by going into the cave where he has been; he in turn ascends the stairs. Speaking of "midsummer madness," King Fisher is angry and uncomprehending.

ACT II   Afternoon. Strephon, dancing alone, is frightened off by the returning friends, on their way to play games. Jack and Bella stay behind. She says it is time they married and settled in a home of their own. Pleased, he leads her off. Strephon returns, summoning the other dancers, who have been disguised as trees. They enact scenes of autumn, winter, and spring. Jack and Bella have been watching the final dance, in which a hawk captures a smaller bird. She cries out in terror, causing the dancers to disappear. Asking Jack to hold her pocket mirror, she composes herself *(They say a woman's glory is her hair)*. Reminding him that King Fisher is still their boss, she runs playfully off, with him in pursuit *(In the summer season the longest day of all)*.

ACT III   As evening approaches, the friends are finishing supper while some dance to a fiddle. King Fisher arrives with Bella and announces he has found a soothsayer, Mme. Sosostris, equal in wisdom to the Ancients. He has Bella summon the Ancients, who accept his challenge, though they say it is Jenifer's own fate, not their power, that holds the girl. Friends bring Sosostris, a veiled figure, whom King Fisher asks to find his daughter. Cautioning that she can describe but not interpret her visions *(Who hopes to conjure with the world of dreams)*, she describes Jenifer in a meadow, where a lion appears—at first threatening, then as lover and protector. Angered by the image, King Fisher smashes her bowl of divination and orders Jack to stop serving as her acolyte. When he tells Jack to unveil the seer, Jack and Bella defy him and quit his service, so he removes Sosostris' veils himself. Underneath the last veil a glow appears, showing an incandescent bud that opens to reveal Mark and Jenifer, posed (as Shiva and Parvati) in mutual contemplation. In order to "free" Jenifer, King Fisher aims a pistol at Mark, but before he can fire, he suffers a fatal heart attack. His body is carried into the temple, from which Strephon emerges with other dancers to surround a ritual fire. A stick in Strephon's hand bursts into flame (chorus: *Fire! St. John's Fire*) and is set above Mark and Jenifer as the petals enclose them again, while the chorus proclaims, "Carnal love . . . becomes transfigured as divine." As Jenifer and Mark sing of "love's perpetually renewed fire," the bud is consumed by flames. After the flames have subsided, the chorus is left wondering, "Was it a vision? Was it a dream?" The voices of Mark and Jenifer are heard; they appear, dressed for their wedding, at peace with themselves after the visionary night. At dawn, the chorus celebrates the resurgence of life *(All things fall and are built again)*.

Giuseppe Verdi
1813–1901

*G*iuseppe Verdi, who began his career as a contemporary of the bel canto composers (Bellini, Donizetti, Rossini) and ended it as a contemporary of Debussy and Richard Strauss, stands tall as the patriarch of Italian opera. Like most important opera composers, he was primarily a dramatist. In the expressiveness of his vocal style and urgent cohesiveness of his pacing, Verdi combined the eloquence and elegance of the bel canto period with a new, more direct form of address that suited changing times.

Though he was not a peasant, as is often erroneously stated, Verdi came from extremely modest circumstances. His parents were innkeepers in Roncole, in the duchy of Parma, at that time under French rule. Apprenticed to the town organist, he showed enough aptitude to be able to pursue studies in the nearby town of Busseto, underwrittten by a fatherly benefactor, Antonio Barezzi, a greengrocer by profession. Barezzi helped him go to Milan, where he was refused enrollment at the conservatory on the grounds that he was too old and not proficient enough at keyboard playing. Despite this humiliation, Verdi was fortunate in studying privately with Vincenzo Lavigna, an accompanist at La Scala, who saw to it that he attended the opera regularly. Through fortuitous circumstances, the young man was able to start at the top, so to speak: his first opera, *Oberto,* was staged at La Scala in 1839. The way was not easy, however, and his second opera, a comedy, *Un Giorno di Regno,* proved a fiasco the following year.

In despair, Verdi, who had lost his young wife (Barezzi's daughter) and two children within a short time, considered abandoning music, but the impresario Bartolomeo Merelli appealed to his dramatic instincts by showing him a libretto entitled *Nabucco.* The resulting opera was very well received when produced at La Scala in 1842. Giuseppina Strepponi, who sang the soprano lead, later became Verdi's mistress and eventually his second wife.

Of Verdi's twenty-six operas, all but four were written in the first half of a fifty-four-year period of activity. Of that first half, it was the "galley years" 1842–53 that contained the most concentrated work, never a year going by without one or two new operas. He was already in his thirties when the works of this first period, notably *Ernani, Macbeth,* and *Luisa Miller,* began to spread his reputation all over Italy. With *Luisa Miller* and *Stiffelio* in 1849–50, the composer reached a turning point. Having earned enough to buy Sant'Agata, a large farm outside Busseto, he began to lead a less pressured existence. And shifting away from bloodthirsty melodrama (often tinged with popular patriotic sentiments), he began to seek out more subtle characterizations and emotions in his librettos.

The years 1851–53 marked a high-water mark of his career, bringing three of his most successful operas one right after the other—*Rigoletto, Il Trovatore,* and *La Traviata.* Though censors of the Austrian and papal governments in Italy had put up with Verdi the patriot, they cracked down on Verdi the depictor of regicide *(Rigoletto)* and of a sexual double standard *(La Traviata).* He was in trouble, again because of regicide, with *Un Ballo in Maschera* (1859), one of the works of his intermediate period (1855–71).

Starting with *Les Vêpres Siciliennes,* written for the Paris Exposition of 1855, Verdi began to enrich and expand the forms with which he worked. Seeing the operas of Meyerbeer in Paris, he adopted and developed some of their procedures, making them his own. *Simon Boccanegra, La Forza del Destino* (written for the Imperial Theater in St. Petersburg), and *Don Carlos* (again for Paris) attest to this growth. Unlike Rossini, Verdi was able to adapt to "modern" public tastes. He was now writing at his own pace, one opera every few years. Five years after *Forza,* he was lured out of what seemed like retirement by a commission (accompanied by a large fee) to write an opera for the opening of the Suez Canal in Cairo. The result was *Aida* (1871), a more advanced work in the French grand-opera format than any other composer had been able to achieve. With its panoramic deployment of the chorus, delicate touches of ballet, and strong face-to-face encounters between the principals, *Aida* has a fluidity that belies its massiveness.

Now Verdi really did retire, attending to the management of his country estate, grumbling—as composers who survive middle age seem to do—that the theaters were going to the dogs, that no one cared about music or singing anymore. It was sixteen years before he was lured by his publisher, Giulio Ricordi, into collaboration with the poet-composer Arrigo Boito on a setting of *Otello,* based, unlike Rossini's opera of the same title, on Shakespeare. When La Scala produced the work in 1887, there was general agreement that the old master had produced something new, an Italian answer to the challenge of Wagner's "music of the future." Its success encouraged the same pair to write *Falstaff*, Verdi's only comedy after the disastrous *Un Giorno di Regno* of his youth. Its premiere in 1893 marked his farewell to the theater he had served so long. During the eight years remaining to him, he wrote next to nothing, living on as a monument to an age of glory in Italian opera.

NABUCCO

(Nabucodonosor) (Nebuchadnezzar)

THREE ACTS
MUSIC: Giuseppe Verdi
TEXT (Italian): Temistocle Solera
WORLD PREMIERE: Milan, La Scala, March 9, 1842
U.S. PREMIERE: New York, Astor Place Opera House, April 4, 1848
METROPOLITAN OPERA PREMIERE: October 24, 1960

CHARACTERS

Abigaille, *Nabucco's supposed daughter* . . . . Soprano
Fenena, *Nabucco's actual daughter* . . . . Mezzo-Soprano
Anna, *Zaccaria's sister* . . . . Soprano
Nabucco, *King of Babylon* . . . . Baritone
Ismaele, *nephew of the King of Jerusalem* . . . . Tenor
Abdallo, *official of Nabucco's court* . . . . Tenor
Zaccaria, *Hebrew high priest* . . . . Bass
High Priest of Baal . . . . Bass
Hebrews, Levites, Assyrians, vestals, soldiers

ACT I   In the Temple of Solomon in Jerusalem, the Israelites bewail their fate: Nabucco (Nebuchadnezzar), king of Assyria, has fallen on them with his hordes and is desecrating the city. As they offer prayers, Zaccaria (Zacharius), their high priest, enters with his sister, Anna, and Nabucco's daughter, Fenena, whom the Jews hold hostage. He counsels his people to be steadfast, as peace is within their reach, and reassures them that the Lord will not forsake them *(Sperate, o figli)*. Ismaele, nephew of the king of Jerusalem and leader of the military, comes in with soldiers to say Nabucco is sweeping all before him.

Zaccaria hopes for a miracle and turns Fenena over to Ismaele for safekeeping. When the others leave, after a hymn *(Come notte a sol fulgente)*, we learn that Ismaele and Fenena are in love, having met in Babylon when he served there as ambassador. Even then they had a difficult time, because her jealous sister, Abigaille, loved Ismaele too. As they talk, Abigaille bursts in wearing warrior garb, leading a band of Assyrians (disguised as Hebrew soldiers) to occupy the temple. She greets Ismaele with scorn, then privately tells him he can save his people and earn a new kingdom if he returns her love *(Io t'amavo! il regno, il cuore)*. Saying he cannot, he offers to forfeit his life for his people, while Fenena prays to the God of Israel to shield Ismaele. The Hebrew crowd reappears, frightened because Nabucco is approaching. As the conqueror enters the temple, Zaccaria confronts him, denouncing his blasphemous arrogance and threatening to stab Fenena. But Ismaele holds back Zaccaria's blow and delivers Fenena to her father. As Zaccaria and the other Jews revile Ismaele, Nabucco orders the temple looted and burned.

ACT II   In Nabucco's palace in Babylon, Abigaille has found a parchment that could cause her ruin, since it certifies that she is not Nabucco's daughter but the child of slaves. She swears vengeance on Nabucco and his appointed eiress, Fenena, but wistfully reflects that the love she felt for Ismaele could have changed her life *(Anch'io dischiuso un giorno)*. The High Priest of Baal comes to say that Fenena has freed the Hebrew prisoners. As a result of her treason, the religious authorities have decided to offer Abigaille the throne instead, telling the people that their king has fallen in battle. She rejoices that the daughter of slaves will now have everyone at her feet *(Salgo già del torono aurato)*.

§ Elsewhere in the palace, Zaccaria prays for the ability to persuade the Assyrians to put aside their false idols *(Tu sul labbro dei veggenti)*. He will begin by converting Fenena, whose apartment he enters. Two Levites, sent for by Zaccaria, appear and are surprised to meet the outcast Ismaele. As they upbraid him, Zaccaria, accompanied by Fenena and Anna, pardons Ismaele, for he saved a fellow Hebrew—the newly converted Fenena. The aged palace adviser Abdallo rushes in to tell Fenena about the reports of the king's death and to warn that her life is in danger. Before she can escape, the High Priest of Baal, followed by Abigaille and the Assyrian populace, proclaims Abigaille ruler and pronounces a death sentence on the Hebrews. When Abigaille demands the royal scepter, Fenena refuses to yield it. At that moment, to the astonishment of all, Nabucco enters, takes the crown, and places it on his own head. Everyone quakes in dread before the irate monarch *(S'appressan gl'istanti)*, who announces he is not only king but god, having overthrown both Baal and Jehovah. As he tries to force Zaccaria and Fenena to prostrate themselves, lightning strikes him and knocks the crown from his head; it also renders him insane. Abigaille retrieves the crown.

ACT III   In the Hanging Gardens of Babylon, the High Priest of Baal and the populace hail Abigaille as ruler. The High Priest presses her to put the Israelites to death, but before she can sign the warrant, the disheveled Nabucco wanders in, hoping to sit once more on his throne. Abigaille dismisses the others and explains to Nabucco that she is serving as regent, since he is not well enough to rule; she gives him the warrant, hoping to trick him into ordering his own daughter's death. When she taunts him for lack of resolution, he signs. Then Nabucco remembers: what of Fenena? She too will die, retorts Abigaille. When Nabucco tries to find in his garments the document proving Abigaille to be an impostor, she confronts him with it and tears it to bits. Nabucco calls guards but learns that they are no longer his servants: their job is to keep him locked up. Reduced to pleading with Abigaille for Fenena's life, he meets with stony adamancy.

§ By the banks of the Euphrates, the Hebrews are resting from forced labor. Their thoughts ascend "on golden wings" to their lost homeland (Và, pensiero, sull'ali dorate). Zaccaria predicts they will overcome captivity and obliterate Babylon with the Lord's help.

ACT IV   In his royal apartment, Nabucco awakens from fitful sleep to hear voices outside calling Fenena's name. He goes to the window and sees her being led to execution. Trying the door, he remembers he is a prisoner. Desperate, he kneels to pray to the God of the Hebrews for forgiveness (Dio di Giuda!), pledging to convert himself and his people. His reason returns, and when Abdallo and soldiers come to see why he is trying to force the door, he convinces them that he is his old self again. Crying for a sword, he rallies his followers to regain the throne (O prodi miei, seguitemi).

§ In the Hanging Gardens, executioners stand ready to do away with Zaccaria and his flock. The old man hails Fenena as a martyr, and she asks the Lord to receive her into heaven (Oh, dischiuso è il firmamento!), but Nabucco arrives and orders the statue of Baal destroyed. As if by supernatural powers, it falls of its own accord. Abigaille takes poison and confesses her crimes, urging that Ismaele and Fenena be reunited; dying, she prays to the God of Israel to pardon her. Nabucco tells the Israelites to return to their native land and rebuild their temple (Torna Israello), declaring that he himself now serves Jehovah. The crowd acknowledges a miracle and renders praises to God (Immenso Jeova).

ERNANI

FOUR ACTS

MUSIC: Giuseppe Verdi

TEXT (Italian): Francesco Maria Piave, after Victor Hugo's French
  play *Hernani*

WORLD PREMIERE: Venice, Teatro La Fenice, March 9, 1844

U.S. PREMIERE: New York, Park Theatre, April 15, 1847

METROPOLITAN OPERA PREMIERE: January 28, 1903

CHARACTERS

Elvira, *niece and ward of Silva* . . . . Soprano
Giovanna, *her lady-in-waiting* . . . . Mezzo-Soprano
Don Juan of Aragon, *alias Ernani,*
  nobleman turned outlaw . . . . Tenor
Don Carlo, *King of Spain* . . . . Baritone
Don Ruy Gomez de Silva, *Spanish grandee* . . . . Bass
Iago, *his esquire* . . . . Bass
Don Riccardo, *Don Carlo's lieutenant* . . . . Tenor
  Outlaws, courtiers, guests, conspirators

ACT I Spain, 1519. Don Juan of Aragon, stripped of title, lands, and wealth after backing the losing side in civil strife, has been banished and has taken to the hills as the outlaw "Ernani." At their mountain retreat, his followers cheer themselves up with a drinking song, but Ernani is beyond cheer: his beloved Donna Elvira may soon have to marry her elderly uncle and guardian, Don Ruy Gomez de Silva. Recalling his love *(Come rugiada al cespite),* the bandit declares she must be rescued. His men are eager for the escapade, so Ernani envisages a happier future with Elvira *(O tu che l'alma adora).* They set out for Silva's castle.

§ In her apartment in the castle that evening, Elvira longs for Ernani to come to her rescue *(Ernani, involami).* When her ladies-in-waiting bring the wedding gifts, she repeats to herself that Ernani is her sole desire *(Tutto sprezzo che d'Ernani).* An unexpected visitor, Don Carlo, King of Spain, appears as the ladies withdraw. He is impatient to see Elvira, whom he too loves. In answer to his summons, she enters. When he protests his love *(Da qual dì che t'ho* *veduta*), she replies that her proud Aragonese blood places her beyond the temptations of the throne, adding that Carlo's threats are unworthy of a king. As he seems about to abduct her, Ernani appears from a secret doorway and is recognized as the notorious outlaw by Carlo, who tells him to escape with his life. Ernani defies the king, but Elvira steps between them, threatening to take her own life rather than submit to force (trio: *No, crudeli*). Suddenly, Silva appears, aghast at finding not one but two rivals. He mocks himself for believing he could win Elvira's heart *(Infelice! et tu credevi),** then swears vengeance, ordering both men to duel with him outside. The arrival of a royal squire, however, makes Silva realize that Carlo is the king, whom he had not recognized. Loyalty overcomes his rage while Elvira and Ernani, aside, despair at this turn of events (ensemble: *Io tremo, sol io, per te!*). To Silva, Carlo confides that he may be named Holy Roman Emperor and will need Silva's counsel. To spare Ernani and get rid of him, Carlo pretends that the bandit is one of his men and dismisses him. At Elvira's urging, Ernani agrees to go, declaring he will be avenged for past disgrace, while Carlo and Silva happily contemplate the king's future as emperor.

ACT II   In the main hall of the castle, some days later, preparations are under way for Silva's marriage to his niece. Ernani, disguised as a pilgrim, is shown in and asks hospitality, which the old man grants. Elvira appears, about to suggest a wedding gift—her life—when Ernani unmasks and offers his instead. Silva, however, will not betray the sacred obligations of hospitality. He sends Elvira out, then leaves. She returns to face Ernani: hearing he had been killed, she was planning to stab herself at the altar. Discovering them together, Silva is furious, but when the king is announced, he still refuses to betray Ernani, preferring to take his own vengeance later (trio: *No, vendetta più tremenda*). As Elvira leaves and Silva hides Ernani, the king appears, declares that he knows that Ernani is in the castle—the bandit's defeated men having been scattered—and orders Silva to turn him over. So fierce is Silva's pride that he offers his own life rather than betray a guest. Carlo orders his men to search the castle *(La vedremo, veglio audace)*, but they return to say they found no one. Carlo now plans to torture Silva's retainers, but Elvira rushes in to beg clemency. Carlo sees an opportunity to take Elvira hostage; Silva, faced with the alternative of betraying his guest, has to allow this. Carlo urges Elvira to come with him and be happy *(Vieni meco, sol di rose)*, while Silva admits to himself that his loyalty to the crown has been shattered. As soon as the old man is alone, he seizes two swords and pulls Ernani out of hiding, ordering him to come outside and fight. In deference to Silva's age and hospitality, Ernani refuses, saying Silva should simply kill him instead. Learning that Carlo has taken Elvira, Ernani proposes a joint effort to stop their rival. To certify that his word can be trusted, Ernani pledges to forfeit his life whenever Silva gives

*In some editions, *tuo* instead of the original *tu*.

the signal with a hunting horn, which he presents to the old man *(Nel momento in che Ernani vorrai spento)*. Silva agrees and calls his men in pursuit of Carlo.

ACT III   In a crypt housing Charlemagne's tomb at Aix-la-Chapelle, Carlo comes to learn the identity of rebels who meet there in secret, plotting against the throne. Meanwhile, electors have convened nearby to choose the next Holy Roman Emperor. Awed by the surrounding tombs of his ancestors, Carlo reflects on the vanity of life and vows to rule wisely if chosen *(Oh, de' verd'anni miei)*. He enters the gate of Charlemagne's tomb as the conspirators draw near, led by Silva and Ernani. Drawing lots for the honor of assassinating Carlo—Ernani is chosen, to Silva's chagrin—the men of the league look forward to happier days for Spain without the tyrant *(Si ridesti il Leon di Castiglia)*. When three cannon shots are heard, Carlo steps out of hiding, announcing the signal of his appointment as Charles V, Holy Roman Emperor. The electors enter, bearing the crown and followed by courtiers, among them Elvira. Carlo orders the conspirators arrested and the nobles among them executed. Ernani reveals his own identity, asking to be executed with them. Elvira throws herself at Carlo's feet, begging him to let contempt be his revenge. Moved by her words and by the responsibility he has inherited, Carlo decides to emulate Charlemagne's virtues *(O sommo Carlo)*: not only will he spare the plotters, but Ernani and Elvira shall marry.

ACT IV   Restored to his palace in Aragon, Don Juan, the former Ernani, is holding a reception in honor of his imminent marriage to Elvira. On a terrace, guests notice a masked stranger in a black cloak. They return inside as Don Juan and Elvira express their happiness. It is short-lived: a hunting horn is heard in the distance. When Don Juan talks wildly about the old man coming to get him, Elvira thinks he is losing his reason. Pleading the effects of an old wound, he asks her to fetch medicine. Alone on the terrace, he confronts Silva, who throws aside his cloak to demand satisfaction. The younger man pleads for a brief stay of execution so that he can enjoy the only happiness that has ever come to him in a life of misery *(Solingo, errante misero)*. Silva replies that he may choose poison or dagger. When Elvira returns, she cries out against Silva, then apologizes, hoping to mollify him—but in vain. As the lovers lament their fate, Silva repeats his demand (trio: *Non ebbe di noi miseri*). After Don Juan stabs himself, Elvira tries to do likewise, but both men stop her. She falls unconscious as her lover dies and her uncle grimly pronounces vengeance.

MACBETH

FOUR ACTS
MUSIC: Giuseppe Verdi
TEXT (Italian): Francesco Maria Piave, after Shakespeare's play, as
    translated by Giulio Carcano
WORLD PREMIERE: Florence, Teatro della Pergola, March 14, 1847;
    Paris, Théâtre Lyrique, April 21, 1865 (revision)
U.S. PREMIERE: New York, Niblo's Garden, April 24, 1850
METROPOLITAN OPERA PREMIERE: February 5, 1959

CHARACTERS

Lady Macbeth . . . . Soprano
Her Lady-in-Waiting . . . . Mezzo-Soprano
Hecate, *goddess of witchcraft* . . . . Dancer
Macbeth ⎫ *generals* . . . . ⎧Baritone
Banco ⎭ . . . . ⎩ Bass
Fleance, *Banco's son* . . . . Mute
Macduff, *Scottish nobleman* . . . . Tenor
Malcolm, *Duncan's son* . . . . Tenor
Physician . . . . Bass
Duncan, *King of Scotland* . . . . Mute
Witches, spirits (dancers), servants, messengers, soldiers,
assassins, nobles, peasants

ACT I   On a barren heath in medieval Scotland, three groups of witches gather to exchange news. Macbeth and Banco (Banquo) appear and greet the witches, who hail the former as Thane of Glamis, Thane of Cawdor, and King of Scotland, adding that Banco will sire a race of kings. Questioned, the witches vanish, leaving the two men perplexed. Messengers arrive with word that the king has awarded to Macbeth the title Thane of Cawdor, fulfilling the witches' prediction. After the men leave, the witches return briefly, agreeing to meet again later.

§ In Macbeth's castle, Lady Macbeth reads a letter from her husband telling of the meeting with the witches. She pledges herself to spur his ambition for the throne (*Vieni! t'affretta!*). When a servant announces that King Duncan is to arrive that very night with Macbeth, she calls on the ministers of hell to aid her plan *(Or tutti sorgete)*. Macbeth enters, and she tells him they must strike that night. Then Duncan arrives, accompanied by attendants, and is shown to his room by Lady Macbeth. Macbeth sees a vision of a dagger before him *(Mi si affaccia un pugnal?)*. Signaled by the night bell, he goes to perform the murder; on his return, he finds his wife waiting. He tells how unnerved he is by his act, while she retorts that he needs courage *(Fatal mia donna!)*. She takes the dagger herself, to smear the sleeping guards with blood and make them seem the murderers. A knock at the castle gate terrifies the guilty Macbeth. Lady Macbeth returns, and they both withdraw as Macduff and Banco enter. Macduff goes to waken the king and discovers the murder, rousing everyone in the castle. Macbeth and Lady Macbeth hypocritically join in the common expression of horror and shock (ensemble: *Schiudi, inferno).*

ACT II   Macbeth has been named king, thanks to the flight to England of Duncan's son, Malcolm, who is assumed to have plotted the murder of his father. Worried about the prophecy that Banco's heirs will rule, Macbeth now plots with his wife to do away with Banco and *his* son, Fleance, that very night. As Macbeth goes to arrange the deed, Lady Macbeth welcomes the approaching darkness *(La luce langue).*

§ In a park outside the castle, assassins gather to carry out Macbeth's orders; they too welcome the darkness to cover their deed *(Sparve il sol)*. They hide as Banco approaches, warning his son of strange forebodings *(Come dal ciel precipita)*. The assassins emerge to ambush him, but his son, Fleance, escapes.

§ In the banquet hall, Lady Macbeth welcomes the court, offering a drinking song *(Si colmi il calice)*. Aside, Macbeth receives word that Banco is dead but that Fleance has escaped. Turning toward the table, he says he regrets Banco's absence and will take his seat—only to find it occupied by the ghost of the dead man. The others inquire what is the matter with Macbeth, as his wife makes excuses, saying he is sometimes prey to seizures. She resumes the drinking song, but soon afterward he sees Banco's ghost again, crying that he must revisit the witches *(Sangue a me)*. Macduff privately vows to leave the country, which is now ruled by murderers, and the courtiers wonder at the cause of Macbeth's behavior.

ACT III   In a cave on the heath, the witches add infernal ingredients to their cauldron, invoking the powers of darkness. Macbeth enters their lair, demanding more prophecies. They conjure up a warrior's head, which warns Macbeth to beware of Macduff, then a bloody child that tells him "no man of woman born" can harm him, then a crowned child carrying a bough, who says Macbeth will be invincible "till Birnam Wood shall come to Dunsinane." Macbeth insists on knowing whether Banco's heirs will rule. A procession of eight future kings is seen, followed by Banco holding a mirror. When Macbeth swoons at the sight, the witches summon Hecate and spirits of the air to revive him (ballet).* Then they disappear, leaving him on the heath, where his wife finds him. He repeats the prophecies, and the pair resolves to kill Macduff and his family as well as Banco's son *(Ora di morte e di vendetta)*.

ACT IV   Near Birnam Wood and the English border, refugees bemoan Scotland's fate. Macduff laments the reported slaughter of his wife and children, wishing he had been there to defend them *(Ah, la paterna mano)*. Malcolm appears at the head of British forces, and all pledge to overthrow the tyrant *(La patria tradita)*.

§ In Macbeth's castle, a Physician and Lady-in-Waiting watch for the nightly appearance of Lady Macbeth, who enters sleepwalking, muttering that there is still blood on her hands *(Una macchia)* and that all the perfumes of Arabia cannot sweeten them.

§ Alone near a battlefield, Macbeth prepares to meet his foes, knowing he will never live to a peaceful old age *(Pietà, rispetto, amore)*. He learns that Lady Macbeth has died and that Birnam Wood appears to be moving. He grabs his arms and summons his followers.

§ Noises of combat are heard, and British soldiers appear, camouflaging themselves with branches. Macduff confronts Macbeth, who says that "no man of woman born" can harm him, whereupon Macduff announces he had a Caesarean birth. The two men fight, and the dying Macbeth falls to the ground cursing the day he met the witches *(Mal per me)*.* Malcolm and Macduff lead in their followers, who rejoice in the usurper's death and the liberation of their land, hailing Malcolm as rightful king *(S'affidi ognun al Re)*.

LUISA MILLER

THREE ACTS
MUSIC: Giuseppe Verdi
TEXT (Italian): Salvatore Cammarano, after Friedrich Schiller's
   German play *Kabale und Liebe*
WORLD PREMIERE: Naples, Teatro San Carlo, December 8, 1849
U.S. PREMIERE: Philadelphia, Walnut Street Theater, October 27,
   1852 (in English)
METROPOLITAN OPERA PREMIERE: December 21, 1929

* Often omitted in performance.

GIUSEPPE VERDI

CHARACTERS

Luisa Miller, *young bourgeoise*. . . . . Soprano
Duchess Federica . . . . Mezzo-Soprano
Rodolfo, *Luisa's suitor*. . . . . Tenor
Miller, *her father, retired soldier* . . . . Baritone
Count Walter, *Rodolfo's father* . . . . Bass
Wurm, *his steward* . . . . Bass
Villagers, courtiers, servants

ACT I   A village in the Tyrol, early nineteenth century. Villagers greet Luisa
on her birthday. Her father, a retired soldier, knows she is in love and cautions
her. But she is impatient to see her "Carlo," a newcomer to the court of Count
Walter, the local lord, saying it was love at first sight (*Lo vidi, e'l primo
palpito*). Soon "Carlo" appears, dressed for hunting, and declares his love for
her in return. Everyone enters the church except Miller and a late arrival,
Wurm—Count Walter's steward—who says he loves Luisa himself. Miller
replies he would give consent only if his daughter returned Wurm's love (*Sacra
la scelta*). Wurm tells Miller that "Carlo" is actually Rodolfo, the count's son.
Miller is now convinced that the intentions of "Carlo" are not honorable.

§ In Count Walter's castle, Wurm tells his master that Rodolfo is in love
with a commoner. Seeking only his son's happiness, the count has tried to
further his marriage to Duchess Federica (*Il mio sangue, la vita darei*). When
Rodolfo appears, Walter says that Federica, whom the youth has known since
childhood, agrees to marry him. Rodolfo is about to tell his father the truth
when they are interrupted by the duchess' arrival. Left alone with her, Rodolfo
tries to explain, but when Federica learns he loves someone else, she is deeply
hurt (duet: *Deh! la parola amara*).

§ Inside Miller's house, Luisa watches for another visit from Rodolfo as hunters pass by. Her father enters, telling her in despair that her lover is really
Count Walter's son. The old man swears vengeance, but Rodolfo appears at
the door and pleads his sincerity, insisting he wants to marry Luisa. Miller
fears the count's wrath, but Rodolfo says he knows a secret about his father
that no one else knows, which will stay the count from doing anything to stop
the marriage. Walter himself appears, however, determined to break up what
he considers an "illicit intrigue." Rodolfo draws his sword, prepared to strike
his own father in defense of Luisa's honor; Miller too is mortally insulted.
Walter orders both lovers arrested. Luisa pleads with him; Rodolfo continues
to wield his sword threateningly, then tells Walter confidentially that he will
reveal how the latter came by his rank. At this, Walter lets Luisa go free.

ACT II   In Miller's house, villagers tell Luisa that they saw her father taken
prisoner by Walter's men. She is about to go to the castle when Wurm inter-

cepts her and orders everyone else out. He tells her that the only way she can save her father is to write a note "admitting" she never loved Rodolfo and was only fortune hunting, also announcing her intention to elope with Wurm that very night. Luisa does as she is told but begs God to forgive her perjury (*Tu puniscimi, o Signore*). She gives Wurm the letter; he makes her promise to defend its contents if questioned, and to come to the castle to declare before the duchess that she loves Wurm.

§ At the castle, Walter tells Wurm he is losing patience with the raving Rodolfo. Wurm reassures him that Luisa has written the letter, which is being delivered now to Rodolfo, and that she will soon arrive at the castle. When Wurm asks why the original plan to arrest Luisa went awry, Walter says that Rodolfo threatened to reveal the secret of his power. He recalls how, with Wurm's help, he conspired in the death of his cousin, the preceding count, hoping to secure his fortune for Rodolfo and his rank for himself. (*L'alto retaggio*). At the moment of death, Walter now reveals, the old count told Rodolfo who had killed him, though everyone else believed the story given out by Walter and Wurm: that assassins did the deed. Federica enters; dismissing Wurm, Walter tells her that Rodolfo will soon recover from his infatuation with Luisa. Wurm returns with Luisa, who denies having loved Rodolfo and says Wurm is the one she loves (quartet: *Come celar le smanie*).

§ Elsewhere on the castle grounds, Rodolfo has received Luisa's letter from a villager. He despairs over Luisa's betrayal, sadly recalling their love (*Quando le sere al placido*). Wurm, sent for by Rodolfo, enters. Showing him the letter, Rodolfo challenges him to a duel and offers him a choice of pistols. Wurm takes one and fires it into the air to bring help; as retainers appear, he flees. Walter offers Rodolfo Luisa's hand after all, knowing he will refuse. Then he urges the young man to show his scorn for Luisa's treachery by going through with the marriage to Federica. Rodolfo says that the altar and the tomb are the same for him (*L'ara, o l'avello apprestami*).

ACT III   In Miller's house, Luisa's friends wonder at the change that has come over her: she says she is already tasting the delights of heaven. The church is lit for Rodolfo's wedding to Federica, but Luisa's friends, to protect her, say the count is celebrating his assumption of power. Miller, set free by Walter, embraces Luisa and tells her he learned from Wurm of her sacrifice to save him. It is true that she renounced her love, she says—but only on earth. She has written a letter to be taken to Rodolfo, asking him to join her in death. Miller pleads with her not to abandon her father in his old age. Guilt-stricken, she tears up the letter; they talk of quitting the village together and wandering as beggars (*Andrem, raminghi e poveri*). Miller leaves to go to bed. As the organ sounds at the church, Rodolfo appears. Finding Luisa in prayer, he takes a vial of poison and empties it into a cup on the table. When Luisa sees him, he shows her the letter and asks whether she wrote it. She says yes. He asks for a drink, which he says tastes bitter, asking her to taste it too, which she does. Still accusing her, he tells her at length that he has poisoned the drink. Knowing she will die, Luisa no longer feels bound by her oath of silence to Wurm, so she tells Rodolfo the truth. He curses the day he was born *(Maledetto il dì ch'io nacqui)*. Miller enters, horrified to learn that the lovers have taken poison. Luisa dies, but when the villagers burst in, accompanied by Walter and Wurm, Rodolfo has enough strength to grab his sword and kill Wurm before joining his beloved in death.

RIGOLETTO

THREE ACTS
MUSIC: Giuseppe Verdi
TEXT (Italian): Francesco Maria Piave, after Victor Hugo's play *Le Roi s'amuse*
WORLD PREMIERE: Venice, Teatro La Fenice, March 11, 1851
U.S. PREMIERE: New York, Academy of Music, February 19, 1855
METROPOLITAN OPERA PREMIERE: January 2, 1885 (in German)

CHARACTERS

Gilda	Soprano
Giovanna, *her nurse*	Mezzo-Soprano
Countess Ceprano	Mezzo-Soprano
Maddalena, *Sparafucile's sister*	Mezzo-Soprano
Duke of Mantua, *libertine*	Tenor
Matteo Borsa, *courtier*	Tenor
Rigoletto, *his jester*	Baritone
Count Monterone, *noble*	Baritone
Marullo, *courtier*	Baritone
Sparafucile, *assassin*	Bass
Count Ceprano	Bass

Courtiers, page, servants

ACT I Sixteenth-century Mantua. During a ball in the Ducal Palace, the philandering Duke tells one of his courtiers, Borsa, that he wants to consummate his flirtation with an unknown girl he has seen in church. He knows where she lives and has seen a mysterious man enter there every night. The

Duke's attention is diverted by female guests, notably Countess Ceprano. He declares he finds one woman as charming as the next and hates the thought of constancy (*Questa o quella*). Rigoletto, the court jester, a sarcastic hunchback, enters and taunts Count Ceprano about the cuckold's horns he is sprouting. To the Duke, Rigoletto suggests either having the Count beheaded or kidnaping his wife. Led by Ceprano, the courtiers say that Rigoletto goes too far and should be punished; even the Duke reproves him. Marullo tells the other courtiers that Rigoletto has a mistress. Attention is diverted when the indignant old Count Monterone, whose daughter has been seduced by the Duke, storms in demanding vengeance. The Duke orders him arrested, and Rigoletto mocks him—whereupon Monterone thunders a father's curse upon the jester.

§ *Later that evening, in a dark alley outside his house, the superstitious Rigoletto is disturbed by Monterone's curse. He is accosted by Sparafucile, a professional assassin, who offers his services to get rid of the swain he has seen spying on the lady in Rigoletto's house. Sending him off, the jester reflects that he and the assassin have much in common: one kills with words, the other with a sword (*Pari siamo!*). He hates his job and the corrupt courtiers; the only happiness in his life is his daughter, Gilda. He unlocks the door to his courtyard, and she greets him affectionately. When she questions him about her origins, he says only that her mother died (*Deh non parlare al misero*), leaving him with no family, no friends, no identity other than Gilda. To himself he admits his fear that the Duke's courtiers, or people like them, might kidnap his daughter. The housekeeper, Giovanna, in response to Rigoletto's orders to keep a perpetual eye on Gilda (*Ah! veglia, o donna*), assures him of her reliability. But when someone is heard in the alley and Rigoletto goes out to investigate, the Duke—disguised in humble clothes—slips into the garden and hides, silencing Giovanna with a bribe. Rigoletto comes back with more instructions, then leaves for his rendezvous with the courtiers, who plan to kidnap Countess Ceprano from her house nearby. Gilda expresses anxiety to Giovanna about the young man who has shown interest in her. At this the Duke steps forth, and Giovanna withdraws. The Duke quickly mollifies Gilda's fear with words about true love (*È il sol dell'anima*). When she asks his name, he says he is Gualtier Maldè, a poor student. Voices are heard in the alley, where Borsa and Ceprano are furthering a plot of revenge against Rigoletto. Fearing discovery, the Duke leaves, exchanging hurried farewells with Gilda (*Addio! speranza ed anima*). Left to herself, she muses on his name and how dear its meaning is to her (*Caro nome*). Meanwhile, the courtiers have been keeping their eye on Rigoletto's supposed mistress. When Rigoletto himself returns, they say they are about to abduct Countess Ceprano and blindfold him. Then they have him hold a ladder for them as they go over the wall into the courtyard, singing softly of their escapade (*Zitti, zitti*). They make off

---

* This scene is often performed as a separate act.

with Gilda, whose cries startle Rigoletto into tearing off his mask and realizing he has been tricked. Stupefied, he cries out, "Ah! the curse!"

ACT II   In a drawing room of the palace, the Duke laments that when he returned to Gilda's house, he found her gone. He imagines her in tears and wishes he could console her *(Parmi veder le lagrime)*. Soon the courtiers come in to tell how they kidnaped Rigoletto's mistress *(Scorrendo uniti remota via)*, and the Duke realizes that Gilda is in the palace; overjoyed, he rushes to the conquest *(Possente amor)*.* Rigoletto appears, trying to hide his distress *(La rà, la rà, la rà)* while looking for clues to Gilda's whereabouts. A page, inquiring for the Duke, is told he cannot be disturbed, and Rigoletto understands what is happening. Beside himself, he rages at the courtiers to give back his daughter *(Cortigiani! vil razza dannata)*; when they do not respond, he resorts to abject pleading. Finally, Gilda rushes out of an adjoining room into her father's arms, and he orders the courtiers to leave. In shame she tells of the young man she trusted, having seen him at church *(Tutte le feste al tempio)*. He comforts her *(Piangi, fanciulla)*. Then, seeing old Monterone being led to prison, he vows to wreak vengeance on the Duke *(Sì, vendetta)*.

ACT III   A run-down inn on the outskirts of town, at night, some time later. Rigoletto has brought Gilda with him to watch through a chink in the wall. The girl protests she still loves the Duke, but her father says she will see something that will change her mind. The Duke, dressed as a soldier, appears inside the inn and asks Sparafucile for a room and some wine. Then he expounds on the fickleness of women *(La donna è mobile)* and is diverted by Sparafucile's attractive sister, Maddalena, in Gypsy costume. Sparafucile steps outside and asks Rigoletto whether he wants this man killed; Rigoletto says he will come back later to close the deal. Alone with Maddalena inside the inn, the Duke tries to make love to her, while she laughs off his advances; outside, at the same time, Gilda cries out in anguish at her lover's betrayal, and Rigoletto plots his revenge (quartet: *Bella figlia dell'amor*). The jester tells his daughter to dress in men's clothes and ride to Verona, where he will join her the next day. Then he meets Sparafucile and makes a down payment, the other half to be paid on delivery of the body, which he wants to throw in the river himself. As he leaves, a thunderstorm comes up. Sparafucile goes back inside, where he tells Maddalena about the deal he has made; she tries to get the Duke to leave and, aside, asks her brother to spare the handsome young man. When the Duke has retired upstairs, Sparafucile tells his sister he cannot go back on a bargain, but she persuades him to substitute as a victim the next person who comes to the inn. Gilda, who has returned and overheard, resolves to sacrifice herself to save the Duke. While the storm rages, she knocks at the door, posing as a beggar, and is stabbed. Rigoletto comes back, gloating, and knocks

*Often omitted.

too, whereupon Sparfucile hands him the sack and locks him out. But as Rigoletto lugs his burden toward the river, he is stunned to hear the Duke upstairs, singing his earlier song (*La donna è mobile*). Tearing open the sack, he finds Gilda, who asks forgiveness and says she will join her mother in heaven and pray for him (*Lassù in cielo*). As she dies, he cries out, "Ah! the curse!"

Il Trovatore

(The Troubadour)

FOUR ACTS
MUSIC: Giuseppe Verdi
TEXT (Italian): Salvatore Cammarano, after Antonio García
Gutiérrez's play *El Trovador*
WORLD PREMIERE: Rome, Teatro Apollo, January 19, 1853
U.S. PREMIERE: New York, Academy of Music, May 2, 1855
METROPOLITAN OPERA PREMIERE: October 26, 1883

CHARACTERS

Leonora, *lady-in-waiting at an*
  Aragonese court . . . . Soprano
Inez, *her companion* . . . . Soprano
Azucena, *Gypsy woman* . . . . Mezzo-Soprano
Manrico, *troubadour, officer in the*
  service of the count of Biscay . . . . Tenor
Ruiz, *his aide* . . . . Tenor
Count di Luna, *Aragonese nobleman* . . . . Baritone
Ferrando, *captain of Aragonese palace guard* . . . . Bass
        Soldiers, Gypsies, guardsmen, messenger, jailer, nuns,
                palace attendants

ACT I (The Duel). Spain, fifteenth century. Nighttime in hall of the Alia-feria palace. Ferrando, a veteran guardsman, keeps his troop of Count di Luna's soldiers awake by telling the story of how the count's infant brother was hexed by a Gypsy hag, who was burned at the stake for it. In revenge, the Gypsy's daughter stole the child and apparently burned him in the remains of the same fire that killed her mother. Unwilling to believe his child dead, the old count charged his other son, the present Count di Luna, with finding the Gypsy's daughter *(Abbietta zingara)*.

§ Elsewhere on the palace grounds, the lady Leonora hopes for a visit from a mysterious troubadour who has been serenading her. She tells Inez, her lady-in-waiting, how she first met the stranger when she crowned him victor in a knightly tournament, but then civil war came and a long time passed before he reappeared one night under her balcony *(Tacea la notte)*. No sooner have the two ladies left than Di Luna appears, bent on serenading Leonora himself. Before he can begin, the distant voice of the troubadour is heard, singing of the melancholy life of the outlaw *(Deserto sulla terra)*. Leonora comes down to meet the troubadour and angers both men—first by running to Di Luna in the darkness, then by recognizing her mistake and running into the troubadour's arms. Challenged by Di Luna, the stranger reveals that he is Manrico, a follower of the rebel Urgel, and under sentence of death. As Leonora urges the count to kill her instead, the two men prepare for a duel (trio: *Di geloso amor sprezzato*).

ACT II (The Gypsy). Several months later, in their mountain encampment, a group of Gypsies wield hammers, plying their tinkers' craft (anvil chorus: *Chi del gitano*). They stop work to hear one of the old Gypsies, Azucena, tell how she once saw a woman burned at the stake *(Stride la vampa)*. When the others have left, she turns to Manrico and gives more details: the woman led in irons to the stake *(Condotta ell'era in ceppi)* was her own mother, Manrico's grandmother. To avenge the death, Azucena meant to throw the old count's child in the flames, but distractedly she threw her own child instead. Manrico, who believes himself her son, is confused by the tale, but she reassures him of a mother's love, reminding him that she nursed him back to life after the recent Battle of Pelilla, where he was felled by Di Luna's forces. She then asks why, in his earlier duel with Di Luna, Manrico had not killed his rival; Manrico replies that some strange force stayed his hand *(Mal reggendo)*. As Azucena mutters about her mother's dying cry for vengeance, another Gypsy, Ruiz, brings word that Urgel's forces have captured the bastion of Castellor and that Manrico must see to its defense. Leonora, deceived by news of Manrico's death, is about to enter a nearby convent. Though Azucena tries to stop him *(Perigliarti ancor languente)*, Manrico insists on going to Leonora's rescue.

§ In the courtyard of the convent, Di Luna appears with his retainers, also intent on carrying off Leonora. Inspired by love *(Il balen del suo sorriso)*, Di Luna declares that not even God can take Leonora from him. The nuns are heard in a chorus of reassurance to Leonora who appears, ready to take her vows. No sooner does Di Luna burst forth from hiding than Manrico arrives, to Leonora's happy disbelief *(E deggio e posso crederlo?)*. As his forces drive back Di Luna's men, he leads her off.

ACT III (The Gypsy's Son). Di Luna and his soldiers set up an encampment near Castellor in order to recapture it. They are eager for attack (*Squilli, echeggi la tromba*), but Di Luna recalls grimly that Leonora is with Manrico in the fortress. Ferrando comes to tell him that a suspicious-looking Gypsy woman has been found near the camp. It turns out to be Azucena, who answers Di Luna's interrogation by saying she survived a miserable existence (*Giorni poveri vivea*) sustained only by love of her son, who has left her, and she is trying to find him. Ferrando, detecting her resemblance to the old witch once burned at the stake, accuses her of having burned the count's infant brother. Di Luna orders her tied up, despite her entreaties (*Deh, rallentate, o barbari*), and when she calls Manrico's name, he exults in having captured his rival's mother.

§ Inside Castellor, Manrico and Leonora prepare to marry, amid preparations for battle. Manrico pledges his love (*Ah sì, ben mio, coll'essere*), but as they exchange words of tenderness, Ruiz runs in with news that Azucena is about to be burned at the stake. Seeing flames, Manrico rallies his men to the rescue (*Di quella pira*).

ACT IV (The Torture). Outside the tower of Aliaferia, where the captured Manrico languishes, Leonora comes, led by Ruiz, in hopes of rescuing her lover. She sends her love to comfort him (*D'amor sull'ali rosee*), and when monks are heard intoning a Miserere for the condemned man, she expresses anxiety, while Manrico's farewell is heard from the tower. She vows to save him or die with him (*Tu vedrai che amore in terra*).* The count comes in, declaring that love for Leonora has driven him to rash acts. Finding her there, he hears her tearful pleas for Manrico's life (*Mira, d'acerbe lagrime*); as a last, desperate measure she offers herself in exchange for Manrico's freedom. Accepting, Di Luna arranges for Manrico's release. Meanwhile, Leonora takes poison concealed in her ring.

§ Inside the tower, Azucena lies resting fitfully while Manrico offers words of comfort. Once more she is haunted by visions of the stake. Feeling herself near death, she imagines going back with Manrico to the mountains (*Ai nostri monti*). Leonora comes to tell Manrico that he is free, but he angrily guesses at what price. She explains she has poisoned herself and is dying (*Prima che d'altri vivere*). Di Luna enters and, seeing the dying Leonora, realizes he has been cheated of his prize. Ordering Manrico beheaded, he drags Azucena to the window to witness the execution—only to learn from her that Manrico was his own brother. Azucena gasps that at last her mother is avenged.

*Often omitted

LA TRAVIATA

THREE ACTS
MUSIC: Giuseppe Verdi
TEXT (Italian): Francesco Maria Piave, after the novel *La Dame
aux Camélias,* by Alexandre Dumas *fils*
WORLD PREMIERE: Venice, Teatro La Fenice, March 6, 1853
U.S. PREMIERE: New York, Academy of Music, December 3, 1856
METROPOLITAN OPERA PREMIERE: November 5, 1883

CHARACTERS

Violetta Valéry, *courtesan* . . . . Soprano
Flora Bervoix, *her friend* . . . . Mezzo-Soprano
Annina, *Violetta's maid* . . . . Soprano
Alfredo Germont, *Violetta's lover* . . . . Tenor
Giorgio Germont, *his father* . . . . Baritone
Baron Douphol, *Violetta's protector* . . . . Baritone
Gastone, Viscount de Letorières . . . . Tenor
Marquis d'Obigny, *Flora's protector* . . . . Bass
Dr. Grenvil, *physician* . . . . Bass
Party guests, dancers, servants, maskers, gardener

ACT I   A salon in Violetta's house in Paris, around August 1850. Welcoming her guests to a party, Violetta remarks that pleasure is a drug that makes life bearable. Among the arrivals are Baron Douphol, Violetta's current lover, who keeps her; Flora Bervoix, a friend of Violetta's; and Gastone, a young man-about-town. Gastone introduces Alfredo Germont, who has admired Violetta from a distance. To make the tongue-tied young man feel at home, Violetta pours wine, and he responds by proposing a toast (brindisi: *Libiamo ne' lieti calici),* in which Violetta and the others join. It is evident from his verses that Alfredo takes love more seriously than does Violetta. A dance orchestra strikes up in the next room, and the guests start for the door, but Violetta feels faint and stays behind. Everyone leaves except Alfredo, who tells her he is deeply concerned. She cuts off his declaration *(Un dì felice, eterea)* with frank advice: romance is not for her, and he should look for someone else. When he starts to leave, she hands him a camellia and asks him to visit her when it has wilted—the next day. Overjoyed, he kisses her hand and goes. The other guests return, saying daybreak is nigh and thanking their hostess.

When they have gone, Violetta questions herself about the strange feelings aroused by Alfredo *(Ah, fors'è lui):* does she dare allow herself a serious affair? After pondering the idea, she rejects it *(Sempre libera),* declaring that the giddy whirl must continue—even though Alfredo, outside, repeats his words of love.

ACT II A country house near Paris, the following January. In the five months that have elapsed since the time of Act I, Violetta has gone to live with Alfredo outside the city. Alfredo enters the drawing room and rhapsodizes about his happiness *(De' miei bollenti spiriti).* When Annina, Violetta's maid, returns from a trip to Paris, Alfredo learns that her mission was to sell her mistress' belongings: life in the country is expensive. The young man resolves to get money of his own to set the situation right *(Oh mio rimorso!).** He has no sooner left than Violetta appears, asking Annina where he went. The news that he is en route to Paris strikes her as odd, but she is interrupted by the servant Giuseppe, who hands her an invitation to a party at Flora's that evening. Having renounced her old life, Violetta puts it aside. Giuseppe then announces a gentleman caller, and Violetta, thinking it is someone on business, asks for him to be shown in. The visitor turns out to be Alfredo's father, who starts to address her harshly, taking her for a common fortune hunter. He is impressed at once, however, by her ladylike manners. To clear up the question of money, she shows him receipts from the sale of her belongings. Aware that he is dealing with a woman of dignity and character, the elder Germont asks rhetorically why her past should condemn her. She replies that her love for Alfredo has redeemed her, but Germont says he must ask a sacrifice. Because the scandal of the liaison makes it impossible for his daughter to make a respectable marriage *(Pure siccome un angelo),* Germont wants Violetta to renounce Alfredo. Violetta says she cannot: Alfredo is all she has, and the loss would kill her *(Non sapete quale affetto).* Germont is sympathetic but persists, reminding Violetta that she is young and can still make a life for herself, and that Alfredo will eventually tire of her *(Un dì, quando le venere).* She finally gives in, asking Germont to tell his daughter of the sacrifice made for her sake (duet: *Ah! Dite alla giovine).* After exchanging farewells with Germont, she decides she can only leave, sending Annina with a note accepting Flora's invitation. As she writes to Alfredo, however, he suddenly appears. She tries in vain to conceal her agitation, begging Alfredo to love her *(Amami, Alfredo)* as much as she loves him, then saying good-bye. Only when the gardener appears with Violetta's farewell note does he realize that she has left him. His father reappears and tries to comfort him, reminding him of their native Provence *(Di Provenza il mar).* Too distraught to listen, Alfredo believes that Violetta has gone back to Baron Douphol; Germont renews his plea, promising forgiveness if Alfredo returns home *(No, non udrai rimproveri).** Instead, Alfredo sees Flora's invitation on the table and rushes to follow her to the party.

*Often omitted

§ Flora's salon, that evening.* When Flora mentions to her protector, the Marquis d'Obigny, that she has invited Alfredo and Violetta, he says that the lovers have separated. Women dressed as Gypsies read fortunes (chorus: *Noi siamo zingarelle*), and Gastone and a group of men dressed as matadors hail the prowess of a bullfighter (*È Piquillo un bel gagliardo*). Alfredo enters alone and starts gambling with forced nonchalance. When Violetta appears on the arm of the baron, the latter orders her not to speak to Alfredo. Tension builds as Alfredo wins at cards and the baron challenges him by joining the game (ensemble: *Qui desiata giungi*). Alfredo's winning streak continues until supper is announced. Violetta stays behind as the others go into the next room; Alfredo appears, in reply to her summons. Warning him of the baron's anger, she succeeds only in intensifying his jealousy: Alfredo forces her to say that she loves the baron. Then he calls the others in to witness the fact that he is repaying Violetta the money she squandered on him (*Ogni suo aver tal femmina*), throwing his winnings at her feet. Germont unexpectedly enters, denouncing his son's unworthy behavior (*Di sprezzo degno*). The baron challenges Alfredo to a duel, and Violetta, near fainting, tells Alfredo she does not deserve his contempt.

ACT III   Violetta's bedroom in Paris, a month later. Abandoned by Alfredo and the baron, almost out of money, Violetta lies dying of tuberculosis. Only the faithful Annina and a friend, Dr. Grenvil, still attend her; the doctor tells Annina that her mistress cannot last much longer. Sending Annina out to give a few coins to the poor at Carnival time, she rereads a letter from Germont (*Teneste la promessa*) saying that Alfredo wounded the baron and left the country but will return to ask her forgiveness, having learned the truth about her sacrifice. Looking in a mirror, she sees how changed she is by illness and realizes that it is too late, bidding farewell to her past dreams (*Addio del passato*). As merrymakers are heard outside, Annina announces that Alfredo is on his way. When he arrives, the lovers dream briefly of a new life away from the city (duet: *Parigi, o cara*), but Violetta falters and cries out against approaching death (*Gran Dio! morir sì giovine*). Annina goes to fetch the doctor, who returns with the repentant Germont. Violetta gives Alfredo a miniature portrait of herself as she once was (ensemble: *Prendi, quest'è l'immagine*) and urges him to marry and be happy one day. Then, feeling her pain stop, she rises as if reborn, only to fall dead.

---

*The second scene of this act if often staged as a separate act.

I VESPRI SICILIANI

(Les Vêpres Siciliennes) (The Sicilian Vespers)

FIVE ACTS

MUSIC: Giuseppe Verdi

TEXT (French): Eugène Scribe, Charles Duveyrier; Italian version by Ettore Caimi

WORLD PREMIERE: Paris Opera (Salle Le Peletier), June 13, 1855

U.S. PREMIERE: New York, Academy of Music, November 7, 1859 (in Italian)

METROPOLITAN OPERA PREMIERE: August 23, 1967 (concert performance at Newport Festival); January 31, 1974

CHARACTERS

Duchess Elena, *sister of Friedrich of Austria* . . . . Soprano
Ninetta, *her maid* . . . . Contralto
Arrigo, *young Sicilian* . . . . Tenor
Guido di Monforte, *French governor of Sicily* . . . . Baritone
Giovanni da Procida, *physician, Sicilian patriot* . . . . Bass
Bethune } *French officers* . . . . { Bass
Vaudemont } . . . . { Bass
Tebaldo } *French soldiers* . . . . { Tenor
Roberto } . . . . { Bass
Danieli } *Sicilians* . . . . { Tenor
Manfredo } . . . . { Tenor
French soldiers, Sicilians, nobles, pages, monks, executioner

Written to a French text as *Les Vêpres Siciliennes* for the Paris Opera, this score has been revived in modern times only in the Italian adaptation, authorized by Verdi. This was the case even in the Paris revival of 1974; therefore the arias are identified here by their Italian first lines.

With the death of Frederick II of the House of Hohenstaufen, Holy Roman Emperor, in 1250, his southern domains fell under the rule of his bastard son Manfred, who was routed by Charles, Duke of Anjou (brother of King Louis IX of France). Charles successfully met the threat of a takeover in Sicily by heirs to the Hohenstaufen dynasty: in 1268 he executed Corradino, Frederick II's grandson, and Corradino's cousin Frederick of Austria. While Charles presided over the French occupation of Sicily, a patriot loyal to the Hohen-staufens, Giovanni da Procida, schemed against his rule from exile in Spain. The rebellion of the Sicilians in 1282, signaled by the incident of the Sicilian Vespers, placed Peter of Aragon on the Sicilian throne; Procida was made chancellor in 1283.

Act I In the main square of Palermo in 1282, soldiers of the French occu-pying forces are drinking, watched sullenly by the Sicilian natives, who think only of vengenace (O vendetta). Duchess Elena appears, in mourning for her brother, Frederick of Austria, executed by the French. Two officers, Bethune and Vaudemont, take respectful note of her, but a drunken soldier, Roberto, challenges the lady to sing for him and his comrades. She offers a ballad about a ship in distress, a veiled exhortation to her compatriots not to lose courage (In alto mare). This message is lost on the French soldiers but not on the Sicilians. Only the appearance of the French governor, Monforte, disperses them. Elena is surprised to see her lover, Arrigo, who says he has been cleared of charges of treason and released from prison. Monforte walks over and asks Elena to withdraw. When he questions the hostile Arrigo, the young man says he prefers death to tyranny, while Monforte, aside, admires his courage and honesty (duet: Castiga l'ardir). When Monforte offers him a place among his officers, Arrigo refuses, and the older man lets him go, warning him to stay away from Elena. Arrigo defiantly goes to Elena's palace.

Act II In the countryside near the Chapel of St. Rosalie, outside Palermo, two men arrive from the sea by longboat. One of them, the patriot Giovanni da Procida, secretly returning from exile, hails the city in the distance, prom-ising it will regain its former splendor (O tu Palermo). After dispatching two of his companions to fetch Arrigo and Elena, Procida tells his followers that the time will soon arrive to strike the blow for Sicily's freedom. When Arrigo and Elena join him, he tells of trying to arouse support in foreign lands for the patriots' cause: help will come only when the whole population of Sicily has the courage to rise against the French. Alone with Elena, Arrigo declares his love (Ah! da tue luci angeliche). She would like to reciprocate but is still in mourning for her brother, whom she asks Arrigo to avenge. Bethune enters with soldiers and gives Arrigo an invitation to an official ball. When Arrigo refuses, the soldiers disarm him and take him by force. Procida returns, and as some young brides and grooms appear en route to their weddings in the chapel, he incites Roberto and other French soldiers to break up the festivities by carrying off the girls. This has the desired effect of arousing the Sicilians' indignation. When a barge passes, carrying French officers and nobles to the ball at the palace, Procida and his henchmen plan to infiltrate the party.

Act III In the study of his palace, Monforte recalls how he once abducted a woman who bore him a son but fled, rearing the child in hatred of his father. On her deathbed, she wrote a note identifying Arrigo as the child. Monforte has sent for Arrigo to tell him the truth (*In braccio alle dovizie*). When Arrigo is brought in, Monforte reminds him that he has been treated with clemency, then shows him his mother's note. Arrigo reacts with horror, realizing he will lose Elena when she learns he is the tyrant's son. Though Monforte offers titles and honors, Arrigo begs to be left to his fate, while Monforte reacts angrily to his rejection (*Insulto mortale!*). Rather than oppose his own father or give up his principles, Arrigo offers to go into exile. Though Monforte pleads with him, he breaks away and rushes out.

§ Festivities are under way in the ballroom, where Arrigo is astonished to find Elena and Procida disguised among the guests. They pin a ribbon to his chest, the identification for the conspirators against Monforte's life. When Monforte enters, Arrigo wonders how to save him without betraying the rebels. He decides to warn Monforte to flee, but just then Procida and Elena attack. When Arrigo throws himself in front of Monforte, they recoil, and Monforte orders them arrested, saying everyone who wears the ribbon will be executed—except Arrigo, a "loyal enemy." Aghast at Arrigo's apparent treachery, the conspirators curse him (*Colpo orrendo, inaspettato!*).

ACT IV Arrigo, allowed by Monforte to visit the prisoners in the palace fortress, laments his new status as an outcast among the Sicilians (*Voi per me qui gemete*), whom he too feels he has betrayed. Elena comes out of the prison and scorns him, but when she learns he is Monforte's son, she believes his claim that he still wants to live or die with the patriots (*Arrigo! ah, parli a un core*). Procida appears and tells Elena that help from Aragon has arrived on a ship in the harbor. When he sees Arrigo, he distrusts the young man's repentance—a feeling borne out by the appearance of Monforte, who orders Procida and Elena executed. When Arrigo demands to share their fate, both Monforte and Procida turn him down. Elena tells Procida of Arrigo's paternity, and Procida now believes all is lost, as voices chant a De Profundis in the background. When Monforte says the rebel pair will die unless Arrigo acknowledges him as his father, Arrigo in despair does so. Monforte then pardons the rebels and even offers to join Elena with Arrigo in marriage. Procida, believing that this will advance their cause, urges Elena to go through with it. Though the populace is relieved by the conspirators' pardon, and Elena and Arrigo briefly contemplate happiness, Procida remains unswerving in his rebellious purpose.

ACT V Outside the palace, preparations are under way for the wedding in the adjoining chapel. Elena, in bridal dress, thanks her friends for their bouquets and sings of her happiness (*Mercè, dilette amiche*). She and Arrigo pledge their love, but when the bridegroom excuses himself for a word with his father, Procida approaches Elena, saying the festivities offer a chance to catch the French off guard. When the wedding bell sounds, the populace will rise in open revolt. Declaring she is also loyal to her husband, Elena finds herself in an impossible position. She decides to tell Arrigo that she cannot go through with the wedding—the memory of her brother prevents it. Both Procida and Arrigo now feel betrayed by her, but Monforte enters and informs Elena that the wedding must proceed, for he sees that their love is genuine. He joins their hands, and the gloating Procida hears the bell ring, summoning the Sicilians to rise and massacre the unarmed French.

SIMON BOCCANEGRA

PROLOGUE AND THREE ACTS
MUSIC: Giuseppe Verdi
TEXT (Italian): Francesco Maria Piave, with later revisions and
   additions by Arrigo Boito, after the Spanish play by Antonio
   García Gutiérrez
WORLD PREMIERE: Venice, Teatro La Fenice, March 12, 1857;
   Milan, La Scala, March 24, 1881 (revision)
U.S. PREMIERE: Metropolitan Opera, January 28, 1932

CHARACTERS

Maria Boccanegra, *alias Amelia Grimaldi* . . . . Soprano
Gabriele Adorno, *Genoese noble, her fiancé* . . . . Tenor
Simon Boccanegra, *corsair, later Doge of Genoa* . . . . Baritone
Jacopo Fiesco, *alias Andrea, Genoese noble* . . . . Bass
Paolo Albiani ⎫ *plebeian leaders* . . . . ⎧Bass
Pietro   ⎭   ⎩Bass
   Commoners, sailors, courtiers, senators, maid, palace-guard captain

PROLOGUE   A square in Genoa, 1339, just before dawn. Paolo and Pietro, members of the plebeian faction, are discussing who should be the next doge. Paolo puts forth the name of Simon Boccanegra, the corsair who has freed the Adriatic of pirates, enabling the maritime state to flourish. Simon himself arrives in haste from Savona, wanting to know why Paolo sent for him. At first Simon shows no interest in being doge, but Paolo reminds him that from such a position he would at last be able to marry his mistress, Maria, daughter of the noble Fiesco family, which has refused to acknowledge Maria's liaison with him. Simon accepts, on the condition that Paolo remain close to him in power. Pietro brings a crowd of seamen and workers, with whom he and Paolo discuss their choice. Looking at the Fiesco palace, facing the square, the men recall the plight of Maria, held a virtual prisoner by her family. They leave to campaign for Boccanegra. Into the deserted square comes Jacopo Fiesco; his daughter Maria has just died, and he curses the seducer Boccanegra, then turns to a figure of the Virgin to pray *(Il lacerato spirito)*. Simon returns, knowing nothing of Maria's fate, and Fiesco repeats his curses while Simon begs for pardon. Fiesco says he will forgive Simon only when Maria's illegitimate child is returned to her family. Simon has to confess that the child, left in the care of an old woman who died, disappeared while he was at sea *(Del mar sul lido)*. Fiesco withdraws, and Simon summons courage to enter the palace to see Maria. Finding the door unbolted, he goes in, only to discover Maria lying on her bier, while Fiesco watches from the shadows in grim satisfaction. As Simon emerges, unnerved and bereft, he is swept on the shoulders of the plebeian mob, which rushes in to tell of his election by popular acclaim.

ACT I   Twenty-five years later, outside a seaside villa near Genoa where Fiesco, under the assumed name Andrea, has lived incognito since the accession of a plebeian doge. His ward, the adopted Amelia Grimaldi, stands looking out over the sea, admiring its beauty and thinking of her lover, Gabriele Adorno *(Come in quest'ora bruna)*. The noble Gabriele is heard approaching, and the two greet each other warmly *(Vieni a mirar la cerula)*. They are disturbed by the appearance of the doge's messenger, Pietro, who says that the doge wants to pay a call. Amelia, sensing that Boccanegra is coming to ask her hand in marriage on behalf of his crony, Paolo, urges Gabriele to get her father's approval at once for their own marriage. Gabriele broaches the subject to Andrea, who says Amelia is actually an orphan of humble birth, but Gabriele reaffirms his love, and Andrea gives his blessing *(Vieni a me, ti benedico)*. As the doge draws near, the two men leave Amelia to greet him. He offers a pardon for her exiled brothers, who have defied him. Surprised by this generosity, Amelia confides that she has a lover whom she wants to marry but that Paolo has designs on her. When she explains that she was an orphan, living near Pisa in the care of an old woman who died *(Grave d'anni quella pia)*, and that the Grimaldis adopted her, Boccanegra realizes that she is his own lost daughter, Maria. The two embrace in joy *(Figlia, a tal nome)*. When Paolo appears, Boccanegra tells him, without explanation, to forget about marrying the girl, then leaves. Paolo confides his frustration to the newly arrived Pietro, and the two plan to kidnap Amelia.

§ In the council chamber of Genoa, the doge is seated on his throne, flanked by patrician councilors on one side, plebeians on the other. He shows a letter from the poet Petrarch, urging Genoa to make a treaty with Venice; though the council is in a warlike mood, Boccanegra speaks for peace. A tumult is heard in the streets; Gabriele Adorno rushes in, announcing that he has just killed Lorenzino, a plebeian favorite who was attempting to kidnap Amelia.

Before he died, Lorenzino admitted that he was in the employ of a "man of great power." Amelia throws herself in front of the doge, describing her abduction and saying that the real kidnapper is in the room. Plebeian and patrician councilors defy each other, but Boccanegra pleads eloquently with them to restore peace (Plebe! Patrizi!). Gabriele offers his sword to Boccanegra, who refuses it, saying he wants only the young man's word of honor. Then he calls Paolo forth and orders him to pronounce a curse on the man behind the kidnapping. In panic, Paolo curses himself (Sia maledetto!).

ACT II   By night in the ducal palace, Paolo sends Pietro to release Gabriele and Fiesco from detention. The discredited Paolo will have to flee Genoa, but first he means to dispatch the man he raised to power—the doge. He puts slow-working poison in the doge's wine goblet, which stands on a nearby table. Fiesco and Gabriele are brought in, and Paolo tries to persuade Fiesco to assassinate Boccanegra. Disdainfully refusing such a dishonorable act, Fiesco is sent back to his cell. Paolo then tells Gabriele to kill Boccanegra or meet death himself, adding that Amelia is the doge's mistress. Gabriele raves with jealousy (Sento avvampar). Amelia enters, but before she can explain that Boccanegra is her father, the doge approaches, and Gabriele hides. Amelia tells her father that she wants to marry Gabriele, whom he declares a traitor. When she says she would rather die than lose her lover, Boccanegra muses on the danger of leniency toward his enemies. He sends Amelia to bed and pours a drink into the poisoned goblet, noting that even pure water tastes bitter to a man who reigns. When he dozes off, Gabriele comes in and is about to strike him with a dagger, but Amelia returns and stays his hand. When the doge awakens, Gabriele at last learns that Amelia is his daughter. Valuing peace above his own safety, Boccanegra forgives him, while Amelia prays to her mother in heaven (trio: Perdon, Amelia). Once more the mob is heard outside, threatening the doge, who tells Gabriele to rejoin the patricians. Gabriele refuses, saying he will try to pacify them or else die in Boccanegra's defense. Boccanegra tells him that Amelia's hand will be his reward.

ACT III   The patricians have been defeated by Boccanegra's forces. Fiesco, set free, encounters Paolo, who joined the rebels and is going to be executed as a traitor. When Paolo confides that Boccanegra will soon die of poison, Fiesco condemns his act. Voices within hail the wedding of Gabriele and Amelia, as Paolo is led off and Fiesco steps out of sight. A herald tells the populace from the doge's balcony that in honor of the fallen, there must be a curfew to the public rejoicing. The doge comes in; starting to feel the effects of the poison, he longs for the ocean of his youthful days and wishes he had found his grave there. Fiesco steps from the shadows, saying he is a ghost from the past, still longing for vengeance. When Boccanegra recognizes him, he offers friendship instead, explaining that Amelia is Maria's lost daughter. The old man weeps at having the truth revealed too late and tells Boccanegra about the poison. Gabriele and Amelia enter and receive the doge's blessing. Naming Gabriele his successor, Boccanegra dies, leaving a sad Fiesco to announce his death to the people and to proclaim Gabriele the new doge.

UN BALLO IN MASCHERA

(A Masked Ball)

THREE ACTS
MUSIC: Giuseppe Verdi
TEXT (ITALIAN): Antonio Somma, after a French libretto (1833) by
    Eugène Scribe
WORLD PREMIERE: Rome, Teatro Apollo, February 17, 1859
U.S. PREMIERE: New York, Academy of Music, February 11, 1861
METROPOLITAN OPERA PREMIERE: December 11, 1889 (in German)

CHARACTERS*

Amelia, *Renato's wife* . . . . Soprano
Ulrica, *sorceress* . . . . Contralto
Oscar, *page* . . . . Soprano
Riccardo, *Count of Warwick, governor of Boston* . . . . Tenor
Renato, *his secretary* . . . . Baritone
Samuel ⎫ *conspirators* . . . . ⎧Bass
Tom ⎭ . . . . ⎩Bass
Silvano, *sailor* . . . . Bass
Judge . . . . Tenor
Courtiers, townspeople, conspirators, party guests

ACT I   Boston, late seventeenth century (colonial period). In a hall of the governor's mansion, officers and civilians wait for a morning audience with Riccardo, Count of Warwick, governor of Boston. Among them are Samuel and Tom, conspirators who bear grudges against him for alleged injustices. Preceded by his page, Oscar, the governor greets the assembled visitors with reassurances that their petitions will receive fair consideration. When Oscar hands him a guest list for the forthcoming masked ball, he muses on the name

*When the original Swedish setting is reinstated, Riccardo becomes Gustavo III, King of Sweden, but the Italian names for the characters are usually unchanged.

of Amelia, his beloved (ensemble: *La rivedrà nell' estasi*). When the petitioners leave, Riccardo receives Renato, his trusted aide, who is also Amelia's husband. Renato warns of the conspiracy and urges Riccardo to be careful, for the colony's sake as well as his own *(Alla vita che t'arride)*. Oscar announces a Judge, who wants Riccardo's authorization to banish a sorceress named Ulrica, but Oscar speaks in her behalf *(Volta la terrea)*. Brushing aside Renato's prudent counsel, Riccardo decides that it would be amusing to visit the sorceress incognito and put her to the test. He summons his courtiers and invites them to join him at her lair that afternoon (ensemble: *Ogni cura si doni al diletto*).

§ At Ulrica's hut, her curious clients watch as she invokes Satan's powers to aid her divinations *(Re dell'abisso)*. Riccardo slips in, disguised as a fisherman, and hears Silvano, a naval sailor, ask for a reading. When Ulrica predicts a promotion, Riccardo writes one and slips it into Silvano's pocket, where the man finds it when he goes to pay Ulrica. At the appearance of a servant of Amelia's, Ulrica dismisses everyone, and Riccardo hides. Amelia comes in through a private entrance and asks Ulrica for help in overcoming her guilty love for Riccardo. The sorceress prescribes a magic herb that is only found growing in a gallows field outside the city *(Della città all'occaso)*. As Amelia leaves, Riccardo vows that he too will be there, late that night. Then Ulrica calls the crowd back, whereupon Riccardo steps forward and asks about his own fortune *(Di' tu se fedele)*. From his palm, Ulrica recognizes that he is someone important, then abruptly tells him to ask no more. When he presses her, she says he will die very soon—not by an enemy's hand, but by a friend's. Riccardo refuses to take her seriously and laughs at the superstitious credulity of the others (ensemble: *È scherzo, od è follia)*. He insists on hearing the rest of the prophecy. Ulrica says the murderer will be the first who clasps his hand, whereupon Riccardo offers his hand to everyone, but none will take it. Only Renato, newly arrived and ignorant of what has transpired, shakes hands with the governor. As the conspirators sigh in relief because Ulrica has not implicated them, Silvano appears and leads the crowd in a hymn of praise to the leader they all now recognize *(O figlio d'Inghilterra)*.

ACT II   On the outskirts of town, late that night. Amelia arrives alone, terrified to be in so desolate a place. She looks for the magic herb. When midnight strikes, she imagines that she sees the ghost of an executed criminal and prays for God's mercy *(Ma dell'arido stelo divulsa)*. Riccardo appears, trying to calm her with declarations of love. Protesting that she belongs to his best friend, she urges him to leave, but his ardent declarations *(Non sai tu che se l'anima mia)* force her to admit she loves him too (duet: *Oh, qual soave brivido)*. Their rapture is cut short by the arrival of Renato, who has followed Riccardo to warn him that conspirators are plotting against him. In the darkness Renato does not recognize his wife, who joins him in urging Riccardo to flee for his life (trio: *Fuggi, fuggi)*. Having promised Riccardo that he would lead the veiled Amelia back to the city without questioning her identity, Renato is confronted by the disappointed conspirators, who hoped to find Riccardo. When they threaten Renato, Amelia removes her veil to save him from harm. He is thunderstruck to recognize his own wife, but Samuel and Tom find this a great joke: they expected to surprise secret lovers, meeting instead a man and wife out for an evening stroll (ensemble: *Ve' se di notte*). Renato orders Samuel and Tom to come to his house the next morning.

ACT III   As night gives way to early morning, Renato at last confronts Amelia in the privacy of his study. He intends to kill her, but she pleads for a last chance to embrace their only child *(Morrò, ma prima in grazia)*, and he lets her go. Then, seeing Riccardo's portrait, he decides it is Riccardo who should die instead *(Eri tu)* for betraying Renato's friendship and shattering the joy of his marriage. Samuel and Tom appear, assuming he meant to prosecute them; instead he declares he wants to join the conspiracy (trio: *Dunque l'onta di tutti*). When the three argue as to who will be the assassin, Renato says fate will decide: they prepare to draw lots. Amelia enters, telling her husband that Oscar has arrived with a message from the governor. Renato makes her draw a name from the urn: to his joy, it is his own. Oscar comes to invite Renato and Amelia to the masked ball that evening, and the conspirators realize that this is their opportunity (ensemble: *Ah! di che fulgor*). The distraught Amelia hopes to warn Riccardo.

§ The governor's study. Wondering whether Amelia has gotten home safely, Riccardo decides he must break off the romance and writes an order sending Renato and Amelia back to England. Signing it, he bids farewell to Amelia in his heart *(Ma se m'è forza perderti)*. Oscar arrives with a note from an unknown lady. Though it warns of an attempt on his life at the ball, he declares that to stay away would be cowardice.

In the ballroom, as maskers mingle, Renato tells his fellow conspirators he is afraid Riccardo will not come. He is recognized by Oscar, who tells him the governor is in fact there but teasingly refuses to describe his costume *(Saper vorreste)*. When Renato insists he has important matters to discuss with Riccardo, Oscar says that the governor is wearing a black cloak with a pink ribbon. Riccardo appears and is taken aside by a masked woman, repeating the warning of her letter. He recognizes her as Amelia and scorns the idea of fleeing, especially if he can be near her one more time. While dance musicians strike up a mazurka, she again admits her love and pleads with him to save himself *(T'amo, sì t'amo e in lagrime)*. He tells her of his decision to send her and Renato back to England. As he bids her a last farewell, Renato steps from the crowd and delivers his own farewell—the fatal blow. The crowd turns on Renato, but the stricken Riccardo orders him left alone, then tells him Amelia is innocent: though he loved her, Riccardo respected her virtue and her husband's honor. As Renato upbraids himself for his rash revenge, and as Oscar and the crowd voice shocked disbelief and prayer, the dying man pardons his enemies and bids farewell to his people and country.

LA FORZA DEL DESTINO

(The Force of Destiny)

FOUR ACTS

MUSIC: Giuseppe Verdi

TEXT (Italian): Francesco Maria Piave, with later revisions by
Antonio Ghislanzoni, after the Spanish play *Don Alvaro, ó La Fuerza del Sino* (1835), by Angel Pérez de Saavedra, Duke of Rivas

WORLD PREMIERE: St. Petersburg, Imperial Opera, November 10, 1862; Milan, La Scala, February 27, 1869 (revision)

U.S. PREMIERE: New York, Academy of Music, February 24, 1865

METROPOLITAN OPERA PREMIERE: November 15, 1918

CHARACTERS

Leonora di Vargas, *Marquis's daughter* . . . . Soprano
Curra, *her maid* . . . . Mezzo-Sopranno
Preziosilla, *Gypsy* . . . . Mezzo-Soprano
Don Alvaro, *noble of Inca descent* . . . . Tenor
Don Carlo di Vargas, *Leonora's brother* . . . . Baritone
Marquis of Calatrava, *their father* . . . . Bass
Padre Guardiano, *Father Superior of the
   convent of Madonna degli Angeli* . . . . Bass
Brother Melitone, *friar* . . . . Baritone
Mastro Trabuco, *muleteer and peddler* . . . . Tenor
Soldiers, peasants, beggars, pilgrims, Alcalde, monks, innkeeper, surgeon

ACT I Seville, middle of the eighteenth century. In his villa, the Marquis of Calatrava bids good night to his daughter, Leonora di Vargas. As soon as he leaves, Leonora talks with her maid, Curra, about her imminent elopement with her lover, Don Alvaro. Hesitant to leave her father, Leonora is nevertheless torn by her love for Don Alvaro, an Inca of royal descent *(Me pellegrina ed orfana)*. When a noise is heard in the courtyard, Leonora panics. Climbing in via the balcony, Alvaro tries to reassure her, then accuses her of not loving him. She agrees to leave, but her father, awakened by the noise, storms in with sword drawn, challenging Alvaro, who throws his pistol to the floor. It goes off by accident and fatally wounds the Marquis, who dies cursing his daughter. Alvaro leaves, taking Leonora with him.

ACT II An inn at Hornachuelos. Amid peasants and mule drivers, Don Carlo di Vargas, Leonora's brother, posing as "Pereda," a student from Salamanca, hunts for his sister and her lover to avenge the Marquis's death. Leonora, disguised in male clothes, comes to the door and recognizes her brother. Separated from Alvaro during their flight, she is traveling with a muleteer, Trabuco, who endures jibes as to the identity and sex of the "little person" he has brought to stay at the inn. Preziosilla, a Gypsy girl, offers to tell fortunes and inspire morale for the upcoming battles of Italy and Spain against the Germans (Al suono del tamburo). She tells Carlo that he is no student, while Leonora wonders how she can escape from her vengeful brother. A group of pilgrims en route to Holy Week arrives, and everyone joins in prayer (Santo Spirto, Signor). Carlo questions Trabuco about his companion but gets no satisfaction. At the urging of the Alcalde (local mayor), Carlo tells the gathering that he is a student, mentioning his friend "Vargas," who is bent on avenging the death of his father at the hands of his sister's lover. Good-nights are exchanged.

§ Outside the church and monastery of Madonna degli Angeli, Leonora, still in male clothes, prays for the Virgin's forgiveness (Madre, pietosa Vergine). Evening prayers are heard from within. She sounds the monastery bell and is greeted gruffly by Brother Melitone, who tries to send her away till next morning. She says she has been sent by Father Cleto to see the Padre Guardiano (Father Superior), whereupon Melitone says he will relay the message. The Padre Guardiano appears, dismisses Melitone, and listens to his visitor say she is Leonora di Vargas, the woman in distress about whom Father Cleto has written. She asks to become a hermit and live in a cave, devoting herself only to God (duet: Più tranquilla l'alma sento). When he learns that her brother is bent on killing her, the Padre Guardiano agrees, sending for Melitone to summon the other monks. When they assemble, they are told the stranger will have inviolate solitude, and they vow to respect "his" isolation (ensemble: La Vergine degli angeli).

ACT III Near a battlefield in Velletri, Italy, soldiers are gambling. Alvaro, now in the military, comes forward alone to lament his outcast state, praying to Leonora—whom he believes dead—to pity him (O tu che in seno agli angeli). Hearing the cries of another officer, he goes to the rescue and returns with Carlo. Neither is aware of the other's identity, and both are using assumed names. Carlo thanks Alvaro for saving his life from soldiers who were quarreling over cards. They swear friendship in life and death, then run off to battle.

§ The wounded Alvaro, borne in on a stretcher, asks Carlo to burn his private papers when he dies (duet: Solenne in quest'ora). Carlo agrees, but when his friend is removed for surgery, he muses on the possibility that Alvaro might be the "cursed Indian" who killed his father and dishonored his sister *(Urna fatale)*. Looking among Alvaro's belongings, he finds a portrait of Leonora. As word comes that Alvaro's life has been saved by surgery, Carlo exults that his enemy will live—to suffer his personal revenge.

A patrol passes by night *(Compagni, sostiamo)*. Alvaro enters, encountering Carlo, who announces he has found out who he is and wants to fight. Alvaro feels betrayed *(Sleale! il segreto fu dunque violato?)** but tries to pacify Carlo by saying that no intentional wrong was done—that Leonora, if still alive, as Carlo says, should be the object of their joint search. Carlo bullies him into a rage, and they fight, but a patrol separates them. Alvaro, repenting of his anger, resolves to enter a monastery. As the sun rises, soldiers and civilians crowd the scene, led by Preziosilla, telling fortunes, and Trabuco, peddling cheap merchandise. Beggars, new recruits, and camp followers join the throng, and a spirited dance gets under way *(Nella guerra è la follia)*. Melitone stumbles upon the motley gathering of people and lectures them on their ungodly ways *(Toh! poffare il mondo!)*. Finally, Preziosilla, wearing a drum around her neck, leads an unaccompanied marching chorus in imitation of a military drummer's sound *(Rataplan)*.

ACT IV   Inside the monastery, back on Spanish soil, beggars wait for Melitone to dole out soup while the Padre Guardiano cautions him against being impatient with the poor, who are dear to God (duet: *Del mondo i disinganni*). The gate bell rings, announcing Carlo, who demands to see "Father Rafaello," Alvaro's assumed name. As he waits, he vows to kill Alvaro *(Ivano, Alvaro)*, then greets him with the news that he has been tracking him down for five years. Alvaro, bound by monastic vows, pleads for peace between them, but again Carlo goads him and they rush off to find a dueling place.

§ Leonora emerges from her cave, disheveled and distressed, to pray for the peace that still eludes her *(Pace, mio Dio)*: in her heart she still loves Alvaro. Hearing a commotion nearby, she retreats into the cave, only to be summoned forth by Alvaro himself: having mortally wounded Carlo, he asks the hermit to give absolution to the dying man. They recognize each other, and Alvaro cries that once again he has the blood of her family on his hands. Leonora goes to Carlo, who with his last strength deals her a mortal blow. The Padre Guardiano enters and silences Alvaro's frustrated rage as Leonora gasps that she will precede him to heaven and seek pardon for him, so that they can find peace there at last (trio: *Non imprecare: umiliati*).

*Sometimes omitted.

DON CARLO

(Don Carlos)

FIVE ACTS; REVISED VERSION, FOUR ACTS
MUSIC: Giuseppe Verdi
TEXT (French): François Joseph Méry, Carmille du Locle, after
Friedrich Schiller's play *Don Carlos;* Italian version by Achille de
Lauzières and Angelo Zanardini, with later revisions by the com-
poser and Antonio Ghislanzoni
WORLD PREMIERE: Paris Opera (Salle Le Peletier), March 11, 1867;
Milan, La Scala, January 10, 1884 (four-act revision, in Italian)
U.S. PREMIERE: New York, Academy of Music, April 12, 1877
(five-act version, in Italian)
METROPOLITAN OPERA PREMIERE: December 23, 1920 (four-act
version, in Italian)

CHARACTERS

Elisabetta di Valois . . . . Soprano
Princess Eboli . . . . Mezzo-Soprano
Voice from Heaven . . . . Soprano
Tebaldo, *page* . . . . Soprano
Countess Aremberg . . . . Mime
Don Carlo, *Filippo's son* . . . . Tenor
Rodrigo, Marquis of Posa, *his friend* . . . . Baritone
Filippo II, *King of Spain* . . . . Bass
Grand Inquisitor . . . . Bass
Friar . . . . Bass
Count Lerma . . . . Tenor
*Courtiers, nobles, monks, Flemish deputies, inquisitors, soldiers, magis-
trates, populace*

ACT I* Sixteenth-century France. In the forest of Fontainebleau, near Paris,
the Spanish infante Don Carlo (Carlos) enters, reflecting on how he left Madrid
at his father's displeasure to visit France and catch a glimpse of Elisabetta
(Elisabeth de Valois), the princess to whom he is betrothed. She enters with
her page, Tebaldo, having lost her way, and Carlo, still unknown to her, offers

*Omitted in the four-act version.

to escort her. Alone briefly, the two discuss peace between their countries, and Elisabetta voices concern about her betrothal to the Spanish king's son. Carlo identifies himself and declares his love; drawn to him, she responds (duet: *Di qual amor*). Tebaldo returns with news that Elisabetta's father, King Henry of France, has for reasons of state promised her hand instead to Filippo (Philip II), Carlo's father. As members of the court appear on the scene with words of congratulations, the Spanish ambassador to France, Count Lerma, tells Elisabetta she has free choice; but she knows she cannot refuse Filippo's offer, because it will ensure peace. The young lovers feel they have heard the voice of doom (ensemble: *L'ora fatale e suonata!*).

ACT II* Inside the cloister of St. Just in Madrid, in sight of the tomb of Charles V, a chorus of monks, led by a Friar, sings of how the great Holy Roman Emperor is now nothing but dust *(Carlo, il sommo Imperatore)*. Having retired as a monk in his last years, he died there. As dawn breaks, Carlo enters in distraction, imagining that the Friar's voice and face remind him of the late Charles V, whose ghost is said to walk the cloister.† He greets his friend Rodrigo, Marquis of Posa, who reminds him they are both committed to the cause of Flemish independence, the Flemings being oppressed under Spanish rule. A bell announces the arrival of the king and queen. Shaken by the sight of his lost fiancée married to his father, Carlo joins Rodrigo in an oath of brotherhood, to live and die for Flemish liberty *(Dio, che nell'alma infondere)*.

§ Outside the chapel, in a courtyard, Princess Eboli offers the ladies of the court a serenade in Moorish style about King Mohammed and his mistress— who, when she raised her veil, turned out to be his queen in disguise *(Nei giardin)*. Elisabetta enters, her sadness noted by Eboli, and receives a message from Carlo, delivered by Rodrigo, who distracts Eboli with small talk (ensemble: *Che mai si fa nel suol francese*). Rodrigo tells Elisabetta that Carlo would like an audience with her. Aside, Eboli remarks that Carlo has seemed upset, but she fancies it might be because he loves *her*. When Carlo enters, the other courtiers withdraw as he addresses the queen, asking her to intercede with his father so that he can gain permission to go to Flanders. She tries to keep the dialogue on a formal level, but he presses her with reminders of their lost love, swooning in near delirium *(Perduto ben, mio sol tesor)*. Unnerved, she tells him he would have to kill his own father to lead his stepmother to the altar. As she calls on God for protection, he runs off crying that he is accursed. Filippo, angered at finding the queen unaccompanied, chastises Countess Aremberg, who was to have been in waiting on her, and orders her back to France. Elisabetta comforts her friend *(Non pianger, mia compagna)*, gives her a ring, and retires with her retinue. Filippo tells Rodrigo to stay behind and asks why

---

*Act I of the four-act version.

†In the four-act version, Carlo sings about his loss of Elisabetta and the brief romance at Fontainebleau.

he has been avoiding him lately. Hesitantly, Rodrigo pleads the cause of Flanders (*O Signor, di Fiandra arrivo*). Filippo defends his policies, calling the Flemish rebellious and pointing to the prosperity of Spain under his rule. Rodrigo cautions against excesses that can lead to tyranny and urges humanitarian aims. Filippo brands this dream unrealistic but says it is the Grand Inquisitor, not the king, for whom Rodrigo must watch out. Then he confides that he suspects his son of being in love with his wife. In effect, he asks Rodrigo to spy on the two, but Rodrigo accepts this as an expression of trust (*Inaspettata aurora in ciel appar!*).

Act III* The queen's garden.† Carlo appears, in response to an anonymous note. He assumes that it is from the queen; in fact it is from Eboli, but since she appears wearing the queen's cloak, he pleads his love. When he discovers who she actually is, he recoils. Saying she herself loves him, Eboli offers to save him from the king's suspicions. Rodrigo interrupts, countering Eboli's threats with his own, but she vows revenge (trio: *Il mio furor*). Eboli now sees the queen as a rival, but when Rodrigo threatens her with his sword, Carlo stops him. Her recriminations continue (*Trema per te*) until she rushes off in fury. Recognizing that Carlo is in danger, Rodrigo asks him for any compromising papers he may be carrying. Carlo hesitates to trust the king's newfound confidant, but Rodrigo reminds him of their oath of friendship.

§ In a square before the Cathedral of Our Lady of Atocha in Madrid, the chorus celebrates while monks accompany a group of heretics condemned by the Inquisition to be burned at the stake. The church doors open to reveal Filippo, who proclaims that he will uphold divine justice. He is interrupted by Carlo, who leads six Flemish deputies before the king to plead for their country. The crowd is impressed, but Filippo and the monks revile the intruders, whereupon Carlo boldly asks his father to appoint him deputy ruler of Brabant and Flanders. Filippo is outraged, the more so when Carlo defiantly draws his sword. Filippo demands that Carlo be disarmed; no one, however, will step forward except Rodrigo. Carlo yields his sword to his friend, who is made a duke on the spot. As the king and his court proceed to the auto-dafé, a Voice from Heaven proclaims mercy on the heretics' souls.

Act IV‡ Filippo, exhausted but sleepless at his desk in the Escorial, broods over the fact that Elisabetta has never loved him (*Ella giammai m'amò*). Aging and lonely, he will find rest only in the tomb. A visitor appears—the blind old Grand Inquisitor, led by two monks. Filippo asks for guidance; his son is openly rebellious. The Inquisitor makes it plain that the death penalty would not be considered too extreme: did not God sacrifice His own Son? The old

---

* Act II of the four-act version.

† In a scene omitted from the standard version, Elisabetta and Eboli trade cloaks.

‡ Act III of the four-act version.

fanatic goes on to denounce Rodrigo as a leader of the growing heresy in Spain.* Threatening Filippo with an inquisitorial trial, he demands the life of Rodrigo, then leaves in anger as Filippo bitterly reflects that the throne must always bow before the altar. Elisabetta rushes in, declaring that her jewel box has been stolen. Filippo hands her the box and tells her to open it; when she refuses, he does so himself and finds the miniature portrait of Carlo that he had given her at Fontainebleau. The king accuses her of infidelity. She faints, and he calls for help; Eboli and Rodrigo enter and ask why the king, who controls half the world, cannot control himself. Filippo realizes that he has been rash; Elisabetta, reviving, laments her loneliness in this foreign land; Eboli feels remorse at having denounced the queen out of jealousy; and Rodrigo, aware that his days are numbered, hopes his death will somehow leave Spain a happier place (quartet: *Ah! si maledetto, sospetto fatale*). When Filippo and Rodrigo withdraw, Eboli throws herself on the queen's mercy, admitting that she stole the casket and that she herself was once the king's mistress. Elisabetta tells her to choose between exile and the convent within the next twenty-four hours, then leaves. Alone, Eboli swears that in the day remaining to her she will try to save the situation, cursing her own beauty, the cause of her vanity and intriguing *(O don fatale)*.

§ In a dungeon, Carlo is visited by Rodrigo, who sadly takes leave of him *(Per me giunto)*. Rodrigo explains that he allowed Carlo's incriminating papers to be found on his person, and thus he has taken the blame for the Flemish insurrection, leaving Carlo free to lead it in reality. Entering the prison from above, a member of the Inquisition points out Rodrigo to a soldier, who shoots him. The dying man tells Carlo to meet his stepmother for the last time at St. Just *(O Carlo, ascolta)*. Filippo, entering with several nobles, tries to give Carlo back his sword, which Carlo indignantly refuses. As Filippo laments the death of the only man he trusted, a crowd, aroused by Rodrigo's death and wanting Carlo made king, tries to storm the prison, but the Inquisitor appears and orders the rebellious mob to its knees.

ACT V† Alone in the cloister, Elisabetta addresses the tomb of Charles V, asking him to carry her prayers to heaven *(Tu che le vanità)*. When Carlo arrives, she pleads the Flemish cause (duet: *Si l'eroismo è questo*). At their last farewell, Filippo enters with the Inquisitor, demanding a "double sacrifice." But as guards seize Carlo, the Friar appears, in the likeness of Charles V. Filippo recoils as the spectre drags Carlo to the safety of the sanctuary.

---

*In Schiller's play, it is explained that Rodrigo is a secret Protestant.
†Act IV of the four-act version.

AIDA

FOUR ACTS
MUSIC: Giuseppe Verdi
TEXT (Italian): Antonio Ghislanzoni
WORLD PREMIERE: Cairo, Egypt, December 24, 1871
U.S. PREMIERE: New York, Academy of Music, November 26,
  1873
METROPOLITAN OPERA PREMIERE: November 12, 1886 (in
  German)

CHARACTERS

Aida, *Ethiopian princess enslaved in Egypt* . . . . Soprano
Amneris, *Egyptian princess* . . . . Mezzo-Soprano
High Priestess . . . . Soprano
Radames, *Egyptian army captain* . . . . Tenor
Messenger . . . . Tenor
Amonasro, *Ethiopian king, Aida's father* . . . . Baritone
Ramfis, *high priest of Isis* . . . . Bass
King of Egypt, *Amneris' father* . . . . Bass
  Priests, priestesses, dancers, slaves, guards, soldiers, Egyptian populace,
  Ethiopian prisoners of war

ACT I   Hall in the royal palace at Memphis, ancient Egypt. The high priest, Ramfis, tells the young warrior Radames that Egypt is threatened once again by the barbaric Ethiopians and that the goddess Isis has named the Egyptian supreme commander. Left alone, Radames expresses the hope that he will be the one chosen, and he muses on his love for the slave girl Aida *(Celeste Aida)*. He is caught off guard when Princess Amneris finds him; her thinly-veiled remarks make it clear that she desires him herself and suspects she has a rival. When Aida enters, the girl's anxiety betrays to the observant Amneris who this rival is. Feigning friendliness she asks Aida to approach and tell what is troubling her. When Aida says it is the idea of war between her own country, Ethiopia, and that of her captors, Amneris wonders whether there is no deeper cause. Radames meanwhile fears that the princess will discover his secret love. The mounting tension is broken by the appearance of the King with his retinue. A Messenger comes to tell of border attacks by marauding Ethiopians led by their king, Amonasro. Aida starts in recognition: Amonasro is her father. As the crowd waxes enthusiastic, the King reveals that Radames is to be supreme commander of the Egyptian forces; he is to go to the Temple of Ptah (Vulcan) for consecration. After everyone calls out that Radames should return victorious, Aida, left alone, reflects in horror at having joined in the cry (*Ritorna vincitor!*), as if wishing her lover's victory over her own father and people. Torn by conflicting loyalties, she prays to the gods for mercy.

§ Inside the temple, a High Priestess' voice is heard invoking Ptah, seconded by priestesses. Ramfis and his priests echo the invocation. Priestesses dance before the altar. To Radames he entrusts the sacred sword, urging him to succeed, and all pray to Ptah to bless his mission.

ACT II   Amneris' apartments in Thebes. Slave girls are grooming her for the celebrations in honor of Radames' victory. Languishing with love, she dreams of his return, and some of the slaves dance for her. She dismisses the servants when Aida approaches, carrying a crown. Again Amneris feigns sympathy for Aida, this time because of the defeat her people have suffered; she tricks the slave girl into revealing her love for Radames by pretending he has fallen in battle. Amneris admits her lie—Radames is alive—and threatens Aida as a rival. Aida pleads that Amneris is powerful and can have whatever she wants, while Aida has nothing but her love (*Pieta ti prenda*). To this Amneris retorts that she will decide what is to befall Aida.

§ The scene changes to an open square by the gates of Thebes. Spurred on by Ramfis and the priests, the people sing a hymn to Egypt and Isis (*Gloria all'Egitto*). The Egyptian army parades by. Radames is borne in, greeted by the King, who says Amneris will crown him victorious. When the King tells Radames to ask any reward, Radames replies that the prisoners should be brought in; among them Aida recognizes her father, who whispers to her not to give away the fact that he is also Amonasro, the Ethiopian king. He pleads with the King to be merciful toward the prisoners, adding that he himself saw their own kind die in the dust (*Ma tu, Re*). Ramfis and the priests insist that the dangerous Ethiopians be stamped out once and for all, but Radames asks for mercy for them. Ramfis tries to intercede (*Ascolta, o Re*), requesting that Aida and her father, at least, be kept as hostages. Accepting this compromise, the King announces the marriage of Radames and Amneris. Amneris relishes her triumph; Aida bemoans her loss of love; Radames realizes that he has been placed in an impossible position, not wishing to offend the King or give up Aida; and Amonasro murmurs to Aida that this is only a temporary reversal for the Ethiopian cause.

ACT III   The banks of the Nile, by night. From the temple of Isis, seen in the background, voices drift out in prayer. Amneris comes by boat to the temple with Ramfis, who tells her to pray for the goddess' favor toward her marriage. When they have gone inside, Aida appears; Radames has agreed to meet her here, and if he does not, she will throw herself in the river. She sings longingly of her homeland *(O patria mia)*. Amonasro springs out of the shadows, telling her she can defeat her rival and be free to see her home again *(Rivedrai le foreste imbalsamate)* if she will ask Radames what road the Egyptian troops plan to take in their next campaign. At first she is horrified at the idea of such treachery, but Amonasro reviles her for her disloyalty and depicts in vivid words the inevitable destruction of Ethiopia. She finally agrees, and Amonasro tells her she will be the savior of a defeated people *(Pensa che un popolo vinto, straziato)*. He hides as Radames appears. Aida asks Radames how he can claim to love her when the might of the state is forcing him to marry Amneris. He replies that the war has flared up again, that he will lead the troops in renewed assault *(Nel fiero anelito)* and be able to ask his own reward— the hand of Aida. She suggests they flee together to her native land *(Fuggiam gli ardori inospiti)*. When he recoils from the thought of betraying his country, she accuses him of not loving her. He agrees to her plan *(Si: fuggiam di questa mura)*, and they start to leave, but first she asks what road will be the safest, avoiding the troops. He replies that the troops will pass through the gorge of Napata, whereupon Amonasro jumps from the shadows. Radames recognizes what he has done, as all three attempt to flee. They are stopped by Ramfis, who comes out of the temple with Amneris and orders Radames arrested. Amonasro escapes with Aida.

ACT IV In a hall of the palace, Amneris paces back and forth, knowing Radames is to face judgment in a nearby chamber. When he is led in, she urges him to defend himself *(Già i sacerdoti adunansi)*, saying she will use her influence to save him if he will marry her. He refuses, saying life has no meaning without Aida. Amneris reviles him, then collapses as he is led away and the priests file past. The charges against Radames are heard being read from within, but each time the priests ask him to defend himself, he says nothing. They find him guilty of treason and condemn him to be entombed alive "below the altar of the outraged god." As they leave, Amneris rails in vain against them, protesting his innocence.

§ Priests in the temple of Ptah seal the heavy stone over the tomb in which Radames has been placed. Thinking of Aida, he discerns her beside him in the darkness: she has chosen to share his fate. He laments that she too must die *(Morir! si pura e bella)*, but she, light-headed from the lack of air, thinks she sees the angel of death, who will liberate them to immortal love. They bid farewell to earth *(O terra, addio)*, as Amneris, kneeling above the tomb, prays for peace.

OTELLO

(Othello)

FOUR ACTS

MUSIC: Giuseppe Verdi

TEXT (Italian): Arrigo Boito, after Shakespeare's play, as translated by Giulio Carcano (Italian) and Victor Hugo (French)

WORLD PREMIERE: Milan, La Scala, February 5, 1887

U.S. PREMIERE: New York, Academy of Music, April 16, 1888

METROPOLITAN OPERA PREMIERE: January 11, 1892

CHARACTERS

Otello, *Moorish general in the Venetian army* . . . . Tenor
Desdemona, *Otello's wife* . . . . Soprano
Emilia, *her attendant, Iago's wife* . . . . Mezzo-Soprano
Cassio, *lieutenant* . . . . Tenor
Roderigo, *Venetian gentleman* . . . . Tenor
Iago, *Otello's ensign* . . . . Baritone
Montano, *Otello's predecessor as Governor of Cyprus* . . . . Bass
Lodovico, *Venetian ambassador* . . . . Bass
Herald . . . . Bass
*Cypriots, Venetian soldiers and sailors, children, servants, Venetian ladies
and gentlemen*

ACT I   The island of Cyprus, late fifteenth century. On a stormy evening, outside the governor's castle, officers and soldiers of the Venetian army join the local population in watching for the return of the Moor Otello, governor of the island, who is expected back from a naval campaign. A sail, then a ship is sighted. The chorus vividly describes the tempest, and Otello steps ashore after a near-shipwreck. He tells everyone to rejoice: the Turkish fleet is defeated *(Esultate!)*. Iago, Otello's ensign, confers with Roderigo, a fop who has come to Cyprus because of his unrequited love for Desdemona, a Venetian beauty recently married to Otello. Promising to help Roderigo, Iago says Desdemona should soon tire of her Moorish husband, adding that he himself has reasons for revenge on Otello, who passed him over for advancement, promoting Cassio instead. The storm has subsided, and Cypriots relax around a crackling fire. Iago proposes a toast; when Cassio declines any more drink, Iago says he cannot refuse to salute Otello's new wife. Cassio consents and grows tipsy as Iago leads him on with a drinking song *(Inaffia l'ugola)*. Iago tells Roderigo to pick a quarrel with Cassio, causing a commotion that will disturb Otello's night of love. Roderigo laughs at the drunken Cassio, who fights with him. When Montano, Otello's predecessor in command, tries to separate the two, Cassio attacks him as well. Otello comes out of the castle to restore order *(Abbasso le spade!)*, then asks Iago what happened. Iago says he has no idea. When Otello sees Desdemona disturbed by the fray, he takes away Cassio's recent promotion. Sending everyone home, Otello turns to his bride and welcomes the return of peace *(Già nella notte densa)*. They recall their courtship and pray that their love will not change. Leading her back into the castle, Otello kisses her.

ACT II   A room in the castle, opening on a garden. Iago tells Cassio that by presenting his case to Desdemona he can be reinstated, because Otello is influenced by his wife. As soon as Cassio is out of sight, Iago declares that Cassio is nothing but a pawn. A cruel God created man wicked, he says *(Credo)*, and life has no meaning. Iago watches as Cassio approaches Desdemona in the garden. When Otello comes in and greets Iago, the lieutenant makes casual remarks to arouse the Moor's suspicion: didn't Cassio know Desdemona before Otello courted her? Otello grows impatient and tells Iago to come to the point. Iago warns him to beware of jealousy, a blind, self-destructive monster *(Temete, signor, la gelosia!)*. As voices are heard serenading Desdemona, Iago tells Otello to keep an eye on her. Women, children, and sailors bring flowers and gifts to Desdemona. Calmed by the sound, Otello greets her, but she brings up the question of Cassio's demotion, annoying him. When she offers a handkerchief to wipe his brow, he throws it to the ground, where her attendant, Emilia, retrieves it. As Desdemona tries to calm Otello, Iago orders Emilia (his wife) to give him the handkerchief (quartet: *Dammi la dolce e lieta parola*). Otello asks to be alone, and the others leave except for Iago, who hangs back to observe Otello's growing suspicion. Otello turns furiously on him as the instigator of vile thoughts: already the Moor imagines his wife in Cassio's embrace. To fan the flames, Iago invents a story about how Cassio spoke lovingly of Desdemona in his sleep *(Era la notte)*. Then he mentions Desdemona's handkerchief, saying he saw it in Cassio's hand. Beside himself, Otello swears to have vengeance, and Iago joins in the oath *(Sì, pel ciel)*.

ACT III   In the main hall, a Herald announces the sighting of a ship bearing Venetian officials. Iago suggests that Otello might learn something important by eavesdropping on the conversation between Iago and Cassio. He also reminds Otello about the handkerchief. Desdemona enters, and Otello speaks calmly until she revives the subject of Cassio. Otello demands her handkerchief—not the one she offers, but the one he gave her during their courtship. Believing he is only trying to divert her pleas for Cassio, Desdemona resumes them, punctuated by Otello's demands for the handkerchief. Finally he tells her that he believes her to be unfaithful. Aghast at the suggestion, she insists she is innocent, but he sends her away, then cries out that heaven could have afflicted him with anything but this *(Dio! mi potevi scagliar)*. Iago returns and reminds him to hide: Cassio is coming. Iago welcomes Cassio and leads him on in banter in such a way that Otello overhears only fragments and thinks they are talking about Desdemona. Cassio then shows a handkerchief that someone left at his house; Iago waves it to be sure Otello recognizes it. A cannon shot announces the arrival of the ship. Iago sends Cassio off, then turns to Otello, who is ready to kill Desdemona immediately, but Iago suggests waiting till night, when he can kill her in bed, "where she has sinned." Struggling to regain his composure, Otello greets Lodovico, the Venetian ambassador, and his retinue. To the assembled crowd, Otello reads their proc- lamation recalling him to Venice and appointing Cassio to govern Cyprus. Aside, he mutters to Desdemona to conceal her grief at being parted from Cassio, then pushes her to the ground. Desdemona laments her injured inno- cence, while Iago urges Otello to kill her promptly, then approaches Roderigo and plots with him to kill Cassio, so that Otello and Desdemona will have to stay on Cyprus. Otello orders everyone out and falls to the floor in a seizure. As voices outside hail the Lion of Venice, Iago gloats over the fallen Moor, crying, "Behold the Lion!"

ACT IV   In her bedchamber, Desdemona asks Emilia to lay her wedding gown on the bed and asks to be buried in it if she should die. She recalls the willow song, which a maid of her mother's used to sing, about a bereaved sweetheart *(Piangea cantando)*. Then she bids Emilia an impassioned farewell and kneels in prayer *(Ave Maria)*. As soon as she has dozed off, Otello enters through a secret door and kisses his wife. This wakens her, and he asks whether she has said her prayers, because he does not want her to die unrepentant. She protests her innocence as Otello charges that she was Cassio's mistress and gave him the handkerchief as a token. Convinced by Iago that Cassio has been killed, Otello says that Cassio cannot defend himself. Desdemona's concern over this enrages Otello, and he strangles her. Emilia knocks at the door to report that Cassio has in fact killed Roderigo; entering, she is horrified to find the dying Desdemona, who murmurs that she is guiltless. When Otello says that Iago was his informant, Emilia says that Otello was a fool to believe him, then cries for help. Cassio, Lodovico, and Iago appear. Though Iago orders her to keep quiet, Emilia denounces his lies. Then Montano rushes in to say that the dying Roderigo also told of Iago's plotting. Challenged by Otello to reply, Iago escapes. Otello seizes a sword, then drops it at Lodovico's com- mand, saying he has come to the end of his road *(Nium mi tema)*. Turning to Desdemona, he laments her ill-starred life and death, then pulls out a concealed dagger and stabs himself. Dying, he kisses Desdemona, wishing "to die upon a kiss."

FALSTAFF

THREE ACTS

MUSIC: Giuseppe Verdi

TEXT (Italian): Arrigo Boito, after Shakespeare's plays *The Merry Wives of Windsor* and *King Henry IV*, as translated by Giulio Carcano (Italian) and Victor Hugo (French)

WORLD PREMIERE: Milan, La Scala, February 9, 1893

U.S. PREMIERE: Metropolitan Opera, February 4, 1895

CHARACTERS

Sir John Falstaff, *down-at-the-heels knight* . . . . Baritone

Alice Ford, *Ford's wife* . . . . Soprano

Nannetta, *her daughter* . . . . Soprano

Meg Page, *her neighbor* . . . . Mezzo-Soprano

Dame Quickly, *another neighbor* . . . . Contralto

Fenton, *Nannetta's suitor* . . . . Tenor

Ford, *wealthy burgher* . . . . Baritone

Bardolfo⎫
　　　⎬ *Falstaff's cronies* . . . . ⎧Tenor
Pistola ⎭　　　　　　　　　　　　　　　　　　　　　　　　⎩ Bass

Dr. Caius, *pedantic French professor* . . . . Tenor

Innkeeper, townspeople, servants, pages, maskers

ACT I Windsor, England, during the reign of Henry IV, early fifteenth century. At the Garter, favorite inn of the stout Sir John Falstaff, the French pedant Dr. Caius storms in to accuse Falstaff of having broken into his house and created havoc there during Caius' absence. The knight confesses, knowing that Caius can do nothing about it. Caius then charges Falstaff's cronies, Bardolfo and Pistola, with getting him drunk and picking his pockets. Falstaff calms them all down and sends Caius away as the other two recite a mock *Amen*. Falstaff tells them that they are clumsy thieves and have a lot to learn. Confronted with the bill and finding his own purse empty, he lectures them on their bad influence: these companions cost too much. They hail "Enormous Falstaff" and hear his latest stratagem: he intends to pay court to Alice Ford, pretty wife of a rich local merchant. "She keeps the money box," notes Pistola astutely. So does Meg Page, says Falstaff, mentioning another attractive matron—and he intends to lay siege to her affections at the same time. When Bardolfo and Pistola indignantly refuse to deliver his love notes, Falstaff gives them to a page boy. Then he scolds his companions. True to their honor, indeed. And what exactly is honor? A word! (L'onore! Ladri!). Concluding that the very idea of honor makes nothing but trouble, Falstaff chases them out the door.

§ In the garden of Ford's house, Alice and her daughter, Nannetta, exchange greetings with Meg and another town gossip, Dame Quickly. Alice says she has just received a love letter from Falstaff, and Meg says that she has too; they compare and find that only the names are different. The women ridicule Falstaff's pretensions and vow to punish him soundly (Quell'otre! quel tino!). They leave but remain in the background as several men approach. Caius, still complaining about Falstaff's abuse, tells Ford of the fat knight's iniquities; so do Bardolfo and Pistola, warning of Falstaff's plan to seduce Alice. In the midst of the confusion, young Fenton steals a kiss from his sweetheart, Nannetta (Labbra di fuoco!). The three Merry Wives return and discuss how to deal with Falstaff: Alice will send Quickly to make an appointment for him to visit. Afraid of being overheard, they leave, and Fenton comes back for one more kiss from Nannetta. As they part, they repeat their password: "Lips that are kissed have nothing to lose / But as the moon does, their pleasure renews" (Bocca baciata non perde ventura).* Ford returns, discussing a plot of his own with Bardolfo and Pistola: they will announce him, under a false name, to Falstaff, and he will take it from there. As they join with Caius in relishing their triumph over Falstaff (Del tuo barbaro diagnostico), the ladies return and recapitulate their own plan at the same time. The men leave, and the ladies laugh over the high-flown poetry of Sir John's love letters.

ACT II Back at the inn, Bardolfo and Pistola return in mock penitence to Sir John's service and introduce Quickly, who bows with exaggerated respect and begs a moment's audience. When he has dismissed the others, she explains that Alice sent her with a message: Ford will be away from home between two and three o'clock, and Sir John may call then. Quickly bears another message, this one from Meg, who says her husband is rarely absent. Falstaff gives Quickly a coin and sends her off, gloating about his fascination for women, despite his age (Va, vecchio John). Bardolfo reappears to announce a certain "Signor Fontana" (Mr. Brook)—Ford in disguise—who mentions his wealth and asks Sir John's help in wooing Alice Ford, who has refused his attentions. The two men join in a little madrigal about the volatility of love (L'amor che non ci dà mai tregue). Accepting some gold from his visitor, Falstaff agrees to help, since

* A quote from Boccaccio.

he has an appointment with Alice between two and three that very afternoon. When he excuses himself to freshen up for the visit, Ford—who was not ready for this news—falls prey to jealousy, cursing matrimony and the horns that symbolize a betrayed husband (*E sogno? o realtà?*). Covering his anxiety when Falstaff returns, he links arms with the fat knight as they leave the inn.

§ Inside Ford's house, the ladies prepare for Falstaff's visit. Quickly describes how the knight received her and took the bait. Their plan is to lure him into a laundry basket and have him dumped into the Thames, which flows past the house. Nannetta enters in tears, because her father has insisted that she marry Caius; the others declare that she will not have to. Alice supervises the arrangement of the furniture and tells her fellow conspirators that their joke will soon begin (*Gaie comari di Windsor!*). All except Alice hide when Falstaff is sighted. As Alice plays a few chords on the lute, Falstaff launches into a love song, then tells her he wishes she were free to marry him. She remarks that he has a great deal of flesh to be tempted by sin, whereupon he launches into a ditty about how slim and agile he used to be as a boy, when he served as page to the Duke of Norfolk (*Quand'ero paggio;*). Alice accuses him of duplicity, charging he also loves Meg. He denies it and tries to embrace her, but Quickly's voice is heard from another room, saying that Meg is on her way. Alice hides Falstaff behind a screen as Meg rushes in to warn her—in earnest—that the furious Ford is en route to the house to catch Falstaff. Alice folds the screen to conceal Falstaff as Ford bursts in, accompanied by a posse of Caius, Fenton, Bardolfo, and Pistola. They check the laundry hamper, then go to search other rooms; Alice and Meg hurry Falstaff into the hamper and cover him with dirty laundry. Nannetta and Fenton step behind the screen as the searchers reenter, looking for other hiding places: suddenly their attention is riveted by the screen, from behind which a kiss is heard. Ford deploys the others for an assault on the screen, as Quickly and Meg keep the suffocating Falstaff hidden in the basket. When the screen is knocked over and Fenton is discovered with Nannetta, Ford tells Fenton to keep away from his daughter. While Bardolfo calls the searchers upstairs, Alice gets the servants to carry out the laundry hamper and empty it in the river. Ford returns in time to look out the window and see the fat knight going overboard with a splash, and he forgets his anger in the general merriment.

ACT III Outside the inn at sunset, Falstaff sits on a bench trying to restore his dampened body and spirits with mulled wine, reflecting on the treachery of man and the decline of civilization (*Reo mondo!*). When Dame Quickly approaches, he is suspicious. With difficulty she persuades him of Alice's innocence in the recent escapade. Then she presents a letter asking Falstaff to meet Alice at midnight in Windsor Park by Herne's Oak. As Alice, Nannetta, and Ford eavesdrop to see whether the plan is working, Falstaff invites Quickly into the inn. She tells him the legend of the Black Huntsman, who hanged himself from the oak and whose ghost is said to reappear. Mockingly, Alice repeats the legend; then she tells Nannetta to prepare a costume as queen of the fairies. They will frighten Falstaff in the forest to chastise him. Meanwhile, Quickly overhears Ford reassuring Caius that he will marry Nannetta.

§ In the woods by Herne's Oak, Fenton addresses a serenade to summon his beloved *(Dal labbro il canto),* whose voice replies in the distance. Nannetta comes in, costumed and accompanied by Alice, who gives Fenton a cloak; Quickly is dressed as a witch. Lacking time to explain their plan, they tell Fenton simply to follow instructions. They all vanish as Falstaff lumbers in, wrapped in a dark robe and wearing stag's antlers on his head. Falstaff is terrified when he hears a distant chime strike midnight, noting, "Love transforms man into a beast," but Alice's appearance turns him once again into a swain. She is in a hurry, because Meg is close behind her, crying that witches are approaching. Knowing that mortals cannot look upon fairies and live, Falstaff throws himself to the ground as distant voices draw closer. Nannetta, as queen of the fairies, invokes her "agile phantoms" to gather around the ancient tree *(Sul fil d'un soffio etesio);* they appear and dance. Led by Bardolfo dressed as an exorcist, the "spirits" chastise Falstaff for his grossness and impurity, as the Merry Wives urge them to pinch and prod him *(Pizzica, pizzica).* Falstaff cries out his repentance, but at the height of the tumult he recognizes Bardolfo and realizes that he is the butt on an all-too-human masquerade. As Ford asks him who now wears the horns, Quickly leads Bardolfo aside and covers him with Nannetta's veil. Ford proposes to crown the masquerade with a wedding for the queen of the fairies. Alice presents a second couple, and Ford agrees to a double wedding. When they have done, Caius sees that he has been "wed" to the disguised Bardolfo, while Ford discovers that he has been tricked into giving Nannetta in marriage to Fenton. Now it is Falstaff's turn to ask who has the last laugh. He concludes that everything in the world is but a jest (fugue: *Tutto nel mondo è burla*), and they all go off to celebrate.

RICHARD WAGNER
1813–83

*C*redit or blame for a great deal of what has happened in modern music has been laid at the doorstep of Richard Wagner. The strength of his individuality was such that he created a revolution not only in music but in the arts generally. In retrospect, however, it seems less a revolution and more a transition. Most great innovators do not invent their materials, only new ways of using them. For Wagner, the ideas developed by his precursors and contemporaries served as grist for the mill of a relentless, didactic mind. As a result, one tends to forget—and it does not matter much—that such tools as chromatic harmony, the leitmotif, symphonic development, large-scale orchestration, and the *durchkomponiert* (through-composed) scene did not originate with Wagner, so indelibly did he stamp them as his.

Living in an age of rampant nationalism, Wagner drew sustenance from the German operas of Mozart and the later works in this genre by Beethoven, Weber, and Marschner. His subject matter came from Germanic history and mythology, which he studied assiduously. A voracious reader, Wagner developed a taste for the classics, especially the Greeks and Shakespeare, as a boy at the Kreuzschule in Dresden, where his family moved for a time from Leipzig, his birthplace. At fourteen he wrote a flowery tragedy in a Shakespearean vein. Wanting to add music to his play, he began to study piano and violin but was frustrated by the long practice required and by his slow progress. When the family moved back to Leipzig in 1827, he studied theory and composition there. Six years later he had learned enough to become chorus master at the Würzburg Theater, which was managed by his brother, Albert, and to write his first complete opera—*Die Feen,* after Carlo Gozzi's fantasy play *La Donna*

Serpente. This work remained unperformed during his lifetime, but when he became an opera conductor himself, at Magdeburg, he wrote *Das Liebesverbot* (1836), loosely based on Shakespeare's *Measure for Measure,* and saw it through a solitary performance. After marrying the actress Minna Planer, he went to Riga, in Latvia, to conduct more opera, meanwhile starting work on a French-style grand opera of his own, *Rienzi.*

It was on the way from Riga by ship that Wagner conceived his nautical opera *Der Fliegende Holländer* (The Flying Dutchman), a personal version of a tale that was popular at the time in various guises. During an unproductive stay in Paris, when Wagner knew terrible hardship and scrounged for hackwork, he sold the *Holländer* text for use by a minor French composer but proceeded with his own musical setting. During this period he met Meyerbeer, who tried to help him with introductions to the musical world but whom Wagner later criticized for "effects without causes" and empty bombast.

Things finally began to improve as Wagner approached thirty. The Dresden production of *Rienzi* in 1842, his first success, showed he had aptitude for the stage. *Der Fliegende Holländer* the following year showed he also had insight and the makings of a personal style. In this work he cautiously began to experiment with the breakdown of set forms for dramatic purposes, a procedure more evident in *Tannhäuser* (Dresden, 1845). The capstone of his early maturity was *Lohengrin,* finished in the revolutionary year 1848, its production delayed until 1850 because of Wagner's political exile to Switzerland.

Having pushed German romantic opera as far as it would go in *Lohengrin.* Wagner entered his most characteristic period with the dramatic poem *Siegfrieds Tod* (Siegfried's Death), which eventually grew into his gigantic, four-evening cycle *Der Ring des Nibelungen* (The Ring of the Nibelung). The evolution of this epochal work was spread over more than a decade, delayed by work on two operas as different from each other as they were from the *Ring*— namely, *Tristan und Isolde* and *Die Meistersinger von Nürnberg.*

In *Tristan* (1865) Wagner reached the outer limits of chromatic harmony, pointing the way toward Arnold Schoenberg's systemization of atonality. Its quintessentially romantic story reflects the composer's susceptibility to the philosophical ideas of Schopenhauer and to the charms of the poet Mathilde Wesendonck, his affair with whom dealt the death blow to his marriage. *Die Meistersinger* (1868), much more diatonic in musical style, reflects Wagner's absorption with Protestant chorales and counterpoint as the structural roots of German music.

During his period of greatest productivity, Wagner was fortunate in the support of two individuals who changed his life and made it possible for him to achieve some of his goals. One was the Bavarian king Ludwig II, who risked the displeasure of his cabinet ministers by supporting Wagner lavishly with state funds. The other was Cosima von Bülow, daughter of Franz Liszt, who ran the gauntlet of social disapproval by leaving her husband, a famous conductor, to become the mistress and in 1870 the wife of a composer twenty-four years her senior.

Part of the concept of the *Ring* was Wagner's own kind of theater, one in which the fripperies of mere entertainment would be forgotten—a temple for the *Gesamtkunstwerk* (total work of art) in which he proposed to join poetry, music, and drama by means of a new alchemy involving "endless melody" and "the music of the future." To accomplish this, a new type of opera house was required; the result was the construction of the Bayreuth Festival Theater in a small Bavarian town. There the first complete *Ring* cycle was staged in 1876. Wagner's final work, *Parsifal,* performed the year before his death, was intended exclusively for the Bayreuth stage. Despite the efforts of Wagner's widow to keep *Parsifal* from being appropriated by other theaters, however, it was soon produced outside the shrine.

One of the paradoxes of Wagner's career is that this iconoclast and renegade, whose daring music and abrasive ego offended so many, was transformed after his death into a pillar of German art, embraced by the most conservative patriots as a spokesman for their national culture. Because Hitler felt the same way, many today persist in holding Wagner somehow accountable for nazism. Though a born polemicist and no stranger to hyperbole, Wagner was willfully misread by the Nazis. Despite the blinders of his own prejudices—he ranted against the Jews, the French, and the Jesuits with equal fervor—Wagner was capable of visualizing a better world, one redeemed by love.

His opera reforms, much more sweeping than those of Gluck, produced further paradoxes, for he was never a slave to his own theories. When a rousing march, chorus, or duet served his purpose, as they all did in *Götterdämmerung,* he used the traditional forms. If an opera seemed to need an old-fashioned potpourri overture or a quintet, as *Die Meistersinger* did, he wrote one. "Exaggeration for the sake of emphasis" seems to have been the key to his theorizing, aided by the notorious Saxon penchant for never saying anything in ten words that can be said in a thousand. Carried over into music, this led to the greatest of all his innovations—the creation of a time scale vastly broader than ever before achieved in opera, yet a scale the willing mind can accept. In the words of Virgil Thomson, "The problem of getting something on the stage is to animate a dramatic action, or the concept of a dramatic action. And Wagner does animate it. His music doesn't start and stop—it goes on. It may go on like a slow stream, but it's there, and not only the music but the play moves from beginning to end."

Though other composers, notably Bach and Mozart, left behind children who were musicians, Wagner was the only one who founded a dynasty to keep alive the cult of his artistic ideas. During Cosima's lifetime (she died in 1930) the Bayreuth Festival was in danger of stagnation: she insisted that the Master's instructions be obeyed without change, and the heir apparent, their son

Siegfried, was not the sort of man to assert dynamic leadership. After World War II, however, Siegfried's son Wieland turned Bayreuth into an experimental theater, pioneering the use of abstract sets and evocative, nonliteral stage direction. The old guard of Wagnerians finds postwar Bayreuth blasphemous. But Wagner's grandchildren and their younger generation of adherents argue that Wagner, always at the forefront of new theatrical ideas, would have understood.

DER FLIEGENDE HOLLÄNDER

(The Flying Dutchman)

THREE ACTS

MUSIC: Richard Wagner

TEXT (German): by the composer, after Heinrich Hein's *Memoirs of Herr von Schnabelewopski* and a novel by Wilhelm Hauff

WORLD PREMIERE: Dresden, Hoftheater, January 2, 1843

U.S. PREMIERE: Philadelphia, Academy of Music, November 8, 1876 (in Italian)

METROPOLITAN OPERA PREMIERE: December 31, 1890

CHARACTERS

The Dutchman . . . . Bass-Baritone
Senta, *Daland's daughter* . . . . Soprano
Mary, *Daland's housekeeper* . . . . Mezzo-Soprano
Erik, huntsman, *Senta's fiancé* . . . . Tenor
Daland, *Norwegian sea captain* . . . . Bass
Sailors, spectres, village girls

According to folklore, a Dutch sea captain, Philip Vanderdecken, who swore that in spite of the devil he would sail around the Cape of Good Hope, even if it took him forever, was condemned to roam the seas for eternity in search of redemption.

ACT I   Norway, eighteenth century. On a ship seeking shelter in the harbor of Sandviken,* Daland, the captain, marvels with his Steersman at the hellish

_____
* Near Oslo, in the Christiania Fjord.

force of the tempest that drove them past their home port, where they tried to land. He leaves the docked ship in the care of the Steersman, who dozes off while singing a sea chantey *(Mit Gewitter und Sturm)*. Silently, another ship docks nearby—the Dutchman's ghostly vessel, with black mast and blood-red sails. The Dutchman disembarks and broods darkly on his fate. Every seven years he is allowed ashore to look for redemption; having failed, he must return to sea for another seven years *(Die Frist ist um)*. In vain he yearns for the peace of death, fearing it will not be his till Judgment Day. Daland reappears and greets the strange man, who offers him rich rewards if Daland will take him to his home. The Dutchman adds that he is looking for a wife, and Daland says he has a daughter, thinking to make a match with this generous stranger. Daland boards his ship to sail on to his home port, not far away, with the Dutchman to follow.

ACT II   At Daland's house, a group of women sing a spinning song while busying themselves with domestic work. Dominating the room is a painting of the legendary Flying Dutchman. Senta, Daland's daughter, is obsessed with the Dutchman's picture, and the others tease her about her suitor, Erik, who will be jealous. Somewhat reluctantly, Senta launches again into the familiar ballad of the Flying Dutchman and his fate *(Johohoe! Traft ihr das Schiff)*. According to the refrain, the Dutchman will find rest only if he meets a woman who will be faithful to him unto death. Senta is convinced she herself is the woman. Erik appears with news that Daland's ship has returned from its latest voyage. He pleads with Senta to make up her mind when she will marry him, but Senta evades the question, saying it is enough for now to welcome her father home. Erik persists, accusing Senta of being infatuated with the Dutchman's portrait; she replies that the poor man deserves sympathy. Erik tells of a dream in which he saw Daland approaching with the Dutchman, who embraced Senta and took her on his ship; Senta has had the same dream. When she declares she would follow the Dutchman even unto death, Erik runs off in horror. Daland steps in the door, surprised to find no greeting from his spellbound daughter, who is interested only in the stranger accompanying him. Daland prattles on about the stranger's generosity and his interest in marrying Senta, while she and the Dutchman stand transfixed by recognition of the mate each has longed for. When at length they find words *(Wie aus der Ferne)*, she plights her troth to the Dutchman, with Daland's blessings.

ACT III   Where the two ships are tied to the dock, Daland's sailors celebrate their homecoming, singing and dancing with local girls. No signs of life are seen aboard the Dutchman's ship, in spite of invitations from the Norwegians to join the party. At length the spectral crew is heard from inside the ship, singing about their voyage of eternal damnation. Uncertain whether it is a joke or something genuinely frightening, the Norwegians withdraw. Erik and

Senta enter, in the midst of an argument: Senta continues to refuse Erik's pleas for her hand. Sensing that she is held by unearthly powers, he feels he has to save her. Passionately, he reminds her of their courtship and her earlier promises *(Willst jenes Tags)*. They are interrupted by the Dutchman, who declares that Senta has betrayed him by consorting with another lover. Over Senta's protests, he whistles his crew on deck and prepares to resume his seven-year cycle of wandering. Erik, imagining he sees Satan himself, stands by aghast as Senta vows she will prove herself true, but the Dutchman replies he alone bears the curse and, by leaving, will spare her from it. She says she knows who he is and knows his fate: by her own choice she will follow and save him. As the Dutchman's ship pulls away, she throws herself into the sea, crying that she is faithful unto death. The ship sinks, and Senta and the Dutchman are seen transfigured, rising toward heaven.

Tannhäuser

THREE ACTS

MUSIC: Richard Wagner

TEXT (German): by the composer, after the Arnim–Brentano anthology *Des Knaben Wunderhorn* (folk verse), *Danhauser* (sixteenth-century ballad), and writings by Eichendorff, Tieck, Heine, and E. T. A. Hoffmann

WORLD PREMIERE: Dresden, October 19, 1845

U.S. PREMIERE: New York, Stadt Theater, April 4, 1859

METROPOLITAN OPERA PREMIERE: November 17, 1884

CHARACTERS

(Heinrich) Tannhäuser, *minstrel knight* . . . . Tenor
Elisabeth, *Hermann's niece* . . . . Soprano
Venus, *pagan goddess of love* . . . . (Mezzo-)Soprano
Shepherd . . . . Soprano
Wolfram von Eschenbach ⎫   ⎧ Baritone
Walther von der Vogelweide ⎬ *other knights* . . . . ⎨ Tenor
Biterolf ⎭   ⎩ Bass
Hermann, *Landgrave of Thuringia* . . . . Bass
    Heinrich der Schreiber, Reinmar von Zweter, knights, ladies, pages,
                            bacchants, pilgrims

ACT I   In thirteenth-century Germany, the minstrel Tannhäuser has found his way to the legendary Venusberg, grotto of the pagan goddess Venus in Thuringia. Sirens' voices lure wayfarers as bacchants, nymphs, and satyrs revel with sensual abandon. Finally exhausted, the celebrants leave. Tannhäuser too is beginning to tire of Venus' delights: he dreams of the real world he left behind. Venus chides him for ingratitude, since she rescued him from world-weariness and despair. He rallies to offer a hymn of praise to love (*Dir töne Lob!*) but ends it with a plea to Venus to release him. Each time Venus complains, he adds another verse, always with the same ending. Livid with anger and still protesting, she lets him go, declaring he will return. He replies that his hope lies with the Virgin Mary. At the mention of this name, Venus' empire disappears, and Tannhäuser finds himself in a valley near the Wartburg Castle, seat of authority of the Landgrave of Thuringia.

§ A Shepherd plays his pipe and sings about Holda, pagan goddess of spring. Pilgrims approach (*Zu dir wall' ich*) en route to Rome. As they pass, Tannhäuser kneels in prayer before a wayside shrine. The Landgrave appears in a hunting party with some of his minstrels, former companions of Tannhäuser. Wolfram von Eschenbach is the first to recognize the minstrel. The group asks Tannhäuser whether he returns as a friend or in the same hostile mood in which he left. He says he is driven to seek salvation and cannot stay, but when Wolfram mentions the Landgrave's niece, Elisabeth, Tannhäuser—who once loved her—is persuaded. According to Wolfram, Elisabeth will no longer listen to the other minstrels' songs, though she used to be enthralled by Tannhäuser's (*Als du in kühnem Sange*). The party leads him toward the castle.

ACT II   Elisabeth greets the minstrels' hall in the Wartburg, jubilant at the news of Tannhäuser's return (*Dich, teure Halle*). Wolfram brings Tannhäuser, who kneels before Elisabeth; she tells him to rise, since this hall is his domain. Questioning him as to where he has been, she hears evasive words about the realm of love, which—being pious—she takes to mean the holy variety. As the reunited pair sings of love as a grace from God, Wolfram stands aside, realizing he must forfeit his own hopes for Elisabeth's hand. The Landgrave arrives with his entourage for the singing contest, which Wolfram opens with an eloquent eulogy (*Blick' ich umher*). Tannhäuser replies with a song in guarded praise of love, though with hints of pagan sensuality (*Auch ich darf mich so glücklich nennen*). Walther von der Vogelweide, the next singer, offers cautionary verses about the fountain of grace at which the soul can drink of salvation—but not slake its thirst for earthly pleasures (*Der Bronnen, den uns Wolfram nannte*). Tannhäuser rises in rebuttal, declaring that God's place is in heaven but that love has an earthly side too (*O Walther, der du also sangest*). Biterolf, a hotheaded knight, calls him a blasphemer and challenges him to combat, and though the crowd agrees with Biterolf's viewpoint, Tannhäuser remains defiant. The Landgrave orders the two to put up their swords, and Wolfram offers a prayer for the inspiration of divine love. Tannhäuser, carried away, replies with his hymn to Venus *(Dir, Göttin der Liebe)*. Understanding at last where he has been during his absence, the women leave the hall in horror as the men prepare to kill him, but Elisabeth throws herself in front of him, saying his soul must not be dispatched without a chance to earn salvation *(Der Unglücksel'ge, den gefangen)*. Returning to his senses, Tannhäuser is seized by remorse and begs forgiveness for having abused Elisabeth's trust *(Zum Heil den Sündigen zu führen)*. Banishing him, the Landgrave offers one hope: Tannhäuser can join the pilgrims on their way to Rome. As their hymn sounds in the distance, Tannhäuser kisses the hem of Elisabeth's dress and cries that he will go.

ACT III Back in the valley near the Wartburg, Elisabeth lies in prayer by a roadside shrine. Months have passed, and now the voices of pilgrims are heard again in the distance, this time on their return. As they troop past the shrine, she looks in vain for Tannhäuser, then offers a prayer to the Virgin, hoping she may die and win forgiveness for Tannhäuser (*Allmächt'ge Jungfrau*). Wolfram offers to escort her to the castle, but she indicates she must go alone. Taking up his harp, he addresses the Evening Star, asking it to guide Elisabeth in her quest for heaven (*O du mein holder Abendstern*). The exhausted Tannhäuser appears, bitter and disillusioned, wanting to find the way back to Venus' cave. Softening somewhat in the face of his friend's concern, he tells of his trip to Rome *(Inbrunst im Herzen)*. There he knelt before the pope, who declared the staff in his hand could as soon burst into bloom as a sinner be forgiven who had visited the Venusberg. Spurned by mankind, he feels he can only return to Venus. In near delirium he sees a vision of the goddess. To save Tannhäuser's soul, Wolfram pleads and struggles with him, finally mentioning Elisabeth, who even now is on her journey to heaven to pray for Tannhäuser. Distant voices announce her death, and the vision of Venus disappears as Elisabeth's funeral cortège draws near. Tannhäuser, feeling his own soul released, falls dying in Wolfram's arms as more pilgrims arrive from Rome with news of a miracle: the pope's staff, which they bear, has burst into bloom.

LOHENGRIN

THREE ACTS
MUSIC: Richard Wagner
TEXT (German): the composer, after an anonymous medieval epic
   and poems by Wolfram von Eschenbach
WORLD PREMIERE: Weimar, August 28, 1850

U.S. PREMIERE: New York, Stadt Theater, April 3, 1871
METROPOLITAN OPERA PREMIERE: November 7, 1883 (in Italian)

CHARACTERS

Lohengrin, *unknown knight* . . . . Tenor
Elsa of Brabant . . . . Soprano
Ortrud of Friesland, *pagan princess* . . . . (Mezzo-)Soprano
Friedrich, *Count of Telramund, Ortrud's husband* . . . . Baritone
Heinrich, *King of Germany* . . . . Bass
Herald . . . . Baritone
Gottfried, *Elsa's younger brother* . . . . Mime
Nobles, pages, attendants

ACT I   The year 933, on the banks of the river Scheldt, near Antwerp. Heinrich (Henry the Fowler), king of the German states, has come to warn his Saxon nobles that the Hungarians threaten the kingdom again, after a peace of nine years. Calling his subjects to arms, he asks Friedrich, Count of Telramund, to explain the feuding he finds among them. Telramund replies that his former ward and fiancée, Elsa—daughter of the late grand duke who ruled Brabant—appears to have murdered her younger brother, Gottfried. Horrified, Telramund instead married Princess Ortrud of Friesland. He now claims his right to the succession and asks Heinrich to judge the case. The king orders his Herald to summon Elsa. Asked to reply to the charge, Elsa tells how her prayers for divine guidance were answered by a vision of a knight in shining armor who would defend her *(Einsam in trüben Tagen)*. Telramund declares he will fight anyone who defends Elsa, but no one steps forward. The king calls upon Telramund and Elsa to submit their case to heaven's judgment, and Elsa repeats that she is waiting for her champion to appear. Twice the Herald issues the call for Elsa's defender, and Elsa kneels in prayer. In the distance a small boat is seen approaching on the river, drawn by a swan and bearing a knight. Arriving at the shore, the stranger bids his swan farewell *(Nun sei bedankt, mein lieber Schwan!)* and announces he will defend Elsa, asking to marry her if he succeeds—on the condition that she never try to find out who he is or where he comes from. She accepts, and the king orders the contest to proceed, leading a prayer that God may show the truth through the outcome *(Mein Herr und Gott)*. The stranger knocks Telramund to the ground but spares his life. Amid general rejoicing, Telramund laments that God has caused him to lose, but the pagan Ortrud hints that the stranger used sorcery.

ACT II   The central square of Antwerp, with the cathedral at one side, the knights' and womens' palaces at the other. Telramund sits glumly in the dark while Ortrud watches the lighted windows of the knights' palace, wondering how to turn the tables on her oppressors. Telramund rails at her for causing his downfall, but she retorts that the strange knight must have some Achilles heel: did he not insist that Elsa never ask his name or origin? Telramund agrees they will have to persuade Elsa to ask the fatal question, and they take an oath of vengeance. Elsa appears on the balcony of the women's palace and thanks the breezes, which have so often borne her laments, for the good fortune that has now come to her (*Euch Lüften, die mein Klagen*). Ortrud sends Telramund away so that she can ingratiate herself with Elsa. Calling toward the balcony, she protests she has never harmed the girl. As the guileless Elsa comes downstairs to commiserate with her, Ortrud calls on the pagan gods for help (*Entweihte Götter!*). Elsa invites Ortrud to accompany her to the cathedral for the wedding the next day. Pretending humility and gratitude, Ortrud plants the seeds of suspicion about the strange knight's origins, suggesting he may vanish by the same magic that brought him there. When Elsa has led Ortrud into the women's palace, Telramund reappears from the shadows and hides. As day breaks, the Herald appears before the assembling nobles and their retainers to announce the banishment of Telramund by royal decree. The king has named the strange knight guardian of Brabant and has assigned lands to him. Today is his wedding day, but tomorrow everyone must go to battle. A few disgruntled nobles question the wisdom of following a stranger on the campaign, and Telramund fans the flames of their suspicion. Not wishing to be caught scheming with the outcast, they lead him aside as the populace hails Elsa. When she approaches the cathedral, Ortrud, who has been following her, suddenly declares that her husband was falsely judged and challenges Elsa to identify the mysterious stranger. When the king approaches, Elsa turns to her knight, who embraces her, but Telramund bursts in, calling the knight an evil sorcerer and demanding to know his identity. King and nobles stand by the knight's right to keep his secret, but Elsa is beginning to doubt him. Seeing Ortrud and Telramund beside Elsa, the knight sends them away and leads his bride into the cathedral.

ACT III   Attendants enter the bridal chamber, singing a wedding song (*Treulich geführt*), and withdraw after the king has led the knight in to meet Elsa. Alone for the first time, the two exchange vows and recall the rapture of their first meeting. In spite of herself, Elsa begins to regret that she cannot call her husband by name. If she did know his secret, she declares, she would never reveal it. Fearing that magic powers brought him and may take him away, she imagines the swan returning. Finally she asks outright who he is and where he has come from. Telramund and the scheming nobles burst into the bridal chamber with swords drawn. Elsa hands the knight his sword, with which he strikes Telramund dead, saying all their happiness has fled. The nobles carry Telramund's body out as the knight calls attendants to prepare Elsa for an audience with the king. There he will tell who he is and how he came there.

§ By the shores of the river, the army gathers as the king prepares for battle. Waiting for the guardian of Brabant to appear, he sees instead Telramund's corpse, followed by the pale and troubled Elsa. When he greets the guardian at last, the knight replies he cannot lead the army. He then asks the king to judge whether he was right to kill the attacking Telramund. Absolved of guilt, the knight says Elsa has been made to doubt him by treacherous counsel. He reveals his secret: in a far-off country stands the temple fortress of Monsalvat,* where the Holy Grail is guarded by knights. His father, Parsifal, is their leader, and his own name is Lohengrin *(In fernem Land)*. Catching the swooning Elsa, he mourns their lost happiness. The swan approaches, and Lohengrin greets it *(Mein lieber Schwan!)*, bidding farewell to Elsa. As he is about to embark, Ortrud bursts in to reveal that the swan is Elsa's brother Gottfried, whom she herself placed under a spell. As Lohengrin kneels in prayer, the dove of the Grail descends, and Gottfried stands in the swan's place. Ortrud swoons. The dove then draws Lohengrin away in his boat, leaving Elsa lifeless in the arms of her brother, the rightful ruler of Brabant.

TRISTAN UND ISOLDE

THREE ACTS
MUSIC: Richard Wagner
TEXT (German): the composer, after a Celtic romance
WORLD PREMIERE: Munich, June 10, 1865
U.S. PREMIERE: Metropolitan Opera, December 1, 1886

CHARACTERS

Isolde, *Irish princess* . . . . Soprano
Tristan, *Cornish knight, Marke's nephew* . . . . Tenor
Brangäne, *Isolde's attendant* . . . . Mezzo-Soprano
Kurwenal, *Tristan's comrade* . . . . Baritone
Marke, *King of Cornwall* . . . . Bass
Melot, *courtier* . . . . Tenor
Sailor . . . . Tenor
Shepherd . . . . Tenor
Steersman . . . . Baritone
Sailors, knights, attendants, courtiers

*Montserrat, near Barcelona.

ACT I The legend of Tristan and Isolde (Tristram and Iseult) takes place during the Middle Ages, when knighthood and the chivalric code prevailed. On board ship from Ireland to Cornwall, a sailor's voice resounds from the rigging. His song about an Irish girl annoys the fiery Isolde, who is being taken by Tristan as bride for his uncle, King Marke. Isolde wishes the ship would sink rather than take her to her hated destination. Her companion, Brangäne, tries in vain to calm her. Instead Isolde is enraged by the knight Tristan, whom she sees standing on the afterdeck, avoiding her: by delivering her to his uncle, he shows no regard for her feelings. She sends Brangäne to summon Tristan, who sends back courtly, evasive replies. His plainspoken companion, Kurwenal, however, tells Brangäne that Tristan is not a vassal to answer Isolde's beck and call. Embarrassed by this outburst, Tristan sends Kurwenal away, but not before the latter has intoned an insolent verse about Isolde's fiancé, Morold, whom Tristan killed in combat some time before *(Herr Morold zog zu Meere her)*. Sailors pick up the refrain as the crestfallen Brangäne returns to the furious Isolde, who recalls that after Tristan came to Ireland to collect taxes for King Marke and killed Morold, she herself nursed him back to health, using her mother's knowledge of herbs and magic. When she realized he was her fiancé's slayer, she bemoaned her charity—but when he looked lovingly into her eyes, she took pity on him. Now he delivers her like a chattel to his uncle. She hurls forth a curse on his head and wishes death for both of them *(Fluch dir, Verruchter!)*. Brangäne tries to tell her that it is no dishonor to marry a king and that Tristan is simply performing his duty. Isolde replies darkly that it shows his lack of love for her. When Brangäne reminds Isolde that her mother charged her with secret arts, Isolde tells Brangäne to prepare one of her mother's potions—the one that brings death. Cries from the deck that land is in sight are followed by the arrival of Kurwenal, who bids the women prepare to disembark. Isolde retorts that she will not accompany Tristan until he apologizes to her for his offenses. Kurwenal takes the message to his lord while Isolde forces Brangäne to pour the potion. Tristan appears, greeting Isolde with cool courtesy. When she announces that she wants satisfaction for Morold's death, Tristan offers her his sword, but she will not kill him. This would violate King Marke's hospitality and her own unwilling vows, she replies. Better that she and Tristan make peace with a drink of friendship. Understanding that she means to poison them both, he drinks, and she does the same. Expecting death, they exchange a long look of love instead, then fall into a passionate embrace. Brangäne admits she mixed a love potion as sailors' voices hail the ship's arrival in Cornwall.

ACT II In a garden outside Marke's castle, distant horns signal the departure of the king and his retinue on a hunting party. Impatient for a rendezvous with Tristan, Isolde believes that the party is far off, but Brangäne cautions her about spies, particularly Melot, a jealous knight whom she has noted watching Tristan. Isolde says Melot is Tristan's friend and urges Brangäne to put out the warning torch so that Tristan can approach. Brangäne knows this would be unwise, but when she laments having switched the potions, Isolde tells her the power of love rules all destiny and guided her hand. Sending the girl to stand watch, Isolde herself puts out the torch and welcomes Tristan rapturously. Both hail the darkness, which banishes the light of everyday reality and false appearances. It was the forces of daylight, Isolde says, that caused Tristan to behave conventionally and bring her from Ireland; the potion, the power of love, has released them from this delusion. Feeling safe in the truthfulness of night, they welcome its embrace (*O sink' hernieder, Nacht der Liebe*). Brangäne's distant voice warns that night will soon fade and danger be revealed, but the lovers equate their oblivion with death, which will give them the total union and safe removal they crave (*O ew'ge Nacht, süsse Nacht!*). Their idyll is shattered as Kurwenal runs in with a warning: the king and his followers have returned, led by Melot, who denounces the lovers. Moved and disturbed, Marke declares that it was Tristan himself who urged him to marry and chose the bride, asking how a knight he so loved could bring dishonor on him. Tristan says he cannot answer, then turns to Isolde and asks whether she will follow him into the realm of death. She accepts, and Melot rushes forward, sword drawn. Wounded, Tristan falls in Kurwenal's arms.

ACT III   Outside Kareol, Tristan's home castle in Brittany, the knight lies grievously wounded, tended by Kurwenal. To a Shepherd who inquires about his master, Kurwenal replies sadly that only Isolde's arrival, with her magic arts, can save him. The Shepherd agrees to change the sad tune he is playing on his pipe as soon as he sights a ship approaching. Stirring, Tristan asks where he is, then in delirium says he has visited the realm of night and will return there. He clings to life only so that he can find Isolde and take her with him. Tristan thanks Kurwenal for his devotion (*Mein Kurwenal, du trauter Freund!*), then imagines he sees Isolde's ship approaching. But the Shepherd still pipes a sad tune: the sea is empty. Tristan recalls the tune, which he heard as a child in connection with his parents' death and which he later associated with his own near-death after the duel with Morold. He wishes Isolde's medicine had given him peace then instead of reviving him to suffer the torments of longing. Once more he swoons, then revives to imagine Isolde's smile as she draws near (*Wie sie selig, heer und milde*). The Shepherd's tune finally changes to a cheerful fanfare, and Kurwenal sees the ship. Tristan rouses himself in growing agitation. For once he blesses the day (*O diese Sonne!*), because it lights Isolde's way to him. Recklessly he tears off his bandages, letting his wounds bleed so that she can heal them—"forever." No sooner has Isolde rushed in than he falls dying in her arms. She exhorts him to live in order that they can share a final hour of reunion, but he is dead. The Shepherd sights another ship, which Kurwenal assumes is bringing Marke and Melot, bent on vengeance. Though Brangäne is with them, Kurwenal will not listen and attacks them, killing Melot and holding Marke's retainers at bay until he himself falls, mortally wounded. Marke, overwhelmed with sadness, sees the dead Tristan, while Brangäne tries to arouse Isolde, telling her the king has come to pardon and unite the lovers. But Isolde, oblivious, has a vision of Tristan beckoning to the world beyond *(Mild und leise)*. Must she alone perceive this and go to meet him? She must. As Brangäne tries to hold her, she sinks, transfigured in death, upon Tristan's body.

DIE MEISTERSINGER
VON NÜRNBERG

(The Mastersingers of Nuremberg)

THREE ACTS
MUSIC: Richard Wagner
TEXT (German): the composer, based on chronicles of the
    Mastersingers of sixteenth-century Germany
WORLD PREMIERE: Munich, Hoftheater, June 21, 1868
U.S. PREMIERE: Metropolitan Opera, January 4, 1886

CHARACTERS

Eva Pogner. . . . . Soprano
Magdalene, *her nurse*. . . . . Mezzo-Soprano
Walther von Stolzing, *young Franconian knight* . . . . Tenor
Hans Sachs, *cobbler and Mastersinger* . . . . Baritone
David, *his apprentice* . . . . Tenor
Sixtus Beckmesser, *town clerk* . . . . Baritone
Veit Pogner, *goldsmith, Eva's father* . . . . Bass
Fritz Kothner, *baker*. . . . . Bass
Night Watchman . . . . Bass
Mastersingers, journeymen, apprentices, burghers, townspeople, musicians,
children

ACT I   Nuremberg, middle of the sixteenth century. As the service concludes in St. Katharine's Church, a newcomer in town, the young knight Walther von Stolzing, seeks a word with Eva Pogner. They have met, but he knows little about the girl and wants to find out whether she is engaged. Her mother being dead, Eva is attended by a young housekeeper, Magdalene, who wants to leave, but she is distracted by the appearance of her boyfriend, David, apprentice to the cobbler Hans Sachs. Eva tells Walther she is to be engaged to the winner of the Mastersingers' contest the next day. But Eva's heart already belongs to Walther, who reminds her of David in Albrecht Dürer's picture of David and Goliath, the Mastersingers' emblem. When Magdalene repeats the name David, her sweetheart thinks she is calling him and comes in, saying he has to ready the church for the Mastersingers' auditions, at which apprentices will try to qualify for tomorrow's contest. Magdalene advises Walther to present himself as a Master for the competition. Meanwhile, Walther tells Eva he will meet her that evening outside her house. Magdalene takes Eva home, leaving David to supervise the other apprentices in setting up benches. Since Magdalene has told him to brief Walther for the singing test, David starts to explain the Mastersingers' rules: a song must be put together with care, its parts in the proper place and proportion. As he catalogues the various kinds of verse and music, his pupil shrugs in confusion but declares he will qualify as a Master, since he is able to compose both words and tune. The apprentices get the place set up just as Pogner the goldsmith enters with the town clerk, Beckmesser, and greets Walther, who says he will seek membership in the Mastersingers' guild. The other Masters have been filing in, and one of them, Fritz Kothner, calls the roll. Pogner reminds the group that tomorrow is Midsummer Day, the annual holiday of all the guilds, saying they have a responsibility to uphold German arts and crafts (*Das schöne Fest, Johannistag*), adding he is offering his daughter's hand to the winner of the singing contest. If she rejects the winner, she must either stay single or marry another Mastersinger. Hans Sachs speaks out in favor of Eva's right to marry whomever she wants, while some of the stuffier Masters (notably Beckmesser) disagree, saying the rules should bind her as well as them. Finally a vote is taken, and Pogner's proposal is accepted. Pogner introduces Walther, vouching for his noble family, and Kothner asks his qualifications to apply as a Master. Who was his teacher? Walther replies that in winter, when his castle was snowbound, he studied the work of Walther von der Vogelweide (*Am stillen Herd*), and in summer he studied the actual "Vogelweide"—the meadows filled with birds. Kothner suggests an auditon, and the grumbling Beckmesser takes his place as "marker," to chalk up the contestant's errors on a slate: seven are allowed. Kothner reads the rules, and Beckmesser cries, "Fanget an!" (Begin). Taking these words as his starting point, Walther improvises about springtime and the jubilation of nature. Beckmesser's chalk is heard scratching inside his curtained booth; when the first part of the song is done, he shows his blackboard filled with errors, to the amusement of the other guild members. Sachs quiets them with a plea for tolerance, requesting that Walther be allowed to finish, but Beckmesser tries to prevent it, citing chapter and verse of the errors. Amid the tumult Walther resumes singing, and though Sachs continues to defend him, the Masters vote emphatically against the newcomer.

ACT II A street in front of Pogner's and Sachs' houses. As evening falls, apprentices close the shutters of the various houses. Magdalene, eager for news of the song trial, learns from David that Walther was disqualified. Sachs arrives and takes David into his house. Pogner comes home with Eva and reflects on the day to come, but she can think only of her rendezvous with Walther. Magdalene announces dinner and tells Eva the bad news about Walther. As they go into the house, Sachs prepares to work at his cobbler's bench in the street, sending David off to bed. Distracted by the balmy air and lilac scent, Sachs reflects on Walther's song, which sounded natural and right despite its departure from the rules *(Wie duftet doch der Flieder)*. Eva comes outside to look for Walther and is surprised to see Sachs instead. She banters with him, revealing that she cannot bear Beckmesser but has often thought of Sachs himself as a husband. He, a middle-aged widower, admits the warmth of his feelings for her but says he is too old. The conversation turns to that afternoon's singing test, and Eva gets angry with Sachs for his feigned indifference to Walther's rejection. When Magdalene calls to Eva, Sachs withdraws. Magdalene warns Eva that Beckmesser plans to serenade her. Just as Pogner calls both girls back inside, Walther appears and exchanges agitated words with Eva, telling her about his afternoon's experience. When the Night Watchman's horn sounds, Eva tells Walther to hide while she prepares to elope with him. Sachs, overhearing, resolves to prevent the pair from making such a mistake. As Eva comes back out, having changed dresses with Magdalene, Sachs sets his lamp so that it casts a bright light into the alley, forcing Eva and Walther to hide. Beckmesser arrives, tuning his lute; though Sachs puts out his light, Beckmesser's presence keeps the young couple in hiding. Sach resumes work outside the shop door, launching into a lusty cobbling song *(Jerum!)* and telling Beckmesser his shoes will be ready by morning. Impatient to serenade Eva, Beckmesser has to endure further verses of Sachs' song, meanwhile noting that "Eva" (Magdalene in Eva's dress) has appeared at Pogner's upstairs window. Trying flattery, Beckmesser says he wants Sachs's opinion of his serenade, but when Sachs declares he will stick to cobbling, the clerk loses patience and delivers a tirade about how Sachs will never become a marker for the guild. "Was that your song?" asks Sachs in mock innocence. Finally they arrange a compromise: Beckmesser will sing, and Sachs will strike a nail only when he hears a mistake. As soon as the clerk begins, Sachs strikes several nails and begins to argue, forcing Beckmesser to begin again. This time he gets through the serenade, with an unnerving barrage of hammer strokes. Sachs pronounces the shoes finished; Beckmesser attributes his slips to nervousness; and David, thinking the clerk has been serenading Magdalene, comes out with a cudgel to threaten his rival. Neighbors appear at their windows, aroused by the increasing racket, and soon the whole population of the quarter is out in the street, fighting and arguing. Walther, trapped in his hiding place with Eva, decides to draw his sword and clear a path through the mob, but Sachs hustles him into his house and Eva into hers. The street empties as rapidly as it filled, the townspeople all being back home by the time the Night Watchman returns on his hourly rounds.

ACT III   Inside his workshop the next morning, Sachs at first ignores David's excuses about the preceding night's melée, then finally asks the apprentice to recite his verses. David does, realizing at the mention of St. John that today is his master's name day, "Hans" being short for "Johannes." He urges Sachs to compete at the festivities and get married. Sachs sends him off to dress as his herald, then muses on the general madness of mankind, brought home to him by the night's events *(Wahn! überall Wahn!)*. Walther appears, and Sachs offers to help him shape his master song, based on a dream he just had, into acceptable form. As Walther describes his dream of Adam and Eve's paradise, Sachs writes down the words, interspersing the verses with comments. Then he takes Walther to get dressed for the contest. Beckmesser arrives, the worse for wear from his beating the night before. Finding the shop vacant, he snoops around, sees the poem in Sachs' handwriting, and exults that he has caught Sachs trying to win Eva. Sachs, returning to the room, denies he will compete and even tells Beckmesser to keep the sheet. When Beckmesser asks whether he can sing the verses, Sachs tells him to use them any way at all, promising he will claim no authorship. Beside himself with excitement, Beckmesser leaves. Sachs' next visitor is Eva, dressed for the festivities but complaining that one of her new shoes pinches. Sachs checks the shoe and finds it a perfect fit. Walther enters, and Eva forgets the shoe, her excuse for coming to Sachs's shop. Prompted by Sachs, Walther offers Eva his song, after which Sachs— noting Eva's rapture—remarks that the poet can set everything right that the shoemaker could not fix. In an outburst of gratitude, Eva thanks Sachs for bringing her to an awareness of womanhood *(O Sachs! mein Freund!)*, adding that if fate had not introduced her to Walther, she would have esteemed Sachs himself as a husband. He reminds her of what happened to another older man, King Marke of legend, who married Isolde and came to grief. Summoning Magdalene and David, Sachs announces the birth of Walther's song and says it should be christened. Since an apprentice cannot serve as witness, Sachs elevates David to journeyman. Then he names the song, after the rules, "Die selige Morgentraum-Deutweise" (The Blessed Morning Dream True Story), asking Eva to be its godmother. To herself she expresses the hope that Walther's song represents, and all the others reflect on their hopes for that day (quintet: *Selig, wie die Sonne*). Then they leave for the festivities.

§ In a meadow near the Pegnitz River, a platform has been raised. The guilds arrive, each carrying its banner and singing the praises of its profession— shoemakers, tailors, and bakers, with their apprentices and journeymen. When they see Sachs, they welcome him. As keynote speaker for the event, he offers thanks for their affection and praises Pogner for offering so rare a prize in honor of art *(Euch macht ihr's leicht)*. Kothner announces the contest—open only to single Masters, in order of seniority—and asks Beckmesser to go first. Shaking with anxiety, the clerk steps onto the singer's mound and makes mistakes in the verses, either changing their meaning or rendering them meaningless, with grotesque effect; snickers from the crowd unnerve him further. Unable to finish, he rushes at Sachs, declaring him the author, and then storms off. Sachs explains he did not write the poem, which in its proper form is a great one and should be sung by its real author. Walther takes his place and sings *(Morgenlich leuchtend)*. Though puzzled by its novelty, the Masters are swayed by the song, and the crowd responds with enthusiasm. At the end, when Walther describes the singer's highest prize—Parnassus and Paradise— he has won by acclamation. Eva crowns him with a wreath, and the Masters urge Pogner to name Walther a Mastersinger, which he does. Walther refuses, but Sachs tells him the Masters' values and dedication are not to be scorned, praising German art for flowering under adversity. With this, Sachs decorates Walther with the chain and medals of his guild, while Eva takes Walther's wreath and crowns Sachs with it, to general acclaim.

DER RING DES NIBELUNGEN

(The Ring of the Nibelung)

CYCLE OF FOUR MUSIC DRAMAS
MUSIC: Richard Wagner
TEXT (German): the composer, after ancient Nordic epics

DAS RHEINGOLD

(The Rhinegold)

FOUR SCENES
WORLD PREMIERE: Munich, September 22, 1869
U.S. PREMIERE: Metropolitan Opera, January 4, 1889

DAS RHEINGOLD

CHARACTERS

Woglinde		Soprano
Wellgunde	*Rhinemaidens*	Soprano
Flosshilde		Mezzo-Soprano
Fricka		Mezzo-Soprano
Freia	*goddesses*	Soprano
Erda		Contralto
Wotan		Bass-Baritone
Donner	*gods*	Baritone
Froh		Tenor
Loge		Tenor
Alberich	*Nibelungs*	Bass-Baritone
Mime		Tenor
Fasolt	*giants*	Bass-Baritone
Fafner		Bass

Nibelungs

According to Nordic mythology, northern Europe in legendary times consisted of three realms: beneath the earth, where the Nibelung dwarfs lived; the earth's surface, inhabited by giants and ordinary mortals; and the cloudy heights, home of the gods. Mortal warriors who died gloriously were taken to dwell with Wotan (Odin), lord of the gods, in Valhalla. *Das Rheingold* tells how Valhalla came to be built.

SCENE 1 In the waters of the Rhine, three Rhinemaidens play and scarcely notice the approach of the dwarf Alberich. Taken with the nymphs, he tries clumsily to catch them as they mockingly lead him on. His attempts to climb the slippery rocks lead only to frustration. Out of patience with their taunts, he starts chasing them angrily, but a gleam of sunlight reveals the Rhinegold on the summit of a high rock. Hailing the treasure they guard, they wonder at Alberich's ignorance when he asks what it is. They reveal that whoever possesses the gold and forges a ring from it will rule the world, though he must forswear love. Since his efforts at love have brought him nothing, Alberich decides to steal the treasure and enjoy power instead. Climbing to where the gold shines, he wrests it from the rock and runs off with it, plunging the scene in darkness as the Rhinemaidens try to catch him.

SCENE 2 On a mountaintop in the cloudy heights with a newly built castle, Valhalla, visible in the background, Wotan and his wife, Fricka, goddess of marriage and the family, lie asleep in a meadow. Fricka rises and wakes her husband, who hails the castle as a fulfillment of his dreams (*Vollendet das ewige Werk!*). Fricka reminds him he will now have to pay the giants Fafner and Fasolt, who built the edifice. The payment was to be her sister Freia, goddess of youth, but Wotan never seriously meant to keep his bargain. Freia runs in, already pursued by the giants, who remind Wotan of the agreement. Wotan says that the offer was made in jest, and that they must settle for other payment. Fafner, realizing that loss of the golden apples tended by Freia would cost the gods their eternal youth, favors carrying her off by force. Wotan, who has sent for the fire god Loge for advice, stalls for time. Meanwhile, Freia's brothers Froh (god of the fields) and Donner (god of thunder) come to her aid, and when Donner threatens the giants with his hammer, Wotan intervenes, saying that all contracts were guaranteed on his spear. When Loge arrives, Wotan reminds him that he promised to find a way out of the bargain when it was made. Loge replies he has searched the earth for a suitable treasure to redeem Freia but has found only one—the Rhinegold, which the Rhinemaidens want Wotan to restore to them. Loge explains that whoever fashions a ring from it, as Alberich has done, will gain world power. When Fricka learns that a wife could use it to keep her husband in line, she urges Wotan to get it for her. Since Alberich stole the gold, says Loge, why not steal it from him? Fafner, who wants the gold as substitute payment and lacks the guile to get it, tells Wotan to use his wits for that purpose. Fasolt, however, still wants Freia and insists on holding her hostage until the ransom is brought. As the giants carry her away, Loge sees the gods beginning to age. Wotan bids Loge accompany him to the nether world.

SCENE 3   In their underground domain, Alberich torments his brother, Mime, with threats: why has he not yet finished forging the gold? Mime reluctantly lets Alberich why the Tarnhelm, a magic helmet made from the treasure. It enables Alberich to become invisible, whereupon he gleefully thrashes his brother. Loge leads Wotan to the cowering Mime, who complains of his brother's tyranny, admitting he had hoped to outwit him and keep both ring and Tarnhelm. The gods, unrecognized by Mime, offer to help him and the other Nibelungs free themselves from Alberich's yoke. Alberich, visible again, returns from terrorizing his minions, whom he drives in ceaseless toil to mine more gold to add to his store of treasure. He confronts Loge and Wotan, whom he recognizes but does not fear, since the ring gives him power. He warns the gods of his plan to overthrow them *(Die in linder Lüfte Weh'n)*. Flattering Alberich for his clever achievements, Loge asks what would happen if someone stole the ring. Alberich gives away the secret of the Tarnhelm, which enables him to rule invisibly, and when Loge incredulously asks for a demonstration, Alberich turns himself into a dragon, then back again. Loge asks whether the Tarnhelm enables him to turn into something smaller—a toad, for instance—so he could hide. Obligingly Alberich turns into a toad, whereupon Wotan traps him under his foot and Loge seizes the Tarnhelm. As Alberich resumes his accustomed shape, they tie him up and lead him back to the gods' abode.

SCENE 4   On the mountain heights, Loge and Wotan tell Alberich he cannot go free without paying ransom. Though outraged at their demand for his entire hoard of gold, he imagines that by keeping the ring he will recoup his fortunes. Loge unties his right hand so he can use the power of the ring to summon his dwarfs, who carry the golden treasure and pile it up. Having delivered the gold, Alberich asks for the Tarnhelm back, but Loge says they will keep it. Wotan adds that the ring must be part of the ransom, reminding the dwarf that it is not rightfully his to begin with. Alberich retorts that Wotan is as much a thief as he, but this does not prevent the god from tearing the ring off his finger. Loge frees Alberich, who lays a curse on the ring: may care, envy, and death befall all who possess it. He disappears as the other gods enter, followed by Fasolt and Fafner. Sad at the thought of losing Freia, Fasolt agrees on the condition that the gold cover her from view. The brothers thrust their staffs into the ground in order to measure the height of the treasure, which Loge and Froh heap up between the staffs. Fafner complains that the gold is not quite enough—he can still see Freia's hair through a crack—so Loge reluctantly adds the Tarnhelm to the pile. Fasolt claims he can still see a gleam of her eye through a chink, so Fafner demands the ring on Wotan's finger. When Wotan refuses, Fasolt says the deal is off and repossesses Freia, but Wotan will not relent. Then, from a rocky cleft, the earth goddess Erda appears, rising from perpetual sleep to warn Wotan not to keep the ring (*Weiche, Wotan!*): it will bring the end of the gods. Wotan wants to learn more, but she disappears. Finally he tosses the ring onto the treasure pile, Freia is released, and the giants begin packing their prize into a sack. Immediately the curse begins to take effect: the brothers quarrel over the division of the treasure. Loge slyly advises Fasolt to let Fafner take the rest of the treasure but to keep the ring for himself. When the two struggle over the ring, Fafner kills Fasolt. Fricka bids Wotan turn his thoughts to their new castle. Donner, swinging his hammer, summons lightning and thunder to clear the mists, and a rainbow forms a bridge to the castle. Noting how the setting sun gilds the building (*Abendlich strahlt*), Wotan leads the gods across the bridge, while Loge muses that they are heading toward their downfall: he would like to burn the place. The voices of the Rhinemaidens below, grieving for their lost treasure, draw no sympathy from the gods but end on an ominous note: only in the depths lie truth and purity, whereas the rejoicing gods are false and weak.

DIE WALKÜRE

(The Valkyrie)

THREE ACTS
WORLD PREMIERE: Munich, June 26, 1870
U.S. PREMIERE: New York, Academy of Music, April 2, 1877
METROPOLITAN OPERA PREMIERE: January 30, 1885

CHARACTERS

Sieglinde, *Wälsung, mortal daughter of Wotan* . . . . Soprano
Fricka, *Wotan's wife, goddess of marriage* . . . . Mezzo-soprano
Brünnhilde, *eldest Valkyrie, daughter of Wotan and Erda* . . . Soprano
Siegmund, *Sieglinde's twin brother* . . . . Tenor
Wotan, *chief of the gods* . . . . Bass-Baritone
Hunding, *Sieglinde's husband* . . . . Bass
Eight other Valkyries

ACT I Legendary times, in the forests of northern Europe. Built around the trunk of a giant ash tree is a rude dwelling. As a storm rages, a stranger opens the door in exhaustion, seeking rest and shelter; finding no one, he collapses on the hearth. There he is discovered by a young woman, who fetches water when he stirs and asks for a drink. Thanking her, he learns she is the wife of Hunding, who will soon be home; the stranger remarks that in his present condition he is no threat to anyone: outnumbered and disarmed by foes, he barely escaped them. The woman offers a drink, and they look at each other with growing interest. When he says he must leave, she urges him to stay, hinting that a sympathetic face is welcome in a home where unhappiness dwells. His own name, he says, is "Wehwalt"—one ruled by woe—so he might as well stay. Hunding approaches and looks inquiringly at the stranger, then says the hospitality of his house is sacred. Sending his wife to prepare food, he looks at the newcomer and notes his resemblance to her. When Hunding asks who he is, the stranger, with prompting from the wife, identifies himself again as Wehwalt, since misfortune has dogged him. Born with a twin sister, he came home one day from hunting with his father, Wolfe, to find his mother killed, their home laid waste, and his twin sister missing. His father's enemies, the Neidings, had done this. He and his father then began years of wandering, dogged by enemies. Hunding says he has heard tales of Wolfe and his wolf cub. The story continues with the disappearance of Wolfe during a skirmish with the Neidings, after which Wehwalt tried to settle down but was treated like an outcast in every community. His most recent adventure involved trying to rescue a girl from a forced wedding: though he killed her oppressors, she would not leave the corpses of her brothers and was finally killed. Hunding says he himself was summoned to that battle but could not get there in time: it was his own tribesmen whom Wehwalt slaughtered. Stonily, he informs the visitor he is a guest for the night but had better arm himself the next day, when Hunding will seek vengeance. Picking up his own arms, he goes to bed, telling his wife to prepare his nightly drink. She takes it to him. Alone, the stranger recalls that his father, whom he now calls Wälse, once promised him a sword in time of need. A ray of light from the fire illuminates a spot on the tree trunk, drawing the man's attention. As he thinks about the attractive woman he has just met, she steals into the room, saying she drugged her husband's drink. She tells of her forced wedding to Hunding, at which a wanderer appeared and thrust a sword into the trunk of the ash tree. Since none of the guests could pull it out, it is still there (*Der Männer Sippe*). She knows that the right person can win the sword, and impulsively the stranger says it is he. As he embraces her, the door of the house blows open, revealing a moonlit night. Wehwalt declares that spring and love are brother and sister, and that one sets the other free (*Winterstürme wichen dem Wonnemond*). She replies that he is the spring, come to free her (*Du bist der Lenz*), adding that his face reflects her own just as surely as did a brook she looked into recently. At length, when he reveals that his father, known as "Wolfe" to cowards, was really Wälse, she is beside herself with the realization that he is a Wälsung—her twin brother, Siegmund—and that the sword in the tree belongs to him. He draws it out, naming the blade Nothung, "time of need." Proclaiming herself to be Sieglinde, she says he has won her along with the sword, and together they rush out into the night.

ACT II   In a wild, rocky place, Wotan summons his Valkyrie daughter Brünnhilde, telling her to make sure that Siegmund wins the upcoming fight with Hunding. With her battle cry (*Hojotoho!*), the girl warns him that his wife, Fricka, is approaching. As goddess of marriage and the family, Fricka has been called upon to defend Hunding's rights. When Wotan claims that compulsory, loveless vows are not sacred, Fricka points out that the Wälsungs are guilty not only of adultery but of incest. When he defends them, she says his indulgent attitude degrades his authority and the standing of all the gods. As Brünnhilde is heard returning, Fricka forces Wotan to withdraw his support from Siegmund, including the magic power of the sword and Brünnhilde's intervention. He sits in dejection as she rides off, then turns to Brünnhilde, relating how he made off with Alberich's treasure to pay for Valhalla, and how Erda warned about the ring's evil power. After that, he descended into the earth to learn more from Erda and become her lover, begetting Brünn-hilde and her sister Valkyries. With their help, he hoped to stem the tide of the gods' decline. But Erda warned that if Alberich regained the ring, he would destroy the gods. The giant Fafner, Valhalla's surviving builder, now guards the treasure, and Wotan cannot get it back without breaking his prom-ise, so he needs a hero to do it for him—someone outside his own control, unaided by his power. Wotan declares that the free create themselves, while he, the god, can create only subservient knaves. Tainted by contact with the ring, he must renounce whatever he loves, betray whoever trusts him, and wait in resignation for the end. Lately he heard that Alberich bought himself a wife and produced a son, born of hate, who will fulfill Erda's prophecy of bringing about the gods' ruin. Brünnhilde now has to make sure Siegmund loses. Seeing Wotan set against himself, she wants to carry out his true wishes and help Siegmund, but he warns her of his wrath. He storms off, leaving her to withdraw as she sees Siegmund approaching with Sieglinde, who is over-come with guilt. Near hysteria, the girl imagines Hunding in pursuit and sees Siegmund fall. As he puts her down to rest, Brünnhilde appears as an angel of death, saying she will soon take him to Valhalla *(Siegmund! Sieh auf mich!)*. When he learns that Sieglinde cannot come too, he refuses. Brünnhilde tells him he must die, and she offers to look after Sieglinde, but he replies he will kill both Sieglinde and himself if need be. At this, Brünnhilde relents and promises to help Siegmund. She leaves, and he prepares to fight the approaching Hunding, while the fitfully sleeping Sieglinde wakes to see the two men preparing to fight. Brünnhilde appears, shielding Siegmund, but Wotan intervenes, pointing his spear, whereupon Siegmund's sword shatters and Hunding kills him. Brünnhilde escapes with Sieglinde. At a wave of Wotan's hand, Hunding drops lifeless. Furious over Brünnhilde's disobedi-ence, the god sets out to catch her.

ACT III   On a craggy mountain, Valkyries bring slain heroes to Valhalla. When Brünnhilde arrives, carrying Sieglinde on her saddle, the sisters hesitate to brave Wotan's wrath by helping the Wälsung to escape. When Sieglinde revives, she asks only for death until Brünnhilde tells her she will bear Sieg-mund's child; then she hails Brünnhilde for saving her *(O hehrstes Wunder!)* and runs off, leaving the Valkyries to shield Brünnhilde from the approaching Wotan. He demands Brünnhilde, who steps forward to hear her punishment. He says she has chosen her own fate: by disobeying him, she has cut herself off from duties and privileges as a Valkyrie and will be left sleeping on the rock, prey to the first man who finds her. He orders the other Valkyries to leave, and Brünnhilde argues that she was true to his real wishes rather than to his outward pronouncements *(War es so schmählich)*. He admits it but must shun her, just as he had to shun his impulse to save Siegmund. In casting her off, he is denying, she says, the most important part of himself—his true, inmost feelings. He retorts that in yielding to love she has condemned herself to live as a mortal wife. Having renounced the Wälsungs, he has no interest in Sieglinde's forthcoming child. Brünnhilde asks one grace: fire should surround her in sleep, so that only a worthy hero can wake her. Wotan bids farewell (*Leb' wohl, du kühnes, herrliches Kind!*) and kisses her eyes with sleep, then calls on Loge to send flames, which leap up around the rock. "May no one who fears my spear's point," he says, "ever step through this fire!" Overcome with sadness, he disappears.

SIEGFRIED

THREE ACTS
WORLD PREMIERE: Bayreuth, Festspielhaus, August 16, 1876
U.S. PREMIERE: Metropolitan Opera, November 9, 1887

CHARACTERS

Siegfried, *son of Siegmund and Sieglinde* . . . . Tenor
Brünnhilde, *eldest Valkyrie, daughter of Wotan and Erda* . . . Soprano
Forest Bird . . . . Soprano
Erda, *earth goddess* . . . . Contralto
Mime, *Nibelung dwarf* . . . . Tenor
Alberich, *his brother* . . . . Baritone
Wanderer *(Wotan in disguise)* . . . . Bass-Baritone
Dragon *(Fafner in disguise)* . . . . Bass

In the years since *Das Rheingold* and *Die Walküre,* the Nibelung treasure (including the troublesome ring) has been in the custody of the giant Fafner, who used the Tarnhelm to transform himself into a dragon and guards the hoard in a cave. Since he sleeps all the time, the gold is out of harm's way, and Alberich's curse on the ring too remains dormant. Sieglinde, rescued by Brünnhilde after Siegmund's death, wandered in the woods and was sheltered by the dwarf Mime; in his cave she gave birth to her child and died. Mime realized that the infant would grow into a hero capable of retrieving the Nibelung treasure. Brünnhilde, locked in sleep and surrounded by protective fire, remains on a mountaintop; the only one who can awaken her is a hero with no fear of Wotan's spear, symbol of the gods' power.

ACT I   In his cave workshop, Mime toils to forge the pieces of the broken sword, Nothung, that he acquired from the dying Sieglinde when he took on the care of her baby, Siegfried, now grown to young manhood. Aware of the sword's power and of Siegfried's invincibility once it is repaired, he has fixed it over and over, only to have it break in pieces whenever the youth tries it. Siegfried appears with a bear he has caught; he playfully scares Mime with it, then sends it off. Impatient for his sword, Siegfried tries it, only to have it break once more. Mime offers him food, which Siegfried refuses. Then he reminds him how he has cared for him, to which Siegfried replies that the one thing he was never taught is how to stand the sight of Mime. Noting that he does not resemble his adoptive father, he demands to know who his real parents were. Mime tells how he found a woman in distress in the woods and nursed her in his cave, where she died giving birth. Her name was Sieglinde, and the baby's father had fallen in combat; Siegfried's name and the pieces of broken sword were his legacy from his mother. Once more Siegfried insists the blade be repaired, so he can leave Mime forever. As he storms out, the dwarf moans he will never be able to forge it. As he sits dejected, a Wanderer (Wotan in earthly guise) appears at his door, asking for hospitality. The Wanderer challenges Mime to a battle of wits: whoever proves deficient in wisdom shall forfeit his head. Mime agrees to ask three questions: what race lives under the earth (the Nibelungs), on the face of the earth (the giants), and on the cloudy heights (the gods)? The Wanderer not only answers but adds information about Alberich's cursed ring, Fafner's guardianship of the treasure, and the origins of Wotan's powerful spear, which he strikes on the ground for emphasis, terrifying the dwarf. Mime now hopes he is rid of his visitor, but the Wanderer insists he too can ask three questions. What is the race that Wotan mistreats but loves most? Mime correctly identifies them as the Wälsungs (Volsungs). What is the name of the sword Siegfried will have to use if he is to kill the dragon Fafner? Nothung, says Mime. And who will repair the sword? Mime cannot answer. The Wanderer tells him it can only be forged anew by one who has never known fear—and Mime's head is forfeit to that same person. He leaves Mime so unnerved that when Siegfried returns, the dwarf is afraid to face him. Recovering his composure, Mime tries to find out whether Siegfried can learn fear. Since the youth seems unable to understand what fear is, Mime decides to take him to Fafner's lair, where he will surely learn. Siegfried declares he will repair the sword himself and sets about it with a will, his unorthodox metalworking methods unnerving and fascinating Mime. Siegfried launches into a massive forging song (*Nothung! neidliches Schwert!*) while Mime thinks ahead: once Siegfried has killed Fafner and recovered the hoard, how to get rid of him and gain the prize? He will have to drug the tired hero and dispatch him with his sword. Siegfried, having shredded the metal and melted it, pours it into a mold and places the glowing blade on the anvil to hammer it into shape. As he tempers the finished steel in water, Mime begins to share his elation, imagining he will turn the tables on his brother Alberich. He falls in terror, however, when Siegfried brandishes the sword and breaks the anvil with it.

ACT II   By night in the forest, Alberich lies near Fafner's cave, brooding about his lost treasure. The Wanderer appears, and Alberich recognizes Wotan at once. Though the dwarf heaps recriminations upon him, the Wanderer replies that he cares nothing about the ring himself, adding that it is Mime whom Alberich should fear: Mime is the only other one who wants the gold. Perplexed that his enemy, the lord of the gods, seems to be helping him, Alberich watches the Wanderer rouse the sleeping Fafner to warn him of approaching danger and urge him to give up the ring and save his life. Fafner mumbles that he will devour any attacker. The Wanderer leaves after telling Alberich it is useless to try to change the course of fate. Alberich hides as dawn breaks and Mime enters with Siegfried. When the youth insists he leave, Mime hobbles off, muttering that he hopes Siegfried and Fafner kill each other. Siegfried listens to the murmurs of the forest, wondering what his mother was like. A Forest Bird warbles a song, which he wishes he could understand. Cutting a reed and blowing on it, he tries unsuccessfully to answer the bird's song. Then he uses his hunting horn to summon the bird but instead awakens Fafner, who lumbers out of his cave. In a brief struggle, Siegfried stabs the monster through the heart. Dying, Fafner warns the youth that whoever put him up to the deed is plotting his death as well. When Siegfried draws his sword from Fafner's breast, he inadvertently licks some of the dragon's blood from his fingers. This enables him to understand the Forest Bird's song, directing him into the cave where the Nibelung's treasure is stored. As Siegfried enters, Mime slinks back, only to meet Alberich, who blocks his path. The brothers argue until Siegfried reappears; then they hide while Siegfried dons the ring and Tarnhelm as souvenirs of his fight with Fafner. The Forest Bird warns about Mime, saying the taste of dragon's blood will make it possible to read Mime's thoughts. When Mime returns, Siegfried hears his real intentions—to trick and destroy Siegfried, then seize the treasure. When Mime proffers a poisoned drink, Siegfried loses patience and kills him, throwing his body into the cave, then pushing Fafner's body into the cave entrance to block it. Resting from these exertions, he calls on the Forest Bird for more advice. She tells him he can win a bride who lies asleep on a fire-encircled rock. He starts toward the mountain, the bird leading the way.

ACT III   By night at the foot of the mountain, the Wanderer calls Erda from her sleep in the depths of the earth, hoping to learn how to interfere with the course of fate and avoid the gods' downfall. Though he pleads with her at length, reciting the events that have brought him to his present pass, she refuses to shed any more light on his destiny, saying only that he should ask Brünnhilde or his other daughters, the three Norns, who weave the cord of fate. Then she sinks back into sleep as dawn approaches, and with it Siegfried. The Wanderer is pleased to meet Siegfried and to see his predictions fulfilled, but Siegfried impatiently draws his sword and breaks the spear with which the Wanderer tries to block his path. Wotan, whose spear once shattered that same sword, realizes that his power is ended and withdraws, leaving Siegfried to climb through the fire.

§ Reaching the summit, Siegfried sees a figure on the rock, asleep. He assumes it is a man, but when he cuts loose the outer layer of armor, he discovers that it is a woman. Experiencing fear for the first time, he calls on his mother for help. Overwhelmed by Brünnhilde's beauty, he kisses her; she stirs from her sleep, greets the sunlight *(Heil dir, Sonne!)*, and hails the gods for letting Siegfried awaken her. When she tells Siegfried she always loved him, even before he was born, he thinks she must be his mother, but she explains she is not. Her words about his parents, and about Brünnhilde's role in their last moments on earth, confuse Siegfried. Though he is frightened by his unfamiliar feelings, and she too feels no longer protected by the weapons and the demigoddess status that used to be hers, Siegfried takes the initiative and declares he must now awaken her completely. She gradually overcomes her shame at this descent to mortal womanhood, until she is content to bid farewell to Valhalla's memory, dimmed by the approaching dusk of the gods. Abandoning all other concerns but their love, the couple feels for the moment invincible, exulting even in the thought of death.

GÖTTERDÄMMERUNG

(Twilight of the Gods)

PROLOGUE AND THREE ACTS
WORLD PREMIERE: Bayreuth, Festspielhaus, August 17, 1876
U.S. PREMIERE: Cincinnati, Music Hall, May 16, 1878 (Act III
   only, concert performance); Metropolitan Opera, March 11,
   1889

CHARACTERS

Three Norns,
   daughters of Erda . . . . Contralto, Mezzo-Soprano, Soprano
Brünnhilde, *eldest Valkyrie, daughter of Wotan and Erda* . . . Soprano

Gutrune, *Gunther's sister* . . . . Soprano
Waltraute, *Valkyrie* . . . . Mezzo-Soprano
Rhinemaidens . . . . Soprano, Mezzo-Soprano, Contralto
Siegfried . . . . Tenor
Gunther, *head of the Gibich clan* . . . . Baritone
Hagen, *his half-brother, Alberich's son* . . . . Bass
Alberich, *Nibelung dwarf* . . . . Bass-Baritone
Vassals, warriors, women

PROLOGUE   On the Valkyries' rock, where Brünnhilde lay in sleep, the three
Norns, sisters of the Valkyries, weave the cord of fate. They recall how the
world ash tree, once flourishing and the source of Wotan's spear, is now broken into logs that surround Valhalla, waiting to be ignited by Loge when the
gods' end is at hand. At the mention of Alberich and the Rhinegold, the skein
they have been winding breaks, signifying the end of their wisdom. They
disappear as the day dawns. Brünnhilde and Siegfried emerge from a nearby
cave, where they live since he awakened her. Having taught him her wisdom,
the former Valkyrie now sends Siegfried off to deeds of valor (*Zu neuen Taten*).
They recall how he killed the dragon and climbed the mountain. Now he
leaves her, still protected by the magic fire, and gives her the ring as a token
of love. His horn resounds as he sets forth into the Rhine valley.

ACT I   In the hall of the Gibichungs, a Rhineland tribe, a discussion is in
progress between two half-brothers, Gunther, chief of the clan, and Hagen,
whose father is Alberich the Nibelung. Hagen envies Gunther his legitimacy,
but Gunther envies Hagen's cleverness: they are trying to combine these assets
in furthering the family fortunes. Hagen knows of a prize—Brünnhilde—that
Gunther should win, but he says that only Siegfried is up to the task. Since it
would advance their plans if Siegfried were to marry Gunther's sister, Gutrune,
Hagen suggests that Siegfried be given a potion that will make him forget he
ever saw any other woman. As they talk, they hear Siegfried's horn. Hagen
sights him in a boat on the river and hails him ashore. After exchanges of
greeting and welcome, Gunther gives Siegfried the potion, causing him to
forget his recent past. He looks at Gutrune with interest. When Gunther says
he has set his heart on a certain bride but cannot approach her fire-encircled
abode, Siegfried offers help by using the Tarnhelm to transform himself into
Gunther's likeness. The two take an oath of blood brotherhood, in which
Hagen does not join, declaring his own blood too impure. As Gunther and
Siegfried leave in Siegfried's boat, Hagen keeps a vigil over the hall (*Hier sitz
ich zur Wacht*). His real motive, he admits, is to regain the ring.

§   This same ring preoccupies Brünnhilde as she sits by her cave, interrupted
by a sister Valkyrie, Waltraute. Wotan's plight and the decline of Valhalla
bring her there (*Höre mit Sinn*). The only remedy for the gods' impending
doom is for Brünnhilde to throw the ring back to the Rhinemaidens, lifting

Alberich's curse. Brünnhilde refuses, declaring Siegfried's love more important than the gods' fate. In despair Waltraute leaves Brünnhilde to her destiny, which appears in the form of the disguised Siegfried. Claiming her in Gunther's name, he takes the ring. As she retreats in shame to the cave, Siegfried draws his sword as witness that he has fulfilled his promise to Gunther.

ACT II   As the sleeping Hagen waits outside the Gibichungs' hall, his father, Alberich, appears as if in a dream (*Schläfst du, Hagen, mein Sohn?*). The dwarf extracts Hagen's promise that he will use his wiles to defeat Siegfried and regain the ring; as day breaks, he vanishes. Siegfried appears on the shore, transported by the Tarnhelm's magic; Gunther is following by boat with Brünnhilde. Hagen sights a distant sail and sounds his horn, summoning the Gibichung men (*Hoiho!*). Answering horns are heard in the distance as the clan congregates. Hagen tells the vassals that their weapons will be needed only to prepare sacrifices and a wedding feast. He asks them to welcome Gunther's bride, adding meaningfully that if any wrong has been done, they should avenge it. When the pair arrives, the vassals offer a greeting (*Heil! Willkommen!*), but Brünnhilde's unhappiness turns to rage when she sees Siegfried. Having no recollection of their past together, he announces he is marrying Gutrune, she Gunther. Seeing the ring on Siegfried's finger, Brünnhilde asks how he got it, since Gunther took it from her. Hagen seizes on this, telling Brünnhilde to be more specific. She charges Siegfried with betrayal, saying he is her real husband. The vassals clamor to protect Gunther's honor as Siegfried protests his innocence, swearing on Hagen's spear that if he has done wrong he will die by that same weapon (*Helle Wehr!*). Brünnhilde joins in the oath. Siegfried leads Gutrune into the hall and calls the vassals to celebrate. Brünnhilde, Hagen, and Gunther remain to plan revenge (*Welches Unhold's List*). When Hagen offers to kill Siegfried, Brünnhilde says the hero is invincible, except for his back, which she never protected with magic, since he would not turn it on a foe. Though Gunther is still hesitant—partly to protect his sister, partly because of his oath of brotherhood with Siegfried— the three agree that Siegfried must die. Hagen suggests that his death be made to appear a hunting accident. While Gunther and Brünnhilde call upon the gods for aid, Hagen invokes Alberich.

ACT III   In a forest beside the banks of the Rhine, the Rhinemaidens call upon the sun to guide Siegfried to them, since he alone can return their gold. He appears, having left the hunting party to pursue a bear, and the maidens tease him for his ring. He is almost inclined to give it to them, but when they tell of the curse and predict his death that very day if he does not give it up, he keeps it in order to show he is not afraid. As they swim away, Hagen and his fellow hunters catch up with Siegfried. As the group stretches out to rest, Siegfried reminisces about his youth, his adoption by Mime, the repair of the sword, his fight with the dragon (*Mime hiess ein mürrischer Zwerg*). Midway in his narrative, Hagen offers him a drink to refresh his memory. Gunther listens in astonishment and Hagen in grim satisfaction as Siegfried, his memory restored, tells of winning Brünnhilde. Two ravens fly out of a bush, and as Siegfried turns to watch them, Hagen takes his spear and stabs Siegfried in the back, announcing vengeance. Gunther and the other men surround the stricken hero, whose dying thoughts are only of Brünnhilde: he imagines her smiling and calling to him *(Brünnhilde! Heilige Braut!)*. The vassals pick up his body and carry it away (Siegfried's funeral music).

§ At the Gibichungs' hall, Gutrune wakes from anxious dreams to wonder what has become of Siegfried. Her question is answered by the arrival of the funeral cortège. Gunther confirms Gutrune's suspicions that Hagen is the real slayer, and when he and Hagen come to blows, Gunther too is killed. As Hagen reaches for the ring, Siegfried's lifeless arm rises threateningly in the air, causing terror among the clamoring throng. Brünnhilde appears, ordering a funeral pyre built on the Rhine's bank *(Starke Scheite schichtet mir dort)*. She eulogizes Siegfried for his purity of heart, even in error, and calls on Wotan to hear her lament, since he too faces his doom. Taking the ring from Siegfried's hand, she cleanses it of its sinister power by throwing it into the river, where the Rhinemaidens await it. She dispatches Wotan's two ravens homeward, telling them to pass by the Valkyries' rock and send Loge to Valhalla to burn the place. Then, throwing a torch onto the pyre, she ignites it and leads her horse, Grane, into the flames, greeting Siegfried in death. Hagen plunges into the river to get the ring back from the Rhinemaidens, who pull him under, as Valhalla is seen ablaze in the distance.

PARSIFAL

THREE ACTS
MUSIC: Richard Wagner
TEXT (German): the composer, after Wolfram von Eschenbach's
    Parzifal and Chrétien de Troyes' *Legends of the Grail*
WORLD PREMIERE: Bayreuth, Festspielhaus, July 26, 1882
U.S. PREMIERE: Metropolitan Opera, March 3, 1886 (concert per-
    formance); December 24, 1903 (staged)

CHARACTERS

Parsifal, *youth, later knight* . . . . Tenor
Kundry, *part sorceress, part mortal* . . . . Soprano
Amfortas, *head of the knights of the Grail* . . . . Baritone

Gurnemanz, *knight of the Grail* . . . . Bass
Titurel, *Amfortas' father and predecessor* . . . . Bass
Klingsor, *sorcerer, former knight of the Grail* . . . . (Bass-)Baritone
Knights, esquires, choirboys, flowermaidens

The legend of Parsifal interested Wagner as far back as his research for *Lohengrin*. Parsifal is mentioned as Lohengrin's father; he is also known to legend as Sir Percival, one of King Arthur's knights. The quest for the Holy Grail, the vessel with which Christ performed Communion at the Last Supper, was a popular subject in medieval folklore and literature.

ACT I Medieval times in the southeastern mountains of Spain. Near the monastery of Monsalvat, a knight of the Grail, the aged Gurnemanz, awakens two esquires from sleep as day breaks. Two knights enter, discussing the affliction of their leader, Amfortas, who will shortly be brought for his daily bath in the waters. Musing that only one person can heal Amfortas' wound, Gurnemanz greets a wild-looking woman, Kundry, who brings balsam from far away. Amfortas is carried in on a litter and reflects on the prediction that a pure-hearted fool will heal him *(Durch Mitleid wissend)*. Amfortas thanks Kundry en route to his bath, but the two esquires speak scornfully to her. Reprimanding them, Gurnemanz recalls how Titurel, their former leader and Amfortas's father, found her almost lifeless in the woods. As if to expiate some sin in an earlier life, she has from time to time helped the knights of the Grail, but neither she nor anyone else could retrieve the Holy Spear, which pierced Christ's side on the cross. Amfortas lost the spear—and was wounded by it—when a sorcerer named Klingsor used a beautiful woman to lead him astray. Gurnemanz further recalls how Titurel became custodian of the Grail and spear and built a sanctuary for them, turning away Klingsor, who brought purification through the holy relics. Frustrated in his quest, Klingsor tried to overcome worldly desire by emasculating himself, then learned black magic, conjuring up a magic garden where he has ensnared erring knights of the Grail. Klingsor captured the spear from Amfortas and wants the Grail as well. Since only this spear can heal Amfortas's wound, there is no hope for their leader—unless, as Amfortas heard once in a vision, an innocent fool should appear who could retrieve the weapon from Klingsor. Gurnemanz is interrupted by cries from the woods as knights and esquires bring a young man they caught shooting a swan that circled the lake as Amfortas bathed. Gurnemanz upbraids the stranger for his heedless act and asks who he is, where he comes from, and how he got there, to which his answer is "I don't know." He does remember that his mother's name was Herzeleide (Heart's Sorrow) and that he grew up in the wilderness. Kundry, who knows about him, says that his father, Gamuret, died in battle and that the mother did not want her son to be a knight. When she adds that Herzeleide too is dead, the youth attacks her and has to be restrained by Gurnemanz, who says Kundry never lies. In hopes that the stranger may be the innocent fool of the prophecy, Gurnemanz leads him toward the Temple of the Grail: if he is pure in heart, the power of the Grail will make itself known to him without prior instruction.

§ In the Temple, the knights prepare for Communion. Amfortas is carried in on a litter, and the covered Grail is placed on an altar. From the background, as if from a tomb, the voice of Titurel calls out for the Grail to be unveiled one more time, so that he can experience salvation and die in peace. Amfortas, agonized by his fall from grace in Klingsor's snare, cannot bear the sight of the Grail *(Nein! Lasst ihn unenthüllt!)*, but Titurel insists that his son perform the office. Acolytes uncover the chalice and place it in front of Amfortas while choral voices repeat the words of the ceremony: bread and wine are taken as tokens of the flesh and blood of the Redeemer. The Grail glows, and Amfortas raises it to consecrate the bread and wine. Acolytes again cover the chalice, and esquires distribute the consecrated bread and wine for a symbolic reenactment of the Last Supper. Amfortas abstains from this part of the ceremony, sinking back in pain while Gurnemanz gestures to the wandering youth to join the knights. The youth shows no understanding, and Gurnemanz sends him on his way, declaring him nothing but a fool after all.

ACT II In his magic castle, Klingsor prepares to ensnare the fool he sees leaving the domain of the Grail. He summons his accomplice, Kundry, who rises from sleep as if in a trance. In spite of her attempts to atone through service to the knights, she is beholden to Klingsor because of sins in her distant past. When he reminds her of this, she taunts him for his own sins, and he rants about the shame that drives him to seek revenge against the knights *(Furchtbare Not!)*. When she refuses her latest assignment, Klingsor tells her she must go through with it, adding that she will find redemption only through a man who can refuse her. He is confident that this will not be the stranger, whom he sees fighting his way toward the magic garden.

§ In the garden, Klingsor's flowermaidens bemoan the injuries inflicted on their lovers, the guardians of Klingsor's domain, by the marauding stranger, who appears in their midst, dazzled by the sight of so much beauty. They chide him for fighting their sweethearts but soon flirt with him *(Komm, holder Knabe!)*. They withdraw when they hear Kundry calling the name "Parsifal." Transformed into a siren, she tells him she learned his name from Gamuret in Arabia: thus the dying father named his unborn son. She relates how she saw him as an infant and watched him grow, then saw his mother die of grief during his long absence *(Ich sah das Kind)*. Parsifal cries out that he unwittingly caused his mother's death. Kundry reassures him that knowledge will be his through love. On his mother's behalf, she brings him his first kiss. As she embraces him, he recoils as if in great pain *(Amfortas! Die Wunde!)*. He remembers the sight of the Grail and the anguished words of Amfortas, declaring he wants to overcome sin and attain grace. When Kundry tries again to lure him, he realizes she did the same to Amfortas and rejects her, but she persists, pleading that she too needs redemption and can achieve it only through his love. Her soul has been accursed through the ages, she says; since she saw Christ on the Cross and laughed, she has tried in vain to find Him again. Parsifal replies that renunciation of desire is the only path to salvation; he can help both of them if she will show him the way back to Amfortas. She lays a curse on him that he shall never find his way, calling on Klingsor for help. The sorcerer appears and hurls the spear at Parsifal; it stops in midair above the young man's head, enabling him to seize it and make the sign of the Cross, thus causing castle and garden to disappear. Parsifal tells Kundry she will know where to find him and sets off to regain the Temple of the Grail.

ACT III Years have passed, and Gurnemanz is living as a hermit in the domain of Monsalvat. Awakened by moans from a thicket, he finds Kundry lying nearly lifeless and revives her. She mutters that she wants to serve, then points out a stranger approaching. It is a knight, who does not return Gurnemanz's greeting but kneels in prayer when told that today is Good Friday. Gurnemanz recognizes him as Parsifal and sees he is carrying the spear. Parsifal recognizes Gurnemanz and relates how he has wandered far and wide, determined to find his way back. Gurnemanz tells how the order of the Grail has fallen on hard times. Amfortas, longing for death himself, has refused to uncover the Grail; deprived of it, Titurel has died, and the knights have lost their spirit. Today is Titurel's funeral, and Amfortas will be forced to perform his office one more time. As Kundry washes Parsifal's feet, Gurnemanz anoints him as new leader of the order. Parsifal baptizes Kundry, freeing her from the curse of centuries. He remarks that the meadows seem transfigured. Gurnemanz replies that this is the Good Friday Spell: though the day is one of sadness, nature is made more radiant by love and regained innocence. As bells signal midday, he leads Parsifal to the Temple.

The knights carry the Grail into the main hall and charge Amfortas with unveiling it. Seeing his father's coffin, he grieves that he has been unable to find death himself. Rather than suffer renewed life through the power of the Grail, he begs the knights to kill him. Unnoticed, Parsifal touches Amfortas's wound with the spear and declares him healed in body and spirit *(Nur eine Waffe taugt)*, then orders the Grail uncovered. As he holds it aloft, a dove descends from the dome of the Temple, and Kundry sinks lifeless as Gurnemanz, Amfortas, and the others kneel in homage to their new leader.

CARL MARIA von WEBER
1786–1826

*T*hough opera may be considered a conservative art form, its adherents thrive on controversy, pitting their favorite singers, composers, or national schools against one another. When Carl Maria von Weber appeared on the scene, Italian opera still held sway, and composers originating in the Germanic sphere, from Handel to Mozart, had embraced it as the vehicle for most of their stage works. But the movement toward a native genre, given powerful impetus by Mozart himself (notably in *Die Entführung aus dem Serail* and *Die Zauberflöte*), was not to be put down. It was easy enough for court audiences and aristocrats, with their travels and multiple languages, to enjoy Italian opera. But the ordinary citizen who liked music had few places to go.

Born at Eutin—not far from Hamburg, which had the oldest and most flourishing tradition of German-language musical theater—Weber became the founding father of German romantic opera, a movement that culminated in Wagner. His mother, a singer, died when he was twelve. His father, an army officer and amateur fiddler, wanted the boy to be another Mozart (Mozart's wife, Constanze, was his niece) and drove him to become a prodigy. An accomplished pianist, the youth developed an interest in composition, studying counterpoint with Michael Haydn in Salzburg, later analyzing the classics with Abbé Vogler in Vienna. Like his father, Weber married a singer, Caroline Brandt. By the time he took over the directorship of the Dresden Opera House in 1817, he was nearly thirty and had acquired a reputation as an opera conductor.

In Dresden he became acquainted with Friedrich Kind, a lawyer, who proposed making an opera of *Der Freischütz,* a tale from a book of ghost stories put together by a friend of his, Johann August Apel. Weber took three years to compose the music, and when his opera was accepted for production in Berlin, he in effect challenged the despotic Gasparo Spontini, director of the Berlin opera and standard-bearer of the Italian-opera establishment. For all its national color and mood, *Der Freischütz* is no chauvinistic work. Weber had absorbed the graceful French opéra-comique style, which shows in some of his arias. Yet the audiences recognized the new opera as theirs, and it became a kind of craze after its premiere, in 1821, surprising many people, including Beethoven, who is said to have remarked, "That usually feeble little man—I'd never have thought it of him."

Weber, now a celebrity, wrote two more romantic operas that were less tumultuously received, *Euryanthe* (1823) and *Oberon* (1826). From age thirteen he had written short chamber operas suitable for amateur performance, starting his official stage career with *Das Waldmädchen* in 1800. *Der Freischütz* was sixth of his nine operas produced in the professional theater—a total that includes the unfinished *Die Drei Pintos,* completed by the young Gustav Mahler for posthumous production in 1888. Never robust, Weber succumbed to tuberculosis in London after the introduction of *Oberon,* written to an English text. He was buried in England, and not until 1844 were his remains transferred to Dresden, where Richard Wagner delivered his eulogy.

DER FREISCHÜTZ

(The Free Shot)

THREE ACTS
MUSIC: Carl Maria von Weber
TEXT (German): Friedrich Kind, after a story by Johann August
   Apel
WORLD PREMIERE: Berlin, Schauspielhaus, June 18, 1821
U.S. PREMIERE: New York, Park Theatre, March 2, 1825
   (in English)
METROPOLITAN OPERA PREMIERE: November 24, 1884

CHARACTERS

Agathe, *Cuno's daughter* . . . . Soprano
Ännchen, *her young relative* . . . . Soprano

Max, *forester* .... Tenor
Ottokar, *Prince of Bohemia* .... Tenor
Kilian, *well-to-do farmer* .... Bass
Caspar, *forester* .... Bass
Cuno, *chief forester* .... Bass
Hermit .... Bass
Samiel, the Black Huntsman .... Speaking Role
Huntsmen, peasants, apparitions, bridesmaids

ACT I Mid-seventeenth-century Bohemia. Outside an inn in the forest, shots ring out, and villagers hail Kilian's marksmanship. The forester Max, a disgruntled rival, stands wondering whether he has lost his own skill. When the victor needles Max with remarks about his bad aim, the forester pulls his knife. Villagers intervene as Cuno, Caspar, and other foresters appear. Cuno, head ranger for the prince of Bohemia, asks what the trouble is and is shocked to hear that Max missed every shot. Caspar, who has sold his own soul to the devil, means to lure Max into a similar compact: taking him aside, he says someone has hexed Max's aim and urges him to invoke the aid of the Black Huntsman, Samiel. Cuno warns Max that if he cannot pass his trial "free shot" at tomorrow's tournament, his daughter Agathe cannot be his. Asked by Kilian to explain the tradition of the free shot, Cuno relates that his great-grandfather made an extraordinary shot but was accused by rivals of having used magic bullets. Kilian recalls the legend of six charmed bullets and a seventh that strikes where the devil wills it. As Cuno reminds Max that tomorrow means win or lose, Caspar repeats his hints about "help." Kilian tries to cheer Max, who is full of foreboding about the next day and stays behind when his comrade goes inside. Thinking of his past good fortune and his love for Agathe, Max feels forsaken by heaven (*Durch die Wälder*). When he sings of the powers of darkness, Samiel puts in a shadowy appearance, followed by Caspar, who plies Max with wine and launches into a drinking song (*Hier im ird'schen Jammertal*). Then Caspar offers Max his rifle and asks him to aim at a bird barely visible in the twilight sky. Amazed when an eagle drops at his feet, Max demands to know the secret of the shot and learns that it was a charmed bullet. More can be obtained, Caspar says, if Max will join him at midnight in the Wolf's Glen. Max agrees when he remembers that he may lose Agathe. As Max leaves, Caspar exults at winning another soul for the devil.

ACT II In Cuno's house, his great-grandfather's portrait has fallen from the wall. Agathe and her relative, Ännchen, hang it back up, the younger girl remarking that though ancestors deserve respect, she is more interested in meeting a young man (*Kommt ein schlanker Bursch gegangen*). Ännchen leaves to go to bed, while Agathe waits for Max, reflecting that love has brought sorrow and anxiety but that Max's victory tomorrow may bring her happiness (*Leise, fromme Weise!*). Max enters, greeting Agathe with news that he shot a large bird. He notes a bruise on her forehead and learns that the portrait fell at seven that evening—the very moment he fired Caspar's rifle. Disconcerted, he excuses himself, saying he shot a stag in the Wolf's Glen and has to retrieve it before the bears find it. Ännchen, who has reappeared, joins Agathe in warning Max against the accursed place, but he says he is not afraid.

In the Wolf's Glen, Caspar awaits Max while spirit voices hail the approach of a new victim. As midnight strikes, Caspar invokes Samiel and asks the demon to grant him another three years of life in exchange for a new recruit, Max. The seventh bullet will be Samiel's to guide to Agathe's heart, claiming yet another victim. Samiel agrees but warns Caspar he must forfeit his life the next day if Max is not won over. After Samiel disappears, Caspar steps inside a magic circle of stones and starts to fan the coals of a fire as Max appears on the rocks nearby, wondering at the spooky surroundings. Stopped by an apparition of his late mother, who seems to be praying for him, Max will not come down into the circle, but Caspar calls upon Samiel, who changes the apparition into one of Agathe leaping off a precipice. Fearing for her life, Max joins Caspar, who instructs him in the ritual of casting the bullets, then calls upon Samiel. As each bullet is cast, weird sounds and apparitions fill the glen, climaxing in the appearance of wild huntsmen and Samiel himself, who disappears as the hour strikes one, leaving the two men bowed to the ground.

ACT III   In another part of the forest the next forenoon, Max argues with Caspar: Caspar kept three bullets and gave him four, but mysteriously three of those have disappeared, leaving Max with a single shot. A forester appears, looking for Max on behalf of the prince, who wants him to make his free shot. As he leaves, Caspar gloats over the fact that he pilfered Max's bullets and fired them, leaving Max with only the fatal seventh, the devil's bullet.

§ In her room, Agathe compares her hopes to the sun that drives away clouds (*Und ob die Wolke*), but when Ännchen appears, Agathe confesses she dreamed she was changed into a white dove and shot by Max, whereupon she resumed her usual form and the dove was replaced by a dead bird of prey. Trying to persuade her that the dream bodes well, Ännchen tells how their aunt was once frightened by a ghostly vision that turned out to be the family dog (*Einst träumte meiner sel'gen Base*). Going to fetch Agathe's wreath, the girl welcomes her bridesmaids, who bring a chain of flowers (*Wir winden dir den Jungfern-kranz*). Ännchen returns, saying that great-grandfather Cuno's portrait has fallen again. When she opens the box she brought, she finds in it a funeral wreath instead of a wedding wreath. Ännchen assumes that the woman who made it gave her the wrong one by mistake, hastily improvising a new wreath while the bridesmaids resume their song.

§ At Prince Ottokar's encampment, hunters hail their sport (*Was gleicht wohl auf Erden dem Jägervergnügen?*). Ottokar approves Cuno's choice of a son-in-law and asks Max to prove his ability by shooting a white dove on a nearby tree.

When he pulls the trigger, Agathe appears among the trees, crying, "Don't shoot! I am the dove!" As the shot rings out, she and Caspar both sink to the ground, he as if shot down from another tree. A Hermit appears behind Agathe and raises her up. As Agathe revives, Caspar recognizes the intervention of heaven (in the person of the Hermit) and knows his own time is up. Seeing Samiel come to claim him instead of Agathe, he dies. Ottokar orders his body carried to the Wolf's Glen, then turns to Max for an explanation. When Max confesses that in his despair he turned to magic bullets, Ottokar orders him banished, but the Hermit intercedes, saying a year of penance should be enough. Ottokar agrees, saying he will allow Max and Agathe to marry after a year, as the Hermit leads everyone in a prayer that penitence will earn forgiveness.

KURT WEILL
1900–50

urt Weill, son of a cantor in Dessau, studied with Humperdinck and Busoni. His early music, astringent in style and tending toward atonality, was programmed alongside the recent works of Hindemith, Schoenberg, and Stravinsky, but in his twenties he found himself at an artistic crossroads. Possessing the aptitude for a more popular musical idiom, and wishing to communicate with a broader audience, he decided to cast his lot with the world of the theater.

This decision was a product of the times. Out of the peculiar blend of disillusion and creativity that characterized Germany (especially Berlin) after World War I, the cabaret entertainment came into its own as an art form. Ironic and satirical, it both expressed and criticized the permissive atmosphere of Germany during the 1920s. Among Weill's colleagues was the leftist playwright Bertolt Brecht (1898–1956), whose "epic theater" was aimed at demolishing sentimental bourgeois entertainment and forcing the audience to face uncomfortable realities. Weill's music, an ideal complement to Brecht's stage pieces, not only enhanced their sardonic moods but also humanized them, giving them general appeal. So successful were the Brecht–Weill collaborations that Brecht came to resent the composer's popularity and turned his later endeavors over to colleagues whose work attracted less attention.

Die Dreigroschenoper marked the first full-fledged joint work of the two men. A year earlier, in 1927, they had written *Das Kleine Mahagonny,* a dramatized group of songs that formed the nucleus of their later "grand" opera, *Aufstieg und Fall der Stadt Mahagonny.*

Die Dreigroschenoper was an immediate triumph, with 10,000 performances

536

all over Europe in five years, plus translations into eighteen languages, before the Nazis came to power and suppressed it in Germany. It owes much of its appeal to the ballad *Morität* (Morality) that opens and closes it, known in English as *Mack the Knife,* a last-minute addition by the authors to please a self-important actor. The plot, faithfully yet freely borrowed from *The Beggar's Opera,* by Gay and Pepusch, is vague as to period, suggesting both Dickens's England and the Berlin in which Brecht and Weill found themselves. Mention of the queen's coronation, presumably referring to Queen Victoria, would place the action in 1837.

In *Mahagonny* two years later, Brecht and Weill lampooned the United States, which they knew only through the movies, as a land of free-for-all rapacity in which only the Almighty Dollar had value. As Patrick J. Smith points out, however, "An underlying aspect serves to bind together . . . the disparate threads of the story. That is the history of Germany—not only the history of the Weimar Republic, established after World War I, but the span of German history from the creation of the unified Empire at Versailles in 1871. . . . The hurricane . . . represents of course the First World War." The premiere was a theatrical scandal to equal that of *Le Sacre du Printemps* in Paris in 1913. Police were posted in the theater to prevent rioting.

Soon thereafter, Weill was on the Nazi blacklist and en route to a different life in the New World. After a stopover in Paris, where he found his German texts and musical vocabulary no longer welcome, he came to the United States in 1934 and began a fruitful career working for the Broadway theater. This was the man who wrote *September Song,* a sunset apostrophe to love, and musicals like the sophisticated *Lady in the Dark* (about a patient in psychoanalysis, played by Gertrude Lawrence) and *One Touch of Venus* (a Mary Martin vehicle). He was a hit composer, but he never gave up his love for the more "operatic" stage, and in *Street Scene* (1947) and *Lost in the Stars* (1949) he led Broadway to new intersections. His folk-song opera *Down in the Valley* (1948) remains a staple of college and conservatory workshops.

After his death, Weill's widow, the singer Lotte Lenya, who had sung in many of his European premieres, encouraged the revival of his earlier works, to the point where they have come to outrank even his Broadway successes in frequency of performance.

DIE DREIGROSCHENOPER

(The Threepenny Opera)

PROLOGUE AND THREE ACTS
MUSIC: Kurt Weill
TEXT (German): Bertolt Brecht, after *The Beggar's Opera,* by John
   Gay (1728)
WORLD PREMIERE: Berlin, Theater am Schiffbauerdamm, August
   31, 1928
U.S. PREMIERE: New York, Empire Theater, April 13, 1933 (in
   English)

CHARACTERS

Polly Peachum . . . . Soprano
Jenny, *prostitute* . . . . Soprano
Lucy Brown . . . . Soprano
Mrs. Peachum, *Polly's mother* . . . . Mezzo-Soprano
Macheath, *gangster* . . . . Tenor
Street Singer . . . . Tenor
Peachum, *Polly's father* . . . . Bass
Tiger Brown, *chief of police* . . . . Bass
   Constable Smith, gangsters, whores, other denizens of Soho

PROLOGUE   On the streets of Soho in London, a Street Singer tells the audience they are about to see a beggars' opera—splendidly imagined, yet done on
the cheap. It will open with the introduction of Macheath . . .

ACT I   . . . also known as Mack the Knife, whom the Street Singer describes
as a nonchalant, ruthless criminal *(Und der Haifisch, der hat Zähne)* who always
covers his traces, though he leaves the mark of his style on every crime. The
Street Singer next introduces the shopkeeper Peachum, who has opened a
haberdashery for the beggars of the neighborhood, enabling them to keep up
appearances. Peachum starts the day with a rousing hymn expressing his low
opinion of human nature *(Wach auf, du verrotterer Christ!)*. When he and his
wife notice that their daughter, Polly, was not home the night before, they
curse the moon over Soho and its romantic spell, which turns young people
into good-for-nothings (duet: *Anstatt dass*). Next comes news of Polly's marriage to Macheath, celebrated by denizens of Soho with a song about the slim

chances that marriage will last in such an environment (*Bill Lawgen und Mary Syer*). Macheath owes his power in the underworld to his friendship with Police Chief Brown, who reminisces with him about their rough-and-ready life together in the army (*John war darunter*) in India, where they made mincemeat of the natives. A change of mood comes with Polly's appearance, as she and Macheath speak of the love they feel now: it may last, it may not (*Und gibt's auch kein Schriftstück*).

§ Inside Peachum's store, Polly reflects that whereas other suitors never had the power to move her, Macheath—a wrong choice in every way—swept her off her feet (*Einst glaubte ich*). Alarmed at their daughter's notion of marrying for love, the Peachums lecture her on the vicissitudes of real life: everyone would like to be good, comfortable, and happy, but circumstances are against it (*Was ich möchte, ist es viel?*). The world, they conclude, is nothing but a junkheap.

ACT II Macheath, wanted by the police, finds it prudent to go away for a while. He and Polly wonder whether their relationship is over so soon. As he leaves, she tells herself to expect nothing more: he is gone for good (*Er kommt nicht wieder*).

§ Mrs. Peachum walks before the curtain with Jenny, a streetwalker, telling her to watch for Macheath, since whoever turns him in will get a reward. Jenny thinks he is too smart to show himself, but Mrs. Peachum says his weakness for women, like that of most men, will prove his undoing (*Da ist nun einer*). Jenny sings a barmaid's ballad: though she works behind the bar and everyone takes her for granted, someday a pirate ship will enter the harbor and storm the town, sparing only her, because she is someone special (*Meine Herren, heute sehen Sie*).

§ Outside the whorehouse where Jenny works, she and Macheath reminisce about the six months they lived there together, he as her pimp and protector (*In einer Zeit*). Jenny covertly signals Constable Smith, who arrests Macheath.

§ In the Old Bailey jail, Macheath daydreams about a life of wealth and ease (*Da preist man uns*). Meanwhile, Polly and Jenny defy each other, arguing as to which of them he really loves (duet: *Mackie und ich*). When she is alone, Polly plans to put rat poison in Jenny's gin.

§ Stepping before the curtain, Macheath and Jenny pose a question: What keeps a man alive? Before discussing morals, they agree, the first order of business is getting enough to eat, and toward this end mankind will do absolutely anything (*Ihr Herrn, die ihr uns lehrt*).

ACT III Peachum lectures a crony, Tiger Brown, about man's inadequacy: no matter what he strives for, it is always out of reach (*Der Mensch lebt durch den Kopf*). Accompanied by an organ-grinder, Jenny tells the fate of Solomon,

540

Cleopatra, and Caesar, done in by their wisdom, beauty, and boldness, respectively; now she and Macheath are done in by their passion *(Ihr saht den weisen Salomon)*. Macheath's voice is heard calling from prison, begging the denizens of Soho to save him before it is too late—he is already practically in the grave *(Nun hört die Stimme)*. He forgives Jenny for betraying him, since this is the way of the world. In fact he asks pardon of everyone, with the possible exception of the police *(Ihr Menschenbrüder)*, saying the imminence of death has humbled his pride. As he starts for the gallows, accompanied by friends and neighbors, Peachum tells the audience that such an ending is to be expected in real life but not in the theater. To show how "for once mercy and not justice carries the day," he calls for a messenger, who appears in the form of Tiger Brown as police chief, announcing that in honor of the queen's coronation she has pardoned Macheath, giving him a title, lands, and a life income of 10,000 pounds a year. Peachum asks for understanding on behalf of the downtrodden, and the Street Singer concludes his ballad, "One sees people who are in the light, not those who are in the dark."

AUFSTIEG UND FALL DER STADT MAHAGONNY

(Rise and Fall of the City of Mahagonny)

THREE ACTS
MUSIC: Kurt Weill
TEXT (German): Bertolt Brecht
WORLD PREMIERE: Leipzig, Neue Theater, March 9, 1930
U.S. PREMIERE: New York, Town Hall, February 23, 1952
   (abridged concert performance); New York, Anderson Theater, April 28, 1970 (in English)
METROPOLITAN OPERA PREMIERE: November 16, 1979

CHARACTERS

Jenny, *prostitute* .... Soprano
Leokadja Begbick, *widow, entrepreneur* .... Mezzo-Soprano
Narrator... Tenor
Jimmy Mahoney .... Tenor
Jacob Schmidt .... Tenor

Toby Higgins . . . . Tenor
Fatty, *bookkeeper* . . . . Tenor
Trinity Moses. . . . . Baritone
Bill (Bankbook Billy) . . . . Baritone
Joe (Alaska-Wolf Joe) . . . . Bass
Whores, drifters, gamblers

ACT I   In a desolate part of Florida in the late 1920s, a battered truck breaks down, disgorging a motley crew of fugitives from justice. As Fatty the Book-keeper and Trinity Moses discuss how they can get farther up the coast, where gold has been discovered, the more practical Widow Leokadja Begbick says they will do better to stay where they are and get the gold an easier way—by fleecing the prospectors, who will be looking for ways to spend their new wealth. The group plans to build a "city of nets," called Mahagonny, to catch these "edible birds." It will be a paradise, where no one works and everyone does what he pleases (*Aber dieses ganze Mahagonny*).

§ The city has risen almost overnight, and Jenny, a prostitute, arrives with six colleagues (*Oh, show us the way to the next whisky-bar!*), leading them in a sentimental ballad (*Oh, moon of Alabama*). As men from the big cities lament the frustrations of their life, Fatty and Trinity Moses extol the virtues of peaceful Mahagonny, where liquor is cheap and morality open (*Doch sitzt ihr einmal bei den Mahagonny-Leuten*). Malcontents from all over begin to arrive, among them four who have made their fortune in Alaska, led by Jim Maho-ney. Widow Begbick welcomes them and offers a choice of girls, who parade their wares (*Wir sind die Mädchen von Mahagonny*). Jacob Schmidt refuses to pay Jenny's price, but Jim takes a fancy to her, and they strike up an acquaint-ance.

§ Some time later, the founders of Mahagonny sit in Begbick's bar, worrying about their enterprise's wavering success: people are starting to leave. They themselves consider leaving, but a warrant is out for Begbick's arrest in the outside world, so they decide to try their luck a little longer.

§ Bored with the easy life and offended by a sign saying that something is forbidden, Jim starts to leave, thinking he will take a drive to Georgia. He insists he will do whatever he wants, even eat his hat. His three cronies lead him back toward the bar.

§ Outside the bar, Jim continues to voice discontent, recalling seven years of hard work at logging in Alaska (*Sieben Jahre hab' ich gebraucht*). Afraid he will make trouble, the prostitutes and other citizens try to mollify him, but he jumps on a table and announces that no one will find happiness in Mahagonny, where there is too much peace and security. As if in answer to his challenge, the lights go out, and warning of an approaching hurricane is heard. The others are terrified, but Jim finds it reassuring that a force of nature like a hurricane, or man himself, makes peace and harmony impossible *(Ruhe und Eintracht das gibt es nicht)*. Jenny tries to calm him, but he steps to the footlights and announces his credo: people should do whatever they want, no matter what it is *(Wenn es etwas gibt)*. Word arrives that the storm has destroyed Pensacola and will do the same to Mahagonny. Faced with annihilation, says Jim, they should do whatever is forbidden, starting with the singing of cheerful songs: he leads one, "As you make your bed, that's how you'll lie in it" *(Denn wie man sich bettet)*.

ACT II   Huddled along a highway outside Mahagonny, the citizens await the destruction of their city, only to find that the hurricane has bypassed it. They hail the miracle of their rescue *(O wunderbare Lösung!)*.

§ Having come so close to destruction, the people accept Jim's credo of "Anything goes" and embark on an orgy of permissiveness. The first casualty is the gluttonous Jacob Schmidt, who eats himself to death, earning praise for having the courage of his convictions. Next, in celebration of sex, Begbick lectures the men on the art of being a good client *(Spucke den Kaugummi aus)*, adding they should be quick about it, so that the wheels of commerce may keep turning. With this marathon of prostitution as background, Jim and Jenny watch a pair of cranes flying, seeing an allegory of the transitory grace of love *(Sieh jene Kraniche)*. Violence is next on the agenda, in the form of a boxing match between Trinity Moses and Alaska-Wolf Joe. Confident of victory, Joe bets all his money on himself and asks his friends to do the same, but only Jim is persuaded. He quickly regrets it when Joe is killed by his opponent. To celebrate the joys of drinking, the men gravitate to the bar, where Jim, in spite of having lost his fortune, recklessly treats everyone to drinks.

ACT III   A court of justice has been set up, with Trinity Moses as prosecuting attorney and Begbick as judge. Toby Higgins, charged with murder, is acquitted when he offers the judge a bribe and no complainant can be found, since the victim is dead. Now Jim stands accused of the worst crime in Mahagonny—having no money. Unable to pay his debts or offer a bribe, he is found guilty and sentenced to death.

§ Longing for a better life, the people plan to move to another city *(Let's go to Benares)*, but they learn that it has been destroyed by an earthquake. Where can they go now?

§ Jim bids a last farewell to Jenny, who says she will never forget their good times together. To the others he says he has no regrets: life is to be enjoyed while you have it *(Lasst euch nicht verführen)*. Seated in the electric chair, he raises the question of God in Mahagonny. Acting the role of God, Trinity

Moses pronounces the people of Mahagonny condemned to hell—indeed, they are already there *(An einem grauen Vormittag).* The execution proceeds.

§ Because of inflation and unrest, protests have raged in Mahagonny, and the city is in flames. Carrying Jim's hat on a stick, men proclaim that even though the hurricane spared Mahagonny, man alone suffices to destroy his own creation. There is no helping anyone once he is dead, others announce. Amid a forest of placards proclaiming various conflicting goals, the citizens conclude that nothing is to be done, either for themselves or for their audience.

RICCARDO ZANDONAI
1883–1944

*I*n the wake of the veristic movement around 1900, Italian composers
turned to poetic drama and the classical or romantic past. Of the
generation that followed Puccini and Mascagni, those who particularly reflected this trend were Italo Montemezzi, Ottorino Respighi,
Ildebrando Pizzetti, and Riccardo Zandonai. All enjoyed their share of success, but because their music was "modern" and their choice of subjects literary, their works held less immediate appeal for a general audience and have
been revived only sporadically.

Zandonai was the publisher Tito Ricordi's choice as most likely to succeed
after Puccini. Zandonai's *Francesca da Rimini,* based on Canto V of the "Inferno"
section of Dante's *Divine Comedy*—which in turn loosely used actual characters
and events of Dante's Florence—embodies the characteristics of the postver-
istic school. Opulently orchestrated in the manner of Richard Strauss, without
Italianate emphasis on purely melodic vocal line, this was considered a pro-
gressive work by opera audiences in its day. The language of Gabriele D'Annunzio's libretto is high-flown and poetic, showered with archaic vocabulary,
but the plot line is old-fashioned violent melodrama. A salient feature of the
score is its genre painting of a historic period, influenced by Wagner's in *Die
Meistersinger.* By stressing the Gothic underpinnings of verismo, Zandonai
tapped a coloristic vein as rich as the geographical wanderings of Puccini.

Of the various composers who set dramas by D'Annunzio to music, Zandonai came the closest to creating an enduring work. Born at Sacco (Rovereto),

544

the only child of a shoemaker and a tobacco-factory worker, he was befriended by Arrigo Boito, who introduced him to Giulio Ricordi, Tito's father, in 1907. For the house of Ricordi the young man wrote *Il Grillo del Focolare* (1908), after Dickens's *A Cricket on the Hearth,* but it was *Conchita* (1911) that achieved performances abroad and made his name known. Based on a Pierre Louÿs story that Puccini had turned down, *Conchita* proved a vehicle for Zandonai's soprano wife, Tarquinia Tarquini. Vocal problems, however, prevented her from "creating" the role of Francesca da Rimini in his most famous work. Of the dozen operas he wrote over a quarter-century, *Giulietta e Romeo* (1922) and *I Cavalieri Di Ekebù* (1925, after Selma Lagerlöf's *Gösta Berlings Saga*) are still occasionally staged.

A modest, serious man, quite opposite in character to the flamboyant D'Annunzio, Zandonai was known for his independence. Symphonic and instrumental music interested him as much as the theater. His last opera staged during his lifetime was *La Farsa Amorosa* (1933), based on the same Alarcón story as Falla's ballet *El Sombrero de Tres Picos* (The Three-Cornered Hat). A posthumous premiere of the incomplete *Il Bacio* took place in 1954. During his last four years, Zandonai served as director of the Conservatory of Pesaro, in the town of Rossini's birth. Administrative contretemps with the Fascist bureaucracy apparently strained his health, and he died in 1944, before the end of the Second World War.

FRANCESCA DA RIMINI

FOUR ACTS
MUSIC: Riccardo Zandonai
TEXT (Italian): Gabriele D'Annunzio, edited by Tito Ricordi
WORLD PREMIERE: Turin, Teatro Regio, February 19, 1914
U.S. PREMIERE: Metropolitan Opera, December 22, 1916

CHARACTERS

Francesca . . . . Soprano
Samaritana, *her younger sister* . . . . Soprano
Garsenda ⎫
Biancofiore ⎬ *her attendants* . . . .
Altichiara ⎭
⎧ Soprano
⎨ Soprano
⎩ Mezzo-Soprano
Smaragdi, *her slave* . . . . Mezzo-Soprano

RICCARDO ZANDONAI

Brothers of the Malatesta family:
Paolo, "The Handsome" .... Tenor
Malatestino, "The One-Eyed" .... Tenor
Giovanni, (Gianciotto), "The Lame" .... Baritone
Ser Toldo, *lawyer* .... Tenor
Ostasio, *Francesca's brother* .... Baritone
Jester .... Baritone
Archers, soldiers, torchbearers, servants, guests, prisoner's voice

ACT I   A courtyard of the Polenta family palace in Ravenna, in the year
1285. Some girls are seen bantering with a Jester, who begs to have his torn
jacket mended; in return he offers to tell stories of King Arthur's knights, of
Tristram's love for Iseult. He has barely begun when Ostasio da Polenta bursts
in, dispersing the gathering, complaining to his lawyer, Ser Toldo, that jest-
ers are just gossips. He does not want their latest plan known—that of tricking his sister Francesca into a marriage of convenience with Gianciotto ("The
Lame") of the Malatesta family. This he means to do by introducing a proxy
suitor, Gianciotto's brother Paolo ("The Handsome"). Ser Toldo agrees that
this is the only way to get around Francesca *(Voi dovete pur sapere),* and he urges
that the marriage contract be signed as quickly as possible. As they leave,
Francesca descends the stairway. Her sister Samaritana, knowing a suitor is
about to arrive for Francesca, laments their impending separation, but Francesca comforts her *(Pace, anima cara),* saying Samaritana will marry too. A
flurry of excitement goes through her entourage as they catch a glimpse of the
arriving Paolo; Francesca is smitten by the sight of him, as her brother planned.
Upset, she asks Samaritana to take her to her room *(Ah, tu ora pigliami),* where
she will try to calm the tumult in her heart. As she turns toward the stairs,
she and Paolo exchange a long, wordless glance, and she hands him a rose.
The other women surround her, offering a madrigal about the month of May
(Per la terra di maggio).

ACT II   In a tower of the Malatesta castle in Rimini, in sight of the Adriatic,
soldiers are engaged in a battle between Ghibellines and Guelphs (Malatesta
being a Guelph). Francesca, now married to Gianciotto, nervously greets Paolo,
whom she accuses of having wooed her fraudulently. He realizes he deceived
her, though he denies having known it at the time, and he adds that peace
has fled his soul. A call to arms brings them back to reality. Removing his
helmet, Paolo recklessly exposes his head to enemy fire, then tells Francesca
to raise the portcullis. Grazed by an arrow, he falls back, saying he is not
wounded by anything but his guilty love. Because he has survived this risk of
death, Francesca considers him absolved of the fraud practiced on her. Gianciotto arrives, and Francesca offers wine to the two brothers. The third brother,
Malatestino, is brought in, struck by a stone in one eye; despite his injury, he

returns to the fray. Archers are heard crying confidently that the Guelph side is winning *(Vittoria a Malatesta!)*.

ACT III   In a room decorated with frescoes showing the story of Tristram, Francesca sits reading, then turns to her maid, Smaragdi, to complain of the wine she poured the day of the battle: was it bewitched? Women and musicians enter, singing the praises of approaching spring *(Marzo è giunto)* while dancing with wooden swallows in their hands. Francesca dismisses them when she learns that Paolo is approaching. Gone since the battle, he reminds her that on that day she offered him wine. She begs for no more recollections: she wants peace from her torment *(Paolo, datemi pace)*. He too has known no peace since their first meeting *(Perchè volete voi)*. He picks up the story she has been reading, as told by Galeoto, a go-between for Lancelot and Guinevere. Francesca reads Guinevere's lines. When she comes to the point where the queen kisses her suitor, Paolo embraces her passionately. In the background, the women are still heard singing their welcome to spring.

ACT IV   Malatestino, now blind in one eye, makes advances toward Francesca in a hallway of the castle. When she says she will call his brother, he tauntingly asks, "Which one?" To silence the screams of a prisoner in the dungeon below, he takes an ax from the wall and leaves. When Gianciotto finds Francesca upset, she says it is because of Malatestino's cruelty. As she questions him about his impending trip to Pesaro, Malatestino knocks at the door, and she leaves, so as to avoid him. Gianciotto admits his brother, who carries the prisoner's head in a sack. Gianciotto demands to know what Malatestino has done to offend Francesca. Malatestino replies that he is loyal but that Paolo is not. The furious Gianciotto swears he will kill Malatestino if he is lying. Malatestino tells him to postpone his departure, wait till nightfall, and see for himself.

§ In Francesca's room at night, she dismisses all her women except Biancofiore, who reminds her of the little sister she left behind in Ravenna. After Biancofiore too has said good night, Francesca hears knocking and calls for Smaragdi, but it is Paolo who enters. As they embrace and declare their ardent love, another knock is heard, along with Gianciotto's voice. Paolo starts to escape through a trap door, but his cloak catches on the bolt, and when Gianciotto enters, he sees his brother still struggling to free it. Gianciotto drags him back up, and Francesca throws herself between them, catching the full force of her husband's sword. As Paolo takes her in his arms, Gianciotto watches their last embrace, then kills Paolo. In disgust he breaks his bloodstained sword over his knee.